Marketing at the Millennium

A historical record of people,
organisations and events that shaped
the marketing profession in Ireland,
1947–2000

About the Author

Harry Woods, author, lecturer and retired marketing consultant, is married and lives in Dublin, Ireland. Mathematics and Cost Accountancy study led him early to a fascinated investigation of Sales Management of which Marketing was a subject in the 1950s.

Having led the first Irish delegation to a European Congress of Marketing and Distribution in Barcelona 1964, he was elected to the Council of the EMC – now known as the European Marketing Confederation. In 1971 he became the first Irishman to hold the EMC Presidency.

A fellow of the Marketing Institute and the UK Incorporated Sales Managers Association (now the Chartered Institute of Marketing), he was vice-chairman of the Publicity Club of Ireland.

His interests include academic reading and ecclesiastic involvement. He has completed twenty-one 42K marathons and participates in walking events. He is past-president of his alma mater, Terenure College.

The Marketing Institute of Ireland distinguished Harry at its AGM 2000 by awarding him Honorary Life Membership of the Institute.

MARKETING AT THE MILLENNIUM

A historical record of people,
organisations and events that shaped
the marketing profession in Ireland,
1947–2000

Harry V. Woods FMII, F.INST.M

Past Chairman of the Marketing Institute of Ireland (MII) and
Past President of the European Marketing Council (EMC)
(now the European Marketing Confederation)

BLACKHALL
Publishing

This book was typeset by Gough Typesetting Services for
Blackhall Publishing,
8 Priory Hall, Stillorgan,
Co. Dublin,
Ireland.

Email: blackhall@eircom.net
Website: www.blackhallpublishing.com

A catalogue record for this book is available from the British
Library

ISBN: 1 842180 29 0

Printed in Ireland by
ColourBooks Ltd

Contents

Appendices

Foreword

Future historians will offer a sincere vote of thanks to Harry Woods for his Herculean efforts in compiling this detailed study of the evolution in Ireland of marketing in general and the role of the Marketing Institute in particular during the latter half of the twentieth century.

For these 'tiger cubs' who now see the virtually unlimited marketing opportunities being offered by the globalising economy, it may be difficult to visualise the historical investment of intellectual capital necessary in order to arrive at our current state. Harry's meticulous work will offer many potential insights.

For those more chronologically advantaged marketers who lived through this period and survived you may wish to open this magnum opus at the index of names, choose one of your friends, acquaintances or indeed your own name and follow the referred pages.

This may well cause you to recall an event which had slipped into the deeper recesses of your memory banks but which at its time was significant and satisfying.

Prof. Anthony C. Cunningham,
June 2001.

Dedication

To Sheila

Preface

Change is the order of the day. Knowledge of technology, growth of education and consumer awareness are just some of the social changes affecting our way of living in the new century.

With an ever-increasing quantity of websites set up by Irish firms, spending is a transformation relative to Ireland's booming economy. The volume of advertising has been reflected by international investment into local agencies.

Marketing communications must pay attention to the rapidly developing website medium. Response devices now appear in more advertisements as the trend is towards direct marketing.

THE INTERNET

Looking back on the internet, it began with e-mail, moved on to the next phase, the world-wide-web and then the development of e-commerce came along, consuming a vast amount of articles, debate and discussion.

ELECTRONIC COMMERCE

Electronic commerce, or e-commerce, is simply defined as 'activities involved in the buying and selling of goods or services'. Spending in this area is expected to increase to over £400m in the year 2001.

To remain competitive, in an e-commerce environment, marketing strategies, relationships and technologies will undoubtedly change in order to plan and conduct business. The role of the marketer is transforming. They must direct growth and take the lead by using the new technologies to win future business, enhance brand loyalty and create customer awareness. That entails knowledge of the market and reaching it profitably by forward planning. It calls for the particular expertise of marketing personnel professionals. Business has become global, because of competitive pressures, and Ireland is an attractive location.

OPENING YEAR(S) OF NEW CENTURY

In the opening year(s) of the new century, Ireland's tourism growth rate seems set to continue at the unprecedented level as that of the nineties. The outgoing decade showed a three-fold increase in the international conference sector of the Irish tourism industry. Delegate numbers rose to over 100,000 in 1999, with earnings of over IR£100m. The Convention Bureau of Ireland, (CBI), the specialist marketing wing of Bord Fáilte, has consistently adapted its approach to the highly competitive overseas marketplace.

CONFERENCE DIRECTORY, 2000

The Minister for Tourism, Sport and Recreation, Dr James McDaid TD, introduced the *Sunday Business Post* 'Conference Directory 2000' at the end of November 1999. The CBI was expanded to ensure dynamic leadership and support to Bord Fáilte in a sustained marketing programme. The programme targets conference and incentive travel.

A millennium edition of a new format of the *Conference and Meetings Planner*, a specialist guide to Ireland, published on a three-yearly basis, was formally launched in the British market. (October 1999 — internet www.conference.Ireland.ie). The strategic conference marketing plan, (1999–2000), was in overseas marketing activity and was unprecedented in intensity and scope.

POWER IN NORTHERN IRELAND DEVOLVED, DECEMBER 1999

On 2 December 1999, direct rule from Westminister, England, of the six northern counties of Ireland, ended after 25 years. Power was devolved to the new North-South Ministerial Council and the British-Irish Council. The first formal meeting of the Northern Ireland Executive took place in Stormont, Belfast. It marked a new beginning for Ireland — peace and prosperity.

In looking forward to long awaited mutual progress and success in trade, enterprise, tourism and goodwill, I extend greetings to marketing colleagues in the Chartered Institute of Marketing, Northern Ireland and United Kingdom, all business professions and, of course, all those in the European Marketing Confederation (EMC).

EURO CURRENCY

'It is the sales and marketing department that must be the driver of the implications, in their company, of the move to the Euro currency, *not* the personnel, *nor* the production *nor* the financial department.' Such was the claim of the chartered accountants, stated Jean-Marie Van Houwe, director-general of the EMC (European Marketing Confederation), in 1998.

MARKETING IN THE NEW MILLENNIUM

Marketing effectiveness in the new millennium must be obtained by tackling the changing requirements. In order to achieve this, new creativity, new skills including design, indeed a true marketing renaissance are needed. Much more investment, however, is required in training company marketing personnel.

Acknowledgements

I am most grateful to the National Millennium Committee, for the enthusiastic support of my initiative and the financial support in compiling and computing the volume *Marketing at the Millennium*. In particular the officers of Dún Laoghaire–Rathdown County Council were very helpful in the application for grant process.

I would like to take this opportunity to thank in advance Mr Seamus Brennan TD, Minister of State and Government Chief Whip, colleagues, friends including co-sponsors and all those present at the book launch in Marketing House, Stillorgan, Co Dublin.

The kind comments and introduction of the book by Professor Anthony Cunningham are an appreciated honour.

The interest, help and financial contribution made by the following co-sponsors encouraged and assured the final production of the book: Bord Bia, Hispano Cars Ltd, Irish Marketing Surveys Ltd, Irish Trade Board (CTT), now Enterprise Ireland, Lansdowne Market Research, optimAS, SDL Exhibitions Ltd, Smurfit Web Press, The Marketing Institute and The Irish Times.

In the wide investigation and preparation of this book, it was with agreement of the Marketing Institute that the writer do so, provided the Institute was under no obligation to contribute financially. Self-supporting being as they are a non-profit body, I would like to acknowledge that the facility allowed me to go through the minute books up to the time they ceased to be hand written. Fortunately I had kept a variety of records, minutes, press cuttings, photographs, conference and other brochures, yearly diaries, books and manuscripts over the half-decade.

Thanks to many colleagues, friends, family and academics. Many persons contributed in discussion and advice and indeed criticism, be it friendly caution, as to the task involved.

It was undoubtedly a labour of love and recalled friends of a lifetime. On review I find that many marketing members and students, having served the Institute or its many committees, are not named. Due to lack of space, data has been confined to MII officers and council personnel.

The following contributed in ways, best known to them, which were of consolation in my perseverance: Robin Addis, Tony Amoroso, Clíona Ní Bréartúin, Seamus Brennan, TD, John Casey, John D. Carroll, Frank Cusack, Peter Corcoran, Louise Coughlan, Prof. Anthony Cunningham, Sylvia Doyle, Maeve Donovan, Philip Flood, Aubrey Fogarty, Ian Fox, the late Bill Fraser, Robert Gahan, Fred Hayden, Michael J. Hayes, Roger Jupp, Raymond I. Joyce, Catherine KilBride, Muiris Kennedy, Maureen Kenneally, Sean Lemass (SDL), Mahon Lee, Hugh Millar, Arthur Moyniham, Michael Moriarty, Norman

McConnell, Alan McDonnell, Dr John McGuire, Anthony Neville, Aidan O'Driscoll, J. Brendan O'Reilly, Dermot Prendergast, Tom Prior, Derek Pullen, Brendan V. Wafer, Derek P. Whelan.

Sincerest thanks to Gerard O'Connor and the team at Blackhall Publishing for their courtesy, patience and editorial assistance in bringing the product to finality.

The media have been gracious over the many years in their reporting and photography of marketing and sales events. It is only fair to thank them now for courtesy and co-operation at all times. The following is a short list of outlets that come to mind: *Business & Finance, Cork Examiner, Cork Marketing News, Evening Herald, Evening Press, Harvard Business Review, IMJ (Irish Marketing Journal), International Newsletter (SME-1, New York), Irish Examiner, Financial Times, Irish Independent, Irish Marketing Review, Irish Press, Marketing, Marketing Journal, Marketing News, Munster Express, News Extracts Ltd, O'Neill's Who's* Who, Radio *Eireann, Radio Telefis Eireann, Salesweek (New York), Strategic Marketing Newsflash (EMC), Sunday Business Post, Sunday Tribune, Tatlor & Sketch, The Irish Times* and *Ulster Television*; and marketing websites as listed in *The Marketing Institute Diary2000* of particular interest to marketers include:

www.kompass.ie
//nsns.com/Syllabits/mar
//internetmarketing.digitalsprings.com/ch01/catshaw.html
www.smartbiz.com
www.wdfm.com
www.marketware-tech.com/marketing/htm
www.marketingsource.com
www.emarketer.com
www.consumerworld.org
www.1to1.com
www.imarketinc.com/products/roicale/index.asp
www.tka.co.uk
www.mii.ie
www.oestat.gv.at

Introduction

This book tells the history of Ireland's development of the Incorporated Sales Managers' Association (ISMA) from the few group members in 1947 to the 2,800 members, representing a wide range of business and 1,300 students registered on the education programme of the Marketing Institute of Ireland (MII) in 1999.

It is my hope that this compilation will give you enjoyable, interesting reading and that the facts and figures will be of assistance to students in their planning and studies, in the broadest sense.

Adam Smith

Adam Smith, The Wealth of Nations 1776, the first great economist said two hundred years ago the sole end and purpose of all production is consumption. The same applies today.

Marketing is not a direct science; it is not some mysterious or magic method of managing a business. Rather it is an umbrella of facets, each rib playing an important and essential part of the whole marketing mix.

Marketing directs all business activities involved in assessing and converting customer purchasing power into effective demand for a specific product or service. Such enables achievement of the profit target and or other objective set by a company.

Undoubtedly marketing is a major function of management, starting by analysing the changes taking place in society. This is often carried out by using a form of market research, and the examination of several alternative solutions to problems, in a rational way.

Measurement

Over years of study and lecturing this author has summed up the need as *measurement*, a word easy to remember and, if fully considered and implemented, ensures a more exacting and, yes, profitable result.

4 P's (Production, Pricing, Planning and People)

To carry out the plan desired, an assessment of all the aspects must be made of the product: Production, in the wide sense, Pricing, Planning and People (4 P's) market, at whom the output is aimed. The essential being to determine the right time, place/area, appeal, price, and also for what period. This particularly relates to new product introduction.

In the case of export, vital to the economy, it is essential to travel to the market to survey and assess the competition and, first hand, measure the potential sale outlet market. This, of course, is related to the population percentage to sell to, to be aimed at in socio-economic groups, teenage, leisure spenders and the now all important senior citizen market.

Taking into account the assessment figures required to decide on size, shape, quality, design of packaging, apart from goods, and the economic method of efficient, on time, distribution being assessed and also seen to be carried out to satisfy the market, one will agree all come under the referred-to *measurement*.

SALES DEVELOPMENT FROM 1900
1900–1950 WAGE COMPARISONS

In 1900 a man's wages in manufacturing averaged one pound eight shillings, one punt forty pence, and the comparison in 1969 was twenty five pounds ten shillings, twenty five punt and fifty pence.

Before the First World War, pre 1914, the average male wage earner was paid only 60 per cent of that given a salaried earner. However, by 1969 the ratio was 79 per cent while in 1991 parity was almost reached, on average comparison.

The situation with women earners goes back to the domestic servant market and the widow, trying to pay for her children's education, who took in washing or became the local dressmaker. By the year 1900 this had changed and certainly by the end of the First World War, 1918, the change was quite rapid. Clerical, typing, teaching and nursing became the occupations of women. It was observed too that middle-class jobs found greatest growth in women employment and particularly so from 1900 to 1950.

Today, probably 50 per cent of employment is engaged in by women. It can truly be said that same is due to the number of married women workers, of which it is estimated 70 per cent is employed.

It can be seen that purchasing power has expanded in the middle class rapidly, as with longevity and the new spending capacity available in disposable income, brought about by investment and pension schemes, the opportunity to travel and higher living standards.

Education has been a considerable factor in economic life, resulting too in more discretionary purchasing, while former household luxuries, such as washing machines, fridges, microwaves, computers etc., are now in standard use, making life easier and increasing buying of stock to fill the shelves and display areas of supermarkets and departmental stores. This, of course, led to the considerable number of shopping centres now in every town. The smaller shops too with facility of late night shopping have provided new convenience for purchases including from service stations, stores, restaurants and fast-food outlets.

Incorporated Sales Managers' Association (ISMA)

Back in 1911, the Incorporated Sales Managers' Association was founded by Mr E.S. Daniells and incorporated in 1921. Formal examinations resulting from planned course education took place from 1931.

The main objectives cited for the association were to promote the interests of its members, by the exchange of knowledge and experience, thus to raise the level of sales management by providing professional status and recognised standards of performance

In producing this volume and telling the history, I have gone back to the year 1947, when some eight gentlemen met in Jury's hotel, then in Dame Street, Dublin, with the late Mr Tom Moran who was acting as both honorary secretary and honorary treasurer. A minute book was produced and it was recorded in it that these gentlemen, described as the Irish resident members of the London based Incorporated Sales Managers' Association (ISMA), be formed into a group of same.

In those days the logo and theme of the ISMA was, 'Honest in Telling, Bold in Selling' and individuals were known and recorded as 'Mr' with no Christian names being shown.

ISMA membership, 1961

By the end of 1961, the fiftieth anniversary of the Incorporated Sales Managers' Association, there were 10,000 members in the 21 branches of the association, of which the Ireland branch, with its headquarters in Dublin and branches in Belfast and Cork, became a strong and active unit. The membership comprised of fellows, members and associates with registered students taking their examinations in Dublin.

Marketing and selling deemed interchangeable until late 1940s

It was not until the late 1940s that the word 'marketing' came into use on the business scene. Up to that time marketing and selling were deemed to be interchangeable. In fact, 'marketing' was a subject part of the Incorporated Sales Managers' Association (ISMA) London diploma course of study.

The market upsurge in customer products' availability became apparent in the late 1940s. Increased disposable income, productivity and consequent employment brought about the need to find out who one's customer was and what, in fact, was their need. This led undoubtedly to increased customer loyalty and profitability.

However, having obtained my diploma in 1951, I became an associate, as I was under age for full membership (a minimum of 30 years). I became active on subcommittees who, out of their individual members' pockets, financed committee expenses such as stationery, postages, meals etc. Meetings were held mainly in the office of a committee member, generally at 6 p.m.

Irish Exporters' Association

The emphasis of this organisation was on export and many group members contributed to its success, particularly Mr Tom Moran in the initial stages. The latter was a delegate to the export committee at meetings of the Irish Exporters' Association for a number of years.

Irish-American sales' conferences

This involvement was to later lead on to the attendance at meetings with both bodies and in the following years with the arrangement of Irish-American sales' conferences.

Marketing Institute of Ireland (MII)

Much has been said and written over the years about the foundation salesmen, i.e. from 1947 onward. The words of Mr John McGuire, chairman of the Marketing Institute of Ireland, in the special Marketing House brochure issue, in his year of office, 1989, give a short explanation of how the Institute owed its birth and foundation to individuals of the Irish branch who were originally members of the Incorporated Sales Managers' Association.
I, therefore, quote:

> They showed great foresight at the time in recognising the need for a professional body to represent marketing practitioners in Ireland. Marketing, a business function, was greatly misunderstood in the 1960s and their establishment of the Institute was a major milestone in giving the profession a new credibility. Great credit is due to the council and pioneering members who laid the foundation of the Institute's current success when there were no support structures available.
>
> Contributions were extremely important in communicating the role of marketing to various publics such as to government, educational institutions and the business community. Such foundations were vital in laying the path and so enabling the Institute to develop through the 1960s and the 1970s particularly.

Today in marketing circles one involves in the innovative process. First of all, the concept of innovation is examined and follows the various types of organisations involved. Here concern is not alone with products but new expansive services such as tourism, health care, leisure and sophisticated processes of catering for all needs.

Research and development

Irish marketing professionals are aware of the available research and development opportunities to give service to research and development groups to identify by way of an 'exploitation manager'. Their responsibility is to produce a market survey to show research and development in relation to the market and strategy, thus ensuring commercially exploited results.

ECU — research and development funding

In ECU the next research and development programme (Framework V 1999–2020) is currently under negotiation. Ireland has received about IR£20m. from EU research and development funding annually over the period 1994 to 1999.

The new wave of marketing thinking is very much being contributed to by Ireland even though it is a small country. This was particularly evident over the decade 1989–99, which saw a change from traditional consumer and mass marketing to new forms and methods of investigating targets and applied research. Ireland has an increasing dominance of services in its economy. Huge strides have been made in the Irish economy by improvement in growth and competitiveness.

Internet marketing opportunity

The Internet Marketing Opportunity (IMO) provides a new marketing perspective while information is the most important method to impress a client. So traditional marketing skills, experience and techniques continue because the end product is to make the customer the king or queen.

However, the internet provides much more information about products and services than previously possible. It provides many advantageous opportunities including customers to customise products on one's website and opportunities for niche marketing in home, overseas and world cities. The internet and other related changes will be dealt with in more detail later.

THE MARKETING INSTITUTE OF IRELAND 1999–2000 ON THE NATIONAL LEVEL

The Marketing Institute of Ireland (MII) is the voice of the marketing profession with government, public bodies, the media and business in all its aspects. Again the Institute presents, at all opportunities, the case of marketing as the essential, integral part of economic development and growth in Ireland.

The professional body representing marketing practitioners in Ireland today is the Marketing Institute of Ireland. It is the only national body exclusively devoted to marketing education and that acts positively and strongly on behalf of the trading sector.

Marketing at the Millennium

The MII is a national non-profit making organisation, an entirely Irish body. Its headquarters is located at:

> Marketing House
> South County Business Park
> Leopardstown, Dublin 18.
> Telephone: 01 295 2355 Fax: 01 295 2453
> e-mail: info@mii.ie, http://www.mii.ie

The mission of the Marketing Institute is 'Leading, Representing, Educating and Servicing'.

The Institute is governed by a constitutionally elected council with a defined limitation of service by its voluntary serving members. The elected executive comprises of President, Vice-President, Chairman, Deputy Chairman, Honorary Treasurer, Honorary Secretary and a Chairman of Fellows. In addition to further council elected members, regional chairpersons sit on councils, i.e. Kerry, the Mid-West, North-East, North-West, South-East, South and West of Ireland. The staff includes a Chief Executive, Director of Education, Secretary/Administrator, Financial Controller, Marketing and Membership Executive and their respective assistants and other personnel (security, etc.).

On the European marketing front

Irish marketing practitioners are represented by the MII on the European Marketing Confederation (formerly Council). Members of MII have served on the EMC in the honour of president twice. I myself, Harry V. Woods, was the first Irishman to hold the office of president and later, Mr William (Bill) Fraser took office. Delegates from Ireland have attended meetings in about fifteen countries since 1964. Dublin has hosted conferences of the EMC and AGMs. The very valuable chain of office of the EMC was presented to the body by Ireland from Mr Aubrey Fogarty in 1972. The 1996 chairman of MII, Mr Roger Jupp of Landsdowne Market Research Ltd, became vice-president of the EMC (he was still serving in 1999) while Mr John Casey, chief executive, represents MII on the EMC Management Board.

The Single European market

With the involvement of life in the single European market, from 1993, membership of the revitalised European Marketing Confederation (EMC) was deemed essential by the Marketing Institute of Ireland. The MII has full membership status, an honour only granted to one national marketing body in each country.

Marketing Association of Australia and New Zealand and Hong Kong Institute of Marketing

The MII members are now automatically individual members of the EMC. A reciprocal arrangement exists for MII paid-up members to be temporary members of the Marketing Association of Australia and New Zealand and the Hong Kong Institute of Marketing, that is to member only events on visits to them.

European Marketing Diploma

A permanent office has been set up in Brussels, with a part-time European Marketing Confederation Chief Executive and an assistant. Activities include the development of a common standard for education programmes in marketing together with registration of same for European Communities' recognition. An agreed European Marketing Diploma is available.

MII membership services

Members of the Marketing Institute of Ireland are offered a most comprehensive range of services. These essentially help members be aware of developments in marketing, advancing their marketing skills through appropriate learning courses, availing of services useful in their workplace, learning of career opportunities and exchanging business experiences.

Professional Development in Marketing

However well qualified, today's marketing professionals need to constantly update their knowledge and skills. How are they to do this? The most effective way is by attending the specialist seminars of the Professional Development in Marketing Programme (PDM) of the Marketing Institute of Ireland. Presented by top calibre national and international practitioners and academics, these seminars are designed for busy professionals who need to keep abreast of developments in both theory and practice.

PDM courses can also be delivered to companies in-house, or to other groups tailored to specific needs. FÁS, the state employment and training authority, will consider giving grant aid for attending PDM courses.

Regional branches of the Marketing Institute of Ireland

The regional branches of the MII national organisation are situated in the south, the west, Kerry, the mid-west, north-west, north-east and south-east of Ireland. Each region plans a series of events designed to cater for the business community in their particular region. Likewise, each has its own officers and committee, with regional branch representatives on the National Council.

The Institute is very fortunate in having voluntary committees, by precedent over the years, who run the functions and also to have the significant commitment by prominent speakers, some of whom give up their valuable time to make a presentation in more than one region.

Activity reporting of MII events

All of the Institute's activities are regularly reported in *MII News*. If a presentation has given an exceptional marketing insight it is reviewed in the newsletter to bring the details to the wider audience of members. Other publications provided for members include the *Irish Marketing Review*, an excellent publication which includes academic articles and articles on marketing theory. The review is an international journal of research and practice and is supplied to MII members as a members' service since 1986.

Education and the training of MII members and students

The most important role of the Marketing Institute of Ireland is that of education. Students are advised that marketing is the way of doing business, which starts with the customer. It involves a broad range of management skills, from research and product design to advertising and promotion, distribution and sales. A career in marketing may involve all or any of these activities.

Graduateship programme of the MII

The graduateship programme of the Marketing Institute offers four separate qualifications at three levels, each representing a stage in professional development.

Foundation Certificate in Marketing

The Foundation Certificate in Marketing is awarded following the successful completion of a course that provides a foundation in marketing and a general grounding in business.

Certificate in selling

As an alternative to the Foundation Certificate in Marketing this course provides a thorough understanding of the selling function in the overall marketing context. Certificate holders can become Associates of the Marketing Institute.

Diploma

The Diploma follows a more advanced course in marketing management. Holders may apply for full membership of the Institute if they have at least two years relevant business experience.

Graduateship

Graduateship is awarded on completion of a further year's study and accredits the holder as a fully qualified marketing professional with the entitlement to use the letters 'MMII Grad.'.

EMC and the graduateship programme

The graduateship of the Institute is recognised by the European Marketing Confederation (EMC), which represents marketing professionals in thirteen countries.

Modes of study

There are two ways of taking the course — by tuition in a college or by distance learning.

Step into marketing

For a number of years the Institute has been offering a programme specially developed for transition year students in second level schools. 'Step into Marketing' is a self-directed learning programme which covers all the core issues in marketing and finally takes the student through some market research and a sales presentation.

For further information on all programmes email: education@mii.ie.

PART 1

First decade of the history of sales management and marketing in Ireland, 1947–1957

THE FORMATION OF THE IRISH GROUP INCORPORATED SALES MANAGERS' ASSOCIATION (ISMA) — INAUGURAL MEETING APRIL 1947, DUBLIN

The inaugural meeting of eight Irish resident members of the Incorporated Sales Managers 'Association (ISMA) London was held at Jury's hotel, then in Dame Street, Dublin, on 14 April 1947. It resulted in the agreement to form a group to be called the Irish Group Incorporated Sales Managers' Association.

An election was held and the first officers of the group were as follows:

• Chairman: Mr H.N.B. Palmer

• Hon. Secretary/Treasurer: Mr Tom Moran

• Committee: Mr D. Bolton Thom, J.M. Patterson, J.F. Kearney, Donald MacKenzie, H.W. Stephenson and J. Parrett.

Future meetings were arranged for 8 p.m. at Jury's hotel, Dublin. These were to be held on a monthly basis with an informal meal beforehand. The hon. secretary was instructed to apply to the London parent body, ISMA, for a contribution of £1 (one punt) per head of a grant towards the expenses of forming the group in Dublin. Meanwhile it was arranged to hold a committee meeting on 21 April at Wallace Brothers, Coal Merchants, D'Olier Street, Dublin, at 6 p.m. by kind permission of Mr D. Bolton Thom.

Tom Moran, hon. secretary, agreed to have membership application forms available for distribution amongst the group. He was also instructed to inform the committee chairman and members of the council of the Northern Ireland group of the ISMA of the proposed Irish group and to invite them to the next meeting in Dublin.

The second monthly meeting of the ISMA Irish group, held at Jury's hotel on Wednesday 21 May 1947, saw additional new members present, Derek Black and Jim Groves, while apologies were recorded for Joe Bigger, George Orme and Bill Chesson. Mr Donald MacKenzie was elected vice-chairman.

The hon. secretary reported his interview with the ISMA director (London), Mr David Griffiths, who suggested directions for the Irish group:

1. Letter headings should not be printed until official approval came from London.

2. The Irish group should move slowly in building up such a group.

The goal to be aimed at was that the Irish group should, from the outset, be representative of the leading sales managers and sales executives in Ireland. Numbers, at first, were not of prime importance. These would come in automatically *if* a sound foundation was laid at the beginning. A list of approximately twelve to sixteen names of leading men in sales management was to be made out and two or three of those would be approached by a member of the executive committee personally and sold the idea of the Incorporated Sales Managers' Association (Irish group). When such men were 'roped' in Mr Griffiths said that he would come to Dublin anytime after 1 July 1947.

Mr Griffiths warned the Irish group to avoid forming a businessmen's club. However, he said that monthly luncheon meetings with interesting speakers would be very helpful.

A letter was read from the London secretary of ISMA congratulating the Irish members on forming the Irish group and confirming that a grant of twenty pounds towards the expenses of forming the Irish group would be forthcoming. The suggestions of London were approved and committee members instructed to proceed with approaching potentially suitable new members.

The method devised was that each member would submit to the hon. secretary a list of outstanding sales executives and sales managers whom they felt would be necessary to have in the Irish group and be representative of Irish business life.

DUBLIN ROTARY CLUB

A number of members of the Belfast group, Messrs McCoy, Cunningham and Wheeler had replied indicating their interest in the Irish group. It was arranged that Mr David Griffiths of London would address the Dublin Rotary Club in the coming autumn.

The hon. secretary was instructed to inform London that all new applications for membership in Ireland must first be passed through the Dublin group executive. Tom Moran, hon. secretary, was congratulated and thanked sincerely for his liaison work in London on behalf of the Irish group.

DOLPHIN HOTEL, DUBLIN

After the summer recess the Irish group met at the Dolphin hotel, Essex Street,

Dublin, on Tuesday, 11 November 1947. Thirteen members were present with apologies from seven others. A proposal was made that it was the considered opinion of the Dublin group that prospective members be entertained to lunch to hear Mr David Griffiths speak. The cost of the luncheon for prospective members would be met out of London funds.

The press would be invited to hear David Griffiths, not so much for publicity but rather for prospective membership purposes, give his luncheon address to the Rotary at the Shelbourne hotel on 24 November 1947.

The next general meeting was held on 26 February 1948 at No.3, St Stephen's Green. There were nine members present with four apologies. The chairman, Mr Palmer, had arranged for Mr Rant of Belfast to lecture at the School of Technology, Belfast, which was appreciated.

Speakers for the March and April meetings of the group were arranged. In addition, it was decided that the first AGM would be held on Tuesday, 25 May 1948. The hon. secretary was instructed to arrange that letterhead notepaper for the Irish group would be printed after obtaining a block, logo, address etc. from London.

IMPORTING AND ADVERTISING COSTS, 1948

Mr J.M. Patterson gave an interesting and provocative paper on importing and advertising costs. He pointed out the difficulty in obtaining statistics as Irish manufacturers were not prepared to give turnover figures to their advertising people. The wide discussion that followed concluded that a very good start had been made on this first paper address to members. An extremely optimistic note was recorded showing that members had benefited very much indeed from the paper and open discussion that followed.

At the 30 March 1948 meeting held at No.3, St Stephen's Green, Mr Donald MacKenzie addressed the group on what he expected from his representatives. Mr Cathcart, who had spoken at the rotary luncheon on the previous day, congratulated Mr MacKenzie on his grasp of the subject. The next speaker, Mr H.W. Stephenson, agreed to read a paper on the current problems of Irish sales managers.

POLICY AND REQUIREMENTS

Before recording the first AGM, it is important to relate how the Irish group of the Incorporated Sales Managers' Association initially organised policy and requirements. Some of the difficulties encountered would today seem trivial but very serious cognisance were taken of them in the 1940s.

A separate minute book of the executive council meetings was maintained, from the meeting of the first officers. This was held at the offices of

Mr D. Bolton Thom, Wallace Bros, Coal Merchants, on 21 April 1947. It contains a compilation of decisions taken following earnest thought and consideration before any implementation. It is worthy to give some highlights of these.

Initially suitable documentation, e.g. a special letter to selected eligible business executives, including sales managers, set out the intended aims, objectives and functions of the association pointing out the benefits available and intended for members. A special letter was sent inviting attendance to a general open meeting, at which personal reception and introductions took place — not however, before very strict investigations of the possible candidates for membership took place. Even as to what should, or should not, be put on the letter heading for such invitations was a decision in each case. Often existing members used the letter heading of their firm.

The composition of the committee type of individual was also considered. The aim was to obtain branch status, rather than remain a group, at the earliest opportunity possible. Liaison with ISMA London was emphasised, as immediate and continuous, by individual attendance at meetings of committees in London when at all possible. This meant financing travel and other costs often from the individual's own pocket. Mutually, London and Dublin agreed that the outlook was for an independent Irish body of sales managers to be created, but not until sufficient executives were members in Ireland. The recognition then of such numerical executive members and of students and their examinations, would be fully agreed before such a change would take place.

Mr David Griffiths (London Director) maintained that from the outset of the group formation, once the Irish members attained a branch status it would be inevitable that this would lead to the formation of an Irish Sales Managers' Association. It was also stated, in June 1947, that to make finance available to the Irish group would inhibit the Irish from having more freedom to adopt their own procedures. Therefore, it should be the aim to embark on events to develop finance in Ireland for its own independence. Nevertheless, London would meet the Irish group regarding study matters in furthering education, which came under the aims and objectives of the association. Mr Griffiths also stated that for sales management to be effective it must naturally be concerned with politics and therefore, if a separate association was necessary it should be formed in Ireland.

O'NEILL'S WHO'S WHO

Comparative methods of recruitment of members were investigated. One in particular was that of the Dundee branch in England, whose effort to solicit had an effective result. On the lines of the Dundee approach a copy of *O'Neill's Who's Who* was obtained in order to provide the list of principal Irish firms to enhance existing research which had provided some information about the top executive sales personnel. In this way the Irish chairman allocated names to be approached by individual council members.

A grant of ten pounds was received from London towards the cost of the special Rotary Club luncheon meeting and its follow-up of all contacts of likely potential members who were guests at same.

MARKETING JOURNAL, UK

It was regretted, on investigation, that the marketing journal had not reported on the Irish group meetings, London having decided that Dublin luncheon meetings were not of general interest. This decision was thankfully reversed later with the inclusion of a programme for the Irish group.

Membership applications recommended from Dublin were rejected in some cases. This gave rise to the obtaining exact reasons which included further interpretation and clarification of the existing rules. One example of this related to the misunderstanding of what was called an 'area sales manager' in Ireland.

FIRST AGM: ISMA IRISH GROUP, 1948

The first AGM of the Irish group of the ISMA was held at No. 3, St Stephen's Green, on Monday, 7 June 1948. There were eight members present with apologies from seven others of the Irish group and that of Mr Graham of the Northern Ireland group. The hon. treasurer reported an account balance in hand of one pound five shillings and four pence. This, however, had only been created by the fact that the committee had personally paid for the debit of one pound nineteen shillings and sixpence for the luncheon held at the Shelbourne hotel, Dublin, November 1947.

The election of officers resulted in Mr Palmer's re-election as chairman of the Irish group, likewise Mr MacKenzie as vice-chairman, Mr Tom Moran as hon. Secretary and Mr Groves as assistant-secretary and hon. treasurer. The committee members were Mr Derek Black, Mr D. Bolton Thom and Mr H.W. Stephenson. Members not on committee at this stage included Messrs Orme, Patterson, Chesson, McMurray, Groves, Fraser, Kilroy, Bigger, Graham, Midgley and Carton.

At this point all records in the minute book show no Christian names. All names were recorded only as 'Mr'. I have, however, endeavoured to provide Christian names through subsequent knowledge and research. It is worthy of mention also that the apparent small numerical attendance at meetings was due in those days to the commercial occupations of the individuals travelling in the country. Sales managers and sales executives found it difficult to be present at committee meetings. For some, Monday evenings were not possible, while others could not be present on Fridays. From personal knowledge later I recall that this was certainly the case and that in no way was absence an indication of a lack of interest in furthering the group.

At this stage, considerable conversation, negotiation and correspondence took place between the chairman (Irish group) Mr David Griffiths and Mr Stanley Talbot, director and general secretary of ISMA, London respectively. It was stated that the Irish group should build up its numbers starting with student members as London felt that Dublin was starting at the top instead of working from the bottom. This opinion varied with that previously outlined to the group. However, the emphasis on education was mutual.

EDUCATION COMMITTEE ISMA DUBLIN, 1948

An educational sub-committee was set up by the Irish group comprising Messrs Palmer, MacKenzie and Patterson. They arranged to meet with Mr George Clampett, Principal of the College of Commerce, Rathmines, Dublin.

The principal objective was to arrange accommodation for classes for the diploma course of the ISMA. The second important factor stressed by Mr Palmer was that the British Institute of Management were affiliated to the ISMA and the BIM accepted the ISMA as the authoritative body speaking on behalf of sales management. The importance of this relationship could not be overstated. Further, in the next five years the BIM would assume even greater importance as it intended to collate all functions and branches of management.

Concern was expressed by the executive of the ISMA (Irish group), at the lack of support at group meetings, by the main body of individual members. It was decided to publish the names of members in Ireland and that activities of the Irish group be published in the marketing journal but that company names should not be mentioned. The hon. secretary was instructed to seek a grant of one pound per member towards expenses for the current year, particularly for rooms for meetings etc. It was agreed that the question of opening a bank account would not be justified for the present. These decisions were reported to the members generally at the meeting held in Jury's hotel, Dublin, on Monday, 1 October 1948.

A float of twenty pounds was sought from London for incidental expenditure of the group. This was mainly required for the hire of rooms for meetings. At this time committee members personally financed such costs as postages and telephone. They also kept their own committee minute book and records for the particular committee.

The float was refused from London but an account was opened by the group at the Munster and Leinster Bank Ltd, Drumcondra Road, Dublin, on an overdraft basis, for twenty pounds. The latter was guaranteed by the current executive committee.

ACCOUNTANCY IN RELATION TO SALES, NOVEMBER 1948

On Monday, 15 November 1948 the members were addressed at a meeting in Jury's hotel, Dublin, by C. Russell Murphy, ACA, on the subject of accountancy in relation to sales. He expressed the importance of the sales manager in any business undertaking and pointed out that it was not enough to say to a sales manager that sales are down unless all relevant figures are at the sales manager's disposal. Furthermore, he said that the main point to watch in any business was the turnover in relation to gross profits and to beware not to overstress the importance of net profit. He also believed that account system changes should always be submitted to the sales manager. A lively question session then ensued including the debating of manufacturing costs and their importance in providing a competitive quality product.

There were five guest potential members. These were Messrs Polden, McConnell, Young, Orme jun. and Dagg. This showed an increased endeavour and co-operation by members. It was also a tribute to the speaker Mr C. Russell Murphy.

PLANNING A SALES CAMPAIGN, 1948

It was recorded at the December 1948 session, held at No. 3, St Stephen's Green, that the change-over from a sellers' to a buyers' market, occasioned by increased supplies of almost all commodities combined with other factors, such as increased costs and income tax, had all been taken into consideration when planning a sales campaign. Mr Bolton Thom in his talk on sales (in 1948) emphasised that technical knowledge of the fuel, coal, turf, briquettes, anthracite etc. that he was selling, was a very important part of a salesman's equipment.

Previously, fuel bills were small in the family budget and as long as the price was right all went well, but greatly increased costs had made the householder more conscious of the efficiency factor. In addition, the introduction of heat storage and slow combustion appliances had made the public more critical of such aspects. Industrial users now also required technical data on efficiency, rather than price, hence the salesman's necessary increase in knowledge and ability to make recommendations. The latter then had to include supportive efficiency figures, BTU output and so forth.

COAL SALESMANSHIP COURSE, 1948

It was gratifying to note, Mr Thom said, that the Coal Utilisation Council was sponsoring a course in coal salesmanship, divided into two categories — domestic and industrial. It was recognised that the housewife was the prime factor in domestic sales. Sales had to be backed by quality and service, it was agreed, otherwise the business would be easily lost to a competitor who gave greater satisfaction. Again, the sales manager had to be conversant with the problem of credit, even though this was mainly the concern of the department of accounts, and also give his opinion and decision on occasions.

DIRECT MAIL ADVERTISING IN THE FUEL INDUSTRY, 1948

In advertising, Mr Thom stated that it was a mistake to make extravagant claims regarding performance, rather it was wiser to recommend an efficiency with confidence. Reputation was built on reliability. Direct mail advertising, based on carefully selected lists, had shown excellent results in the fuel industry. Colourful attractive literature produced better results than long circulars, which were often unread. He further found a 15–20 per cent response was not unusual in his experience.

OPENING MEETING ISMA, 1949

The opening meeting of the year 1949 was held at Jury's hotel, Dublin, as usual. It was specially convened to have present visitors including Mr Smyth of the London Council of the ISMA, Mr Bowden from Belfast, Northern Ireland, Mr Tweedale, Mr Ronayne, Mr Murphy and Mr White. The importance of the ISMA was stressed by the Irish group chairman, Mr Palmer, and in particular its need and importance in Ireland. The group hoped shortly to be in a position to achieve full branch status.

ECONOMIC FUNCTION OF ADVERTISING

Mr Bill Chesson, in his address to members, gave what was described as a 'masterly paper' on the economic function of advertising. He went on to say that during and after the emergency (Second World War), public attention had been focused on distributive costs and particularly advertising brands which were discarded in favour of advertised goods before the emergency (1939–45) as they were found to be cheaper and just as satisfactory as branded goods.

Advertising: economists' criticism

Advertising came in for adverse criticism because of the methods used and, as an example, Mr Chesson referred to the fear motive. Economists of the time had drawn certain conclusions, e.g. that school children should be inoculated against the wiles of advertisers and that advertising cheapened production costs, cheapened distribution, promoted inventions and improvements and created new wants.

Mr Chesson felt the truth lay somewhere between these two statements. In Ireland, hitherto, advertising had been left out of the economic picture but it was beginning to be realised that the mass distribution necessary for mass production could only be obtained through advertising. In assessing the economic function of advertising the questions to consider were:

1. Does advertising tend to increase the demand for goods as a whole?

2. Does advertising tend to increase or decrease distributive costs?

3. Are there similar reproduction costs?

4. Does advertising create semi-monopolies for individual manufacturers?

5. Does advertising tend to cause rigidity of prices?

Advertising: variety of gainful results

Collectively the answers would reply to the question: Has modern advertising any economic function and if so, what is it? Opinion on advertising at that time (and most likely today also) held that:

• advertising was the great educator of the consumer through an organised technique of persuasion

• advertising claimed to have contributed to the rise in standards of living, during the past 50 years, without claiming to have created it

• advertising had cheapened many consumer goods by enabling them to gain sales large enough to justify mass production

• advertising had improved standards of cleanliness, sanitation and, to some degree, health

• advertising had built up an efficient newspaper and periodical press throughout the world.

Finally, every government department was using advertising on a considerable scale. In short, modern government practice dictated that advertising could be an indispensable technique for public information and education.

EDUCATION OF SALES EXECUTIVES, 1949

On the subject of the education of sales executive personnel the speaker at the Jury's hotel March 1949 meeting, was F.D. Tweedale (Irish Correspondance College). He stated that personality was important and that schoolboys were frequently classed as good or bad, funny or pugnacious, bookworms or sports. He stressed that personality should be classed as the first requirement of a sales executive. This, added to the essential training and actual experience would gain the best results.

The Institute of Industrial Administration was registered in 1922 as a specially authorised society for the promotion of education in their administration. The main aims of the Institute were to formulate standards of knowledge, training, conduct and experience to practice. Those qualified promoted the education of students.

Mr Tweedale posed the all important question: Where are the theoretically trained salesmen of the day to be given the practical experience considered necessary by firms advertising vacancies? It was agreed that the formation of a students' group in Dublin would be most welcome and that the members of the Dublin group would give the students every assistance in obtaining practical experience. Now, the important position was the professional training of entrants to the field of sales management. Mr Thomas, of Cambridge branch of the ISMA was made most welcome at a further meeting in March 1949. The speaker then was Mr Exley, manager for Éire of the British Tabulating Machine Company, who gave an absorbing paper on how the Hollerett Punch Card System could produce sales statistics. Forms were handed out to members, demonstrated and used, showing fully how they could be used by sales managers. Mr Exley stated that to be effective a sales manager had to be able to discover from the invoices all the statistics he required quickly.

SECOND AGM OF ISMA IRISH GROUP, 1949

The second AGM of the Irish group of the ISMA was held at Jury's hotel on Monday, 2 May 1949. It was presided over by Mr H.N.B. Palmer with ten members present and apologies from three others. Mr Thomas, of the Cambridge branch, attended as a guest. Again it was hoped to reach branch status during the coming year. Membership at this time was: Fellow 1, Members 25, Associates 8, a total of thirty-four. The work (over a period of two years) of the outgoing chairman, Mr H.N.B. Palmer, was highly praised. He could not be persuaded to continue in office, though he would retain an active interest. Mr Donald MacKenzie was then elected chairman. He aspired to:

• increase the membership to enable branch status to be obtained

• secure an increased attendance at regular monthly meetings

• secure top speakers to stimulate the imagination of sales managers.

Through the widely issued and read journal, *Marketing*, he appealed to all members, north, south, east and west to attend the opening meeting of the new session on Monday, 3 October 1949. Mr Derek Black was elected vice-chairman, Mr Thom as hon. secretary, Mr Parrett as hon. treasurer and the committee comprised of Mr H.N.B.Palmer, Mr T.A. Moran and Mr H.W. Stephenson. A proposal by Mr Tom Moran that the group co-operate with the Minister of Industry and Commerce in his efforts to counter the objections to Irish manufactured goods was agreed by all present.

It was reported in September 1949 that the London executive committee had agreed to deposit the required twenty pounds in any bank nominated by the Irish group, on condition that a monthly finance statement be submitted to the national finance committee on a petty cash float basis.

IMPRESSIONS ON SELLING IN IRELAND, 1949

Mr Derek Black presided, in the unavoidable absence of the chairman, at the opening meeting, 3 October 1949 of the new session at Jury's hotel, Dublin. Visitors present were Mr Leslie Whitehead, Bristol branch, Mr Thomas and Mr Ibberston. Mr Whitehead spoke on the subject: 'My Impressions on Selling in Ireland', as compared with marketing in England. Thanking the group for the opportunity to address them he first emphasised the importance of student groups and the quality of membership for the success of any branch. On taking up his position in Ireland he found that business was not highly organised and that dealers throughout the country were 'happy-go-lucky', while after sales service was lacking. He was struck with the small populations in scattered areas. Dealers appeared to offer very few listed price lists and allowances of 10–15 per cent seemed to be a common procedure. Mr Whitehead considered that service was not given owing to these special allowances. Why, he asked, should a trader reduce his profit? Selling here in Ireland was on price and not on quality and service, proving the necessity for fixed prices. Mr Ibbertson (visitor) said he was now three months in Ireland and agreed that traders allowed too many allowances, because most Irish people knew someone whom they got an allowance from. He believed that this was all wrong. Delays in quotations, deliveries etc. also contributed to the loss of business.

Mr Bill Fraser said Irish products, in his experience, sold in good quality but agreed that difficulties arose occasionally over fixed-price articles. He reminded members that they were in the first generation of industry and that salesmen were perhaps slow on making their reports. Mr Black stated that where a trader was found making special prices, he immediately cut off supplies, as he was very particular regarding price-cutting. Also a new member, a Mr Brennan, said he did not agree that in Ireland, firms were any different to overseas firms, as in his experience he could get several prices for the same fixed-price commodity from ten or twelve English firms. He considered that advertising was the source of a lot of trouble and the English did not understand the Irish temperament, as could be observed in their advertising. Mr Whitehead, replying, appreciated the importance of advertising in Ireland being written by Irish publicity agents who knew their readers.

In proposing a vote of thanks to the speaker, Mr Patterson thought one most important point had been missed — that we in Ireland were first and foremost of the clay, agriculture and cattle dealing people, and that we were only one generation from the clay. This, he felt, counted for our distrust of Irish goods. Furthermore, he stated that we were a suspicious people.

PERSONNEL MANAGEMENT CONFERENCE: BRIGHTON, NOVEMBER 1949

At the evening meeting for open members at Jury's hotel on 7 November 1949, Mr Palmer reported on his visit to the personnel management conference in Brighton. Mr Whitehead referred to the British Institute of Management statement current. This stated that there were some 50,000 unemployed people in Dublin. Mr Tweedale wondered what the causes were — lack of salesmanship, leadership or marketing? He also enquired if it was in the power of the Irish group of the ISMA to influence those responsible for industry and the welfare of the population. The members believed that the establishment of a student group and the obtaining of branch status were of first importance. They felt there was a lack of material to help salesmen (indoor and outdoor) as well as a need for the the increased output of goods at home, rather than imports, and to conversely increase exports. It was agreed that industry must produce goods competitive with imported goods. Certain Irish manufactured products were named as needing improvement urgently. It was known that at this time good sales must commence with the sales director setting policy and drawing the attention of the powers that be to the general trend of affairs.

PRINTING: SUPPLY DIFFICULTIES, 1949

Printing came in for serious comment. According to one member present, it was not being produced in Ireland within a reasonable time. This was discounted somewhat by another who said that, after certain difficulties, he was now getting work done most satisfactorily and it was also being delivered to him within the time stated and honoured by English printing firms. However, it was agreed that unfortunately trade union restrictions were crippling the printing trade. It was found that it was better to manufacture good products rather than to produce many articles.

This, deemed a most satisfactory and progressive meeting, resulted in the following decisions to be investigated:

• the formation of a small committee to meet members of the Dublin Chamber of Commerce for general discussion

- the production of goods and articles to be of good quality
- the status of sales management
- to invite representatives of the Federated Employers to consult with on production
- to invite members of the press to be present at specific meetings.

Mr Murdock, a visitor at the meeting, felt that the group should stimulate agricultural labourers and farmers to be progressive. Mr Blair, a member, said industry must be developed in the rural areas.

In Roberts Cafe, Grafton Street, Dublin, on Thursday, 24 November a special luncheon meeting of the executive took place to arrange a programme of speakers for member meetings, over the period from January to the end of the session of May 1950.

REMUNERATION: SALES PERSONNEL, 1949

The end of 1949 found thirteen members and three visitors at the 5 December meeting at Jury's hotel. The question was posed: What was the opinion of sales managers regarding the remuneration of their salesmen? Was it better to pay salary plus commission, salary or commission only, or some other method? It was also debated how to cover expenses, car, subsistence etc. One opinion was that a salary sufficient to cover normal living expenses plus commission would be the best incentive. Another speaker felt that firms who paid commission only were somewhat shady. An enlightened trend of thought was produced by another member. He stated that the essentials were that the representative should have economical security, goods of good quality to sell and a superannuation pension scheme to provide for his retirement.

Members were in agreement that it was essential that a pension scheme and salary sufficient to keep an individual in comfort and without worry were the ideal to aim for.

On the commission front, it was stated that it should not be paid until the sale was completed to the purchaser's satisfaction. In order to be different another individual was of the opinion that speciality selling demanded good commission and a small salary. However, he failed to see why a pension should be provided when one could save instead. Salesmen should be retired at 65 years it was felt, but with an appropriate pension. Mr McMurray, a member, referred to the K.C.A. scheme whereby unemployed or sick members could draw five pounds for a week or even two pounds ten shillings for three days, while on reaching 65 years they would draw a lump sum plus compound interest. This would show a gain of one-third of the original investment sum paid in, but unfortunately the scheme did not operate in Éire.

A question was raised about a salesman, a junior at that, who was earning more on commission than the remuneration of the sales director. Caution was also expressed regarding the best way to handle a situation where a trusted salesman was getting too old to cover his territory and resented an assistant being appointed.

Tact was required by the sales director to produce the right approach to ensure little trouble arose. Each member was asked to procure a new member for the group to ensure that branch status would be attained in 1950. It was satisfying discussing sales management problems but then other functions arose, particularly in relation to numerical growth. It was decided that the first thing to do should be to organise a student society to assist students during their training.

MEETING OF ISMA, JANUARY 1950

The decade of 1950 started well on 2 January. The chairman, Donald MacKenzie, had a reply from David R. Griffiths, director of ISMA London, regarding the Irish group obtaining possible branch status in the near future. Also Mr MacKenzie proposed the formation of an educational committee to view steps to meet the principals of the technical schools so that the ISMA examinations would be included in their syllabus. At this time students could still only avail of correspondence courses. The desired committee was agreed on and formed as: R.J. Blair, J.M. Patterson, H.N.B. Palmer and Leslie V. Whitehead.

SALES AND PSYCHOLOGY, 1950

An open discussion took place on the subject of sales and psychology. It was the opinion of Leslie Whitehead that in the study of the mind, it was important to appeal to the emotions. He provided examples of this for example, when envy of one's neighbours' possessions was sufficient to procure a sale. Mr Palmer believed that an appeal to the senses was necessary. Nevertheless, Mr Patterson considered that goods do not require selling, but that one had to sell oneself by sound of the voice, appeal to sense of taste, etc. Mr Black agreed to the presentation of oneself as a subject for much discussion as well as the appeal man-to-man, the difficult buyer, etc. On the other hand, Mr Parrett referred to the finding out about the buyer's outside interests as paving the way for future more smooth interviews. Finally, Tom Moran added that it was his belief that salesmen must keep their ears open and mix well with people.

SALESMANSHIP CAREER FOR A MAN

A book entitled *Salesmanship Career for a Man*, by Martin E. Perry, was recommended for study. Leslie Whitehead had read it in Bristol and recommended it to all interested in sales.

Mr Blair reported on the educational committee progress. He stated that a meeting had been arranged with Mr Clampett of the technical schools for March 1950.

At the 6 March 1950 meeting of members, Mr Parrett reported that, in response to an appeal for funds in connection with the conference, 'How America Sells', to be held in London, he had received six pounds and ten shillings which he sent to London.

AER LINGUS TEO (IRISH AIRLINES) EXPANSION, 1950

The speaker at this Irish group meeting in Dublin was Felix O'Neill, sales representative of Aer Lingus Teo (Irish Airlines).

He gave members a picture of the difficulties that had to be overcome in order to make Irish people 'airminded' and related the history of the build-up of Aer Lingus. His figures of expansion were most impressive. The approach to freight developments was appreciated by the attendance and the statistics, relating to some fourteen years, were declared phenomenal.

Questions to him concerned custom clearance, advertising, private hire, special terms for business executives etc. during the winter months, insurance against delays as well as many others.

Mr Blair reported at the meeting of 3 April 1950 that Mr Clampett, principal of the College of Commerce, Rathmines, was willing to co-operate in providing classes for students. However, Mr Blair considered that it would be some time before any definite arrangements would be forthcoming. Nevertheless, members should encourage any available students to enrol. Secondary schools should be advised of the course and ISMA members should consider producing individuals from their own staff. On enquiry of those present at the meeting, four members said a total of five students would come from their firms. One of the delegates, over for the 'How America Sells' conference, a Mr Donald Sloan of Portland, Oregan, had visited Mr Derek Black in Dublin and the latter reported on this to the meeting.

It was concluded that not enough publicity was being sought by the ISMA Dublin group to put it on the map. Advertising meetings in the daily press, the printing of a list of members and the holding of a ladies night at the commencement of the next session were all considered.

THIRD AGM: ISMA IRISH GROUP, 1950

The third AGM of ISMA Irish group, was held on 1 May 1950 at Jury's hotel as usual. There were fourteen members present and an apology given for Mr Bill Chesson. The outgoing chairman, Donald MacKenzie, referred to weaknesses of the group's activities akin to the aims and objects of the association. However, progress items included the appointment of an educational officer and sub-committee with hopeful development in the near future. Membership had increased but inadequately. Mr Palmer said London had now officially authorised the opening of a bank account and advanced the sum of twenty pounds for such purpose.

The Dublin group members' contribution of six pounds ten shillings towards the expenses of the American sales executives' visit, was very satisfactory and appreciated. Mr Derek Black was elected new chairman. Mr Thom, vice-chairman, Mr Blair as hon. secretary, while Mr Parrett agreed to re-election as hon. treasurer. After a ballot election the committee was announced as Messrs Whitehead, Palmer and Patterson. In order to increase membership, Mr Palmer suggested contacts be made at the forthcoming Royal Dublin Society spring show at Ballsbridge.

Further luncheon meetings were suggested while the day of the week to have them and/or evening meetings required survey. Failing agreement at this AGM, it was agreed that a questionnaire be sent to members as well as appointing a programme sub-committee.

FIRST ISMA DIPLOMA EXAMINATIONS IN DUBLIN, JUNE 1950

The High School of Commerce, Rathmines, Dublin was considered for holding examinations for the diploma and these were duly held there for the first time in June 1950. Mr George Clampett, the principal at Rathmines, was thanked for his assistance in making this possible.

ISMA STUDENTS FIRST AGM, JUNE 1950

At this time also a students' AGM was held at which its officers were duly elected. They were:

- Vice-Chairman: Mr Dawson

- Hon. Secretary: Mr Daly

- Librarian: Mr Kelly.

No christian names were recorded while the chairman of the group education committee was automatically chairman of the student society. All student study was by correspondence courses. Contact with members of the group not attending open and monthly meetings was met with individual members of the executive making a personal call on them, a suggestion originated by Mr Leslie Whitehead.

FIRST IRISH ISMA EDUCATION COMMITTEE, JUNE 1950

It was Mr Leslie Whitehead who also announced the first executive education committee. This comprised of Messrs Bill Fraser, Tom Moran, Stephen Doyle and H.N.B. Palmer. Students meetings were held in the early years in what was described as 'outside centres'. This meant a premises where no charge was made for accommodation, generally an office, as no finance was available. The education committee also invited firms to send representatives to such meetings, with a view to providing students for the diploma course.

Mr Peter Colley, member of the ISMA group, volunteered and was accepted as Press Officer. As students were spread over a wide area this made it impossible to get them together and consequently resulted in poor attendance at meetings.

STUDENT LIAISON WITH NORTHERN IRELAND, JUNE 1950

Mr C.R.O. Morrison, ASMA, of Belfast undertook membership liaison with students in the Northern Ireland group and for the provision of a suitable meeting place.

Mr William Wilson likewise offered such. In acceptance of these offers, an invitation was extended to either of them to serve as deputy chairman of the Irish group education committee.

LAW IN RELATION TO SALES: GORE-GRIMES, OCTOBER 1950

Mr Gore-Grimes, Solicitor, gave a most interesting and entertaining talk on the subject, the law in relation to sales, at the October 1950 meeting. The hon. treasurer, Mr G.A. Parrett, had unfortunately been injured in the Holyhead mail-boat crash, a rail accident en route to the vessel, but was fortunately progressing favourably.

The holding of a Ladies' Night was seriously discussed and a social sub-committee formed to explore their possibilities and make recommendations. Mr Bill Chesson offered the use of the Aspro Hall for the purpose. Mr Vic Adey was elected to the social committee, to which it was hoped Mr Bill Chesson would join.

TRAINING OF SALESMEN OUTLINED, NOVEMBER 1950

Mr Leslie Whitehead proposed the formation of a students' society. He spoke on the subject of 'training salesmen to close sales' in considerable detail and under the following headings:

• representative or salesman

• preparation and presentation

• the prospect does not give a hoot about you

• sales are made by agreement not arguments

• enthusiasm is infectious

• when to ask for the order

• the secondary decision

• action gets action

• how to apply pressure.

However, there was disagreement as some members thought of difficulties, e.g. how to get interviews and that more use of the telephone should be made. It was said by Mr Whitehead, speaker, that the issue of prepared statements, doctrine he meant, to salesmen, would be a good way of training salesmen who would learn to remember and use but not to sound parrot-like. Those present voiced their appreciation of the amount of time and preparation put into the talk.

FINAL MEETING, DECEMBER 1950

Members present at the December 1950 final meeting totalled twelve plus seven apologies recorded, and three guests welcomed. An increase in activity and achievement was felt. Those present included regular supporting members such as Joe Bigger, Stephen Doyle, A. Vic Adey, D.M. Milmo, P.G. Kilroy, H.J. Hawley, P.J. Kavanagh and members of the executive.

Arrangements for the holding of the first Ladies' Night were well in hand and booking forms for an expected outstanding event had been mailed to members. The date of the function was to be the 12 January 1951 at Jury's hotel, Dame Street. This was later changed to Aspro Ltd, Naas Road, (Dublin premises).

A change of office of hon. secretary became necessary due to the transfer of Mr Blair to England. This resulted in Mr A. Vic Adey being co-opted in his place until the next AGM.

The Dublin group secretary was instructed to obtain twenty-five copies of the aims and objects of the association from London. At the same time members of the recently formed group student society were invited to the members' luncheon meeting of 9 February 1951, at Jury's hotel, Dame Street, Dublin. The cost to members and their guests was seven shillings and six-pence each.

Mr Leslie Whitehead reported on the first meeting of the students' society and of the officers elected to its committee. Future society meetings would be held on the third Friday of each month, commencing on 16 February 1951. Members of the group would be welcomed at such meetings.

To help the formation of a library, members were now asked to donate suitable books for the benefit of students.

SELLING 'RECORDS', 1951

A paper on the subject 'Selling Records', was given by Mr R.J. Blair. He said successful business must have adequate sales control and complete and up-to-date selling records. Mr Joe Bigger voiced the difficulty of recruiting suitable persons to maintain such 'records'. Others agreed but said it was a full-time important job and not a part-time occupation, as most firms thought.

ISMA HISTORY OUTLINED, 1911–51

It is worthy to emphasise the enhanced attendance at the 9 February 1951 group meeting luncheon at Jury's hotel, as new names of members appeared. Those present were Messrs Palmer, Whitehead, Doyle, Stephenson, C.J. Orme, Moran, Kavanagh, Milmo, McClune, Fraser, Parkinson, Hanley, Tweedale, Thorn, Wilson, MacKenzie, Thom and Adey (eighteen), with some 22 guests, an overall total of 40.

Apologies were recorded for Messrs Chesson, Moffett, McMurray, Kilroy, Paine, Rant, Midgley, Parle, Graham, McGuinness and McConnell (eleven). The speaker was Mr J.B. Barker, FSMA, RSA, the vice-chairman and chair-man-elect of the London branch of the ISMA. The latter gave a very interesting paper on the ISMA's history, activities and achievements. He outlined the history of the ISMA during the 40 years since its foundation (1911). At that time he suggested that sales managers were virtually managers of salesmen rather than administrators of sales and sales policy. He referred to the development of the association's functions, and to the general growth of policy, whereby recognition of its usefulness had been obtained both in industrial, commercial and government circles. He stressed the importance of education as being one of the highest duties of any branch and so that, as a result of examinations and the constant flow of qualified men and women, they would, in due course, become full members of the association. The most successful branch was the one that remained most faithful to the original aims of the association, i.e. to provide for members, and visiting sales managers, a forum at which problems attached to sales technique could be fairly and freely discussed. Meetings which had no concern with selling should be, he went on to say, discouraged and it must always be the aim to arouse interest in the association's activities and to give the member the best possible service.

SALES OFFICE ORGANISATION, 1951

Mr A.G. Stock, FCIS, gave a talk on the place of the sales office in commercial organisations. The sales department was only one of the many departments of a company formed primarily to provide for the shareholders, he told his audience. Friction often took place between sales and accounts offices and, he suggested, that at times sales managers believed that their department was the pivot around which the whole organisation revolved. On the other hand, accountants on occasions could see no reason for a sales department at all. He said each department should have its own responsibilities clearly defined and every effort should be made to understand the other's point of view to avoid friction at all costs. It would be a good idea for a sales manager to spend time in the accounts department and for the accountant to spend time on the road.

The sales office job was to get business, in close harmony with the works and within scope of general policy laid down by the board. Further he stressed that the sales office should not be bogged down with paper work which the accounts department could readily handle.

All staff should be informed of new lines, bearing in mind they could become salesmen during their normal social activities. The sales office could often provide information to the accounts department on the question of credit, not normally available through business channels. In other words, accounts and sales departments should liaise with one another. This applied particularly to a decision before final action was taken to enforce payment of an account, or in the event of a complaint being received from a customer. Advertising must be considered by the sales office with other departments contributing to advantage. Staff should be used as salesmen, with paperwork being left to the accounts department. The sales office should concentrate solely on the all-important sales.

Members voiced their opinion that those in a sales office should be chosen more advantageously by the sales manager. The question also arose as to whether advertising brought in the orders, and not whether it suited individual tastes.

TREATY OF PARIS, APRIL 1951 (ECSC)

The Treaty of Paris, signed on 18 April 1951, created the European Coal and Steel Community (ECSC). It was signed by Belgium, France, Germany, Italy, Luxembourg and the Netherlands. This resulted in increased trade in such products at this outset.

Also in April 1951, the next student examinations were reported as arranged for 24, 25, 26 of May at the High School of Commerce, Rathmines, Dublin, and that an invigilator had been appointed. In the meantime, a student society meeting would take place at the Grosvenor hotel, Westland Row, Dublin, to which group members were encouraged to attend, to support the students. ISMA London proposed increasing membership subscriptions while the Irish group did not enjoy the same facilities as branches in the UK. However, in view of the intention to apply for full branch status, it was considered unwise to comment on the proposed increase.

DIRECT MAIL SELLING, 1951

On the subject of selling by direct mail, an open discussion took place, producing many interesting viewpoints and methods of usage to produce best the impact and consequent ascending market share.

FOURTH AGM OF ISMA IRISH GROUP, 1951

The fourth AGM of the Irish group of the ISMA was held on 11 May 1951 at Jury's hotel. There were twelve members present with apologies of four recorded.

ISMA LADIES' NIGHT FIRST IRISH FUNCTION, JANUARY 1951

The first Ladies' Night had been held the previous January and much appreciation was expressed of the gesture by member Bill Chesson and his co-directors in Aspro Ltd, in making available their large hall on the Naas Road, Dublin, and the other facilities afforded in such generous manner. This was endorsed by the members present. The social committee was congratulated on the organisational success of the evening.

Mr D.M. Milmo agreed to act as hon. treasurer during the absence of Mr Parrett while Mr A.V. Adey would substitute, for the remaining part of the session, for Mr Blair, who had been transferred to Birmingham, England, by his company.

Urgency now was for a new membership drive and to get the right type of salesman for student registration. Derek Black, the chairman observed that only properly trained salesmen could achieve full recognition amongst the profession. The acting hon. treasurer presented a report showing that the total expenditure for the year was thirty-two pounds twelve shillings and five pence. Due to the generosity of the directors of Aspro Ltd, no loss had incurred on the first Ladies' Night, in fact three pounds one shilling and eight pence remained to the credit of the gift scheme and was so carried forward. This was the surplus on donations and gifts collected for the ladies' gift bags presented to them on the night.

Mr D. Bolton Thom became the new chairman with Mr Tweedale as hon. secretary and Mr Parrett as hon. treasurer. After an election, the following were announced as committee members: Messrs Milmo, Fraser, Adey, Kavanagh, Patterson, Moran, Chesson, and McClune (eight). Leslie Whitehead was unanimously declared as education chairman. The programme chairman would be Derek Black, membership chairman A. Vic Adey and social chairman Bill Chesson.

RDS, RECRUITMENT VENUE FOR NEW ISMA MEMBERS, 1951

It was agreed to again take a room at the Dublin Horse Show in Ballsbridge and also at the Spring Show there, to aid the recruitment of suitable new members. The new membership committee would give this matter their attention. Emphasis would in future be on luncheon meetings rather than evening meetings as the former would provide a better opportunity to do membership propaganda work.

At the September 1951 luncheon meeting the speaker was Mr William Thompson. A lively discussion took place following his paper which related to the role of public relations in business, its organisation and implementation.

DIRECT MAIL ADVERTISING: PETER OWENS, 1951

The next group meeting was held on 12 October 1951 at No. 3, St Stephen's Green. The guests included Mr and Mrs Peter Rackow (Cinema and General Publicity), Peter Colley (Sydney Barton Ireland Ltd) and Mr Hingerty and Mr O'Sullivan (courtesy of Rory Barnes). Mr Peter Owens addressed the meeting on the subject of direct mail advertising. He made the point that very few firms in the Republic of Ireland were using direct mail successfully, while it could be used to advantage under proper instruction. Mr Bill Chesson in reply and thanking the speaker, agreed that direct mail advertising was in its infancy in Ireland.

PEPSI-COLA SALES PROMOTION, 1951

The Metropole Ballroom, O'Connell Street, Dublin was the venue for the 9 November 1951 luncheon meeting. The speaker was Mr Leslie V. Swalby of Pepsi-Cola who gave a presentation on sales promotion. The members present also provided a lively contribution about their experiences. The vote of thanks to Mr Swalby was elegently delivered by Mr W. Wilson, of the Northern Ireland group, after he had made a summary of remarks, following his own contribution.

ISMA LONDON TIGHTENS STATUS

At a 7 December 1951 specially convened executive committee meeting of the Irish group, Mr Leslie Whitehead reported that London was generally tightening up on the number of groups and indeed branches. In the Irish group situation they now stated they were not prepared to grant branch status to them unless members had ten to twelve years membership of ISMA. As a comparison, ISMA secretary, Mr R.J. Morgan, said that branch status had not been granted yet to South Africa or Australia and went on to say that the Irish group had a choice to either remain as a group of ISMA or form their own association. In the event of the latter, the situation relating to applications for membership from Ireland would be that associate rather than membership would be the UK ruling. In view of the above, the council of the Irish group sought further replies as to status recognition, particularly in the event of the formation of its own independent association. London's opinion was also sought as to what was best for sales management in Ireland.

Applications for membership in Ireland were being very rigidly scrutinised and in some cases being referred back for student study. The ruling of London at that time was, that even though an applicant had only one or two subjects to pass in his final examinations, he would have to wait until all papers were passed before being considered for associateship. This was so even though the candidate had qualified through work experience, etc. Similarly, in the case of what was referred to as 'young age', despite having the experience, one would have to await the age minimum of thirty years before being eligible for full membership status in the ISMA.

LET'S DO AN AD!: D.M. PATTERSON, 1952

The 11 of January 1952 saw Mr D.M. Patterson MSMA as the speaker. This was the first occasion when the members title of MSMA was used in the minute book. The subject was 'Let's do an ad!' Sales managers were advised to use an advertising expert if they wanted to advertise. The speaker gave a most thorough demonstration of how to do an advertisement. Members appreciated the detail outlined. Some new members were present at the meeting including Messrs Saunders and Kelly.

Mr Morrison of Belfast duly joined the education sub-committee from 8 January 1952. Hence an education meeting was arranged for Belfast to be held on 8 February 1952. This meeting was, however, subsequently postponed.

FIRST CORK ISMA MEMBER, 1952

A special executive committee meeting was held at the offices of the Mercantile Credit Company at Dame Street, Dublin on 1 February, 1952. Welcomed particularly at the meeting was Mr Bob Moffett, the only Cork member of the group. On the question of the application for branch status, it was then understood by the chairman (Irish group) that Belfast members were seeking to retain their group status. London individual executive members had divergent views on the future of the Irish group. Taking into account various comments of individuals, it was finally felt that, just as the Institute of Secretaries and the Advertising Association had expanded in Ireland by running their own affairs, the formation of an Irish association, working in co-operation with London, would initially be the best answer to the problem. It was again agreed to apply for branch status and to press the issue.

ISMA JOINT MEETING BELFAST, 1952

A joint meeting was held in Belfast on 10 March 1952 with a combined satisfactory agreement on the branch issue situation. It must be recorded that at this time much executive and committee work was organised and progressed, notably by Leslie Whitehead, Bill Chesson, Don MacKenzie, H.N.B. Palmer, Stephen Doyle, Norman McConnell, Bill Fraser, A. Vic Adey, Derek Black, Leslie Thorn, D.M. Milmo, J.B. Thom, W.S. Kelly, Joe Bigger and Tom Moran, all of whom in my knowledge, were stalwarts in the endeavours of many years following.

MEMBERSHIP OF ISMA AGE LIMIT, 1952

An appeal about the minimum age limit for associate membership failed, as London insisted on the thirty-year minimum. The test case put forward lost a considerably experienced applicant who would have added knowledge and enhanced the group membership.

HIRE PURCHASE, 1952

Visitors at the March 1952 meeting of the group were introduced and included Michael Coote, Fred Ward, Jack Simpson, and Messrs Conway and Lonergan. The speaker was A. Vic Adey, MSMA, Mercantile Credit Company and the subject was hire purchase. The subject, he said, was complex but he provided headings and explanations about such important items as, why purchase should be hired, its relationship to various trades and the mechanics of successful use. The statistics were revealing and covered an extensive period up to the current time.

AMERICAN SALES TECHNIQUES, 1952

At the evening meeting in the Royal Hibernian hotel, Dawson Street, Dublin on 25 April 1952, the response to a circular to members regarding branch status was widely discussed. Mr Leslie Whitehead gave his personal impressions, gathered whilst attending the conference in London last autumn, on 'How America Sells'. This was arranged by the ISMA London in conjunction with the Sales and Marketing Executives Inc., New York. The differences between American sales methods and Irish sales techniques were then fully outlined and considered.

FIFTH AGM OF ISMA IRISH GROUP, 1952

The fifth AGM of the Irish group of the ISMA was held at 16 St Stephen's Green, Dublin on 9 May 1952. Mr B.D. Thom presided with fifteen members present including myself (Harry Woods) who was formally introduced to colleagues. I had obtained my diploma while not quite having the minimum 30 years of age but had given support to branch meetings and to the education committee during the previous year.

The outgoing chairman said it was a matter of regret that branch status had not been achieved during his term of office. While the education committee, who had met twelve times during the session, had progressed considerably, the membership committee had encountered difficulties. He also stated that London failed to realise that the conditions in Ireland were quite different to those applying in England.

MEMBERSHIP OF ISMA IRISH GROUP, 1952

Following a further intended application for branch status, if it again failed, the question of a separate Sales Managers' Association for Ireland would arise. Current membership stood at forty-five. Congratulations were extended to the committee chairmen for the work they had done during the year, and in particular to Leslie Thorn who acted as MC on Ladies' Night 1952, for such a successful evening. The profit on Ladies' Night had amounted to twenty-six pounds and ten shillings.

BUSINESS REPLY ENVELOPE INTRODUCED, 1952

It was announced that the GPO had agreed to institute the business reply envelope shortly. This would be a great facility for use by members. A tribute was paid to Major Wilson, of the Presbyterian Association, for placing the meeting room at disposal at short notice.

The new chairman was announced as Mr Leslie Whitehead. The officers being: vice-chairmen (three for the first time) Bill Chesson, A. Vic Adey and Stephen Doyle, hon. secretary, Mr W.S. Kelly and the hon. treasurer, Mr D.M. Milmo. Serving members of the executive committee were re-elected en bloc, while the number was increased by the addition of the newly elected Stephen Doyle, Norman McConnell, Joe Bigger, Leslie Thorn and Max Moffett. In addition to the previous committees for programme, social and membership, a new committee, export, was created. Its first chairman, Tom Moran, announced its member content.

By a unanimous decision it was agreed that the group become members of the Dublin Chamber of Commerce. The possibilities of having a golf outing were being explored and it was decided to make it open to members, friends and potential members to play. The executive committee was asked to investigate the provision of a chairman's badge of office for the group.

ISMA SYLLABUS, 1952–53

The syllabus of 1952–53 referred to the fact that, in the development of sales management, the codifying of best practices, most of the work had been done at branch meetings in the course of free discussion between members drawn from different sections of industry. It was also agreed that the asscociation, in totem, had been fortunate in the number of its members who regularly and consistently supported meetings. This sense of loyalty, which compelled a man to take a keen interest in the activities of his professional association, had been referred to by many eminent men. Two comments were set out (the first by Emerson and the second by Sir Alexander Carr-Saunders) from different centuries which taken together, explained why those who founded the association were so willing to work for it and so determined that it should succeed:

The high prize of life, the crowning fortune of a man, is to be born with a bias to some purpose which finds him in employment and happiness.

Briefly, one problem facing the modern world is how to preserve personal freedom and dignity when industry and commerce are highly organised. In part the solution is for each man to belong to an association composed of those who follow the same vocation as himself, no matter by whom they are employed. Membership of the association gives status. From it he goes out to serve some organisation, to it he returns when he wishes, or is obliged to change employment. In this way the independent status of the freelance worker, which all envy, may in some measure be transferred to the salaried worker.

Incorporated Sales Managers' Association (Irish group) — Syllabus 1952–53

All meetings will be held at the Royal Hibernian hotel, Dublin, at 7.30 p.m. except the luncheon meeting on October 10 and dinner on 12 December.

Chairman: Mr L.V.Whitehead MSMA,
hon. Secretary: Mr W.S. Kelly ASMA.

12 Sept. Speaker: D.R. Griffiths, Esq., Director of ISMA
Subject: 'Forming a Branch'

10 Oct. Luncheon
Speaker: Major General H. McNeill, Executive organising officer of 'An Tostal': Ireland at Home.
Subject: 'Climb a Tree'.

He who whispers down a well,
About the goods he has to sell,
Will not make as many dollars,
As he who climbs a tree and hollers.

14 Nov. Speaker: E. Mullane, Esq., Managing Director, Waterford Metal Industries Ltd
Subject: 'Industrial Transport Facilities'

12 Dec. Dinner (provisional)
Inauguration of branch

1953

9 Jan. Speakers: Walter Smithwick, Esq., Smithwick's Brewery, Kilkenny
R.G. Moffett, Esq., MSMA, Cork Iron and

Hardware Co. Ltd
An executive of CTT – Córas Tráchtála Tta
(Government body organised to promote Irish
exports to the dollar area)
Subject: 'What about Export?'
Joint meeting with Irish Exporters' Association

13 Feb.   Speakers: Max Moffett, Esq., Managing Director,
Max Models Ltd
J. Webb, Esq., Manager, *The Irish Times* Ltd
Subject: 'Selling by Science'

Joint meeting with Advertising Press Club of
Ireland, the Publicity Club of Ireland and
Association of Advertisers

13 Mar.   Speaker: T.A. Moran, Esq., MSMA,
Gateaux Ltd, Finglas
Subject: 'Marketing a New Line'.

10 Apr.   Speakers: S.S. Stephenson, Esq., AIAC, Secretary,
Short Bros and Harland Ltd, Belfast
Cathal Loughney, BL, Secretary, RGDATA
Subject: 'Are Distribution Costs Too High?'

8 May   AGM

The ISMA Students' Society (Irish group) — Syllabus 1952–1953

All Meetings will be held at the Royal Hibernian hotel, Dublin
at 7.45 p.m.

Chairman: Mr H.N.B.Palmer, FSMA
Hon. Sec.: Mr T. Doolan, 44 Grove Road,
Finglas, Dublin

19 Sept.   'Economic Aspects of Sales Management'

17 Oct.   'Legal Aspects of Sales Management'

21 Nov.   'Psychological Aspects of Sales Management'

5 Dec.   'Financial Accounting and Cost Accounting'

16 Jan.   'Statistical Method'

20 Feb.   'Office Organisation and Method'

20 Mar.   'Brains Trust'

| 17 Apr. | 'What the Examiners are Looking For' |
| 15 May | AGM |

Incorporated Sales Managers' Association (Northern Ireland Group) — Syllabus 1952–53

Chairman: Mr William Wilson, Hon. Sec.: C.R.O. Morrisson

1952	Evening meetings
5 Dec.	Friday at 7.00 for 7.30 p.m.
	Subject:'Company Representation' Speaker:Group-Capt. G.W. Williamson, OBE, MC, MICE, FRAeS, productivity adviser to Short Brothers and Harland, Ltd
1953	
9 Jan.	Friday at 7.00 for 7.30 p.m.
	Subject: 'Cash Control' Speaker: Mr C.A. Knill District Manager, National Cash Register Co.
6 Feb.	Friday at 7.00 for 7.30 p.m.
	Subject: 'Speciality Selling' Speaker: Mr E.E. Rant, District Manager, Hoover Ltd
6 March	Friday at 7.00 for 7.30 p.m.
	Subject: 'Cost Accounting' Speaker: Mr S.A. Harding, FCA, Director Harding & Harding Ltd
10 April	Friday at 7.00 for 7.30 p.m.
	To be arranged
12 May	Tuesday, Reception 7.30 p.m
	Carriages midnight, dinner
	Friday, 22nd at 7.00 for 7.30 p.m. AGM
	Venue for all meetings: The Imperial Restaurant, Donegall Place, tel: Belfast 20954

1952 Luncheon meetings

6 Dec.   Tuesday at 12.30 for 1.00 p.m.

1953

20 Jan.   Tuesday at 12.30 for 1.00 p.m.

17 Feb.   Tuesday at 12.30 for 1.00 p.m.

17 March   Tuesday at 12.30 for 1.00 p.m.

21 April   Tuesday at 12.30 for 1.00 p.m.

STUDENT SOCIETY EXAMINATION SUBJECTS, 1952–53

The ISMA Irish group student society programme (as detailed already) set out the meetings being held at the Royal Hibernian hotel, Dawson Street, Dublin, monthly. The subjects were all akin to the examination course for the diploma. These included the economic, legal and psychological aspects of ISMA sales management, financial and cost accounting, statistical methods and a 'brains trust'!

ISMA IRISH BRANCH STATUS ACHIEVED, SEPTEMBER 1952

At the council executive meeting held at the Anchor hotel, Parnell Square, Dublin on 5 September 1952, the chairman read what was described then as a wire, i.e. a telegram from ISMA London. It informed the council of its approval of branch status application, subject to certain conditions. It was agreed that the branch would be known as the Ireland branch. The national chairman (London) also said that a very fine job of salesmanship had been done in recent presentations of the case from Dublin.

In appreciation of the considerable work and achievement for the advancement of students and their programme in particular, Mr Joe Bigger was appointed deputy chairman of the education committee.

The director, Mr David Griffiths, and Mr Baines, national executive ISMA London, visited Dublin concerning the branch formation and expressed their appreciation of the hospitality and welcome they received.

An interview panel was set up to screen students seeking admission to the student society. The charge for the luncheon meeting at the Metropole Ballroom restaurant, 10 October 1952 was agreed on as six shillings and sixpence for members while the cost of guests was covered from branch funds.

PRESS OFFICER ISMA IRELAND BRANCH, 1952

Mr P.C. Kavanagh became the press officer of the Ireland branch with a duty to prepare press releases for the branch. He was advised that reimbursement would be made to him for the entertainment of press officials. The new branch notepaper cost three pounds and ten shillings for 1,000 sheets.

It was considered that pending legislation and the demands of the trade unions, there seemed to be a call for a federation of different bodies of professional workers.

FIRST GENERAL MEETING IRELAND BRANCH ISMA, SEPTEMBER 1952

The 1952–53 session commenced at the Royal Hibernian hotel, Dawson Street, Dublin, on 12 September 1952. At that evening meeting there were thirty-seven members and guests present with apologies of nine noted. Mr Leslie Whitehead, chairman, opened the discussion by welcoming the director of ISMA, Mr David Griffiths and Mr Baines, past national chairman, who had come to Ireland to report on the situation about the Irish group's most recent application for branch status.

Mr Griffiths congratulated the officers of the Irish group on what he described as one of the best set of applications he had the pleasure of reading for a very long time. The question of the status of members was raised by Mr Griffiths, as was the quality of such persons. Several examples were given in reply by naming individual members present, their important positions and the esteem to which they were held in the business life of the community in Ireland. The title of the proposed branch was then referred to. Mr Griffiths stated that it should have the name of the city in it and therefore should be called the 'Dublin Branch of the Incorporated Sales Managers' Association', rather than the 'Ireland Branch' as in the application. Members did not agree however, saying that the 'Dublin Branch' would carry no weight in Ireland and that all other professional bodies attended by members were defined as Irish and not confined to a county. Mr Griffiths rose and said that he had heard nothing to change the UK council's attitude. Mr Chesson then pointed out that a number of businessmen could band together and call themselves Irish Sales Managers' Association and be accepted as such by the community. Mr Tom Moran pointed out that from the important point of education it would be ridiculous to tackle the problem using Dublin in the title. The chairman, Mr Leslie Whitehead, then put the proposal to the meeting that the branch be known as the 'Dublin Branch', resulting in no vote being cast. Conversely, the subsequent proposal for the body to be known as 'Irish' or 'Ireland Branch', resulted in a unanimous vote in favour with every member present exercising their right to vote. Consequently, Mr Griffiths was asked to convey this decision to the council in London. Mr Baines then stated that he believed that the

Irish group was trying 'to run before it could walk' and was in too much of a hurry. Mr Chesson, in his vote of thanks to Mr Griffiths and Mr Baines and appreciation of their attendance at the meeting also listening to the views of the executive and members, said that the sincere wish of all in the group was to do what was best for sales management in Ireland and the profession. Mr Griffiths replied that Mr Baines and himself would convey the situation to the council in London.

IRELAND BRANCH ISMA: RECORD ATTENDANCE, 1952

The increased interest and effort of the branch to progress resulted in an attendance of almost 100 members, students and guests at a luncheon meeting on 10 October 1952 in the Metropole Ballroom, O'Connell Street, Dublin. Included were Senator McGuire, Mr David Frame (Hammond Lane Group) Alderman Doyle, TD and Mr Cooper, president of the Irish Exporters' Association. Apologies recorded included Senator George O'Brien, Sir Basil Goulding and Mr R.G. (Bob) Moffett, Cork.

AN TÓSTAL: IRELAND AT HOME EXPLAINED, 1952

The chairman introduced Major General Hugo McNeill as principal speaker at the luncheon. He as executive organising officer of An Tóstal (Ireland at home) said that his organisation would greatly benefit business and conversely he sought members help to ensure its success. An Tóstal was brought about in 1952 to extend the Irish tourist season, in order to bring more people to Ireland, hence more revenue for the country and increased business all round. It would also ensure that Irish people should move more around the country.

The event was expected to be a yearly one and was being organised on a long-term basis. The traditional Irish welcome of Céad Míle Fáilte was a true invitation to all and aimed to spread the news of good value for money. Tourism was everybody's business, the Major General went on to say, and the tourist everyone's guest. Mr T. O'Gorman who was in charge of the programme and publicity for An Tóstal outlined its goal in relation to the American and Canadian markets, for which campaigns had already been established. Publicity and a welcome of course was also extended to the United Kingdom market. (Indeed I myself well remember participating in crossroad Irish dancing and the festivities of An Tóstal in Leitrim, Donegal and Cork particularly during some years of my travels).

The syllabus programme for the said luncheon described the subject as 'Climb a Tree' and went on to set out the following poem:

> He who whispers down a well
> about the goods he has to sell

will not make as many dollars
as he who climbs a tree and hollers.

A combined conference had been held comprising airways, shipping and other major transport organisations. Full support had been pledged by each body. Naturally people like Major General McNeill were travelling to the various tourist markets to sell the entire idea of what was envisaged as the greatest event of modern times in Ireland. The commencement in 1953 would be the only springtime national event.

Talking tourism and making people aware of its value was how business-men could contribute to much of the anticipated success. Ireland was back now in normal times and business must be stimulated by each one contributing to successful promotion. Mr Leslie Thorn said the requirement was salesmanship to which Mr David Frame concurred.

IRISH-AMERICAN SALES CONFERENCE, NOVEMBER 1952

A special meeting of the executive on 10 October 1952 at the offices of Carthorn Ltd, (compliments of Leslie Thorn) heard the announcement of a forthcoming Irish-American sales conference.

The leader of the American team was Mr Edgar Kruger and the venue the Metropole Ballroom, O'Connell Street, Dublin with Monday, 3 November 1952 being the agreed date. The conference was organised in association with the National Sales Executives Inc., New York and was entitled 'Operation Enterprise III'. A list of the American team speakers and their subjects is set out below. This was indeed a most important venture for the Ireland branch of the ISMA to undertake at that time. The brochure was entitled 'How America Sells'. It told that it was now known that skill in salesmanship did not return automatically with competitive conditions. A long list was made of companies which had been in sharply competitive conditions for many months.

It was asked whether these companies had increased their sales efficiency or whether they had been able to generate sufficient selling power to adjust themselves satisfactorily to the then changed conditions. The answer of many sales managers was no, it was not nearly good enough yet. Re-training a sales force which had no real selling to do for years was an alarmingly slow job.

The Americans described this situation as a need 'to jerk one out of all remembrance of the past dozen years and force oneself into new standards of performance'. They asked if Ireland was exporting their products to the dollar area. Those who were should have a refresher course on American sales methods resulting in probable increased orders. Alternatively, planning dollar exports and contemplating the most efficient manner in which to do so was recommended by the Irish branch of ISMA as a tie-up now with the An Tóstal programme.

The four subjects agreed for the conference were:

- the selection and training of salesmen
- the supervision and control of salesmen
- salesmen's compensation and incentives
- demonstration selling.

The official welcome of the friendly American delegation was extended by the Rt. Hon. Lord Mayor of Dublin, Senator Andrew S. Clarkin.

A film entitled 'The Importance of Selling' was shown. This depicted sales case studies and role playing.

Accommodation was limited and it was a pleasure and a worthwhile experience for myself to be present at the conference and functions arranged therewith. The cost of attendance for the conference day was: 12/6d (62p today) for the luncheon, conference and buffet tea or 6/- (30p today) for the conference and buffet tea only. Below is the programme for the Irish-American sales conference.

Programme of the Irish-American Sales Conference, 3 Nov. 1952

  a) Elmer R. Kruger, Indianapolis
     President, Paper Art Co.
     Subject: Chairman – Operation Enterprise (moderator)
  b) Charles Alling, New York
     President, Hils-Demroth Inc.
     Subject: Demonstration Selling (use of visuals in selling)
  c) Winfield Cook, Pennsylvania
     President, Vita Craft Sales
     Subject: Supervision and Control of Salesmen
  d) William Gove, Minnesota
     Director of Sales Development, Minnesota Mining
     Subject: Salesmanship in Keen Competition (inspirational)
  e) C.B. Larabee, New York
     President, Printers' Ink
     Subject: Advertising and Sales Promotion Today
  f) Charles Love, Rochester
     Executive Vice-President, Commercial Controls Corporation
     Subject: Selection and Training of Salesmen – for Sales Management Positions
  g) Eugene Mapel, Penn.
     Vice-President, Methods Engineering, Pittsburgh
     Subject: Salesmen's Motivation and Incentives

I well recall the various fast moving, demonstrative, enthusiastic delivery of several of the presenters. One for example, demonstrated how ice can go on fire while another literally sold the shirt off his back to the audience and proceeded to take off his jacket and show that of the shirt he literally had only cuffs and collar with a mini-front.

Not to be outdone however, the Irish committee pre-arranged entertainment for the visitors from the USA. On arrival at Dublin Airport on the Saturday preceding the conference a luncheon was held (1 November 1952). A tour took place through the Wicklow mountains on Sunday 2 November following with a luncheon at Hunter's hotel, Wicklow. After the conference on the Monday the evening was spent at the Abbey Theatre, Dublin. Transport was provided at all times. Finally, the American team and guests were seen off by members of the executive at Dublin Airport on Tuesday, 4 November.

The result of this conference was very satisfactory particularly from the business and educational aspect. Socially it was also very beneficial and resulted in new friends and connections being made. Letters were subsequently received and read to the executive at its meeting on Tuesday, 11 November from the Irish Exporters' Association. Senator McGuire, Mr Bernard Roche, sales director of Irish Ropes, Newbridge and Mr W.J. Milne, director of Gouldings, expressing their appreciation of the opportunity afforded and the benefits accrued them by their attendance at the Irish-American conference. They and others congratulated the Irish branch executive on the excellent manner in which everything had been organised.

'MADE IN IRELAND': E. MULLANE, 1952

Mr E. Mullane, managing-director of Waterford Metal Industries Ltd gave an interesting talk to members of the ISMA on the subject 'Made in Ireland' at a combined speakers' meeting on 4 November 1952. This was a campaign to encourage the purchase of Irish goods. He gave a wide account of the various procedures experienced in the metal manufacturing industry from raw material to the finished sale product.

CÓRAS IOMPAIR ÉIREANN (IRISH RAIL), 1952

At the 4 November meeting Mr Stewart, traffic manager of Córas Iompair Éireann (Irish Rail), spoke about industrial transport facilities. The various services were fully explained and he provided an insight into the effort being made to overcome problems and provide a really efficient public service.

FIRST PRESIDENT OF THE IRISH BRANCH OF ISMA

To close the year 1952 a meeting was held at the Hibernian hotel, Dawson Street, Dublin, on 12 December. At this event it was with great pleasure that the announcement was made that Senator E.A. McGuire (Brown Thomas and Co.) had agreed to be the first president of the Irish branch of the Incorporated Sales Managers' Association. On his introduction to the members he said he would do all in his power to further the aims of the Irish branch. The chairman, Mr Leslie Whitehead, then reported on his recent visit to the council in London and answered questions from the members present. Thanks were especially expressed to the chairman and to Mr R.G. Moffett (Cork) who had accompanied him, for giving up so much of their personal time particularly considering the amount of travel involved.

IRISH EXPORTERS' ASSOCIATION/CTT DOLLAR AREA AIM, 1953

On 9 January heralding in the new year, 1953, there was a combined meeting with guests of the Irish Exporters' Association — Córas Trachtála Tta (CTT). The latter was the government body organised to promote Irish exports particularly to the dollar area.

Mr Bill Chesson chaired the meeting in Mr Leslie Whitehead's absence (he was on business). 'What about Export?' was the subject of a paper prepared by Mr Walter Smithwick of Smithwick's Brewery, Kilkenny, and as he was unable to attend it was read by Mr Leslie Thorn. The second speaker to address the meeting was Mr Bob Moffett of Cork. He spoke about the difficulties encountered on a sales tour of the continent, while a third contributor, Mr Bill Walsh CTT, spoke about the dollar market. He mainly concentrated on the American supermarkets and their requirements. Every facility was available to investigate further markets and the usage of Irish goods and products abroad. Irish sales managers were encouraged to avail of the services now rather than later.

Members of both ISMA and the Irish Exporters' Association joined in with various questions and the ensuing discussion was to fruitful advantage.

(It will be noticed that the use of 'Mr' still prevailed in written records.)

FIRST LADIES' NIGHT OF ISMA IRELAND BRANCH, JANUARY 1953

The first Ladies' Night function of the branch was held on 13 January 1953. It was a very successful social evening. While the donation to the benevolent fund was deferred, it was agreed to meet the financial deficit on the Irish-American sales conference (twelve pounds eighteen shillings and four pence (£12.92) out of the social fund account. A further decision was made to circulate a copy of the minutes of executive committee meetings to members from May 1953. This was a new departure.

INAUGURAL DINNER OF THE IRELAND BRANCH OF ISMA, FEBRUARY 1953

The inaugural dinner of the Ireland branch of the Incorporated Sales Managers' Association was held at the Royal Hibernian hotel, Dawson Street, Dublin, on Monday, 2 February 1953. The guests included the Minister of Industry and Commerce, Mr Seán Lemass, TD who replied to the toast of Irish industry, ably responded to by Senator E.A. McGuire, president of the Ireland branch. Many of the leaders of Irish industry were present at the dinner including Major-General Sir Charles Harvey, CV, CVO, CBE, MC, chairman of the Irish Management Institute who responded to Mr Michael Coote's toast of the guests.

The Incoportated Sales Managers' Association toast was proposed by the Rt. Hon. Lord Mayor of Dublin, Senator Andrew S. Clarkin, to which Mr David Griffiths, director of ISMA, London suitably responded. Mr Joseph Atack, a member of the London council, proposed the new branch toast to which Senator McGuire, its president, replied. He again stated that he was honoured to be the first appointed and would do everything possible in his power to help promote the aims and objectives. He also stated that he was looking forward to working with the chairman and executive committee. He outlined the advantages to Irish industry and export in the quality of the members of the Incorporated Sales Managers' Association and the future programme and targets to be aimed at. The branch chairman, Mr Leslie Whitehead, seconded the response and said he accepted the challenge ahead and the futherance of the Irish branch of the ISMA. He stated that he believed the newly appointed executive committee would work together in harmony to enhance the branch by widening its membership and education of members and students alike for the benefit of Ireland. He further thanked Mr Atack for his sincere wishes and support for the Ireland branch.

The entertainment at the dinner was provided by some of the leading artistes at the time — Jack Cowle, Al Thomas, R. McCullagh and Seán Mooney. They suitably concluded a most enjoyable and historic evening.

Brochure of historic inaugural dinner, 1953

The brochure of the inaugural dinner recorded the history of the association's growth as the development of sales management being the codifying of best practices. It went on to outline:

The practitioners of sales management must keep in touch with other sales managers, must help to form opinions on all matters affecting the profession and must be sensitive to those opinions as and when they are formed. Membership of ISMA affords practically the only opportunity to a progressive sales executive to do all these things by a free exchange of knowledge and experience through discussion with other sales executives. The association's magazine *Marketing* reports the proceedings of over twenty branches and groups of the association. Most of the work is done at branch meetings in the course of free discussions between members of different industries.

IRELAND BRANCH ISMA: FIRST OFFICERS, 1952–53 SESSION

The first officers of the Ireland branch of the Incorporated Sales Managers' Association who took office for the 1952–53 session were:

- President: Senator E.A. McGuire
- Chairman: Leslie V. Whitehead
- Vice-Chairman: C.W. Chesson
- Hon. Treasurer: D.M. .Milmo
- Hon. Secretary: W.S. Kelly.

The executive committee were composed of the following: Messrs H.N.B. Palmer, D. MacKenzie, D.A. Black, P.J. Kavanagh, W.D. Fraser, J.C. Bigger, A.V. Adey, S.J. Doyle, R.G. Moffett, T.A. Moran, B.D. Thom, L.C. Thorn, W. Wilson and N. McConnell.

The sub-committee chairmen were:

- Education: Mr J.C. Bigger
- Programme: Mr L.C. Thorn
- Membership: Mr W.D. Fraser
- Export: Mr T.A. Moran
- Social: Mr A.V. Adey.

FIRST IRELAND BRANCH COUNCILLOR TO ATTEND ISMA LONDON MEETINGS

Mr Leslie Whitehead, branch chairman, was appointed the first branch councillor to attend meetings in London. It is now possible to disclose that a number of prominent Irish citizens were considered before putting forward Senator McGuire as president of the Ireland branch of the ISMA. Of course his consent to accept the position had been diplomatically obtained prior to this. A further appointment made was that of Mr D.M. Milmo to the important education committee.

MEMBERS OF ISMA (IRISH GROUP) TRANSFER TO IRELAND BRANCH

At this juncture the members of the Irish group were transferred to the Ireland Branch of the ISMA. An invigilator was appointed for the 1953 examinations in Dublin and future arrangements for Northern Ireland students sitting them were undertaken. Formerly these were the responsibility of London.

The national membership committee meetings in London were now attended by Mr Bill Fraser and Mr Joe Bigger who likewise attended the monthly education meetings there and reported back to the Ireland branch council. An example showed that agreement came about whereby no Irish student would in future be in any way penalised as a result of examiniation questions which had an applicability to English students rather than Irish students — particularly legal questions.

The Ireland branch secretary secured additional copies of the booklet *Professional Career in Sales Management* for distribution to potential students.

Additional vice-chairmen were then appointed to the Ireland branch — Mr Tom Moran and Mr W. Wilson, chairman of the Northern Ireland group. The student education programme was aimed particularly at the subjects for the final examinations now with added subjects and a 'brains trust' evening. During the session arranged visits were made for students to go to various businesses and manufacturing concerns to observe goods in process right through to actual sales outlets.

ADVERTISING PRESS CLUB, PUBLICITY CLUB OF IRELAND, ASSOCIATION OF ADVERTISERS: ISMA MEETING, 1953

A joint meeting comprising members of the Advertising Press Club of Ireland, the Publicity Club of Ireland, the Association of Advertisers and the Irish branch of the ISMA was held at the Royal Hibernian hotel, Dawson Street, Dublin, on 13 February 1953. The speaker was Mr Max Moffett, managing director of Max Models Ltd. The subject dealt with the notion of selling being a science. In the production of his art he demonstrated the use of perspex particularly for advertising. He produced for viewing actual models he that he had made and which had been used already as advertising aids. He also showed a special model — that of the Irish stand at the Toronto Fair. Mr J. Webb, manager of *The Irish Times* spoke also on the subject and amplified the work of Mr Moffett while complimenting him on the creativity design and usage to which the products were put to considerable advantage.

It was announced that Mr Stephen Doyle had been elected to the chair of conference committee at an executive meeting on 17 April 1953. Among the accounts passed for payment that meeting was an interesting one for the 1953 smoking concert, having had an outlay of one pound eleven shillings and sixpence. The financial loss on the inaugural branch dinner of thirty pounds five shillings and seven pence was kindly met by London. They at the same time congratulated the Ireland branch on the excellent organisation in every respect and the outstanding success achieved.

DISTRIBUTION COSTS, 1953

'Are Distribution Costs Too High?' was the subject of the evening meeting on 10 April 1953 at the Royal Hibernian hotel, Dublin. The speaker was Mr Stephenson, secretary of Short Bros and Harland, Belfast, who provided a series of statistics involving much general discussion. Apparently the figures and other detail were retained by the then sub-committee as they do not appear in the council minute book of the time.

At the same meeting Mr Cathal Loughney BL, secretary RGDATA, Retail Grocers' Association, gave his experiences particularly on price margins and illustrated his examples from the grocery trade experience. Contributing views on the types of variences in many other trades were made by those present which included Mr Val Edmunds of the Northern Ireland group.

NEW MEMBERS ELECTED TO ISMA, APRIL 1953

A special executive committee meeting was held on April 29 1953 at which some new members were elected. However, at the same time recruitment of students was considered slow and attendance of members at meetings poor. Various steps were initiated to improve both. Address plates had now been procured and were handed over to the hon. secretary to improve mailing procedure.

Mr Leslie Luke was appointed press officer. Before submitting the accounts of the branch to London it was decided to appoint internal auditors. Consequently A.V. Adey and C.W. Cheeson were given the task as hon. auditors. It was emphasised that there was no problem with the accounts which had already been fully approved by the council.

Mr Brian Murphy became the new hon. secretary of the branch from 1 May 1953. It was noted with satisfaction that Mr Joe Bigger had been honoured by election to the council of the Association of Advertisers in Ireland in June 1953.

MEMBERS ATTEND FIRST STUDENT SOCIETY MEETING, MAY 1953

Branch members of the ISMA now became welcome to attend student society meetings and in particular to hear speakers on examination subjects. Warm appreciation was expressed to Senator McGuire by the council on his offer to allow the use of the cinema/theatre of Brown Thomas, the leading fashion store on Grafton Street, Dublin, as the occasion would arise. Mr Leslie White-head attended the chairman's conference in London and contributed by ask-ing certain questions requiring clarification regarding the situation in Ireland.

The education chairman Mr Joe Bigger reported that the booklet — *A Professional Career in Sales Management* — had been well received by vari-ous firms, public bodies etc. He was congratulated on the improved student results consequent to the excellent speaker education programme he devised for them.

FIRST ISMA STUDENT EXAMINATIONS HELD IN DUBLIN, MAY 1953

The first examinations for Irish students were held in the Rathmines Techni-cal Institute on the 14, 15 and 16 of May 1953. Two students sat for qualifying and three for the final examinations. The completed papers were duly trans-mitted to London immediately after the examinations. The student AGM was held on 15 May 1953. Mr J.D. Cleary was elected chairman, Miss E.J. Lloyd, hon. secretary and Messrs T.B. Fortune, B.M.Kinsella, T.W. Doolan and J.R. Richardson, committee members. Miss E.J. Lloyd was the first female stu-dent of the ISMA student society.

MEMBERSHIP APPLICATION PROBLEMS, LONDON 1953

The national members' committee meeting of the ISMA, held in London, June 1953, was attended by Mr Michael Coote, secretary of the Ireland branch membership sub-committee. Following his presentation of the applications from Ireland he found the ISMA London national committee in a difficult humour. An example of this showed that if a company director was sole dis-tributor for say Frigidaire, Bendix or Colombas-Dixon he would be consid-ered for membership but if he were merely one of the distributors he would not be considered. A Mr M.F. Ross, late of India now residing at a given address in Dublin, was transferred from the UK to the Ireland branch and welcomed.

IMPROVEMENT OF ISMA STUDENT FACILITIES, 1953

In August 1953 Mr Joe Bigger, chairman of the student education committee, reported considerable advancement in the arrangements and provisions for students. A syllabus had been prepared for the student society for the next session and would be printed into the general syllabus for the branch. A new qualifying course had been prepared and introduced for the examinations in introductory subjects and a full course was being edited and prepared for the main subjects. It was hopeful that demand would be sufficient to have from ten to twelve students attend actual classes. The subject, psychological aspects of industry and commerce, was arranged to be taken in conjunction with the Institute of Personnel Management and by courtesy of Mr Byrne, their secretary.

ISMA STUDENT REGISTRATION FIGURES

A new student residing in Kilkenny had been added to the list of the Ireland branch and also registered in London. The latter's figure for 1952–53 Ireland branch registrations was 238 of which 30 were re-registrations. These were compared to previous figures — 1948–49: 258, 1949–50: 310, 1950–51: 328 and 1951–52: 291. The downward trend was being investigated, particularly London figure explanations as to the number of student applications rejected and the actual reasons for same.

ISMA EXAMINATIONS

The ISMA examination results in the overall branches of the Institute were not encouraging. For the few that sat from Ireland the result was considered fair. Only one student had failed in all subjects while two had passed with distinction in a particular subject. However, on the marking of papers, London indicated that they would be even more severe in future years. The Pickup medal and first distinction in the final examinations had been won by a Mr A.H. Davies of London with an achievement of 70.66 per cent. In future, awards would be limited to candidates who secured 80 per cent of total marks. The manual of sales management had been stencil copied and was an outline of the broad principles of the course. Copies were sent to principals of technical colleges, while no charge was made for same. In printed form it was made available at four shillings per copy (twenty pence today) to the Ireland branch.

NEW SESSION OF ISMA IRELAND BRANCH, 1953–54

The new session of the Ireland branch commenced in September 1953 and was formally opened by Senator E.A. McGuire, president, voicing the many and varied duties of sales managers. His remarks were considered of value to both members and students alike. Mr Leslie Whitehead, chairman, concurred and said the president had taken an unfailing interest and co-operated in every way in furthering branch effort. The guest speaker was Mr George Gamlin of McConnell's Advertising Service whose paper was on the subject of market research. He gave much emphasis to the method adopted and in particular to the branding, marketing and advertising of various types of products. The use of samples, press advertising, personal contacts and desk research were some of the methods used in market research and given as an example by him.

ISMA NORTHERN IRELAND GROUP PROGRAMME

The Northern Ireland group programme received from Mr Edwards, then hon. secretary, was acclaimed as excellent and copies obtained were sent to members and students of the Ireland branch with encouragement to attend a meeting or meetings any time they were in the Belfast area. Finance was very limited and committees were generally not receiving any allocation other than for some exceptional necessity. The minute of accounts passed for payment for the Northern Ireland group (totalling three pounds and twelve shillings) and to the Ireland branch (of one pound and ten shillings to petty cash account) highlighted the meagre situation at the time. However, a budget was sought from the Northern Ireland group to combine with that prepared for the Ireland branch and this showed an improved organisation to substantiate financial requirements for 1953–54.

INTRODUCTION OF MEMBERSHIP BADGES, OCTOBER 1953

A new member Jack Simpson, who would figure prominently in years to come, was introduced to the branch membership in October 1953. Membership badges now became available at general meetings, provided from a special board at each meeting place, while they were returned after each such get together.

'GOODWILL, THE NEGLECTED ASSET', OCTOBER 1953

At the meeting of 9 October 1953 at the Royal Hibernian hotel, Dublin, there were eighteen members and guests present to hear Mr Leslie A. Luke,

McConnell's Advertising Service Ltd, speak on his selected subject — 'Good-will, the Neglected Asset'. He emphasised that the importance of goodwill included appropriate advertising. It was difficult to assess the value of good-will as an asset, a most important point in all business, he stated, no matter how big or small. Goodwill should emanate from the managing director down to the lowliest salesman but should not of necessity be personal. The firm's representative should reflect the goodwill of the firm he represented. Members present felt that public relations was closely linked with goodwill in general. Irish manufacturers as a whole, it was said, had not launched an effective campaign to enlighten the public on the merits of most Irish made goods.

HIGH SCHOOL PRINCIPAL CO-OPTED TO EDUCATION COMMITTEE

Mr Joe Bigger attended the London national council education meetings and sought all the printed student recruitment information available. Contact was made with Mr Sean Ó Ceallaigh, principal of the High School of Commerce, Rathmines, Dublin, who was co-opted to the education committee of the branch. It was agreed to circulate students regarding the Ladies' Night of 1953 to which they were for the first time invited.

FILMS AS AN ADVERTISING MEDIUM

The speaker at the Little Theatre of Messrs Brown Thomas and Co., Grafton Street, Dublin, on 13 November, 1953, was Mr W.J. Collins, director of Pearl and Dean Ltd, London, a title screening sales promotion. Felicitations having been conveyed by Mr Collins from the London branch, he went on to stress the importance of films as an advertising medium. He described films as the mass demonstration of an article particularly for items requiring actual demonstration. He believed that much more ground was covered by such a medium than could possibly be made by salesmen or demonstrators. Commodities such as sweets could be advertised to more advantage but in such case screen advertising was used as posters. He explained in detail how advertising films were prepared and gave examples of the complex intricacies of advertising film making. He showed a series of films both talkie and silent some of which were then destined for the American market. The future of 3D cinemascope and warner-scope films particularly in relation to advertising being processed, were of the utmost interest to those present.

PUBLICITY CLUB AND ADVERTISING ASSOCIATIONS ATTEND ISMA OPEN MEETINGS

The ISMA branch were pleased to have at this meeting members of the Publicity Club, Association of Advertisers and Advertising Press Club all of whom were invited to attend future open meetings of the ISMA Ireland branch. Senator McGuire provided a cocktail party for those present which was much appreciated.

IRISH MANAGEMENT INSTITUTE (IMI) LIAISON, 1953

Mr Sean Ó Ceallaigh, principal of the High School of Commerce, Rathmines, Dublin, was welcomed to the executive branch meeting of 20 November 1953. He was complimented for his outstanding interest and co-operation in the matter of the student society educational requirements. Liaison with the Irish Management Institute (IMI) was fully discussed and it was agreed to encourage working together as much as possible. The opportunity would arise and be conveyed to Sir Charles Harvey, chairman IMI, in the next month when he would be addressing a branch members' meeting of the ISMA to which the council of the IMI and its members were also invited.

Mr Tom Moran agreed to investigate the situation arising in regard to the Income Tax Commission and report back to the council.

Mr Joe Bigger stated that in future students would receive a copy of the *Marketing* publication. Mr Ó Ceallaigh spoke of concern regarding the standard of students requiring improvement in the subject English. He further suggested that a leaflet be issued by the Ireland branch showing the advantages of sales management. Likewise he would welcome lectures given by experts on sales organisation. He agreed to serve on the education committee to further its aims.

LADIES'NIGHT AND PRESIDENT'S NIGHT, ISMA

Regarding the 1954 Ladies' Night, Mr Norman McConnell reported that already some 140 tickets had been sold and there was a waiting list of twelve. Also there was a record number of tickets (104) sold for the benevolent fund ballot. For the President's Night the theme would be education. The national chairman, Mr Mauwle (London) would be one of the invited guests for the night which was to be 11 February 1954. It was agreed also that students would be invited to attend the function at a concession amount of one pound one shilling each. In the meantime Mr Leslie A. Luke was welcomed as a newly elected member of the executive committee.

MANAGEMENT DEFINED

To conclude the year 1953 the December branch meeting was addressed at the Royal Hibernian hotel Dublin by Sir Charles Harvey, Chairman Guinness Group and also of the Irish Management Institute. His subject was divided into four parts: 'What is management?', 'What Does Management Entail?', 'What Is Being Achieved by the Irish Management Institute?' and 'How Does the IMI Affect ISMA?' He stated that one of the objects of IMI was to make work interesting. Its aim was also to obtain better results and to improve working facilities while enlarging existing markets and developing new ones. Good management was an intimate knowledge of one's profession and not necessarily technical. One required knowledge of accounting, statistical methods, the economy, valuation etc. he went on to say.

Continuing, Sir Charles Harvey stated that a complete knowledge of products being marketed was essential as indeed was proper staff control. The Irish Management Institute encouraged the growth of management and recommended conferences and lectures with discussions following. Student groups and carefully selected literature were also of great help in promoting good management.

The IMI had an advisory panel in co-operation with the universities and technical institutes. Their combined aim was to get the whole machinery of management running smoothly in the shortest possible time. Sales management was related to the IMI from the sales promotion point of view, as was advertising, public relations etc.

The speaker concluded by saying that sales managers should have a knowledge of general management methods and production management. Most importantly sales managers should co-operate with one another and learn to know of each others problems.

The ISMA branch president Senator McGuire spoke of the necessity of co-operation between the IMI and ISMA, from which both would gain knowledge for their members.

Mr Leslie Thorn then posed the question — Are we selling what we make and are we making what we can sell? Sales managers must study the market as much as production managers and their ideas be carefully considered by production and works managers. He believed that customer reaction must be understood by works managers. Over-selling via the over-loading of customers' stocks for the sake of getting an order must be avoided. Regular orders and goodwill did not restrict the buying or indeed payment of accounts.

Mr Bill Chesson then stated that he felt that a market survey was the best method of determining what the market could take. Mr Joe Bigger raised the question of the situation regarding the value of the pound at present. This, he believed, was making it impossible for some business houses to stock in sufficient quantities. The need to sell wisely to get the maximum turnover and sale of products was emphasised.

EDUCATION ADVANCE FOR ISMA STUDENTS, 1954

To the executive meeting of January 1954 the education chairman Mr Joe Bigger reported the possibility of publicity in the *Marketing* journal for student activities and that progress had been made in recruitment in Ireland. Weekend courses would take place in England soon but it was difficult for Irish students to avail of the opportunity offered to partake. A new motion had been passed in London declaring that a finalist, i.e. graduate member who held an important business position for seven years, could be recommended for fellowship of ISMA.

The average attendance of students in Ireland at meetings was 75 per cent compared to only 10 per cent in the UK. It was now agreed to circulate papers read at student meetings to all students while a folder of such papers, directed to both students and members, would be made available at a nominal cost.

The Ireland branch had £36 to credit in the social fund while the branch account balance was £5. Mr Edwards of the Northern Ireland group was co-opted to the membership committee.

It was recorded that Senator J. O'Brien BA, BL gave a most interesting, informative and enlightening address entitled 'Free Enterprise and Government Intervention' at the luncheon in the Metropole Ballroom, O'Connell Street, Dublin on Tuesday, 21 March 1954. However, no written detail is forthcoming on this.

EXPORT HOUSE FUNCTION, 1954

An evening meeting saw Mr Norris Marsden Ml. Ex. address his remarks on the function of an export house. Export houses were described in 1954 as mediums to enable a manufacturer place his goods overseas. Export houses had to know the foreign markets and whether a manufacturer's product was suitable. A product suitable on the home market did not necessarily mean that it would be accepted as alright for the different export markets in which an export house could place it. Examples were given on such an operation in the Argentine.

A confirming house operated with a series of agents and correspondents who put business through a particular export or confirming house. The latter was responsible for payment for shipping charges. Usually charge was made for buying commission from 1.5 per cent to 5 per cent depending on the size of the order. Although an agent might not pay for six months the manufacturer got paid (at the latest 30 days) by the confirming house.

As distant travel was too expensive at that time for the normal manufacturer, the funding of the export or confirming house became extremely important. The textile business used a collective marketing organisation. The speaker outlined the example of twenty manufacturers combining to make a range of goods, each manufacturer making up those parts of export orders most suitable for his plant and resources.

Regarding finance Mr Marsden stated that if an export house could not give extended credit, which sometimes ran into three years on certain export markets, they made necessary credit arrangements with banks. Individual manufacturers found it very difficult to convince the banks but banks were more co-operative with export houses.

Questions were then asked as to how this could be applied to Ireland and whether it would be possible to establish an export house in Ireland. Members wondered if it was the opinion that the banks in Great Britain helped an export house and the manufacturer who was engaged in export, more fully than the banks in Ireland. Mr Marsden replied by saying that export credit guarantees operated in England through banks and also through the Board of Trade. However, he would not venture an opinion as to the relative merits of Irish banks in comparison to English banks.

It was further stated that over 50 per cent of all British exports passed through export houses. Any advantageous rates obtained for the shipment of bulk lots were passed on to the manufacturer by the export house. The export house did not reckon that its shipping department should make a loss merely to cover its outgoings.

BRAINS TRUST STUDENT MEETING, 1954

At the executive meeting on 26 March 1954 the first students 'brains trust' get together was discussed and considered to be a very successful exercise.

THE SALESMAN, HIS HEALTH AND PSYCHOLOGY, 1954

Dr J.F. Eustace was introduced by Leslie Whitehead as speaker at the evening meeting of 9 April 1954, in the Royal Hibernian hotel. The subject being presented was: 'Salesman, His Health and Psychology'. Straight away he stressed that the most important point in the selection of a suitable salesman was stability. By that he meant that the prospective salesman should be at ease, have adaptability and come from a good home environment. He also stressed the need to have stable parents.

He went on to say that the sales manager who was interviewing the prospective salesman must like the person being interviewed. Likewise, the salesman himself must like people as otherwise he would not be a success in his job.

A salesman had to be a good mixer, be physically fit and intelligent. Too much imagination and over ambition were not always desirable attributes. Another important point in a salesman, he mentioned, was that he should possess temperate habits. Domestic harmony was essential and domestic responsibilities were often proved to be advantageous to salesmen. In fact, he stated, it applied to any man in a business profession.

According to Dr Eustace the method by which a man was handled determined his morale and furthermore, the salesman must be aware himself of the value of his job and must feel that he is part of a group striving towards the good of the firm. Security to a man was one of the most important things possible towards making him happy, contented and successful.

It was essential, Dr Eustace said, that the salesman's employer or company be aware of his prowess. In recognising ability it gave the man the required incentive to give of his best. Recognition of good work and using the proper means of selecting a man for due promotion were essentials. Furthermore, emphasis was a vital consideration in seeing that favouritism be deplored, as it broke down a man's morale very quickly.

Dr Eustace concluded by saying that he believed the success of a salesman depended on the type of leader or boss he had, while leaders and bosses must also be stable themselves.

EXPORT MARKET, PRODUCTS SUITABILITY, 1954

Bill Fraser suggested to the executive committee that they should inform the government Department of Industry and Commerce that the Ireland branch of the Incorporated Sales Managers' Association was in a position to advise on possible suitable types of products for the export market and the sales organisation of same.

FIRST AGM, IRELAND BRANCH ISMA

The first AGM of the Ireland branch of the ISMA was held on 14 May 1954, at the offices of Aspro (Ireland) Ltd, Naas Road, Dublin (courtesy of Bill Chesson). Historically it is worthy to note the exact attendance recorded.

There were twenty-five present in all and these were: Senator F.M Summerfield, Senator, E.A. McGuire, Mr David Griffiths (director of ISMA London) and Messrs C.W. Chesson, L.V. Whitehead, D.M. Milmo, F. Napier, J.C. Bigger, C.A. Knill, S.J. Doyle, H.V. Woods, H.N.B. Palmer, W.D. Fraser, P. Duggan, J. Parle, A.J. O'Reilly, J. Douglas, D. Black, L.A. Luke, N. McConnell, A. Saunders, D. MacKenzie, D.J. Targett, J.R. Nimmon and B.M. Murphy.

APPOINTMENTS, IRELAND BRANCH, 1954

The outgoing President, Senator E.A. McGuire, introduced his successor, Senator F.M. Summerfield, to whom he paid tribute.

On his installation, with the chain of office, Senator Summerfield said that he would do everything he could to help further the branch. Realising the vital importance to the economy, he referred to manufacturers and distributors, saying they must work properly within a regulated sales organisation. At that time export and conference committees were endeavouring liaison with the Irish Exporters' Association.

Mr Bill Chesson, in accepting the chairmanship of the branch and badge of office, in turn presented Leslie Whitehead with a past-chairman's insignia. A general discussion followed on the possibility of funding a group of ISMA in Cork during the coming year. Mr David Griffiths was thanked for coming to Ireland for the AGM and a special welcome was extended to him to attend future meetings of the branch.

MEMBERSHIP OF ISMA IRELAND BRANCH, APRIL 1954

Bill Fraser reported an increase in branch membership from 53 in 1952, 73 in 1953, while in April 1954 the figure stood at 81. The target aimed at for the end of 1954 was 100.

STUDENT ACTIVITIES

The education chairman, Joe Bigger, gave a very comprehensive report on student activities. At that time there were 28 students in the Republic of Ireland and eleven students in Northern Ireland registered for the ISMA diploma examinations

ISMA IRELAND BRANCH, SESSION 1954–55

The initial executive meeting of the session 1954–55, held on 21 May 1954, heard of a request from a Mr Porteous, chairman-elect of the Preston branch of ISMA. It was agreed to accede to his request and send him names of the most prominent speakers heard at Ireland branch meetings during the previous year.

A report was submitted by Tom Moran to the Industrial taxation committee on behalf of the branch. Mr Bill Chesson arranged to attend the ISMA London chairmens' conference. An idea of the agenda at the conference can be felt when indicated that some sixty-four points were raised for possible question, comment or discussion.

The grade of Associate Member of the Association was discussed at length. This was in view of the general remarks from branches that the national membership committee were not granting full membership as freely as Associate grade. It was pointed out that, in due course, the combined number of Members and Fellows would be less than that of Associates.

OUTLINE OF *MANUAL OF SALES MANAGEMENT*, JULY 1954

The first part of the ISMA *Manual of Sales Management* was published in July l954. It was described then as an outline of the broad principles of sales management and for the guidance of tutors and lecturers at technical institutes and colleges, which had courses based on the association's examination syllabus.

On a wider scale, it was recommended for use as a training aid for those sales managers who wished to put into the hands of their assistant executives a clear explanation of sales management function and a means of putting them into effect.

(I myself have original copies of Sections I, (the above outline), III (*Sales Organisation and Control*), V (*A Manual of Sales Management — Salesmanship Part I*) and VI (*Salesmanship Part II*), purchased at the then cost of 6/-, each, which would be 3Op today).

At that time there were still no formal classes for teaching the ISMA subjects in Ireland, while learning was available from correspondence colleges.

MARKETING PUBLISHES MEMBERSHIP AND APPLICATIONS, AUGUST 1954

In the August 1954 issue of *Marketing* journal, (I have a copy of this), it showed that the total membership of ISMA at that time was 4,418, of which the Ireland branch number was 84. The London branch alone had a membership of 1,617, while the remaining members were in the other twenty branches and the number included 144 individual overseas members

In the same issue of *Marketing* it listed applications for new members, including some from Ireland: H.A. Gardner, F.H. Steele and G.G. Stuart. Associateship were also listed and included: F.L. Cox and A. Craig.

Procedure being then that names must be published for fourteen days and if no objection lodged, the membership in the grade published would be deemed approved.

SALES MANAGEMENT: TEN-YEAR PLAN, 1954–64

Again, in the same volume of *Marketing*, under the heading of 'The Next Ten Years' a Mr O. Bertoya indicated, to an ISMA meeting at the Flying Horse hotel, Nottingham, that 'during those years ahead' sales managers 'would have to disclose more information, provide more statistical data, plan scientific approach and further give more attention to training sales staff '.

Next to the setting of targets came briefing, particularly in the field of selling. He stated that it was no use spending vast amounts on research if some junior was to throw it all away by not caring at the point of sale. He also hoped that impediments would be reduced, e.g. that trains would run on time, that there would be faster, earlier and later trains so that salesmen could do a full days' work.

APPOINTMENTS, AUGUST 1954

In August 1954, the chairman of the Northern Ireland group, Mr Val Edmunds, was made a member of the Ireland branch of the ISMA executive. Mr Bill Chesson was officially appointed a branch councillor of ISMA and took office at the ISMA London AGM on 4 November 1954, to serve for one year.

For the benefit of the Northern Ireland group, it was decided that, if they submitted their accounts by the second Friday each month, they could now have a petty cash float of five pounds.

APPROACH TO NATIONAL SALES EXECUTIVES INC., NEW YORK, 1954

The hon. secretary was instructed to write to the National Sales Executives Inc., New York, with a view to having their Mr Whitney include Ireland in the European itinerary for their next programme.

IRISH STUDENTS ISMA: EXAMINATION DISTINCTIONS, 1954

Suitable publicity recorded the success of three Irish students in the ISMA final examinations 1954, they being Miss Evelyn Lloyd and Messrs Lawson and O'Sullivan.

Two distinctions, obtained from the total of five for the entire ISMA examinations, including the UK and overseas, was acclaimed by the executive and members as a very meritorious result.

Miss Lloyd was the first Irish lady student to pass the final diploma examinations.

MARKETING LIQUID ENERGY: ESSO, 1954

An evening meeting on 17 September 1954 brought together 29 members, students and guests. The speaker was Mr W.J. Delaney of Esso Petroleum Ltd, who gave his talk on 'Marketing Liquid Energy'.

In his speech he made the point that oil was found and taken from the ground but that in earlier days a company might have bored ten potential oil wells but found that only one contained oil. Mr Delaney compared the situation then, 1954, when 50 per cent of wells were fruitful. The average cost of drilling wells bored was approximately £75,000 in the USA. The deepest well bored was stated to have been 17,800 feet or, compared to the example given by Mr Delaney, 165 times the height of the then Nelson's Pillar in O'Connell Street, Dublin, (the said Pillar was blown up many years later).

Mr Delaney went on to describe the method of disposing oil for refining and treatment which was by long pipelines to a refinery or by transporting the oil by rail. An alternative was to build the refinery near the well. It was interesting to note, went on Mr Delaney, that a 1,700 mile stretch of pipeline, in the Middle East, had cost some £71m. Refineries were very costly items, one built by Esso, for instance, had cost over £40m. while on the other hand, refineries were a vital necessity as crude oil was merely waste without them.

He also pointed out that oil comprised hydrogen and carbon, and so one of the most important requirements in the oil industry was, undoubtedly, fire protection.

The members of ISMA were invited to visit the new Esso terminal at Dublin docks. Solo sites were a method of economising as they enabled increasing loads to one particular address. While 1945 saw an average of 290 gallons provided to a petrol station, in 1954 one station would take 600 gallons or more. There was no question of monopolies, he said, while solo sites were an advantage to the oil industry.

In 1954 the price of petrol in Ireland was lower than in most European countries. Some 50 per cent of the wholesale price of petrol went in taxation in Ireland. The rise of 25 per cent in petrol prices since 1914 (forty years previous) was much less than that of numerous other products. World sales amounted to 960 million barrels per day. The major part of world industry and general living would, Mr Delaney said, come to a standstill if petroleum products were not available.

He summed up his address by stating that 'petrol makes a better way of living'.

ISMA EXECUTIVE MEETING, SEPTEMBER, 1954

Mr Bernard Roche (Irish Ropes Ltd, Newbridge, Co. Kildare) was welcomed onto the executive committee of the Ireland branch in September 1954. Mr Leslie Whitehead reported that London hoped to consider Ireland as the venue for a conference in 1960 (six years hence). All booking dates in England were already committed, i.e. for the years up to and including 1959.

In the meantime a tentative agreement had, however, been decided on to hold the Irish-American conference in Ireland. The Northern Ireland group chairman, Mr Val Edmunds, recommended the postponement of an Ireland north/south conference until 1955.

Mr George La Niece, chairman of the National Education Committee (London) forwarded a copy of *ISMA-Student*, then issued four times a year and made available to all students registered .

STOUT SELLING (GUINNESS) FROM 1759 ONWARD

Stout Selling was the subject of the speaker, J.A. MacKeown, of Arthur Guinness Son & Co. (D) Ltd, at an evening meeting in the Royal Hibernian hotel, Dublin. He said that St James's Gate brewery in Dublin had been operating since 1759, the original brewery covering just four acres. At this time (1954) the area amounted to some 66 acres.

In its early days Guinness had no particular technique of advertising but, as more people continued to ask for Guinness, wholesalers and agents were set up. Guinness sold itself and quickly acquired a reputation, lasting all that time right up to the present. Mr MacKeown mentioned that while other small breweries closed down through the years Guinness became more and more popular.

Mr MacKeown informed those present that the first Guinness advertisement appeared in a national newspaper on 2 February 1929. The product was, of course, well known before that — the company had been in operation since 1759. Indeed since 1887, records had been kept of the number of people who had visited the brewery and been shown around the Guinness premises.

In 1949 the millionth visitor passed through the brewery. Approximately 50,000 visitors called each year. In Mr MacKeown's opinion this created a valued medium of advertising.

More money was spent in England on advertising Guinness than in Ireland. This was due to a greater percentage of the population partaking of the product in Ireland. Hence so much of the advertising allocation was spent in England to stimulate sales there. Examples of Guinness advertisements were read out while others were on view for the observation of members at the meeting.

Finally, Mr MacKeown stated emphatically that he believed that unless one had a good product, advertising alone would not keep up the volume of sales.

ISMA LADIES' NIGHT, DECEMBER 1954

The December 1954 ISMA Ladies' Night was held at the Royal Marine hotel in Dún Laoghaire. Tickets were, by necessity, limited to the first 120 persons.

VISIT TO *THE IRISH TIMES*, OCTOBER 1954

An invitation was issued by *The Irish Times* newspaper to members of the ISMA Ireland branch to visit the premises. They would be able to see firsthand the production process. It would take place on an evening to midnight basis. The invitation was gladly accepted. During the visit the entire process involved in organisation, from the procurement of news and 'copy', editorial, photography, layout, final proofs and print, was shown and explained. This, of course, included the output of the newspaper to the street, city and the total country distribution conveyances.

At the same time, their advertising executive (and a most active member of the ISMA branch) Mr Merville Miller, kindly made a room available on the premises where discussion took place between the ISMA members present at the visit and the various press staff.

I myself was one of those privileged to avail of the opportunity of such a visit and concurred with the general opinion that it afforded an outstanding insight and educational opportunity. In addition, the hospitality extended to all present was also exceptional.

AMERICAN SALES CONFERENCE — A SUCCESS

Mr Leslie Whitehead conveyed to the ISMA London council that the success of the American sales conference, held in Dublin, had substantiated the efforts made and resulted in several applications from prominent personnel, for membership of the Ireland branch. Excellent press and radio coverage had also been obtained.

PHYSICAL FITNESS, NOVEMBER 1954

Dr J.F. Eustace MB, BCh. DPH, gave a lecture relating to the 'Cult of Physical Fitness' at the evening meeting of 12 November 1954.

In it he stated that health could be defined as a state of physical well-being. The body was a piece of complicated machinery requiring fuel in certain quantities and of certain types. He maintained that vitamins were most important, particularly A and D.

Following a bad summer, Dr Eustace went on to say, it would be most necessary to supplement one's diet with the said vitamins. Fluid was also most important and it was recommended that each person should take 2.5 pints per day. However, he did make the point that much of the necessary fluid was consumed in a concealed way via potatoes, fruit and so forth.

Dr Eustace agreed with the opinion of several world experts of the time that alcohol taken in moderation was desirable. Eating methods, and times, were also of much importance. If one did not feel like eating a full meal, the advice was to not take it but to take just enough to satisfy oneself. Eat to savour, otherwise acute indigestion could occur was the message.

Dr Eustace continued by saying that suitably insulated clothes kept the body from being cold, a layer of cotton next to the skin gave the best insulation. In footwear no difference arose when comparing rubber to that of leather soled shoes.

Dr Eustace then stated that he believed that sunlight was not of particular advantage to the body, the gains being largely psychological. During sunbathing any benefit gained was from the air exposure of the body rather than from the sun.

Regular exercise was most desirable to keep one in physical condition. Reviewing the mental aspect, he said there are two systems in the body, the nervous and the symptomatic. The latter ran the body, i.e. blood pressure etc. Continual worry greatly damaged one's physical health and constant strain invoked various types of ailments.

Dr Eustace concluded his speech by mentioning religion. This, in his opinion, was most important for mental stability. He believed that if a man lost faith in religion he lost faith in everything.

FELLOWSHIP OF THE ISMA AWARDED TO IRISHMEN, NOVEMBER 1954

Four members of the Ireland branch were honoured from London by being elevated to the Fellowship of ISMA. They were: C.W. (Bill) Chesson, Tom A. Moran, Donal MacKenzie and Leslie V. Whitehead. The announcement was greeted with acclamation by members at the 12 November 1954 meeting.

SPECIAL MOTION TABLED, NOVEMBER 1954

The executive met on 19 November 1954 to hear a special motion tabled by Mr Leslie Whitehead and seconded by Mr Milmo: 'that in view of the growth of the ISMA association and the extension of the number of countries in which its members reside, ISMA Ireland branch suggested that the national council consider whether the title 'Irish National Chairman' was correct. It was considered in Ireland that the title 'chairman', without further qualification was more appropriate.

FORMATION OF NORTHERN IRELAND STUDENT GROUP

Whilst more students had been enrolled in Dublin for ISMA study, a Northern

Ireland student group was formed, to the surprise of the Ireland branch. It was decided to seek comment from the chairman of the group.

EXPORT TRADE AND CTT ASSISTANCE, NOVEMBER 1954

On the 26 November 1954, a luncheon meeting of ISMA members, at the Metropole hotel, O'Connell Street, Dublin, were addressed by Mr Tim O'Driscoll, director, Córas Tráchtála Teo (CTT). The subject was: 'Export Trade Vitally Necessary to the National Economy'.

Mr O'Driscoll stated that CTT would soon be in a position to give assistance to exporters in non-dollar areas. He then outlined the success of CTT in those areas. Personal contact with potential markets was necessary, although CTT would have previously explored the market, interviewed possible agents, distributed samples and so forth, for potential exporters.

In certain cases CTT gave financial aid to exporters. They also provided full market information and experienced advice on markets, packaging and advertising, inter alia, to all interested parties. Sales managers were now advised to explore constantly the possibility of supplying their goods abroad and should liaise with the Irish Exporters' Association.

Mr O'Driscoll concluded by saying he believed that a firm having confidence in its products and methods, would succeed in widening its business associations both at home and abroad.

DESCRIPTIVE PRICE MERCHANDISING, DECEMBER 1954

The concluding meeting for 1954 was held on 10 December at the Royal Hibernian hotel, Dublin. The speaker was Mr C.A. Knill, ASMA of Sweda Cash Registers and the subject was: 'Descriptive Price Merchandising'.

Mr Knill began by saying that he believed that the quality of goods largely determined the volume of trade. In addition, he said that he was sorry to have to point out that the quality, of some Irish goods, was inferior and certainly not helping trade on the home and export markets. He gave an example of that as being in the manufacture of garden tools, where large quantities were now being imported, particularly garden forks. The average retailer in that business admitted that the imported fork was far superior and although double the price of the Irish one, it sold very well.

Mr Knill maintained that Irish manufacturers could, and indeed must, make goods comparable in every way to those that were imported. Examples of good descriptive merchandise, which in itself advertised goods, helped to promote sales of the commodity.

Packaging was most important, being in effect descriptive merchandising. Retail salesmen, in the opinion of Mr Knill, had generally little or no knowledge of the products being marketed and they were the very people on whom the manufacturers relied. Anything that could be done to further the description of goods and the methods of improving products was a most important factor in expanding a business.

He went on to say that sales people must attend customers promptly and courteously. Details of the product manufactured (regarding the materials, services and benefits to the retailers) must also be given and issued by the manufacturers. The latter in turn should instruct their staff accordingly.

Too much emphasis was given to price and if more care was taken by manufacturers to produce well finished and durable articles, an increase in price would not be detrimental to sales. He contended that, on the contrary, it would widen sales, particularly in the export trade.

Finally, Mr Knill concluded by stating that if manufacturers realised the importance of descriptive price merchandising, sales would increase and so too would standards. However, he added that he did not mean that badly made articles should be sold in fancy packages.

NORTHERN IRELAND ISMA GROUP LIAISE WITH IRELAND BRANCH, 1954

Mr Val Edmunds, chairman of the Northern Ireland ISMA group, agreed that their group committee meetings should be held on Tuesdays to facilitate the presence of branch executive members at Belfast meetings. Mr Leslie Whitehead accepted an invitation to address the Northern group on 17 January 1955.

ISMA EDUCATION REPORTS, 1955

An education report of Mr Joe Bigger was given at the Ireland branch executive committee meeting on 21 January 1955. He had attended the national education meeting in London, where the formation of a Northern Ireland group student society had been discussed but finally deferred.

Suggestions were made by Mr Bernard Roche regarding Ireland branch courses for salesmen to be held in Dublin.

Mr Tom Moran had written an excellent article on education which was published in *The Irish Times*.

'ASTHETICS IN INDUSTRY', FEBRUARY 1955

'Asthetics in Industry' was Senator E.A. McGuire's subject at the monthly meeting of members, February 1955. His opinion was that sales management should hear about the virtues and desirability, where possible, of introducing the principles of design and good taste into business life.

Industrial design was not the special concern of any one group of special-ists or technicians but was a matter of general public interest. There was, then, a noticeable improvement in public taste due to the higher standard of living and the good efforts of wireless and television in particular.

Good taste should provide goods needed at a price people could afford. The speaker also said that he believed that Ireland was rather backward in that field and art was still considered by many businesses as unpractical.

Senator McGuire maintained that art was the efficient producing of what was needed, whether it applied to an item of furniture or to the painting of a landscape. He also believed that to strive after beauty was to strive after good work and workmanship. No good businessman should fail to appreciate the desirability and advantage of applying art to business activities.

Asthetic principles, applied in business, had both material and spiritual advantages, they gave pleasure to the creator, spectator and customer. The character of methods employed were suitable to the object of publicity.

The problem of art in industry was to learn to apply the principles of art to the industrial and commercial work of making and selling goods, and services.

An improvement in the art of advertising had been noticeable over the previous twenty years, both in the use of design and methods of presentation. Good design was good economics and therefore good business.

It was a fallacy that no special training or qualification was required to exercise good taste. Ireland needed effort, by those in a position, to produce articles of good taste. Hence a definite leeway had to be made up.

Some ISMA members did not entirely agree. Mr Joe Bigger (Hammond Lane Foundries) said he believed that all Irish industries were not lacking in design and manufacturers were proud of their products. The Senator con-curred but said there were, however, a great number who were still apathetic in their outlook on design and good taste.

MARKETING RESEARCH, W.V. KINGSTON, 1955

Mr W.V. Kingston of A.C. Nielson and Co., Oxford, gave an enlightening talk on 'Marketing Research' at the ISMA monthly meeting on 11 March 1955. He said, it was his opinion that it would aid Irish farmers considerably if they would avail of marketing research. He appreciated that this would create some difficulties but they could be overcome later.

Giving a concise description of the methods employed in marketing re-search, he showed various charts to emphasise his points. He also submitted information relating to the lines of distribution in which his particular market-ing research organisation worked. In his opinion, the main fundamentals re-quired were:

- knowledge of the size of the market
- the trend and relative importance of one's own and competitive product(s).

Mr Kingston went on to state that he believed all research techniques depended on samples and the type and number depended on the goods being marketed. Original marketing research methods were by:

- main questionnaire
- consumer interview
- consumer panel
- pantry checks
- store audit technique.

In order to prove that marketing research provided essential information for manufacturers, Mr Kingston explained various methods of arriving at the points outlined. He was ably assisted by his colleague, Mr Brook, in answering queries put to him by seven ISMA members, representing a variety of industries.

LORD LUKE IN DUBLIN, 1955

A luncheon meeting at the Metropole Ballroom, O'Connell Street, Dublin on 15 April 1955 was addressed by Lord Luke, National President ISMA London, and recorded as a most interesting and informative occasion.

Present were some sixty-eight members and guests of the Ireland branch, including the chairman of the Irish Management Institute (Sir Charles Harvey) and chairmen of the Irish Exporters' Association, Chamber of Commerce and Córas Tráchtála. The Lord Mayor of Dublin also graced the meeting by his presence.

I recall that his Lordship (Lord Luke) outlined the history of the Incorporated Sales Managers' Association, from its foundation to membership success over a period of some forty-four years. The ISMA was recognised as the authority in all sales and marketing facets of education and business. He congratulated the Ireland branch on its progressive success.

The cost of the luncheon to members was seven shillings and sixpence, (37p), while all guests were sponsored by the branch.

AGM ADVICE FOR NORTHERN IRELAND ISMA GROUP, 1955

Mr W. (Bill) Edmunds, chairman Northern Ireland group, sought guidance regarding the holding of their AGM. He was advised that the procedure was for 50 per cent of committee to retire annually, by rotation, and that election of those nominated take place at their own AGM.

SELLING THE PRODUCT, (HOOVER), 1955

Mr R.T. Griffiths, Hoover Ltd, addressed the ISMA members on 'Selling the product'. This was certainly a very wide subject indeed but he condensed it into the most important aspects.

He began by stating that he believed that the personnel within the sales organisation must be able to sell goods apart from their design. To gear the sales organisation to the job of selling the product, often in face of fierce competition, was undoubtedly sales training. This was a fundamental basis for success in the field.

Senior, and indeed junior, area managers had first to be made fully aware of the training to be given, not only to new recruits but the retraining of existing representatives. The breakdown of a salesman's job provided the decision for a particular basis of training.

Sales force, headed by sixty sales managers, 1955

Mr Griffith's sixty sales managers comprised of men previously on the road selling and were the result of intensive training for each specific job in the organisation. It was his opinion that someone had to make a sale just as someone in a specialised job or profession must perform his complete and efficient function, e.g. a doctor, barrister, accountant, etc.

Sales training methods (Hoover), 1955

Hoover's methods of training were outlined as follows:

• the product — confidence in it, in *all* aspects

• a real understanding of the fundamental principles of everything sold

• knowledge of buying machines and how to handle prospective buyers

• training to sell through dealers and directly on behalf of dealers

• training to be efficient in approach work

• the 'training man' must understand all appplications of equipment to be demonstrated and sold

• the explanation of policy, as to the necessity for decisions regarding the trainee, must rest with the instructor, irrespective of who engaged him, from general manager down

- if passed, after five weeks of intensive training, the trainee went out in the selling field, under the guidance of an area manager

- the special grading of staff for future promotion advancement.

The experience of Mr Griffiths showed that the success of any company rested on the sales manager, who must have been suitably and fully trained for his job. This did not mean just through previous experience, gained the hard way as a salesman, but trained additionally in the fundamental functions, being the fully trained profession of sales management

SECOND AGM, IRELAND BRANCH ISMA, 1955

The second AGM of the ISMA Ireland branch was held at the offices of Aspro Ltd, Inchicore, Dublin on 3 June 1955. There were 30 present. These were: Bill Chesson, chairman, Brian Murphy, hon.secretary, D.M. Milmo, hon. treasurer, Lord Killanin (president designate), Messrs D. MacKenzie, L.V. Whitehead, S.J. Doyle, H.N.B. Palmer, J.C. Bigger, A. Brownlee, P.K. Duggan, N. McConnell, J. Kierans, L. Maude-Roxby, E.C. Lawson, L.C. Thorn, A. O'Reilly, T. Watson, A.H. Harrison, J.W. Gorman, H.E. McCormack, P. Rackow, D. Targett, G. Stewart, J.S. Henderson, W.D. Fraser, T.A. Moran, D.A. Black, H.V. Woods and Mr David Griffiths, director ISMA London.

The chairman, Bill Chesson, said ISMA was becoming a power in business circles in Ireland. He recalled highlights of the previous session, both in the quality of speakers at meetings and their selected subjects. In particular, he referred to the Ireland-American conference, the taxation commission meetings and the visit of Lord Luke.

Ireland branch executive members had, as far as was possible, attended the Northern Ireland group committee and other meetings there. The furtherance of education was also importantly related.

The badge of office was presented to Lord Killanin, by Mr David Griffiths, on his Lordship's installation as president of the branch for 1955–6 session.

Branch officers of ISMA elected for 1955–56

The newly elected officers were then announced:

- President: Lord Killanin

- Chairman: Mr C.W. (Bill) Chesson

- Vice-Chairmen: Messrs W.W. Wilson, T.A. Moran and W.D. (Bill) Fraser

- Hon. Secretary: Mr Brian Murphy

- Hon treasurer: Mr D.M. Milmo.

The executive committee appointed was:

J.C. Bigger, L.C. Thorn, D. MacKenzie, D.A. Black, S.J. Doyle, R.G. Moffett, M.H. Coote, A.H. Harrison, B. Roche, C.V. Edmunds, D.J. Targett, N. McConnell, H.N.B. Palmer, L.A. Luke and L.V. Whitehead.

Fellowships, Ireland branch ISMA, 1955

Fellowship certificates were presented by Lord Killanin, president, in recognition of their length of service and contribution to sales management and marketing to: Bill Chesson, Donal MacKenzie, Tom Moran and Leslie Whitehead.

It was announced then that forty-three students were registered and studying for the ISMA diploma.

THOM'S BUSINESS DIRECTORY, 1955

With the use of Thom's business directory, Michael Coote prepared a comprehensive list of potential ISMA members from various business categories. His proposal to personally contact a selected few, whom it would be considered to be of advantage to the branch by their experience, was accepted with appreciation. However, caution was expressed that quality must not be sacrified for quantity.

Mr Bill Chesson, branch chairman, explained the meaning, interpreted by ISMA, of the 'family tree' in relation to membership. He stated that it was like the seniority of individuals in a company.

Mr Sean Ó Ceallaigh was thanked for all the work he had done in helping the student society and for his continued interest.

MEMBERSHIP OF ISMA GLOBALLY, JUNE 1955

Addressing the AGM, Mr David Griffiths said while ISMA generally was finding no problem regarding the number of members, now standing at 4,700, there was still an insufficient number of students registered. Only 1,500 were registered for Britain, Ireland and overseas. He asked for an increase in effort to obtain student registrations by means of an earnest recruitment drive.

DECISION RE QUALIFICATIONS OF SPEAKERS, JULY 1955

An innovation, at the executive committee meeting of 15 July 1955 was the decision taken to cite the qualifications of speakers at meetings and including same on the programme syllabus cards being prepared for printing.

SALES MANAGERS'CONFERENCE, PARIS 1955

The Department of Industry and Commerce drew attention to a sales managers' conference which was to take place shortly in Paris.

Also, it was agreed that in future newly elected members and associates be introduced to the branch chairman by their proposers.

AWARD TO ISMA IRISH STUDENT, 1955

London advised that at the final ISMA examinations Mr T. Brendan Fortune, a student of the Ireland branch, had won the overall special prize for market research examination. It was decided to honour him at the President's Night dinner, with suitable press publicity, in February 1956.

NORTHERN IRELAND GROUP ISMA, MEMBERSHIP DRIVE 1955

A membership recruitment meeting was organised by the Northern Ireland group of ISMA and held at the Grand hotel, Belfast on 27 September 1955.

In addition to the association members there were several prominent speakers present in support, including Lord Glentoran, David Griffiths of London and J.R. Price. At this stage the membership of the Ireland branch of ISMA had reached 100.

THE IRISH TIMES VISIT RECALLED, SEPTEMBER 1955

At the evening meeting of 29 September 1955 members of the Ireland branch recalled, and once again expressed appreciation, for the action of *The Irish Times* newspaper management, in affording the opportunity of visiting the works and having an excellent tour and production explanation. Two separate groups of ISMA members had visited the works. It was agreed that it had been a most instructive and informative get-together and, in every way, a memorable occasion.

As a follow-up to the works visit, ISMA member Merville Miller, advertising manager of *The Irish Times*, and P. Campbell, works manager, addressed members in the Royal Hibernian hotel Dublin.

In his address Mr Miller said management welcomed such visits of business executives. The main purpose of the invitation had been to give some idea of the happenings in a newspaper organisation during the course of an average twenty-four hours. He said that he specially welcomed, at all times, businessmen and advertising agents who brought along their problems for discussion, though 'explanation sometimes resulted in ulcers rather than answers'.

Going over some of the various points made during the tours, Mr Miller again stressed the importance of 'copy' being correct when passed to his department. In relation to that he explained that their 'copy' deadline was mid-day, so that the newspaper dummy could be made up each day by 2.30 p.m. Unfortunately it happened, too often, that corrections had to be made last thing before printing, mainly due to the 'copy' being incorrect.

He explained the technicalities of block-making, production of 'mats' and so forth. He also mentioned the differences between coarse and fine screen blocks and showed that '65' screen blocks were the most suitable for use in Irish newspapers, to ensure the best possible reproduction.

Mr D.J. Targett, an ISMA member, posed a question about circulation sales surveys. He was informed that while such were made, an agreement existed between the newspapers not to disclose the actual breakdown of circulation figures. The rule applied to both parts of Ireland, as it did to sales on specific days. Mr Miller agreed that circulation was actually very consistent from day to day. He personally considered it doubtful whether any survey gave a true assessment of any market. This was in view of the many angles considered and bearing in mind that they often had no relation to circulation figures.

Congratulations were extended to Mr Derek Black, at the meeting, on having been awarded a Fellowship of ISMA.

ADVERTISING PRESS CLUB 'BRAINS TRUST' MEETING, OCTOBER 1955

At the invitation of the Advertising Press Club, the executive and members of the ISMA branch were present at the Shelbourne hotel, Dublin, on 14 October 1955 at a joint meeting.

For a first meeting it proved to be very successful and consisted of a 'brains trust' made up of two teams, of three members each, from the Advertising Press Club and ISMA. The latter panel comprised of Bill Fraser, Bill Chesson and Tom Moran.

RECOGNITION FOR THE ISMA STUDENT SOCIETY, 1955

At the 23 September 1955 meeting of the council, the hon. secretary was instructed to announce, at each future monthly meeting of members, details of forthcoming student society meetings.

For the benefit of student education it was pleasant to find that a booklet, concerning the ISMA student society, had been compiled by Mr David Griffiths. Arrangements were made to obtain a supply for Irish student distribution.

Mr Joe Bigger reported that he attended a London meeting which discussed educational courses generally, the availability of sales films and special weekend courses organised there. He also advised the executive that he had accepted an invitation, for November 1955, to present a short address at the Cork conference.

LADIES'NIGHT, NOVEMBER 1955

Ladies' Night, 26 November 1955, was held at the Royal hotel, Bray, Co. Wicklow. It proved yet again to be an outstanding success. The attendance was 161 (someone without a partner?!) and stupendous gift parcels were given to the ladies. Much publicity was obtained in both the *Marketing* (managing editor Stanley Talbot of London) and *Social & Personal* magazines.

RATHBORNE/CTT INVESTIGATION OF AMERICAN MARKET, 1955

Mr H. (Eimear) McCormack, MD of J.G. Rathborne Ltd, (the oldest manfacturing organisation in Ireland, having been established in 1488 and still very much in operation at present) addressed ISMA meeting of members on 11 November 1955. His company manufactured candles. The subject he was to speak on was 'The American Market as Seen by an Irish Exporter'.

On the home market, output for candles was then mainly for ecclesiastical use with the balance for special social and domestic household requirements. Mr McCormack felt that the use of candles, particularly in decorative shapes and colour, should be in considerable demand in the future in other countries.

He decided he could not offer any magical formula for successful selling in America but outlined some of the personal experiences he had in that country. He then went on to give his impressions of the market.

Córas Tráchtála Teo, market research, 1955

Córas Tráchtála Teo (CTT), the Irish export board, had been of great assistance and carried out a preliminary market investigation for Rathborne's.

Mr McCormack said he initially made a visit to America in 1954 and obtained a substantial amount of business then. Success warranted a full-scale investigation into the potential market. The latter covered the gleaning of information regarding new techniques, and so forth, and he discussed same with CTT.

Mr Mc Cormack stated that he believed that anyone travelling to the USA with the export trade in mind had to have an overall picture of production and sales. Only in that way could all questions, covering both functions, be answered without reference back to one's firm.

The selection of suitable agents in the areas, in which sales were anticipated, was most important. He found that all prospective American agents said they required exclusive rights for handling any important product. That was so, whether they had nationwide distribution facilities or not. He did not grant a sole agency to any individual agent.

Mr McCormack continued on to say that CTT had developed to a stage where they went practically all the way towards selecting potential agents for any manufacturer in Ireland to choose from. However, that as it was, the manufacturer had to make the final decision.

He also stated that he believed the full use of a firm's cost accountant in financial assessment was vital, because, unless a completely up-to-date costing system was used, it became impossible to meet the day-to-day variations required in the American market.

It was his opinion that selling in America involved the use of trade display centres. These he felt should be used in Ireland also, as for example, so many business people living outside of Dublin visited the capital throughout the year. He maintained that to achieve the sale of any product in America it was essential to use the following discovered factors:

1. Goods must be first class quality, preferably original in design and packaging.

2. Price must be, at least, competitive.

3. Delivery promises must be fulfilled, no matter what complications had to be overcome.

It is reasonable to suggest that the above basics are as true today as then.

The US statistics showed that in 1955, £8m. (sterling) worth of candles were manufactured in that country. They certainly had a high standard of quality in America and descriptive colour catalogues would have had to have been seen to be believed.

Rathborne's efforts in the US markets were rewarding, both from the sales and valuable findings made in market research surveys. I myself well remember Eimear McCormack relating that, after the first orders were shipped and delivered from Rathborne's to the States, a more than normal period of time took place in receipt of repeat/new orders. He then travelled again to the market and found that there was a particular reason for delay. The Americans had found Irish candles to be too heavy. This was due to the avoirdupois differential (being only fourteen ounces to the pound weight in the States, compared to sixteen ounces in Ireland).

This resulted, obviously, in less material content for further production for US export and also consequent saving in freight costs. The double benefit to Rathborne's also brought a subsequent increase in the all important export profitable sales.

CORK ISMA CONFERENCE, DECEMBER 1955

An important conference was held at the Imperial hotel, Cork on 8 December 1955. The Lord Mayor of Cork, Alderman P. McGrath, Lord Killanin, president of the Ireland branch ISMA, C.W. Chesson, chairman, fourteen members of the executive and some branch members from Dublin were included in the attendance of forty-eight.

Mr R.G. (Bob) Moffett welcomed everyone to the conference and to Cork with a view to forming a group of the association there. He introduced the Lord Mayor and the Ireland branch chairman.

Mr Chesson said that the executive committee and himself had travelled specially to Cork to sell the idea of a Munster group of ISMA. Furthermore, sales management being one of the most important branches of industry, he believed that there was no doubt that when sales managers were branded together outstanding benefits accrued.

At that time (December 1955), Cork had two recent graduate members of ISMA. They were a Mr O'Sullivan and a Mr B. Cronin. The Lord Mayor, Alderman P. McGrath, considered that an ISMA group in Cork would be a great asset to Munster when formed and said he was pleased to see such an important gathering, representing the business community of Cork, at the conference.

Sales management emphasis, Lord Killanin, December 1955

Lord Killanin spoke on the subject of 'sales management' and said that, in his opinion, Cork had become an important centre of industry in Ireland. Undoubtedly a need for an ISMA group in Munster was apparent. On the suggestion of Lord Killanin, it was agreed that Mr Bob Moffett act as convenor of a meeting to officially form a group of ISMA in Munster. Considerable publicity, organised by George O'Toole, PRO, followed the Cork conference meeting.

Sales management had become a scientific part of industry and his lordship said he was wholeheartedly in favour of the creation of the proposed group.

Heavy industry was engaged in at Cork, while ISMA was and would play an important part in its development in Ireland. It was then agreed that the theme of 'sales management examination subjects' be concentrated on, for general member meetings in the coming year (1956).

History and aims of ISMA

Mr Chesson then went on to say that the Incorporated Sales Managers' Association, (ISMA), was a professional body of sales managers.

Founded in London in 1911, it was the oldest professional management body. Mr Leslie Whitehead, past branch chairman, said the only surviving member of the original foundation meeting of ISMA was Mr Stanley Talbot, editor of the *Marketing* journal. The aims and objects of the association were the provision of sales promotion, market research, advertising and economic distribution. Mr Whitehead suggested that a history of the ISMA (Irish group) from its formation in 1947 through to branch status should be compiled. (The history was, however, never compiled until this production).

The monthly magazine *Marketing* was distributed to each member free, as part of the service of the association. A library was available in London also for the mailing use of members, including Ireland. Important meetings and conferences organised in Ireland were recalled, including with Córas Tráchtála Teo, the Irish Exporters' Association and National Sales Executives-Inc., New York.

Student activities, entrusted in the Ireland branch, involved the education and training of the student groups in Dublin and Belfast. A student's journal was free to members of the student groups.

The ISMA theme at that time was: 'Nothing happens until someone sells something'. Selling had become a key part of business and it was extremely important that sales managers came together to discuss problems and provided education for the up-and-coming personnel, whether they were connected with large or small firms.

By 1921, when incorporation took place, a great deal of work had been done. Members had set about, by the systematic study of their profession, sifting the good ideas and methods from the bad ones, determining what a sales manager should know, in order to do his job effectively.

SUBSCRIPTION FOR ISMA MEMBERSHIP, 1955

The subscription in 1955 for full membership was £5.5.0 (£5.25 in punts today) associate £3.3.0 and student £2.2.0 with an entrance fee of £2.2.0.

STATISTICS, DR R.C. GEARY, 1956

The opening meeting of 1956, held at the Hibernian hotel, was addressed by Dr R.C. Geary, Director of Statistics at the Department of the Taoiseach.

Dr Geary stated his belief that close co-operation between firms and the statistics office was essential to the systematic running of a business concern. He felt that statistics were essential in order to keep up-to-date with modern business trends. Irish firms would be well advised to set up their own statistical system like that in use at the Central Statistics Office. He offered advice from his department, on request, to make suggestions to individual firms.

The necessity for each firm to make returns requested by the statistics office, and promptly, was emphasised. He described how the statistics office worked and gave interesting data and also explained the census report and maps, and presented copies to those at the meeting.

ISMA PRESIDENT'S NIGHT, FEBRUARY 1956

The guests at the President's Night on 9 February 1956 included the vice-chairman of the Irish Management Institute, editor (Mr Stanley Talbot) of *Marketing*, president of the Chamber of Commerce, Mr Martin Gleeson, Vocational education committee, (VEC), the Lord Mayor, president of the Federation of Irish Industries and president of the Irish Exporters' Association. The overall attendance at the dinner was ninety-seven.

Unfortunately the formation of a Munster group of the ISMA had to be postponed as a sufficient number of members had not been obtained.

BRANCH OFFICERS OF ISMA, 1956–57

Officers elected for the 1956–57 session at the executive meeting of 7 March 1956 were:

- President: Lord Killanin
- Chairman: Mr C.W. Chesson
- Vice-Chairmen: Messrs T.A. Moran, W.D. Fraser and M.H. Coote
- Hon. Treasurer: Mr S. Miller
- Hon. Secretary: Mr Brian Murphy
- Press Officer: Mr George O'Toole.

A new lady member of the Ireland branch of ISMA, Miss Anna Fox, was welcomed in the Royal Hibernian hotel, at the monthly meeting of 9 March 1956. Lord Woolton was announced as being the new president of ISMA globally.

MECHANISED ACCOUNTING, MARCH 1956

The speaker for the March 1956 evening meeting was Mr M.J. Appleby, Manager of Powers-Samas (Ireland) Ltd. He illustrated his talk by showing films on mechanised accounting using punched cards. Much appreciation was expressed for his detailed demonstration of the beneficial results achieved by such varied use.

The executive was asked by members to provide a solution to their position relative to the Irish Management Institute, (IMI). They were asked if members of the ISMA considered themselves affiliated to IMI or not.

SELLING ELECTRICITY, APRIL 1956

The subject of the address by Mr E.A. Lawlor, PRO of the Electricity Supply Board at the meeting of 13 April 1956 was: 'Selling Electricity'. A film shown by him covered detail of electrical power stations throughout Ireland.

An educational discussion on electrical provision and uses took place following an interesting question and answer session.

THIRD AGM OF THE IRELAND BRANCH OF ISMA, MAY 1956

Aspro-Nicholas Ireland, Naas Road, Dublin, housed the Ireland branch of the ISMA AGM of May 25, 1956. There were twenty-five members present. These were C.W. Chesson, chairman, and Messrs L.V. Whitehead, M.H. Coote, C.A. Knill, N. McConnell, L.C. Thorn, H.V. Woods, A. Brownlee, J.W. Gorman, D. Targett, E.K. O'Brien, D.A. Black, P.J. McGeeney, M. Kennedy, H. Doolan, S. Millar, T.K. Watson, C.C. O'Dowd, S.J. Doyle, A.H. Harrison, J.S. Henderson, P. Ryan, G. O'Toole, D.M. Milmo and B.M. Murphy. Apologies numbered fourteen. Mr D.M. Smallbone (London) hon. secretary of the ISMA parent body was also present.

It was with pleasure that Lord Killanin consented to remain in office, as president of the branch. Mr Michael Coote was elected as vice-chairman and Mr Chesson thanked all sub-committee chairmen for their earnest work and co-operation.

The executive committee for the branch (1956–57) was announced as: Messrs J.C. Bigger, D.A. Black, C.V. Edmunds, (N. Ireland), A.H. Harrison, H.N.B. Palmer, L.C. Thorn, B. Roche, S.J. Doyle, J.S. Henderson, J.P.D. Kierans, N. McConnell, D.M. Milmo, R.G. Moffett, (Cork), D.J. Targett and the past-chairman (ex officio) L.V. Whitehead.

A visitor from the Bermingham ISMA branch, Mr Donald Hewsen, was made welcome. As usual refreshments were provided by kindness of Mr Chesson, for which he was sincerely thanked.

The next executive committee meeting, 20 April 1956, noted that the Irish Management Institute (IMI) had deferred a request for representation of the Ireland branch of ISMA on their council, even though it was known that ISMA London were so represented on the British Institute of Management (BIM).

SALES APPROACH TO THE NATIONAL FARMERS' ASSOCIATION, JUNE 1956

It was decided to communicate with the National Farmers' Association, (NFA), regarding agricultural productivity and selling aspects.

CHAMBER OF COMMERCE JOURNAL, 1956

Mr Joe Bigger complimented Mr Leslie Whitehead on articles he had prepared which were published in the Chamber of Commerce journal. Mr George O'Toole, branch press officer, was appointed to the editorial committee of ISMA London. Mr Smallbone, hon. secretary of the latter, sent copies of the course for junior executives to be used in the Ireland branch.

IMI/ISMA JOINT SEMINARS, JULY 1956

The Irish Management Institute, (IMI), made a proposal that they and the Ireland branch of the ISMA should organise seminars on marketing, merchandising and other relative subjects — one seminar to be in Dublin and another to be held in Cork. It was consequently intimated, to Mr Brian Quigley (IMI), that the branch would give full support provided the latter was not financially responsible.

MANUEL OF SALES ORGANISATION (UK), SEPTEMBER 1956

The third section of a manuel of sales management, related to sales organisation and control, was published by ISMA London in September 1956. It was priced at 6/- (30p) per copy and contained 48 A4 pages.

The manual dealt with company organisation, particularly in relation to the executive structure of industrial and trading companies. It stated it was the responsibility of the managing director to see that the board's policy and directions were implemented. To do so effectively it required departmental managers appropriate to the nature of the business. Only in such a way could every function be properly provided for and co-ordinated in relation to the respective departments.

The three main functions were defined as finance, production and distribution. It was essential to recognise the sales manager as a senior company executive. He had to be prepared to meet his fellow executives, from the production and finance branches, with facts and figures on the progress of sales. He also should be prepared to co-operate with them in producing the best possible results in prevailing conditions.

Furthermore, the sales manager had full responsibility for his sales staff and the control of all those answerable to him. In other words he became an administrator.

Inter alia, the contents necessary for an efficient sales manual were detailed. Very diverse subjects were dealt with in the volume. These included:

* implementing a sales programme

* the recruitment and training of a sales force

* the statistics of sales

* territories

* incentives

* reports

* remuneration

* advertising

* the handling of complaints.

At that time the compilation was considered a very useful guide manual and a reference for sales trainers and sales managers alike.

ISMA CORK GROUP INAUGURATED, SEPTEMBER 1956

Arrangements were made to officially inaugurate the ISMA Munster group, from 1 September 1956. A very successful meeting resulted in the first officers being elected. These were:

* Chairman: Mr R.G. (Bob) Moffett

* Hon. Treasurer: Mr B. Scally

* Hon. Secretary: Mr B.J. Cronin.

Mr Leslie Whitehead addressed the new Cork group on behalf of the council and members of the Ireland branch. A number of Dublin members were also present to convey their sincere wishes and support.

Mr R.G. (Bob) Moffett became the first Cork group chairman. This was a tribute to his outstanding work over previous years in the Ireland branch.

Mr Harry Woods submitted the education committee programme arrangements for 1956–57 session. He reported that there were now fifty-two students enrolled for the ISMA diploma course.

AGRICULTURAL BUYING AND SELLING, SEPTEMBER 1956

On 14 September 1956, Dr Louis P.F. Smith, Ph.D., economic advisor to the National Farmers' Association, (NFA), addressed the branch members on the subject of: 'Buying and Selling Agriculture'. The discussions following this prompted many questions in a wide range of aspects.

DEVELOPMENT OF MOTOR FUELS, OCTOBER 1956

A very interesting talk, updating the development of motor fuels, enhanced by an explanatory film, was provided by Mr W.S. Ault, manager of the technical department of Shell-Mex & BP Ltd (London) on 12 October 1956 at the Hibernian hotel, Dublin.

AMERICAN SALES METHODS: IRISH ADAPTATION, NOVEMBER 1956

Mr A.H. Harrison, Colgate-Palmolive (Ireland) Ltd, having addressed the members' monthly meeting on 9 November 1956, prompted twelve questions about his subject: 'American Sales Methods — Adaptation to Irish Marketing'.

DIRECT MAIL, NOVEMBER 1956

Mr Brian Clancy, Aer Lingus Teo, an ISMA member, advised the executive that an association to foster and study the practice of 'direct mail', as a medium for use in advertising and salesmanship, was contemplated. It was agreed that the ISMA branch would help in any way suitable and that Mr George O'Toole, press officer, would attend a meeting of the direct mail organising committee.

Mr Tom Moran pressed for representation of the ISMA branch on the National Farmers' Association, (NFA), following the recent successful ISMA agricultural conference arranged with Dr O'Donovan.

Mr Don Bevan of Cork was appointed liaison officer for the communication of the affairs of ISMA between Cork and Dublin.

CREATION OF CHAIRMAN'S CHEST FUND, NOVEMBER 1956

At the suggestion of ISMA London, the raffle proceeds of the Ladies' Night function (£60) were allocated to a newly created benevolent fund of the ISMA Ireland branch. The fund became known as the 'Chairman's Chest Fund'.

As in London, it was agreed that the fund would be reserved for the provision of financial aid in the case of a member's circumstantial need. A specially formed sub-committee was formed to confidentially consider and decide on such cases if and when they arose

Ladies' Night was held at the Grand hotel, Malahide, Co. Dublin on 24 November 1956 and a very enjoyable time was had by all. The tickets were 30 shillings each (£1.50 today). Over 200 attended the function.

PETROL RATIONING, DECEMBER 1956

In December 1956 members were circularised, as was the public generally, that it was proposed to ration petrol. The scheme proposed the enforcement of rationing from 1 January 1957.

Views of members were sought as to how rationing would affect employment in their companies. A survey was made and sent to the Department of Industry and Commerce, emphasising the need for supply to keep to the required standards of commercial business. Otherwise, it was stated, the economy would suffer.

PHOTOGRAPHY — ITS USES IN SELLING, 1956

Mr Rex Roberts gave a very informative and most interesting talk on the subject of 'Photography and its Uses in Selling'. The evening meeting was held at the Royal Hibernian hotel, Dublin, on 7 December 1956. Adding to the enjoyment, a series of well-produced films were shown by him.

DIRECT SELLING, JANUARY 1957

Opening the year 1957, at the ISMA branch evening meeting, member Mr Jack Feldman, was deemed as having given a 'forceful, well illustrated and highly interesting' talk entitled: 'Direct Selling — the Organisation and Planning of Salesmanship Schools'.

A lively discussion then took place, summed up by Mr M.P. Kavanagh.

In the course of his vote of thanks, he stated that 'the paper was most constructive, presented in an excellent balance, between instructional essentials and some amusing touches of humour'.

I myself can well remember Jack Feldman telling the story of how one of his salesmen had called a number of times on a certain large potential customer, without obtaining an order. The product in question was fire-extinguishers.

Remuneraton to the sales force was by payment of commission on ascending scale, depending on the size of the order. However, the said salesman eventually obtained an unusually substantial order which entailed supplying an entire factory and office areas with new fire exinguishers. This proved good sales follow-up endeavour and confirmed his training.

Unfortunately, when the salesman promptly received his considerable commission cheque, he did not turn into work again for several weeks. That, of course, was not the object as the company required the continuous effort of sales. The sales manager took cognisance then and made a new basis of agreement to pay representatives commission spread over a reasonable mutual agreed period. It was to the benefit of salesmen, as very large orders were exceptional, so a more even flow of remuneration was the ideal to aim for.

MEMBERSHIP FIGURES FOR IRELAND BRANCH ISMA, JANUARY 1957

Membership of the ISMA Ireland branch was 142 in January 1957.

CATTLE MARKETING, FEBRUARY 1957

Mr Tom Moran, having attended a prior meeting of the National Farmers' Association, (NFA), was appointed to represent the ISMA Ireland branch at their future meetings. In February 1957 he informed the executive of a scheme, submitted by the NFA, in connection with cattle marketing.

Mr Michael Coote was of the opinion that the proposed European Union and marketing had a direct link. Consequently, it was arranged to ask Mr J.J. Stacey and Dr Louis P. Smith to address a full meeting of members.

CUSTOMS UNION AND FREE TRADE AREAS, FEBRUARY 1957

A special meeting of the Ireland branch of ISMA was called and held on 18 February 1957 at the Royal Hibernian hotel, Dublin.

Mr Tom Moran opened discussion on the proposed 'Customs' Union and Free Trade' areas. He introduced Mr J.J. Stacey, director-general of the Federation of Irish Manufacturers, (FIM), and Dr Louis P. Smith, economic adviser to the National Farmers' Association. These gentlemen addressed the meeting giving a full outline of what was intended and answered many questions.

Mr Tom Moran drew attention to the rebate of income tax applicable to exporters. He expressed the hope that the new government would make provisions satisfactory to exporters in general.

The council appointed the following officers for 1957–58 session:

- President: Lord Killanin
- Chairman: Mr Tom A. Moran
- Vice-Chairmen: Messrs Bill Fraser, Michael Coote and Stephen Doyle
- Hon. Treasurer: Mr S. Miller
- Hon. Secretary: Mr Brian Murphy
- Press Officer: Mr George O'Toole.

MANAGEMENT, APRIL 1957

At the meeting of members on 12 April 1957 the speaker was Mr W.K. Holden, Urwick, Orr and Partners (Ireland) Ltd. He spoke on the subject of 'Management — Organisation for Maximum Sales Efficiency'.

Mr Holden gave a very wide discourse covering production, research, sales control and personnel. Ireland needed better sales management, he stressed, and also sound company organisation

The IMI/ISMA conference had been very successful. Mr Harrison's paper was deemed very factful, instructive and well presented, said Mr Bill Chesson, branch chairman.

An interesting decision then made (April 1957) was an announcement that students be invited to take part in the annual golf outing of ISMA members.

Second decade of the history of sales management and marketing in Ireland, 1957–1967

FOURTH AGM, ISMA, MAY 1957

The fourth AGM of the Ireland branch of ISMA was held on 24 May 1957 at the offices of Aspro-Nicholas (Ireland) Ltd, Inchicore, Dublin. There were 33 present. Those were: Mr C.W. Chesson (outgoing chairman), Lord Killanin (president), Messrs T.A. Moran, S. Miller, J.S. Henderson, W.F. Keys, L.V. Whitehead, S.J. Doyle, J.W. Gorman, H.C. Browne, L.C. Thorn, P. Greville, J.T. Wood, D. Ryan, W.P. Cavanagh, F.L. Cox, J.J. Carmody, N. McConnell, H.E. McCormick, C. Barnes, A.G. Brownlee, R.L. Thompson, G.G. Stuart, A. O'Reilly, D.M. Milmo, H.V. Woods, G.F. Orme, J. Feldman, F.W. Armstrong, A. Grimston, D. MacKenzie, T.B. Fortune and Brian Murphy.

By this time the membership of the Ireland branch of ISMA had reached 152. Under the chairmanship of Bob Moffett the Munster group progressed, while the well-established Northern Ireland group had shown very progressive results and attainment.

Lord Killanin, president, was thanked sincerely for his unfailing interest, support and help in the success of the branch. Outgoing chairman, Bill Chesson, reminded members that his successor, Tom Moran, had been a founder member of ISMA, Ireland, a graduate, who recently obtained his BL (Bachelor of Law) degree.

The newly elected executive committee members for 1957–58 were: Messrs R.G. Moffet (Cork), J.C. Bigger, N. McConnell, A.H. Harrison, H.V. Woods, H.E. McCormack, D.J. Targett, W.J.C. Milne, J.S. Henderson, H.N.B. Palmer, D.M. Milmo, L.C. Thorn, W.P. Cavanagh, L.V. Whitehead and C.W. Chesson (ex officio).

Mr Bill Chesson, having been presented with his past-chairman's badge, was thanked for arranging the hospitality (courtesy of his company Aspro-Nicholas) by providing refreshments after the AGM.

Harry Woods then gave a detailed report on education and student activities, while for the export committee, Michael Coote reported on a letter sent to the Minister of Industry and Commerce, offering ISMA support for the 'free trade' proposals. Regarding the programme, Tom Moran said that it was London policy for future meeting addresses to members that they centre on the European Union.

EUROPEAN FREE TRADE, (EFTA), 1957

It was considered essential that a paper be prepared on the marketing of agricultural produce, within the scope of the European Union, and included in the coming syllabus programme.

From my own records, it is worthy here to recall the position of Ireland regarding the European Free Trade Area (EFTA) situation.

The following countries were then members of the OEEC: Austria, Belgium, Britain, Denmark, France, Western Germany, Greece, Iceland, Ireland, Italy, Luxembourg, the Netherlands, Norway, Portugal, Sweden, Switzerland and Turkey. Six countries (referred to as 'the six', Belgium, France, Germany, Italy, Luxembourg and the Netherlands) decided to form a Customs and Economic Union of their territories.

The OEEC established a working party to consider the possible forms and methods of association on a multilateral basis between the proposed Customs and Economic Union and member countries not taking part therein. The working party considered the creation of a 'free trade area' to include the Customs and Economic Union of member countries.

A 'free trade area' was defined as 'an area in which the member countries abolished trade barriers (tariffs and quantitative import and export restrictions etc.) against one another'. At the same time each country, it was said, retained its freedom to maintain individual trade barriers with regard to countries outside the area. In a Customs and Economic Union trade barriers were abolished between the members but there was a common tariff in relation to countries outside the union.

Again, if the free trade area was established it would apply to industry only, as at that stage agriculture was being left out of the plan. The system for the removal of restrictions under consideration by the Customs Union of 'the six' was established.

At the same time it was considered desirable to have a common system for the customs union and free trade area. In effect, it meant that unless Ireland, in common with other countries in the process of economic development, was granted special treatment, she would, if she joined the free trade area, have to refrain from granting new or additional protection to her industries. It would be against countries within the area and Ireland would have to withdraw her existing protection gradually, within a proposed transitional period of twelve to fifteen years. Similarly, other countries would have to remove any existing measures aimed at the protection of their own industries.

It was clear that the economies of the countries of the free trade area would become increasingly interdependent as trade barriers were removed. Certain member countries expressed to the working party the view that the establishment of the area should involve more than the mere abolition of import and export barriers to trade.

There were indications then that measures would have to be considered to harmonise regulations relating to certain conditions of employment. These would include wages, over-time, paid holidays and so forth. It would also be vital to solve, possibly by means of investment and re-adaptation funds, the problem of granting assistance to countries or industries which were adversely affected by the establishment of the area.

In Ireland's case, it was necessary for the government to take into account, not only economic considerations but to consider many factors, including that of national policy affecting the question of the country's participation in a movement towards the closer association of the countries of western Europe in their common interest.

The formation of a free trade area and the emergence of an integrated western European market, of some 250 million people, were developments that would have significant implications for Ireland's economy. Fundamental re-appraisal of economic plans and policies was required.

Consideration by government was given to:

1. The effects of assuming an obligation to remove existing protection progressively, over a period of years and of foregoing the right to impose further protection against countries within the area.

2. The possibility of the inclusion in the agreement of establishing the area of provisions for:

    *   escape clauses related, for example, to the balance of payments' difficulties

    *   special arrangements modifying the obligations in favour of member countries, like Ireland, whose economies were not fully developed

    *   investment and re-adaptation funds

    *   measures to avoid unfair competition (dumping for example)

    *   the benefits to accrue to Irish exports from the removal of tariffs and other trade barriers in the countries of the area.

SPEAKER REQUEST, 1957

Mr Alex Harrison (Palmolive-Colgate) ISMA member, received a personal invitation from Messrs D. E. Williams, Tullamore, Co. Offaly to address their executives and sales representatives.

PROS AND CONS OF THE PROPOSED COMMON MARKET, SEPTEMBER 1957

In formally opening the 1957–58 session, Tom Moran, Ireland branch chairman, introduced the speaker Mr E.C. Lee, FSMA, national chairman, ISMA London, whose subject was entitled: 'Some of the Pros and Cons of the Proposed Common Market'.

A number of illuminating details on the problems of free trade were offered for consideration. With the subject foremost in the minds of sales executives at the time, Mr Lee's contribution was much appreciated.

It was announced then that a conference on free trade would be held at the Royal Festival Hall, London, on 28 October 1957. Members in Ireland were urged to attend, if at all possible.

FOUNDER MEMBER ISMA, IRELAND, H.N.B. PALMER, RIP

It was learned, with sincere regret, that one of the founder members of the ISMA in Ireland Mr H.N.B. Palmer had passed away. Deepest sympathy was expressed to Mrs Palmer.

STUDENT SOCIETY REQUESTS

Mr Harry Woods reported that future meetings of the student society would be held in Wynne's hotel, Abbey Street, Dublin. At a recent student meeting the formation of a small library had been discussed. Students asked respectfully for:

1. Members to donate books on sales subjects and copies of the journal *Marketing*, to help their study.

2. Facilities for visiting factories and businesses where they could be shown an insight into same.

Messrs George O'Toole, Eimear McCormick and Tom Moran said that students would be very welcome at their firms, at suitable times which could be arranged. There were then twenty-two students registered for the diploma examinations.

FINAL EXAM SUCCESS FOR NORTHERN IRELAND STUDENTS

London advised of the success of Northern Ireland students, Messrs Pattison and Atkins, who had completed the ISMA final examination. It was arranged that Mr Harrison would present the diplomas when he was in Belfast addressing the group.

EDUCATION FOR MARKETING, 1957

Details of a conference arranged for 1 November 1957 were given by Mr Harry Woods. The theme of the conference was: 'Education for Marketing'. It would be opened by Mr Sean Lemass TD. Mr Woods outlined the extensive mailing coverage undertaken and reported arranging for a radio talk on the day of the conference The programme was approved and Mr Bill Cavanagh agreed to help with the arrangements.

It was also noted at the meeting that Mr Michael Coote had been elected to the council and executive of the Irish Management Institute.

AGRICULTURAL MARKETING ADVISORY COUNCIL, OCTOBER 1957

The Minister for Agriculture, in appointing a Marketing Advisory Council, accepted the nominee of ISMA Ireland branch, Mr Michael Coote with Mr Bill Chesson and Mr Bill Fraser as substitutes. Mr Milmo was co-opted to expand the export sub-committee.

EUROMART, OCTOBER 1957

The subject of Mr Colm Barnes' address to members on 11 October 1957 was: 'Euromart — its Industrial and Agricultural Implications to Ireland'.

Mr Barnes' detailed replies to a number of questions posed by members were much appreciated.

Mr A. Kehoe, M.AgrSc, H.Dip.Ed., concerned with agriculture, felt it a great advantage that the sales managers of Ireland were taking an interest in the agricultural aspect of the country. He dwelt on exports, and particularly agriculture, which made up two-thirds of the total exports. He also submitted details regarding the production of dairy products in various European markets and was concerned with the total effects relating to Ireland's position in a free market.

Mr Colm Barnes said he believed that from the industrial point of view, regarding free trade, one must assess what was best for Ireland. Products must be subject to careful investigation and decisions made as to what types were most suitable for marketing in the free trade area. Various problems arose but he indicated the part that sales managers could play in the success of Ireland's participation in the common market.

A new member of the branch was welcomed at the meeting, he being Mr George Bowen, Urney Ltd, Tallaght, Co. Dublin.

Mr Michael Coote had to resign his seat on the advisory council of the Department of Agriculture due to pressure of work. By agreement Mr Bill Fraser took his place.

CÓRAS TRÁCHTÁLA TEO, OCTOBER 1957

Mr Peter Greville was appointed to take the seat offered on the consultative committee of Córas Tráchtála. The subject of export guarantees was under consideration by CTT.

New rules and a constitution were produced for the student society, bringing them under the guidance of the executive committee.

Copies of *A Manual of Sales Management — Salesmanship Part 1*, (Section V) became available produced from London. This was priced at 6/- (30p today) per copy. The London manual sub-committee comprised of E.S. Baynes FSMA, G. La Niece FSMA, J. Atack FSMA and J. Neilson Lapraik DSO, OBE, MC, TD, FSMA. These gentlemen were household names to members of the Ireland branch executive, myself included.

At the outset of the manual, the question posed was 'What is salesmanship?' and the reply given as: 'The art of persuading someone to do something'.

Furthermore, it stated that a missionary was a salesman and that a diplomat seeking a treaty with a foreign country was also a salesman. However, the main message was that: 'A salesman endeavours to persuade someone to buy products or services'.

The success of the recent 'Education for Marketing' conference resulted in a hearty vote of thanks to the committee chaired by Mr Harry Woods.

Collated copies of the speakers' papers were mailed to the Minister for Education, Mr J.J. Stacey (Federation of Irish Employers), National Chairman ISMA London and also to ISMA branch members and students.

ECONOMIST CONTRIBUTION IN BUSINESS, NOVEMBER 1957

The monthly meeting of 15 November 1957 was addressed by Dr John Baxter, B.Com. Ph.D. (Econ). His topic was: 'The Contribution of an Economist in Business'. Defining the functions of such an individual, he outlined various problems that would have to be faced by non-participation of Ireland in the free trade area, which he felt, would be economic suicide.

He went on to say that there was a great future for agricultural produce and he listed five fundamental problems to be considered by members of the Free Trade Area (FTA):

1. Agriculture.

2. Origin of produce.

3. Institutions to control the FTA.

4. The question of colonial possessions.

5. France, whose objections were apt to mar the success of FTA.

Lord Killanin, branch president, who was present at the meeting thanked everyone saying that it had been a very stimulating and interesting evening.

DIRECT MAIL ADVERTISING, DECEMBER 1957

To conclude the year, the speaker at the monthly meeting of members on 13 December 1957 was Mr I.M. Woodburn, vice-chairman, Irish Direct Mail Association. The latter was also the general-manager of Gestetner (Éire) Ltd. His subject for the meeting was: 'Direct Mail Advertising'.

Mr Woodburn stated that he felt that the importance of direct mail was seen by its excellent medium of keeping the name of the firm to the forefront. It also acted as an introduction for salesmen. Direct mail established good relations between producer and consumer. As an advertising medium it was accepted as being of great value. In conclusion, he stated that one could also sell directly to consumers by that method and that direct mail was used for market research.

Mr Woodburn considered that a good sales letter should have an effective opening, a factual description and a closing paragraph requesting an enquiry or order. It was vital to keep sales letters brief, while a great deal of thought must be put into each letter, before being dictated.

Mailing lists were available, and Mr Woodburn named these, while interesting data regarding mail order advertising was presented to each of those present at the meeting.

ISMA IRELAND BRANCH EXECUTIVE REVIEW MEETING, 1958

At the initial 1958 executive meeting of the ISMA branch on 10 January a number of progress reports were given. Tom Moran outlined position with the Department of Agriculture. An up-to-date list of members was distributed.

Mr Joe Bigger, education chairman, confirmed the formation of a library for students and stateded that they sought a joint meeting with their counterparts in the Northern Ireland group. He also reported that the education vice-chairman, Mr Harry Woods, had done excellent work for students and a decision was made to have a second vice-chairman appointed to spread the workload. Mr Brian Clancy agreed to undertake the task, while the committee was enlarged by the co-option of Bill Cavanagh, Bill Chesson and A. H. Harrison. It was realised that an increase in student numbers was vital to the future of the Ireland branch.

EXPORT COSTINGS, JANUARY 1958

The evening meeting of 10 January 1958 was addressed by Mr Eddie Mullen, FCWA. His subject was: 'Export Costings'.

The application of the cost accountant to particular problems in industry with the export trade in mind was explained. Costing was defined as were the types of market with which one had to contend with.

Mr Mullen submitted details of products and costing techniques covering application to exports and market problems. He also referred to management policy *vis-à-vis* surplus stocks, expansion of business and tax remissions. He particularly defined cost factors involved in such situations by giving typical examples.

In February 1958, ISMA, London, was concerned with the interpretation of the association's function, particularly in light of the then economic and business position. A summary of the concern was given to each executive member of the Ireland branch and opinion and recommendations forwarded to London.

GOVERNMENT GRANTS, 1958

Mr Michael Coote said government grants were being made available for a portion of consultants' fees in business. It was agreed to apply for grants for marketing consultancy. Peter Greville, Michael Coote and Bill Cavanagh were delegated to follow up the matter.

APPOINTMENTS OF ISMA MEMBERS, 1958

Mr Bill Fraser was appointed chairman of the meat sub-committee of the advisory council on marketing agriculture and Mr Tom Moran became chairman of the section covering dairy produce. Mr Bill Cavanagh was congratulated on his appointment as president of the Association of Advertisers and a letter of congratulations and support was sent to Dr J.I. Fitzpatrick on his election as president of the Federation of Irish Industries.

In addition, Mr Bill Chesson was appointed ISMA branch councillor for three years, 1958–61. This involved travelling to London for meetings of branch officers representing Ireland on the 'National Council'.

The ISMA officers elected for 1958–59 were:

- President: Mr David D. Frame

- Chairman: Mr Bill Fraser

- Vice-Chairmen: Messrs Norman McConnell, Michael Coote and Stephen Doyle

- Hon. Treasurer: Mr Peter Greville

- Hon. Secretary: Mr Brian Murphy.

THE PORT OF DUBLIN, MARCH 1958

Mr D.A. Hegarty, general manager of the Dublin Port and Docks board, addressed the monthly meeting of members on 14 March 1958. His subject was: 'The Port of Dublin'. The history of the port of Dublin had begun 250 years previously (about 1700) and Mr Hegarty gave an outline of this.

He explained that the first organising body was known as the Ballast Commissioners. This was where the name of the then Port and Docks board headquarters, the Ballast Office, in Westmoreland Street, Dublin had originated.

The port authorities had excellent relations with the Department of Industry and Commerce observed Mr Hegarty. He said the port had 22 acres of warehousing accommodation, the largest such area in Ireland and he gave details about available transit sheds, cranes and port facilities in general.

To supplement his talk, an enjoyable film was shown illustrating his points.

FIFTH AGM OF ISMA IRELAND BRANCH, MAY 1958

Present at the AGM of the ISMA Ireland branch on 16 May 1958 at the Royal Hibernian hotel, then in Dawson street, Dublin, were: Mr Tom Moran (outgoing chairman), Lord Killanin (president), Messrs W.D. Fraser, M.H. Coote, A.H. Harrison, W.P. Cavanagh, L. Bowers, C.W. Chesson, J. Feldman, S.J. Doyle, P. Ryan, P.K. Duggan, W.F. Keys, J.S. Henderson, C.J. Orme, M. Willis, M. Miller, R.W. Harvey, A.G. Brownlee, D.M. Milmo, H.V. Woods, A.H. Crawford, T. McMurray, F. Ward, N. McConnell, J.W. Gorman, E.K. O'Brien, W.F. Roe and Brian Murphy (hon. secretary).

A report was given on the activities of the sub-committee that was formed to consult with the Ministry of Industry and Commerce regarding grants for firms employing marketing consultants.

Mr Coote reported on his activities as the ISMA's representative member on the executive committee of the Irish Management Institute.

Mr David Frame was invested with the chain of office, as president. Having also been welcomed to office, Mr Bill Fraser took his place as chairman of the branch for 1958–59.

The newly elected officers to the executive committee were: J.C. Bigger, W. Good, A.H. Harrison, W.P. Cavanagh, H.E. McCormick, J.S. Henderson, W.J.C. Milne, M. Miller, L.C. Thorn, R.G. Moffettt, L.V. Whitehead, A.G. Simon, C.W. Chesson, F.J. Ward, D.E. Beaven and T.A. Moran (past chairman).

It was announced at the meeting that official ISMA ties would become available for member purchase in September 1958.

The chairman, Mr Bill Fraser, then introduced Mr David Chatt, hon. secretary from headquarters, London. Mr Chatt congratulated the branch and, in particular, the chairman and executive committee for their earnest endeavour. He stressed the need for the education and training of good sales managers, which he knew to be the aim of the Ireland branch.

IRISH TRANSATLANTIC AIR SERVICE, APRIL 1958

On 11 April 1958 the chairman, Bill Fraser, introduced the speaker, Mr J.F. Dempsey, general manager Aer Rianta Teo. His subject was: 'The Irish Transatlantic Air Service'.

Mr Dempsey outlined the story of the growth of Irish aviation and the position of Ireland in the air age. He mentioned the numbers of passengers carried during the previous nine years showing the amazing increase in air traffic on the North Atlantic route. The proof was that air travel had become more and more popular and availed of for business and pleasure alike.

Mr Bill Cavanagh, education chairman, reported that at the student society AGM of 6 June 1958, students had stated that they were opposed to the idea of joint meetings with branch members during the coming session. The branch executive decided that the future monthly meetings of members be addressed alternatively at luncheon and evening meetings.

INGERSOLL SPONSOR GOLF CUP, 1958

Mr Norman McConnell was congratulated on his usual dedicated work ensuring the success of the ISMA golf outing. It was appreciated also that Mr Bill Fraser, together with a member in England, had organised the sponsorship of a cup from Ingersoll Ltd to be competed for annually. Northern Ireland group colleagues were also informed of the Ingersoll Cup.

ISMA STUDENT RECRUITMENT DRIVE, SEPTEMBER 1958

The education chairman, Mr Bill Cavanagh, reported to the council meeting on 5 September 1958 that a recruitment drive for student membership had been organised. A brochure had been sent to firms throughout Ireland to stimulate interest in providing students for registration of the student society.

Meanwhile students were invited to the members' luncheon meeting of Friday 12 September.

Furthermore, it was agreed that Mr Sean Ó Ceallaigh, Principal of

Rathmines College of Commerce, be invited to attend executive council meetings whenever special matters arose in connection with the student society.

PUBLICATION OF SECTION SIX OF *A MANUEL OF SALES MANAGEMENT*, 1958

Section six of *A Manual of Sales Management — Part 2*, was made available to members at a cost of 6/- per copy. The manual covered selling to industry, the wholesale and retail trades, the professions and the home.

It was said then that the specialist salesman sold directly to the customer and helped him to buy those products which really benefited him. Further, he aimed to create customers by solving their problems and by satisfying their needs. The term 'specialist' replaced the then outmoded, even discredited, term 'speciality'.

The manual also covered notes on special forms of organisation, such as mail order, direct mail and the credit trade. Exhibitions were referred to as 'the spice of life' to the direct salesman as they gave him a shop window to the buying world. The opportunity to show and demonstrate a salesman's products to their best advantage made prospective buyers his guests on his premises. This was considered a psychological advantage.

HONORARY MEMBERSHIP OF ISMA, IRELAND BRANCH

Consideration was given to having an honorary membership of the ISMA Ireland branch granted to Mr D.M. Milmo in recognition of the very valuable service he had given during his term as hon. treasurer and executive committee member. It was decided to suggest this to Mr David Chatt, hon. secretary, London. This was done and the granting of the honour was subsequently agreed.

METROPOLE BALLROOM LUNCHEON, SEPTEMBER 1958

At the Metropole ballroom luncheon on 12 September 1958 there were fifty-four present, including fellows, members, and guests.

The new president, Mr David D. Frame, was pleased to congratulate two students who successfully passed their final diploma examinations. They were Miss Elizabeth J. Lloyd and Mr Brian Clancy.

Mr J.J. Stacey, director-general and secretary of the Federation of Irish Industries, gave an interesting talk concerning the up-to-date position of plans being made for the free trade area.

UCD AND TCD LIAISON, OCTOBER 1958

Investigations were undertaken in October 1958 regarding the liaison with UCD (University College Dublin) and TCD (Trinity College Dublin) in the recruitment of students.

FIRST LADY OBTAINS ISMA DIPLOMA, OCTOBER 1958

Miss Elizabeth J. Lloyd, having obtained her ISMA diploma, by completing the final examinations, became the first lady to do so in Ireland. Her membership application was accepted with pleasure.

COMMERCIAL TELEVISION, 1958

The luncheon meeting at the Metropole ballroom, O'Connell Street, Dublin, on 14 November 1958 was a combined meeting of the members of ISMA and the Association of Advertisers. The attendance of seventy-two at the luncheon included ISMA president, Mr David Frame.

The arrangement was made by Mr Bill Cavanagh, MSMA, in his dual capacity (he was an ISMA member and also president of the Association of Advertisers). Mr Cavanagh presented a very interesting paper concerning commercial television and the advantages pertaining to sales and management organisation. The definition comprised aspects of financial rates, timing, budgeting and the return effectiveness of television advertising.

At the branch council meeting that evening a welcome was extended to Mr Don E. Bevan, chairman of the Munster Group, on his first attendance at such an executive ISMA meeting.

PURCHASING OFFICERS' ASSOCIATION AND ISMA MEETING, NOVEMBER 1958

In November 1958 a combined evening meeting with the Purchasing Officers' Association took place at the Royal Hibernian hotel, Dublin. In appreciating the 'get-together' of members of both bodies, Mr Larkin, chairman of the Purchasing Officers' Association, outlined the aims and practical objectives of their group. With thirty-seven present there followed a lively discussion.

EDUCATIONAL FILMS, DECEMBER 1958

A number of excellent films were presented by Esso Petroleum Co. (Ireland) Ltd, while Gestetner (Ireland) Ltd, provided printed handouts and general co-operation at the monthly evening meeting of 12 December 1958.

MR D.M. MILMO, RIP

At the end of year executive meeting, held earlier that evening, it was announced with sincere regret that Mr D.M. Milmo, first honorary member of the ISMA Ireland branch, had died. Deepest sympathy was expressed and conveyed to Mrs Milmo.

FEDERATION OF IRISH INDUSTRIES, DECEMBER 1958

A meeting took place between Mr Tom Moran and Mr Bill Fraser of the ISMA Ireland branch and Dr J.I. Fitzpatrick, president of the Federation of Irish Industries.

The matter to be discussed was the proposal that various associations should be 'centralised'. A policy sub-committee was formed, comprised of the honorary officers, fellows and past chairmen of the branch, to consider the situation.

ISMA, PAST, PRESENT AND FUTURE, 1959

Opening the new year (1959) Mr Bill Chesson announced a most satisfactory social result of Ladies' Night, which also brought in £115 for the benevolent fund.

The meeting was a luncheon one held at the Metropole ballroom, O'Connell Street, Dublin, on 9 January 1959. The chairman, Bill Fraser, gave a talk concerning: 'ISMA — Past, Present and Future'.

Mr Joe Bigger became a Fellow of the Association and was presented with his certificate at the meeting. He was complimented for his contribution to branch progress.

The dinner for President's Night was held on 29 January 1959 at the Hibernian hotel on Dawson Street with an attendance of 102.

INCOME TAX PROBLEMS, G.M. WHEELER, FEBRUARY 1959

The discussion subject of Mr G.M. Wheeler, FCS, FCIS, at the evening meeting of 13 February 1959 was 'Income Tax Problems'.

Mr Wheeler gave in-depth examples and case studies from his own practical experience and members declared that it had been a most enlightening, interesting and informative evening.

THE JOB OF SELLING, FEBRUARY 1959

The monthly meeting of the Irish Management Institute, (IMI), held in the chemistry theatre of University College Dublin in Upper Merrion street, was addressed by Michael H. Coote, MSMA, Sales Advisory Service. He spoke on the subject of: 'The Job of Selling'.

In his speech Mr Coote made the point that there was a lack of good salesmen in Ireland and he attributed this lack to the Second World War when there had been nothing to sell. He believed that the aftermath of the war, when goods came in such quantity that they only had to be passed off to the customer, left the customer vaguely dissatisfied after purchasing.

Selling was a professional task and he was, he said, proud to be a professional salesman. Salesmanship was just as important as the other recognised professions which, he thought, depended on the success of good management. He further said that at that time there were no standards of professional salesmanship though he hoped that there soon would be.

Mr Coote then went on to state that he felt that salesmen and selling were the only credit on the balance sheet and that they produced the money needed to pay everyone else in the rest of their organisation. A good salesman needed the right mental approach, a genuine enthusiasm and also had to be a good listener. He concluded by saying that he believed that the main problems in selling in Ireland were caused by bad management in the firm's themselves.

Mr Peter Greville, MSMA, told the audience of 200 that it was his opinion that every new salesman should be required to undergo thorough training on joining a company. After that, training should become a continuous factor through regular visits to each man in the field, sales conferences, courses and training sessions. In addition, he recommended the judicious use of the written word.

For his part Mr Dermot A. Ryan stated that he felt that success in selling related to a study of the other side's position and entailed knowledge not only of what one was doing but also of what one was thinking.

Dr L. Dillon Digby, who presided, said it was his opinion that the whole process would be liable to collapse unless the person who handled the sale of the goods persuaded the customer to buy.

BUILDING CENTRE, DUBLIN, MARCH 1959

Mr Michael Scott the well-known architect and chairman of the new building centre outlined to members and guests his plans for the centre. This took place at a luncheon meeting in the Metropole ballroom on Friday 13 March 1959. It was generally agreed that such a centre was badly needed and Mr Scott further emphasised this making the point that it was essential especially for educational purposes.

INNOVATION FOR ISMA AGM, MAY 1959

Arrangements were made for the May AGM resulting in new thought being evoked. The outgoing chairman, Bill Fraser, suggested, and the executive agreed, that each of them choose a member of the association and nominate him, provided he was suitable, to go forward for election to the executive committee.

The following ISMA Ireland branch officers elected for session 1959–60 were:

• President: Mr David D. Frame (outgoing)

• Chairman: Mr Stephen J. Doyle

• Vice-Chairmen: Messrs Michael Coote, Norman McConnell and A.H. Harrison

• Hon. Treasurer: Mr Peter Greville

• Hon. Secretary: Mr Brian Murphy.

Mr Sean Ó Ceallaigh also announced at this meeting that a course in foreign trade would be available shortly at Rathmines College of Commerce, Dublin.

SIXTH AGM OF ISMA, MAY 1959

At the 1959 AGM on 29 May there were thirty-four in attendance. Mr David Frame agreed to his re-election as president. He said he was pleased at the growth in the number of members and the importance in which the association was held. This, he felt, was reflected in the considerable influence the body had in the business life of the country.

The new executive committee comprised: Messrs D.E. Bevan, J.C. Bigger, W.P. Cavanagh, B.A. Clancy, J.S. Henderson, R.F. Hatch, M. Miller, W.P. O'Donoghue, R.G. Moffett, L.C. Thorn, A.G. Simon, K.E.J. Tyrrell, F.J. Ward, L.V. Whitehead and C.W. Chesson (past chairman). The ex-officio members were Messrs W.D. Fraser and T.A. Moran.

Mr Stanley Talbot, editor of *Marketing* publication, came from London especially for the meeting and was introduced to members by Stephen Doyle, branch chairman. Mr Talbot stated that from what he had heard and seen about the Ireland branch it augured well for its future.

SHANNON CONFERENCE, JULY 1959

Arrangements for a conference at Shannon, Co. Limerick were reported on by Michael Coote. The subject of the conference was: 'Freedom to Trade' and it was to be organised by the Incorporated Sales Managers' Association in conjunction with the Irish Exporters' Association.

Thousands of circulars, giving in-depth information about the conference, had been sent to ISMA in England, NSEI, (National Sales Executives Inc., New York), the Irish Management Institute, the Irish Exporters' Association and members of the Ireland branch of ISMA.

PRESIDENT'S NIGHT DINNER, OCTOBER 1959

The Minister for Industry and Commerce and the Lord Mayor of Dublin were both present at the dinner for President's Night at the Zoological Gardens, Phoenix Park, Dublin on 22 October 1959.

The large attendance of guests, from other associations and members of the branch, enjoyed both the scenic setting and the encouraging speeches regarding the association's future.

It is also interesting to note that the No. I menu was selected at a cost of 21/- per person, (£1.05).

Mr Bill Fraser became branch councillor for the year commencing 1 November 1959.

He announced that he would represent ISMA at a conference being held in Berlin. Later he gave a summary to the executive committee.

STUDENT ACTIVITIES, OCTOBER 1959

In October 1959, Mr Brian Clancy reported on a special meeting that was held with students of the universities in Dublin. This concluded with a film show on sales. The result of this was that several new students enroled for the ISMA course.

The student education sub-committee met with the Irish Management Institute when it was agreed to form a study group relating to the Institute of Marketing. IMI agreed to call for a representative of each association and a member of the faculty concerned from each of the Dublin universities.

Mr Norman McConnell attended several meetings of the sub-committee of the Federation of Irish Industries, the trend of which were to investigate their inclusion in the Institute of Marketing study group.

CHANGE OF TITLE FOR BELFAST GROUP, OCTOBER 1959

The Belfast group of ISMA circularised an appeal for new members stating that a prize would be given to their members who obtained certain quotas. The Ireland branch executive, however, did not think that was in the best interests of the association. It was also observed that the Belfast group were then describing themselves as the Northern Ireland group.

Mr Hatch, representing the Belfast group, agreed to discuss such matters with their executive committee and report back to the Ireland branch executive meeting on 16 October 1959 in Dublin. Mr Leslie Whitehead subsequently attended a group meeting of ISMA in Belfast. A majority of members there favoured the name 'Northern Ireland group' and sought agreement of same from the Ireland branch.

Mr Stephen Doyle stated that it was the wish of the Ireland branch to co-operate in every way possible and so there was no objection. Nevertheless, the executive required a copy of the minutes to be sent to Dublin.

BEHIND THE GUINNESS BRAND NAME, NOVEMBER 1959

The guest speaker at the evening meeting of ISMA members on 13 November 1959 was Ken E.J. Tyrrell MSMA, Advertising Manager of Arthur Guinness Son & Co. Ltd. His subject was: 'Behind the Guinness Brand Name'. He replied to the many questions in a most efficient and professional manner.

ULSTER TELEVISION LTD, DECEMBER 1959

Mr Basil Lapworth MSMA, Sales Manager of Ulster Television Ltd, was the guest at the luncheon meeting on Friday 11 December 1959. Instead of giving an address to ISMA members he elected to answer their questions and indeed many were put to him regarding wide aspects of television.

STUDENT EDUCATION MATTERS

Regarding student education Mr Brian Clancy reported an increase in student attendance at meetings, 67 being present recently. It was also noted that student membership had exceeded the figure of 100 for the first time. This, it was stated, had been achieved by the keen interest taken by the branch and the chairman, Mr Stephen Doyle, the education chairman, Mr Bill Cavanagh, and the hard-working education committee were praised for their efforts.

Mr Clancy also reported that there had since been a joint meeting with the Exporters' Association and he had attended a national education committee meeting in London, where he submitted points particularly in regard to the proposed changes in the study syllabus.

Mr Leslie Whitehead stated that when the course cost of £6.6.0 was taken into consideration it should be available at £2.2.0 entrance fee — £1.1.0 for first year and the balance settled at £1.1.0 per year to completion. It was noted that sales trainees could apply for exemption from the qualifying entrance examination.

Mr Bill Fraser reported on the progress made with the Irish Management Institute liaison particularly regarding library facilities.

NATIONAL SALES EXECUTIVES: PROPOSALS, MARCH 1960

A conference with the National Sales Executives, (NSE), New York, was proposed for a Dublin venue. They sent a special form for distribution and completion by ISMA Ireland members to enable an assessment of requirements.

In the meantime Mr Michael Coote proposed that consideration be given to forming an affiliated club of NSE in Dublin. NSE would make available sales management and other literature and books for Irish students. At that time there were 122 registered students studying for stages of the ISMA diploma.

The School of Commerce in Rathmines, Dublin issued an *Education for Marketing* syllabus. Prizes for examination subjects were established. It was agreed that the president's prize would be a medal and the branch chairman's prize an academic book or books. These would be presented to the best qualifiers in the examination stages.

ELECTION OF OFFICERS FOR AGM, 1960

The council elected officers for the AGM of 27 May 1960. These were:

- President: Sir Basil Goulding
- Chairman: Mr Michael Coote
- Vice-Chairmen: Messrs Norman McConnell, Brian Murphy and Peter Greville
- Hon. Treasurer: Mr Peter Greville

- Hon. Secretary: Mr Brian Murphy.

At that time the executive committee meetings were held at 111, Pearse Street, Dublin (the premises of the Hammond Lane group) at 5.30 p.m.

The social committee organised a fork supper and entertainment (12/6d per head) to be held at the Zoological Gardens on 8 July 1960. A golf outing was arranged for the following week.

It was also reported that Mr Smallbone, hon. secretary of ISMA London had agreed to Mr Brian Clancy's suggestion, at their national executive meeting, that the question of a separate examination for Irish students on the legal examination paper be favourably considered.

DECORATIVE MEMBERSHIP IDENTITIES

All members now had membership badges to wear at meetings. A gavel (chairman's mallet) was obtained and it became the responsibility of the membership committee to have it available at all branch meetings. ISMA ties, cufflinks and tie-clips were placed on view for sale at meetings. These decorative membership identities had been obtained from London.

ROLE PLAYING, APRIL 1960

A special meeting of members and students of the ISMA branch took place at the Hibernian hotel, Dawson Street on the evening of 26 April 1960. The subject for discussion was 'Role playing'. Its physical and practical use in sales training was especially concentrated on. With many of the members and students present taking part, it was considered a very beneficial and educational experience.

SEVENTH AGM OF ISMA, MAY 1960

The AGM of the Ireland Branch of ISMA was held at the Shelbourne hotel in Dublin on 27 May 1960. Mr Stephen Doyle was in the chair with the outgoing president, Mr David D. Frame and thirty-nine Fellows, Members and Associates present.

Awards and appreciations

Mr David Frame presented Mr Bill Fraser with the Fellowship of ISMA. He declared that the award was for his outstanding service to the association over the years from its formation in 1947. Sir Basil Goulding was invested with the chain of office as president. In accepting he stated that he was very conscious of the honour bestowed on him and promised to work to further the interests of the association.

Sincere thanks were expressed to Mr David Frame for the help and guidance he had given during his term of office as president. In presenting Mr Stephen Doyle, outgoing chairman, with his past-chairman's badge, Mr Michael Coote spoke of how appreciative all his colleagues were of his energy and untiring enthusiasm. Compliments were also paid to Mr Michael Coote, who had chaired the successful conference at Shannon and to Mr Harrison, membership chairman, who had brought the number of members to 200.

Thanks were also expressed to Mr Harry Woods who, due to Mr Harrison's illness, had taken over the membership chair and subsequently contributed to the membership expansion.

It was reported that the registered number of students had exceeded 100 and Mr Brian Clancy was congratulated for his efforts.

Editor of *Marketing*

The editor of *Marketing* journal, Mr Stanley Talbot of London was then introduced. He gave details of the early days of the association and mentioned that next year ISMA would hold their fiftieth anniversary celebration in the Festival Hall, London.

Examinations update

For the next examinations it was reported that eighteen Irish students would be sitting for various stages of the diploma.

It was also mentioned with regret that at this stage the proposed revised syllabus for the ISMA examinations (legal aspects) had not been finalised.

ISMA, IRELAND BRANCH SESSION, 1960–61

The executive meeting of 15 July 1960 saw the commencement of the 1960–61 ISMA Ireland branch session.

Having taken up an appointment in England, Mr R.F. Hatch, (Scribbans-Kemp) of Northern Ireland announced with regret his resignation from the executive committee.

Mr J.A. McCarroll of Baxter Ltd, Ballymoney, Co. Antrim, was co-opted to the executive to replace Mr Hatch in representing the Northern Ireland group.

Mr George Bowen reported that it was hoped that a conference at University College Cork would take place in January or February 1961.

Mr Harry Woods, reporting on education stated that a luncheon meeting had been held with Mr Sean Ó Ceallaigh and a new syllabus arranged for lecturers at Rathmines. There would be 28 lectures in each subject for night classes. Lecturers were sought for market research, salesmanship and advertising in particular.

The students' conference was arranged for the 28 and 29 of October 1960 at the Claremont hotel, Dublin. The fee for participation was £2.10.0. (£2.50).

ISMA NATIONAL MEMBERSHIP, LONDON, JULY 1960

Mr Harry Woods had travelled to London for the usual monthly national membership meeting arranged for 2.30 p.m. However, on his arrival he was surprised to find that the meeting had started at 10 a.m. and the Ireland branch had not been advised of the change. In any case, Mr Woods gave a full account of what had apparently transpired including other association changes.

With regard to the Northern Ireland group applications for membership, the national committee insisted they would publish in the *Marketing* journal 'whatever was on an application for a membership form'. The Northern Ireland group had said that they did not want company names published.

A new 'increased membership target' was indicated for the Ireland branch, numbering 60 new members for the session.

At the policy sub-committee meeting in London, Mr Bill Fraser asked for a national conference be held in Dublin. Nevertheless, he was told that this was not possible, at least until 1963, as conference areas had already been reserved including Eastbourne for 1962.

LECTURERS APPOINTED FOR ISMA CLASSES, SEPTEMBER 1960

The panel of agreed lecturers for the ISMA evening classes at Rathmines was announced as: Messrs Bill Chesson, Bill Fraser, Peter Greville, Miss Elizabeth Lloyd, Tom Quinn and Harry Woods.

Mr Tom Quinn was presented with the Ireland branch chairman's prize for exceptional merit. At the same time it was announced that classes, for study of ISMA course subjects, were then booked out. Over 100 students had registered.

PRESIDENT'S NIGHT, ISMA, OCTOBER 1960

The banquet for President's Night was held at the Zoological Gardens, Phoenix Park, Dublin on Saturday 8 October 1960. The column of *The Irish Times* newspaper 'An Irishman's Diary' reported on the President's Night dinner of the Ireland branch of ISMA. It stated that it was an extremely 'stag affair'. The one exception was that of the solitary sales manageress, Miss Elizabeth Lloyd of Gateaux. It was stated that: 'she kept a brave upper lip when confronted with the monstrous regiment of men'.

The columnist reported that so intense was the concentration of high-powered persuaders on that Thursday night that he was convinced any one of them could have sold an unwanted article to the most difficult customer.

Minister's speech

In his speech that night the Minister for Transport and Power, Mr Erskine Childers, said that in given circumstances the employment target was not beyond the national capacity. He stated that material economic progress was hardly questioned by the public but that efforts must be made if Ireland was to become a modern, fully developed country.

He spoke about increased exports, particularly the selling of agricultural machinery to New Zealand and the Argentine and he complimented the splendid work of Córas Tráchtála (Irish export board). He told of his own personal pride as he had sold agricultural machinery in his earlier career. He also described his life as a travel agent (his first job) and likened it to 'selling something invisible in advance'.

Mr Childers went on to say that the field for exports had been only barely tapped and that some of the new undeveloped exports, to hitherto unexplored markets, should be a source of inspiration to industrialists and industrial promoters. Radio receivers had been exported to Pakistan and South America; cars to Chile and Uruguay; books to Ghana and sisal carpeting to 40 different countries.

In his opinion sales management was a highly technical science and in relation to the fiercely competitive world of the future, the idea that Irish geniality and the national gift for putting over a deal meant that full training was unnecessary was completely outdated.

President's speech

The President of ISMA Sir Basil Goulding made a stirring speech at the dinner that night. Referring to the 'island of saints and scholars' motif, he said that many who attempted one of those two ladders found the going a trifle sticky. However, he now knew there was a country of saints, scholars and salesmen. He agreed that salesmen in the export market would make the greatest contribution towards the progression of their country.

According to Sir Basil the time was coming when schools, such as the Rathmines School of Management Studies, would be seen as the real progressives who recognised future trends. It would be a great day, he said, when such schools could not meet all the demands on them.

On the lighter side, he compared the salesman to a pale pink prawn and the sales manager to a large red lobster, adding that sales managership was as different from salesmanship as Stephen Potter's brinkmanship was from lifemanship.

Sir Basil Goulding continued by stating that Irish universities had not yet been able to bring themselves to investigate courses in sales management. It was possible funds were not available for such courses but he felt that while university authorities should not be hustled some pressure should be put on them.

In concluding, he mentioned his pleasure at the fact that there were now over 100 students enrolled at Rathmines for the new Diploma in Marketing course

Prizegiving

At the dinner a number of awards were presented. The student of the year award (gold medal) was presented to Mr Michael Quinn the sales manager of Irish Art Publications, Coolock, Dublin and the Bowden prize for marketing was presented to Mr W. Maher who had gained second place in the association's examinations.

FIRST STUDENT ISMA CONFERENCE, OCTOBER 1960

The ISMA students' society organised their first marketing conference for 28 and 29 of October 1960. It was held at the Clare Manor hotel, Coolock, Co. Dublin. This was an outstanding success, achieved its objectives, created considerable interest and resulted in student recruitment.

The speakers at the conference were all members of the Ireland branch of ISMA. They included Mr Ken Tyrrell, advertising manager of Arthur Guinness Son & Co. Ltd; Mr Bill Chesson, managing director of Aspro Nicholas (Ireland) Ltd; Frank Sykes, sales manager of W.R. Jacob and Co. and Mr Bernard Prendiville, director of A.C. Nielsen (Ireland) Ltd.

Delegates at the conference comprised 110 students, 100 of these were registered ISMA student members and potential students, who came mainly from Cork, Limerick, Waterford, Belfast and Dublin. Others who were present at the conference included members of the education committee (Ireland branch). These were: Mr Brian Clancy, chairman, Mr Harry Woods vice-chairman, Mr Sean Walshe and Mr Bill Cavanagh. In addition, the assistant director of studies at the College of Marketing, London, Mr Taylor, was also present for the occasion.

Speaking at the conference the chairman of the Ireland branch of ISMA, Mr Michael Coote, said that the aim was to put marketing in its proper perspective and to stimulate the interest of participants through exchange of views and experience. In such a manner, aspiring executives would return to their employment equipped to do a better job.

Inauguration of new courses

In his speech Mr Michael Coote stated that two developments gave the conference even more added importance. The first was the inauguration of the new Diploma in Marketing, it being established as the professional qualification in sales and marketing management. The second was the initiation of the first comprehensive course in marketing in Ireland. The ISMA education committee had organised the course in co-operation with the Rathmines School of Management Studies.

Sales promotion

In his address, Mr Ken Tyrrell ASMA, MAA said he believed that sales promotion was the co-ordination of personal selling and advertising, a vital cog in the machinery of marketing. In planning sales promotion it was his opinion that its success depended on the time and thought put into it. It was also, he stated, necessary to ensure that sales promotion backed up adequately the efforts of one's production team, salesmen and advertising. It was, in effect, the cornerstone of modern marketing.

Irish student achievement, October 1960

Mr Taylor of the College of Marketing, London, speaking at the evening dinner, said that he had visited all the student societies of the association in Britain and Ireland during the previous twelve months. He found the Ireland branch to be the most enthusiastic and most successful particularly with regard to student progress and achievement.

At that time there were about 1000 students enrolled in the new diploma course between the two countries while no other branch had as many students registered as Dublin.

Evening Press report

The *Evening Press* report of the student conference cited that 'it was superbly mounted — the kind of thing that one sees laid on for American presidential elections'. Furthermore, it stated that two of the worksheets, shown to them by Sean Walshe, PRO, made fascinating reading. One of these had been prepared by the indefatigable Mr Bill Chesson of Aspro and the other by Mr Frank Sykes of Jacobs.

The *Evening Press* also mentioned the location for the conference, the Clare Manor hotel. It reported that it would not be opened to the public for a further fortnight but having been refurbished would arouse pleasantly astonishing comment,

Selection and training of salesmen

At the conference Mr Frank Sykes, sales manager of W. and R. Jacob Ltd, spoke extensively on the 'Selection and Training of Salesmen'.

ADVERTISING POSSIBILITIES ON IRISH TELEVISION, NOVEMBER 1960

The ISMA monthly members' meeting of November 1960 took place in the Metropole ballroom, Dublin and was addressed by Mr Bill Cavanagh, chairman of the Association of Advertisers in Ireland. His subject dealt with the advertising possibilities of an Irish television service. The increased sales of products following television exposure on the BBC and UTV stations were outlined and discussed.

LADIES' NIGHT ISMA, NOVEMBER 1960

In October 1960, as the number of bookings for Ladies' Night had reached 316, it was necessary to announce that the final issue was limited strictly to 350. The usual successful function took place on 18 November 1960 with the cost for double tickets being £3.10.0 (£3.50).

STUDENT SOCIETY FOR CORK

Regarding Cork, a meeting was held on 29 November 1960 arranged with Mr Farrar (Harrington's). The education committee considered that there was the nucleus of a student society in Cork. At that stage student class registration at Rathmines had come to 120.

APPOINTMENTS

Mr Stephen Doyle was appointed councillor for the Ireland branch to be present at London executive meetings. Mr Don. E. Bevan was congratulated on his appointment to the Cork Harbour Board.

SUPERMARKET BUSINESS, DECEMBER 1960

At the concluding executive meeting for 1960 (16 December), appreciation was expressed regarding a very interesting student society meeting. There had been an attendance of 80 to hear Mr John J. Quinn, MSMA, MD of the H. Williams, Irish supermarket chain. The talk had given an exposé of the food, drink and tobacco business in buying, shelf stocking and sale to the taste and habits of the discerning public.

IRELAND BRANCH ISMA, 1961 ACTIVITY

The 20 January 1961 executive branch meeting decided that a deputation from Ireland, consisting of the chairman and two past chairmen, attend the next London executive meeting.

Amongst the matters for discussion was the situation where London had seen fit to have a membership drive by sending application forms direct to some individuals in Ireland. It was, however, pointed out to Mr David Chatt, hon. secretary (London), that this could not be accepted, particularly as the Ireland membership drive continued to have considerable success. At that point in time membership of the Ireland branch of ISMA had reached 248. The future of the Ireland branch was widely discussed by its council with unanimous agreement on the points raised.

EGM OF ISMA, MARCH 1961

On 10 March 1961 following a special executive committee meeting of the Ireland branch at the Royal Hibernian hotel, Dawson Street, Dublin, an EGM of ISMA members took place at 7.30 p.m. The current position of the branch and its future were outlined. Mr D.A. Chatt was present, representing London.

MR GEORGE O'TOOLE, RIP

A most sincere vote of sympathy was expressed on the death of the branch's friend and executive member, the late George O'Toole, (press officer), RIP.

ASPECTS OF MARKETING, MARCH 1961

The Publicity Club of Ireland invited ISMA members to a joint meeting with their members. The subject discussed was: 'Aspects of Marketing'. The panel representing ISMA comprised of Mr Peter Greville and the branch chairman, Mr Michael Coote.

ISMA MEMBERSHIP DRIVE, APRIL 1961

Mr Harry Woods, membership chairman, reported an increase in membership to the executive meeting of 13 April 1961. Targets had been set by the membership committee. The aim of the membership committee had been and was, that intake substantially enhances membership quality. At the same time it was possible that the drive would result in obtaining the greatest increase in members of any branch of ISMA for the year 1960–61.

Over the previous year research had been carried out in all categories of business, trade and service professions in Ireland to bring ISMA to the notice of marketing and sales management executives. Invitation to apply for membership had been made to such personnel. Assessment had been made ascertaining the length of time involved in having an application for membership accepted. The procedure combined final approval from London, who published the name, business and applicant's position in *Marketing* and allowed a further month before acceptance and final approval (or rejection) at their next meeting of branch membership chairmen.

PROPOSED INDEPENDENT IRISH MARKETING ASSOCIATION, APRIL 1961

Policy executive meetings continued to be held and reports presented to the council in London by Mr Michael Coote. In turn he gave detailed accounts of what transpired at such meetings and was gratified to find that headquarters were very anxious to help the Ireland branch form its own independent association. Mr Coote was congratulated on his presentation of the Irish case.

MEMBERSHIP FIGURES OF ISMA (IRL), APRIL 1961

Details on membership figures in the Ireland branch of ISMA from 1 April 1961 showed the following:

	Irish Republic	Northern Ireland
Fellows	7	1
Members	115	27
Associates	68	44
Graduates	1	1

Branch total = 191 plus 73 = Grand total 264

London set up a 'Stanley Talbot Testimonial Fund' (named after the editor of *Marketing* journal), a most worthy recognition, to which the Ireland branch were pleased to contribute a cheque for £15.15.0 (£15.75 punts today).

SALESWEEK REPORT, MAY 1961

On 1 May 1961, the issue of *Salesweek*, the professional magazine of the National Sales Executives Inc., New York, made very interesting reading. For example, in the office equipment world, it was recorded that while the basic tasks performed by their products remained relatively constant, competition was not with new products but with new features, thus making office work easier.

It was reported that some 77 members of the Office Equipment Manufacturers' Institute (OFMI) moved into New York's Coliseum to show the product achievements of more than 4 billion dollars worth of equipment and a number of factors emerged that marketers were watching closely. It was found that companies were then competing for office personnel in much the same way as they once competed for customers. There were relatively few 'new products'. A typewriter, for instance, served the same purpose then as it did, say 50 years previously. However, manufacturers did revamp the old models constantly in order to meet competition.

PUBLIC RELATIONS MAY 1961

Automation, essentially the industry's stock-in-trade, had, it then stated, caused considerable problems. The individual often felt his job security threatened.

To counter the notion that the worker was being 'replaced by a machine', the industry poured its resources into public relations, stressing the idea that new streamlined methods actually mean that the worker's time and skills are free for more productive, creative work.

Competition, in the United States, from low-priced imports had been keen in nearly every sector of industry. Steps were outlined showing how the incorporation of ancillary items — desks, chairs, tables, lighting and partitioning — created style and colour while also providing attractive surroundings as well as being more functional.

EUROPEAN SALES AND MARKETING EXECUTIVES' MEETING, MAY 1961

The ISMA London director, Mr David Griffiths, invited the Ireland branch to send a delegate to the buffet luncheon and meet members of the contact group of the European Sales and Marketing Executives' Association. Mr Bill Fraser represented the Ireland branch.

INQUIRIES REGARDING HISTORY OF ISMA, IRELAND BRANCH

Mr Leslie Whitehead sought information from executive members of the ISMA Ireland branch as to its history from group status in 1947. Meanwhile he would continue his own investigations and report back at a later meeting. (However to the best of my knowledge no compiled record transpired.)

Plans to form an independent Irish association were further investigated, discussed and drafted, as were policy procedures. It also involved meetings with London, culminating in a draft document being received from Mr David Chatt. Following adjustments it was read to the Ireland branch executives.

The normally held AGM (May), of the Ireland branch of ISMA was postponed sine die.

'WILKINSON GOLD SWORD' AWARD TO IRELAND, JUNE 1961

Membership was the highlight of the executive committee meeting of 30 June 1961.

Mr Harry Woods, membership chairman, reported that on returning from a business trip (four weeks Hardwood research in Ghana, West Africa, May/ June) he had attended a London ISMA membership meeting. He was advised that further membership applications he submitted before his departure had been approved.

The end of session figure for Ireland branch membership had now reached 286.

Mr Michael Coote announced that he had received a letter from Mr A.L. Benzing of London informing the Ireland branch of its success in winning the 'Wilkinson Sword of Honour' for the highest branch increase in membership for the session 1960–61.

Mr Benzing stated that not only had the Ireland branch exceeded their target performance, which had been raised considerably from the previous session, but the excess was such that it left them a clear and convincing winner of the contest.

He further thanked the chairman, officers and in particular, the chairman of the membership committee, Mr Harry Woods, for the consistent excellent work done. The help of all concerned had been appreciated by ISMA. Mr' Michael Coote, endorsing the congratulations, thanked the membership committee and the individual members of the council for their concentrated effort. The joint runners up in the award endeavour were Birmingham and the Royal

Counties, while Nottingham took third place.

Student examinations

At the same meeting Mr Brian Clancy reported that examinations for students had been successfully held and a record number of students had presented themselves.

Appreciation

It was decided that a letter of appreciation should be sent to Sir Basil and Lady Goulding for making available the use of their magnificent gardens for an association function.

EXECUTIVE COMMITTEE MEETING, AUGUST 1961

It was confirmed at the August 1961 executive committee meeting, that luncheon and evening member meetings would, in future, be held at the Central hotel, Exchequer street, Dublin.

A finally agreed letter regarding the formation of an independent Irish association was sent to all members. Replies to a questionnaire in the letter were to be returned by 31 August 1961.

Mr Joseph McGough BL spoke about future branch policy and the important legal aspects in particular. A lively discussion followed.

The changes to be considered in eligibility for ISMA membership were outlined by Mr Harry Woods. It was also observed that the achievement of winning the 'Wilkinson Sword' had a rather pointed lack of publicity in *Marketing* journal. This was disappointing, as the Ireland branch had increased its membership number by over 25 per cent compared to the previous session.

It was also reported that over 100 students were present at their ISMA society meeting that month. The number of registered students, 153, meant an increase of 60 per cent on the previous year.

STUDENT SOCIETY CONFERENCE, SEPTEMBER 1961

The attendance at the student society second annual conference, held in September 1961 at the Clare Manor hotel, Dublin, included the president of the ISMA branch, Sir Basil Goulding, Mr Jack Lynch, TD, Minister of Industry and Commerce, and the association chairman, Mr Michael Coote.

The students, numbering 114, were divided into team groups and participated in an interesting Harvard case study.

STUDENT VOLUME, SEPTEMBER 1961

Overcrowding for the diploma course at Rathmines College of Commerce in September 1961 resulted in some 70 extra students awaiting class places. However, alternative accommodation was later arranged for their enrolment and class participation. The increase in numbers seeking class enrolment was due to the student conference.

A third class was formed for diploma students at the High School of Commerce, Rathmines and enabled 170 to participate from November 1961.

The branch education committee submitted a report to the Commission for Higher Education.

DEVELOPMENT OF MOTOR VEHICLES, NOVEMBER 1961

The general sales manager, Mr John Wyer of Henry Ford and Son Ltd, Cork, addressed the association members in Dublin on Friday 10 November 1961. He gave a graphic outline of the development of the motor car from the earliest production, by Henry Ford of the model T, to the luxury transport of 1961.

ISMA IRELAND BRANCH OFFICERS, 1961–62

The officers elected for Ireland branch ISMA session of 1961–62 were:

- President: Sir Basil Goulding, Bart.

- Chairman: Mr Brian M. Murphy

- Vice-Chairmen: Messrs Norman McConnell, Peter E. Greville and Harry V. Woods

- Hon. Treasurer: Mr Peter E. Greville

- Hon. Secretary: Mr Harry V. Woods.

LADIES' NIGHT, ISMA IRELAND BRANCH, NOVEMBER 1961

Ladies' Night was reported in the media as *the* function of Dublin on the night of 25 November 1961. It was held at the Shelbourne hotel ballroom. The record attendance of 372 and the social success were attributed to the hard work of the social committee.

As always, each lady was presented with a bumper bag of member company products consisting of perfumes, groceries, cosmetics and various household items, which included detergents.

PUBLIC RELATIONS COMMITTEE ISMA, NOVEMBER 1961

To enhance the image and expand the knowledge of the Ireland branch of the ISMA association, the outgoing chairman, Mr Michael Coote, decided that a public relations committee would be essential. This resulted in the unanimous election of Mr Jack Carmody, press officer, with Mr Sean Walshe and Mr Harry Woods making up the committee.

At the executive committee evening meeting of 8 December 1961 at the Central hotel, the increased membership achievement was honoured.

AWARD CEREMONY AT THE EIGHTH AGM, DECEMBER 1961

On 9 December1961 the *Irish Times* and *Irish Independent* newspapers reported that the Irish branch of the Incorporated Sales Managers' Association had won the award of 'Wilkinson Gold Sword of Honour'. It had been presented at the institute's AGM the previous evening to Mr Harry Woods, ISMA Ireland branch membership chairman, by Mr A.L. Benzing (Ingersoll Ltd) chairman of the national membership development committee, London.

He stated that the 'Sword' was awarded to the ISMA branch in the British Isles that had achieved the highest increase in membership during the year. The award bearing the inscription, 'The power that numbers create', had taken place for the previous three years. It was the first time it had gone to the Irish branch and Mr Benzing expressed his pleasure at that fact.

In his reply and report, Mr Harry Woods said that membership of the branch had reached 286, an increase of 72 on the previous year (34 per cent). He stated that the increase reflected the amount of work, which his sub-committee and council members had put into researching suitably qualified members. Furthermore, the activities of the branch, in holding conferences and encouraging educational progress, had meant that the principles of marketing and sales management were made more widely known.

LAUNCH OF TELEFÍS ÉIREANN, DECEMBER 1961

The official opening of Telefís Éireann (Irish television) took place in the Gresham hotel, Dublin on New Year's Eve, 1961. The Irish government had set up the Radio Éireann authority with the inauguration of a television station as its responsibility.

The authority chairman was Mr Eamonn Andrews, a well-known television presenter with BBC television, London. He had been with Radio Éireann some ten years previously. The first transmitter of the new television was located at Kippure, Co. Wicklow.

The exciting evening was attended by individuals from all walks of life, industry and entertainment. It marked a new and significant era of life in Ireland and around the world regarding aspects of sales promotion and other forms of advertising.

The first day's programme on Telefís Éireann began at teatime on 1 January 1962. There were many commercial advertisements transmitted that evening, particularly before and after the 9 o'clock news.

ISMA IRISH BROCHURE, DECEMBER 1961

The Irish branch of ISMA issued a brochure at the end of 1961 declaring the association to be an internationally recognised organisation catering for salesmanship.

Its objectives included the exchange of knowledge and experience, and raising the level of sales management by providing professional status and recognised standards of performance. At that time there were 10,000 members of ISMA globally.

The Ireland branch, with its headquarters in Dublin and groups in Belfast and Cork, was a strong and active unit. ISMA's influence was being felt more and more in Irish commercial life and the importance of marketing, in its widest sense, was receiving ever-increasing recognition.

The brochure described the ISMA student society functions concerning educational lectures, meeting sales specialists, monthly student meetings and the provision of ISMA student journal and library access. In this way assistance was provided and given to students, from aid in completing their courses to the attainment of the diploma and membership of the association.

ISMA NEW YEAR, JANUARY 1962

Opening the year 1962 on 5 January, Mr Brian Murphy took the chair. The newly elected council then comprised of: Messrs Peter Greville, hon. treasurer, Harry Woods, hon. secretary, Joe Bigger, Jack Carmody, Fred Ward, Brian Clancy, Bill Chesson, Jim McCarroll (N. Ireland), Leslie Whitehead, Ray Nickels, Michael Coote, Stephen Doyle, George Bowen, Ken Tyrrell and Bill Cavanagh, all of whom were present at the meeting.

'EDUCATION FOR MARKETING SUBMISSION', JANUARY 1962

The submission on 'Education for Marketing' to the Commission on Higher Education was approved and forwarded to the authority.

TELEVISION ADVERTISING, 1962

Speaking on the subject of television advertising, at the ISMA meeting in the Hibernian hotel on 10 January 1962, Mr C. Gordon Lambert, sales director, W. and R. Jacob and Co. (biscuit manufacturers), stated that he believed the three elements of selling were quality, presentation and price. It was his opinion that the main aim of advertising was sales and that the quality must be right and live up to what was claimed. In addition, the presentation should be attractive and the price acceptable to the viewer/customer.

Mr Mack Kyle, (Royd's Advertising) also spoke and reported that 50 per cent of the cost of television advertising was spent on production. The advertising agencies were pressing Telefís Éireann for a rating service and if it was established it would provide a report on the viewing pattern during the first week of Irish television (January 1962). He maintained that the agencies had to be sure that the film produced was the right one, presented at the right time and they could only know that by proper audience measurement.

Mr Niall Sheridan, the first advertisement sales manager of Telefís Éireann, then stated that television was not a commercial venture in the real sense and that any profits made went back either into the taxpayers' pocket or into an improvement of programmes. He concluded his contribution by stating that to provide a reasonable and acceptable service to some three million viewers would cost as much, in effort time and money, as it would to provide a service for 50 million. Success depended on acceptance of programmes, which had proved very good during the previous week.

It was stated then that programmes originating in Ireland were the ones that were 'really pulling' the audience to view television on Telefís Éireann.

TAXATION, JANUARY 1962

On January 12 1962, Mr G.M. Wheeler FCA addressed the ISMA members' luncheon meeting on taxation with special reference to its position with regard to expenses. The subject was described as being very important for marketing executives and salesmen. All present agreed that they had learnt a lot from Mr Wheeler about their allowance entitlements and restrictions.

The London National Council indicated to the treasurer of the Ireland branch that the expenditure budget granted for the new year was £148.

EXECUTIVE COUNCIL MEETING, FEBRUARY 1962

Mr Sean Walshe was co-opted to the members' executive committee and in particular to join the public relations committee. In the absence of Mr Jack

Carmody, Mr Walshe undertook to make the press aware of particular forth-coming member meetings.

The branch chairman, Mr Brian Murphy, referred to the *Marketing* journal (February 1962 issue, p. 99), which had mentioned that Mr Reg Bowden's memorandum had been accepted by the London council. It quoted him as saying that 'the clearest way to satisfy the majority would be to classify all in membership in Southern Ireland as overseas members and for the proposed Irish association to make their own subscription rate to cover their requirements'.

POLICY COMMITTEE PROGRESS, FEBRUARY 1962

Following discussion, a proposal was agreed unanimously at the executive meeting to proceed with the formation of an Irish association. It was further decided to co-opt the education and membership committee chairmen to the policy committee. The latter comprised of Messrs Brian Murphy, Bill Cavanagh, Michael Coote, Leslie Whitehead, Stephen Doyle, Peter Greville, Brian Clancy and Harry Woods.

The policy committee meeting was held on Monday 12 February 1962 at the Central hotel, Dublin at 5.30 p.m.

Mr Joseph Bigger was congratulated on his appointment as Chairman of the Association of Advertisers in Ireland.

At 111, Pearse street, Dublin (Hammond Lane offices) the executive met on Friday 2 March 1962. Mr Leslie Whitehead acted as chairman, while Mr Harry Woods, hon. secretary, Messrs Michael Coote, Jim McCarroll, Sean Walshe, Brian Clancy, George Bowen, Joe Bigger and Fred Ward were all present.

Regarding student education, Mr Brian Clancy drew attention to certain members of the executive — Messrs Peter Greville, Bill Cavanagh, Harry Woods and Miss Elizabeth Lloyd, a graduate member of the branch. He praised them for having given up so much of their own time lecturing to the institute students studying for the various stages of the diploma course.

Council member, Mr Jim McCarroll of Baxter Ltd, Ballymoney, Co. Antrim, suggested that members of the group in Northern Ireland be given a copy of the proposed draft Memorandum and Articles of Association of the proposed Irish institute.

Mr Leslie Whitehead was pleased to say that such had already been provided for and that comunication of every kind would continue to be sent to all members north and south. He went on to say that the draft memorandum was then with the solicitors.

Regarding a proposed name for the Irish institute, Mr Sean Walshe suggested 'The Institute of Marketing and Sales Management in Ireland'.

EUROPEAN COMMON MARKET, 1962

Mr J. J. Stacey, Director-General of the Federation of Irish Industries was the guest speaker on the subject of 'the Common Market' at the evening meeting of 9 March 1962 at the Central hotel, Dublin.

Mr Stacey said that the slogan for the future must be: 'Produce what we can sell rather than sell what is produced'. In previous years, he said, firms that had been strongly engaged in exports agreed that the idea of exporting surplus production did not provide a lasting basis for success on either the export or home markets.

Mr Stacey went on to say that the necessity for good marketing, particularly in a large common market of 200 or 300 million people, presented very serious problems for a country whose industry was composed of very small firms in the main, such as in Ireland. He further said that this demanded the necessity for immediate co-operation, especially between firms in the same industry and suggested the idea of co-operation between complementary industries.

Mr Stacey was of the opinion that if Ireland's application to join the Common Market was accepted, their tariffs would begin to lose their effect within four or five years — a very short time in which to adapt to a completely new regime. In concluding, he stated that he felt an immediate start was necessary.

MR R. MCCUTCHEON, RIP

The death of Mr R. McCutcheon, (RIP), a prominent active member of ISMA, was announced with sincere regret. Mr Jim McCarroll, a Ballymoney, Co. Antrim council member, conveyed sincere sympathy to Mr McCutcheon's family and to the members of the Northern Ireland ISMA group.

IRISH INSTITUTE OF MARKETING AND SALES MANAGEMENT

A special executive meeting was held at Hammond Lane, Dublin, on 25 April 1962.

Present were: Messrs Brian M. Murphy, chairman, Harry V. Woods, hon. secretary, Peter Greville, hon. treasurer, and Joe Bigger, George Bowen, Stephen Doyle, Michael Coote, Bill Fraser and Sean Walshe. In attendance also were Mr Joseph McGough BL and Mr Desmond Moran, solicitor.

No motion otherwise having been received by the hon. secretary, the business set out in the notice of 19 April 1962 proceeded, as follows:

1. Amendments made to the draft Memorandum and Articles of Association of the proposed Irish institute were read, finalised and approved.

2. It was unanimously decided that the name of the Irish body be the 'Irish Institute of Marketing and Sales Management'.

IRISH STUDENT GROWTH, 1951–62

The growth of the student society was recorded by the education committee. It can be observed from the table below that the rapid increase in the number of registered students, particularly in the Republic, took place from 1960 onward:

Year	Republic of Ireland	Northern Ireland	Total
1951	6	5	11
1952	14	13	27
1953	27	11	38
1954	28	11	39
1955	29	11	40
1956	31	12	43
1957	41	21	62
1958	48	20	68
1959	55	20	75
1960	102	33	135
1961	167	33	200
1962	235	35	270

CORK — FACILITIES FOR STUDENT LECTURES, MAY 1962

A special open meeting took place at 8 p.m. on Friday 18 May 1962 at the College of Commerce, Morrison's Island, Cork. The chief executive of the college, Mr Parfrey, arranged the facilities.

Prior to the public meeting, members from the Ireland branch executive met with Mr Parfrey to arrange ways and means of providing student lectures on the ISMA diploma subjects so that a course may commence at the next session (autumn 1962). Hon. secretary, Mr Harry Woods, had arranged press advertising for what would be the first entity of a school of management in Cork.

There were 52 present (including one lady) at the public meeting. Many students expressed a desire to enrol for the diploma course at the Municipal College of Commerce, Cork in September 1962. The *Cork Examiner* of Saturday 19 May 1962 reported that Mr Harry Woods, hon. secretary and vice-chairman of the Ireland branch of ISMA, had presided at the inauguration of a Cork branch to cater particularly for the diploma course and examinations in marketing.

The education chairman, Mr Brian Clancy, and vice-chairman, Mr Tom Mullen, were among the large number of management personnel from Cork and Dublin who attended and contributed to the meeting. The expansion of the institute and details of submission to the government Commission on Higher Education, making the case for education in marketing, were explained. It stated that it was imperative to help Ireland compete in the situation arising relative to the European Common Market.

In reply Mr Parfrey suggested also that students of the diploma course take a foreign language. He went on to say that in the future marketing executives would not alone be marketing for Ireland but also for the Continent.

As a result of the meeting some forty persons indicated their desire to enrol for the course.

JEFFERS CANDELABRA AWARD, 1962

Having obtained the highest percentage of student registrations for the diploma course of ISMA in the British Isles, the education committee of the Ireland branch was awarded the 'Jeffers Candelabra'. The presentation was formally made in October 1962.

Meanwhile, in the absence of any premises of the Ireland branch, it was appreciated that the honorary librarian, member Mr Frank Young, had accepted such an appointment in Dublin. He was thanked sincerely for the time he gave and the service and control he organised over the distribution of text books to registered students. Many members had contributed books and some had given financial assistance so that more books could be purchased.

In a letter (dated 24 May 1962) to Mr David Griffiths of London Mr Harry Woods reported on the successful Cork meeting. However, he pointed out that the usual complication arose with regard to obtaining suitably qualified lecturers thus requiring ISMA members to provide evening lecturing. Dublin agreed to keep in close contact and provide assistance.

Additional quantities of literature etc. were requested particularly as a student recruitment meeting was organised for Limerick Technical Institute on Wednesday 13 June.

HARVARD CASE STUDY, DUBLIN 1962

During the winter period of 1962/63 classes for all stages of the Diploma in Marketing were organised. They catered for approximately 200 students. The third year marketing class made use, for the first time, of the Harvard case study technique.

It was deemed most successful.

The task of the founder member lecturers was eased due to the availability of some graduate students who helped by giving some of the lectures to students. Appreciation was expressed to Miss Elizabeth Lloyd, Messrs Tom Mullen, Michael Quinn, Sean Walshe, and Harry Woods for lecturing on the specialised subjects of the course.

In Cork the first year examinations were catered for at the College of Commerce with the co-operation and help of the principal, Mr Goggin and the chief executive officer, Mr Parfrey. As the attendance at classes was very good, the inauguration of a new examination centre for the Cork students was established for 1963.

NEW DIPLOMA IN MARKETING, 1962

A new diploma in marketing was established in October 1962. The old syllabus of the Diploma in Sales Management Studies continued to operate though it was being gradually phased out. Four students passed the final Diploma in Sales Management Studies in 1962 and were then studying for the transfer examination to obtain the Diploma in Marketing.

On the new course thirteen students completed part 1 and five were successful in part 2 — the first opportunity to sit such examinations. The part 3, Diploma in Marketing, final year examinations were held for the first time in 1962. This heralded an increasing flow of incoming members qualified by examination.

KURT ALTSCHUL IN DUBLIN, 1962

Mr Kurt Altschul, international co-ordinator of the National Sales and Marketing executives, New York, addressed a meeting of 120 ISMA students at the Hibernian hotel, Dublin, in October 1962. He also went to three of the evening classes at Rathmines and there he explained to students the importance of studying marketing subjects and encouraged their progress and perseverance.

STUDENT CONFERENCE, CASE STUDY, 1962

A most successful conference was held at the Clare Manor hotel, Dublin, in October 1962. A feature of the conference was the use of a special case study, set up by an experienced group of senior members: Peter Greville, (Albright & Wilson), Gerry Rooney (Neilson Research) and Mack Kyle (Royd's Advertising). The case study comprised a full day marketing exercise, which tested the knowledge of the students in team participation, incorporating decision making following the practical use of marketing criteria.

NEGOTIATIONS WITH UK EDUCATION COMMITTEE

The 'break' with London was recorded by the education committee as having caused problems in the organisation of study in Ireland. The British diploma was still accepted as a qualification for membership of the Irish Institute. The formation of the latter had, however, 'cut-off' the educational committee in Ireland from participating in the National (UK) Education Committee (NATEDCO) meetings in London. Much negotiation took place resulting in a solution for the best interests in marketing education by an agreed long-term co-operation between the British and Irish Institutes.

EXPANDED SYLLABUS OF I.INST.MSM

As the Irish Institute of Marketing and Sales Management grew from strength to strength, closer liaison with the universities, Irish Management Institute, Federation of Irish Industries and Irish Exporters' Association was established.

The expanded syllabus of the I.Inst.MSM programme, Marketing I lectures, included such diverse concerns as:

1. Typical patterns of departmental organisation in industry.

2. The contribution of marketing and its responsibility.

3. Distribution channels and distribution methods.

4. Designing the marketing organisation.

5. The Common Market.

6. Capital goods markets.

7. Export markets.

8. Pricing and the stocking and physical distribution of goods.

SUPERMARKET IMPACT ON TRADE, 1962

Mr John J. Quinn, managing director of H. Williams & Co. gave a talk in February 1962 on the supermarket and its impact on the grocery trade and relevance to the housewife.

He explained that self-service was a labour-saving device, giving the customer more leisure time. Anyone could do their shopping in three or four minutes in this type of shop. He also expressed the desire to improve supermarket facilities still further by providing more and more pre-packed goods, to include prepared goods and clean vegetables.

He emphasised the point that with a rapid efficient service this would ease the buyer's job and save time. It would lead to better value in price, quality, weight and hygiene. He concluded by saying that Irish housewives would respond quickly and appreciatively to the new change and appreciated the service provided.

COMMON MARKET IMPLICATIONS FOR IRISH INDUSTRY, 1962

At the members' meeting on 9 March 1962 in the Central hotel, Dublin, Mr J.J. Stacey, Director of the Federation of Irish Industries, warned that the conditions under which industry was operating would be drastically changed within the following few years. If Ireland's application for Common Market membership was to be accepted, its tariffs would begin to lose their effect in four or five years. That was a short time to adapt to a completely new regime, hence an immediate start was necessary, felt Mr Stacey.

Mr Stacey stated his belief that the Irish Institute had, therefore, to examine itself critically and the need was to investigate the possibilities of specialisation in different products. That would mean intensifying efforts to improve productivity and ensure that equipment was up-to-date. The necessity of good marketing presented a serious problem for Ireland, where industry was composed of small firms. Mr Stacey stressed the urgent need for co-operation 'particularly between firms in the same industry'. Mr Stacey concluded by stressing the fact that industry had to realise, that in Common Market conditions, it would have to export more not only to develop industries at home but to make up for the loss of home markets to imports.

IRISH INSTITUTE OF MARKETING AND SALES MANAGEMENT (I.INST.MSM) ESTABLISHED 1962

It was no coincidence that the establishment of the autonomous Irish Institute took place against the backdrop of the first Irish programme of economic expansion. This was masterminded by Mr Sean Lemass, TD and Dr Ken Whitaker, secretary at the Department of Finance (later governor of the Central Bank and afterwards a director of the Bank of Ireland).

The inaugural meeting of the Irish Institute of Marketing and Sales Management, (I.Inst.MSM) was held at the Royal Hibernian hotel, Dublin, on 20 July 1962.

It was an honour that Mr Tom Murray, chairman of the Electricity Supply Board, agreed to become the first president. Mr Murray presided at the meeting and Mr N. Brownlee, chairman of the Northern Ireland branch ISMA, attended.

Mr Norman McConnell, a vice-chairman, M.Inst.MSM, informed those present that up to the night before the new Institute had received 105 applications for membership, while 25 more were in transit. Most of the applicants had also applied for 'overseas membership' of the London Institute. Mr McConnell said that the executive of the new Irish Institute were expecting many more applications in the immediate future.

The Irish Institute concentrated on meeting the demands from an increasing number of firms who were then realising the benefits of sound marketing education. It was the aim to establish more branches and increase educational facilities.

At Rathmines Vocational College, Dublin and also in the Cork Vocational College, a diploma, following a three-year course of lectures, attendance and study, was operating. There were then 167 students enrolled at Rathmines, College of Commerce, while supplemental study was provided by seminars, lectures and short-evening courses. Other centres were to be established later. The diploma was the only professional marketing qualification in Ireland at the time and included the subjects of economics, advertising, salesmanship, office organisation, company law and psychology.

Mr Stephen Doyle, M.Inst.MSM, Irish representative to the UK Institute, read a report on a recent council meeting in London. He had been asked to convey to the executive and members, the good wishes for the success of the new Irish Institute.

MEMORANDUM AND ARTICLES OF ASSOCIATION, 1962

The Irish Institute of Marketing and Sales Management Ltd was registered under the Companies' Acts of 1908–1959. Its objectives included the organising, watching over, maintaining, promoting, protecting and assisting by all lawful means the rights and interests of those who were sales or marketing managers, proprietors or directors of businesses and others engaged in the professions of marketing and selling, who wished to become sales managers in Ireland or elsewhere, particularly those who were members of the Institute.

The subscribers to the Memorandum and Articles of Association, dated 27 July 1962, were:

- Mr Leslie V. Whitehead, company director

- Mr M.H. Coote, marketing consultant

- Mr Charles W. Chesson, company director

- Mr William P. Cavanagh, company director

- Mr Norman McConnell, marketing director

- Mr Joseph C. Bigger, marketing director

- Mr W. Raymond Nickels, sales manager

- Mr H.V. Woods, company director

- Mr B.M. Murphy, company director

- Mr W.D. Fraser, managing director

- Mr Sean A. Walshe, salesman.

The signatures were witnessed by Mr Stephen J. Doyle, Peace Commissioner, who in doing so, precluded himself from being a subscriber, (to which he would otherwise have undoubtedly been).

The rules and regulations for administering the Institute, cited above, the powers and regulations of the council, including the provision of examinations for intending members had been carefully drawn up over a considerable period of time. The limited liability of members was £2 and the solicitors were Moran & Ryan, Lr Ormond Quay, Dublin.

FIRST OFFICERS AND EXECUTIVE, I.INST.MSM, 1962

The first appointed officers of the I.Inst.MSM were recorded as:

- President: Mr Thomas Murray (ESB)

- Chairman: Mr Brian M. Murphy (Hammond Lane Industries)

- Vice-Chairmen: Mr Norman McConnell (Aspro Nicholas of Ireland)
          Mr Peter E. Greville (Goodbody and Albright & Wilson (I) Ltd)
          Mr Harry V. Woods (Mart-Woods Ltd)

- Executive: Mr M.H. Coote (M.H. Coote & Co.)
          Mr Leslie C. Thorn (Car-Thorn)
          Mr K.E.J. Tyrrell (Arthur Guinness & Son Ltd)
          Mr Brian Clancy (Aer Lingus)
          Mr W.R. Nickels (Irish Ale Breweries Ltd)
          Mr J.J. Carmody (Irish Farmers' Journal)
          Mr J.C. Bigger (Hammond Lane Iron founders Ltd)
          Mr Leslie V. Whitehead
          Mr Bill Cavanagh (Chivers)
          Mr C.W. Chesson (Aspro)
          Mr F.J. Ward (Mercantile Credit Co.)
          Mr Stephen J. Doyle (Dollards)
          Mr W.D. Fraser (Jeyes)
          Mr T.A. Moran (Park Cake Bakeries, Kent)
          Mr J.A. McCarroll (Baxter Ltd, Co. Antrim)
          Mr Sean A. Walshe (Dakota Ltd).
          Mr George Bowen

The new offices of the Irish Institute were located at No. 90, St. Stephen's Green, Dublin, while Mr Harry Woods, the managing director of Mart-Woods Ltd, became the first hon. secretary.

MARKETING DEFINED, 1962

Marketing was defined then as:the creative management function which promoted trade and employment by assessing consumer needs, initiating research and development to meet them by:

1. Co-ordinating the resources of finance, production and distribution of goods and services.

2. Determining and directing the nature and scale of the total effort required to sell profitably the optimum production to the ultimate user.

The directors of the Institute felt that the concept of marketing was at the heart of any dynamic economic system.

AFFILIATION OF IRISH INSTITUTE TO SME-I, NEW YORK, 1962

The Irish Institute of Marketing and Sales Management became affiliated to the Sales and Marketing Executives International (SME-I), New York. The Institute was recognised internationally as the organisation responsible for the development of marketing in Ireland, as it was also a member of the European Marketing Contact Group (later known as the European Marketing Council — EMC). A number of things resulted from this:

• membership increased, as did student registrations

• monthly lecture meetings were provided in Dublin and Cork

• courses for the Diploma in Marketing were held at the School of Management Studies, Rathmines, Dublin

• vocational guidance lectures were introduced for prospective students at Rathmines

• actual participating case study histories (a Harvard University technique) were provided at the Annual Student Conference.

It was observed that a principal factor which influenced growth in student educational activity was that companies, in all fields, became aware of and recognised the Diploma in Marketing as essential for training marketing personnel, junior and senior alike. The course, of three-year duration, was the only recognised professional qualification in marketing management in Ireland at that time.

DUBLINER'S DIARY, JULY 1962

In the *Evening Press* Terry O'Sullivan wrote in the 'Dubliner's Diary' column about the 'christening party' (inauguration of the new Irish Institute). He reported that 'all the top brains, of all the top virile industries, were at the inauguration meeting of the Irish Institute of Marketing and Sales Management, in one group, managing directors and marketing directors'. He described it as 'half-way between the payroll of CIE (Irish Railway) and the next on the list, Arthur Guinness (Brewery)'.

INAUGURAL BANQUET, I.INST.MSM, NOVEMBER 1962

The inaugural banquet of the Irish Institute of Marketing and Sales Management took place at the Shelbourne hotel, Dublin, on 7 November 1962.

MINISTER'S SPEECH, NOVEMBER 1962

Mr Jack Lynch, TD, Minister of Industry and Commerce, in congratulating the Institute on its achievements, stated that he believed that in future, exports would form a major element in plans for product policies, for pricing structures and for selling arrangements. It was his conviction that some Irish firms had already shown what could be achieved, while others would do well to follow their example.

Concentration on production techniques, Mr Lynch felt, was inevitable during the formative years of Ireland's new industrial expansion structure. However, he also felt that the enormous increase in Ireland's exports over the last ten years, from £80m. to £180m. a year, was tangible evidence that progress had been made in marketing.

EEC and EFTA areas, 1962

Continuing his speech Mr Lynch stated that conditions were changing rapidly from those that had prevailed even during the last decade. Competition was everywhere, increasing under the impetus of tariff cuts with the EEC and EFTA areas. It was his opinion that Ireland was losing many of the advantages she had formerly enjoyed in export markets. Ireland would have to face the fact that her manufacturers were going to lose many of the privileges enjoyed on the home market.

The Minister said in such changed conditions the fullest range of marketing talents and experience was needed as a vital contribution to the important management decisions which would be taken in the years ahead and which, in some cases, were likely to be taken more urgently.

Marketing men must help to choose the products to concentrate on, Mr Lynch said, and they must give a lead in determining the priorities in products, presentation and development. They must keep in close touch with rapidly changing distribution systems, at home and abroad. Also they would have to work within tightening profit margins to get the maximum value from promotional expenditure.

In the management plans there had to be positive acceptance that exports were a necessity. He finished his speech by mentioning the fact that the days were rapidly disappearing when exports were a convenient addition to a structure that was based on the home market.

Scandinavian Design Group criticism, July 1962

In reference to the then report of the Scandinavian Design Group, which criticised industrial design in Ireland, Mr Lynch stated that an organising consultant for design had been appointed to the National College of Art. To date 14 firms had been assisted by Córas Tráchtála in the recruitment of designers. Design goods had been manufactured by about 15 firms. In addition arrangements had been made for a nucleus of young Irish designers to work with others abroad. Many other design improvement projects were also in the course of preparation.

TAOISEACH CONGRATULATES INSTITUTE, JULY 1962

In a special message of congratulations, read at the inaugural dinner, An Taoiseach Mr Sean Lemass, TD, said that the future held out the challenge of more intense competition on the home market, coupled with greatly increased opportunities on the Continent.

In the work of discovering such opportunities and making the best of them, efficient marketing management was indispensable. It was, therefore, of vital importance for the future of Irish industry to have at the highest levels of management an awareness of the problems and a full knowledge of the techniques with which the Institute would be concerned.

With the co-operation of its members and through its educational programmes, the Institute would, he was confident, foster a dynamic approach to marketing and make a significant contribution to the industrial and commercial development of Ireland.

Among the speakers at the inaugural dinner were the first president of the Irish Institute of Marketing and Sales Management, Mr Tom Murray, the first

Institute chairman, Mr Brian Murphy and a vice-chairman, Mr Norman McConnell, the Lord Mayor of Dublin, Alderman J.J. O'Keeffe TD and Mr T.N. Brownlee, M.Inst.M.S.M, (chairman of the Northern Ireland group).

Other dignitaries present at the dinner were the deputy-president of the Insurance Institute of Ireland, Mr James Beggs; the president of the Incorporated Law Society of Ireland, Mr G.G. Overend; the chairman of the Irish Association of Advertising Agencies, Mr M.B. Kenny; chairman of the Dublin Port and Docks Board, Mr Davy Frame, Mr J.K. McPhie, chairman of the Institute of Marketing and Sales Management, London, and Mr J.O. Leet, vice-president, Sales and Marketing Executives International, New York.

FELLOWSHIP AWARDS, OCTOBER 1962

It was recorded on 1 October 1962 that the existing Irish Fellows of the Incorporated Sales Managers' Association (ISMA) became the first Fellows of the Irish Institute of Marketing and Sales Management, (F.Inst.MSM,). They were Messrs Bill Fraser, Leslie Whitehead, Bill Chesson and Tom Moran.

GUIDE TO CAREERS, NOVEMBER 1962

On 21 November 1962 the *Irish Independent* newspaper published a *Guide to Careers — How to Become a Salesman.* It contained a very lengthy article covering the expanding field of marketing and sales management, which they commented, was such an important part of the whole structure of business and commerce. The article referred to marketing research as a continuous process and the liaison with other departments, such as costing, packaging, design, advertising and, the timing and economics of distribution.

It pointed out that the salesman was only one of the many individuals who comprised the sales and marketing force of the modern company. Salesmanship was one of the stepping stones leading to the highest positions of responsibility while there were also other ways that promotion could be gained within an organisation.

It mentioned that the ability to drive a car was necessary to become a salesman and that knowledge of a continental language was a distinct advantage in obtaining a top sales position, thereby ensuring better remuneration and future prospects. A Leaving certificate standard of education was required. Night classes were advised for trainee salesmen aged between 19 and 25 years. Trainees, it was said, could expect about £7 or £8 per week when starting off.

The marketing managers were key figures who co-ordinated the work of supervisors and salesmen and were responsible for the successful and profitable operation of the sales and marketing department.

Fringe benefits were outlined. Salaries, varying greatly, anything from

£750 to £1,250 per annum, for the experienced salesman or area supervisor. Higher executive positions would command upwards of £2,500 per annum.

It was also recorded that a recognised marketing qualification was essential and that the Irish Institute of Marketing and Sales Management had provided the Diploma in Marketing. This, it reported, was the professional qualification in Ireland covering the whole field of marketing management.

CHALLENGES IN UK MARKETING, 1962

Recorded in my own copy of the UK *Marketing* journal of December 1962, are the sound words of their Institute chief administrative officer, Mr R.F. (Bob) Collischon, when addressing the annual dinner of the Bristol branch of ISMA on 9 November 1962.

He recalled that over 50 years ago a handful of men sought each other's company because they were employed in the task of selling. Such men were on the crest of the prosperity wave of the industrial revolution. Everything made by the great power of the machine was new and exciting in their country. 'Made in Great Britain', he said, was a hallmark all over the world.

Mr Collischon described how change had taken place and mentioned that in 1961 ISMA, in UK, had taken the big step forward to show that they were determined to meet the new challenge of change. ISMA then became known as the Institute of Marketing and Sales Management (instead of Incorporated Sales Managers Association).

He warned that the honeymoon period of fat order books had passed and that good salesmen, backed up by good production, were required to ensure continuity of selling. His speech finished with the thought that while it was fine thinking in terms of a great new market in Europe, what people did not realise was that the marketing men of Europe had plans. European employers, with highly trained marketing men, were just waiting to come over and secure a share of the very lush market in the UK.

MR TONY O' REILLY'S SPEECH, FEBRUARY 1963

An evening meeting with its theme of: 'Ireland and the International Consumer' was held on 15 February 1963 in the Russell Hotel, St. Stephen's Green, Dublin. Mr A.J. (Tony) O'Reilly, general manager, Bord Bainne (Irish Milk Board) was the speaker.

Writing in the 'Dubliner's Diary' in the following *Evening Press* issue, Mr Terry O'Sullivan said that in all the years of his experience he had never, until then, been at a press conference/lecture in the sophisticated Russell Hotel. The Russell hotel, Mr O'Sullivan observed, was one of those places to which newspapermen never went, unless most formally asked to, so it was with an air of surprise that he went to the Russell to hear Mr Tony O'Reilly, 'the biggest milkman in Ireland', lecture to the students of the Institute. Students, he wrote, was a misnomer as the room was packed with senior executives and senior salesmen, all of whom were anxious to learn from someone else's success.

Mr O'Reilly told his captive audience at the Russell that an additional 18 million gallons of milk (equivalent to 3,500 tons of butter or £2,000,000) was taken in at creameries throughout the year. The result of the year's trading showed a total of 15,547 tons of butter sold at £296 per ton in 1962, compared to the 1961 exports of 14,819 tons at £253 per ton.

He informed those present that cheese manufacturing in Ireland had secured approximately 9 per cent of the total imports of Colby cheese into the United States. Of the 6,000 tons of Irish butter, which found a market in the Liverpool and Manchester areas, 5,000 tons went into the blenders packs, with a consequent decrease in the premiums available to the Irish farmer.

Mr O'Reilly also outlined Bord Bainne's four main aims which he said were implicit to their marketing plan. These were the following:

1. To increase the revenue from the sale of Irish butter in the restricted UK market by obtaining a price premium for a promoted branded Irish pack.

2. To help build up favourable associations in the UK for Irish food products.

3. To confer protection for the future by marketing a branded pack which could command its price much more readily than butter, which was primarily used for blending purposes.

4. To reduce wholesaler/agent dependence by developing consumer awareness and demand.

Attendance at the meeting, chaired by Mr Brian Murphy, included Mr Melville Miller, managing director of Rowntree Mackintosh (Irl) Ltd, who proposed a vote of thanks, Mr Jack Jones, Market Research Bureau of Ireland, Mr Jack Carmody Farmers' Journal and Mr David Dand, directorof Gilbey's (Irl) Ltd.

It is interesting to note that one of the 'students' at the meeting was Mr Harry Christmas, director of EMI in Ireland, who at that time sold enormous quantities of records, referred to by the press as being 'under a dazzling multitude of labels'. It was said that record sleeves probably cost about 10 per cent of the cost of each record and that good classical music could be sold in any wrapper paper.

RESEARCH IN MARKETING STRUCTURE, APRIL 1963

Mr Jack J. Jones, managing director of the Market Research Bureau of Ireland Ltd, was the speaker at the April 1963 luncheon meeting in the South

County hotel, Stillorgan, Dublin. His subject was: 'Research — Its Place in the Modern Marketing Structure'.

He informed those present that the final criterion of the successful marketing of a product was the attainment of a satisfactory degree of continuing consumer acceptance. Mr Jones told the members and guests that the gradual removal of import tariffs, the continued growth of self-service and supermarket types of retail outlets, and television as an advertising medium would eventually mean a greater variety of products for the Irish consumer.

He also pointed out five basic marketing errors that could be eliminated. They could be got through provision of appropriate data, obtained via conventional market research and by over-estimating one's share of the market.

Further error showed the over-estimation of the percentage of public awareness of the product, failure to grasp opportunities to increase the market for products and again under-estimating the sales potential and resourcefulness of competitors. Finally, failure to assess values of promotional and advertising methods and media was observed. There was no point in producing a product that did not sell.

Mr Cecil McQuiston the general manager of Switzer & Co. Dublin, in proposing thanks to the speaker, said that if one was going to sell outside Ireland, as it moved towards free trade, market research would be essential.

WINES, MAY 1963

The renowned wine taster, Mr Tom Whelehan from Mullingar, Co. Westmeath, was asked by Gilbey's Wine Merchants to pass on a few tips to members of the Institute. Mr David Dand of Gilbeys was the host to fellow Institute members, at 46/7, Upper O'Connell Street, Dublin, on 3 May 1963.

The subject of Mr Whelehan's speech was: 'The Right Wines for the Right Occasion'. He informed those present that the enjoyment of wine, like music, did not call for any particular knowledge of the subject. The development of an appreciation of wine was acquired through regular sampling or tasting. In addition, he stated that the three most important things about a wine were the bouquet, colour and taste.

Mr Whelehan, who was a wholesale manufacturing chemist by profession, told those present that he had found he had a palate and a fantastic sense of smell so he took up wine-tasting. It was more or less a hobby and he said he had no time for snobs who pretended to know the quality of a wine, merely by smelling the cork, or who cribbed at the temperature of a room.

Before finishing Mr Whelehan advised his audience to drink young white wines while they retained acidity. However, red wines should age, as young red wine had an excess of tannin and a drawing effect on one's gums.

STUDENT RECRUITMENT, SEPTEMBER 1963

In the Town Hall, Rathmines, Dublin, a recruitment meeting of the students' society of the Insitiute was held on 6 September 1963.

The attendance included Mr Sean Ó Ceallaigh of the College of Commerce and speakers Messrs Stephen Doyle, (Dollard Printing House), Bill Fraser (Jeyes Ltd) and Harry Woods (Mart-Woods Ltd), honorary-secretary of the Institute, who gave a history of marketing education and the prospects for the future employment of students.

DANIEL AWARD, SEPTEMBER 1963

The Irish student branch of the London Institute won the Daniel Award Prize (the annual award for recruiting the most students in Britain and Ireland) for the second successive year.

At that stage some 400 students were studying for the diploma course.

APPOINTMENTS TO THE INSTITUTE, 1963–64

Mr Norman McConnell, marketing director of Aspro-Nicholas Ireland Ltd was elected as chairman of the Irish Institute of Marketing and Sales Management for the year 1963–64. Mr Tom Murray agreed to continue as president, while all the other officers were re-appointed.

MARKETING CONFERENCE OF THE FEDERATION OF IRISH INDUSTRIES, OCTOBER 1963

Mr Brian Murphy, immediate past-chairman, and Mr Harry Woods, hon. secretary, represented the Institute along with some members of the executive, at the third national marketing conference of the Federation of Irish Industries on Thursday 3 October 1963.

PRESIDENT'S NIGHT DINNER, NOVEMBER 1963

The annual President's Night dinner of the Institute took place in the Shelbourne Hotel on 6 November 1963.

The principal speaker was the Minister for Transport and Power, Mr Erskine Childers, TD. In his speech he mentioned that there was still negative reaction to the need for expertise in Ireland and a belief that in 1963 sales and marketing required only bright Irish genius and the gift of the gab. He also felt that there was a belief that education in designing, packaging and marketing was not essential.

Irish Exports had greatly increased since 1956 but the 'Second Programme for Economic Expansion' had set a very high target for industrial exports, which had to expand by 150 per cent between 1960 and 1970. The minister stressed the need for dedicated action and ambitious endeavour on the part of Ireland's manufacturers.

He went on to say that he believed that the Institute along with the Irish Exporters' Association had to be the leading influence in persuading the country to remember the target and prepare for the second upward explosion of exports, so essential to the national prosperity.

The Minister was aware that evidence had been submitted by the Marketing Institute, to the Commission on Higher Education and which recommended evening courses on marketing take place in eight towns. They could take place at commercial colleges, and at summer schools, establishing marketing as a major subject and also marketing research at universities.

Finally he said, that if the Institute and allied organisations, pressed for better facilities, he felt the Minister for Education would meet the case with sympathy.

MR SEAN Ó CEALLAIGH, FIRST HONORARY MEMBER, NOVEMBER 1963

The principal of the College of Commerce, Rathmines, Mr Sean Ó Ceallaigh, became the first honorary member of the Irish Institute of Marketing and Sales Management. This honour was in recognition of the valuable work he had done over the previous fifteen years, particularly in the field of the education of marketing.

LADIES' NIGHT, NOVEMBER 1963

The Ladies night held at the Shelbourne hotel on 23 November 1963 proved yet again to be an outstanding social evening. Each lady was presented with an assortment of products in a special gift bag from member companies.

MARKETING DIPLOMA ATTAINMENTS, JANUARY 1964

The results of the diploma examinations were reported in the *Evening Herald* of 15 January 1964. Seven students had passed the final examinations and in doing so qualified for the three-year diploma marketing course. Three students obtained a distinction in advertising. They were: Messrs J.P. Corcoran,

T.K. Francis and F.J. Young. The other finalists to be awarded the diploma were: Messrs Cartan Finnegan, H.L. Drew, M.D. Glynn and A.O. Kelly, all from Dublin.

It is gratifying to record also the list of those who passed the second year stage of the diploma course: Messrs P.C. Costello, C.A. Curran, S.L. Forde, J Forsyth, T.V. Francis, D.A. McCormick, P.M. O'Malley and P. McGee. The number who passed in first year study was fourteen, of which three were from Cork, with one each from Wicklow, Meath and Louth, S. Dato Ahmad (Trinity College) and seven from Dublin.

There were approximately 250 students studying for stages of the diploma, at Dublin and Cork at that time.

BUSINESS GIFTS, JANUARY 1964

On 17 January 1964 the sales director of Irish Goodwill Novelties Ltd, Mr Phil. E. Thomas, when addressing a luncheon meeting of members in the Crofton Airport hotel, Dublin, told his audience that the increasing growth of advertising confirmed his adage 'Business gifts aid promoting sales of products in Ireland'.

He also expressed the opinion that on the continent no firms of any standing would neglect the sending of some goodwill gift at Christmas to their overseas customers.

In Italy and Spain buyers expected such gifts not only at Christmas but at Easter also. In the case of Holland gifts were expected for the Feast of St. Nicholas on 6 December. The easy way of sending gifts, such as whiskey or cigarettes, was rapidly being abandoned. A carefully chosen article, particularly if it was of a novel nature, would be kept, used and greatly appreciated. Mr Thomas finished up by reminding members that the man behind the counter, as well as the boss, should not be forgotten either.

IRISH DIRECT MAIL ASSOCIATION, FEBRUARY 1964

On the evening of 17 February 1964 the Irish Direct Mail Association at 9, Pearse Street, Dublin, introduced Institute members and guests to an aspect of sales management which the *Evening Press* reported as being 'not generally aware of'.

The talk given by Mr Eric Thomas, advertising superintendent of British European Airways (BEA) had been arranged by the Irish Direct Mail Association (IDMA) in conjunction with the Irish Institute of Marketing and Sales Management. A member of the executive of the Irish Institute, Mr Brian Clancy (who was also chairman of the IDMA) was also present as was hon. Secretary of the IDMA, Miss Oona McWhirter.

The large interested attendance included guest, Jiri F. Vranek, BA, Ph.D. who contributed to the subsequent lively discussion.

In the next issue of the *Evening Press*, Mr Terry O'Sullivan ('Dubliner's Diary'), recalled that every day apart from the normal incoming mail from all over Ireland, and other countries, the *Evening Press* recieved personally addressed commercial material from London or New York. Regular packets also arrived particularly from the governments of South Africa and Spain, and from UNESCO, and UNICEF, to name a few. Very expensive calendars were also sent to him from the major airlines of the world.

Mr O'Sullivan pointed out that the name and address of individuals were usually supplied by an advertising agency. From his own experience in Ireland he said that the IDMA was simply a group of executives using direct mail services. Further, he believed such business executives were not interested in just sending circulars to an enormous mailing list taken in large chunks from directories.

Sales literature being sent out, through the medium of direct sales, was then so expensive that the value of every name and address had to be weighed. Miss McWhirter said that some of the pieces, sent out by London firms, cost between £2 and £3 per unit. On the demonstration panel, prepared for the speaker there was one classical example of what she meant: a BEA strip of film in colour with a viewer supplied.

The slim and irresistible piece of direct mail showed, in film strip, the attractions of the *Trident* aeroplane, while each strip had cost over £2. The common bond was to study the economics of direct mail and decide to whom one should mail.

IRISH MANUFACTURERS CRITICISED, FEBRUARY 1964

Irish manufacturers criticised for failure to co-operate with their retailers, was the subject of concern of two major retailers in Dublin. They were Mr John J. Quinn, managing director of H. Williams & Co. (Irish owned supermarket group) and Mr Cecil McQuiston LLB, general manager of Switzer & Co. the leading fashion store.

The meeting was held at the Royal Hibernian hotel on 21 February 1964. Members of the Institute sought comment regarding servicing the retailer and consumer. Mr McQuiston said that whilst Irish manufacturers had the home market to themselves, they should be getting together with the retailers to discuss the basic problems of delivery, mark-up, pricing and styling.

At that time pricing had become far more important and the old idea of adding 25 per cent to all costs was quite dead. Successive wage rises, increased expenses and the need to modernise stores had made a bigger mark-up essential for a store to keep its head above water.

It was incredible to say that, truthfully, he knew more British and

Continental manufacturers by name than he did Irish manufacturers. The reason for this, Mr Quinn believed, was because Irish manufacturers did not come into his office and he added that Irish manufacturers were depending too much on small traders to support them. He ended his speech by warning those present that the small man was finished and would not have a ghost of a chance in a few years time.

GOODWILL ENCOURAGED, APRIL 1964

Goodwill towards Irish products in the British market would not be encouraged by the blowing up of Customs posts on the Irish border said Lt.General M.J. Costello, general manager of the Irish Sugar Company, at the evening meeting of 25 April 1964. He disclosed that the 'barometer of goodwill' had dropped a few points immediately following raids in Northern Ireland. However, he said, that feeling against products manufactured in the Republic of Ireland had not continued for long.

Lt. General Costello referred to the fact that the Prime Minister of Northern Ireland, Captain Terence O'Neill, had allowed himself to be photographed drinking some soup at the Erin Food stand at a food fair in Britain, a few days previously. That was the sort of thing that would not have won any votes in County Down, Northern Ireland, a few years ago, stated Lt. General Costello.

It was, however, an indication that the goodwill which existed was growing and should be promoted. Lt. General Costello also mentioned in his speech that his company had been greatly surprised at the amount of goodwill it had found in Britain for Irish products. Trade was a two-way venture, he believed, and if Ireland wanted to hold its volume of trade with Britain and increase its volume with America, it would have to give more than formal recognition to English and American goods.

Stressing the importance of selling Irish products, under an easy identifiable brand name, he said he felt that the brand image had to be 'burned' into the brain of the housewife. Irish firms who wanted to succeed in the export markets would do well to choose from a limited number of brand names.

A brand image needed to be backed up by a good sales force operating in the market and a merchandising team which could ensure that the goods found their way, from the shop shelves, into the housewife's basket. Lt.General Costello urged exporting firms to consider ways in which they could reduce costs and improve efficiency by co-operating with each other, particularly in fields such as market research and distribution.

EUROPEAN MARKETING CONGRESS, BARCELONA 1964

The 24 April 1964 issue of the *Evening Herald* reported that the Irish Institute of Marketing and Sales Management would be represented 'by a number of prominent marketing executives' at the V1 International Marketing and Distribution Congress to be held in Barcelona in May 1964.

The congress was organised by the European Contact Group of Marketing, later known as the European Marketing Council and still later (1999), known as the European Marketing Confederation (EMC). It was agreed by the executive that the Institute delegates be led by Mr Harry V. Woods, hon. secretary and vice-chairman. Mr Woods was then managing director of Mart-Woods Ltd, a hardwood and timber products firm based in Dublin. Delegates personally financed their travel, hotel and fees to participate in the congress.

STUDENTS' QUIZ, APRIL 1964

The AGM of the students' society of the I.Inst.MSM was held at the Royal Hibernian hotel, Dublin on 29 April 1964. At the same meeting two teams of students, all in their final year of the Diploma in Marketing and Sales Management, took part in a marketing quiz. Each member of the winning team was awarded a briefcase, donated by Elley & Son, Aungier Street, Dublin.

Officers elected for student executive for the year 1964–65 were:

- Chairman: Mr Brian A. Clancy (Aer Lingus)
- Vice-Chairmen: Mr P. Quinn, James Fitzgerald and Mr Frank Young
- Hon. Secretary: Mr P.C. Costello, (Greenmount Oil Co.)
- Assistant Secretary: Mr Ian Thompson (Cooper, McDougall and Robertson).

MARKETING CONGRESS REPORT, BARCELONA, MAY 1964

Eight Irish delegates took part in the Vl International Marketing and Distribution Congress. This was held over four full days from May 6 to 9 1964 in Barcelona.

The participants were asked to arrive a day early to see the wonderful city of Barcelona for themselves.

Institute delegates comprised of Mr Bill Cavanagh (Chivers), Mr Tony Corduff, (National Board and Paper Mills), Mr Ronnie Bates (Jacob Biscuits), Mr Stephen Doyle (Dollard Printing House), Mr Michael O'Reilly (Mace Food Group) Mr Des Fennessy (Fennessy Shoes), Mr Tom Manweiler (Guinness) and Mr Harry Woods (Mart-Woods).

Also accompanying the party were Mrs Cavanagh, Mrs Corduff, Mrs O'Reilly and Mr Stephen Doyle's friend, Mr Tom Quinn. The ladies enjoyed partaking in the special tour programme and social events provided for them as well as meeting those from the host and other countries.

Having arrived on the pre-congress commencement day (as suggested by the organisers, Club de Dirigentes de Ventas, Barcelona), the Irish delegates went along to see the congress building. All were fascinated with the number of congresses medical, engineering and others that were being held at and around that time in the city.

The Irish were, however, very disappointed to find that, while flags of innumerable nations flew outside the Palace of Nations, there was no Irish flag. The Irish delegation contacted the Mayor of Barcelona and informed him that unless the Republic of Ireland flag was flown they would not be attending the proceedings the next day. Arrangements were made to go to a major department store where on the top floor the material for the flag was selected and the flag produced. The finished product was then brought to the Palace and hoisted.

The distinguished patron of the congress was the Spanish Chief of State, H. E. Don Francisco Franco. The souvenir book (252 pages) issued to participants, sometime following the proceedings, gave credit to the Spanish government, official institutions, different committees, organisations who gave collaboration, speakers and in general delegates from many countries taking part as well as the large number of Spanish participants.

The international honour committee was headed by Mr Lawrence D. Doyle, president of the Sales and Marketing Executives International, New York. The president of the European Contact Group, Mr John McPhie, UK, and presidents of the various Institutes of Belgium, France, Germany, Denmark, Sweden, Norway, Finland and Spain together with Sir Edwin Leather, MP, were also present.

Introductory remarks were made by Sr Abraham M. Buxaderas, president of the Barcelona Club, who said that the Spanish marketing clubs were very young but concerned with learning, improving and applying marketing techniques. Such required a liberalised economy, a free market, in order to provide the best results in favour of the development of the economy of any enterprise.

SME-I defined

Mr Lawrence Doyle said that the International Sales and Marketing Association, New York (SME-I) was recognised as the greatest organisation of sales and marketing executives in the world. He brought greetings from thousands of fellow members in the United States and from headquarters in New York. SME-I had at that time 30,000 members in 42 countries of the free world.

Communication — the Japanese view

On the subject of communication Mr Haryo Yoneda, director of Dentsu Advertising, Tokyo, said that in such an age when a Japanese advertising man like himself, was, without dwelling much on it, attending a conference in Spain, it was all too easy to assume that all one's problems of communication were solved. This, he stressed, was not the case.

It was also, he believed, wrong to assume that all nations spoke the common language of modern advertising. Again this was not so. It was a similar situation in the case of methods. It cannot he stated be expected that what would work in France or the United Kingdom would work in, for example, Southeast Asia.

Invitation of council seat

All in all, the congress had been very successful and very well attended. The Irish presence was observed, due to their active participation in all sessions, and resulted in an invitation to have a seat on council of the Contact Group of Marketing (now known as the European Marketing Confederation — EMC). Mr Harry Woods took the seat offered and participated in the council's meeting in Barcelona following the close of the congress.

AGM, I.INST.MSM, MAY 1964

The AGM of the Irish Institute of Marketing and Sales Management (I.Inst.MSM) was held in the Royal Hibernian hotel, Dawson Street on 22 May 1964.

FELLOWS ELECTED, MAY L964

Four newly admitted Fellows of the I.Inst.MSM were named and congratulated at the AGM. These were: Mr Michael Coote (M.H. Coote & Co.), Mr Stephen Doyle, (Dollard Printing House Ltd), Mr W.P. (Bill) Cavanagh (Chivers Ireland Ltd) and Mr Brian M. Murphy (Hammond Lane Industries Ltd).

BUSINESS STUDIES (MARKETING) DIPLOMA, MAY 1964

Following meetings with the representatives of the Dublin Vocational Education Committee (VEC), members of the Institute were pleased to report that Mr Sean Ó Ceallaigh (College of Commerce, Rathmines) had arranged a special day course. The course was for students seeking a Diploma in Business Studies (marketing).

Hon. secretary, Mr Harry Woods, who also held the 'management' seat on the College of Commerce Council, reported on the details of the new course.

Three distinct terms were arranged and it would be necessary to have the co-operation of member firms straight away, by supplying suitable students for the course. Firms would also need to provide employment for such students when they were not on the training course.

NEW APPOINTMENTS TO THE INSTITUTE, MAY 1964

The executive and members welcomed the new president of the Institute, Mr John Haughey, chairman of Córas Tráchtála, and the new chairman, Mr Harry V. Woods, managing director of Mart-Woods Ltd. Both were presented with the official ribbon and medal of office. The vice-chairmen elected for 1964–65 were Messrs Joseph Bigger, Peter Greville and Fred. Ward. Mr Brian Murphy (outgoing chairman) agreed to act as hon. secretary and Mr Jack J. Jones (MRBI) as treasurer.

PUBLIC RELATIONS, COMMANDER WHITEHEAD, JUNE 1964

The Irish Times column, An Irishman's Diary, reported an overflow attendance of Marketing Institute members and guess at the South County Hotel, Stillorgan, Co. Dublin on 9 June 1964. (Indeed chairing the meeting myself, I well remember the unprecedented and unexpected number who arrived for lunch to hear the speaker. Some 50 or 60 persons had to be accommodated in adjoining areas.)

The occasion was to hear Commander Edward Whitehead, OBE, president of Schweppes USA Ltd, give an address and recall his experiences on the subject of public relations.

The press correctly recorded that there were, in fact, two Commander Whiteheads present, the other being the Institute programme chairman, Mr Leslie Whitehead, a Fellow of I.Inst.MSM.

Schweppes, Indian tonic water, 1964

The speaker had been a Lt. Commander in small boats during the last war (1939–45). He was, in his own words, just half a rank junior to the man who made Indian tonic water famous and fashionable in the United States of America. That, of course, was a reference to the speaker (who the newspaper reported as being 'spiky-bearded') Mr Edward Whitehead OBE whose photograph was known to millions in America.

Mr David Ogilvie said that he was 'like the man in the Hathaway shirt and the girl who dreamt she walked down Broadway, in her maidenform bra'. Since he had gone to America tonic-water, particularly Schweppes, was the 'in' mix for summer drinks.

The first advertisement, featuring Commander Whitehead appeared in 1953. It showed him stepping off an aircraft, complete with briefcase and umbrella. Since then he had been very much a part of the American scene and had even won a television prize as personality of the year.

Prior to Schweppes, the Commander had held a Treasury post under Sir Stafford Cripps and had been responsible for interpreting Britain's economic needs to industry in the hard and early days of the Crippsian era.

He was of the opinion that if an advertising campaign was successful there was no reason why it should be changed and as the public became accustomed to and liked it, they bought more of the product advertised so the campaign should be continued. The same principle had applied to Schweppes advertising over the previous ten years.

Commander Whitehead gave a brief outline of the history of his company since its foundation in 1794 and stated his belief that publicity was a valuable and inexpensive tool in the field of marketing and distribution. He also showed a series of television commercials and slides of newspaper and magazine advertisements. All of these had been used in the United States and it was observed by those present that he had appeared in most of them himself.

COMMON MARKET OF CENTRAL AMERICA, 1964

Having a particular interest, as a buyer of Hardwoods for my own business, *inter alia*, I myself specialised in exotic types of wood for particularly good furniture, joinery, and shop-fitting. In such I found excellent quality, including reliable dimensions, in Central America. I recall, in particular, Honduras mahogany, cedar and rosewood, also Guatemala and Nicaragua pine.

In the summer of 1964 I made a study of the market data of Central America. In fact I also obtained the volume *A Guide to Market Data in Central America* by Dr Lawrence C. Lockler, Professor of Business Administration, University of Santa Clara, compiled in collaboration with other specialists. It was issued by the Central American Bank for Economic Integration, Tegucigalpa, Honduras.

The guide brought together the marketing information then available for the five Common Market countries of Central America which were industrially maturing rapidly — Guatemala, Honduras, El Salvador, Nicaragua, and Costa Rica.

It was apparent that agriculture and exports of crops, coffee, bananas and sugar, which had given a modest standard of living over generations, would not provide a higher standard for a greater number of families envisaged.

Industry required mass markets to make possible the use of mass manufacturing. Tabulated statistics for varied economic strata were gathered, compiled and analysed. Channels of distribution and other marketing functions were investigated.

Export output was concentrated on a small group of landowners. Luxury items were imported by agents rather than available from stores.

In Honduras resources were not adequately surveyed or developed, while timber was the third largest foreign exchange earner of that country. Forests were abundant and capable of being profitably developed. Exports of timber in log and sawn form amounted to 9.3 per cent of the Honduras figure in 1962. A land study indicated that about 44 per cent of the country's area was forest land.

RECRUITMENT FOR MARKETING DIPLOMA, SEPTEMBER 1964

Young men interested in the sales management/marketing courses at Rathmines attended a briefing meeting there. This was jointly arranged by the Institute and the City of Dublin VEC. The chairman of the recruitment committee of the students' society, Mr Patrick Costello, was responsible for getting such an enthusiastic group of serious young men together.

The *Evening Press* reported the meeting thus:

> Last night, the keener students, (who are studying for the Diploma in Marketing, a three-year course, prescribed in London), were met and addressed by Mr Harry Woods, chairman of the Irish Institute of Marketing and Sales Management, and some of his experienced colleagues. The integration between the experienced professional and the eager student, in such context, was a happy example of the liaison existing between both.

PRESIDENT'S DINNER, OCTOBER 1964

The president's dinner of the Institiute took place at the Shelbourne hotel, Dublin on 1 October 1964. The guests included Mr J.J. Stacey, director general, Federation of Irish Industries, Mr G.L. Pearson, British Trade Commissioner, and Mr Robert F. Collischon, F.Inst.MSM (London), past national chairman, UK.

Dr P.J. Hillery, TD, Minister for Education was the principal guest at the dinner. In his speech he stated his belief that the greatest problem facing Irish industry then was the training and equipping of management for the transition from a small protected home-market to conditions of unrestricted competition at home and abroad.

Second Programme for Economic Expansion, October 1964

Dr Hillery continued by saying that Ireland was going through a revolution in its attitude to education, which was particularly reflected in the reference, in the 'Second Programme for Economic Expansion, to education as being an investment. Such an investment would be expected to yield increasing returns on the economic as well as social side.

The Minister expressed his appreciation in relation to the work of the Institute in the field of business education. He stated that the training and equipment of management was essential to meet competition from abroad and added 'we have long since cast aside the amateur approach to business matters'.

He also pointed out that Irish people welcomed the new approach to business, through knowledge, and said that in recent years they had shown an intelligent interest in everything that contributed to the country's economic progress and development.

In reply Mr John Haughey stated that marketing and selling had a great and growing role to play as tools of export promotion. He felt that viewed from that perspective their importance could hardly be overstated.

The press reported that, in introducing the minister, Mr Harry Woods, chairman, stated that Ireland had progressed at as rapid a rate, and in fact ahead of many other countries in the training of students, particularly in the application of the techniques of marketing. In such a way members were being fitted and students trained to meet the challenges which were undoubtedly arising in the joint marketing and integration of firms manufacturing similar products or components of a major article.

Mr Woods went on to say that since 1960 some 400 students had attended classes for the Diploma in Marketing at the Rathmines School of Management Studies, while over 100 had studied at the Municipal College of Commerce, Cork, where the course started in 1962.

Mr Woods concluded by stating that he believed efficient marketing meant looking at a product from the customer's point of view and then initiating research and development to meet it.

ADVERTISING, OCTOBER 1964

Mr C. Mack Kyle, managing director of Royd's Advertising and Marketing, spoke on the subject of advertising at the Royal Hibernian hotel on 14 October 1964.

He told those present that although it was said that pharmaceutical advertising was too expensive he did not agree. Most research in that field had been carried out by private firms financed by sales and which were partly financed by advertising. Adding to Mr Kyle's remarks, Mr Luke Mahon, managing director of Arks Ltd, stated that it was not the cost of advertising that mattered but the efficient way in which advertising was carried out.

TRAINING FOR MANAGEMENT, OCTOBER 1964

The deputy director of the Irish Management Institute, Mr Brian Whelan, addressed Institute members on the topic of 'Training for Management' at the evening meeting on 16 October 1964 in the Royal Hibernian hotel, Dublin.

German Productivity Committee, October 1964

Fresh from a European conference on training directors, Mr Brian Whelan disclosed that Germany boasted a National Productivity Committee to which were affiliated no less than 78 Institutes. Ireland was in 'slightly' different company, he said, for like remote, and according to the *Evening Press* 'undeveloped Iceland', Ireland had only one marketing institute. On the serious side, however, the fact was that Ireland may make some of the best goods in the world but after that they had to sell them and according to Mr Whelan marketing and sales management were essential for that.

Writing in the *Evening Press* Mr D.F. Moore reported that Mr Harry Woods had told him that his organisation had 300 young sales managers, registered students, preparing for their examinations. 'That,' wrote Mr Moore, 'is a start but with the world market as a battlefield, it is still a mighty small army'.

Management and marketing courses, 1965

During his speech Mr Brian Whelan announced that some 1,700 persons from all over Ireland would participate in the 100 courses organised by the Irish Management Institute for the training of managers. These were to be held in Dublin during 1965.

A panel of experts had been organised as lecturers and a marketing specialist would be appointed to make the final arrangements. Mr Whelan said that the courses, organised by the two Institutes (Management and Marketing) would commence in the New Year.

STUDENTS' SOCIETY CONFERENCE, NOVEMBER 1964

Mr John Haughey, chairman of Córas Tráchtála and president of the Irish Institute of Marketing and Sales Management, opened the one-day conference of the student society. This was held on 14 November 1964 at the Clare Manor hotel, Coolock, Co. Dublin.

Exports affected by British levy, 1964

Mr Haughey said the British levy put an onus on every Irish exporter to fight back, not only to hold, but to extend each individual's share of the market.

Last year (1963) exports had reached the highest level, in value and volume, in Ireland's history.

Mr Haughey told those present that it was even more encouraging to note the further progress recorded in the first half of 1964, from figures just then published. The upward trend had continued up to October 1963, halted only by the levy. Given the necessary degree of determination, he firmly believed the levy could be beaten and that 1964 would be another record year for Irish exports.

Personal selling

Mr Hector Grey was the second speaker at the conference. A well-known figure to the Irish public, he stood and sold 'bric-a-brac' wares on Sunday mornings at the corner of Liffey Street, Dublin. He was very much travelled and had a number of retail outlets in Ireland, especially Dublin. Again he was an importer/exporter and travelled to do all his buying personally.

Mr Grey opened his lecture by saying that he urged the necessity to investigate new markets further afield than England. He felt that many small markets were better than one or two very large ones. One of the most important changes he would like to see happen was for the government to subsidise freight charges for any firm that was exporting. This, he said, was one of the bugbears of selling abroad. Subsidising of freight was done in Australia and worked well. Mr Grey further said that he would like a board set up in Ireland to inspect manufactured goods and set certain standards.

MARKETING, NOVEMBER 1964

Mr Garrett Fitzgerald, TD, economist and parliamentarian, spoke on factors influencing the role of marketing in the 'Second Programme for Economic Expansion'. He told those present that the second programme made one look at markets at home and abroad to try to assess future trend. People had been made more growth conscious than ever before. However, he felt that there was now a vast improvement in statistical data available to manufacturers.

THE COMPUTER — ARTILLERY OF MARKETING, NOVEMBER 1964

Mr Paul Cremins of International Business Machines (Ireland) Ltd, gave an address on the application of 'The Computer — the Artillery of Marketing'. He spoke of the advantages of the computer and its usefulness to those engaged in marketing and illustrated his remarks by showing two related films.

The attendance of 110 at the conference was made up of sales and marketing representatives from the north and south of Ireland. A survey which was undertaken later showed both an appreciation of the organisation and the excellence of the speakers.

LADIES' NIGHT, DECEMBER 1964

Ladies' Night at the Shelbourne hotel, Dublin in December 1964, had an attendence of 350. It was described by Terry O'Sullivan in the *Evening Press* as 'a big, glittering affair' at which the Institute members — 'the country's big sellers', graciously devoted the evening to their womenfolk in style. Each lady received a gift which included foodstuffs, toilet requisites and dry goods, anything from biscuits to perfume.

An unusual elaborate seating plan and setting was provided by Mr Aubrey Fogarty of Fogarty Advertising and was the object of great interest. It was said that the model was devised to make it easy to find individual Institute members, considering the large attendance.

CONTRIBUTION OF ACCOUNTANCY TO MODERN BUSINESS, JANUARY 1965

The 1965 session opened on 13 January with Mr Eric S. Cooke of W. R. Jacob & Co. propounding the importance of a knowledge of computers and mathematical techniques. He maintained the former were vital in order to retain position in providing and interpreting management information.

The title of Mr Cooke's speech was: 'The Contribution of Accountancy to Modern Business'. Students and members alike were present at the informative and successful evening. Other speakers at the meeting were Mr D. Rowe (Forsythe & Co.) and Mr J. O'Sullivan (Arnott & Co.). Both of whom added further helpful advice and replied to questions.

MARKETING DIPLOMAS, JANUARY 1965

On 16 January 1965, in the town hall, Rathmines, Dublin, the president of the Institute, Mr John Haughey, presented diplomas to 34 successful students of marketing and sales management. At that time about 300 students were studying for various stages of the diploma in Dublin and in Cork.

On presenting the diplomas he stated that marketing was the most important development in modern business and in his opinion, the people with the most foresight were those making the most progress.

The chairman of the Institute, Mr Harry Woods, added his congratulations to the new diploma holders and to all those studying for diplomas. He also announced that the Irish Institute of Marketing and Sales Management was seeking recognition for a Chair in Marketing at University College, Dublin. The first such Chair was that at the University of Lancaster in England which had been established the previous year.

Goodbody award

The most outstanding performance by an Irish student had been achieved by Mr P.J. Hendrick of Cork in the May 1964 final examinations. He was presented with the Goodbody award donated by Mr Peter Greville, their marketing director and a vice-chairman of the Institute.

SALES ORGANISATION METHODS, JANUARY 1965

Mr Michael Coote was the guest speaker at the monthly luncheon in the Montrose hotel, Dublin on 15 January 1965. He gave a very interesting talk to members and guests on the subject of sales organisation methods and marketing objectives.

SUPERMARKETS, FEBRUARY 1965

The Publicity Club of Ireland held their monthly luncheon on 12 February 1965 at the Metropole Ballroom, O'Connell Street, Dublin. The guest speakers were Mr C.A. Morris-Cox, hon. treasurer of the Association of Advertisers in Ireland and managing director of Beecham Sales Ltd, and Mr Harry Woods, chairman of the Irish Institute of Marketing and Sales Management and vice-chairman of the Publicity Club.

It was the view of Mr Morris-Cox that price cutting in supermarkets and self-service stores had got so much out of control, in recent years, that it was deemed necessary for manufacturers to produce to a price rather than to a quality. He believed that in the future there would be a movement to build such stores out of the city and further intimated that they would take the form of a large shopping centre.

Supermarkets, he felt, would cater for all the needs of the shopper. Such a movement would undoubtedly be for the benefit of the customers as they would be able to buy a large selection of goods in a relatively small area. In addition, they would also avoid having to travel long distances and suffer the lack of parking space in a city.

Mr Woods foresaw the likelihood of 'one-stop' shopping with much more development in the field of hypermarkets, supermarkets and larger self-service store outlets. (In fact at the time, a large shopping complex was under consideration for the Ballymun area of north Dublin.) There would also be fast food, drive-in availability, thereby having every facility to entice the shopper. This would not only include food, pharmaceutical goods, drapery and footware but also areas as diverse as sports goods, jewellery, hardware, travel agencies and so forth.

CORK AIRPORT MEETING, FEBRUARY 1965

If Ireland was to become integrated in its own right into the European Common Market by 1970, it was essential that men, qualified in modern marketing techniques, be ready to size up the opportunities which would undoubtedly be forthcoming.

The Lord Mayor of Cork, Senator A.A. Healy spoke at the Irish Institute of Marketing and Sales Management, Cork student society meeting held at Cork Airport on the evening of 18 February 1965. He told those assembled how gratifying it was to have in Cork an excellent vocational educational authority whose purpose and aim was to provide the right training for all aspects of commerce.

Continuing on, the Lord Mayor spoke of how pleased he was that well attended lectures were being held at the College of Commerce, Cork, preparing students for the Marketing Institute examinations. The subjects in those courses were marketing, market research, advertising, economics, accountancy, statistics and most importantly, salesmanship. The diploma, he said, had international recognition.

Mr E.J. (Ted) Jenner, BA (Hons), M.Inst.MSM, the registrar of the Institute of Marketing, London and also editor of *Marketing Forum* (excellent student Journal) spoke of the aims for education in marketing for the years ahead.

Mr Jenner indicated important changes directed to the raising of standards and that wider study of techniques was also imminent. He said the Institute needed to win a royal charter so that marketing studies would become formally recognised. In that way an important contribution would be made to the achievement of greater prosperity in Britain and Ireland.

The chairman of the Cork student society, Mr M.J. Hanrahan, replying to the Lord Mayor, said that it was gratifying to record that though the society in Cork had difficulties in establishing itself at the outset, it had gained ever-increasing support and recognition by Cork industrialists.

Mr R.T. O' Shea, a member of the Cork branch of the Institute, thanked the Lord Mayor for his interest and encouragement to students and also those expressed by Mr Jago and other guests, by their presence at the meeting. Mr Jago replied that Ireland had a lot to learn, having been an insular nation for so long it had always provided for its own needs. While producing enough for itself, it then had to learn to sell and to sell more and more abroad. Ireland had to decide whether it would sell quality and small quantities at home or go all out and sell quality first and a large amount abroad.

Mr M.A. Goggin, principal of the College of Commerce, Cork, paid tribute to the Irish Marketing Institute and its foresight in organising lecturing in Cork and also praised the efforts of the Cork student body. He stressed that marketing was the final link in the chain of production and facilities by way of education were and would be provided.

Mr Harry Woods then took the floor and said how pleased he was to have presided in Cork at what was a very well attended and important meeting.

SALES MANAGERS' ATTITUDE, FEBRUARY 1965

The monthly member's meeting was addressed by Mr C.A. Morris-Cox of Beecham Sales Ltd who spoke on the subject of 'The Sales Managers' Attitude to Marketing'. The meeting was held at the Montrose hotel, Dublin, on Friday 19 February 1965.

Born in London, Mr Morris-Cox had, at the time, been in Dublin for over three years. He informed those gathered that Beechams had been founded in 1880 and been in Ireland for 25 years at that stage. Their products numbered such 'essentials' as Lucozade, Brylcream, McLean's toothpaste, Silvikrin and the famed 'Beecham's pills'.

A revolution was taking place in the consumer goods field, he said, and he cautioned that by defining a number of shortcomings that they should be aware of:

• lack of understanding

• breakdown in communications

• inter-departmental prejudice and rivalry

• ultra-concern over status

• lethargy and unused powers of observation

• conservatism

• failure to take account of modern materials, packaging and production techniques.

MARKETING, ADVERTISING AND PUBLIC RELATIONS, FEBRUARY 1965

The Publicity Club of Ireland arranged a joint meeting at the Hibernian hotel, Dawson Street on Friday evening, 26 February 1965. The topics for discussion were sales, marketing, advertising and public relations.

Mr Billy King, Chairman, Publicity Club of Ireland, chaired the very informative meeting, comprising open discussion and question time. Speakers were Mr Peter Rackow, M.Inst.MSM, Managing-Director, Cinema and General Publicity Ltd, Mr Jerry F. Kearney, Chairman, Association of Advertisers in Ireland, Mr Llew Price, Director, Pearl & Dean, Mr Leonard Citron, secretary, Screen Advertising Association and Mr Harry Woods, Irish Institute of Marketing and Sales Management.

Mr Albert Price, hon. secretary of the Publicity Club, renowned as usual, ably organised the proceedings of the largely attended and press reported, significant get-together.

At that time, particularly, the writer recalls the insistence of Mr Sean Lemass, An Taoiseach, that the national advancement had to continue so to ensure the programme engaged in chartering the nation's course to prosperity. Hence the co-operation of business and management were sought, defined as being essential to play their part in the continuing progress of the previous eight years.

ECONOMIC EXPANSION PROGRAMMES, MARCH 1965

The *Irish Press* feature issue on 9 March 1965 was headed: 'Ireland's Plan for Expansion Commended'. It outlined the progress since the introduction of the 'First and Second Programmes for Economic Expansion'.

Mr Patrick Perry, an economist for the previous four years in the European Department of the Industrial Monetary Fund, had written about modernising Ireland's economy. He described the 1950s as a time of economic stagnation for Ireland.

Population had fallen and output only risen by 1 per cent per annum. In a Europe that was economically moving then Ireland had stood still.

A much needed attempt to stimulate the growth of industrial and agricultural exports, reinvigorate the economy and reverse the decline in employment and population, related to the first programme. Such an attempt had been successful. In fact, more had been achieved than planned.

Ireland's gross national product rose between 1959 and 1963 at an average annual rate of nearly 4 ½ per cent in real terms. By 1963 the rate of expansion, in non-agricultural employment, was sufficient to absorb the exodus from agriculture so the decline in the labour force was curtailed. Unemployment was reduced and emigration fell to a level lower than the national rate of growth in the population, so the population, in fact, increased.

In 1963 exports were over 50 per cent higher than in 1958. Industrial exports, in particular, were 90 per cent higher. Prices were reasonably stable and while the balance of payments in 1962 and 1963 showed a deficit on current account, reserves continued to increase. That was provided by an inflow of capital, more than offsetting the deficit.

In short, the Irish economy had ceased to stagnate and moved freely and vigorously. Much of the success was due to incentives, introduced to encourage agriculture and industry, to increase output efficiency and exports' provision. As the requirements of the economy changed, revision and amplification was made.

The second programme was a more ambitious, detailed and comprehensive exercise in economic programming than the first. It called for a reshaping of the entire economy and a greater willingness to abandon traditional ways of life and accept substantial changes.

HARVARD INTERNATIONAL PROGRAMME, APRIL 1965

The Intercontinental hotel (now Jury's hotel) Ballsbridge, Dublin, was the venue for the Minister for Industry and Commerce, Mr Jack Lynch, TD, to speak to a large attendance of members and guests of the Irish Institute of Marketing and Sales Management.

Opening the meeting on Monday, 12 April 1965, Mr Lynch said it was generally accepted that in Ireland, in the past, and perhaps in other countries, marketing had to play a role secondary to other elements of management. More attention had been paid to productive skills than to market research or selling, in the narrow sense of the word.

The meeting and reception took place in connection with the Harvard International Marketing Programme, the first occasion that it was held outside of Harvard University, while under the sponsorship of the Irish Institute of Marketing and Sales Management.

Harvard Business Review, April 1965

The American university sent to Dublin all the members of the Marketing faculty, headed by Professor James Hagler, Professor David Leighton and Professor Edward Bursk, editor of *Harvard Business Review.*

Thirty-nine businessmen, many of them members of the Marketing Institute and others connected with marketing, were then attending the Harvard Programme in University College, Dublin, continuing until 29 April.

Irish exports — record level reached in 1964

Mr Jack Lynch, TD, further said that concentration on production techniques was inevitable during the formative years of their new industrial structure. The fact was that Irish exports reached the record level of £222m. the previous year (1964).

That was just double what they had been ten years previously and was tangible evidence that progress had been made in marketing.

Competition was increasing everywhere under the impetus of tariff cuts in the Common Market and EFTA. Many of the advantages were therefore being lost compared to those formerly enjoyed in export markets. This, he said, was at a time when prosperity depended more and more on the expansion of exports.

The fact had also to be faced up to, that manufacturers were going to lose many of the privileges enjoyed in the home market. In such changed conditions the fullest range of marketing talents and experience were needed. These were necessary to make vital contributions to important management decisions, which would undoubtedly be taken in the coming years.

Mr Lynch stated that he was pleased with the increasing facilities available for the training of management as this was a very necessary development. The bringing of the Harvard International Marketing Programme to Ireland, he believed, served a very useful purpose in further helping to meet the need for trained personnel to handle marketing operations at a high level.

He paid tribute also to the authorities of University College, Dublin, for their part in organising the very useful exercise in international co-operation. In particular he referred to Mr Michael McCormac, director of the Department of Business Administration, and his assistants for the work they put into the organising the programme.

In conclusion, Mr Lynch said the original target of 150 per cent increase in industrial exports, by 1970, envisaged in the 'Second Programme of Economic Expansion', had recently been increased to 300 per cent, following on discussions with industry.

He stressed the critical importance attached to exports as a condition of growth in Ireland's economy, a fact that he had referred to in practically every speech he made since he became Minister for Industry and Commerce.

IRISH EXPORTERS ADVISED TO LOOK TO COMMON MARKET, APRIL 1965

At the April 1965 luncheon of the Institute the speaker was Mr Colin Hodgkinson, chairman and managing director of Hodgkinson Partners Ltd, London.

He informed those present that Irish exporters would have to look much more to the Common Market countries, than to England, where 75 per cent of Irish exports had until then being going. Further he told delegates at the meeting that Germany, Italy, Holland, and Belgium were constantly trying to attract English and Irish exporters to their markets. The continentals were eating much more beef and were prepared to pay more for the beef that they consumed. He felt that Irish marketing firms should now be directing their attention more to the Common Market countries. England itself was being forced to look to the Common Market, more than to the Commonwealth, to do business and it was, therefore, more logical for Ireland to try to open up greater markets in Europe.

STATUS PERSONNEL, SALARY INCREASES, APRIL 1965

The *Irish Independent* of 13 April 1965 highlighted an explanation of the 'status' salary increases awarded to civil servants and other state-paid personnel, given by the Minister for Finance, Dr Ryan. He had said that the process of determining, on an individual basis, the pay of the many civil servants had been a long one but worthwhile.

A need for adjustments in the pay of civil servants arose from the protracted period during which the eighth round revisions had been effected. As a result disparities and anomalies had arisen when later settlements diverged.

ROYAL DUBLIN SOCIETY LIBRARY, APRIL 1965

In the same issue of the *Irish Independent* the opening of the new Royal Dublin Society Library by President Eamonn de Valera was reported. The large attendance included Mr James Meenan, president of the RDS. At the opening Mr Meenan mentioned that the library contained approximately 250,000 books that had been accumulated over 200 years dating back to 1877.

EUROPEAN MARKETING CONGRESS, MAY 1965

The AGM of the European Contact Group of Sales and Marketing Associations and Congress, was held in Milan, Italy, in May 1965 over a four-day period. It was attended by delegates from fourteen countries. The participating members of the Irish Institute of Marketing and Sales Management were led by Mr Harry Woods.

At the AGM, under the rules and regulations pertaining, only one delegate from each member country was allowed to speak.

Ireland's industrial expansion outlined

Mr Harry Woods, as an executive member of the European Marketing Group Council, accepted the privilege of addressing the congress participants. His paper, given at the Chamber of Commerce, Milan, was entitled: 'Ireland's Industrial Expansion and export potential'.

It contained an impressive report of industrial expansion while outlining the preparation for Ireland's future and possible entry into the European Common Market. On concluding Mr Woods presented the Mayor of Milan with a scrolled message of greeting from the Lord Mayor of Dublin, Councillor John McCann.

FORMATION OF DEVELOPMENT COMMITTEE, JUNE 1965

To further develop and promulgate the concept of marketing, the Irish Institute of Marketing and Sales Management formed a development committee with precisely those aims.

It was the initial announcement of the chairman, Mr Harry Woods, at the AGM in the Hibernian hotel, Dublin, on 25 June1965. He was sure that the special committee, having been given its wide task, would, in its findings, lead to a raising of the status of the marketing profession in Ireland.

FELLOWSHIP AWARDS, JUNE 1965

The Fellowship award of the Institute of Marketing was made to:

• Mr Norman McConnell: Aspro-Nicholas of Ireland Ltd

• Mr Jim McCarroll: Baxter Ltd., Ballymoney, Co. Antrim

• Mr Harry Woods: Mart-Woods Ltd.

The citations said the awards were for outstanding service given in furthering the interests of marketing in Ireland. In the case of Mr Woods, mention was also made of his successful marketing involvement and representation of the Institute in Europe.

The executive elected for 1965–66 was declared as:

• President: Mr John Haughey (re-elected)

• Chairman: Mr Harry Woods (re-elected)

• Vice-Chairmen: Mr Peter Greville
                 Mr Joseph Bigger
                 Mr Brian Clancy

• Hon. Secretary: Mr Walter Connolly

• Hon. Treasurer: Mr Jack Jones.

The executive committee chairmen were:

• Mr Michael Quinn (Education)

• Mr Brian Murphy (Programme)

• Mr Stephen Doyle (Social)

• Mr Michael Coote (Conference)

• Mr Gerry Maher (Membership)

• Mr Sean Walshe (Public Relations)

• Mr Pat Walsh (Development).

The members of council (in addition to the officers and executive) were as follows:

• Mr N. McConnell

• Mr L.V. Whitehead

• Mr C. Faughnan

• Mr J. McCarroll

• Mr G. O'Shaughnessy

• Mr A. Fogarty

• Mr J.C. McGough

• Mr J. Simpson

• Mr J. Sandford.

EXPORTS FOCUS, AUGUST 1965

The *Waterfront News* of August 1965 published a full A4 page report of a lecture given in Milan by Mr Harry Woods. It was entitled: 'Focus on Exports — The Life-Blood of the Nation'.

The Irish exports' record figure of £222m. for 1964 was made up of:

	Million £
Live animals	67
Food, drink and tobacco	73
Manufactured goods	55
Raw materials	11
Miscellaneous small exports	11
Total domestic exports	217
Re-exports	5
	222

Of the increase, compared to 1951, almost one-third related to industrial goods, while foodstuffs, drink and tobacco accounted for an improvement of 30 per cent.

CÓRAS TRÁCHTÁLA DEFINED AUGUST, 1965

Mr Harry Woods referred to the fact that the Irish government had set up Córas Tráchtála in 1952. The state-sponsored organisation was responsible for the promotion and development of exports. It had offices then in New York, Montreal, London, Manchester, Frankfurt, Port of Spain (Trinidad) and San Francisco.

The board provided co-operation and assistance to exporters in the provision of marketing and general information, (other countries' distribution methods, sales procedures, packaging preferences, and Customs duties and import regulations, *inter alia*).

Grants for marketing research, consultancy, design projects and in certain circumstances, for advertising, were outlined in detail. At that time Ireland offered the one holiday that manufacturers needed — no taxes on export profits for ten full years, with five additional years of reduced taxes. Industries using air freight were encouraged to come to the Shannon Free Airport Industrial Estate, where tax exemption, until 1983, was granted.

Manufacturers setting up subsidiaries in Ireland also enjoyed:

1. Outright cash grants covering a substantial percentage of the cost of building and machinery to equip it.

2. Reasonable labour costs — a plentiful supply of willing workers and plenty of young scientists, engineers and marketing men.

PRESIDENT'S DINNER, SEPTEMBER 1965

The President's Night dinner took place at the Shelbourne hotel, Dublin on 30 September 1965. Guests present to honour the Institute president, Mr John Haughey, included Mr Erskine Childers, TD, Minister for Transport and Power and Mr Alfred F. Colborn, director of the Institute of Marketing, London as well as chairmen of various professional institutes and asssociations in Dublin.

Speaking to those assembled Mr Childers said he wondered how many appreciated the fact that of every £1 freshly circulating in the economy, 8/6d (42½p) was spent on imports. Even if the 'Buy Irish' campaign effected the minimum expected, the final result would not fundamentally alter the situation.

No large deposits of raw materials in Ireland

There was no escape from the '8/6d' because there were no large deposits of ores, no oil, cotton or other essential raw materials found in Ireland. Governments, Mr Childers said, were compelled to take whatever action was required to cut down spending in order to balance the national accounts.

Seeking increases in prosperity not yet earned only resulted in economic difficulties.

Mr Childers went on to say that increases in agricultural output were accompanied everywhere by reduced rural employment, save in the specialised horticulture field. An increase in farm exports created more demand for home-produced goods but the relentless import urge remained and could only be met by the triple farm, tourist and industrial export expansion.

Membership of the organisations concerned with exports and the re-equipment of industry constituted Ireland's then 'new dynamic world'. However, membership of such organisations had to be representative of the whole industrial community. It had been observed that in some European countries over 80 per cent of the firms, in a given industry, participated in such activities.

Export targets

Ireland's latest exports increase to faraway countries made an impressive list. However, Mr Childers warned that neither housing nor social objectives could be achieved in the 'Second Programme for Economic Expansion' unless the export targets were achieved at the same time.

One of the most serious obstacles to fast economic expansion was the shortage of trained marketing executives, maintained Mr Childers. He knew the Irish Institute of Marketing and Sales Management was fully aware of this and was filling an important national need by sponsoring courses.

Mr John Haughey, president of the Institute and also chairman of Córas Tráchtála, reassured the minister that the Irish Institute felt fully confident it would measure up to the task ahead and also spare no effort in fulfilling its contribution towards the achievement of the targets set out in the second programme.

In conclusion he paid tribute to the honorary officers, whose work he described as 'dedicated' to advancing the interests concerned.

Free Trade Area

Mr Harry Woods in reply said that the Free Trade Area (FTA) was of such vital importance to marketing men and the future of Ireland that the Institute realised it would have to be in continuous touch with the commercial problems of the country in an official capacity.

Such engagement had, in fact, been activated by the Institute executive, in preparation for meeting the implications that faced it when the inevitable would happen. The introduction of the FTA would undoubtedly create even more competition for a share of the existing market. Mr Woods stated that the Institute was internationally recognised and had a complete understanding with friends and neighbours in the Institute of Marketing in London.

Mr Woods told those present that the Irish Institute was affiliated with the Sales and Marketing Executives, International, New York, and at the Sixth International Marketing and Distribution Congress, in Barcelona last year he himself had been elected to a seat on the executive committee of the European Contact Group of Sales and Marketing Associations.

CÓRAS TRÁCHTÁLA APPOINT MARKETING OFFICER, OCTOBER 1965

A 'Special Notice' advertisement appeared in the Irish daily newspapers on 7 October 1965. Córas Tráchtála/Irish Export Board were inviting applications for the new post of Industrial Marketing Officer to be based at its head office in Dublin.

The advertisement stated that the appointed officer would have responsibility for advising manufacturers of engineering and allied products on all aspects of export marketing. He would also be required to undertake market research surveys and establish sales contacts, at a senior level, with potential overseas customers. This would include foreign government agencies.

The age of applicants sought was in the range of 30 to 40 years and a degree in mechanical or electrical engineering and a successful record of achievement in industrial export marketing were also desirable. The starting salary to be not less than £2,000 per annum, and reviewed annually. CTT worked a five-day week and had a pension scheme in operation.

INDEPENDENT NEWSPAPERS INTERVIEW MR HARRY WOODS, OCTOBER 1965

Mr Harry Woods, chairman of the Marketing Institute of Ireland, was interviewed by Mr Sean O'Conaill of Independent newspapers on 8 October 1965. Mr Woods told Mr O'Conaill that negotiation for facilities to lecture a marketing course at the College of Commerce, Rathmines, went back to 1958. The Institute was then known as the Incorporated Sales Managers' Association (ISMA), Ireland branch. The examinations were set from London.

An educational sub-committee of the Irish ISMA group (before branch status) was set up in Dublin in 1951. There were, at that time, six students registered in the Republic of Ireland and five in Northern Ireland who were studying by correspondence for the diploma.

Education lecturing provision for marketing and sales management students was a paramount goal of the Institute founders but could not have been implemented without the help, in 1958, from the then Rathmines Technical Institute. Thanks to the co-operation of Mr Sean Ó Ceallaigh, principal, aided and abetted by Mr Martin Gleeson, they were persuaded to allow the first class of ten 'young men' to study.

It was hard to realise how it had been difficult then to get the aimed for twelve students to attend those first evening lectures. The ten enrolled for the first diploma classes in marketing and sales management included some very active and prominent persons in the Institute in later years — Messrs Jim Culliton, Cartan Finegan, Frank Young and the late Capt. Oliver Walsh, to name a few. Subsequently a full-day course, supplementing evening classes, was introduced at the School of Commerce and Retail Distribution in Parnell Square, Dublin.

The Irish group function was to organise, supervise and provide an examination premises. At the same time the Institute, while being the examining body, did not directly undertake the provision of qualified lecturers. Fortunately suitable lecturers became available from experienced qualified Institute members and these were later supplemented by some graduates of the diploma.

In the intervening years the number of students had grown to the180 registered students last year (1964) who were following the three-year course leading to the final examinations set from London. Unfortunately the problem was that many 'would-be' students could not be accommodated at Rathmines in 1965. Over 100 seeking to join the course did not get a place. Endeavours were made to get extra space or alternative accommodation.

In addition, the Irish Institute hoped to set its own examination papers as soon as possible. The subjects were outlined while the very high standard required was emphasised. An example was given pertaining to direct selling and staples selling.

DIRECT SELLING TO INDUSTRY, 1965

Direct selling to industry demanded field trainers. Good direct salesmen were in short supply, hence training was the answer. To produce a profitable business required highly trained experienced top sales managers. It was the undertaking and agreed responsibility of the Institute to ensure members knew of all new published work on training material and methods. This was done by organised knowledgeable lecturing and role-playing sessions.

As sales management was just one facet of marketing, it had been agreed unnecessary to continue the former in the title of the Institute, which was renamed the 'Marketing Institute of Ireland, (MII)'. Amendment had been duly made to the Memorandum and Articles of Association to such effect.

The Institute defined marketing then as:

> The creative management function, which promotes trade and employment by assessing consumer needs and instigating research and development to meet them.
> It co-ordinates the resources of production and distribution of goods

and services and determines and directs the nature and scale of the total effort required to sell profitably the maximum production to the ultimate user.

He said the theme of the annual conference, June 1966, of the European marketing bodies, would be 'Marketing and Civilisation'. Some 1200 delegates were expected to attend at Paris, including a strong representation from Ireland.

INGERSOLL WATCHES, OCTOBER 1965

A reception was hosted by Mr Henry Spring, MII member, and managing director of H. Spring & Co., Pearse Street, Dublin, for Mr A.L. (Jack) Benzing, managing director of Ingersoll Ltd at the Shelbourne hotel, Dublin, on 15 October 1965.

Mr Benzing told his marketing friends and associates in Dublin that Ingersoll Ltd then turned out 30,000 watches a week in their South Wales factory. The firm had been founded in Waterbury, Connecticut at the beginning of the century by one Robert H. Ingersoll. In 1905 the output was transferred across the Atlantic to England and reached Ireland shortly afterwards.

MARKET RESEARCH, 1965

Mr John Lepere, MMII, joined P.J. Carroll & Co. (cigarette manufacturers) and was in charge of their marketing. He had spent his earlier career in market research in London. He brought enthusiasm to his new job, particularly in scientific market research. He became a director of Irish Marketing Surveys, in which Carrolls and Guinness were major shareholders.

With the growth of television, market research came to the forefront and Mr Lepere then engaged in providing what was described as 'a more accurate approach to advertising', including the use of full colour advertisements for Carrolls in newspapers. Carrolls were clients of the Peter Owens advertising agency. At the time there were less than 30 such agencies in Dublin.

A new brand of Carroll's cigarettes, cork-tipped, called Major, comes to mind. While a lot of money was invested in its advertising, the result brought about an extraordinary share of the cigarette market — almost 25 per cent. The launch took place in 1966.

STUDENT CLASSES IN LIMERICK, JUNE 1966

At the instigation of Mr Noel T. McComish of Limerick, a meeting was arranged for 27 June 1966, at Cruise's hotel, Limerick. The objective was the getting together of already registered and potential diploma students to substantiate the need to have classes established there.

Mr Brian Clancy, education chairman, arranged for the Institute chairman, Mr Harry Woods and Mr Stephen Doyle, a former chairman, who met the principal of the Limerick Technical School, students and other interested parties.

EUROPEAN COMMON MARKET REVIEW, 1966

In 1966 the European Common Market (ECM) having been in existence five years was the richest and most rapidly growing market outside of the United States of America. In the six-nation group membership of ECM (Belgium, France, Holland, West Germany, Italy and Luxembourg) there were some 171 million people. Over the previous ten years the gross national product of the six had increased by 66 per cent.

Products considered as luxury, even a few years previously, were then being bought universally and, what was unknown a generation previously, services were being paid for even by average income families. No longer was it a consideration to buy the cheapest available product or mere necessities of life. Quality and good design became a must for everyone. In other words, possession of services and goods denoted the new status symbol.

Much more and longer distance travel became the norm, including to foreign countries, and was coupled with new living standards. A boom in durable consumption was created by enhanced use of household appliances. It was felt that it would continue to widen among populations. On the cautious side however, the French were concerned about the future for farmers.

Prior to 1966 domestic servants were badly paid. However, the situation changed when they became well paid, were in demand and expensive to have. Household domestic work became the work of middle-class housewives in Europe when they procured automatic machines for washing clothes, electric floor polishers and electric food mixers. They never had these items previously, nor bought them while maids were economically available.

Former domestics got employment in factories and offices and earned money to purchase added electrical conveniences, such as vacuum cleaners and fridges. Even at that time there was considerable competition in the types of detergents advertised.

Frozen foods came on the market providing more convenient availability of ready to consume products. It was researched, however, that only a small percentage of persons used frozen foods then but that they appreciated canned foods. Over 30 per cent of the vegetables consumed in the Common Market came out of tins and 20 per cent of purchasers bought canned fruit. It was also interesting to note that canned soup had at the time (1966), little sale, home cooked being preferred.

In the United States some 75 per cent of families had at least a car, while in the ECM only 30 per cent had such luxury. Payment of wages in ECM also lagged behing the USA — they paid about four times that of an Italian worker, or three times the ratio of a German employee.

International marketing took cognisance of market trends envisaged, possible saturation and design appeal for the intended consumer. Income was naturally a very serious factor for consideration, bearing in mind also changes in world markets for goods. It became obvious too that some markets were unevenly divided. Colour was seriously considered in packaging and advertising in view of religious beliefs, particularly in Asian and American markets.

The European Common Market had been created to unite Europe again, as it had been in the Middle Ages and Roman Empire days. Western Europe had shown the world its destiny, in culture and commercial achievement over some 2,000 years. Hence the aim to expand and bring more countries, like Britain and Spain, into the one market.

Constant attention was given to the environment in different countries. The realisation of doing business in any nation became more researched and concentrated on. Decision-making was the concern of companies' marketing output programmes. Three out of every ten top advertising agencies had their control from the USA and/or were owned by them. Domestic advertising, cinema and poster advertising were more highly developed in Europe. Nevertheless, investment in advertising showed great variance nation to nation, particularly per capita, for example:

1964	Volume spent in advertising (millions)	Volume spent in advertising (per capita)
United States	14,500	77
Britain	1,475	27
West Germany	1,300	23
Japan	950	10
France	520	11
Australia	260	23
Switzerland	170	30
Finland	110	24
Ireland	3	1

(figures in US dollars)

It can readily be seen that Ireland was too low in advertising investment in the mid 1960s (It was, in fact, thirtieth out of 100 countries). Africa had no daily press and a distribution of only one newspaper per 100 of population, compared to 50 per 100 in the United Kingdom.

ELECTRONIC COMPUTER USES, 1966

There was an acceptance then of the role of the electronic computer and the disciplines attached to it. It had been used for reporting marketing information, sales trends and forecasting, and order processing, inventory control, market analysis and so forth. It was forecast (correctly) as becoming an important tool of marketing management.

At that time there were reservations as to marketing decision making with some saying it was being reduced to mathematical formulas. The use of the computer in promotional decision making was in the experimental stage. Factual quantitative data was scarce and large amounts of judgement input were required when it came to decision making.

MR JOSEPH C. BIGGER, CHAIRMAN MII, 1966-67

The newly elected chairman of the Marketing Institute of Ireland, Mr Joseph C. Bigger, marketing director of Hammond Lane Ironfounders Ltd, took office from June 1966. Mr John Haughey agreed to continue as president and appreciation was expressed to him for his considerable contribution to Institute affairs. The chairman, Mr Joe Bigger, recalled that he became an Associate of ISMA (Incorporated Sales Managers' Association) in 1947. He had phoned Mr Derek Black, who had come to Ireland sometime in 1948, to take up an appointment with Lewis Berger & Co., paint manufacturers. In *Marketing* journal, the ISMA London magazine, Mr Black's photograph had appeared with the statement that he intended to start a group of ISMA in Dublin. Mr Bigger met him in Roberts' Cafe and invited along a few friends who were also interested in forming the ISMA Ireland group. These included Messrs Leslie Whitehead, J. Bolton-Thom and Donald MacKenzie.

The president, Mr John Haughey and chairman, Mr Joseph Bigger, were invested with the new Institute chain of office (replacing the former insignia — ribbon and medal).

At that time the MII offices were located at No. 43, Kildare Street, Dublin.

MARKETING PROBLEMS JULY 1966

Mr Peter Owens, MMII, governing director of Peter Owens Ltd, advertising and marketing, spoke on the subject of: 'The Application of the Creative Process to Marketing Problems' at the members' luncheon meeting in the Montrose hotel, Stillorgan, Co. Dublin. It was an unusual but interesting topic and was appreciated by members and their guests.

BOOK LAUNCH, OCTOBER 1966

A research report for the Irish Management Institute was carried out by Mr Breffni Tomlin, their research executive, and resulted in him writing the book entitled: *The Management of Irish Industry.* This was launched in October 1966.

The Joint Committee on Education and Training for Management IMI report had been published in 1956. The Report of the Review Committee, successor to the joint Committee, was published in 1962. The Review Committee was representative of the organisations in Ireland concerned with management education and training. In summary, the Committee felt that long-term development of management education and training had to be based, not on a consensus of opinion but on objective research into the educational and training needs of Irish management.

Thanks were particularly recorded to Dr Max Adler, director of education of the College of Marketing and Mr Dermot Harrington, acting head of the Statistical Department of An Foras Talúntais, for their assistance at two crucial stages of the project.

The Marketing Institute of Ireland was pleased to be able to supply all the information and experience it had that time about education and training for management generally and in doing so contribute to the book.

In the foreword Mr Rigby-Jones, chairman of IMI (Irish Ropes Ltd, Newbridge, Co. Kildare) stated that the book was the first study of such scope to be undertaken in any country and should be read widely, not alone in Ireland, but by all those concerned with the development of the science and practice of management. He also thanked An Foras Talúntais for use of their computer and the Central Statistics Office for providing essential lists of firms.

Mr Ivor Kenny, director of the Irish Management Institute expressed written thanks for the help given to Mr Breffni Tomlin when he sought information about the facilities for education and training for management from the Marketing Institute.

The project

In December 1960 the Irish Management Institute had set up a further committee to implement recommendations. The review committee issued a report in 1962. It recommended, among other things, an identification of needs in educational management in Ireland.

A sample survey ensued to collect information. The only feasible way found was to sample the population of Irish managers. Resources were limited and so the survey sample was confined to firms with over twenty employees. It was later decided to limit coverage to industry and omit all other business activity.

Method of assessment

The book details, in its technical appendix, all the approaches tried and rejected before the decision to use the sample of firms visited to estimate how far some of the more widely applicable techniques of management were being used in Irish industry.

Finally it became necessary to do individual interviews, usually to the chief executive. Information was collected on their existing facilities and preferences indicated for various suggested ones. A structural questionnaire was produced to obtain the desired information.

In 1961 the total number engaged in employment, by sector of economy, concerned some 1,052,539 divided into employment in: agriculture 376,272; manufacturing 179,43; and in categories down to entertainment and sport 10,986, while electricity, gas and water accounted for 10,172.

The 472 pages in the book volume covers all aspects of management function, participation in management training, functional areas, age, nationality, etc.

A particular interest to marketing personnel relates to the training facilities and education outlets.

It also stated that industry was highly diversified, not technologically advanced and largely concentrated in Dublin. Most Irish firms were family owned, while over 75 per cent of firms with more than 500 employees were public companies.

MR AUBREY N. FOGARTY, CHAIRMAN MII, 1967–68

Mr Aubrey N. Fogarty MMII, MIAPI (Fogarty Advertising) was elected chairman of the Marketing Institute of Ireland for the session 1967–68.

The vice-chairmen were announced as:

- Mr Leslie C. Thorn

- Mr Gerry F. Maher

- Mr Pat N. Walsh.

The hon. secretary was Mr Bernard V. Woods (my brother) and Mr Walter Connolly, hon. treasurer.

AGM, JUNE 1967

At the AGM of 16 June 1967, Mr John Haughey, outgoing president of MII had the pleasure to introduce his successor, Mr Sean Lemass, TD who, he recalled, had masterminded the 'First Programme of Economic Expansion' along with Dr Ken Whitaker, government Department of Finance.

In turn, Mr Lemass said he had observed the progress of the Marketing Institute of Ireland and looked forward to its continued success and achievement, particularly regarding student education. He continued to realise that Ireland needed to prepare well to ensure successful entry into the European Common Market (ECM) and he referred to the vital part that the Institute must contribute in this.

The hard working committees on industrial organisation had been delayed because of General de Gaulle's veto of Britain's entry to the ECM back in January 1963.

The chairman, Mr Aubrey Fogarty, asked members to co-operate with greater attendance at Institute meetings and functions organised by dedicated council members. He stated to all present that the Institute *is* the members, each working towards one goal via self-help. Furthermore, he believed that any Institute was only as good as the members made it, no more, no less.

It was also announced at the meeting that much effort would be put into organising an international symposium to be held in Dublin in the autumn.

Mr Harry Woods, chairman of the education committee, informed members that it was proposed to form a regional education committee shortly. He recommended that the council consider further facilities be made available for specific lectures, group discussion sessions and courses, abreast with developments current and changes envisaged.

ADMINISTRATOR APPOINTED TO MII, JUNE 1967

Mr Fogarty announced that the Institute had acquired new office premises at 44, Lower Leeson Street, Dublin 2. In addition, it was that Mr Harry V. Woods would take up office there, having been appointed by council as MII administrator. His particular function would be to carry out a number of additional services to council, members and students alike, and co-ordinate committee activities and Institute expansion in the coming year.

MEMBERS' EDUCATION PROGRAMME, 1967–68

The first lecture in a new series was given by Mr Martin Rafferty of the Irish Management Institute. He outlined very dynamically the important role of finance in modern business and especially the use of techniques to assess project investment.

He was very clear in his views on the role of the accountant and the need for management to obtain financial information. It was required in the form in which it could contribute to the effective planning and control of the total business operation.

Mr M.D. Corbett, financial director of P.J. Carroll & Co. developed the theme in the second lecture of the programme with the role of finance in the marketing plan.

Such lectures were aimed at bringing, to the MII members, the latest information on the management techniques that had been developed over recent years.

BIBLIOGRAPHY ON FIELD SALES MANAGEMENT, 1967

As a European Director of Sales and Marketing Executives International (SME-I), New York, Mr Harry Woods received a 42 page annotated *Bibliography on Field Sales Management*, edited by Albert H. Dunn, Professor of Business Administration, University of Delaware.

The content covered books, magazines and American government publications relative to all aspects of sales management, promotion, motivation, training, research, and effects on the 'suburbanisation of the marketing function'. All in all seventeen major areas of field sales management was covered by the bibliography.

The faculty who wrote the bibliography comprised of Professors Albert Dunn, author, and F.R. Durr, both of University of Delaware, C.L. Lapp, Washington University, D.C. Rogers, Harvard Business School, J. Schiff, Pace College, M. Schiff, New York University, W.J. Stanton, University of Colorado and A.D. Van Nostrand, Brown University.

The publication stated that the management of field selling was not an exact science. Rather it was a complex and demanding art but an art that was discernibly on the move toward the status of a science.

INNOVATION IN MARKETING, THEODORE LEVITT

One of the books referred to under the marketing management concept 'a philosophy of management' is the universally known volume *Innovation in Marketing* by Theodore Levitt, New York published by McGraw-Hill in 1962. The book distinguishes between selling and marketing. Many examples are given to emphasise that the survival of a business hinges upon the acceptance of the customer-oriented approach.

Third decade of the history of sales management and marketing in Ireland, 1967-1977

EUROPEAN MARKETING COUNCIL AGM, JUNE 1967

The Marketing Institute of Ireland (MII) was represented at the AGM and conference, of the European Marketing Council (EMC), held at Oslo, Norway on 20–23 June 1967, by Mr Harry V. Woods FMII, spokesman, and Mr Stephen J. Doyle FMII as observer.

MARKETING EDUCATION, OSLO REPORT, JUNE 1967

One of the main items discussed was the special MII report *Marketing Management Education in Ireland*. This was distributed to the delegates in Oslo. The executive officers of the EMC verbally considered the council's policies, procedures and future aims and from that produced a draft constitution, to be reviewed at future quarterly meetings, until completed and adopted.

MR HARRY V. WOODS FMII, FIRST VICE-PRESIDENT, EMC JUNE 1967

Mr Harry Woods FMII (Ireland) was elected as the first vice-president of the European Marketing Council (EMC) which was made up of fifteen countries. In addition he also secured a major EMC international conference for Dublin in May/June 1969.

The fact that there were then (1967) some 850 students studying for various stages of the diploma in marketing in Ireland was considered an outstanding success by other Europeans at the Oslo meeting.

Press reports referred to the strong new link with Europe for Irish marketing executives and marketing students that had been forged by the MII, following executive election to the internationally constituted European Marketing Council. The development, they stated, would give Ireland access to a pool of marketing knowledge and experience among the fourteen European member countries.

At a press conference and reception at the Hibernian hotel, Dublin on 3 August 1967, Mr Aubrey Fogarty, Chairman of MII said that the Institute had been honoured by the EMC recognition and would continue to work for combined aims.

INTERNATIONAL STUDY OF MARKETING EDUCATION, AUGUST 1967

Professional marketing associations around the world had joined together and formed the International Marketing Federation (IMF) back in 1961. The book report: *International Study of Marketing Education* covering some 21 countries was published in August 1967 by the IMF. It contained 638 pages.

The IMF constitution listed the furtherance of marketing education among its basic objectives.

The first formal meeting of the Federation Assembly (Board of Directors) was held in Evian, France. An IMF committee on marketing education was established with a basic programme to:

1. Determine the attitudes toward the prevailing marketing education programme in each country on the part of :

    • professional marketing men

    • officials of colleges and universities, both those who provided education in marketing and those which did not

    • officials of institutes or other management training centres

    • leaders in the general business community

    • government officials.

2. To appraise the need for marketing education in general.

3. To prepare and issue an analytical and objective report on marketing education throughout the world.

4. To hold conferences or seminars on marketing education in appropriate locations, in the world.

5. To stimulate the introduction of courses of study in marketing in colleges and universities, in management institutes and other organisations devoted to the improvement of business management.

The committee began its work shortly afterwards under the chairmanship of Professor D. Maynard Phelps, University of Michigan, a past-president of the American Marketing Association (AMA). A decision was quickly reached to carry out a comprehensive survey among IMF association countries to determine the state of marketing education in each and the educational trends evidently at work.

Mr Bertil Liander, executive secretary of the IMF education committee, as a marketing leader and consultant in Sweden, in France (with the organisation of European Economic Co-Operation) and in Italy, as a marketing executive, became the project director of the survey. The survey was carried out under Professor D. Maynard Phelps, chairman of the International Marketing Federations' education committee, Marketing Science Institute, Philadelphia, Pennsylvania.

The book presents the findings in 21 countries including the 'Republic of Ireland', (pp. 219–33). It includes education at primary and secondary schools, universities, Irish Management Institute, School of Management Studies, College of Commerce, Rathmines and details of the diploma awarded by the UK Institute of Marketing.

It pointed out that while identically the examination subjects were those sat for in the United Kingdom, a study of the syllabus had been undertaken by the Marketing Institute of Ireland with the aim of adapting those parts (e.g. Industrial Law) that required different treatment in Ireland.

The report indicated that Rathmines had some 110 students studying for the first year of the diploma, 40 for the second and 30 for the final year. The diploma course was also provided for at the College of Commerce, Cork.

A 1962 survey had revealed that only a handful of firms in Ireland (generally large ones) operated management development programmes. The conclusion reached was that the pre-dominance of small-scale business operations did not make in-house training practical.

MARKETING EDUCATION IN INFANCY, EUROPEAN REPORT, 1967

At the time of the 1967 European report many of the respondents had stated their belief that marketing education in their countries was in its infancy. Such comments came from all continents and from many countries. However, chairs in marketing had been set up at some leading institutions, including the new University of Lancaster while Manchester University had already had a chair in marketing since 1965.

With regard to the Republic of Ireland, it was stated that there were reasons for the mitigation of need to take steps towards establishing higher level marketing courses, until recently. Recollection was made that during Eamonn de Valera's administration as Taoiseach (Prime Minister), all but six years between 1932 and 1959, the predominant economic policy was isolation and self-sufficiency. High tariff barriers against foreign trade had been introduced to promote home industry, thereby discouraging foreign investment in the Republic of Ireland.

Irish exports had a ready-made market in the United Kingdom (75 per cent of the Republic's 1964 exports) in which almost all Irish goods were exempt from custom duties. Further it was concluded that business firms in Ireland were predominantly small-scale operations.

SOCIO-STATISTICAL DATA, IRELAND (1964 FIGURES)

The socio-statistical data figures for Ireland according to Business International Annual Market Indicators, Parts I and II (Nov.–Dec. 1965) were as follows:

- total exports f.o.b. 1964, 623 million dollars: 24 per cent of GNP, 1964

- total imports c.i.f. 1964, 974 million dollars: 37.5 per cent of do.

PRESIDENT'S NIGHT BANQUET, SEPTEMBER 1967

The Marketing Institute of Ireland President's Night banquet was held at the Shelbourne hotel, Dublin on Thursday 28 September 1967 and proved a successful and enjoyable evening. The function was distinguished by the presence of the American Ambassador and many leaders from Irish professional Institutes, to honour Mr Sean Lemass, TD, Institute president.

INTERNATIONAL SYMPOSIUM, OCTOBER 1967

'Target Europe', the first Irish international marketing symposium, was held in Dublin at the Intercontinental hotel, Ballsbridge, (now Jurys), on 6 and 7 of October 1967. It attracted 93 delegates, considered a most encouraging number at the time. However, of the number, only eighteen were members of MII (not including the organising committee). Later the chairman, Mr Aubrey Fogarty, in his end of year report, expressed disappointment at the apathy of Institute members not participating at what had been a tremendously successful conference. Nevertheless, The organising committee was complimented for the work it had done, including obtaining important European speakers so conversant with happenings in the EEC.

When Mr Fogarty spoke of this two-day international marketing 'working' symposium he stated his belief that in modern business the most powerful weapon was efficient marketing. The intention was to learn, as much as possible, about the Common Market. For several years back the Marketing Institute had been concerned regarding its readiness for possible membership of the EEC. Survival against the high efficiency of Ireland's competitors meant being more proficient than ever before.

A radio interview had also been conducted, relating to the conference, with Mr Tom Brady MMII, secretary of the conference committee and Mr Harry Woods FMII, vice-president of the European Marketing Council. They conveyed the importance of Irish industrial and agricultural interests being represented at the conference and the importance of being able to hear authoritative speakers give up-to-date views. As a result of this interview, bookings were made for 46 extra delegates, mainly from the country and Northern Ireland, and particularly from agricultural bodies.

Irish EEC entry favoured

In his address at the symposium dinner, Mr Sean Lemass TD, president of MII, remarked that the holding of the symposium under the auspices of the Marketing Institute was part of the total national effort to prepare Ireland for membership of the EEC. All planning had to be made on the assumption that membership of the EEC was inevitable.

Mr Lemass went on to say that he was wholeheartedly in favour of Ireland acquiring membership of the EEC and as quickly as possible. For his part he regarded the setting up of the EEC as the beginning of a new era in European and world history and believed that the crown of achievement would be completed when Ireland and those other countries seeking membership ultimately obtained it.

He wanted to see Ireland fully committed, not merely fully involved but fully committed, to the idea. He regarded the opportunities for economic expansion that it would present as even less important in the long term than the moral benefits of participation in such a great challenging enterprise.

The symposium had added something to the pool of knowledge and understanding of the problems and opportunities to arise in the era of free trade. There, he felt, lay the future. He complimented the Marketing Institute of Ireland for recognising the part it had to play in preparing Ireland for the new era.

Choosing your market

Mr John Lepere MMII, director and marketing manager of P.J. Carroll & Co., addressed the symposium on the topic of 'Choosing your Market'. He said the policy of import substitution, induced by quota restrictions and tariff protection, created its own industrial structure. Given the very limited size of the domestic market and the Irish cultural background, the pattern of small proprietor managed firms, with production emphasis on an extended range of goods, was a direct corollary.

In Mr Lepere's view, a free trade economy implied a considerable change in Ireland's industrial structure, with the consequential economic and social problems of transition. It could not be argued that protection was the first step in a planned evolution to free trade, especially in a market the size of Ireland.

It had been recognised, for some years, that free trade would involve the loss to Irish industry of a very substantial, even major, part of the home market. Despite the success of the adaptation grant programme in stimulating greater production efficiency, losses in the domestic markets would be heavy.

Price competitiveness and the impact of free trade on subsidiaries of foreign companies, established under protection, the tenure of foreign owned licences and the impact of variety on consumer demand, had to be considered.

In conclusion, Mr Lepere stated that the key to Ireland's industrial prosperity in the future was one of basic product development on a national scale. Extensive marketing research in the Western European markets was essential. Capital and marketing minded management of the right calibre were scarce. New types of incentives were urgently required to stimulate and facilitate such process.

EEC opportunities

Dr M.T.G. Meulenberg, Professor of Marketing at the Agricultural University of Wageningen, Holland, provided a widely informative paper entitled: 'EEC — Opportunities for Ireland'.

He explained the challenge to western European countries whether they were members of the European Common Market or not. However, he felt that participation in a huge market not hampered by tariffs and quotas between member countries was highly attractive. Free movement of persons, capital and services between member countries was a feature. Another factor of the Treaty of Rome was a common transport policy, also a stimulant to economy. Dr Meulenberg said that it was his opinion that one of the most important issues for Ireland related to the common agricultural policy.

Of great importance to the Irish export basket was a restriction contained in the 'Second Programme for Economic Expansion of Ireland' confining Irish exports of £156.7m., of agricultural origin, in 1970 of a total export of £385.0m. of said origin, in the same year.

In the (38-page) paper, he covered many aspects of the characteristics of the then Common Market (comprising the six countries), particularly in demand and supply situations. Marketing policy was paramount with regard to product, price, promotion and the distribution system. He stated that Common Market membership for Ireland would have repercussions on the Irish traditional market in the UK. Therefore, special attention would also have to be made regarding export opportunities for Ireland, and especially to the UK.

Common Market demand

To every marketer, the market of 182 million consumers (in the six countries) opened up wide vistas for more sales. It would be made so because the projected population in 1975 was 193.5 million and in 1985 about 200 million. It was envisaged that the gross domestic product (GDP) per head, at constant factor cost, would increase at an annual compound rate of between 2.8 and 4.2 per cent during 1965–75 and further between 2.5 and 4.6 per cent during the period 1975–85.

Yet, it was well known that food expenditure formed a decreasing pro-portion of total expenditure when income increased. An example related was that in 1962 about 40.4 per cent of total family expenditure in the Common Market countries was for food, while the figure was 51.5 per cent in Italy, but at the same time only 26.2 per cent in the United States. There would, how-ever, be an expected increase in demand for animal protein in the Common Market, very important to Irish agriculture, whose main export products had a high content of such protein and were cattle and beef, pork, mutton, lamb and dairy products. Comparisons were given to the position particularly in West Germany, France, the Netherlands, Belgium and Italy.

The Belgian example of Dalhaize and Brothers demonstrated that bar-gaining problems, as faced by Dutch horticultural growers, might appear also in the selling of beef cattle. Concentration on supply would be recommended, as larger sellers would have many other competitive advantages. A better service could be given by them and consequently products could be handled more efficiently.

Exporters' problems in the EEC

Mr Peter Needham MMII, while referring to the title *Problems Experienced by Exporters Already Trading in EEC*, appearing in the brochure, said that his talk would be taken from his own personal experience during four years in Germany. He had carried out a survey for Córas Tráchtála Teo and the committee on industrial organisation and set up the German office of CTT.

Mr Needham segregated his talk into areas relating to elements he con-sidered were sometimes forgotten or neglected by exporters. He referred to the market itself, product planning, knowing one's market, languages, pric-ing, freight situation, channels of distribution and advertising and promo-tion.

An example given by Mr Needham was that of quoting price. To give the potential buyer an idea of the build-up of a price, from cif in the foreign currency, to the retail price in the buyer's currency, he gave graphic explana-tory figures. Brand name had to be always stated, not alone on the product but in correspondence and pertaining literature. Language translation also had to be checked to make sure the brand name did not mean something else altogether when translated into the language of the foreign market.

The importance of wholesalers, co-operative buying groups and agents was clearly explained. Trade fairs had become an important medium for ex-port promotion in Europe but he warned that to succeed an exhibitor must decide to participate on a continuous basis to gain full benefit. The same applied to repetitive advertising.

Display was an intrinsic part of the marketing function, particularly with the development of supermarkets and easy-to-serve types of outlets. Shelf-space therefore came to the fore and the ability of a product to command such. The successful use of symbols in France, for example, 'Sopexa' originally for cheese, was extended to other products and 'Berliner Chic' for ladies outerwear in West Berlin was explained. The population of West Berlin was similar to the Republic of Ireland then, i.e. 2.8 million.

Advertising in the EEC

According to Mr Helmut Knaupp of H.K. McCann Co., Germany, the European Economic Community had changed everyone — consumers, dealers, manufacturers, politicians (with a few exceptions) and of course, himself and his colleagues in the international marketing-communications field. He spoke on the subject: 'Advertising in the EEC Marketing Mix'. Mr Knaupp said that, after a transition period of ten years, six national markets in western Europe would become one single home market on 1 July 1968. That was assuming that the UK and Ireland had not participated before then, as he hoped they would have.

The new Common Market had changed those in the international advertising world, perhaps more than others. Big advertising agencies, mostly of US origin, had been in international business for more than 50 years. Export was changing into home market business.

Mr Knaupp believed that the Common Market was expected, in the long run, to bring extended specialisation, with large enterprises, so that less products would be produced in larger quantities. Integration would reduce production costs but increase the amount of money being spent for distribution and advertising. Sales force co-operation was called for.

An interesting example of co-operation was that of a German champagne producer with the famous French champagne company Chandon. A special marketing problem was solved by the licence production of a German 'Sekt' under the brand name M. Chandon; while the German company became the distribution agent for top quality champagne, like Dom Perignon, for the German market.

Vertical marketing examples

In the United States the problem of reducing production and marketing costs was often solved by mergers. European integration induced independent enterprises to join in their marketing and advertising efforts. Such integration led into 'vertical marketing', already being followed in the textile industry.

From the advertising world-view, it was interesting to relate expenditure, for body-care products in France. Per capita, this was twice as high as that in Italy while Germany, the Netherlands and Belgium maintained a medium level.

The share figures given then for television advertising expenditure were:

• Italy: 15 per cent

- France: 2 per cent
- Netherlands: 1 per cent
- Germany: 11 per cent.

However, the percentages did not reflect advertising demand for the media but rather developments in legislation and policy of mass communication media. In Germany, for example, the planned television advertising expenditure for 1968 had to be booked a year in advance. Only half of the bookings, at some stations only one-third, were granted. In the Netherlands television advertising was at a very early stage.

Other comparisons, given by Mr Helmut Knaupp, related to newspaper/magazine advertising and to the legal restrictions in certain product areas, particularly pharmaceutical. Medical products in Germany could only be offered from pharmacies, while in other countries they were available from varying outlets.

Marketing skills for Europe

Mr M.J. O'Shea, chairman of Unilever (Ireland) said his experience included being advertising director of the Unilever detergent company in Sweden, head of the Scandinavian offices of Lintas advertising agency and advertising director of Savonneries Lever in Paris. He had spent the previous seven years as managing director of the Lever company in Italy.

Mr O'Shea posed a question in relation to the state of marketing on the continent of Europe. The problem, he maintained, was how to sell goods profitably, even on the home market, while import tariffs still provided protection from outside competition. It was his belief that this could not continue for much longer. The lowering of tariffs annually was seeing to that.

Industry was under considerable pressure to produce goods more economically and to learn how to market them more successfully. Hence marketing skills for Europe could be summarised as the skills needed by the foreigner marketing his brand internationally on the continent of Europe. He needed the same range of skills and the same measure as other marketing men concerned with their home markets in highly developed countries

Product design

The final speaker at the symposium was Mr Alexis G. Joseph, Frankfurt/M.

His talk concerned 'Product Design and Development — the Critical Path to Form'.

He covered many important areas such as the evolution from product-centred to market-centred industrial thought.

He spoke about the importance of change, declaring a truly great man as one who shows his scope by accepting change and incorporating it in his thought. He declared that no system was good forever or even for any length of time. As soon as a system belonged to the past it had to be jettisoned and replaced by a better one.

He described the four 'infernal C's' of marketing' as:

1. Costs: rising.

2. Competition: tougher.

3. Complexity of markets: increasing.

4. Cycles of methodology: shorter as technological progress becomes faster and faster.

Regarding the complexity of markets, Mr Joseph said it was:

1. On account of tougher competition.

2. On account of fashion and new inventions, technological and sociological obsolescence.

3. Because the consumer was:

   • more numerous

   • more affluent

   • more educated or at least better informed

   • more cosmopolitan or wider travelled.

Systematic methods for designers covering function, manufacture and marketing were described in detail as were classes of design-factors and their relevance.

The sponsors for the symposium lectures were: Mr P.J. Dillon-Malone, chairman of the Marketing Research Society of Ireland; Mr Don Davern, parliamentary secretary to the Minister for Agriculture and Finance; and Mr Guy P. Jackson, president of the Federation of Irish Industries.

STUDENT GOLF OUTING, OCTOBER 1967

A student society golf outing was held at the Curragh Golf Club Co. Kildare on Saturday, 28 October 1967. Twenty-six players teed off and the best card was returned by Mr J.M. Archer of Dublin who received the Sinalco Cup and two tickets for the forthcoming first student gala ball in December.

The Cork team (Messrs Flor O'Leary, J. Glynn, Mahon-Lee and Eddie Moriarty) were rewarded, after their long journey, with victory in the team competition and received the Fennessy Cup.

STUDENT CONFERENCE, NOVEMBER 1967

An MII student conference entitled 'Blue Print Europe' was held at the La Touche hotel, Greystones on Saturday 11 November 1967. An innovation was the introduction of the Harvard case-study technique and it achieved very successful and beneficial results.

Harvard case study technique, November 1967

The case used was that presented for the previous year's Part 3 diploma examinations and it kept all students fully occupied throughout the day-long exercise. The president of the Institute, Mr Sean Lemass TD, who was introduced by Mr Jack J. Jones, vice- chairman of MII and chairman of the student education body, opened the proceedings. Mr Lemass stressed the fundamental importance of scientific marketing based on sound marketing education then and in the even more competitive years ahead.

Mr E.J. (Ted) Jenner, education chairman of the Institute of Marketing, London, attended and was suitably welcomed by the conference committee chairman, Mr Tom Prior. At the conference dinner, Mr Lemass presented the prizes to the winning student group led by Eddie Moore of M.H. Coote and Co. The speakers included Mr Kieran Sweeney, chairman of the hard working students' committee and Mr Paddy Dillon-Malone of Irish Tam Ltd, an adjudicator. Other conference adjudicators were Messrs R.A. Price, ICI Fibres Ltd, C. Mack Kile, Irish International Advertising and Marketing Ltd and F.C. Palmer, Reckitts (Ireland) Ltd.

CORK REGIONAL GROUP MII AGM, NOVEMBER 1967

The AGM of the Cork regional group of MII was held on 14 November 1967. The MII chairman Mr Aubrey Fogarty, administrator Mr Harry Woods and the hon.secretary Mr Bernard V. Woods made a special journey from Dublin.

Mr F.E. James, southern regional manager of Guinness Group Sales was elected chairman of the Cork group, Mr Flor O'Leary of Dwyer's became hon. secretary and treasurer and a small committee comprising of Messrs J. Glynn, then chairman of the students' society Cork, P. Hendricks of F.H. Thompson & Son Ltd and Tom Heffernan of Harrington & Goodlass Wall Ltd was formed.

In his report, the new chairman referred to the work done by Mr John Wyer (Fords) who had achieved marketing success for Cork. He regretted that John had to resign as he had been chairman since the group was inaugurated in July 1966 and also related to the student division, since it was formed five years previously.

Five Cork students had received their diplomas in 1966. Some thirty-two members of MII lived in or near Cork, the nucleus of a strong regional group. Mr James appealed for support from members in all activities organised.

MANAGEMENT CONSULTANTS IN MARKETING, NOVEMBER 1967

A luncheon meeting was held at the Intercontinental hotel (now Jurys) Cork on Tuesday 28 November 1967 and addressed by Mr T.G. Flynn, P.A. Management Consultants Ltd. He spoke on the subject of: 'The Place of the Management Consultant in Marketing Today'.

FELLOWSHIP AWARDS UK INSTITUTE, DECEMBER 1967

The Institute of Marketing, London and overseas, presented Fellowship awards (F.Inst.M.) to Irish members, Messrs Norman McConnell and Harry Woods. The honour was for outstanding contribution to the UK Institute's work of 'making the principles of marketing and sales management more widely known and more effectively practised over many years'. The certificates of election are dated 5 December 1967.

FIRST GALA BALL OF STUDENT SOCIETY, DECEMBER 1967

The first gala ball organised by the MII Students' division was held at Jury's hotel, Dublin on Wednesday 6 December 1967. It was deemed a most enjoyable and well attended function.

CANDLEBRA AWARD, DECEMBER 1967

By December 1967 there were over 1,000 Irish students registered with the Institute of Marketing, London, studying for the marketing diploma. Ireland emerged as runners-up for the Candlebra award, an award given yearly to the group with the highest proportional increase in student membership. As the system obviously operated in favour of the smaller new groups in these isles, it was considered to be a notable achievement to have obtained such a high placing.

CORK ANNUAL MII DINNER, DECEMBER 1967

The Cork branch MII dinner dance was held on 8 December 1967 in the then named Intercontinental hotel. The attendance included the Lord Mayor of Cork, Ald. Pearse Wyse, TD, Mr Aubrey Fogarty, chairman of MII and Mrs Fogarty, Mr and Mrs Ted. Jenner, College of Marketing, London, Mr Harry Woods, MII Administrator and Mrs Woods and the president of the Cork Chamber of Commerce and Mrs Nolan. It was once again a really wonderful evening, bringing together a record gathering of marketing personnel and friends.

MARKETING IN IRELAND — PEOPLE, PLANS, PROFITS, DECEMBER 1967

Mr Desmond O'Rourke AMII, had written a book entitled *Marketing in Ireland — People, Plans, Profits*. This became available from the MII office at the concession price of 14/- (70p) post paid, for members and students. It had been published in September 1967 at 16/- (80p) net. Commenting on the book, the MII chairman, Mr Aubrey Fogarty MIAPI, MMII said it was highly informative and 'fills a long-felt want . . . by students and practising marketers alike'.

The book contains a historical survey, reminding us that marketing and markets have been an integral part of human society since the dawn of civilisation. In my current review (1999) I observe that Desmond O'Rourke said that the then definition of marketing used (1967) was 'The planning, pricing, distribution and selling of goods and services to consumers at a profit'.

EUROPEAN COUNTRIES DEFINED BY OECD, JANUARY 1968

The OECD statistics of Foreign Trade, Series A January 1968, defined Europe as:

1. Western Europe:
    (a) EEC countries: Belgium, Luxembourg, Netherlands, Germany, France and Italy.
    (b) EFTA countries: United Kingdom, Norway, Sweden, Denmark, Austria, Switzerland and Portugal.
    (c) Other countries: Iceland, Ireland, Spain, Greece, Turkey and Finland.

2. Eastern Europe:
    (a) USSR, East Germany, Poland, Czechoslovakia, Hungary, Romania, Bulgaria, Albania and Yugoslavia.

US TRAVEL RESTRAINTS, FEBRUARY 1968

A reassurance that there was no need to panic in the Irish tourist industry, despite the threat of President Johnson's intended curb on US travellers, was given in Dublin by Mr Raymond I. Joyce MMII, tourism division manager of the Shannon Free Airport Development Co.

Mr Joyce stated that the proposed American legislation and the tightening of British belts called for the skilful use of all the most available modern marketing methods to ensure that even if the total number of tourists leaving such areas should decrease, Ireland's share would be increased.

In addition, Mr Joyce, speaking at an MII luncheon meeting on 22 February 1968, said that additional funds would have to be ploughed into marketing because the production of Ireland's tourism plant, in terms of accommodation, amenities and visitor facilities, was then just gaining momentum to provide for the earnings from the respective markets. Concluding his address he remarked that the next two seasons would be difficult.

SHANNON'S ROLE IN TOURISM MARKETING, 1968

Mr Joyce's theme, 'Shannon's Role in Tourism Marketing', dealt with the history of Shannon Airport from its pioneering transatlantic days. He stated that it was expected that in 1968, over 500,000 passengers would pass through the airport compared to 557,000 the previous year.

Tours were specifically designed for Shannon at the non-ethnic element of the transatlantic market. They were used as 'bait' to attract US and Canadian visitors to include an Irish stopover in their European itineraries.

EXPORTERS TOLD HOW TO TACKLE US MARKET, MARCH 1968

Exporters hoping to succeed on the American market were told to concentrate all their 'fire' on a particular segment of that market. This advice was given by Mr Winslow Martin, joint managing director of Arthur D. Little, international management consultants, when he spoke to MII members on 14 March 1968. His chosen topic was:

'How Exporters Should Tackle the US Market'.

Mr Martin believed that any exporter who thought of the US as one vast homogenised market of 200 million people who spoke the same language, read the same periodicals and saw the same television was heading for trouble. The fact was that the US was a highly segmented market divided by all sorts of consideration. American manufacturers directed their efforts at particular areas and exporters hoping to succeed had to do the same. However, these areas were by no means small and because of the size of the population as a whole they were often as large as European markets.

Mr Martin felt that the key to success on the American market was new ideas and innovation for there the emphasis was on change. Brand loyalties were dying and the move was towards things new. However, Mr Martin stated that for those who faced up to the real demanding nature of the US market there was an unparalleled profit opportunity.

DIPLOMA AWARDS PRESENTED, APRIL 1968

A Dublin man, Mr Owen P. Keane, was presented with the Goodbody award for first place in Ireland in marketing, at the Royal Hibernian hotel, Dublin, on Tuesday evening 23 April 1968.

The *Irish Independent* reported that Mr Keane, a married man with four children, had received his award, plus a marketing diploma, from the president of the Marketing Institute of Ireland, Mr Sean Lemass, TD. Mr Keane had received part-time evening training at the Rathmines College of Commerce for his diploma and worked as an area representative for Calor Gas (Ireland) Ltd, when the company started in 1954.

Other awards were presented to:

• Mr T.J. Meaney, for advertising, (presented by Adsell Ltd)

• Mr D.R. Miller, Kosangas-McMullans Ltd, for marketing case study (Part 3) (presented by Fogarty Advertising Ltd)

• Mr R.K. Sheehan, for market research (presented by the Market Research Bureau of Ireland Ltd).

SPECIAL LECTURE ON MARKETING, MAY 1968

As a part-time marketing lecturer at the School of Management Studies, College of Commerce, Rathmines, Mr Harry Woods prepared and gave students advice and a special extra pre-examination talk. He described the marketing concept as a comparatively new meaning in business management, while by its function, it produced a more scientific attitude to selling.

Marketing, he said, essentially became a co-ordinating function. The success of any marketing operation depended on the efficient co-ordination of all the different elements which it comprised. Clearly it was marketing's function to find out what the market required in shape, form, type, taste, quantity and so forth, relative to the product.

Business in industrial goods and services of all kinds was calculated then as being almost four times that of consumer goods. While industrial marketing had been equated with the selling of capital equipment, the term also covered a vast number of transactions related to manufacturers' processors and finishers in the production and sale of intermediate products and components. It also covered services from as wide a range as management consultancy to office cleaning. Customers were not only in manufacture, constructional and processing industries but in agriculture, central and local government and commerce in general.

The situation of buyers and a written marketing plan of campaign were clearly defined and explained. This covered forecasting, market research, sales training, sales outlets, advertising and measurements of performance. A statement of variable goals for a marketing plan, for a coming year, was shown in objective percentage detail.

UNIVERSITY OF LANCASTER, DEPARTMENT OF MARKETING, 1968

A Department of Marketing was established at the University of Lancaster through the generosity of companies and individuals who subscribed to a fund organised by the Institute of Marketing and Sales Management, London. Lancaster was unique in that it had a separate department for marketing studies.

The first postgraduate marketing course at Lancaster took place in October 1966. Of the twenty students generally, one half had previous business experience with the remainder being from first degree studies. The one-year full-time programme at postgraduate level led to an MA degree in marketing on the successful completion of the course. The academic staff at University of Lancaster was led by Professor R.J. Lawrence, MA (Cam.), MBIM, M.Inst.MSM. In 1968 the visiting American Professor J.H. Wieland, MBA, Ph.D. (Michigan State), joined the staff faculty to run the company marketing part of the course. Fees were £82 for the twelve-month course or £262 in the case of overseas students. The sum included fees for registration, tuition, examination and graduation, as appropriate, and official college and society charges.

In the prospectus, 1968–69, the definition of marketing was said to fall into four divisions:

1. Company marketing.

2. Buyer marketing.

3. Marketing intermediaries.

4. Macro-Marketing.

It is of interest to recall a few statements made in the prospectus, e.g.:

- 'The study of marketing has grown up in the shadow of economics … '
- 'Marketing is concerned with the firm and some of its operations in their real complexity, organisation theory, sociology, etc.'
- 'Marketing (relating to buyer behaviour) is concerned with human needs and behaviour as they are expressed in the buying decisions which people make'.

Macro-Marketing defined in 1968

Macro-Marketing was described as being concerned with marketing operations treated as a single system, rather than as the activities of separate individuals and firms. It was stated that the effects of government legislation (UK), for example in discouraging resale price maintenance, of balance of payment difficulties and technological change, on the structure of manufacturing companies and intermediaries came under the heading of macro-marketing.

COMPUTERISED BUSINESS GAME, MAY 1968

The first 'computerised business game' organised by the Marketing Institute of Ireland was held over a full Saturday on 25 May 1968 at University College, Dublin.

On the three previous Saturdays teams had met and studied the elaborate case prepared by Professor A.C. (Tony) Cunningham. There were nine teams participating and excitement was intense as to which team would come out with the best result. A certain team, I recall, stayed at Jury's hotel on the Friday night, so keen were they to organise themselves to prepare and hopefully come out winners on that final day.

The actual length of time for completion of the 'business game' was not given beforehand, rather at a moment's notice each team received an ultimatum to cease operations.

The other eight teams participating in the 'game' came from manufacturing, retail and industrial firms. However, the MII team consisting of Messrs Jack Jones (Market Research Bureau of Ireland), Frank Young (Wilson Hartnell, Advertising and Marketing) and Harry Woods, had produced the best result according to the adjudicating team.

Each member of the winning team was presented with a special certificate, signed by the president Mr Sean Lemass TD and Mr Aubrey N. Fogarty, chairman of the Marketing Institute of Ireland at a dinner that evening in the Montrose hotel, Stillorgan, Co. Dublin.

HARVARD UNIVERSITY GRADUATE SCHOOL, JUNE 1968

A group of members of the MII participated in the ninth annual session of the International Marketing Institute at Harvard University Graduate School of Business Administration in June 1968. It consisted, as usual, of a six weeks' case study and lectures. The individual fee was $900. Lodging and meals at Harvard were $475 and meals at weekends plus return travel also had to be paid by the participants.

The objective of the course was to increase worldwide understanding of the dynamic aspects of marketing and distribution. Its emphasis was practical rather than theoretical, action-oriented rather than academic. The hours were quite long and each day packed with activites. According to the brochure a typical day began at 7.15 a.m. with breakfast and ended after 7.00 p.m. with occasional extra guest lectures, special seminars and study.

The Irish participants in 1967 were:

• Mr Richard Birchall: W. & C. McDonnell (Unilever)

• Mr Anthony Cunningham: University College, Dublin

• Mr Con Denvir: Irish Ropes Ltd

• Mr Frederick Jackson: George A. Mansil & Co.

• Mr Peter Needham: John Power & Son Ltd

• Mr Thomas Wall: Canadian Laundry Machinery

• Mr Michael Woods, An Foras Talúntais.

MARKETING TEACHERS FIRST EUROPEAN SEMINAR, JUNE 1968

Marketing Forum, journal of the College of the Institute of Marketing London, reported on a seminar held in Antwerp from Monday 10 June to Wednesday 12 June 1968. The seminar in question was the first European seminar of marketing teachers held throughout western Europe. The planning and organisation of the seminar was undertaken by the University of St Ignatius, Antwerp which was hosting the event.

The seminar was well supported. Forty-three representatives from universities and business schools in twelve different countries attended. Ireland was represented by Dr A.C. Cunningham, University College, Dublin, Mr Eddie McDermott, Irish Management Institute, Mr Philip Flood, School of Retail Distribution (VEC), Dublin, and Mr Harry Woods, Marketing Institute of Ireland.

The problems of the marketing executives of the future were explored and their educational needs identified. The facilities for marketing education in each country were reviewed and the needs for additional facilities, to close the gap between then resources and needs, were evaluated. Delegates also exchanged views on the problems of teaching the subject of marketing.

A controversial paper by Professor Ray Lawrence of Lancaster University on: 'Management Education as a Continuous Process — the Role of Postgraduate and Post-experience Courses', led to an interesting discussion in which delegates from all countries participated.

Another paper, that of Mr N.T. Scott, University of Nottingham, Careers and Appointments Board, related to the image of a marketing career amongst university students. He left delegates in no doubt about the misgivings that many students had about entering a career in marketing.

Many other contributions were made by speakers from the United States and countries in western Europe, including Ireland.

IRISH WINNER OF THE DREXLER OFREX SCHOLARSHIP, 1968

The 1968 award for the Drexler Ofrex travelling scholarship was presented to Mr Austin M. O'Malley, a 40-year-old general manager of the automotive division of Pinchin Johnson and Associates Ltd, who completed the diploma in marketing examinations in November 1967.

Mr O'Malley was born in Dublin and after service in the Merchant Navy and the RAF, had been a sales representative in the steel industry. He transferred to the paint industry in 1952 and worked for a time in the USA. In 1960 he joined Pinchin Johnson engaging in market surveys and investigations.

The scholarship, for which competition in 1968 had reached an exceedingly high standard, covered the 'cost of a return passage to America and a minimum of four weeks' travel and maintenance during a study tour'.

NEW APPOINTMENT TO MII, 1968–69

Mr Aubrey Fogarty, outgoing chairman, was presented with his past chairman's badge and thanked sincerely for his achievements during his term of office. He then introduced Mr G. (Gerry) F. Maher, marketing director of Remington-Rand (Ireland), as his elected successor, presenting him with the chain of office. Mr Sean Lemass TD kindly agreed to continue as president for the coming session.

BRITISH INSTITUTE OF MANAGEMENT, EFFECTIVE TEST MARKETING, SEPTEMBER 1968

The British Institute of Management (BIM) issued a 46-page document free to their collective subscribers in September 1968. The title *Effective Test Marketing* referred to an evaluation of risk reduction procedures for the introduction of new products. The volume was based on a series of BIM seminars conducted by the authors: Roy Hayhurst and Gordon Wills of the Management Centre, University of Bradford. It recognised that a test market could be regarded as an optimising process, i.e. in seeking the best possible mix of marketing components, rather than simply furnishing data on which a 'Go, No Go' decision could be made, with a 'Go' often being at a sub-optimum level.

At the time an analysis was made of a series of new product launches, most of which involved test marketing. Fieldwork was still in process while a factor emerged very clearly as to the importance of planning before a product entered a test market. When effective packaging and advertising were developed, the job of identifying and correcting any reasons for deviation from objectives during test marketing was made more feasible.

A cost benefit analysis of a test market provoked a new approach. This was described as qualitative and sought to identify the determinants of buyer response in a laboratory situation, away from the test market. One direction sought a relationship between the results of product placement tests and eventual sales levels. A second sought to test market new products through mail order panels or through direct mail promotion and severely limited distribution. In such way it established an understanding of the reasons why a buyer behaved in the way he/she did and so provided the basis for a quantitative assessment of the broadscale market before any national launch took place.

SALES AND MARKETING INTERNATIONAL UPDATE, OCTOBER 1968

Correspondance dated the 25 October 1968 from Mr Kurt J. Altschul, secretary of the Sales and Marketing Executives International (SME-I) New York, contained some useful volume reports and data.

Motivation of salesmen, 1968

Extracts from the correspondance included a research report brought out by SME-I entitled *Motivation of Salesmen through Compensation and Sales Quotas*. This was edited by Gilbert J. Black. In it he stated that although one lived in the age of marketing 'nothing happens until somebody sells something'. In addition, it was also pointed out that with the days of the 'inspirational' manager gone, quantitative tools now occupied the centre stage.

EUROPEAN MARKETING COUNCIL, NOVEMBER 1968

Apart from attending the quarterly meetings of the European Marketing Council (EMC), each in a different country, Mr Harry Woods also travelled to Brussels on Sunday 24 November 1968 to meet Mr Albert Brouwet, president of EMC, for a full discussion of future plans. That included arranging for a meeting of professors/teachers of marketing with delegates of EMC to take place in Dublin in 1969.

The Eighth European Marketing Congress took place in Brussels, commencing on Monday 25 November 1968. It was addressed by several important European speakers. The council meeting following it discussed and considered the agenda for its Dublin meeting in 1969. The MII was represented at the meetings by Messrs Aubrey Fogarty, Derek Trenaman and Harry Woods.

Tentative arrangements to hold a further meeting of professors and teachers of marketing was agreed for the entire day of Wednesday 11 June 1969. Dr Anthony C. Cunningham, lecturer in marketing, University College, Dublin had agreed to provide the accommodation at the college. An outline of the aims of the meeting and names selected to form the working group was agreed.

A letter from Mr William Driscoll, managing director of Sales and Marketing Executives International, New York, indicated their desire for future co-operation on an international basis. It was decided to allocate an hour or two, during the Dublin meeting, to have the EMC working committee meet Mr Driscoll and discuss ways and means of better communication, including a future joint Europe/America Marketing Conference.

SALES AND MARKETING EXECUTIVES INTERNATIONAL, DECEMBER 1968

SME-I, New York, celebrated its thirty-second anniversary in 1968, having its head office in New York. In 1968 it had 240 affiliated sales/marketing executive clubs in 47 nations, including Ireland, and a membership of over 25,000. It organised the annual travelling exhibit of prizewinning marketing case histories: the Top 20 Gold Medal Awards. It also provided many services including facilities for job exchanges between participating clubs and comprehensive education courses.

The aim of SME-I was to co-operate with other bodies in marketing and the main emphasis was placed on the operation of incentives within a free enterprise economy, believed to be the key to secure economic growth.

COMPUTERS NOT USED IN DECISION MAKING, DECEMBER 1968

A report in December 1968 by *Harvard Business Review* stated that computers had not so far affected the way decisions were made or the kind of decisions reached, although they had provided more time in which to make decisions, more choice and other indirect advantages. According to the report, enquiries among 100 top managers revealed that none of them made direct use of the computer for decision making.

Computers were used mainly by middle management to support analyses or recommendations to top management. Nevertheless, by 1975 it was expected that they would be substantially used in defining possible courses of action. The use of simulation models would also increase significantly, particularly in evaluating alternative long-range plans, product lines and pricing decisions.

RETAILING CHANGES IN THE UNITED STATES, DECEMBER 1968

The December 1968 issue of the *International Newsletter* of SME-I, New York (edited by Mr Kurt Altshul) detailed retailing changes in the United States. The fifteenth Annual Study of Audits and Surveys concerned a 'National Sample Census of Retail Distribution'. It showed that during the previous ten years (to 1958), some 72,000 retail stores had vanished from the US marketplace. Specifically, 14,170 had disappeared during 1967 alone.

Furniture/furnishings stores, eating and drinking establishments and food outlets decreased most substantially. Department stores, however, almost doubled. And discount stores in 1968 accounted for almost half of the department store total.

The drop in the numbers of outlets in the retail community, amounting to about 4 per cent over the previous ten years, was portrayed by the 'store-to-people' ratio which then stood at one store for every 115 persons. In 1958, it had been one for every 97 persons.

US Department/discount stores increase strength

One of the developing trends was the increasing concentration of retail strength, characterised by the impressive build-up of department and full-line discount stores. In ten years the department stores had increased in number from 3,457 outlets to 7,010. The discount phenomenon was even more remarkable. The food store classification was experiencing the greatest shrinkage of any group. More than 5,000 food retailers had fallen by the wayside during the previous year.

Mr Solomon Datka, president of Audits and Surveys, suggested that these changes would cause many prominent consumer goods manufacturers to reassess their distribution procedures.

Brand loyalty under heavy pressure, USA, December 1968

Pressures that worked against brand loyalty had never been more powerful, according to *Grey Matter*, the newsletter of Grey Advertising. These included: product similarity; an increase in advertising quality and quantity; lack of salesmanship in the retail selling floor; greater importance of 'impulse buying' as brands proliferated; modern retailing display techniques; and inter-company competition.

Attitudes about brands people use were in a state of flux and a study indicated that during a three-month period, on average, 52 per cent changed their attitude about brands. Some became more positive, some more negative. Depending on the extent of their usage during a six-month period as many as 80 per cent of the consumers changed their opinions about the brands.

Grey Matter suggested that the primary road to increasing a brand's franchise was in trying to change the public attitude toward brands. It was crucial to learn more about the psychological mechanisms that triggered consumer actions and reactions.

PUBLICATION OF PRINTED STUDY NOTES, JANUARY 1969

An excellent handbook, declared as a new form of printed study notes, designed to help students prepare and revise for professional and other examinations was written by G.B. Giles, a college lecturer, and published by MacDonald & Evans Ltd, London, in the M. & B. Handbook series in January 1969 at 13 shillings (65p).

The book was carefully programmed so as to be a self-contained course of tuition in marketing subjects. It contained detailed notes, self-testing questions and hints on examination technique. It was written to provide a vade-mecum for mature students undertaking their first course in marketing and recommended for those preparing for the examinations of the Institute of Marketing and other professional bodies.

APPLIED STATISTICS, FEBRUARY 1969

Published in February 1969 by MacDonald & Evans Ltd London, *Applied Statistics for Management Studies* was written by David Croft, MA, BSc, AIS, senior lecturer in management statistics and operational research at Slough College of Technology.

The introduction related to the ideas and methods of statistics for students on courses such as the then post-graduate diploma in management studies. It dwelt on the application rather than the theory of statistics. Chapter two covered the introduction of statistical symbols and some mathematical reminders.

CONTAINERISATION TRANSPORT SAVING, FEBRUARY 1969

Addressing Marketing Institute members in Cork on 19 February 1969, Mr George W. Hollwey, managing director of the George Bell Group, suggested that the economics of scale would drive the main pipeline deep-sea container services away from Irish ports. It would follow, of course, that they might also be driven away from many British ports, while there would certainly be a tendency to concentrate on one or possibly two main continental container port capitals.

Ireland, he pointed out, had a population of three million compared with 50 million in Britain and 200 million in western Europe. Those population figures alone were fair evidence that Ireland's next generation of overseas trade would be at the end of a feeder service to and from all markets and not on direct deep-sea shipping lines.

Containerisation would give a real saving of up to about 40 per cent in total transportation cost Mr Hollwey believed. Furthermore, it would enable many trades to develop which were simply not viable before.

HARVARD COMES TO IRELAND, FEBRUARY 1969

An international marketing symposium, 'Harvard Comes to Ireland', was held from 28 February to 1 March 1969 at the Intercontinental hotel, Dublin. The chairman of the MII, Mr Gerry Maher, explained the importance of the conference to Ireland at that time.

MARKETING TERMINOLOGY, MAY 1969

The *Irish Press* column, 'The Press Diary', in its issue of Monday 26 May 1969 reported that yet another technical language was about to be born. And Dublin, where the best English was supposed to be spoken, had been chosen as its birthplace.

It stated that, according to sources, it would be the new 'marketing terminology' for the member countries of the *Conseil European du Marketing* organisation.

The article went on to say that with the EEC becoming more of a probability than a possibility, the meetings in Dublin the following month would create a livelier interest. Nobody was more conscious of this than Mr Albert Brouwet, president of the EMC, who had flown into Dublin specially to check on the conference arrangements.

Mr Albert Brouwet was quoted as saying that perhaps not enough emphasis was being placed on the cultural and human aspects of EEC. Headlines tended to harp on trade, duties and taxes, but a cultural benefit would ensue from the new marketing terminology.

SALESMANSHIP FOR SALES ENGINEERS, 1969

A Fellow of the Institute of Sales Engineers and also a member of the Institute of Marketing, UK, Mr J.B. Windsor, FISE, M.Inst.M., AMMRS, wrote a booklet on the subject: *Effective Salesmanship for Sales Engineers*. It was published by the Institution of Sales Engineers in 1969. Mr Windsor was a regular contributor to *Sales Engineer*, the monthly journal of their Institute.

The introduction was by one Mr Thames Ditton, who stated that the pocket reference was not a kind of 'Sales Engineer's Holy Grail' which would solve all his problems. He tried to condense the practical experience of many men who had made a very fine living from selling products which needed to be applied to a customer's problem.

Mr Ditton said it was an endeavour to supply and so provide for members, the professional training in selling that seemed so curiously absent from the British engineering industry. He had been training men to sell succesfully and giving views on company management. Hence he wrote the first chapter which Mr Windsor felt should be captured in print for the members benefit.

Communication was deemed to be the key to learning. The importance of having a goal to aim at, and achieving it with the responsibility of attaining it, brought out many directions in which decisions were vital. From a certain fall-off level, he believed that even some fixed assets would have to be liquidated. The latter could mean no new cars, no further equipment, cancelling programmes and so on. Such would inevitably lead to a delay, at least, in improvements in manufacturing operation and expansion.

MARKETING FOR THE DEVELOPING COMPANY, JUNE 1969

The publishers Hutchinson of London sent a copy of a book due for publication in June 1969, to the Marketing Institute of Ireland for review. The book was written by John Winkler and entitled *Marketing for the Developing Company*. I myself took up the challenge of reviewing the book with my interpretation being published in the *Irish Press* of Saturday 7 June 1969. The book was made available to the public at 45/- (£2.25).

The author, John Winkler, then aged 33, had considerable experience with manufacturers and advertising agencies. He handled marketing problems for over 230 companies operating in different markets. He was then marketing director of a food company, which from a small base five years previously, had developed into a multi-million pound market leader in the catering industry. He had for six years previously been a freelance journalist, including writing for *The Times*, and made television appearances discussing marketing topics.

In my review I wrote that John Winkler had provided a ready reference of both theory and varied examples of actual business cases. Directed to a consumer market of 54 million in the UK, the marketing advice and experience so freely written, in such a 'development' book would equally apply to Irish companies.

Suggestions, encouragement and idea contributions had been given to John Winkler by two well-known marketing brains, Messrs Aubrey Wilson and Franklin (Col) Colborn (editors of the Hutchinson Marketing Library — a series of integrated books on marketing subjects). Mr Winkler acknowledged their contribution, writing that without their encouragement his book would have been abandoned halfway. He also stated that their suggestions vastly improved the book and that it was as much theirs as his.

Marketing men then started by analysing the changes taking place in society, often using some form of market research. They then attempted to find the gaps in demand. This was not to mean merely making quantity available to meet such demand at its 'seasonal' variance. Warning was given against emotion in the use of the decision-making process. Instinct as well as intellect, one was told, played their part in the final decision. Instinct was defined as 'the product of a man's previous experience'. One must be concerned with the behaviour of people, the basis of good marketing.

EUROPEAN MARKETING COUNCIL CONVENTION, JUNE 1969

Dublin was the venue for the annual convention of the European Marketing Council, held from 11–13 June 1969. The EMC (later known as the European Marketing Confederation) was the official co-ordinating body for marketing institutes in Europe.

Over 80 delegates from fourteen European countries (representing some 26,000 senior marketing personnel) attended the convention sponsored by Bord Fáilte, P.J. Carroll & Co., Colorprint Ltd, Heinz/Erin, Navan Carpets and United Distillers of Ireland Ltd.

An official state reception was hosted by the Minister for Industry and Commerce, Mr George Colley TD, at Iveagh House, St Stephen's Green, Dublin, on the evening of Wednesday 11 June. Mr Albert Brouwet, (Belgium), president of EMC, chaired the council meeting at the Intercontinental hotel on Thursday 12 June 1969.

The officers elected for 1969–70 under the constitution were:

- Mr Albert Brouwet (Belgium), president

- Mr Harry Woods (Ireland), (re-elected), vice-president

- Mr Pierre Hazebroucq (France), vice-president

- Mr Arndt Freisleben (Germany), vice-president

- Mr Fred Th. Witkamp (Holland), secretary-general.

The chairman of the Irish organising committee was Mr Jack Simpson who was ably assisted by Messrs Bernard Woods, Leslie Thorn, Walter Connolly, Robert Gahan, Derek Trenaman, John Wilson, Gerry Maher and Harry Woods.

The main subjects for discussion were marketing management and the marketing approach to company management as a means of improving living standards in Europe. The voices of Belgium, Finland, France, Germany, Great Britain, Italy, Norway, Sweden, Switzerland and Ireland were heard while Denmark was represented by Norway and Spain by France. A very welcome observer in attendance at the proceedings was Dr Jaroslav Marcha of Czechoslovakia.

Wilkinson Sword of Honour presented to MII, June 1969

The 'Wilkinson Sword', part of which is made of solid gold, was given to the European Marketing Council in 1967 by the Wilkinson organisation. It is the symbol of office of the host country and was presented to Mr Gerry Maher MMII, chairman of the Marketing Institute of Ireland, by Mr Roy Randolph, the Institute of Marketing, UK. The sword would remain in Ireland for one year. The following year it would go to Italy.

The executive committee of EMC reported its recognition by the European Common Market and EFTA and on the future relationship of the EMC with such international bodies as SME-I and the IMF (International Marketing Federation).

The president of EMC, Mr Albert Brouwet, gave an outline of the thinking, objectives and group spirit in exchange of European marketing surveys and education, particularly to create a bank of specially selected marketing case studies.

EUROPEAN MARKETING CONSTITUTION RATIFIED IN DUBLIN, JUNE 1969

The founding constitution of the European Marketing Council, drawn up at the Oslo meeting in 1967, was explained to delegates. It was fully reviewed, marketing terminology agreed on and ratified at the EMC Dublin council meeting on Thursday 12 June 1969.

At the Oslo meeting in June 1967, the spokesmen delegates from the thirteen countries and their organisations had unanimously agreed on the formation of the European Marketing Council. The countries, known as founder members were: Belgium, Denmark, Finland, France, Germany, Ireland, Italy, Netherlands, Norway, Spain, Sweden, Switzerland, and United Kingdom.

The EMC had been formed to provide a forum for the advancement of those aspects of marketing which were or could become of common interest within Europe. It was declared a non-profit making organisation. The 22-page constitution of the EMC ratified at Dublin, June 1969, included:

Policy of EMC

1. To propogate the concept of marketing management in the conviction that:

   (a) it brings about new thinking and opportunities in management

   (b) it calls for the development of marketing technicians in the compilation and implementation of company plans

   (c) it needs the setting up of marketing education at all levels.

2. The marketing approach to total company management is wholly compatible with a necessary prerequisite of human dignity because honestly and vigorously carried out at all levels, it promotes rising standards of living for the peoples of the world by accelerating the exchange of goods and services.

Objectives of EMC

The objectives listed included:

- the establishment of a European Diploma in Marketing Management

- the encouragement of research

- the establishment of contact relations with other European organisations concerned with aspects of marketing

- contact with similar organisations outside Europe, e.g. IMF, SME-I, etc.

- all officer positions to be held by members from different countries.

The official languages of EMC were agreed as English and French.

Heinz-Erin Irish case study, June 1969

Mr F.J. McCarthy, group marketing co-ordinator of Irish Sugar Company/ Erin Foods Ltd, presented the 'Heinz-Erin Irish case study', at the EMC Congress in Dublin on 13 June 1969. He indicated that the component companies worked well together without losing their individual identity. The combination was just two years old but he believed that Heinz-Erin was a unique marketing experience with regard to the entry by companies and products into new mass markets.

Carroll Irish case study, June 1969

Mr John Lepere, MMII, marketing director of P.J. Carroll & Co., introduced 'Carroll's Irish Case Study', covered its marketing and advertising as Ireland's largest tobacco concern and drew a number of questions from delegates.

On market breakdown of gender, Mr Lepere said that women smokers were covered by the nuances in the tobacco promotional field, and furthermore in his experience, a cigarette aimed solely at women had never been a successful marketing proposition.

He also referred to certain areas where it was policy to maintain sales rather than increase them.

EMC receptions and tour

In 'Dubliner's Diary', Mr Terry O'Sullivan reported on the serious business by day of the European Marketing Council executives and the not so serious by night. At the Abbey Tavern, Howth, he said, they were entertained to dinner and polished off 'sole by candlelight'. The senior host was Mr Gerry Maher, chairman of the Marketing Institute of Ireland. Mr O'Sullivan also wrote that Mr Harry Woods, MII treasurer and Irish vice-president of the EMC, had been active at quarterly meetings of EMC for the past six years and had eaten many dinners indeed on the European circuit.

On Thursday 12 June 1969, the EMC lady delegates were entertained by the Marketing Institute of Ireland ladies, initially to coffee at Brown Thomas, followed by a visit to Switzer & Co. for a cosmetic presentation. Both of the aforementioned were leading fashion stores in Dublin. In the afternoon the ladies went on a tour of local beauty spots in Dublin and Wicklow and had afternoon tea. The ladies were also invited to the state reception and lunches as guests of the MII.

An optional weekend, 13–15 June, took place at Clare Inn, Co. Clare. A full complement ended up going in a luxury bus. The functions there included a medieval banquet and sightseeing of the beautiful Burren, famous for unsurpassed scenery. It was deemed by all to be a truly memorable occasion.

Special brochure of the Dublin EMC Congress

A special brochure of the Dublin European Marketing Congress was printed by Colorprint Ltd, Dublin. The delegates were wished a 'Céad Míle Fáilte go hÉireann' — a hundred thousand welcomes to Ireland. It extended sincere wishes for a fruitful and enjoyable visit and urged them to take the opportunity to see something of the beauty of Ireland and make new friends.

Media coverage of the EMC Congress

The Council of the Marketing Institute of Ireland unanimously recorded its appreciation to the media for much coverage of the events, speeches and functions. Appreciation was extended in particular to *Independent Newspapers*, *Irish Press Group*, *The Irish Times*, *Cork Examiner* and *Business & Finance* magazine.

Sincere appreciation was also extended to Radio Éireann for live coverage by 'It Says in the Papers', on Thursday 12 and 13 of June and to 'Day to Day' on Friday 13 June which carried an interview with Miss Anna Kessman, Swedish delegate to the EMC Congress.

FOUNDER MEMBERS OF THE MARKETING INSTITUTE REMEMBERED, JUNE 1969

The AGM of the Marketing Institute had been held on 19 June 1969 in the Hibernian hotel, Dublin. The outgoing honorary treasurer, Mr Harry Woods, began his report by paying tribute to two outstanding members who were no longer with their colleagues. They were the late Institute Fellows, Messrs Tom Moran and Stephen Doyle, both of whom had contributed so much, for so many years, to the status and success of the Marketing Institute of Ireland. A one-minute silence was observed and the tribute recorded in the minute book.

The elected officers for year 1969–70 were as follows:

• President: Mr Sean Lemass TD

• Chairman: Mr Leslie Thorn

• Vice-Chairmen: Messrs John Lepere, Peter Needham and Bernard V. Woods

• Hon. Secretary: Mr Aubrey Fogarty

• Hon. Treasurer: Mr Harry V. Woods (re-elected).

Sincere thanks were expressed to Mr Sean Lemass for all he had contributed to the continued success of the Marketing Institute of Ireland. His agreement to continue as president for a further year was also much appreciated. In accepting the office as chairman, Mr Leslie Thorn, complimented Mr Gerry Maher, outgoing chairman, on the various successful achievements during his year of office.

BEA MARKET GUIDE, 1969

Published by Queen Anne Press Ltd and British European Airways (BEA), the *BEA Market Guide Book* of 1969 was compiled from sources indicating the latest information on trade statistics of the European Economic Community (EEC) and other non-member countries. It also contained the economic reports of banks, research organisations and marketing specialists.

The EEC countries at that time were Belgium, France, Italy, German Federal Republic, Luxembourg and the Netherlands (known as the Six). Greece and Turkey were associated with the community with a view to eventual membership. In addition, eighteen countries in Africa and Madagascar were in association with EEC. The EEC was then was one of the fastest growing major economic areas of the world. Between 1958, the year in which the Community began, and 1966 its gross product increased in volume by 51 per cent compared with 45 per cent for the USA and 30 per cent for the UK.

The countries analysed in the book are, in alphabetical order: Austria, Belgium (including Luxembourg), Cyprus, Denmark, Finland, France, Gibraltar, Greece, Holland, Israel, Italy, Lebanon, Luxembourg, Malta, Norway, Portugal, Republic of Ireland, Spain, Sweden, Switzerland, Turkey, United Kingdom and West Germany, (i.e. German Federal Republic, but not the German Democratic Republic, as the latter's trading potential was to be examined later in 1969).

It was pointed out that some figures quoted were in American dollars that was because it was generally accepted to be the currency for establishing competitive financial values and was the then method followed by both EFTA and EEC countries.

The latter two also used the American version of the word 'billion' meaning 1,000 million.

Republic of Ireland statistics

The Republic of Ireland section stated that the Irish pound was at par with Sterling. Progress in trading was continuing and was based on the expansion of exports.

The position followed the deflationary period in the years 1965–66, which had been introduced to correct a long-standing deficit in the Irish Republic's balance of payments. Industrial production had increased by 8 per cent in 1967, as against a 2 per cent rise in 1966.

Close trading links existed with the United Kingdom, which supplied half of the Irish Republic's imports and bought approximately two-thirds of its exports. Despite an Anglo-Irish free trade area agreement, licences were required for certain imports.

However, there were no difficulties with payments for imports to the Irish Republic.

The population in the Republic of Ireland was quoted as 2,884,002 in the 1966 census, of which 732,000 were in the capital, Dublin.

The GNP (million Irish pounds) showed: 1966 — 1,018; 1967 —1,103; 1968 — 1,224.96 (Nov.). Income per capita was given as 806 dollars (£288) in 1966. Statistical information was available at the Central Statistics Office, GPO Arcade, Dublin, where unpublished material could be obtained by payment of a fee of 11s.9d. (59p) an hour. However, most government statistics were published. Wages in manufacturing were 5s.4.5p per hour (27p) in 1966.

Many other avenues are recorded in the book, defining banking, price indexes, revenue, standard of living and so forth.

SALESMANSHIP REFRESHER COURSE, 1969

In 1969 MDI Publications, Management Development Institute, Pennsylvania, produced for Sales & Marketing Executives- International, New York, a 300 page (A4) book entitled: *Salesmanship: A Refresher Course in Salesmanship*. Edited by Earle R. Conant and Charles L. Lapp, the twenty-four study units in the volume, they stated, were the result of a combination of 75 years of making a living by selling and showing others how to sell. It comprised the amalgamation of every suggestion, every idea, every concept and every technique that came from the hard, practical, on-the-job experience of the authors.

Mr Earle R. Conant had, since 1956, been a member of the Associate Faculty of the Graduate School of Sales Management and Marketing. With Mr Charles L. Lapp he had developed two texts for the marketing course offered by the International Correspondence Schools of Scranton, Pennsylvania. Mr Lapp with 30 years of teaching experience behind him, including assignments at four universities, since 1951, spent part of every summer working in the field, actually selling with and observing different types of outside salesmen. In the past ten years he had surveyed more than 50,000 buyers and obtained their reactions to the salesmen with whom they had come in contact. In April 1963 he had been named marketing educator of the year by the Sales and Marketing Executives of St Louis. Finally he had been selected as the editor-in-chief of a selling and marketing management series for SME-I.

In Part One it is stated that the term 'sales training' was one that should be replaced by 'salesmanship education', not only in the vocabulary of the sales executive but in his approach to that portion of his duties that concerned him with the self-improvement of the men under his direction. 'Education' they wrote, conversely, implied the cultivation and improvement of the mind through teaching, a process parallel to that of helping a prospect to arrive at a buying decision through the exercise of sales techniques. Further, like 'good selling', 'good teaching' started with a plan.

For self-improvement activity, multiple-choice questions are given to each unit. Certainly I myself found the volume a most useful reference, in my lecturing over some years.

IRISH CASE STUDIES — BELGIAN PRESENTATION, NOVEMBER 1969

The Marketing Institute of Ireland jointly presented the Heinz-Erin and P.J. Carroll 'Marketing in Action' case studies at the l'Auditorium Mail, Brussels with the Marketing Executives' Association of Belgium on the 28 November 1969.

IRELAND AND THE COMON MARKET, NOVEMBER 1969

Many EMC associates and guests met at Brussels to hear an address given by
H.E. Mr Sean Morrisey, Ambassador of Ireland to the European Communities, on 'Ireland and the Common Market'.

NATIONAL ADULT EDUCATION SURVEY, 1969–70

The then Minister for Education, Mr Brian Lenihan TD, announced the appointment of Mr Con Murphy to carry out a survey of the needs of the community in the matter of adult education and to indicate the type of permanent
organisation to be set up in order to serve those needs. Accordingly eleven
persons, representing a wide spectrum of organisations, were appointed to
act as an advisory committee. A time limit of six months was allowed to
produce a report.

An interim report was published in April 1970. The fact that it was interim was explained by the committee finding that, while adults who enrolled for classes were reasonably well provided for, they only formed a small
percentage of the total adult population. It was estimated that only about 10
per cent of the total adult population in Ireland engaged in adult education
annually. However, some of the remaining 90 per cent were being served in a
way that was not generally regarded as adult education. If the latter type of
service had been more developed, it was believed, the remaining 90 per cent
would have many of their ambitions for personal fulfilment resolved. Examples of the 90 per cent being serviced with formal education included agricultural advisory services in the building construction industry taught by vocational education personnel, social workers, social services from councils
and residents' associations.

Reports were received from many Irish bodies and from Europe and
America, and these were carefully studied.

EDUCATION PERMANENTE, 1970

The Council of Europe, Council for Cultural Co-operation, had given much
thought to *'education permanente'* and defined it as:

> The concept of permanent education as the organising principle of all
> education implies a comprehensive, coherent and integrated system
> designed to meet the educational and cultural aspirations of every per-
> son in accordance with his abilities.

Attention was drawn to the fact that a very large proportion of vocational teachers, particularly those recruited in the recent past, even though charged with responsibility for educating adults, received no formal preparation for that part of their work. Vocational Education Committes were the main providers of adult education courses for many years since the obligation was laid on them by the 1930 Vocational Education Act to develop such education.

It was recommended that the Council of Adult Education be made responsible for allocating research projects in defined areas and for financial provision. Meanwhile a directory of agencies and voluntary bodies engaged directly and indirectly in adult education was published in the interim report.

NEW APPOINTMENT TO MII, APRIL 1970

The Marketing Institute of Ireland appointed Mr Joseph C. Bigger as chief executive. This would take effect from 1 April 1970. One of the founder members of the Institute, he had served as a council member for more than twenty years. In 1967 he had been elected chairman.

EUROPEAN MARKETING COUNCIL AGM, MAY 1970

The fifteenth AGM of the European Marketing Council was held in May 1970 in Nice, France. The Marketing Institute of Ireland was represented by Mr Joe Bigger, FMII, chief executive, and Mr Harry Woods, FMII, as spokesman delegate.

On live television at Cannes, Mr Harry Woods representing Ireland, formally handed the 'Wilkinson Sword of Honour' to Mr Pierre Hazebroucq, president of DCF, (Federation des Directeurs Commerciaux et Economiques de France et d'Expression Française) who was representing the French hosts of the European congress meeting.

The programme of speakers at the congress covered many subjects including social and economic factors and government regulation comparisons in the various member countries. The French said they worked hard and had opportunities for greater expansion while their government aided exports. The mentality of workers was considered in aspects, as broad as imagination, individualism, failure to delegate and dislike of follow-up involvement. They claimed to be less unionised in France, while they never had a liberal economy. Banks in France were government controlled and education was socialistic. Years of individual education had a wide span, as much as a 9/10-year period.

A bound report of the very succesful EMC congress and AGM held in Dublin in June 1969 was presented to delegates by Mr Harry Woods. Highlights included a report of increased government recognition of the work and activity of the Marketing Institute of Ireland.

At the Brussels council executive meeting, Mr Harry Woods was elected senior vice-president of EMC and president-elect for the next AGM, to be held in Milan in June 1971.

NEW MII APPOINTMENTS ANNOUNCED, 1970–71

The Marketing Institute of Ireland press announced that the new chairman elected for 1970–71 was Mr W.D. (Bill) Fraser of North Dublin Growers. Messrs Harry Wyer, Walter J. Connolly and Leslie V. Whitehead were elected vice-chairmen. Mr Aubrey Fogarty became honorary secretary and Mr Ernest K. Kent, honorary treasurer. Mr Sean Lemass TD kindly agreed to continue as president. The recently appointed chief executive, Mr Joe Bigger, was also welcomed.

AN ANALYSIS OF MARKETING, 1970

Mr Patrick Dillon-Malone, MA, Ph.D., managing-director of the marketing consultancy firm, Colin McIver Associates (Ireland), was well known. In the course of a varied career in data processing, management education, shipyard management, and industrial and consumer marketing research, he had worked in Britain, Malta and continental Europe. He was a former senior scholar of Stoneyhurst College and of Exeter College, Oxford.

His book, *An Analysis of Marketing*, relates to the strategy of business firms in an open environment and deals with the ways in which alternative choices were opened up and pursued and how individual managers determined the future course of their business.

Agroraphilia

The word 'Agroraphilia' was invented by Mr Dillon-Malone, to describe the process for such determination of choices, referred to above — a market-oriented attitude.

He was instrumental in bringing forth the thinking of many successful Irish managers, and in particular the interview technique.

In his review of the volume, Mr Ivor Kenny, director of the Irish Management Institute, stated that the theme set it apart from a lot of management thought and action which was traditionally directed at the essential, but sometimes subsidiary, problems of improving operational efficiency and the ratio of achievement to effort.

The study was a pioneering one and while based on Irish experience, the results got attention in other European countries. The Irish Management Institute decided to publish the book because it reflected and dissected the thinking of a large and representative sample of practical and successful Irish managers. Mr Dillon-Malone executed his study between 1967 and 1969.

In the text, questionnaires are wide and cover all aspects of industrial and consumer production and output, transport in every form, tourism, finance, energy uses and so forth. Irish performance in exports was described as inadequate. Mr Dillon-Malone however, gave suggestions and advice from experience. Further, he explained medium and long-term strategies of attitude change; the age factor; corporate objectives; opinion sample surveys; and research objectives. These he dealt with in extensive detail.

Reference was made by the author to the difficulties in arriving at a satisfactory probability sample of Irish undertakings, as described in Breffni Tomlin's 'meticulous' study of the *Management of Irish Industry*. The major problem was to arrive at a satisfactory sampling frame in which every existing undertaking (not 'establishment') would have an equal or known probability of selection.

Tomlin, the author said, had restricted his enquiry to transportable goods industries over some 1,249 firms. However, Tomlin, had brought categories from over 500 employees in steps to a 20–99 category, only to find that a considerably larger sample should have been allocated. Neither was it so possible for Tomlin to provide for a breakdown by industry groups. Hence he (Patrick Dillon-Malone) had decided to eliminate firms employing less than 100 and concentrate on the 300-or-so manufacturing firms left.

Register of Undertakings, Trinity College, 1970

The Administrative Research Bureau of Trinity College had compiled a Register of Undertakings over the previous four years, based particularly on references in the press. That register gave the name, industry and general size-category, in terms of employment. Using such it had been possible to interview firms with 400+ employees and a random selection of those in the 100–399 category. Hence a survey of firms other than, but including transportable goods industries had been possible. The sample over the variety of twenty types covered 179 firms.

Mr Dillon-Malone's volume was most seriously studied by managers then (and since), particularly marketing executives in the 1970s.

McConnell Research Marketing Fellowship, 1967–69

The generosity of McConnell's Advertising Service Ltd in founding and awarding the first Research Fellowship in Marketing at Trinity College, Dublin and by the equal consideration of Irish TAM Ltd and the Attwood Group of Companies in permitting him to take it up, was gratefully acknowledged by Mr Dillon-Malone.

SALESMEN UNDER THE MICROSCOPE, 1970

In February 1970 the then chairman of MII, Mr Leslie Thorn, negotiated with PA International Management Consultants Ltd through IPR (Irish Public Relations Consultants), to carry out a survey, 'Salesmen under the Microscope'. It was agreed that it be initiated by a special questionnaire to be sent to all MII members. The survey was to be carried out, at no cost to the MII, in July/August 1970.

PA Management Consultants had already conducted the same survey in Britain, in conjunction with the Institute of Marketing there, and findings had created a great deal of interest and discussion. Almost a quarter of the Institute members directly responsible for salesmen in Britain completed their survey. The 3,060 who replied (total membership being 14,000) covered repeat consumer goods (762 companies representing 25 per cent of replies), intermediate goods (265 companies, 9 per cent of replies), durable consumer goods (385 companies, 13 per cent), repeat industrial goods (744 companies, 24 per cent) capital equipment (689 companies, 22 per cent) and services (215 companies, 7 per cent). The average sales force, for which the replying sales manager was responsible, was 23.

SALESMEN'S REMUNERATION IN BRITAIN, AUGUST 1970

The highest paid salesman in the sales force, according to replies to a survey in 1968 in Britain, got on average £2,200 p.a., the lowest £1,250 p.a. and the average £1,600 p.a. The average amount of commission or bonus was £330. The basis of payment for commission/bonus had many variances.

Mr W.D. Fraser FMII, newly elected chairman of the Marketing Institute of Ireland, said that disagreement between management and its middle income group staff personnel, appeared to be running into difficult times, as indicated by other sections of the group.

IRELAND'S LARGEST INDUSTRY — AGRICULTURE, 1970

In the past, Mr Bill Fraser said, the lack of communication had been one of the greatest shortcomings. He believed that while in industry it would appear that there had been a very considerable improvement in recent years, he was a little disappointed on returning to the agricultural community to find that the progress in that area was not keeping pace. It was his aim, as chairman, to endeavour to integrate more closely the industrial thinking on marketing to what was the largest industry in Ireland based on the wealth of our own countryside — agriculture.

ANTWERP EMC EDUCATION SEMINAR, SEPTEMBER 1970

A specially convened European marketing meeting was held at St Ignatius University in Antwerp, Belgium from 24–26 September 1970. The meeting was sponsored by the European Marketing Council and the Belgium Marketing Executives' Association. It was attended by experts in different aspects of marketing education.

Ireland was represented by Mr Philip Flood, Head of Marketing at the School of Retail Distribution and Mr Harry Woods, Fellow of the Marketing Institute of Ireland and vice-president of EMC.

Education for the Seventies, case studies, 1970

'Education for the Seventies' was among the subjects discussed at the meeting while two days were devoted to creating a bank of European case studies. One of these was 'Cake Mix Europe'. It was, in fact, aptly named as it related to a bakery.

The problems concerned increasing the output to reduce overall costs, thereby increasing profitability. The bakery had further output production capacity. The result was a recommendation to manufacture a decided percentage increase *and* to have delivery vehicles leave at 4 a.m. (instead of 5 a.m.) and thereby avoid traffic conjestion delay. That enabled vanmen to have a wider span of territory in which to seek and supply new customers. Simple but realistic when finely considered.

PRESIDENT'S DINNER, JANUARY 1971

At the MII President's Night dinner on 12 January 1971 at the Gresham hotel, Mr Sean Lemass remarked that the Taoiseach, Mr Jack Lynch, had had a difficult year. There was no such thing as a soft easy year but 1970 was a little bit tougher and rougher than usual and he was glad to see that Mr Lynch had emerged from the end of it 'with only a slight patch over his eye'.

In his address the chairman of the MII, Mr Bill Fraser, stated 'it is here we shall live or die in 1971 and I am quite certain that I can speak for all the members of our Institute in saying that our chief guest, An Taoiseach, Jack Lynch, has our full support in the very difficult year that lies ahead. 'Unless we, each and everyone, face up to the critical decisions of this year, everything that has been done from 1922 to 1932 and to date, could be lost in 1972, or when we re-enter the larger trading community'.

Mr Sean Lemass, architect of the Irish economy, January 1971

The response to the toast of 'Our Guests' was delivered by Mr Colm Barnes, chairman of Córas Tráchtála who paid tribute to Mr Sean Lemass, as the 'architect of the Irish economy'.

Guests including Mr John Haughey, former MII president, Mr Frank Lemass, chairman of the Irish Management Institute, Mr J. O'Sullivan, new industry manager of the IDA and Mr E.J. Gray, director general of the Confederation of Irish Industries, were welcomed at the dinner.

EUROPEAN MARKETING CONSULTANTS, JANUARY 1971

A sales lecture and sales film show was presented by the European Marketing Consultants. I myself was the managing director and lecturer at the Player-Wills Conference Centre on the South Circular Road, Dublin, on 25 January 1971. I referred to the then recent Congress of European Sales' Consultants and Sales' Trainers, held in Venice, at which the following conclusions were arrived at:

- traditional selling is dying out fast
- marketing is really here
- a great *new* future for salesmen lies ahead
- fewer order takers will be needed
- real salesmen will have:

  (a) more training

  (b) more scope

  (c) more importance.

Following my address to the members and sales people present, when I outlined the methods and opportunities for: 'Successful Selling in the Seventies', via new thinking and ideas, a sale film entitled 'Sam's Secret' was shown. This proved that research, organisation and work provided the necessary ingredients for success.

DECIMAL CURRENCY INTRODUCED, FEBRUARY 1971

Decimalisation (D-Day), 15 February 1971, saw the changeover to the decimal system of currency when Britain, Ireland, Jersey and Guernsey implemented it.

Already 95 per cent of the world's population used decimal currency and the final operation ranked as the world's biggest coinage changeover.

It was proposed to accept dual currency, old and new, as legal tender, for a period of 18–24 months to enable the changeover to be completed. The change was naturally a costly affair to implement. However, the advantages were considerable. Calculations became simpler in decimal.

For teaching and learning calculations were brought into line with ordinary arithmetic.

Examples of the new coins showed that five new pennies compared to one shilling in old value, ten new pennies to two shillings and 50 new pennies to ten shillings.

By 1975 it was envisaged that most industries would change weights and measures to grammes, litres and metres, and their derivations.

IRISH ON PAR WITH BRITISH SALESMANSHIP, FEBRUARY L971

An *Irish Press* headline of 25 February 1971 read: 'Irish on Par with British Salesmanship'. It was commenting on a major report then released which stated that the work of Irish salesmen could be very favourably compared with that of their British counterparts.

The report, published by the Marketing Institute of Ireland, gave full details of a survey carried out among 1,200 leading Irish companies. PA Management Consultants had carried out the report during the latter part of 1970. It was an extension of a similar study of British salesmen that had been carried out in 1968.

REMUNERATION OF SALESMAN IN IRELAND

The turnover, per Irish salesman, was impressively high and compared favourably with Britain. The highest pay for a salesman in Ireland was £2,500 p.a. and the lowest £1,325. The average rate agreed for a successful salesman was approximately £1,700.

The survey also revealed that salesmen selling the more expensive products, such as industrial machinery and luxury items, tended to receive somewhat higher pay. There was little recruitment from outside Ireland, while many companies seemed to employ and train people who had no previous selling experience.

EUROPEAN MARKETING COUNCIL, AMSTERDAM, MARCH 1971

A special meeting of the executive of the European Marketing Council was held in Amsterdam on 19 March 1971. Those present included the following:

• Mr Albert Brouwet: president

- Mr Fred Th. Witkamp: secretary-general

- Mr Pierre Hazebroucq: vice-president

- Mr Harry Woods: vice-president.

In his opening remarks the president, Mr Albert Brouwet, stated that the European Marketing Council might, in a decentralised way, organise activities for large groups like the European Marketing Congress and for small groups like the educational meeting in Antwerp or the advanced marketing discussion group in Sweden. However this could only be done by the courtesy of the members as the secretariat was not equipped to organise international activities.

On behalf of the Marketing Institute of Ireland, Mr Harry Woods, EMC vice-president, said that the MII had created an Irish Marketing Diploma drawn from advanced thinking and research, not alone from their own executive educationalists and members, but in collaboration with the universities and other relevant professional institutes. The Institute of Marketing, London, was included in the latter.

The European Association of Advertisers' Agencies informed EMC of their aim and wish to have further co-operation with EMC.

Election of officers

It was again confirmed that 1969 (Dublin) was the first year that officers were elected under the constitution. According to same the president could not be re-elected in 1971. The rules also set out on page twelve of the constitution that: 'The general council shall appoint the president from among the vice-presidents' and the president shall remain in office for two years. The importance of such a method of election will be observed later.

SUPERMARKET CONSUMERISM CONVENTION, MAY 1971

The annual Supermarket World Convention was held at the Astrohall, Houston, Texas, during the entire first week of May 1971. The subject, on this occasion was 'Consumerism'. This was the industry's biggest 'get-together' and the venue accommodated up to 100,000 people.

Delegates started at a working breakfast and attended various seminars on each of the five days. All aspects of marketing were covered, right to the final buyer/consumer.

A number of seminars were held concurrently each day. Delegates selected the particular one, of each session, that he/she wished to participate in. However, due to the thousands of participants, it was not always possible to get into the desired zone, rather one had to accept an alternative.

I myself participated as group planning/marketing executive of the Irish owned H. Williams & Co. supermarket chain of stores and Hafner meat factory. The knowledge gained from Asian, European and American speakers was of undoubted value, particularly relating to the market trends (then and now) for hypermarkets and supermarkets.

MR SEAN F. LEMASS, TD, RIP, MAY 1971

Owing to the death of its esteemed president, Mr Sean F. Lemass, TD, as a mark of respect and deepest sympathy, the offices of the Marketing Institute of Ireland were closed all day on Thursday, 13 May 1971. Indeed all over Ireland many other institutes and business firms did likewise.

JOINT MEETING OF EMC AND SME-I, MAY 1971

A joint meeting of delegates from the European Marketing Council and the Sales and Marketing Executives International, New York, took place in Dusseldorf, Germany on 17 May 1971. Mr Henry W. Beardsley, SME-I, vice president, welcomed the following:

- committee members (SME-I):
  - Mr Paul Berry, Wichita, USA
  - Mr Donald de la Chapelle, New York, USA
  - Mr C. O. Erickson, Stockholm, Sweden
  - Mr Guy Levrier, Paris, France representing
  - Mr Tedd Joseph
  - Dr F. Th. Witkamp, Amsterdam, Holland representing Dr J.A. van Kamp
  - Mr Harry Woods, Dublin, Ireland.

- guests:
  - Mr Albert Brouwet, Brussels, Belgium, representing the European Marketing Council
  - Mr Heinz Franke, Hannover, Germany
  - Mrs L. Wagner, Dusseldorf, Germany, representing Vereinigung Deutscher Marketing Clubs

- SME-I staff:
  - Mr Kurt J. Altschul, New York, USA.

The minutes of the previous meeting of 4 December 1970 were approved. It had been the first international committee meeting ever held outside of the United States. The main aim was to foster closer co-operation and personal relations between SME-I representatives in the USA and Europe. Of the meeting (May 1971) the subsequent minutes recorded some 5-A4 pages of activities discussed and decisions made. A synopsis of this was recorded as follows:

1. A desire to provide more and better services for marketing executives had led to the formation of The Management Council (TMC).

2. The economy situation conversely was discussed.

3. Regarding education, the formula proposed to bring seminars to Europe and/or bring groups to the USA. The Japanese were doing so.

The well-renowned 'Top Twenty'marketing programme, brought by SME-I to Europe, had not been able to make a break even financially. Endeavours were being made to get a grant from the Ford Foundation this and was under consideration. In the meantime they suggested having small groups of approximately three or four cases, (over a three- or four-hour timing) rather than the twenty cases.

Mr Erickson of Sweden considered that activities geared towards keeping a product viable in the marketplace should be a successful marketing aim. Mr Woods of Ireland observed that salesmanship was servicing the customers while marketing also had the responsibility of identifying needs and setting policy.

APPOINTMENTS TO MII, MAY 1971

Dr J.F. Dempsey was elected president of the Marketing Institute of Ireland and welcomed at the AGM of 27 May 1971. He succeeded the late Mr Sean F. Lemass TD, who had given much help and guidance to the Institute during the years he had been president. Mr H.A. Wyer (Armstrong Cork Ltd) became chairman for 1971–72:

Officers elected to the executive council were:

*   Hon. Secretary: Mr Desmond Isle

*   Hon. Treasurer: Mr Ernest K. Kent

*   Vice-Chairmen: Messrs Walter Connolly, Leslie Whitehead and Harry Woods

*   Chief Executive: Mr Joseph C. Bigger.

A record number of eighteen other Fellows and Members were elected to complete the council. After completing the agenda the chairman announced that Mr Harry Woods had been elected president of the European Marketing Council in Milan that afternoon.

EUROPEAN MARKETING CONGRESS, MAY 1971

The official title of the ninth European Marketing Congress, held in Milan from 27–28 May 1971 was: 'The Consumer in the Seventies'. It was sponsored by the president of the Italian Republic, Giuseppe Saragat. There were twelve speakers in all. Below is a selection of their comments.

Burmah Oil

Speaking about marketing oil-fired central heating in the 1970s, Mr W.J. Hill of Burmah Oil Trading Ltd, said the oil industry while having usually high past success, was nevertheless extremely product oriented. It faced direct competition from other fuel industries and technical improvements had halted the growth of automobile lubricants.

He termed the idea of selling a complete solution to customer's problems, rather than individual products, as 'systems marketing' and a form implementing by method as 'vertical marketing'. An illustration of a total integrated oil company, he announced, would be one that carried out each of the various stages of production, shipping, refining, distribution and retailing. He concluded by examining in detail the activities of the Burmah Warmlife Heating Services.

Newspapers

The director and general manager of *The Times* Newspapers Ltd (formed in 1967 from the merger of *The Sunday Times, The Times, The Times Educational Supplement* and *The Times Literary Supplement*) Mr Geoffrey C. Rowett spoke about success in his field. His topic was entitiled: 'Newspapers — Will They Change?'.

He said editorial flair, market research and other management science techniques had been used. However, neither would replace flair in the creation of the continuously changing product. The newspaper industry was poised to meet changes of tomorrow's society with investment in new technologies, while considering the implications, especially in scrapping centralised printing. Diversification possibilites and new methods were available, from automation and data banks, to colour and home printing. Society's needs were changing and newspapers were adapting to them.

Electronics industry

A native of North Dakota, USA, Mr Thomas A. Reed had become the new president of Honeywell Europe Inc. in July 1970. Its headquarters were in Brussels. His purpose was to combine the marketing efforts of Honeywell in the United Kingdom and Scandanavia with those extended by the company all over Central and Southern Europe including the Middle East.

Mr Reed stated that the electronic industries were ahead of time and in fact needed to be, in order to serve other industries and the consumers. Identifying customer needs was the real difficulty and this was where the marketing expert, who could translate them into products by spelling out specifications for the design engineers, came to the fore.

He believed that consumers demanded that the electronics industry make their lives easier. This was required both on the domestic front and also in the pursuit of any scientific, industrial or commercial projects. These could range from the automatic dishwasher to the automatic landing of a lunar module on the moon.

Services advertising

Amongst the many many achievements in his varied academic, army and sporting career, Dr Rudolf Farner had chaired congresses of the IAA. In fact, in 1963, he had also been awarded 'Advertising Man of the Year' and was 1964–68 world president of the IAA.

He presented a case study on 'How to Advertise Services in Modern Marketing' and provided discourse on: marketing communication for services; competitive market personality; marketing formula; the creative process; how to determine target groups; penetration; usage pull; concept; unit selling proposition; reason why. In addition, he also provided highlights of success stories: airline; banking; insurance; leasing and tourism.

Three keys to profit

For a company to respond to opportunity as a single aggressive force one had to be sure that the 'corporate body' was in good health and responsive. So said Mr Robert A. Whitney, management consultant and president of the Management and Marketing Institute since 1957. Recognising the need for graduate business training, he had founded and for five years was chancellor of the Graduate School of Sales Management and Marketing at Syracuse University.

Mr Whitney said the three keys to profit in the 1970s were: people, products and productivity. For ten years he had been president and chief executive officer of National Sales Executives International (now Sales and Marketing Executives). During his tenure in office that association had grown from 6,000 members to over 30,000 members throughout the world.

Italian marketing man

Fieldwork Milan presented the findings of an inquiry into 'The Italian Marketing Man: As They Would Like Him To Be'. It had been carried out on 389 advertisements for personnel recruitments during the year 1970 on the daily newspaper *il Corriere* Della Sera (338) and on the weekly magazine *il Mondo* (51).

Experience showed confusion in the description of different functions in company organisations. Hence the inquiry decided on categories such as commercial director, sales director and director of promotion for inclusion.

For the specific activity of marketing they defined: marketing director (or equivalent), assistant to the marketing director, product manager, retail marketing, expert in marketing research and professors in marketing. In seven of the advertisements a marketing man with 'activity at European level' was specified. An interesting finding was that all the advertisements reviewed clearly referred to male elements. One only request for a marketing director stated 'also a woman'.

EUROPEAN MARKETING COUNCIL AGM, MAY 1971

The AGM of the European Marketing Council was held in Milan on 26 May 1971. This preceded the congress. Delegates from ten countries were present (Belgium, Finland, France, Germany, Ireland, Italy, Netherlands, Norway, Spain and the United Kingdom). Apologies were received from Sweden, Switzerland and Denmark. The 'voice' for Sweden was represented by Finland.

The meeting was presided over by Mr Albert Brouwet, with Messrs Pierre Hazebroucq and Harry Woods, vice-presidents, and the secretary-general Dr Fred Witkamp, in attendance. An apology for the vice-president Mr Arndt Freiesleben, (Germany) was recorded. A number of non-voting observers were also present.

According to page ten of the constitution under the heading 'Procedure at Meetings of the General Council', it stated that 'Additional delegates may attend meetings of the General Council as observers. Such delegates shall not speak to or vote on any matter under discussion'.

Dr Emilio Zara welcomed the EMC members to Milan. He reminded delegates that fifteen years previously, the first European Marketing Congress had taken place, also at Milan. He stated that he was proud to once again show the progressiveness of Italian marketing at this congress.

The outgoing president, Mr Albert Brouwet, thanked Dr Zara for his kind words, the organisation of the congress and the meeting. He reminded the participants of the important contributions of the Club Dirigenti Vendite e Marketing of Italy and in particular Dr Zara, to the development of marketing in Europe and in Italy.

The secretary-general, Mr Fred Witkamp, was sincerely thanked for communications and attendance at meetings including his trip to Norway where he took part in the Seventeenth Annual Conference of International University Contact for Management Education (IUC) at Bergen.

It was announced that a special brochure concerning EMC, citing policy, objectives, organisation and membership qualifications (one representative body only per European country) had been drafted. When produced it would be in English and French, and made available to member countries for distribution.

First European marketing case studies, 1971

Regarding education, the Brussels meeting had been the first seminar to include case studies. The EMC participants were Denmark, Holland, Ireland and the United Kingdom. Co-operation with other bodies included EAAA (European Advertising Association), Zurich and SME-I, (Sales and Marketing Executives International, New York).

EMC elections, May 1971

The chairman, Mr Albert Brouwet of Belgium introduced Mr Pierre Hazebroucq of France for the presidency. Mr Jacobsen of Norway while stating that he was fully aware of the abilities of Mr Hazebroucq, he nevertheless intended to propose Mr Harry Woods of Ireland, vice-president, as a candidate for president.

Mr Botellico of Italy asked if Mr Woods was available for such election to which Mr Woods replied that he was and if elected would serve. He was the senior vice-president having been the first elected to such a position at the Oslo meeting in 1967.

It was he, in fact, who had recommended, in 1968, that there be three vice-presidents, to spread the 'work-load' across Europe.

Furthermore, under the heading of 'Election of President and other Honorary Officers', on page twelve of the constitution, it clearly stated that: 'The General Council shall appoint a president from among the vice-presidents and the president shall remain in office for two years'. Consequently voting *must* come from the delegates entitled to vote at the meeting. These rules were the result of a working party, appointed at the Oslo meeting in 1967.

Mr Roy Randolph, UK, proposed electing Mr Hazebroucq, while Mr Toussaint, speaking for the French delegation, urged this election, saying Mr Hazebroucq had worked hard for the European cause and had the ability to do the job. Much comment took place as to the procedure of the election of a president with the spokesman of each country giving his views. This provoked a lengthy and heated discussion.

As Mr J.C. Toussaint was the appointed 'voice' (spokesman) for France at the meeting, it was however, agreed, following suggestion of Mr Roy Randoplh, UK, that Mr Hazebroucq be permitted to make an address. He did so at great length, in French, criticising the size of Ireland stating that it was 'a dot of an island, on the periphery of Europe'. He further asked, on the matter of voting, whether a country not present could have a vote counted in the tally.

The situation, not explained at the meeting, was that under page sixteen of the constitution,'alterations and/or additions to the constitution', reads as follows:

> The constitution may be altered or added to by the general council upon a proposal by a member organisation who with the support of one-third of the members submits a proposition. Approval of such propositions shall be effective upon receiving a two-thirds majority assent of the voting members. At this meeting voting *by proxy* is to be allowed.

The secretary-general asked the president, Mr Albert Brouwet, for a short adjournment, to discuss the matter informally and refer to the constitution. Adjournment, as later minuted, was not granted by the chairman (outgoing president) as it was felt that enough voices had been heard and voting should take place.

Consequently, Mr Roy Randolp, UK, referred to his proposal for Mr Hazebroucq and called for a seconder and Dr van Nouhuys (Netherlands) did so. Mr Ainamo of Finland seconded the Norwegian proposal of Mr Woods and wanted to end the discussion by a vote being taken. He announced that he (Mr Ainamo) would also vote for Sweden.

The following tellers were then nominated: Mrs L. Wagner (Germany) and Mr J.M. Martinez-Candial (Spain). Eleven votes were cast, Finland having voted for Sweden, of which six votes showed the name of Mr Harry Woods (Ireland) and five votes the name of Mr Pierre Hazebroucq (France).

(As paragraph 9, page 12, of the constitution states 'Where a ballot is necessary it shall be conducted in secret at the meeting'. It was therefore an enormous surprise when the tellers announced the voting result by naming each country and who they had voted for — probably unprecedented.)

Mr Harry Woods of Ireland elected, May 1971

Following the result of the ballot, Mr Harry Woods of Ireland was declared elected as the new president of the European Marketing Council. Mr Hazebroucq stated that he would withdraw from the executive committee and would not attend the remainder of the meeting. Mr Heinz Franke of Germany regretted to hear such a declaration and urged Mr Hazebroucq to stay. Mr Ainamo, of Finland again stressed that, in his view, a fair and open democratic procedure had taken place.

Having taken written notes of the entire proceedings and as a considerable time had elapsed since the voting took place, Mr Harry Woods took over the seat as president of the European Marketing Council. He stated that each EMC member country had an entitlement to one vote and that he was proud of the contribution he had made over the previous seven years. This, he felt, could not be measured by the size of one's country.

Mr Woods went on to say that he had a prepared programme and would also continue to implement the good work which had been been done or was in process. He was supported by those he represented, able to travel and would spend much time in his position as president. He then asked for the total support of the executive and members of EMC. It would, he said, be his intention to meet many of the EMC members, preferably in zone meetings.

The three vice-presidents elected for 1971–72 were:

• Mr Roy Randolph: Institute of Marketing, London

• Mr Matti Ainamo: Markkinointijohdon Ryhma, c/o Markkinointi-Instituutti, Helsinki-25

• Mr Rafael Camps: Federación Española de Clubs de Dirigentes de Ventas y Marketing, Barcelona-8.

The council officers and members of EMC were entertained at a cocktail reception in the evening, hosted in the name of the Club Dirigenti Vendite e Marketing-Italia, by Martini and Rossi at their Terrazze Martini. The president received many congratulations from delegates at the function, including those from France.

EMC COUNCIL MEETING, MAY 1971

The first council meeting of the new executive met in Milan on 29 May 1971. Present were the president, Mr Harry Woods, Dr Fred Witkamp, secretary-general, Messrs Roy Randolph and Matti Ainamo, vice-presidents.

It was agreed that the organisation of a European-American marketing seminar, for a small group of dedicated marketing men, be negotiated. It was also proposed that in future a past-president should be kept on the executive for an agreed period after completing his official term of office.

TV interview in Sardinia, May 1971

On Saturday evening, 29 May 1971, Mr Harry Woods and his wife, Sheila, flew to Sardinia for the weekend as guests of the Club Dirigenti Vendite e Marketing-Italia.

On arrival, as the new president of EMC, Mr Woods was interviewed on television.

The discussion concerned politics and European economics. Mr Woods was accompanied by car to the press conference by Mr Geoffrey Rowett of *The Times* Newspapers Ltd, London, who had addressed the Milan congress.

Congratulations extended to new president

Mr Kurt Altschul, New York, sent a letter to Mr Woods on 1 June 1971 in which he wrote:

> your dedication, Harry, to the cause and your hard work over the years have well earned you the recognition you have received and as your friends, we, in SME-I, are naturally sharing some of the satisfaction with you.

In a letter to all members of the EMC executive, Mr Harry Woods stated that, with their individual support, it would create awareness of the importance of marketing to the benefit of national economies and encourage contact between marketers throughout the member countries. The result would provide a better standard of living, to which each one was entitled.

SEAN LEMASS AWARD, ANNOUNCED, JUNE 1971

Mr Harry Wyer, chairman of the Marketing Institute of Ireland, and his council gave a very pleasant reception for the press at the Moira hotel, Trinity Street, Dublin, on the evening of 10 June 1971. It was reported that there were 400 members of the Marketing Institute who collectively spoke with a powerful voice.

Mr Bill Fraser, immediate past-chairman of MII, announced that to perpetuate the memory of the late Sean Lemass, former President of MII, the Sean Lemass award had been established.

CORK MARKETING CAMPAIGN, JUNE 1971

Mr F.E. James, chairman, announced that the Cork regional branch of MII was to mount a recruitment campaign aimed at businesses in the region that were interested in marketing. He was speaking at their AGM in Silversprings hotel on 14 June 1971.

Mr James went on to say that one of the difficulties of recruitment was the plethora of organisations to which businessmen were expected to belong and support. He gave a wide-ranging report on the success of the branch and said that the next MII examinations would be set and the diploma given by the Irish Institute, with the complete recognition of that formerly obtained from Great Britain.

The MII national chairman, Mr Harry Wyer, said that it was intended to assist the Cork and Limerick branches while establishing further branches throughout the country. It was also proposed to create a marketing consultative panel, comprising of experts in their own field who would be available to give guidance to any member or member firm on a problem associated with marketing.

The Cork MII branch officers elected for 1971–72 were: Messrs F.E. James, chairman; W. Deegan, hon. secretary; T. Browne, hon. treasurer. The committee members were: Messrs D. Mahon Lee, D. Murphy and S. Foley, and the chairman of the students' society was Mr C.D. Seymour.

IRISH BANKING, JUNE 1971

Following his recent election as hon. secretary of the MII parent body, Mr Desmond Isle, group publicity manager of Allied Irish Banks, said that his appointment was a fine indication of confidence in the forward policies of Allied Irish and other Irish banks. He was speaking at an MII members' evening meeting.

Furthermore he said that in the past banks had not been noted for their marketing but orientation existed. A quiet revolution had taken place and banking institutions were among the leading exponents of marketing in Ireland. A new climate of keen competition existed, one in which developments would arise to benefit the customer.

MII COUNCIL MEETING, JUNE 1971

The newly elected council of MII met at 44, Lower Leeson Street, Dublin on Thursday 24 June 1971. The election of committee was announced:

Committee	Chairman	Company
Programme	D.I. Hogg	Mercantile Credit Co.
Graduate	E.B. Moore	Thos. Thompson & Co.
Conference	Nial Darragh	Aer Lingus
Membership	W. Connolly	DCA Product Marketing Ltd
Trade Convenors	D. Fitzgibbon	Auto Union Distributors
Awards	W.D. Fraser	North Dublin Growers Ltd
Finance	Ernest Kent	Ernest Kent & Co.
Reg. Development	L.V. Whitehead	Partitions & Ceilings Ltd
Student Education	P.R. Flood	School of Retail Distribution
Publicity	S. Walshe	Colorprint Ltd
Social	L.C. Thorn	Agent
Special Projects	P.A. Carroll	Philips Scott & Turner Ltd
EMC	Harry Woods	H. Williams & Co.

Education of MII members

Regarding the education of members, the chairman, Mr Harry Wyer, proposed that a committee be formed consisting of the of the programme conference, EMC, awards, graduates and traders' convenors' committees, to meet and consider education and a conference theme.

New management headquarters

Mr Harry Woods referred to a special offer concerning a certain new building proposition (a site for a nominal price) which would economically house the MII and other institutes, if they were willing to combine in and build such a management headquarters. He urged those present at the council meeting to consider this, as the lease on the present MII offices, at 44, Lower Leeson Street, would expire in about eighteen months.

HONORARY MEMBER OF MII

At the same meeting a proposal from the Cork regional branch of the Marketing Institute that Revd. Professor Peter Dempsey, OFM, Cap., be made an honorary member was approved unanimously. The formal proposal was made by Mr Joe Sandford and seconded by Mr Harry Woods.

EMC EXECUTIVE MEETING, AUGUST 1971

Present at the executive committee meeting of EMC in Amsterdam on 9 August 1971, were Mr Harry Woods, president, Dr Fred Witkamp, secretary-general, Mr Matti Ainamo, vice-president and Mr Rafael Lopez-Vivie, replacing Mr R. Camps Ubach, who, for health reasons, could not be present. Due to bereavement it was regretted, with sincere sympathy, that Mr Roy Randolph could not attend.

The president, Mr Harry Woods, presented and handed out a new roster of the Marketing Institute of Ireland membership. Amongst other items, the merger of International University Contact for Management Education (IUC) and the European Association of Management Training Centres (EAMTC) was discussed. The secretary-general said he would be present at the congress of IUC in Brno (Czechoslavakia) from 29 August to 2 September 1971.

Mr Woods explained again what led to his election. He also mentioned important contacts with Northern Ireland, which should also be of interest to EMC in the future.

A progress review and decisions of the many projects on hand was made. This included: 'Marketing Leaders in Europe' case studies. Spain had presented six in 1970 and would present ten in 1971. Examples in Spanish and English were provided.

It was decided to accentuate the importance of public relations activities, particularly with the European Economic Community (EEC), via EMC Belgian member contact.

It was desired to get together with the past-president, Mr Albert Brouwet and therefore, the next meeting would be in Brussels on 16 November 1971

LONDON DIAMOND JUBILEE DINNER, JULY 1971

In his dual capacity, as president of EMC and a Fellow of the UK Institute of Marketing, Mr Harry Woods had been a guest at the Diamond Jubilee Dinner in the London Hilton on 8 July 1971. As president of the EMC, he had accepted an invitation to be the Institute's guest speaker at a luncheon meeting on 8 March 1972, when the subject would be 'The Role of the European Marketing Council'.

The Institute of Marketing UK celebrated its Jubilee Year with the theme 'The World is Your Market'.

Programme of EMC president, August 1971

Stating it was his aim to continue and further the objects of EMC, through the executive committee, Mr Harry Woods outlined his programme, under the following headings:

1. Projects, 1–18, review, communication and encouragement (too lengthy to enumerate here).

2. European-American marketing seminar, each member country to be encouraged to participate.

3. Business meeting in Germany in 1972, plan programme.

4. Tenth European Marketing Congress, 1973. As reported in correspondence, an offer of certain sponsorship had been made to Mr Harry Woods by Mr Geoffrey Rowett, director and general manager, of *The Times* Newspapers Ltd, London. As president of EMC, Mr Woods had discussed this subsequently with Mr Ray Tarrant, national chairman of the Institute of Marketing, UK, who informed him that as result, the venue and standing of the congress would be upgraded.

5. Marketing Institute of Ireland: Mr Bill Fraser, immediate past-chairman of the Marketing Institute of Ireland had been appointed as spokesman delegate for the 1972 meeting at Nurnberg. The North of Ireland group of the Institute of Marketing had promised to send delegates.

6. Institute of Marketing, UK.

GOLD CHAIN OF OFFICE FOR EMC PRESIDENT

As president, Mr Harry Woods had accepted an offer of a gold chain of office, with the EMC logo on the medallion, to be presented by an Irish company. The chain would be inscribed with the past-president's name and year(s) of office and past-president's badges would also be provided. It would be the intention to have the gold chain and badges officially presented to the EMC at the AGM in Nurnberg in 1972.

MII'S OWN MARKETING EXAMINATIONS, SEPTEMBER 1971

The Marketing Institute of Ireland announced their first own programme of examinations for qualifications in marketing. Mr Philip Flood, chairman of the MII education committee, said that students had up to then, September 1971, sat for the examinations conducted by the Institute of Marketing, London.

MII had taken over the responsibility for a new two-tier four-year programme of examinations to be prepared in Ireland. A certificate in marketing would be awarded after completing parts 1 and 2. Students who completed parts 3 and 4 would receive a Graduateship of the Institute.

Arrangements had been made to introduce part 1, commencing immediately in various colleges. Part 1 comprised of marketing (including advertising and salesmanship), business organisation, principles of economics and elementary statistics. Part 2 comprised of marketing 2 (including market research), accounting, applied economics and commercial law. The latter would be introduced in September 1972, with the gradual phasing out of examinations for the Diploma in Marketing, awarded by the Institute of Marketing, London.

COMMON MARKET OR COMMON SENSE, OCTOBER 1971

The author of a 245-page volume, *Common Market or Common Sense*, was Mr Henry L. Wilson, a brother-in-law of Mr Joe Bigger FMII. It was published by De Vere Publications in 1971 and printed in Glasgow. Mr Wilson was well known as a writer and lecturer, having travelled throughout Europe, North America, the Middle East, North Africa and Scandinavia. He was also one of the survivors from the *Lakonia* shipping disaster in 1963.

In his analytical study of the Common Market, and its international effect on trade liberalisation and harmony, Mr Wilson made an important contribution to the public discussion on the European Economic Community that was going on at the time. He referred to Ireland's and Britain's possible entry into that community as having possible 'alleged benefits'.

Mr Wilson referred to Ireland as being an island with a small population and some of the best land in Europe. He said that it was a case of 'too much land and too few people'. While Irish farmers would benefit over a short period he felt, on balance, that he could not acclaim the EEC as an 'economic lifesaver' or recommend it as a viable long-term solution to Irish and British trade problems.

He detailed his evidence and findings, and mentioned that family life, as it was then, would in his opinion, disappear under the structure of continental government.

PRESENTATION OF MARKETING DIPLOMAS, NOVEMBER 1971

The Minister for Education, Mr Brian Faulkner TD, in addressing the Marketing Institute of Ireland at the presentation of diplomas and awards on 11 November 1971, stated that:

> Marketing is no longer confined to selling, but embraces skills in organising, distributing, sales promotion and advertising, production, purchasing, design, research and development, together with knowledge of business organisation, economics, accounting and law.

The minister complimented the Institute on its facilities and readiness for the EEC. He further said that the greatest need then was for high calibre people, well educated and experienced to undertake the responsibility of leadership in a complex and fast changing business world.

Mr Harry Wyer, chairman of MII, said that in the EEC marketing would play an even greater part in Irish business, not alone in the export field but also in the home market, where competition from associates within the community would increase. Absence of tariff barriers would not, in itself, generate sales so it would be up to MII members to ensure, by preparation, that they were ready for change.

The marketing awards and recipients were:

• Albright & Wilson Trophy: Daniel F.M. Lee, Cork (Student of the Year)

• Fogarty Advertising Trophy: Edmund Hayes, Mallow, Co. Cork (1st place, marketing)

• Adsell Trophy: Declan M.K. Bruen, Dublin (1st place, advertising)

• Market Research Bureau of Ireland Trophy: Raymond B.F. Behan, Dublin (1st place, marketing research)

LADIES'NIGHT, DECEMBER 1971

Toast of 'The Ladies' was ably made by the well-known Denis (Din-Joe) Fitzgibbon, at the outstanding Ladies' Night social function in the Shelbourne hotel in December 1971. Some100 company contributors provided the astounding tombola for the ladies, each receiving a wonderful box of gifts. However, it was mentioned that 'with a ticket for two costing £8.40, it must be one of the most expensive dinners of the year'.

IDEA-CONFERENCE, SWEDISH MARKETING FEDERATION, 1971

The 'Idea-Conference', organised by the Swedish Marketing Federation, was held in Stockholm from 11–14 October 1971. It was programmed as 'the considered most efficient way to be up-to-date with constant changes of marketing methods'.

Fifty-nine seminars were run over the three days (including selected duplication) of which twenty-four were in English or German language. Participants selected four different seminars. Here are the English titles and content summary of a few interesting ones:

1. 'Shop for Tomorrow' by Alcan (UK) Ltd, London, related to aluminium and increasing its use for shop-fronts. It included the marketing plan, results obtained and an example of a creative shop.

2. 'Advice against "TV Alcoholism"', an information campaign to increase people's activities at their leisure time.

3. 'TV Cassettes — their Coming of Age', by Gunnar Bergvall, planning manager at Esselte Bonnier, Stockholm. The latter gave a technical description of television cassettes and CATV. He described the development, marketing and competitive devices, and further explained new services offered such as electronic shopping and alarm systems.

On the final day of the conference a study programme took place. This included visits to the Swedish Farmers' Meat Marketing Association. It provided information about promotion of a brand called Scan (a common brand for the total product line) and visits to the Agricultural Experimental Kitchen.

In the afternoon a visit was made to ALFA-LAVAL, whose extensive production programme was divided into farming, thermal, dairy and industry, such as milking machines, separators, heat exchanges and pasteurisers, evaporators, hydraulic gears, etc.

EEC ENLARGEMENT STUDY, OCTOBER 1971

P.A Management Consultants proposed to carry out an extensive 'Study of Comparative Preparedness for an Enlarged EEC', for the European Marketing Council. PA offered to carry out the study concurrently in all the then EEC countries, plus Britain, Ireland, Spain, Denmark, Norway and Sweden.

The report showed that the economic advantages of an enlarged EEC would only be secured when the individual companies throughout the area took advantage, through marketing action, of the diminishing internal tariffs. Perfect understanding did not exist, at company level, of the consequences in two directions. Only a small percentage of European companies had become involved in written marketing plans, in physical and financial terms.

ACCESSION OF IRELAND TO THE EUROPEAN COMMUNITIES, JANUARY 1972

The Accession of Ireland to the European Communities was laid by the government before each House of the Oireachtas, in January 1972. The White Paper was published by the Stationery Office and the book form, priced at 25p, contained 214 pages.

Negotiations for the enlargement of the European Communities (EC) to include the four applicant countries, Ireland, UK, Denmark and Norway, resulted in the treaty being signed in Brussels on 22 January 1972. The Irish signatories were the Taoiseach, Mr Jack Lynch TD, and the Minister for Foreign Affairs, Dr P.J. Hillery TD.

On the same day, the Council of EC adopted a decision concerning the accession of the four applicant states to the European Coal and Steel Community. The treaty was subject to ratification by Ireland and the other signatory states, in accordance with their respective constitutional requirements. The council decision was subject to the deposit of instruments of accession by the four applicant states.

The purpose of the White Paper was, firstly, to put before the Oireachtas and the general public the outcome of the negotiations and the terms agreed and secondly, to give the government's assessment of accession on these terms.

In order to give widest dissemination of information, the Minister for Foreign Affairs, issued a booklet dealing with the terms of accession and the implications of membership. It was made available *free* of charge from post offices.

A supplement to the White Paper was issued in February 1972. It dealt with agriculture. In particular regarding animal health, certain important derogations were expressed to run for five years following accession. Trade between Ireland and the United Kingdom until 31 December 1977 was defined.

Fresh meat (beef and pigmeat) allowed Ireland, Norway and the United Kingdom, in respect of Northern Ireland, being authorised to retain their existing import controls, to guard against the introduction of foot and mouth disease. A sugar production quota was also agreed.

EFFECTS OF WHITE PAPER IN RELATION TO FARM PRODUCTS

Mr Harry Woods carried out an urgent analysis of the effects, relating to the operation of supermarkets, in particular for his employers, the H. Williams & Co. supermarket chain and F. Hafner & Co., meat and pork factory. Here is a brief summary:

Fruit and vegetables: common standards were set out, however, the aim was to keep products of unsatisfactory quality off the market. Specific grades were nominated. Regarding Irish apples and tomatoes, special arrangements were agreed.

Dairy produce and bacon: Irish dairy produce and bacon export subsidies and beef export guarantee payments would be replaced by the common pricing, market intervention and export subsidy arrangements of the common agricultural policy.

Marketing boards: Board Bainne and the Pigs' and Bacon Commission would have to shed their export monopolies for dairy products and pigmeat respectively. The Irish Potato Marketing Company would have to shed its monopoly position in respect of exports of seed.

Value added tax, 1972: the Community had adopted a uniform system of value added tax (VAT) thereby replacing the various forms of turnover tax.

Customs duty of a revenue nature, EEC Treaty: the EEC Treaty required that customs duties, designed to produce revenue, be eliminated, in the same way as protective duties.

Harmonisation of excise duties: as in the case of turnover tax, the Community proposed to harmonise the excise duties in operation in the European Community.

Company taxation: no measures had yet been adopted regarding income tax or taxation on companies.

Israel: the Preferential Trade Agreement between the Community and Israel had come into operation on 1 October 1970 and would last for a five-year period (up to 1975). Under the agreement, more than 85 per cent of all Israeli industrial products, which were liable to customs duties in the Community, would benefit from a tariff concession. That would build up to a 50 per cent tariff reduction (of which 30 per cent had been granted on 1 October 1970).

MOTIVATION MARKETING, FEBRUARY 1972

Mr Terry O'Sullivan wrote in his 'Dubliner's Diary' column of the *Evening Press* of 16 February 1972, that the previous evening he had listened to one who went 'from one aphorism to another, from one paradox to another, from one abstraction to some acid drop of a remark'. He was referring to Revd. Professor P.J. Dempsey, OFM Cap., author of two books, *Psychology for All*, and *Psychology of Satre*, and editor of the journal, *Manpower and Applied Psychology*. He was also a Fellow of the British Psychological Society, a Fellow of the Irish Psychological Society and a Fellow of the American Association for the Advancement of Science.

'With such an appalling load of millstones around his neck', Mr O'Sullivan stated, the lecturer proceeded to give the kind of entertainment that only a genius could achieve without effort. Revd. Professor Dempsey was addressing the MII members at the Shelbourne hotel (in the famed Room 116) and went on to say that in Ireland one needed less Marx and more marketing, and not a workless Republic. The poorest man in Dublin, he said, was better off than a professor in Moscow.

The report concluded by stating that it was as though the members of the Marketing Institute would have to admit to a rare sense of having their brains washed ... and all by a diffident man in a friar's habit who apparently rejected his notes with contempt and brought each one down to size.

HUMAN VALUES, FEBRUARY 1972

Dr J.F. Dempsey, president of MII, speaking at the President's Night dinner in the Shelbourne hotel in February 1972, stated that as a nation we had raised ourselves to higher standards of living in the last ten years, but that our progress must be based on values related to the requirements of human nature. He asked if the progress made during that decade had been purely mechanical as he felt that it had been measured by the wrong yard-sticks. He referred at length to the under-privileged, the mentally handicapped, the old people and so forth.

The Minister for Foreign Affairs, Dr Patrick Hillery TD, disputed the anti-marketeer case that our influence in the EEC, as a small member of the community, would be insufficient. It was his belief that if that were so then our influence as a small non member would be non-existent. It was clearly better to have a veto than have no vote at all.

Agricultural exports fall

Dr Hillery went on to recall that agricultural exports from Ireland to EEC countries had fallen from £12m. in 1965, when the EEC first began to charge levies on cattle and beef, to £2m. in 1970. He warned of an economic depression in Ireland, 'such as we have not seen in this country', if anything on that scale happened to our trade with Britain when they joined the community.

Fellowship awards

At the dinner Fellowships of the Marketing Institute were presented to:

- Mr Walter Connolly: vice-chairman of MII
- Mr Leslie Thorn: past-chairman
- Mr Edward James: past-chairman of the Cork regional branch.

Monumental News

In an article headed 'Monumental News' in February 1972, a report was given of a discussion with Mr Noel Lemass, son of Sean Lemass, which stated that Noel 'runs the Board of Works with an efficiency and drive that was frankly not expected of him'. It stated that Mr Noel Lemass had announced that up to the last count in Ireland, which was far from over, the Board had totted up 2.5 million pre-twelfth century ruins, lioses, forts, standing stones and a mass of archaeological treasure. When it was finished it was certain there would be enough national monuments to go round.

It was also reported that Mr Noel Lemass was trying to coax Irish Lights to yield up the Skelligs off the Kerry coast. He was also convinced that there was great tourist potential in the relics of the historic past, which could be considered to equal the more publicised splendours of Egypt.

The Stephen Doyle award for the late Mr Sean Lemass, February 1972

Dr Dempsey presented the Stephen Doyle Memorial award and replica to Mr Noel Lemass TD, parliamentary secretary to the Minister for Finance, who accepted it on behalf of the late Mr Sean Lemass TD, former president of the Marketing Institute of Ireland. The award was made particularly for his 'meritorious service to marketing' and was the first presentation of this award.

The chairman of MII, Mr Harry Wyer, gave a short oration and presented a citation. He recalled the achievements of the late Mr Sean Lemass in relation to the Institute, particularly during his four years of office as its president.

(The Stephen Doyle award was created in memory of Stephen, as a perpetual reminder of the continuous effort and work he had done, from the early days of his membership and committee involvement in the Incorporated Sales Managers' Association, up to his demise. He had, *inter alia*, travelled as aide-de-camp to Mr Harry Woods to the European Marketing Annual congresses, from the first Irish participation in Barcelona in 1964 and the following years to Milan, Paris, Oslo and Brussels. Stephen had always been most enthusiastic about helping students in their endeavours.)

EUROPEAN ODYSSEY, FEBRUARY 1972

An important conference of the Marketing Institute of Ireland was held at the Intercontinental hotel, Dublin on 22 February 1972. The theme of the conference was 'A European Odyssey — the Challenge to Irish Industry in European Trading Conditions'.

Dr Herbert Gross told the one hundred delegates at the conference that when Ireland entered the Common Market it would not be giving up its home market to ousiders rather it would get a new home market. Dr Gross, a lecturer in marketing at the University of Wurzburg and founder of *Handelssblatt*, the West German financial daily, said in order to be a good nationalist it was necessary to become a good internationalist. His speech was reported in the 'Business and Finance' page of *The Irish Times* on 23 February 1972.

Borrowing the late John F. Kennedy's words he stated 'we are living in an era of rising expectations'. Dr Gross went on to express the opinion that many companies in Europe were then looking for reliable foreign production sources to enable them to shift production away from home factories burdened with high wages and increasing labour shortages.

From his extensive research Dr Gross had many important points to make. Listed below are some of the main ones which I recall:

1. Irish industrial plants could relieve bottlenecks arising in Common Market (CM) industries, as there would have to be a shift to countries outside.

2. Mutual supply sources and export bases, including Ireland, would expand greatly within the CM. Such a multinational integration would become a continuous and ever-widening activity.

3. He suggested that Irish marketing strategy in Europe should be guided by three leading considerations:

    (a) the marketing of Irish brands

(b) co-operation with European manufacturers, wholesale, retail agencies, food brokers, etc.

(c) the provision of a workshop or export base for continental corporations anxious to shift part of their production to factories abroad.

Irish images and designs

Dr Gross stressed that the promotion of branded high quality Irish goods would be identified with Irish images and designs. People like to identify for example, Italian shoes, Danish furniture, French wine and Dutch vegetables.

He recommended the development of an 'Irish food basket', which should contain Guinness, whiskey, smoked salmon, lobster and other sea-food, meat and dairy products. In addition, an 'Irish week' displaying Irish food, retail chain buyers, (supermarkets, departmental stores and voluntary chains) should be considered. Cash and carry wholesalers, such as the famous 'Ratio' C & C markets, should organise special Irish shows, attracting retailers and caterers. He said 'Ratio' frequently organised Bulgarian, Danish and other national food expositions. The same should apply to textiles, home furnishings, glassware, pottery etc.

Wavin Pipes

Mr Frans van der Werff, managing director of Wavin Pipes, told the conference that all people desired a good standard of living, 'that meant education, motor cars, clothing, food and the like'. He referred to extremes, for example in the United States the income per head of population was twelve times higher than in Turkey. For Switzerland the figure was twice as high as in Italy. For Ireland the amount was less than half of that in Western Germany.

Again the percentage of working population in Ireland was only 30 per cent as against 50 per cent in the aforementioned countries. He felt that the industries which would be most interested in Ireland were in the chemical, electronic and engineering sectors.

Dr Thomas Walsh, director of An Foras Talúntais, while stressing that there was no satisfactory alternative to EEC entry, pointed out that an ability to adopt and take advantage of the opportunities offered would be important qualifications for the survival of individual industries. As an example, he cited the new price structures for agricultural raw materials which could have a fundamental effect on the economics of certain industries. Processed foods, whose raw material might be considerably more expensive, might no longer be competitive on some markets. Furthermore, if Irish beef prices rose to the EEC level, he believed it might no longer be appropriate to export beef to the US.

SCHOOL DEBATE ON EEC, FEBRUARY 1972

At a 600 strong Dublin students' EEC meeting, participants were encouraged to ask 'awkward' questions regarding EEC entry. They were attending an unusual education adventure in the Drimnagh Parish Hall, which was organised by senior economics students at the 350 pupil Our Lady of Good Counsel secondary school, Mourne Road, run by the Sisters of Mercy.

Guidance had been given by a teacher, Mr Hugh Mulrooney, in planning the debate and in inviting pupils from many other city schools. In welcoming those present, one of the pupils, Patricia Burke, Mourne Road, said that the convent had 'never expected so many participants'. She then introduced the four political speakers: Senator Neville Keery (FF), Mr Michael Sweetman (FG), Mr Justin Keating (Labour) and Mr Tony Heffernan (SF Gardiner Place). Each speaker was allowed a few minutes talk, after which the question and answer session began.

Another pupil, Deirdre Cray, Our Lady of Good Counsel School, wanted to know if the four members of her family in the motor assembly business should get out of it, in view of the proposed Common Market membership. Mr Sweetman, who was also chairman of the Irish Council of the European Movement, replied stating that protection was guaranteed for the industry up to 1985, but even after that, there need not be any undue worry as the country could specialise in particular sections of the car business.

Regarding voting matters, an assurance was given to David Mullins, a pupil from one of the local secondary schools, that Ireland would not be swamped by Italy, France and Germany, as he had inferred from a section of the Treaty of Rome.

Senator Keery told Antoinette Hickey that the government's concern for redundant workers was shown by their educational programme which was geared towards EEC requirement. Anco, the industrial training authority, had recently opened its biggest training centre in Ballyfermot, Dublin, and the Regional Technical Colleges would turn out the kind of technicians the Common Market needed.

Mr Mulrooney was of the opinion that whether or not Ireland went into the Common Market, her future was assured with the type and calibre of young people that they had in the country.

GALWAY IFA MEETING, FEBRUARY 1972

In the opinion of Mr T.J. Maher, president of the Irish Farmers' Association, 'time was rapidly running out' for the western areas of Ireland. He was addressing a meeting in Galway and also stated that the absence of a well thought out development programme would mean that funds available from the EEC for such purpose would go to other countries and not to Ireland. Mr Maher added that all the money spent on research was wasted unless we were prepared to take action on the information produced by the research.

MARKETING AND RESEARCH SEMINAR, MAY 1972

The Market Research Bureau of Ireland (MRBI) held its tenth anniversary seminar, 'Marketing and Research' in May 1972. Legally incorporated in April 1962, it was the first Irish owned market research company to be set up.

Analysing and presenting the results of Córas Iompair Éireann's (CIE) 'Great Train Robbery', Mr Sean J. White, public relations and publicity manager of CIE, stressed that 'using market research was at least a third of the battle already won. Mounting any marketing campaign without market research is like going into a boxing ring blindfold, with one hand tied behind your back'.

The seminar, held at the Intercontinental hotel, was attended by an audience of 200 executives from the public and private sectors of industry. It was presided over by Mr T.J. Garvey, general manager of Córas Tráchtála. Mr Garvey stated that the range of market research services available in Ireland was instanced in the three cases presented at the seminar. Cases had been chosen out of the hundreds that MRBI Ltd had worked on over the ten years of its existence. The three cases presented were:

- a public transport company, (CIE), experimenting with a reduced price structure in the test market area as if it were a supermarket

- a religious order ascertaining its corporate image, as if it were a business, for its own spiritual ends

- a supermarket chain using research to obtain a profile of its customers as a basis for promotional strategy.

The basic problems in each case were outlined personally by the clients and the three studies were presented by Mr Jack J. Jones MMII and Miss Áine O'Donoghue of MRBI Ltd. The cases were reviewed by an independent panel of marketing specialists. This included Mr A. Cook, marketing administration, University College, Dublin and Mr J.P. McMahon, managing director of Munster Chipboard Ltd.

Revd. F. Sheridan CSSp stated that Vatican 2 not only changed the whole environment of the Catholic Church but it also required religious orders to examine their own roles relative to the spirit of the founders. To define ourselves we had to determine whether we were primarily seen in a missionary or educational role. He felt an objective answer could only be obtained by a corporate image survey conducted by an independent company like MRBI.

Mr Feargal Quinn, managing director of Superquinn Ltd described the customer characterisation survey which his company had commissioned. He told those present that 'it has a twofold effect, telling us not only the type of people who use our stores but it also supplied us with positive points to use in our advertising and promotional campaigns'.

In conclusion Mr Jack Jones said that market research was not a substitute but a basis for decision taking in management.

PRESENTATION OF GOLD CHAIN OF OFFICE, JUNE 1972

The *Evening Herald* of Wednesday 7 June 1972 displayed a picture of the presentation of a gold chain of office to Mr Harry V. Woods FMII, F.Inst.M., the first Irish president of the European Marketing Council.

The reception and presentation took place at the new Burlington hotel in Dublin and was hosted by Mr Aubrey Fogarty, managing director of Fogarty Advertising. Those present included Mr John D. Carroll, chairman, and executive members of MII, the Prior of Mr Woods' alma mater, Terenure College, and the press.

It had been Mr Fogarty's idea to create a marketing chain for Europe. It incorporated Connemara marble in the base setting of each link. A link was inscribed 'Harry Woods, MII, Ireland, 1971–72', while the medallion bore the large initials 'EMC' in the logo. Individual links were also provided for future presentation to past-presidents. *Business & Finance* magazine reported that the presentation was made on the completion of Mr Woods's year of office as EMC president after many years association with the Marketing Institute of Ireland. He would, in turn, present the chain to his successor at the European Marketing Council meeting in Nuremberg on Saturday 10 June 1972. It reported that the strength of the EMC could be seen from its membership in thirteen countries. In Germany alone there were 22 marketing clubs, comprising 3,200 members.

EUROPEAN MARKETING COUNCIL, JUNE 1972

The AGM of the European Marketing Council was held in Nuremberg, Germany on 10 June 1972 at the Carlton hotel. It was chaired by myself (Mr Harry Woods) as president of EMC. It was a pleasure to have the support of the Irish delegation comprising Messrs Bill Fraser, Aubrey Fogarty and Mike Mitchell, among the many delegates. Souvenir copies of a special brochure prepared in Ireland (sponsored by Interprint) were made available to all delegates.

During my year of office I had attended executive EMC meetings in Europe and represented the council at the Europa hotel in Belfast at the Institute of Marketing annual dinner. In the discharge of many duties, and procedure, I was particularly pleased to formally accept, from Mr Aubrey Fogarty FMII, the magnificient chain of office for the presidency of EMC.

The chain, designed by Mr Fogarty's company, was a combination of Irish gold and Connemara marble and depicted the rich traditions of Irish creativity and Ireland's links with the continent. It would be worn at all future formal occasions at which EMC were represented. The exceptional generosity of Mr Aubrey Fogarty was greatly acclaimed by all present.

It was agreed to accept the Irish proposal to organise a European Marketing Congress to be held in Dublin in 1977.

EMC gold chain presented to Finland

Mr Matti Ainamo of the Finnish Marketing Executive Group, Markkinointijohdon Ryhma, became the new EMC president for 1972–73. The EMC chain of office was formally handed over by me to Mr Matti Ainamo, who then presented me with a past-presidents' link. I had previously presented Mr Albert Brouwet of Belgium (my predecessor and first president under the constitution) with his well-earned similar link.

NEW APPOINTMENTS OF MII, 1972

Mr John d'Arcy Carroll MMII, was elected chairman of the Marketing Institute of Ireland and took office from 9 June 1972. In his speech he referred to the unfortunate situation in Northern Ireland in recent years and the inability of people abroad to accept the situation differently in the Republic. He reminded members that over six million people 'over-flew' Ireland every year, between October and February and wondered how we could attract them to stop over, even for a night, and show them that Irish hospitality had not changed. The Dutch, he said, had the theme 'use Holland to visit other areas', and perhaps that was the theme to adopt and show the world the peace and tranquility of Irish life.

His second point concerned the slowing down of Ireland's economy. This, he said, had been crippled by a number of industrial strikes in the last couple of years. With European Community membership then a fact, exporters had to have the freedom to negotiate abroad, knowing that they could deliver on time and at the price quoted.

Dr J.F. Dempsey agreed to a second term as president, which was sincerely appreciated. Other officers and council elected for 1972–73 were:

- Vice-Chairmen: Messrs Leslie Whitehead, Sales Advisory Services Ltd, Mr Walter Connolly, DCS Product Marketing Ltd and Mr Nial Darragh, Aer Lingus

- Hon. Treasurer: Mr P.J. McLoughlin, Australian Embassy

- Hon. Secretary: Mr Joseph W. Sandford, National Engineering Ltd

- Council: Messrs T.J. Barry, T.A. Brady, A.F. Corduff, D.J. Fitzgibbon, P.R. Flood, A.N. Fogarty, W.D. Fraser, D. Hogg, D.E. Isle, R.I. Joyce, Mahon Lee, J.A. McCarroll, E.B. Moore, R.G. Tennant, L.C. Thorn, H.V. Woods and H.A. Wyer

- Chief Executive: Mr Joseph C. Bigger

- Auditors: Butler Chance & Co.

- Solicitors: Moran & Ryan.

MARKETING INSTITUTE COLLEAGUES LOSE LIVES IN LONDON AIR DISASTER OF JUNE, 1972

It was with deepest shock, and sympathy for the relatives and friends, to learn of the tragic London air disaster of 18 June 1972. A group of Irish industrialists, including members of the Marketing Institute of Ireland, were en route to an important meeting in Brussels when the *Trident* aircraft crash-landed, killing many on board. Those representing the Confederation of Irish Industries who lost their lives included their president, director general, council members and staff.

Mr Melville (Sandy) Miller MMII, then managing-director of Rowntree Mackintosh, Ireland (formerly of *The Irish Times*) and Mr Guy Jackson MMII, Guinness Group, past council members of the Marketing Institute, were sadly amongst the deceased.

Mr John Carroll, chairman of MII stated that the Marketing Institute of Ireland would be the poorer with the passing of these gentlemen and their colleagues. Further, he said, in all of his twenty-five years of association with the business world, he could not remember receiving such a shock as that of the tragic news of the loss of so many friends. The Institute offices, and many others, were closed all day on Tuesday 20 June 1972, as a mark of respect to the bereaved wives and families.

Other tributes were given by: Mr T.J. Maher, president of the Irish Farmers' Association; Mr James O'Keeffe, president of the Irish Creamery Milk Suppliers' Association; Mr Robert Nolan, president of the Electrical Industries' Federation; Mr J.B. O'Connell, secretary of the Dublin Chamber of Commerce; Mr John C. Farrell, secretary of Drogheda Chamber of Commerce; Mr Michael Waldron, president of Newbridge Chamber of Commerce; Mr Louis Smith, UCD, former chairman of the European Movement and Mr G.P.S. Hogan, chairman of Irish Steel Holdings Ltd.

MARKETING INSTITUTE'S UPSURGE IN STATURE, JUNE 1972

In a leading article on 22 June 1972 in *Business & Finance* magazine it was reported that the Marketing Institute was one of the most recently established bodies in the sphere of Irish commerce which enjoyed an upsurge in both its membership and public profile of late. It further stated that:

> The success of the activities of the Institute was fairly quantified in the election of one of its members to the position of President of the European Marketing Council. Additionally the Institute announced the formal implementation of its own four-year programme of examinations for students in Ireland.
>
> The recognition of the Irish qualifications, being an acceptable equivalent by the British Institute, is certainly something of which the Irish members can be justifibly proud. There are quite a few other Institutes, in various spheres of commercial and business activity, which have failed to convince their British counterparts of the adequacy of their educational programme.

MARKETING SOCIETY DINNER, JUNE 1972

The second annual dinner of the Marketing Society was held in June 1972. The guest speaker was Mr Nicholas Leonard of *Business & Finance* magazine. The chairman, Mr John M. Lepere MMII, welcomed members and guests, including Mr Harry Wyer MMII, chairman of the Marketing Institute of Ireland.

MQ SYSTEMS, JUNE 1972

Ireland's computer bureau industry was increased by one, with the introduction of MQ Systems. It claimed to be a company with a difference. It was reported that apart from normal bureau facilities it would also design, implement, review and re-organise clerical procedures in any organisation without committing it to a computer bureau.

INDUSTRY OFFERED HELP, JUNE 1972

Following an MII council meeting on 28 June 1972, Mr John Carroll, chairman, stated that members must create an atmosphere to encourage industries to look to the Institute for help in establishing marketing systems as good as the Europeans. Home markets were exposed to international competition, hence industry needed assistance to rationalise marketing procedures.

From January 1973, Irish marketers would become students in Europe and it would be many years before graduating. If one worked hard, however, industry would be able to meet European competition. He finished up by stressing the need to work hard like the rest of Europe and if that meant starting at 7 a.m. so be it. It was the aim, he said, to persuade Ireland's best businessmen to represent us in European trading relations.

MARKETING BODIES TO JOIN FORCES?, JUNE 1972

In the business and finance feature page of *The Irish Times* Mr Con Power referred to a meeting, the previous night, 28 June 1972, of the MII Council. This had been chaired by Mr John Carroll who said the possibility of a 'united' marketing front was mooted. It was an obvious reference to the Marketing Society.

The Marketing Society which had been formed in November 1970, the successor of the Marketing Research Society of Ireland, was stated to have a current membership of approximately 60 corporate and 115 individual members. The amalgamation did not, however, take place.

CORK SEEKS MARKETING COURSE, JUNE 1972

Mr Mahon Lee, chairman of the Cork branch of the Marketing Institute, made an appeal for a 'better deal' for marketing as a part of university training. He was supporting the remarks made on the previous Tuesday of 27 June 1972 by the president of University College, Cork, Dr Donal McCarthy.

At that time there were 40 students attending the College of Commerce in Cork taking the marketing diploma. From studies he had made in the Commerce Faculty of UCC, however, he believed that it was important to have marketing included as a subject on the Commerce course. Later he would hope to see a Chair of Commerce included in the structure of UCC.

CASE STUDY OF GERMAN BREWERY, JULY 1972

On Saturday 1 July 1972, a day-long seminar was held for MII students. It took the form of a competition among the participants, who were split up into ten working syndicates. At the morning plenary session the various groups were given details of a case study of a German brewery faced with some important marketing decisions. Each team had to present a brief to an adjudicating panel.

The marketing decisions were based on the introduction of a table beer, a premium beer, and finally the situation which presented itself, after such decisions had been made. Each team had to explain, in its final report, the marketing and financial implication of their decisions.

The panel included: Dr Tony Cunningham, Economics Department UCD, Mr Colm Lyons, general manager of SPAR, Mr Frank O'Neill general manager of Bristol Meyers and Mr John Murray also of UCD.

Prizes for the winning syndicate were presented by the guest speaker of the evening, Mr Charles Haughey TD.

The executive committee of the students' society were the organisers of the seminar. They were: Messrs F. McDermott, M. Kennedy, F. Garland, P. Geoghegan, T. Comerford, F. Pfeiffer, G. Deegan and A. Murray.

PRACTICAL MARKETING EDUCATION, AUGUST 1972

Members of the Marketing Institute were given a special address by Mr J.J. Sweeney, B.Sc., Marketing Department of Red River Community College, Manitoba, USA. He spoke on the subject: 'Practical Marketing Education', and provided some interesting innuendos, at the Intercontinental hotel on the evening of 3 August 1972. A lively question and answer session ensued.

MARKETING EXAMINATION AWARDS, SEPTEMBER 1972

Dr T.P. O'Raifteartaigh, chairman of the Higher Education Authority, presented the awards, in Dublin, to 21 successful students of the 1971 diploma examinations of the Marketing Institute.

Speaking at the presentation, he said the importance of marketing in industry was too often lost sight of. Production was always stressed but without marketing, production would soon stop.

The awards were as follows:

- Albright & Wilson award: Mr Kenneth Andrew McCullagh, Dublin (Student of the Year)

- Aubrey Fogarty Associates award: Mr Richard C.G. James, Cambridgeshire (Best Marketing Student)

- Market Research Bureau of Ireland award: Mr Frederick P. Whelan, Dublin (Best Marketing Research Student)

- Adsell award: Mr Thomas J. Murphy, Cork (Best Student in Advertising).

A diploma was awarded to the above and to a further seventeen students. These included: Messrs K.P. Barry, P.B. Behan, G.W. Burgess, B. Conway, M. Cunningham, J. Duffy, J.A. Goss, L.A.B. Flynn, L.M. Hughes, M.F. Killeen, M.T. McKenna, P.J. Mulrooney, D.J. Murphy, W.F. O'Byrne, O. O'Sullivan, B.C. O'Toole and D.W. Townsend.

Mr Kenneth McCullagh of Ballinteer Road, Dublin, had a distinction in six of the seven subjects and obtained an average of 86 per cent overall. He was then employed in British Leyland.

LIMERICK BRANCH OF MII, SEPTEMBER 1972

The Limerick branch of MII announced that its winter programme would commence on Wednesday 11 October 1972, at Plassey House. The initial lecture was to be: 'Marketing in the Mid-West region — A Newcomer's View'. It was to be given by Professor Roy Hayhurst, who as senior lecturer, was in charge of business studies at the new National Institute for Higher Education in Limerick.

On Thursday 26 October 1972, Mr Peter Needham, general manager of Livestock and Meat Commission, would address the Limerick MII members on the subject of the marketing drive for the sale of Irish meat in Great Britain.

Mr Bob Chalker, United States Chamber of Commerce in Ireland, was to give a talk on the relative marketing problems in the US and in Ireland at the 30 November 1972 meeting.

NEW MII HEADQUARTERS, NOVEMBER 1972

On 13 November 1972 the MII moved to new headquarters at 73, Orwell Road, Rathgar, Dublin 6.

BASIC MARKETING, DECEMBER 1972

Mr Peter Blood, director of the Institute of Marketing in Britain, told a marketing Institute luncheon meeting in Dublin on 1 December 1972, that if manufacturers would adhere to the basic tenets of marketing, then 'consumerism', as the militant expression of dissatisfied customers, could not and would not exist today.

Sir John Peck, British Ambassador to Ireland, was a guest at the luncheon attended by the president of MII, Dr J.F. Dempsey, chairman, Mr John D. Carroll and a large number of members and guests.

LADIES' NIGHT, MII, DECEMBER 1972

The Ladies' Night function was held on Friday 8 December 1972 at the Burlington hotel, Dublin. The social evening, with a gathering of 800 people, was reported fully in *Tatler's Social Round*. Mr Leslie Thorn, social chairman, recalled the very first evening that was held at Aspro on the Naas Road, twenty-five years previously.

Mr Thorn said that over the years the entertainment had included dancing girls, pipe bands, trumpeters and cabaret acts of all types. He also recalled the 'Two Leslies' act — Mr Leslie Whitehead and himself in a double miming act which lasted for several yearly events! It had featured himself playing the xylophone and violin to cover periods when the 'other Leslie' had to change costumes.

Chrysler SIMCA prize, December 1972

For the first time at Ladies' Night the top draw prize was a Chrysler car, a Simca 1000 L.S. It was won by Mrs W.J. O'Toole, wife of the group brand manager of Irish Biscuits Ltd. The keys were presented to her by Mr Malcolm Freshney MMII, managing director of Chrysler Ireland. All proceeds of the raffle were in aid of the Institute development and benevolent fund.

CHILDREN'S PARTY, DECEMBER 1972

The annual Christmas party for MII members' children, always a sell-out, was held at the Zoological Gardens, Phoenix Park, Dublin, in December 1972.

TRADE CONVENOR'S COMMITTEE, DECEMBER 1972

A special committee was formed with Mr Thomas J. Barry as chairman, termed the 'Trade Convenor's Committee', to promote the image of the Institute.

It was necessary to make it evident that the MII was well aware of the marketing problems confronting the economy as a whole, and was actively engaged in attempting to find solutions to them, with particular reference to entry into the EEC.

CORK REGIONAL BRANCH OF MII, DECEMBER 1972

In a review of the calendar year, the Cork regional chairman, Mr Mahon Lee MMII, reported an increase in their membership from 28 senior members to 42. That was the result of important communication between the Chamber of Commerce, Trade Union movement, other professional bodies, University College, Cork and senior school authorities and students.

On the Cork student front, it was gratifying to recall successes in the May 1972 examinations. In particular Mr John P. Cowman was congratulated for having three excellent papers and achieving a wonderful standard.

Also, enough students had registered to form a second year class, in addition to the existing first year class, at the Cork College of Commerce.

DO MARKETING EXPERTS FUNK REAL ISSUES?

What marketing man could fail to have his curiosity aroused by the headline 'Do Marketing Experts Funk the Real Issues? This was the comment of Mr Michael McDevitt MMII, Marketing Executive of the CIE (Transport) outdoor advertising department.

The author, Mr Maurice Vassie, put forward the premise that marketing theory, as it then stood, funked the issues. It suggested no definite courses of action, with the result that the marketing statistics commercially available were no more than records of the effects of hedging ones bets.

To Mr Michael McDevitt that meant that a terribly naive suggestion, somewhat akin to saying that marketing experts, per se, could never make mistakes, or conversely that being marketing experts, and therefore presumably infallible, they should always take such carefully calculated decisions, as to invariably come out on top. Mr McDevitt stated that to him that was 'sheer and utter nonsense'.

Marketing was a highly speculative enterprise, operating in a world of uncertainty. It faced ever-intensifying competition and it was absolutely essential that all progressive companies wishing to survive had to forge and formulate new and dynamic marketing strategies. One had to think in terms of concentrating on a particular product market. Mr McDevitt concluded by saying that it related to the characteristics of the buyers and potential buyers for such product(s).

Worldwide Marketing

The Marketing Institute's honorary member, Professor Anthony C. Cunningham of UCD was referred to by Mr McDevitt as being 'a veritable gold mine of knowledge'. The professor's book, *Worldwide Marketing,* was to be published shortly. Its chapter on 'The Marketing Scene' in particular was said to contain a crystallisation of every single facet necessary for any would-be marketer in Ireland.

While it was known that the population of the Republic of Ireland was then approaching three million inhabitants, it was not realised that, despite a 50 per cent lower per capita income than most industrialised western European countries, the Republic was rated among the 30 richest nations in the world.

Dr Cunningham by no means suggested complacency but adumbrated that, despite the vast improvements in overall economy in the previous decade, Ireland would have to move into top gear, if she was to seriously catch up with the fantastic economic growth in western Europe.

MARKETING TOPICS PROMOTION, JANUARY 1973

The Irish Times announced a series of meetings to be held in the library of the Kildare Street club from 6–8 p.m. These were to commence on Monday 15 January 1973. Everyone who was interested would be welcome whether they were a member of the Marketing Institute or not.

It was announced that the first meeting, 15 January 1973, would be addressed by Mr E.A. Goulding, managing director of Irish Pensions Trust. He was to speak about new legislation in pensions and the prospects of the transferability of pension rights.

On Tuesday, 30 January the first subject was to be: 'What Are the Added Values of Languages?' The speakers would be Dr W.A. Ryan (who had represented Ireland on an EEC committee for general medical practice) and Mr Franz Isemann of the German Culture Institute, Dublin. In addition Mr Steen Jensen of G.M. Foss Electrical (Ireland) Ltd was to speak on: 'Selling Danish Creamery Equipment to Ireland'.

On Monday, 12 February Mr Martin Rafferty, Belvedere Trust, was to speak on the topic of: 'The Role of Finance Companies in the Modern Business Context'. On Tuesday February 20, Mr Michael O'Keefe, managing director of Motor Manufacturers Ltd along with his colleague, Mr D.J. Fitzgibbon MMII, would be discussing: 'The Future for Assembly Industries in Ireland'. On Monday, 12 March Mr Bob Clarke, personnel manager of the Brooks Thomas Group, was due to give his views on: 'The Relevance of Personnel Management to Marketing'. Finally, on Monday 9 April, a 'free-for-all forum' would take place as a finale in this series of 'talk-abouts' with four guest panellists, each to fight his own corner. The guest panellists were:

• marketing: Mr Richard Pollard, Jeyes

• selling: Mr Tony Woodhouse, Albright & Wilson

• production: Mr Terence O'Sullivan, Rowntree Mackintosh

• distribution: to be named later.

PRESIDENT'S DINNER, FEBRUARY 1973

The social occasion of the night of 15 February 1973 set in a thrilling setting as though in an Austrian or Bavarian valley, was that of the president's dinner of the Marketing Institute of Ireland. This was how Mr Terry O'Sullivan described it in his column 'Dubliner's Diary' in the *Evening Press*. He went on further to describe that:

> a still moon was shining on the snow white slopes of the Opperman Country Club, Enniskerry, County Dublin, while the cars of all the

best known names in the wonderful world of salesmanship, crunched over the snow and frozen sleet, and carefully prepared for an elegant night.

Mr O'Sullivan referred to the fact that the 130 men who came to dinner included 'almost the entire diplomatic community' and the of all the leading professional bodies — the top brass of the Marketing Institute. He went on to say that the Institute sustained a most elegant information and training centre at 73, Orwell Road, Rathgar, Dublin 6 and described the Institute president, Dr J.F. Dempsey, as slim, elegant and though retired, youthful looking.

ICTU concern about Common Market

The principal speaker at the dinner, Mr Stephen McGonagle, president of the Irish Congress of Trade Unions, (ICTU), said that though they had opposed entry into the Common Market, they had accepted the people's overwhelming vote for EEC membership. The policy of the ICTU was not one of sudden and unexplained acquiescence. It was one of participation, because it was better to participate than to sulk in the corner. However, participation would be both militant and critical.

The Irish Times reported that Mr McGonagle had stated that the ICTU would especially direct itself among the people in Europe against those who represented the dominance of capital over the rights of labour; the power of bureaucratic decision-making over democratic procedures; and the priority of monetary and economic integration over social welfare and regional amelioration.

Mr McGonagle went on to inform those present of the ICTU's concern in relation to the harsh effects that free trade would have on employment in large traditional non-growth industries. He stated that the ICTU was concerned about the lack of democracy and social movement in the Common Market.

He added that full employment meant not only providing job opportunities for some 80,000 unemployed individuals, but also for those made redundant in 'lame duck' industries. In conclusion he stated that the key for Ireland was in closing the technological gap between this country and the European mainland.

THE STEPHEN DOYLE AWARD TO MR HARRY WOODS, FEBRUARY 1973

The awards committee, chaired by Mr W.D. (Bill) Fraser, announced the unanimous nomination of Mr Harry Woods FMII, for the Stephen Doyle award for 1972.

The presentation citation stated that Mr Woods was chosen for his contribution to marketing in Ireland, in many spheres, since the foundation of the Institute and particularly for his recent achievement in becoming president of the European Marketing Council (EMC), on which he had held executive office, continuously at quarterly meetings, since 1964.

The chairman, Mr John D. Carroll, said that Mr Woods had concluded his year of office as president of EMC, 'with a flourish, while the many tributes paid, made him (John), realise just how well Mr Woods had projected the image of the Marketing Institute of Ireland abroad.

Mr David Frame, chairman of Hammond Holdings, a past-president of the Institute of Marketing and Sales Management, and Mr Archie McCullough, chairman of the Institute of Marketing, Northern Ireland, were amongst the guests at the dinner.

Dr Dempsey, president of the Institute, referring to the EEC, said that the members of the Institute should aim at not being secondhand or reflected in their attitudes, but original in the sense meant by Carlyle when he said: 'The essence of originality is not novelty but sincerity'.

INTO EUROPE, FEBRUARY 1973

The *Belfast Telegraph* reported on a meeting in Dublin in February 1973, held mainly to discuss the marketing strategy 'Into Europe'. It was inevitable that, if Ireland was to increase or even maintain its foothold in the British food market, more and more emphasis would have to be placed on marketing strategy. This was highlighted by Mr Peter Blood, director general of the Institute of Marketing, London. The British Ambassador, Mr Victor Chambers, Ulster Bank Ltd, Mr Harry Woods, past-president of the European Marketing Council and Mr John McCormack of John Thompson & Sons Ltd, Belfast, were amongst those who contributed to the discussion findings.

ADVANCED MARKETING COURSE, MARCH 1973

According to the cover story of *Business & Finance* (5 April 1973) entitled 'Marketing: The Irish Advance on Harvard', membership of the EEC had prompted many professional organisations, as well as firms, to assess their strengths in the context of a market larger than that of the United States. It stated that the Marketing Institute of Ireland had pulled off quite a 'coup' by organising an advanced marketing course for 73 top Irish executives in the birthplace of the marketing concept, Cambridge, Massachusetts, which harbours Harvard University. The training programme of the Harvard course covered the period 16–22 March 1973. Mr James Milton, editor of *Business & Finance,* accompanied the participants and fully reported on the course and the use of the case study method.

The party included fifteen managing directors, two chairmen, sixteen sales directors, ten general managers and over twenty managers (marketing, sales, advertising etc.). Among the participants were:

- Mary Crotty: public relations officer, Jury's Hotel Group
- Tony Corduff: sales director, National Board & Paper Mills
- Peter J. Gleeson: sales director, Castle Hosiery Co.
- D.J. Fitzgibbon: managing-director, Auto Union Distributors
- Kevin A. Murphy: director, Shell Composites (Ireland) Ltd
- H.A. Wyer: director, Armstrong Cork (Ireland) Ltd
- Finan Blair: marketing manager, Roadstone Concrete
- Bill Fraser: general manager, North Dublin Growers
- R.L.T. Hudson: sales controller, Irish Dunlop Co.
- Michael Coote: chairman, Coote Group
- Roderic O'Shea: sales engineer, Coote Group
- Dermot Larkin: Young Advertising
- Neville O'Connell: retail manager, Irish Sugar Company
- Peadar Pierce: sales group head of RTÉ
- J. Pollock: sales manager, Carreras of Northern Ireland.
- Mahon Lee: chairman, Cork Group MII and three of their members.

Ms Mary Crotty of Jurys had the distinction of being the only Irish lady on the course.

Mr James Milton of *Business & Finance* reported that against the backdrop of St Patrick's Day, in Boston, with its green beer, green plastic bowler hats and large black gentlemen wearing badges with the invitation 'Kiss me I'm Irish', more than 70 sons of Erin, who actually hailed from the fair land of Ireland, sat down in a hotel across the common from Harvard University, to start an intensive training course, organised by the Marketing Institute of Ireland.

PROFESSORSHIP OF MARKETING, APRIL 1973

In April 1973 P.J. Carroll & Company bequeathed a professorship of marketing to University College, Dublin, to be attached to the Faculty of Commerce. The endowment was valued at £35,000.

Mr J.H. Ryan, managing director of Carroll announced the move saying that his company was conscious of the importance of a marketing approach, if as a country we were to avail fully of the opportunities of larger markets created by the EEC.

LANGUAGE BOOM, APRIL 1973

A report of the British Institute of Management advised that language courses having been fully booked from November 1972, created a rush of businessmen to learn foreign languages. British firms had suddenly realised that the EEC was upon them, and panicked. Since Britain entered the Common Market, language demand increased rapidly for French, German and to a lesser degree, Spanish. The difficulty was to find teachers.

In Japan it was reported that 56,000 businessmen students, were 'grinding away' at English language courses, one of which comprised of some 50 hours a week over a six-week training period. Generally these courses were expensive. One of the Tokyo-based language schools cost $1,200 while the Berlitz fee was £847 in London, compared to $2,000 in the United States.

NEW JURY'S HOTEL, APRIL 1973

On the return of the delegates from the advanced marketing training course in the school of business studies, in Harvard Boston, a reception and reunion was held on Wednesday 18 April 1973 in the new Jury's hotel in Ballsbridge, Dublin.

The chairman of the Institute of Marketing, Northern Ireland, Mr Leslie Kyles, and Mr R.G.D. Heather, marketing operations manager of Irish Distillers, were received by Mr John D. Carroll, chairman of the Marketing Institute of Ireland. Other guests included Mr Harry Percival, sales manager of Clarnico-Murray Ltd and Mr Con Murphy, sales manager of Avis. Mr Terry O'Sullivan, in his column, 'Dubliner's Diary', wrote that 'it was a happy thing to have Mr Leslie Kyles of Belfast present these days so finding that professional links still existed between north and south'.

ANNUAL MII MEMBERS' GOLF OUTING, MAY 1973

The annual MII members' golf outing took place at Woodbrook in May 1973. It broke yet another record in relation to the numbers participating, the prizes and evening dinner. Undoubtedly the success was due to the untiring efforts of Mr Norman McConnell who, once again, had organised everything in his own inimitable manner.

The Chairman's Prize and the Ingersoll Challenge Cup (courtesy of Mr

Henry Spring, MMII) was presented by Mr Walter Connolly, vice-chairman of MII, to the overall winner, Mr Hugh O'Donnell of O'Keeffes Advertising.

MR JIM MCCARROLL FMII, HONOURED, MAY 1973

It was gratifying to learn that Mr Jim McCarroll FMII had been elected president of the N.I. Wholesale Merchants and Manufacturers Association Ltd at their seventy-eighth AGM in Belfast. Mr McCarroll had been a most enthusiastic MII supporter, over many years, and an attender at MII council and member meetings in Dublin. He had just previously been appointed president of the National Federation of Wholesale Grocers and Provision Merchants. The managing director of Tobacco Sales Ltd, Mr McCarroll was then a member of the board of the Gallagher Wholesale division.

SHOCK FOR THE BOSSES, MAY 1973

In Colm Rapple's, business report headed 'Shock for the Bosses on Way' in the *Irish Independent* of 4 May 1973 a study of Irish Management was outlined.

The Irish Management Institute chairman, Mr R.S. Nesbitt of Arnott, had told a gathering of the country's top managers in Killarney, at the conference opening the dinner the previous night, that a major research project to get some hard data on the then state of Irish management was being undertaken. The results would be available to everyone, even critics, even though it would not be a cosy report.

This was the 21st national IMI management conference. Mr Nesbitt commented on recent criticism that their Institute's independence had been lessened by the substantial funds it got from the government. For the IMI, he said, the essential independence was freedom to research, to comment and to teach, uninfluenced by the need to avoid offending any particular group.

Prospects: dimension in economic growth, May 1973

The theme of the conference was: 'Prospects: the Human Dimension in Economic Growth'. The formal speakers included:

- Mr Herman Kahn: the American futurologist

- Dr Alexander King: director general of the Organisation for Economic Co-Operation and Development

- Dr Patrick Hillery: Ireland's EEC Commissioner

- Mr Nicholas Leonard: managing director of Fitzwilliam Securities.

Ireland to host 1977 European Marketing Congress

On 4 May 1973 the media reported that the honour to host the twelfth (in 1977) European Marketing Council Congress and AGM in Dublin, was granted to the Marketing Institute of Ireland. The decision had been finally confirmed at the tenth congress in London in May 1973. In the meantime, the 1975 congress would be held in Amsterdam.

Negotiations had taken place between the Irish delegation, led by MII chairman, Mr John D. Carroll and Mr Manuel Caragol, leader of the Spanish group. These resulted in the Spanish accepting to wait and hold the thirteenth congress in Barcelona 1979.

MR BILL FRASER FMII, ELECTED VICE-PRESIDENT OF EMC, MAY 1973

At the London AGM of the European Marketing Council, the proposal of Mr Harry Woods, Ireland, past-president of EMC, resulted in Mr W.D. (Bill) Fraser, managing director North Dublin Growers, being elected a vice-president of EMC for the following two years.

EMC CHAIN OF OFFICE, TO INSTITUTE OF MARKETING, MAY 1973

Originally presented from MII, by the kindness of Aubrey Fogarty Associates, the EMC chain of office was formally handed over, in London, to Mr Austin Nunn, chairman of the Institute of Marketing, UK, by Mr Heinz Franke, Deutsche Marketing-Vereinigung e.v, to hold for the term 1973–74.

WILKINSON 'MINI' SWORD, MAY 1973

Mr Roy Randolph the newly elected president of EMC presented a 'Mini' Wilkinson Sword (contained in an inscribed mahogany box) to Mr Harry Woods as a keepsake. This he said was 'in recognition of the continuous contribution to the work and progress of the European Marketing Council over many years'.

(Mr Roy Randolph informed me later that a similar presentation had been made to each director of Wilkinson, to commemorate the company success, 1772–1972.)

AGRICULTURAL MARKETING COMMITTEE FORMED IN CORK, MAY 1973

Mr Mahon Lee, chairman of the Cork Group of MII, formed a working committee with special responsibility for agricultural marketing.

DUBLIN REGIONAL BRANCH OF THE MARKETING INSTITUTE, JUNE 1973–FEBRUARY 1979

A Dublin regional branch of the Marketing Institute was formed in June 1973 and continued to its dissolution in February 1979.

(In order to explain the origination and reason for cessation, it has been necessary to confine the 'happenings' of the said branch to that below and the immediate following pages, and thereafter, continue with the National Council reports, meetings and so forth, from May 1973, covered prior to this paragraph, to 1999.)

While the Dublin Branch was given Institute authority to arrange certain meetings and functions, their minutes mainly recorded events rather than the factual details. However, I have researched and endeavoured to cover the latter under the National Council heading later.

FORMATION OF DUBLIN REGIONAL BRANCH OF MII

In his outgoing report to the members at the AGM of the Marketing Institute of Ireland on 25 June 1973, Mr John D. Carroll, national chairman, said that it seemed quite remarkable that a year had gone by since he was honoured with election to the Chair. While so much still needed to be done, he had found it a pleasure working with the most active and enthusiastic group he had ever known.

In his review, he went on to say that progress had accelerated, with many new projects requiring particular attention, hours of study and deliberation. He referred in particular to the establishment of the Dublin branch earlier that month (June 1973). It was hoped that it would allow Dublin members greater areas of local marketing interest to explore. He believed it was a forward step and congratulated the national vice-chairman, Mr Leslie Whitehead, on his smooth and highly efficient handling of the branch establishment.

It was felt that, with the Dublin branch ongoing, council could more actively concern itself with national and international affairs, thus allowing greater effort to be made on broader aspects of Institute business.

FIRST MEETING OF THE DUBLIN REGIONAL BRANCH OF MII

The first meeting of the Dublin regional branch of the Marketing Institute of Ireland, was held at the Institute's offices at 73, Orwell Road, Rathgar on 11 June 1973. The national chairman of MII, Mr John D. Carroll, and the chairman of the regional development committees, Mr Leslie Whitehead, attended the inaugural meeting, ex officio.

There were ten MII branch formation members present. These were: Messrs Walter Connolly, Michael H. Coote, Patrick J. Costello, Nial Darragh, Hugh E. McCormack, William C. Milne, Kevin Murphy, Bernard Sawier, Michael P. McDevitt and Brendan Byrne. Election of Officers was declared as:

- Chairman: Mr Kevin Murphy

- Vice-Chairman: Mr Walter Connolly

- Hon. treasurer: Mr Bernard Sawier

- Hon. Secretary: Mr Brendan Byrne.

In accepting office, the branch chairman, Mr Kevin Murphy, stated that he expected, with the assistance of the committee and national council, to play a valuable part in the business life of the country.

SECOND MEETING OF DUBLIN BRANCH

At the second meeting of the branch on 19 June 1973, the chairman, Mr Kevin Murphy, said the national council had decided on a policy of regional development, to have long-term effect on the Institute growth through branches. It would also free the council from detailed operations in any one part of the country and allow more time to organise further branches and groups. Power was granted to co-opt further members onto the committee, to a total of fifteen. Other rules and procedures, in accordance with the Memorandum and Articles of Association, were outlined.

Mr Michael Coote became chairman of the membership sub-committee, while Mr Hugh McCormack agreed to act on same with special reference to members' welfare, employment and redundancy. Mr Patrick Costelloe agreed to chair the programme committee and likewise for education, Messrs Nial Darragh and Walter Connolly for social and Mr Michael McDevitt, publicity.

DUBLIN BRANCH MEETING, JULY 1973

The recently elected national chairman of MII, Mr Denis J. Fitzgibbon, attended, ex officio Dublin branch meeting of 30 July 1973. It was agreed to order a chain of office and past-chairmen's badges, for future use. A Christmas party for the children of members and friends was arranged to be held at the Zoological Members' Restaurant, Phoenix Park, Dublin on 18 December 1973.

A draft set of rules and regulatons for the branch were produced by Mr Joseph McGough, BL, MMII.

NEW CHAIRMAN OF DUBLIN BRANCH, SEPTEMBER 1973

Due to pressure of business commitments, the founder Dublin branch chairman, Mr Kevin Murphy had to resign the chair, which was accepted with regret. Mr Walter Connolly FMII, was elected chairman from September 1973.

INAUGURAL LUNCHEON OF DUBLIN BRANCH, MII, SEPTEMBER 1973

The inaugural luncheon of the Dublin Branch of MII was held at the Burlington hotel, Upper Leeson Street, Dublin, on Friday 28 September 1973. The guest speaker was Mr Liam Connellan of the Confederation of Irish Industries.

DUBLIN BRANCH APPOINTMENTS, SEPTEMBER 1973

The chain of office of chairman of the Dublin branch of the Marketing Institute was formally presented to Mr Walter Connolly by the national chairman, Mr Denis J. Fitzgibbon. Mr Joseph McGough was elected branch vice-chairman. Due to the hon. Secretary's (Mr Brendan Byrne) illness, Mr Michael McDevitt was unanimously elected to that position.

The co-option of Mr Geoff Beggs to the branch committee enabled him to take over the social committee organisation, a position which he had considerable experience of already, having organised the Ladies' Night of MII.

BOSTON REUNION SOCIAL MEETING, OCTOBER 1973

A full report on the Boston Harvard course participation was presented at the evening meeting of the Dublin branch on 22 October 1973. This included a fifteen-minute film, *The Boston Flashback.*

MANAGEMENT CHANGE, OCTOBER 1973

Mr Ivor Kenny, director of the Irish Management Institute, addressed the MII students on current management change and gave them the benefit of his experiences aa well as an outline on future trends.

BUSINESS GAME BENEFIT, OCTOBER 1973

At the members' monthly luncheon on 26 October 1973, Mr Jim Crossan of International Computers Ltd gave an insight into the benefit of using the 'business game'. He freely replied to many questions.

LADIES' NIGHT, DECEMBER 1973

The Ladies' Night function was held at the Burlington hotel on 14 December 1973. The cost for a double ticket was £10.80. Valuable prizes were presented at the benevolent fund raffle, while each lady, as usual, received a stupendous gift bag packed with goods donated from members' firms.

MARKETING IN LOCAL GOVERNMENT, JANUARY 1974

An insight on marketing in local government was given by Mr Denys F. Hodson, MA, at the Player Wills theatre meeting on 24 January 1974. Students, consumer guidance bodies and the marketing society were subsequently sent bulk copies of Mr Hodson's paper for distribution to their members. National dailies and *Business & Finance* magazine gave detailed coverage of the meeting.

Approximately sixteen trade category groups of MII members were defined and a convenor for each decided on by the branch committee. Mr Harry Glynn and Mr Michael Maguire (chairman of the student society) were co-opted to the branch committee. The national conference was held in Wexford on the 4, 5 and 6 April 1974.

TROPHY CREATED FOR SEAN F. LEMASS AWARD, MAY 1974

The Sean F. Lemass award, consisting of a specially designed trophy by artist Brian Clarke and a scholarship for the study of marketing abroad, was officially presented to the Marketing Institute of Ireland on 1 May 1974 in the presence of the Lemass family.

A presentation was made to Mrs Sean Lemass, at a reception in Jury's hotel, Dublin. Also at the unique occasion were: Mr Justin Keating TD, Minister for Industry and Commerce, Mr Jack Lynch TD, Mr Charles Haughey TD and Dr J.F. Dempsey, past-president of MII, together with Mr Denis J.

Fitzgibbon, chairman of MII, executives and members of the Institute. More detail is recorded later in this book under the national MII coverage.

NATIONAL APPOINTMENTS, 1974

A new Irish marketing journal carried some good publicity on the affairs of the Institute and in particular of Dublin branch activities. Mr Joseph McGough was congratulated on his election as national chairman of MII and also his election to Fellowship at its AGM of Monday 29 July 1974 held at the Burlington hotel. Messrs. Philip Flood and Harry A. Wyer were also praised for their deserved election to Fellowship.

FIRST AGM OF DUBLIN BRANCH, SEPTEMBER 1974

Thirty-five members attended the first AGM of the Dublin branch on 30 September 1974 at the Burlington hotel. The chair was taken by Mr Mahon Lee, chairman of the Cork branch. He deputised for the national chairman, who in turn was doing the same for him at a Cork function. He read a brief prepared statement setting guidelines for the future of the Dublin branch. In a recess to elect officers, a marketing film entitled: *The Competitive Spirit* was screened.

The results of the election were as follows:

- Chairman: Mr Walter Connolly
- Vice-Chairman: Mr Nial Darragh
- Hon. treasurer: Mr Eimear McCormick
- Hon. secretary: Mr Michael P. McDevitt.

The committee were:

- Education: Mr Pat Nolan
- Membership: Mr Harry Glynn
- Programme: Mr Brendan Carolan
- Social: Mr Geoff Beggs.

The programme theme for 1975 was 'Marketing in an Inflationary Environment'.

A joint evening meeting was held with the Marketing Society on 5 November 1974. The guest chairman was Mr John Meagher of Irish Marketing Surveys and an excellent attendance of 146 was recorded.

Taking into account the time consumption, in the preparation and reading of lengthy written minutes, it was decided for the future to note 'decisions only' for the branch records.

The Christmas party for members' children was held at the Zoological Gardens, Members' Restaurant on 1 December 1974. Santa (Mr Leslie Thorn) as usual, arrived in his sleigh with gifts for all to great excitement. Profits were donated to the Irish Cancer Society.

FIRST WORKSHOP PROJECT, APRIL 1975

The first workshop, a well worthwhile project, was organised and held in April 1975. A good mix of members (21) and students (22) participated. Considering the successful beneficial participation, it was decided to hold further workshops during the year.

MARKETING AND QUALITY CONTROL, MAY 1975

A joint meeting with the Irish Quality Control Association took place on 13 May 1975 at the Shelbourne hotel, Dublin. The subject was: 'Marketing and Quality control — Friend or Foe?'

Chaired by the vice-chairman of the Consumers' Association of Ireland, the speakers were Mr John Roche, Galway University and Mr Larry McMahon, Irish Management Institute.

The overall theme for evening and luncheon meetings of the Institute to the end of 1975 was declared as being: 'Pragmatic Marketing — the Path to Recovery'.

A joint meeting, with the Marketing Society members, was held at the Carroll's theatre on 14 October 1975.

SECOND AGM OF DUBLIN BRANCH, JANUARY 1976

The second AGM of the Dublin branch of MII was held at the Shelbourne hotel on 5 January 1976. Following successful voiced reports, it was considered that a better corporate image had been projected for the Institute. The Diary/Planner that had been produced was deemed to have especially contributed.

Following a postal ballot the declared officers of the Dublin branch council for 1976 were:

• Chairman: Mr Walter Connolly (re-elected)

• Vice-Chairman: Mr Nial Darragh

- Hon. Treasurer: Mr Matt Collins

- Hon. Secretary: Mr Michael McDevitt.

The committee members were: Messrs Geoff Beggs, Brendan Carroll, Harry Glynn, P.D. Lynch, Pat Nolan, P.N. Pierce, Fergus Plunkett, Donal Shaw, Brendan Rooney and Harry Wyer. Mr J. Brendan O'Reilly was co-opted to the committee.

   The committee chairmen were:

- Programme: Mr Geoff Beggs

- Social: Mr Pat Nolan

- Education: Mr P.D. Lynch

- Membership: Mr H. Glynn.

CASE STUDY, J.J. CARROLL CATERING COMPANY, MARCH 1976

A successful marketing workshop on 4 March 1976 was attended by fifteen members and six students. An actual case study had been submitted, of which the client agreed to release the company name. It was that of J.D. Carroll Catering Company.

   Two follow-up luncheon meetings ensued, at which conclusions were formally presented. Mr John D. Carroll MMII hosted the luncheons.

SLIDE PRESENTATION, APRIL 1976

The theme 'Positioning', with a slide presentation, was declared to be 'the newest concept in advertising'. The presentation was made at a luncheon meeting on 6 April 1976 in association with the Cost and Management Accountants.

WEATHERGLAZE WORKSHOP, NOVEMBER 1976

A workshop meeting held on 20 November 1976 concerned a marketing 'live problem' posed by Weatherglaze and resulted in conclusions being forwarded to them. The feedback was considered good.

THIRD AGM OF DUBLIN BRANCH, APRIL 1977

The third AGM of the Dublin branch was held at Broc House, Donnybrook,

Dublin. A special committee, chaired by Mr J. Brendan O'Reilly, had engaged at re-establishing executives who, for reasons outside their control, had no gainful employment.

The officers of the Dublin branch elected for 1977–8 were:

- Chairman: Mr Patrick Nolan

- Vice-Chairman: Mr Brendan Carolan

- Hon. Treasurer: Mr Fergus Plunkett

- Hon. Secretary: Mr J. Roche-Kelly.

Japanese ambassador addresses MII, April 1977

His Excellency, Nobuyasu Nishimiya, Ambassador of Japan, was the guest speaker following the AGM.

MEMBERS' WORKSHOP, MAY 1977

A workshop for members took place at Irish Biscuits on Saturday 21 May 1977. Three separate groups took part in actual 'official' finding presentations.

SHANNON CRUISE WEEKEND, JUNE 1977

Mr P. Noel Quirke, organised a very successful Killaloe/Shannon cruising weekend. It was well attended, enjoyed and appreciated by members.

MR TOM BRADY MMII, (RIP), SEPTEMBER 1977

After the summer recess a branch committee meeting was held at Twining House, courtesy of Mr Pat Nolan. It was with deep shock that a vote of sympathy was passed, recalling the untimely death of Mr Tom Brady MMII who had given very valued service on Institute committees.

OPENING MEETING, JANUARY 1978

An opening meeting of the Dublin branch was held on January 10, 1978 at Confederation House, Kildare Street, Dublin. The meeting was chaired by Mr Pat Nolan who announced that a new syllabus had been produced for students. Case studies were also made available and a development report was distributed to members.

FOURTH AGM OF DUBLIN BRANCH, OCTOBER 1978

The newly elected Dublin branch chairman, Mr P. Noel Quirke, presided at the AGM in Confederation House, Kildare Street on 16 October 1978. Officers present were: Messrs J. Brendan Carroll, vice-chairman, and joint hon. secretarys, Messrs Brian M. O'Farrell and J. Brendan O'Reilly.

The need for a full-time executive was stressed, 'to enable the Institute be a force to be reckoned with, in the business world'.

DISSOLUTION OF DUBLIN BRANCH OF MII, FEBRUARY 1979

An agreement was reached with the MII national council that, with some members of the Dublin branch accepting to join committees of council, the branch be dissolved as and from 8 February 1979.

NATIONAL AGM OF MII, JUNE 1973

The outgoing national chairman, Mr John D. Carroll, reviewed the previous year at the AGM June 25 1973. He outlined the successes obtained from the MII participation in the European Marketing Council and the Advanced Marketing Programme at Boston. He particularly referred to the continution of a most welcome relationship with colleagues in Northern Ireland. A number of joint meetings had been held, to mutual advantage, and he commented on the extent of the marketing expertise and enthusiasm displayed by Northern colleagues in the face of their political difficulties.

To cement success it had wisely been found appropriate to invest financially in allocating funds for publicity, the furthering of public relations and in member and student education.

Officers elected for 1973–4 session were:

- President: Dr T.J. O'Driscoll

- Chairman: Mr Denis J. Fitzgibbon

- Vice- : Messrs W.J. Connolly, A.F. Corduff and N. Darragh

- Hon. Treasurer: Mr H.V. Woods

- Hon. Secretary: Mr J.C. Bigger.

Elected to the council were: Messrs T.A. Brady, J.D. Carroll, P.R. Flood, A.N. Fogarty, W.D. Fraser, Mahon Lee, P.J. McLoughlin, A.J. Neville, R.E. Reid, J.W. Sandford, L.C. Thorn, B.V. Woods and H.A. Wyer.

Sean F. Lemass trophy, June 1973

Commissioned in 1973, the Sean F. Lemass trophy award, cut from EEC silver, was exhibited at the AGM. The awards' committee, chaired by Mr Bill Fraser, had received valuable assistance from Mr Brian Clarke, who designed and produced the trophy.

It had been agreed that the award would take the form of a perpetual memorial award. This would be made to an outstanding person in the marketing field who then would either nominate, or assist in the nomination of a recipient for cash support.The cash would be to further some emerging marketeer from the Institute graduates or the universities, or a member who would be given financial support from the capital sum invested for the purpose. The sum totalled £3,000.

The perpetual trophy epitomised the contribution made by the Institute's late president, Mr Sean F. Lemass, in the fields of industry, youth education and Europe. It was not intended to be awarded on a regular basis, but rather as the council and the awards' committee considered appropriate.

For their consistent and outstanding record in the export field over the years, the MII awards' committee nominated Waterford Glass Ltd to be the first to earn the honour, (the presentation was to be made in 1974).

SCHOLARSHIP FOR MARKETING DIPLOMA AWARDED, JUNE 1973

Mr Philip Flood, chairman of the education committee, announced that courses for the certificate in marketing were then being offered at ten colleges throughout the country and that graduate courses would begin September 1974.

It was announced that Miss Brid McGhee of Gweedore, Co. Donegal had been awarded a scholarship for the three-year Higher Diploma in Marketing. Miss McGhee was the first female to take the course. Over the previous two years a total of 420 students had been registered.

MR TOM GARVEY, CTT, CHAIRMAN OF MARKETING SOCIETY, JULY 1973

At the third AGM of the Marketing Society, Mr Tom Garvey, general manager of Córas Tráchtála, was elected chairman. The meeting also elected Mr J.F. Meagher as vice-chairman, Mr J.J. Jones as hon. secretary and Mr B. Halpin as hon. treasurer.

EEC SHARE MOVE RECOMMENDED, SEPTEMBER 1973

At the MII meeting on 28 September 1973 Mr Liam Connellan, director general of the Confederation of Irish Industries, stated that the time was opportune to establish a foothold in the new affluent markets of the EC partners. He said exports to the old EEC had grown by 106 per cent in 1972 over 1971 and by 160 per cent so far in 1973, compared with the previous year. He warned that the bouyancy would not continue indefinitely. Already a growth rate of 5 per cent was forecast for the EC in 1974, compared with 6 per cent that year (1973).

Mr Connellan pointed to the Northern Ireland market for a major growth of export. Only 10 per cent of export went there from the Republic of Ireland, while in return they exported 3 per cent to the south.

He also said there was a shortage of top professional marketing executives to deal with the development of trade. It was the marketing executive who was the major link in the chain, identifying what the customer wanted in clearly defined market areas and segments.

MARKETING, *NOT* INCLUDED IN UCC, SEPTEMBER 1973

Complaints that University College, Cork, had not recognised the need to have the subject of marketing included in the commerce class at the college, was made by Mr Philip R. Flood FMII, chairman of the educational committee of the Marketing Institute of Ireland, at an enrolment meeting in Cork on the evening of 9 September 1973.

Mr Flood said that not only had Trinity College, Dublin University and Galway University now got a study of marketing in their courses, but the new Regional Institute in Limerick had also included marketing on their programme.

STUDENT STARTS OWN BUSINESS, SEPTEMBER 1973

Student of the year, Mr Edward J. McEleney, Balally Park, Dundrum, Co. Dublin, was among 22 students who received diplomas at the annual presentation of the Marketing Institute on 12 September 1973. Mr Sean O'Connor, secretary of the Department of Education, presented the awards and diplomas.

Mr McEleney had started his own business, in the sale and distribution of electrical consumer goods, earlier in the year. He also won the Albright & Wilson award for 1973.

The best student subject awards went to Mr G.T. Locke, Caherdavin, Limerick, who received the Aubrey Fogarty Associates award for marketing, Mr C. Kelly, Ennis Road, Limerick for advertising and Mr A.J. Hazley, Clontarf, Dublin, for market research.

IMPRESSIVE GROWTH OF IRISH ECONOMY, OCTOBER 1973

The impresssive growth of the Irish economy, which had taken place over the previous decade, was largely due to the rapid expansion of industry over the period. Industrial exports rose from a level of £51m. in 1960 to an expected level of £425m. for 1973.

The expansion resulted from the realisation (first enunciated in Dr Whitaker's well- known paper) that to provide and maintain a rising standard of living would increase levels of employment, it was necessary that capital expenditure would be directed to productive enterprise and also that considerable capital would be required. The implementation of that policy resulted in much new industry having been established in Ireland.

Significant development took place within the economy, including the emergence of new financial techniques and institutions to service the expansion in enterprise, the development and growth of merchant banking in Ireland, the amalgamation of the domestically controlled clearing banks into large groups and the growth of the influence of the Central Bank.

Assets of the Irish merchant banks (March 1973) totalled almost £200m. and represented 16.9 per cent of all the associated banks in Ireland, as against 12 per cent, a mere two years previously.

TAX RELIEF ON EXPORTS, 1973

New manufacturing firms setting up in Ireland at that time enjoyed full relief from taxes on profits derived from exports for fifteen years.

ASSOCIATION OF CERTIFIED ACCOUNTANTS, NOVEMBER 1973

At the invitation of the Association of Certified Accountants, I prepared a lecture on the Marketing and Business Administration section of the revision course for their December 1973 examinations. The lecture, given on Friday evening 16 November 1973, related to the London set examnination syllabus. My content included:

- Introduction to marketing
- Organisation and control
- Channels of distribution
- Industrial marketing
- International marketing
- Salesmanship

- Role of advertising
- Sales promotion and public relations
- Controlling the marketing operations
- Co-ordination with other elements.

The latter included the marketing committee, research, design, advertising, financial experts, etc. I also included a full organisational chart, with explanatory detailed sub-headings, in my handouts to students.

RETAIL SALES RISE, DECEMBER 1973

Figures published in December 1973 by the Central Statistics Office, for retail sales in the first nine months of 1973, showed a 19 per cent higher value than in the comparable period of the previous year.

The largest retail sales value rise was 35 per cent in chemists, where a significant rise was due to state subsidised prescription charges. Other major rises were in vehicles and garages 28 per cent; fresh meat 23 per cent; department stores 22 per cent; and tobacco, sweets and newspapers 19 per cent.

FIRST VICE-PRESIDENT OF MII, DECEMBER 1973

The appointment of Mr Basil Lapworth MMII, as first vice-president of the Marketing Institute of Ireland, took place at the Burlington hotel on 12 December 1973. Mr Basil Lapworth was then managing director of the radio interests of Ulster Television and Sales Manager of Ulster Television (UTV).

A past chairman of the Institute of Marketing, Northern Ireland, he was also a founder member and former treasurer of the Publicity Association of Northern Ireland. A more popular choice for the new position could not have been made, as Mr Lapworth was very well liked by the MII council members, and members generally. It also marked a step in the policy of recognition of goodwill, to forge links with business interests in Northern Ireland.

BUSINESS & FINANCE CRITICISES CORK BRANCH, DECEMBER 1973

Although the Marketing Institute had been particularly active in the Cork region in training future business executives, in the 13 December 1973 issue of *Business & Finance* it pointed out that Cork businesses had not returned the compliment by supporting the Institute.

However, hopes of the Institute to increase their Cork membership had been enhanced, the article observed, by the fact that the national chairman,

Mr Denis J. Fitzgibbon, was a Corkman, the first chairman from Leeside.

MARKETING LOCAL GOVERNMENT, FEBRUARY 1974

How does an ex-marketing man, who previously sold the world's second most expensive suits, get to be in charge of 33 playgrounds, 11 libraries, 39 football pitches, 2 theatres, 3 museums and 2 cemetries? — and that was not all. That is what happened to Mr Denis Hodson, controller for arts and recreation, Swindon Borough Council. Mr Hodson came to Dublin to talk to the MII members and tell them that marketing was not just selling.

Swindon then had a population of 100,000 in the borough, and the catchment area would shortly expand to include 50,000 extra people. A growth of 50,000 was predicted within ten years.

It was reported in *Business & Finance* on 7 February 1974 that Mr Denis Hodson said that his marketing experience had helped him in estimating supply and demand on a logical basis while he had an annual budget 'winging around' the £1m. mark.

CORK MII DINNER, FEBRUARY 1974

The annual dinner of the Cork regional branch of MII was held at the Metropole hotel, Cork on 8 February 1974. Diplomas in marketing were presented by the Minister for Transport & Power, Mr Peter Barry TD, to Messrs Pat Murnane, Aiden Harte on behalf of Ken Murphy, T.M. Howard, John Cowman and also to Mr Denis O'Sullivan on behalf of Mr T. Healy.

The Lord Mayor of Cork, Senator Pat Kerrigan, was among the principal guests, while Mr Denis Fitzgibbon, national chairman and Mr Mahon Lee, chairman of the Cork branch, were in attendance

Oil situation spelt out, February 1974

Speaking at the dinner the Minister, Mr Peter Barry TD, said he rejected suggestions that the oil companies or Whitegate refinery had hoarded stocks of oil or had tanks so full that tankers had to be turned away, at the end of the previous year.

Furthermore, he stated that immediately before the oil crisis commenced, the oil importing companies and the Whitegate Refinery had stocks of 387,000 tonnes. By 31 December last, the stocks had fallen to 358,000 tonnes. The storage capacity of the refinery and of the companies combined amounted to 700,000 tonnes. The petrol price increases, he believed, were a direct result of price rises in Britain.

PRESIDENT'S NIGHT, FEBRUARY 1974

The annual President's Night of the MII was held at the Shelbourne hotel on Tuesday 26 February 1974.

FELLOWSHIP AWARD, FEBRUARY 1974

The presentation of the award of Fellowship was made, by Dr T. O'Driscoll president of MII, to Mr Aubrey Fogarty of Aubrey Fogarty Associates Ltd, following a citation read by Mr Harry Woods, hon. treasurer and chairman of the Fellows' committee.

A summary of the considerable contribution made by Mr Fogarty to the development of marketing in Ireland and in furthering the Institute was outlined by Mr Woods.

THE STEPHEN DOYLE AWARD, FEBRUARY 1974

The Stephen Doyle Memorial award was presented to Dr A.C. (Tony) Cunningham, Acting Head of the Department of Business Administration at University College, Dublin.

Dr Cunningham received his B.Comm. from the National University of Ireland in 1955, took a Master's Degree in 1959 and in the same year was awarded a Fellowship in Salsburg, Austria. He later spent four years with the American Embassy in Dublin, on market research and development. Dr Cunningham's career in marketing in Arizona, Harvard and Queen's University, Belfast was in addition to being an external examiner to many universities.

His truly magnificient contribution to development was sincerely felt by the MII members and students, and particular reference was made to his contributions to the many conferences held by the Institute over the previous few years.

The citation for the award to Dr Cunningham was read by Mr Bill Fraser FMII, vice-president of the European Marketing Council. The guest speaker at the dinner was Mr William D. Finlay SC, deputy governor of the Bank of Ireland.

Speaking at the ceremony, Dr O'Driscoll, president of MII, said that consideration should be given to a Marketing Organisation of Ireland, which would embrace all Ireland, including the Marketing Society, while retaining a special relationship with the Institute of Marketing, UK.

EMC MEETING IN WEXFORD, APRIL 1974

A council meeting of the European Marketing Council, which was held for only the second time in Ireland, took place in Wexford on Friday, 5 April 1974. The thirteen countries represented, in addition to the nine in the EEC, were Switzerland, Spain, Sweden and Norway.

In attendance were Messrs Roy Randolph, president of EMC (also chairman of the Wilkinson Sword), Bill Fraser FMII, vice-president, Manuel Carragol (Spain), vice-president, Fred Witkamp (Holland), general secretary of the council and Harry Woods FMII, a past-president.

Mr Aubrey Fogarty FMII, said that the holding of the EMC Congress in Dublin 1977, would impress upon marketing executives, many of whom had never been to Ireland, the importance of the country as a 'backdoor' entry, both to EEC and US markets. The emphasis at the 1977 Congress, Mr Fogarty continued, would be on multi-national marketing, the adoption of marketing policies that would be as successful in Spain as in Ireland. The opportunity would be taken to stress the suitability of Ireland as a test market for the products being launched throughout Europe. The size and dispersion of the population and the range of attitudes all favoured the increased use of Ireland as a test market.

The 1975 EMC Congress (eleventh) would be held in Amsterdam as they would be celebrating their 900th anniversary. The programme would be themed: 'Marketing's Challenge Today'.

FINANCIAL TECHNIQUES IN MARKETING, APRIL 1974

The Irish Times extensively reported on the Marketing Institute of Ireland conference/training programme 'Financial Techniques in Marketing'. This was held at the Talbot hotel, Wexford on April 4/5/6. Visitors, at the well-attended presentation, included the executive of the EMC led by their president, Sir Roy Randolph, who were guests of honour at the dinner on the Friday night.

The IT report of Mr Paul Tansey declared that financial control was traditionally weak in marketing according to Mr David Senton, operations director of Marketing Improvements Ltd London and Brussels. It also stated that while there had been a growing acceptance of financial terminology, it had not produced any real changes in marketing policy. Mr Senton believed that financial control could be improved by setting clear profit goals and by using analytical techniques to quantify marketing performance.

Furthermore as markets became more competitive, and marketing more expensive, marketing men must improve their decision-making. Most companies would accept that return on capital employed was the ratio most indicative of management's performance within a company. That, he defined, as the relationship between net profit before tax (management can hardly be held responsible for tax) and capital employed, total assets minus current liabilities. Thus the ratio would show how effectively the management was using the net assets of the company. For the general manager (as opposed to the accountant) the distinction between fixed costs, 'overheads' and variable costs was not always clear.

In the marketing implications of costing systems within business, Mr Colin Norton, also of Marketing Improvements, said that the three marketing dynamics within any business were:

1. The price of the product.

2. The volume of sales.

3. Production costs, both fixed and variable.

The treatment of costs was of great importance. The realistic manager should analyse the way costs had moved in the past, and whether such would change in the future, and then make a decision which most nearly reflected the truth, as he measured it.

The working sessions of the training programme were over three days (Thursday, Friday and Saturday) and comprised of ten group teams (77 delegates). They represented marketing, advertising, industrial manufacturers, agriculture, training colleges, retail concerns, brewing, motor trade, the media, transport, catering, packaging, government trade boards and others

The MII conference committee was chaired by Mr Anthony J. Neville MMII, who later was pleased to report to the council that some non-members of the Institute, who participated in Wexford, had applied for membership. The programme method was designed not only to impart information through lectures but also to involve the maximum of participation, group discussion and case studies.

EUROPEAN MARKETING COUNCIL AGM, ZURICH 1974

The EMC AGM and conference was held in Zurich, Switzerland in May 1974. The Marketing Institute of Ireland was represented by Mr Bill Fraser, vice-president of EMC and Messrs Derek Trenaman and Harry Woods, past-president of EMC.

NCEA STUDY, JUNE 1974

In 1973 the National Council for Educational Awards (NCEA) commissioned Dr Enda Hession, Associate Professor, Department of Business

Administration, University College, Dublin, to undertake a study on business education in Europe. It was the equivalent of that for the National Certificate and National Diploma in Business Studies awarded by the NCEA in Ireland.

The volume report, published in June 1974, contains 211 A4 pages. It was defined as 'a contribution to literature and general discussion on business education'. The report examined and reported on the position of business education, equivalent to the NCEA Certificate and Diploma, in Belgium, Denmark, England, Wales and Northern Ireland, France, West Germany, Netherlands and Scotland.

The description of institutions dealing with business education in the different countries is related to various models of short-cycle institutions, a term used by OECD to describe non-university, post-secondary colleges providing terminal and, for the most part, vocationally oriented education.

The general function of the NCEA, as formulated by the Minister of Education, was to promote, facilitate, encourage, co-ordinate and develop technical, industrial, commercial, technological, professional and scientific education and, in association with same, liberal education. The particular functions of the council are widely set out in Dr Hession's report.

In preparing the report visits were made to a number of institutions dealing with certificate and diploma education in Ireland, in order to give the necessary base of familiarisation, before visiting other countries. Visits were then made to England, Scotland, Holland, Belgium, France, Denmark and Germany. An impressive degree of co-operation was encountered in every institution both at home and abroad.

MR HARRY WOODS JOINS NCEA BOARD, 1974

I myself accepted an invitation to sit on Board C (Business Studies) of the NCEA for a period of two years.

Among the professional institutions, at home and abroad, who accepted NCEA award qualifications, were: The Association of Certified Accountants; The Institute of Chartered Accountants in Ireland; The Institute of Chartered Secretaries and Administrators; The Institute of Cost and Management Accountants; The Institution of Engineers in Ireland; The Institute of Building; The Institute of Biology; and the Marketing Institute of Ireland (MII).

With regard to the MII, a National Certificate in Business Studies exempted the holder from Parts 1 and 2 of the four-part examination leading to graduateship of the MII, provided that marketing had been taken as a subject by the student. In addition, a National Diploma in Business Studies exempted the holder, on a subject-for-subject basis, from appropriate subjects in parts 3 and 4 of the examination leading to graduateship of the MII.

SEAN F. LEMASS AWARD FOR WATERFORD GLASS, JULY 1974

The Sean F. Lemass award, to be presented to the firm considered by the Marketing Institute of Ireland to have contributed most through marketing to the Irish economy, was won by Waterford Glass. The late Sean Lemass had been president of the Institute 1967–71.

Dr T.J. O'Driscoll, president of MII, presented a number of awards in the Martello room of Jury's hotel, Ballsbridge on 23 July 1974. The Special Sean F. Lemass Perpetual trophy, in the presence of Mrs Sean Lemass was presented to Senator P.J. McGrath, chairman of Waterford Glass. Later on the Scholarship award (a basic investment of £3,000) was presented to Mr Kenneth McCullagh, market development manager of Ever Ready Garage Ltd.

The latter was provided for 'a person who wished to develop their marketing ability by further study or visiting some other area, particularly Europe'. Mr McCullagh, aged 26 and married, had passed all his examinations at the first attempt and had obtained the Student of the Year award in the 1971 examinations.

The designer of the Silver trophy, Mr Brian Clarke, said that he had tried to embody three things in which the late Sean Lemass was especially interested — youth, Europe and industry.

Senator McGrath stated that he was greatly honoured to accept the award on behalf of Waterford Glass Ltd. When the manufacture of Waterford Glass commenced 25 years previously, it was the belief that the Irish, as craftsmen, managers and later, learned marketers could compete with those in any industry in the world. Marketing had become the key to the future of Irish industry as a product, however good, had to be presented by good marketing.

The reception was attended by Mrs Sean Lemass, Senator McGrath, also the Minister for Industry and Commerce, Mr Justin Keating TD, Mr and Mrs Jack Lynch, Mr and Mrs Charles Haughey, Mr Jack Haughey and Dr J.F. Dempsey, past-presidents of MII, Mr and Mrs Noel Lemass, Mr Denis J. Fitzgibbon, chairman of MII, Mr Basil Lapworth, vice-chairman of MI and executives and members of the Institute.

MCCONNELL AWARD TO JIM NOLAN, ARKS, FOR 1974

The 1974 McConnell award, the highest award in Irish advertising, was presented in the Burlington hotel at a luncheon reception. The recipient was Mr Jim Nolan, deputy managing director of Arks Advertising Ltd. Of Mr Nolan, it was said: 'quietly and efficiently, he has consistently supported industry organisation, practiced responsibility and is a senior advertising man of depth and experience'.

ANNUAL REPORT OF MII, 1973–74

The outgoing chairman, Mr Denis J. Fitzgibbon, presented his very detailed report of the happenings in the year 1973–74. He referred to the very attractive brochure issued. This was entitled *A Career in Marketing*. It set out the Institute's four-year examination course, which was progressing favourably. Thanks were extended to Mr Phil Flood, chairman of the education committee, for the issue which was produced under his very capable guidance.

Submission on third level education, 1974

At the request of the government, a submission, on third level education had been made (February 1974) to the Higher Education Authority. Again Mr Phil Flood and his committee were responsible for this.

One of the future objectives was to establish a 'Marketing House' and he (Mr Denis Fitzgibbon) asked oncoming councils to work manfully towards that aim.

The chairman of Fellows, Mr Harry Woods, reported that a new set of rules and regulations had been sent to all Institute members, together with a copy of the new Articles of Association.

A member of five years' standing would, in future, be considered for the award of Fellowship. This had previously been seven years.

Mr Mahon Lee was congratulated for his excellent work during the year, which had resulted in an increase in the Cork group membership. So too were Mr Noel Smithwick, Galway group and Mr Donal Scanlan, new branch chairman in Limerick, ably assisted by Ray Joyce, who had also arranged a very ambitious programme of events.

In Waterford Mr Edward James had been working hard to establish a group and some very succesful meetings had been held.

NEW CHAIRMAN OF MII, JULY 1974

Mr Joseph C. McGough, managing director of An Bord Bainne (Irish Dairy Board), was appointed chairman of the Marketing Institute of Ireland for 1974–75, at the AGM in the Burlington hotel on 29 July 1974.

FELLOWSHIP AWARDS, 1974

Following citations, well-earned Fellowship awards for the promotion, marketing and advancement of the Institute were presented to Messrs Philip R. Flood, Joseph C. McGough and Harry A. Wyer.

Dr T.J. O'Driscoll kindly agreed to continue as president of the Institute.

The officers declared elected were:

- Vice-Chairmen: Messrs Nial Darragh, Mahon Lee and Walter Connolly

- Hon. Treasurer: Mr Harry Woods

- Hon. Secretary: Mr Joseph C. Bigger.

The council comprised of Messrs Tom Brady, Philip Flood, Aubrey Fogarty, Tony Neville, Richard Reid, Donal Scanlan, Leslie Thorn, Bernard Woods, Michael Hayes, Denis Fitzgibbbon, Michael Maguire, Rod O'Shea, Eugene Quigley and Bernard Sawier.

AGM OF CORK MII BRANCH, SEPTEMBER 1974

Speaking at the AGM of the Cork regional branch, Mr Joseph McGough, national chairman of MII, called for restoration of the sense of buoyancy in the Irish industrial scene, which had been obvious in the early sixties. He said it was up to the members of the Institute to ensure that the old tempo was reached and indeed increased.

In the changing circumstances, faced in the years ahead, Mr McGough felt the argument could be made that it was difficult to plan for more than the immediate future. That being so, the alternative was not to abandon planning but to constantly review the basic plan, up date it, and by means of market research, not only keep abreast of the times but ahead of the times in the marketing of one's products.

GRADUATE AWARDS, SEPTEMBER 1974

Dr T.J. O'Driscoll, president of MII presented 38 marketing students with their graduate certificates and diplomas at a reception in the Shelbourne hotel on 9 September 1974.

FIRST MII DIPLOMA IN MARKETING EXAMINATIONS, 1974

Twenty-eight students had taken the UK Diploma in Marketing examinations whilst the other ten successfully passed the first Irish MII Diploma in Marketing examinations. The examinations had been held at the School of Retail Distribution in June 1974.

1. October 1960. First Marketing Conference. Organised by Students' Society of Incorporated Sales Managers' Association. Clare Manor Hotel, Coolock, Co. Dublin. *Front row, L to R: Mr Stephen Doyle, FSMA; Mr Brian Clancy, MSMA; Sir Basil Goulding, President; and Mr Michael Coote, FSMA, Chairman.*

2. November 1963. Presentation of the first Honorary Membership of the Irish Institute of Marketing and Sales Management by Mr Thomas Murray, President, to Mr Sean O'Ceallaigh, Principal of the High School of Commerce. *L to R: Mr Thomas Murray, President; Mr Erskine H. Childers, Minister & Power; and Mr Norman McConnell, Chairman.*

3. November 1963. First Ladies Night function.

4. May 1964. Irish Delegation to European Contact Group of Marketing present Letter of Felicitation from Sean Moore, Lord Mayor of Dublin to Mayor of Barcelona.

5. May 1964. *L to R: Newly elected President of the Irish Institute of Marketing & Sales Management, Mr John Haughey, Chairman CTT; Dr P. Hillery, TD, Minister for Education; and Mr Harry V. Woods, Chairman, Irish Institute of Marketing and Sales Management.*

6. June 1965. Mr Harry V. Woods, past Chairman, Irish Institute of Marketing and Sales Management, receives Fellowship award form Mr Gerry Maher, Chairman, in presence of Mr Sean Lemass, TD, Mr Jack Lynch, TD, Mr Sean O'Ceallaigh, Mr Leslie Whitehead, Mr Basil Lapworth, Mr John Meagher and other dignitaries.

12. November 1969. Mr Albert Brouwet, President European Marketing Council, introduces Prince Albert of Belgium to Mr Harry V. Woods (Ireland), vice-President of EMC.

13. May 1970. Mr Pierre Hazebroucq, President, DCF (France) formally accepts Wilkinson Sword of Honour from Mr Harry V. Woods (Ireland) in presence of Mr Albert Brouwet (Belgium) at EMC Annual General Meeting, Nice.

14. June 1972. Mr Harry V. Woods, FMII (Ireland), Outgoing President European Marketing Council Addresses AGM at Nürnberg with Mr Fred T. Witkamp (Holland), Secretary-General EMC, noting for minutes.

15. June 1972. Official handing over of the EMC Sword of Honour to the hosts of the EMC conference, 8 to 10 June 1972, at Nürnberg, W. Germany. *L to R: Mr Harry V. Woods (Ireland), President EMC 1971/1972; Professor G. Tartara (Italy); and Dr R. F. Bossle (Germany).*

16. 1972. Mr John D. Carroll, Chairman Marketing Institute of Ireland and Chairman and Managing Director, John D. Carroll Catering Ltd.

17. 1972. Presentation of the McConnell Trophy. The team from the Marketing Institute won this trophy in competition with other Clubs and Associations. *L to R: Mr C. E. McConnell; Ms E. Ball, Chairman, Publicity Club Ireland; Mr W. Connolly, Captain MII team.*

18. 1973. *L to R: Mr Denis Fitzgibbon, Chairman National Council Marketing Institute of Ireland; Mr Liam Connellan, CII Guest Speaker; and Mr Walter Connolly, Chairman, Dublin branch, MII.*

19. June 1974. The Sean F. Lemass Award, officially presented to the Marketing of Ireland. *L to R: Mr D. J. Ftizgibbon, Chairman, Marketing Institute of Ireland; Mr Charles J. Haughey, TD; Mr Brian Clarke, artist; Mrs C. J. Haughey; and Dr T. J. O'Driscoll, President, Marketing Institute of Ireland.* Source: *Tatler & Sketch*, June 1974.

20. August 1974. Mr Joseph C. McGough, Managing Director, An Board Bainne – Irish Dairy Board, appointed Chairman of the Marketing Institute of Ireland, 1974/1975. Source: *Tatler & Sketch*, August 1974.

21. August 1974. Sean F. Lemass Award presented by Dr Timothy O'Driscoll, president, MII, to Senator Patrick McGrath, Waterford Glass.

22. September 1974. Ms Mary Kearns, first woman marketing award winner in Ireland, received Aubrey Fogarty Award for case study marks in Diploma examination.

23. 1976. *L to R: Mr Anthony J. Neville, Chairman; Dr T. J. O'Driscoll, President; Mr Basil Lapworth, vice-President, Marketing Institute of Ireland.*

24. March 1976. Fellows of the Marketing Institute of Ireland at meeting chaired by Mr Joseph C. McGough. *Front row, L to R: Mr Joseph Bigger, Mr Walter Connolly, Mr Joseph C. McGough (Fellows Chairman), Mr Leslie Whitehead and Mr Leslie Thorn. Standing, L to R: Mr Norman McConnell, Mr Harry V. Woods, Mr Derek Black and Mr Aubrey Fogarty.*

25. September 1978. Mr William D. Fraser, President, European Marketing Council, 1978 & 1979. Source: *Marketing News*, September 1978.

26. May 1979. Mr George Priestley, Chairman of the NI branch of the Institute of Marketing, addressed a Tuesday Club luncheon of the Marketing Institute at Jurys Hotel, Dublin.

27. 1986. Mr Brendan Wafer, Chairman Marketing Institute of Ireland.

28. September 1987. Mr Philip Kotler addressing 'Marketing for the 1990s' seminar at Trinity College Dublin.

29. 1987. Marketing Conference. L to R: Mr Tom Hardiman, President, MII; Mr Seamus Brannan, TD, Minister Trade & Marketing; Mr Alan McDonnell, Chairman, MII; and Mr David Manley, vice-Chairman.

30. October 1987. The President's Night at the Royal Hospital, Kilmainham.
*L to R: Professor Michael J. Baker, Chairman, Institute of Marketing, and
Mr T. P. Hardiman, President, Marketing Institute of Ireland.*

31. 1989. The Council of The Institute gathered for a two-day meeting at Tulfarris
House, Blessington, Co. Wicklow to chart the development of The Institute in 1989 and
beyond. *L to R: Mr Tony Treacy, Mid West; Ms Mary Donoghue, South East; Mr John
McGuire, Chairman; Mr Eddie Pierce, Cork; and Mr John Carroll, Galway.*

32. 1988. Mr Jim Culliton, President, Marketing Institute of Ireland, 1988/1999

33. 1992. Mr David Kennedy, President, Marketing Institute of Ireland, 1989/1992.

34. October 1992. Mr Alan McCarthy, MII, Bord Trachtala, Chairman of National Marketing Conference.

35. October 1993. National Marketing Conference in Cork. *L to R: Dr Paddy Galvin, Waterford Crystal (Speaker); Mr Jim Quinn, Chairman (panellist); and Mr Hans Hijlkema, President of the European Marketing Confederation (EMC).*

36. February 1994. Members of The Marketing Institute and the Chartered Institute of Marketing who attended a joint luncheon in Belfast.

37. May 1994. Mr David Dand, President, Marketing Institute with Mr Michael Conlon, Chairman, Bord Gais, who received his Fellowship of the Institute from Mr John Meagher, Chairman of the Fellows, at the Presidents Dinner in the Royal Hospital, Kilmainham.

38. May 1995. Presidents Night. *L to R: Mr David Dand, President, Marketing Institute; Mr Garry Hynes; Mr Anthony Neville, Chairman-Fellows; Mr Pat O'Mahony; and Dr Cathal Brugha.*

39. June 1995. Mr Philip Flood, FMII, first person to be admitted to The Marketing Institute's newly established Role of Honour.

40. June 1995. The Marketing Institute's seminar 'Credit Control: an essential part of marketing', held in the Derryhale hotel. *L to R: Ms Suzanne Carden, Marketing & Membership Exec with Mr Michael McElroy, Chairman, NE Region; Mr Ivor Deane, French & Associates (Guest Speaker); and Ms Jacqueline O'Connell.*

41. July 1995. The Marketing Institute/Cork Examiner Publications seminar 'How to Use Public Relations Effectively'. *L to R: Ms Sandra O'Reilly, President, Network; Mr Derry O'Keeffe, Promotions Manager, Cork Examiner Publications; Mr Matt Moran, Regional Chairman, The Marketing Institute, (Guest Speaker); Mr John, McMahon, Joint Managing Director, McMahon, Sheedy Communications; and Mr Paul Cogan, Secretary, The Marketing Institute, South Region.*

42. October 1995. Speakers at the National Marketing Conference at Royal Marine hotel, Dun Laoghaire, Co. Dublin. *L to R: Ms Barbara Patton, Irish Permanent, Head of Marketing; Ms Adrienne Murray, AIB Group, Conference Patron; Mr Redmond, O'Donoghue, Conference Chairman; and Mr Roger Jupp, Chairman, The Marketing Institute.*

43. April 1997. Mr Martin Sorrell, Chief Executive, WPP Group plc, speaker at a Top Marketing Forum.

44. June 1997. North-West Region Student Essay Competition. *L to R: Ms Emer Ward, Sligo RTC; Miss Rebecca Strain, 1st place, Loreto Community School, Milford, Co. Donegal; Mr Pat Scanlon, Chairman, NW Region; Mr Richard Kilfeather, 3rd place, Sligo Grammar School, The Mall, Sligo; Mr Seamus Bree, Head, NW Region, Forbairt; Miss Elaine Giblin, 2nd place, St. Patrick's College, Lacken Cross, Ballina, Co. Mayo.*

45. June 1997. Top Marketing Forum 'Ireland: Playing a Leading Role with the World's Hotel Industry Leader'. *L to R: Mr Daniel P. Weadock, Senior vice-President, ITT Sheraton Corporation (Speaker), with Mr Alan Corbett of Telecom Eireann.*

46. November 1997. Graduation Day. Mr Finn McGrath, winner of the International Marketing Management and Strategy award with Mr Peter Nash of Guinness Ireland, sponsors of the award, and Mr John Bourke, President of the Institute.

47. November 1997. Graduate of the Year, Ms Susan Jesper, with Ms Aoife Duncan, Irish Trade Board, sponsors of the award, and Mr Ciaran Conroy, who presented her with a crystal bowl compliments of Waterford Crystal.

48. December 1997. 'Sponsorship: Two Sides of the Coin'. *L to R: Mr Bernard O'Keeffe, The Kerryman; Mr Pat Daly, GAA Games Development Manager (Speaker); Mr Niall O'Loingsigh, Chairman, Kerry Region; and Mr Frank Hayes, Director, Corporate Affairs, Kerry Group plc.*

49. February 1998. Inauguration of New Members of The Marketing Institute West Region. *Back row, L to R: Mr Tony McVerry; Ms Adrienne Lynam; Mr Sean Gavin; Mr Declan Monaghan; Mr John Ryan; Mr Niall J. McNeills; Mr Padraig O'Raighne. Front row, L to R: Mr Jack Harty, Membership Officer, The Marketing Institute, West Region; Mr David Nea, National Chairman, The Marketing Institute; Mr Joe McDonagh, President, GAA (Guest Speaker); Mr Norman Rochford, Chairman, The Marketing Institute, West Region.*

50. May 1998. Receiving Fellowships for their contribution to marketing. *Standing, L to R: Mr Richard Martin, Sales & Marketing Director, Bell Advertising; Mr Tony Brophy, Marketing Manager – Stout, Guinness Ireland Ltd; Mr Bobby Gahan, Chairman, Fellows Committee; Mr Neville Galloway, Chief Executive, RNAN Ltd; Mr Pat Howard, vice-President – Sales & Marketing, Thermo King Europe. Seated, L to R: Mr David Nea, Chairman, The Marketing Institute; Mr Chris Molloy, Director Sales & Marketing Radio Telefis Eireann; Mr John Bourke, President, The Marketing Institute; Ms Sheila Gahan, Director, Wilson Hartnell Public Relations; Dr Patrick Keenan, Group Managing Director, TP Whelehan Son & Co.*

51. May 1998. Mr Bobby Gahan, Fellows Committee, John Bourke, President, The Marketing Institute, presenting Mr Michael Hayes, DIT – Aungier Street, with the Stephen Doyle Award 1998 for his contribution to the development of the Institute.

52. May 1998. Mr John Bourke, President, The Marketing Institute with Sir George Bull, Joint chairman, Diageo plc, the British Ambassador, Her Excellency Veronica Sutherland, Mr David Nea, Chairman, The Marketing Institute and Mr Bobby Gahan, Chairman, Fellows Committee.

53. June 1998. Minister for Education, Mr Michael Martin, making a presentation to Mr Sean Cowman. Also included are Mr Ray Walsh, Chairman, The Marketing Institute, South Region, and Mr Gerry Owens, vice-Chairman, The Marketing Institute, South Region.

Every year Ireland The Food Island produces more than we actually eat and drink.

That's why we always think big.

Ireland - The Food Island has always looked beyond its borders to see the bigger picture on an international front and the result has been a huge success.

The success is based on our natural environment and our long tradition as a food producing country. We've now combined this with innovation and flair to bring you world famous meat, dairy, drinks, consumer and speciality food products.

Today over IR£5 billion (€6.3 billion) worth of Irish food and drink is consumed in 170 countries world-wide, which is just as well - because the quality of food is so good, we'd only end up eating twice as much as we already do.

For further information contact Bord Bia - the agency that promotes Irish food and drink and works with industry to develop export markets.

Part financed by the European Agricultural Guidance and Guarantee Fund (Guidance Section)

Bord Bia

Irish Food Board

Bord Bia, Irish Food Board, Clanwilliam Court, Lower Mount Street, Dublin 2.
Tel +353 1 668 5155 Fax +353 1 668 7521 http://www.bordbia.ie

Ireland
THE FOOD ISLAND

The new SEAT Leon.
When it comes to powerful good looks, we've got a head start.

The all new SEAT Leon is a car to make your head turn and your pulse race no matter what side of the steering wheel you are on.

Visit **seat.ie** for the name of your nearest dealer o▮ See Aertel 2, page 3▮

One look at its musclebound exterior will tell you that. Its dynamic design is matched only by its incredible power, delivered courtesy of an impressive range of engine options.

And with 4 airbags, ABS, and much more as standard, there's only one person with the time to tell you all about it. Your local SEAT Dealer. So arrange a test drive today and experience the SEAT Leon for yourself.

A car that doesn't hide its strengths.

SEAT
auto emoci▮

Re-mixed.
Daily.

optimAS: A PROFESSIONAL NETWORK OF OVER 30 REGIONAL PARTNERS BASED IN SWITZERLAND, GERMANY, AUSTRIA, IRELAND & UK

PROFESSIONAL SERVICES INCLUDE:

SALES PROCESS OPTIMISATION
- Critical appraisal of your sales process to eliminate weaknesses, build on your strengths and improve the effectiveness of your sales team.

INTEGRATED MARKETING
- Tailoring clear marketing campaigns to suit your company. Key areas include Direct Marketing, Database Management and Call Centres.

BUSINESS DEVELOPMENT
- Customer Relations/Development strategies to generate more customers for your business and more business from your customers.
- Franchise System Development
- Benchmarketing & Audit

PARTNER NETWORK IRELAND:
- **Pat Cahill,** Limerick, Mobile: +353-86-833 3149
  E-Mail: patcahill@optimas-ireland.com
- **H. Grattan Donnelly,** Dublin, Mobile: +353-87-225 2737
  E-Mail: hgrattandonnelly@optimas-ireland.com
- **Harry Laird,** Dublin, Mobile: +353-86-269 2241
  E-Mail: harrylaird@optimas-ireland.com
- **Declan Mooney,** Man. Dir., Dublin, Mobile: +353-86-241 3299
  E-Mail: declanmooney@optimas-ireland.com

optimAS Ireland
optimAS International Management Centre
8 Priory Hall, Stillorgan, Co. Dublin, Ireland
Internet: www.optimas-group.com
E-Mail: info@optimas-ireland.com
Phone: +353-1-278 4445, Fax: +353-1-278 4446

ADWATCHING – GILES LURY

Each and every one of us will see over a thousand advertising messages today and on each and every day for the rest of our lives. We are, and will continue to be, 'bombarded' from our television sets, radios, computers, magazines and newspapers. We are all adwatchers.

Adwatching defines advertising and its role in modern-day business and modern-day society. It explores the origins of advertising and how it has developed into the multi-billion pound industry it is today

BRANDWATCHING – GILES LURY

Brandwatching explores the phenomenon of branding from its origins and through its development to its current position as the pre-eminent model for adding value in business. It examines how brands are created, named and how they grow. It explains why we buy brands and how and why they use advertising.

This revised and enlarged second edition includes new chapters on how branding has spread across different market sectors and whether branding on the web is really that different.

SALES AND SALES MANAGEMENT – JIM BLYTHE

Sales and Sales Management will give students on courses in selling and sales management a concise overview of the techniques of selling, the theories underlying selling, the relationship between selling and other business functions (including marketing) and the role, techniques and responsibilities of the sales manager.

Sales and Sales Management provides a sufficient 'real world' text to suit students while giving undergraduates or even masters level students enough further reading and academic references.

The above books are available in all good bookshops or directly from Blackhall Publishing.

For further information on any Blackhall Publishing titles please email us at blackhall@eircom.net

FIRST IRISH WOMAN TO OBTAIN MARKETING AWARD, 1974

Ms Mary Kearns, a Sligo born pharmaceutical chemist employed by Glaxo Laboratories in Dublin as a sales co-ordinator, became the first Irish woman ever to receive a marketing award for the UK Institute of Marketing diploma course. She was one of four students from Irish companies to receive special awards. Ms Kearns was presented with the Aubrey Fogarty Associates award for best student in marketing.

The other Irish awards were:

• Albright & Wilson award: Mr Patrick Moriarty (Best Student of the Year)

• Adsell award: Mr David A. Leech (Best Student in Advertising)

• Market Research Bureau of Ireland Ltd award: Mr Richard Tallon (Best Student in Market Research)

ECONOMIC EMERGENCY, SEPTEMBER 1974

The business and finance page of *The Irish Times* of 10 September 1974 quoted the Minister for Finance, Mr Richie Ryan TD stating that Ireland was experiencing an economic emergency. In the article Mr Ryan said that co-operation between all sections of the community aimed at restraining income demands was 'essential' if worsening inflation, a widening balance of payments and a further deterioration in Ireland's economic international competitiveness was to be avoided.

The Minister, addressing the Rotary Club, said that while the economy was basically sound, resources were limited and were considerably depleted by the rise in oil and commodity prices.

MARKETING IN AN INFLATIONARY ENVIRONMENT, OCTOBER 1974

The 'doomsday prophets', of the then inflationary environment, were strongly criticised by Mr Brendan M. Carolan MMII, director of the Jefferson Smurfit Group, when he addressed the members at Tuesday Club luncheon on 29 October 1974.

He announced that he was pleased to see some members of the Marketing Society at the meeting and stated that he felt that Ireland was too small not to have a common united platform for the development of marketing principles and practice.

According to him inflation was 'an economic bogeyman' and he said that all were aware of the ravages it had brought. It had fathered a 'whole new race of doom and gloom merchants whose sole purpose in life was the spreading of a gospel straight from "panicsville"'. Mr Carolan stated his firm had always tried to work on a basis of 'true volume, true value'. That was how they discounted inflation.

The theme of his paper was in accordance with the Institute programme for the year: 'Marketing in an Inflationary Environment'. He asked his audience not to talk themselves into depression and said he believed the Irish economy to be well founded.

The Smurfit Group were continually looking for new product development opportunities, whether by exclusive development, imitation or substitution. An example given by Mr Carolan related to replacement of the traditional chip basket for tomatoes with an attractive corrugated tray and lid. That development had won, for his company, a top industry award in Europe the previous year known as a Eurostar.

It also managed to sell a few million units.

STUDENT SEMINAR, DÚN LAOGHAIRE, NOVEMBER 1974

The Allied Irish Banks' award winning team at the MII students' one-day seminar, held at the Royal Marine hotel in Dún Laoghaire on 2 November 1974, was led by Mr J. McCauley.

With the president of the MII, Mr T.J. O'Driscoll, chairman of the Institute, Mr Joseph McGough and other members present, a uniformed Aer Lingus hostess, Ms Helen Byrne, had the honour of presenting the award.

FIRST ISSUE OF MARKETING INSTITUTE'S *DIRECTORY AND DIARY*, 1975

The first issue of the Marketing Institute's *Directory and Diary* was produced for 1975. Congratulations were extended to the editor, Mr John Kenna, and the publications committee under the chairmanship of Mr Richard Reid, for the excellent design and content of the volume.

In introducing the directory Mr Joseph McGough stated that marketing was playing an increasingly important role in the daily business life of the country and especially in the context of recent entry into the European Economic Cummunity (EEC). He believed that the ability to prosper in free trade depended on marketing skills and the ability to sell Irish products effectively in open competition.

IMPORTANCE OF SALES FORECASTS, JANUARY 1975

Mr Joseph McGough, managing director of Bord Bainne and chairman of

MII, told the Hotel Sales Management Association, Irish Chapter, at Jury's hotel, Dublin on 13 January 1975, that the basis of effective marketing management was good sales forecasts. He said that the main job was to ensure that opportunities were turned into sales.

PRESIDENT'S NIGHT DINNER, 1975

A small but perhaps significant piece of history was made when the President's Night dinner of the Marketing Institute of Ireland, held at the Shelbourne hotel in Dublin on 21 January 1975, was graced with the presence of a woman.

The chairperson of the government commission on the status of women, Dr Thekla Beere, a former secretary at the Department of Transport and Power, became the first woman ever to attend the annual MII president's function.

The President of Ireland, Mr Cathal O'Dalaigh, who was the guest of honour, said that the ability to speak a second or third language signified 'added value' in marketing terms.

He found that the Institute had come to recognise that the ability to speak the customer's language was a real asset in selling Irish goods abroad and he recommended young executives to engage in short study courses abroad to asssimilate other people's language and culture.

Membership of the EEC had given Ireland a distinct financial gain in the previous two years, while other gains, in opening up new horizons and new interests to add to Irish marketing knowledge and experience, were detailed by Dr O'Driscoll, president of the MII.

THE STEPHEN DOYLE AWARD, JANUARY 1975

The Stephen Doyle Memorial award, for meritorious service to marketing and the Institute over many years, was presented to Mr Michael H. Coote FMII, in January 1975.

CMC KLEBETECHNIK (IRL) MARKETING AWARDS, MARCH 1975

On 14 March 1975 *The Irish Times* reported that three of Ireland's 'new breed' of dynamic marketing executives were the toast of industry chiefs. Awards had been created for international marketing and selling. The recipients were:

- Mr Patrick F. Murphy (34), head of marketing, Aer Lingus, who wrote about 'Physical Distribution in International Marketing'

- Miss Ursula Schmeling (23), international sales manager, Electrical

Industries of Ireland, for a paper on 'International Exhibitions as a Marketing Tool in Opening up New Markets'

- Mr Brendan O'Kelly (22), assistant brands manager, W. & C. McDonnell Ltd, who wrote on 'Export Marketing for the Confectionery Industry'.

The CMC awards, worth £350 each, were presented at a function in Dublin by Mr Heinz Pollmeler, managing director of CMC Klebetechnik (Irl) Ltd, a Waterford based insulation and adhesive tapes firm who were the sponsors.

EEC SEMINAR, MAY 1975

Speaking on 27 May 1975 at a seminar in Dublin entitled 'Ireland and the EEC', Mr Michael Killeen, managing director of the IDA stated that new job approvals would probably fall in the range of 15,000 to 20,000. That represented a decrease in the target set the previous December.

The reasons given by Mr Killeen for this were the deteriorating state of the world economy together with a spiraling inflation rate on the domestic front. Moreover he said that Ireland's rate of inflation was almost certain to exceed the forecasted 25 per cent in 1975.

Mr Tom O'Donnell TD, Minister for the Gaeltacht, added his voice to warnings on inflation. He said that as world trade began to pick up again, recovering from the deflationary effect of the oil crisis, Ireland's competitive trading position would be whittled away, not just slowly but quite rapidly. Continental members of the EEC had been relatively successful in bringing their inflation rates under control in the recent months, but Mr O'Donnell said that in Ireland and Britain the rate of increase to consumer prices had continued to accelerate.

EEC LOAN, £18M., MAY 1975

On 28 May 1975 an agreement signed in London for the provision of project finance to the extent of £18.2m. between Midland Bank Ltd and Cement Ltd Co. Meath was published. The loan was negotiated through the Export Credit Guarantee Department and was the largest EEC guaranteed loan then made to Ireland.

The finance was to assist Cement Ltd in concluding contracts with UK suppliers for plant, equipment and associated services for Cement's extension to its works at Platin, Co. Meath. The main feature of the extension was a one million ton per annum rotary cement kiln. The plant extension was scheduled to be completed by early 1978 and to produce an extra 3,000 tons of cement each day, when in full production.

DEFENCE OF THE MEAT INDUSTRY, MAY 1975

A spirited defence of the meat industry was made by the general manager of Clover Meats, Mr Michael Collins, when he said that in the latter half of 1974 and since the new intervention price was negotiated in March 1975, the trade had been subjected to extreme and, in fact, unjust and unfair criticism.

Mr Collins was speaking at the seminer on 'Ireland and the EEC, 1975', organised by the Marketing Institute. He referred to the 'big glut of cattle' that went on the market in 1974. A rapid increase in the national herd had reflected in a massive total kill in meat factories of 1, 071,000 head in 1974 and coincided with an unanticipated world glut of beef.

Mr Collins stated that the introduction of the Green Pound in September 1974 had resulted in an immediate increase of 5p per lb. in the intervention price for beef, and that was at a time when the meat trade warned that it would be impossible to market beef commercially.

The managing director of An Bord Bainne, Mr Joseph McGough (chairman of MII), said that the latest figures for milk production showed an increase of 11 per cent over the same period the previous year. If that trend continued Bord Bainne would be close to reaching its target, a 10 per cent increase at the commencement of the campaign.

He went on to say that 'we are keenly aware of the value of our investment in the Kerrygold brand name, estimated at £10m. in the UK market alone'. That investment, he stated, had come from the dairy farmers of Ireland.

Allegations made by the EEC Agriculture Commissioner, Mr Petrus Lardinois, that Irish cattle were unsuitable for the continental trade and that they were predominantly dependent on the British market, were flatly rejected by leading figures in the meat industry in Ireland. Mr Gus Fitzpatrick, general manager of Premier Meat Packers, accused Mr Lardinois of attempting to promote Dutch calf exports to Italy at the expense of Irish exports. Mr Collins agreed and stated that there was no foundation whatsoever for this statement.

Mr Thomas J. Garvey, general manager of Córas Tráchtála was of the opinion that Ireland must diversify. He believed that, within a period of five years, Ireland could substantially change its level of dependence. It could be changed to a position where Britain constituted only one-third of Ireland's markets, the rest of the EC another one-third and the remaining third taken by North America and the rest of the world. However, he stressed that major changes in attitudes were necessary and felt that training must be provided to participate actively in the management process.

Dr Sean O'Ceallaigh, director of business policy, Confederation of Irish Industries, and Mr David Kennedy, chief executive of Aer Lingus, also spoke at the seminar.

FINANCIAL YEAR TO BE CHANGED FROM JANUARY 1975

A decision was made by the national council of MII to change their financial year to the end of December from January 1975. This would bring the year into line with the other members of the Common Market.

Consequently it was agreed that the 1974–5 chairman Mr Joseph McGough, officers and council should continue in office until December 1975 (instead of June).

REVIEW OF EXAM PAPERS, 1975

A review of the examination papers, set for students in 1975, shows the subjects covered:

* Certificate in Marketing: Part I

  Elements of Statistics; Principles of Economics l; Business Organisation; Marketing I

* Certificate in Marketing: Part 2

  Marketing 2; Commercial Law; Applied Economics; Accounting

* Graduateship examination: Part 3

  Financial Management; Marketing-Sales Management; International Marketing; Quantitative Methods-Marketing

* Graduateship in Marketing: Part 4

  Marketing 4; Consumer Motivation and Behaviour; Computer Science; Theory of Business; Case Study.

FIRST IRISH GRADUATION OF MII STUDENTS, SEPTEMBER 1975

The Minister for Education, Mr Ray Burke TD, presented the first ever 'completely Irish' graduateships in marketing for 21 MII marketing students in Dublin on 15 September 1975. A number of awards were presented. These were:

* President's medal: Mr John Cowman, Cork (Best Student of the Year)
* Silver award: Mr Anthony Cahill, Dublin
* Albright & Wilson award: Mr Patrick Murnane, Cork

- Aubrey Fogarty Associates award: Mr Thomas Hayes, Dublin

- Adsel award: Mr Albert Murray, Dublin.

Some 836 students had registered with the Institute in the four years since the programme began. Courses were being held in Dublin, Cork and Limerick as well as in the regional colleges in Athlone, Carlow, Dundalk, Galway and Waterford. It was hoped to have courses in operation also in Sligo and Tralee by the beginning of the next academic year.

EUROPEAN MARKETING CONGRESS, MAY 1975

Amsterdam, Holland, was the venue for the eleventh European Marketing Congress and AGM from 28–29 May 1975. Representing the Marketing Institute of Ireland were Messrs Bill Fraser, vice-president of EMC, Harry Woods, past-president and Joseph Bigger, administrator of MII.

Dr I. Samkalden, Burgomaster of Amsterdam, in the preface to Jules B. Farber's pictorial book, *Amsterdam-City of the Seventies,* wrote that it was a portrayal of the most fascinating aspects of life in that city as viewed by a foreign journalist. He became an Amsterdammer. He incorporated the views of all of their kind, adding impressions of his own, on life in the Dutch capital. A copy of the book was kindly presented to the officers of EMC.

It is interesting to recall that the business history of Holland goes back to a charter in 1275 (by Floris V. Count) giving those living near the Dam in the Amstel the freedom to trade throughout Holland.

The Nederlands Centrum van Directeuren (NCD) celebrated their fourth lustrum (decade) in marketing in Holland on 23 March 1973 and to celebrate this the officers of EMC, including myself, were presented with an inscribed glass candleholder.

MARKETING CONFERENCE IN WEXFORD, 26–28 OCTOBER 1975

The 1975 MII annual marketing conference was held at the Great Southern Hotel, Rosslare, Wexford, over two full days, 27 and 28 October 1975. (The dates coincided with the Wexford Opera Festival).

The Irish Times reported that the first day was spent 'learning how to learn'. The title of the conference was: 'Change: Let's Get to Grips with it'. The benefits and implementation of the Coverdale learning system were fully considered. The benefits were learned from Mr Milo Lynch, who attended to Coverdale's affairs in Ireland. Delegates attempted the implementation and formed themselves into syndicates, following Mr Lynch's address.

Later an example of implementation was given by Mr Andrew Dare of the Wexford Creamery, who had introduced a great deal of Coverdale thinking into his company's operation and planning. The system permitted individuals to develop self-monitoring systems by analysing their own thinking process. It was defined as a system of planned experience by which a person could discover for oneself certain benefits and learn from the experience.

An industrial psychologist, Mr Dermot Egan, of Allied Irish Bank said the Coverdale style of learning permitted the systematic application of relatively simple ideas throughout a company. He suggested it could offer a greater total benefit than the injection of an extremely sophisticated technique at top management level.

On the second day of the conference the 40 delegates considered social aspects of marketing and analysed the motivation of the consumer. They also looked at the markets of the world and learned to evaluate the market potential for new industrial products. However, it was pointed out that they, the delegates, were found to be wanting. That was the result of a paper given by Mr John Methven, director general of the UK office of Fair Trading. The paper was read in his absence by Mr Jim Beale of PA Management Consultants. In fact, the paper startled the delegates by the intricacy of its detail and the power of far-reaching effects.

The advantages of a voluntary code of practice were debated and compared to the imposition of government legislation.

Dr Patrick Kehoe MMII, director of Irish Pensions Trust and Hong Kong management consultant, said that the contemporary marketing executive had left behind the old notion of marketing as 'pushing products'. He further said that those involved in any marketing exercise must be very cognisant of a social conscience, particularly with regard to marketing to low income consumers in the expanding urban areas.

Mr Colm Regan, head of the new project identification section of the IDA, in his paper highlighted the creation of new business opportunities in the changing industrial environment in Ireland. Three key opportunity areas lay, he said, in manufacturing products (presently imported), in specific spin-off development from the establishment of big foreign factories in Ireland and in the rapid rate of Irish industrialists creating new opportunities in the supply of building components and equipment.

IMI STUDY, OCTOBER 1975

A published study by the Irish Management Institute (IMI), revealed a significant co-relation between management planning and the return on equity. Of all techniques, planning was found to be the weakest, particularly in medium sized and small companies. The survey showed that market planning rated at an all time low. The challenge to marketing managers was made when judged as planners.

The Marketing Institute of Ireland chairman, Mr Joseph McGough was of the same opinion. He declared that marketing without planning was just not acceptable because one must have a complete concept of demand. No single area could be disregarded or isolated. He maintained that a total marketing plan was a basic essential. It was necessary to first investigate the market, then to construct an appropriate product. Too many companies still seemed to make things first then attempt to sell them and realisation, he felt, only came with the establishment of targets

Mr Jerry Liston, chairman of the Marketing Society, expressed surprise at the facts. However, he respected the IMI and accepted their findings and stated that he was convinced of the basic necessity of planning. He was critical of five-year planning but suggested a two-year plan instead of a one-year plan, then favoured a three-year plan as being most realistic

MARKET RESEARCH, OCTOBER 1975

Addressing members of the Institute of Directors, Mr Bernard Audley of AGB Research, said that market research was not just a matter of asking questions, it required all the right questions. Referring to research made by motor manufacturers in Detroit, he recalled that in their questions to consumers they had not thought to enquire about attitude to cars with an engine of less than 2,000 c.c. Toyota, he stated, did its research completely and resulted in producing the Toyota Corolla, then the world's third best selling car.

ELECTRICITY, STRATEGY REVEALED, FEBRUARY 1976

Mr P.J. Moriarty, director of personnel, Electricity Supply Board (ESB), addressed MII members at the Jury's hotel luncheon on 24 February 1976. He announced that the ESB, who employed 11,600 people, hoped to break the price increase by a combination of measures. He outlined a six-point strategy of which the main three were:

1. Improve the overall economic performance of the business, through load management and load shaping.

2. Make the best use of costly imports of oil, which up to 31 March 1976 had cost £38m. compared to £13.5m. the previous year.

3. Get the share of any new markets which might develop with the national emergence from the economic recession.

In relation to load management and load shaping Mr Moriarty explained that the ESB would endeavour to achieve less use of electricity at peak periods and greater use at slack periods. The board would use bigger units, e.g. the

740 megawatt unit in Tarbert, Co. Kerry, which would be the biggest power station in the Irish Republic.

The latest stage was costing £41.5m., while Poolbeg, Dublin, was also being extended

NCEA AWARDS FIRST DEGREES, FEBRUARY 1976

In February 1976 the director of the National Council for Educational Awards (NCEA), Mr Padraig MacDiarmada, advised Mr Harry Woods FMII, that he had been elected to act on the panel of assessors in marketing for two years.

Submissions from Regional Technical Colleges were provided for consideration. In the meantime, during 1975, the NCEA council had conferred its first degrees (48). The degree of Bachelor of Arts was conferred in two categories:

1. Students who had successfully completed a degree programme at St Mary's College, Twickenham, Middlesex. The students (eleven) had attended the course on scholarship from the Irish government.

2. Students who had successfully completed a degree programme at the National College of Physical Education (NCPE), Limerick.

First NCEA degrees from Irish college, 1975

Awards made to students at NCPE were the first degrees awarded by the NCEA to students graduating from a College of Higher Education in Ireland. The study programme contained a number of interesting features. Besides being the first co-educational teacher training programme in Ireland, it was also the first degree level teacher training course in the Republic of Ireland which followed a concurrent, rather than a consecutive pattern.

The four-year course at NCPE embraced the study of Physical Education *and* one other subject. Together with the study of education it included a period of supervised teaching practice each year.

MII appointments, 1976

Dr T.J. O'Driscoll agreed to continue as president of MII, with Mr Basil Lapworth as vice-president. Mr Anthony J. Neville, MII.Grad., became chairman for the calendar year 1976. He was the youngest person to be elected to that position to date. The officers appointed were:

• Mr Richard E. Reid: Senior Vice-Chairman

• Mr Philip R. Flood: Vice-Chairman of Finance

- Mr Patrick Kehoe: Vice-Chairman of Membership

- Mr Eugene P. Quigley: Vice-Chairman of Education

- Ms Elizabeth Lloyd: Hon. Secretary.

The members of the executive committee in addition to the officers were: Messrs Joseph Bigger, Bill Cavanagh, Nial Darragh, Aubrey Fogarty, Norman McConnell, Harry Woods and Harry Wyer.

AGM OF EUROPEAN MARKETING COUNCIL, MAY 1976

The twenty-first AGM of the European Marketing Council held in Oslo, Norway from 5–6 May 1976, was chaired by the president Mr Manuel Caragol of Spain. The officers present were: vice-presidents, Mr William D. Fraser (Ireland), Dr Leo van Nouhuys (Holland), immediate past-president, Mr Roy Randolph (UK) and the secretary-general, Dr Fred Th. Witkamp. Spokesperson delegates were present from nine countries. These were Germany, Finland, Spain, France, UK, Ireland, Netherlands, Norway and Sweden. Mr Tony Neville, chairman of MII, delegate spokesman and Mr Harry Woods, past-president of EMC, also represented Ireland.

In attendance were non-voting members from the countries mentioned, also nine past-presidents of the host countries.

Mr Leif V. Ruud, president of Salglederklubben (Norway), welcomed the participants. He was presented with the ceremonial 'Wilkinson Sword of Honour' by Mr A. van Eesteren, on behalf of Nederlands Centrum van Directeuren, Amsterdam, where the 1975 AGM had taken place.

The minutes of the Oslo AGM are quite lengthy therefore only some of the highlights can be mentioned.

EMC appointments

The president of EMC Mr Manuel Carragol of Spain asked the vice-president Mr Bill Fraser of Ireland to take the chair. The acting chairman, Mr Bill Fraser, proposed to re-elect Mr Caragol for a second year. Delegates unanimously approved with applause. Mr Tony Bellm (UK) was elected a vice-president.

Arrangements in hand for the twelfth European Marketing Congress, to be held in Dublin in 1977, were reported on by Mr Tony Neville of Ireland.

EMC awards, May 1976

The Robert Collischon award was presented to Mr Peter Blood, director of the Institute of Marketing (UK) for his contributions made to the work of

EMC and in furthering good relationships with other marketing associations in Europe.

The Publications award was accepted by Mrs Liselotte Wagner on behalf of the Deutsche Marketing Vereinigung. The president stated that the magazine, *Absatzwirtschaft*, was important not alone to the German organisation but also because of the influence it had in Europe. It was known as a voice in marketing.

For the considerable efforts made in organising the eleventh European Marketing Congress in Amsterdam in 1975, Mr Abraham van Eesteren was presented with the International Activity award.

EMC registration proposal

Mr Bill Fraser of Ireland explained the 'set-up' in Brussels, in the EEC, including that for marketing education to the delegates. He asked the meeting to approve a letter to be sent to President Ortoli, EEC Commission and that EMC member countries should do the same, through their Commissioner in Brussels

The final decision was that Mr Fraser's letter would go out to the EEC under the names only of those EMC countries who are members of the EEC. Mr Fraser again also urged that the meeting consider and at least have EMC registered in Brussels.

Mr Pirot (France) strongly supported the proposal, as did Holland. Certain minor changes to the wording were agreed on and the letter would be posted on 18 May to the EEC Commissioners

Irish report

Mr Tony Neville gave a broad outline of activities of the Marketing Institute of Ireland, contained in a paper submitted. He also handed each delegate a copy of the study by Dr Enda Hession: 'Business Education — Europe'.

AER LINGUS 40TH ANNIVERSARY, MAY 1976

The Irish Times in its special six-page supplement report of May 28 1976 reported that on May 27 1976 Aer Lingus marked the 40th anniversary of its first flight 'against a background of recession and serious difficulty; yet the airline now has grounds for hope'. Mr Jack Fagan, air correspondent of *The Irish Times*, went on to outline the problems. He said that after two disastrous years, during which Aer Lingus lost over £10m., the future of the North Atlantic service was in the balance. Aer Lingus, however, expected to return a profit in 1977–78.

Mr David Kennedy, chief executive of Aer Lingus, in an interview with

Mr Henry Kelly of *The Irish Times*, stated that 'Airlines don't just run their business as they like. There are rules and laws, ordained by governments, which restrict our operations'. He went on to refer to the autumn of 1973, when there was an oil crisis. He said that for the year ended April 1974 the Aer Lingus fuel bill was £4m., while for the following year the bill for the same amount of fuel was £10.5m. The reason the company had diversified into the hotel business was to 'earn profits to underpin the running of the airline'.

The airline's birthday celebrations took place in style at Dublin Airport reported the *Irish Independent*, with a special reception for passengers on the Bristol bound flight EI-2364. Two of the five passengers, who were on the inaugural commercial flight were at the function. They were Mrs Sheila Martin, Rathfarnham, Dublin and Dr T.J. O'Driscoll, former director general of Bord Fáilte, and a director of the airline.

It had been 40 years previously (1936) that Irish Sea Airways started the first scheduled service from Baldonnel to Bristol, using a solitary five-seater De Haviland Dragon-84, named Iolar. The service had been extended later in the year to London.

IRISHMEN IN TOP BUSINESS LEAGUE, JUNE 1976

Three Irishmen, well known for their work in Irish agriculture, business and marketing, were included in an élite list of European heads published by the exclusive International business magazine, *Vision*. They were Messrs Joseph McGough, Tony O'Reilly and Michael Smurfit.

The list showed 80 top international business executives from fourteen western European countries, as 'men who would be a major asset to the board of a big international company'. The enumeration had been drawn up by international bankers, management consultants and *Vision* editors in the European countries.

PRESIDENT'S DINNER, JUNE 1976

The president's dinner of the Marketing Institute was held on 29 June 1976 in the presence of the chairman Mr Tony Neville, vice-president Mr Basil Lapworth, members and many guests.

The guest speaker, Mr David Orr, chairman of Unilever Ltd, said that pressures from small groups of dedicated consumer advocates, or from bureaucrats, could lead to increased costs without compensating benefits. As an example he cited that if Unilever were to state the exact percentage of each ingredient of the oils and fats used in its margarines it would deprive the company of the flexibility to take advantage of the changing price of raw materials. It would result in the company being unable to use its skill in the interest of the consumer, in producing quality at minimum cost.

THE STEPHEN DOYLE AWARD, JUNE 1976

The Stephen Doyle award, for meritorious service to marketing over many years, was presented to Mr Philip Flood, head of the Marketing Department, College of Marketing, Dublin.

It was awarded particularly for his dedicated work in establishing marketing courses throughout the country. There were now 1,100 students registered at ten colleges in Dublin and the provinces.

MII STUDENT AWARD, 1976

The Student of the Year award was presented to Mr Brian More O'Farrell in the presence of the chairman, president of MII and members. Mr T.J. Garvey, chief executive of Córas Tráchtála made the presentaion on behalf of sponsors, CTT.

MARKETING SOCIETY/MII LIAISON GROUP REPORT, SEPTEMBER 1976

The executive council meeting of 2 September 1976, held at the Royal Hibernian hotel, Dublin, heard a report of discussions between the Marketing Society and the Marketing Institute liaison group.

An examination of the Articles of Association of both bodies anticipated the drawing up of a discussion document, to cover a possible constitution and membership criteria for a single marketing body. (At the end of 1999, such a decision had not materialised.)

UNIVERSITY COLLEGE CORK APPOINT MARKETING LECTURER, 1976

Following a full report of activities from the Cork branch, Mr Philip Flood added that University College, Cork, had decided to establish a Management Department. The first appointment would be a marketing lecturer.

LACK OF USE OF MARKETING TECHNIQUES, OCTOBER 1976

The chairman of MII, Mr Anthony Neville, addressing a Rotary Club luncheon on 26 October 1976, said that the lack of use of marketing techniques was certainly one of the factors contributing to the serious difficulties experienced by some industries in recent years.

He said tariff barriers had resulted in management being production orientate and stated his belief that planning was one of the fundamentals of good marketing practice but he felt the need had not been fully recognised. The purpose of business, he stressed, was to make and keep customers.

MII APPOINTMENTS, NOVEMBER 1976

It was announced at executive meeting of 4 November 1976, that the president, Dr T.J. O'Driscoll, had agreed to continue in office for a further year and that Mr Basil Lapworth and Mr Bill Fraser had agreed to be vice-presidents of the MII for 1977.

At the meeting the continuity committee (Messrs Harry Wyer, Leslie Whitehead, John D. Carroll and Nial Darragh, chairman) reported on four recommendations:

1. Seanad nominations: MII to nominate certain named members.

2. Memorandum and amended Articles of Association: registration and printing to be completed by the end of 1976.

3. Rules and Regulations (of MII): to be brought up-to-date and promulgated, as deemed necessary.

4. Arrangement to be made of a special meeting with the council to discuss issues felt contentious by members.

CONFERENCE OF LECTURERS AND EXAMINERS, NOVEMBER 1976

A conference of MII lecturers and examiners was held at the Green Isle hotel, Dublin on 20 November 1976. Over forty lecturers attended representing the two Dublin colleges, and those of Carlow, Cork, Limerick and Athlone.

BUSINESS & FINANCE SUPPLEMENT, NOVEMBER 1976

An excellent, 28-page supplement entitled *Marketing in Ireland* was produced by *Business & Finance*, in association with the Marketing Institute of Ireland. This was published in November 1976.

It is only possible, due to space limitation in this book, to recall some statements from the variety of articles in the supplement.

Social area and the consumer, November 1976

Mr Pat Kehoe, vice-chairman of MII, wrote that in the 1970s it was clearly evident that marketing methods and practice were not merely technical matters that concerned only the marketing executive. They were, he said, matters of deep concern which demanded from all executives a responsible social sensitivity to the functioning of the company in the marketplace. The attitude to marketing, he felt, may no longer be deemed sufficiently comprehensive.

Marketing Overseas, November 1976

Mr John Kenna, CII, council member of MII and chairman of the Irish European Marketing committee, pointed out that in the ten-year period up to 1973 the value of exports had grown by 40 per cent per annum. At that time over 75 per cent of exports from Ireland came from four main industrial sectors. They included food, drink and tobacco; machinery and transport equipment; chemicals; textiles, clothing and footware.

New product development v old, November 1976

New product development versus old product development was the subject dealt with efficiently by Mr Peter Owens, governing director of Peter Owens Advertising and Marketing. He referred to Mr David Luck, Professor of Marketing at the University of Southern Illinois and quoted him saying:

> The product manager is probably the most misunderstood and most controversial figure in modern marketing. Yet it is the product manager who literally made possible the growth of many businesses over the previous twenty years.

Research in a recession, November 1976

The managing director of Irish Marketing Surveys and past chairman of the Marketing Society, Mr John Meagher, emphasised that there seemed to be general agreement that the slow economic recovery of Ireland to modest prosperity must be tackled particularly from market research.

It was hoped that the tripartite talks, on foot of the government's Green Paper, would produce a consensus among what was fashionably called the social partners. It had to be accepted that the role of business, in bringing about a return to real growth and fuller employment, was a crucial one.

Ireland's product range, November 1976

The product development manager of Córas Tráchtála, Mr A.D. Suttle, pointed out that CTT had been increasingly aware of the fact that many Irish companies were in trouble, in both the home and export markets. Their products were becoming obsolete. Programmes to identify new products to fit into existing ranges were not being identified by companies. It meant that products new to the companies concerned would enable them to maintain a competitive position in their markets. In addition to the tax rebate outlined, financing schemes should be examined

Ireland's membership of the EEC made it attractive to small and medium-sized overseas manufacturers in developed non-EEC countries (e.g. USA and Japan) who were selling successfully in their own markets but who did not want to extend their operations into Europe. Such companies could obtain royalty revenue from Europe by licensing production and marketing to an appropriate Irish company.

STUDENT CASE STUDY, NOVEMBER 1976

In the Victor Hotel, Dún Laoghaire, Co. Dublin, the annual MII case study took place with 132 students (twelve teams of eleven) taking part. The panel of adjudicators for the day comprised: Professor Tony Cunningham (UCD), Dr John Murray (UCD), Dr Frank Bradley (UCD) and Mr Joseph McGough, BL, FMII.

MEMBERSHIP OF MII, NOVEMBER 1976

The membership total of MII had reached 486 (Dublin 423, including overseas members), Cork branch 26, Galway 13 and Limerick 24) in November 1976.

The final meeting of 1976 was held on 7 December at Orwell Road, Dublin. It was noted with regret that the Marketing Society had decided to discontinue discussions regarding the establishment of one marketing body. They felt concern that the style and content of the services they provided to their members would be affected by the large number created by one body. It was agreed that future liaison would be between the Chairmen of the two bodies. Joint meetings should continue to take place and likewise in respect of joint statements on marketing topics.

Dr T.J. O'Driscoll, president of MII, had been invited to the inauguration of the President of Ireland, Dr P. Hillery. It was a significant fact that the invitation had been accepted for Dr O'Driscoll, in his capacity as president of the Marketing Institute of Ireland.

An Institute member, Mr Bob Gahan, deputy-chairman of Radio Telefís Éireann, became the recipient of the McConnell award. Congratulations were extended to him.

EXECUTIVE COUNCIL MEETING HERALDS NEW YEAR, 1977

The new year, 1977, saw the MII first executive council meeting being held on 26 January at Orwell Road, Rathgar, Dublin.

Representing the Auditors, Butler Chance & Co., Mr Paul Wallace was present to discuss the draft accounts and financial situation of the Institute. It was felt necessary to increase the annual subcription to £20.

Mr Phil Flood asked for guidelines for the charity and scholarship funds, and suggested some form of fundraising should take place.

It was reported that there was a possibility of a group of the Institute being formed in Waterford, through the efforts of member, Mrs Delia Burke.

AGM OF MII, FEBRUARY 1977

At 73 Orwell Road, Rathgar, Dublin, the fifteenth AGM of the Marketing Institute of Ireland was held on 14 February 1977 at 6.30 p.m.

The attendance of 54 included Mr Paul Wallace (Butler, Chance & Co. Auditors) the president of the Institute, Dr T.J. O'Driscoll and Mr D. Moran, Institute solicitor.

The outgoing chairman, Mr Tony Neville, referring to progress during the past year, expressed the need for continuity of purpose and action in the long-term development plan, initiated two years previously.

Concern was expressed about the financial deterioration shown in the Institute accounts. Rigorous controls had, however, been put in place to ensure future satisfaction.

New members of the council, Messrs Nial Darragh and Aubrey Fogarty, were declared elected.

NEW APPOINTMENTS OF MII, 1977

The president, Dr O'Driscoll, announced the new chairman as Mr Richard Reid and presented him with the chain of office. Mr Reid then declared the names of the new officers:

* Senior Vice-Chairman: Dr P. Kehoe
* Vice-Chairman, Services: Mr Jack Downey
* Vice-Chairman, Finance: Mr Nial Darragh
* Vice-Chairman, Education: Mr Eugene Quigley

Mr Richard Reid was pleased to announce that Dr O'Driscoll had agreed to continue as president and Messrs Basil Lapworth and Bill Fraser, as vice-presidents. Miss Elizabeth Lloyd was unanimously elected hon. secretary.

It was announced that the Institute of Marketing, London, had kindly agreed to the free inclusion (to their 22,000 members) of a special leaflet prepared by MII, regarding the forthcoming European Marketing Conference to be held in Dublin.

LIMERICK BRANCH OF MII, MARCH 1977

Dr Barra O'Cinneide reported that the Limerick branch had made progress, since its revival in December 1976. Monthly meetings had been planned there and much support had come from the NIHE (National Institute of Higher Education) while they hoped to have a one-day seminar later in the year.

CORK BRANCH OF MII, MARCH 1977

Mr Michael McKenna said that Cork branch also had revived activity and priorities were in membership, student education, facilities and service for all.

The Cork regional branch held their Ladies' Night function on 11 March 1977 at the Imperial hotel. The concept of presenting all ladies with a gift bag of many food, luxury and advertising items, was promoted in the circular to members. This followed the established practice in Dublin. The guest speaker was Mr Albert Gubay a well-known supermarket entrepreneur.

INSTITUTE OF MARKETING, N. IRELAND BRANCH, APRIL 1977

The annual dinner of the Northern Ireland branch of the Institute of Marketing was held at the Culloden hotel on 19 April 1977, at which their new chairman, Mr Eric Pollock, presided. The MMI president, Dr T.J. O'Driscoll, chairman of the Dublin branch, Mr Pat Nolan and the chief executive of MII, Mr Joseph Bigger, were pleased to attend.

The Northern Ireland branch was particularly interested and keen to co-operate with the MII in student affairs and welcomed initiatives from the Institute.

PRESIDENT'S NIGHT, MAY 1977

The speaker for the President's Night dinner on 10 May 1977 at Jury's hotel, Dublin, was Mr John Mann, of Irish National Trading Corporation. It was his first address in his new role. The chairman of the Marketing Society, Mr Finbar Costello, was a guest at the function.

FELLOWSHIPS, MAY 1977

Dr O'Driscoll presented the scroll of honour to Mr J.D. Carroll and Mr D.F. Mahon Lee on their deserved election to Fellowship of the Marketing Institute of Ireland.

The Stephen Doyle award

On the same occasion as the fellowship awards, the president of MII presented the Stephen Doyle award, for meritorious services to marketing, to Mr Joseph C. Bigger.

Mr Bigger retired shortly afterwards from his position as chief executive of the Institute, which he had held since 1970. He was wished a long and happy retirement by his many friends.

STUDENT EXAMINATIONS, MAY 1977

The total number of students who sat the May 1977 examinations was 483. That represented an increase of 87 over that of 1976. The breakdown was: Dublin 379, Cork 56, Carlow 22, Dundalk 12, Limerick 8 and Galway 6.

SEANAD ÉIREANN NOMINATIONS, MAY 1977

The Marketing Institute of Ireland was notified as having been entered on the Register of Nomination Bodies of Seanad Éireann, under its acts. This meant that one candidate could be nominated by MII for election to the Seanad on the appropriate panel, i.e. the industrial and commercial panel.

IFA, BORD BAINNE AND MII MEETING, MAY 1977

The Irish Times of 19 May 1977 reported that a three-way meeting took place between representatives of An Bord Bainne, the Irish Farmers' Association (IFA) and the MII.

Dr Pat Kehoe, who participated, was complimented with regard to statements accredited to the Institute. Much work had been put into organising the European Marketing Congress to be held in Dublin, regarding programme, speakers, sponsorships, bookings, publicity and financial control,

MURPHY'S BREWERY, MAY 1977

On 26 May 1977 a very successful luncheon meeting was held at Silversprings hotel, Cork. The guest speaker was Mr Michael Long, managing director of Murphy's Brewery, Cork, who spoke on the subject: 'Murphy's — the Marketing Story'.

It was a well-attended function and there was a very favourable reaction to the speaker's address. The *Cork Examiner* afforded good coverage the following morning, showing the text of speaker's remarks on its business page.

MR DEREK WHELAN CHAIRS EMC COMMITTEE, MAY 1977

The chairman of the MII European Marketing Council (EMC) committee, Mr Derek Whelan, reporting on the congress in Dublin, 25–27 May 1977, said the EMC held its AGM the first day when two reports were delivered by the Irish delegation.

The first concerned the development of the MII within the previous year, while the second was concerned with the current marketing problem in Ireland ('the influence of foreign controlled companies on marketing in Ireland').

The standard of contribution from delegates of other EMC member countries was impressive and quite a lot was learned also of their problems.

EMC EUROPEAN MARKETING CONGRESS IN DUBLIN, MAY 1977

The two-day EMC twelfth European Marketing Congress held at the Gresham hotel, Dublin, was attended by members from nine of the twelve EMC member countries: Finland, France, Germany, Netherlands, Norway, Spain, Sweden, United Kingdom, and Ireland. Observers were present from Luxembourg and Portugal. Members and students from Ireland taking part numbered 66.

It was agreed that the Marketing Institute of Ireland had benefited in terms of prestige, both within Ireland and among fellow members of the EMC. Letters subsequently received from the latter conveyed appreciation of a worthwhile and enjoyable three-days. It was also gratifying that the final account would show no financial loss on the congress.

BUSINESS & FINANCE SPECIAL SUPPLEMENT, MAY 1977

A special *Business & Finance* EMC Congress supplement (32 pp.) in association with the Marketing Institute of Ireland, was declared a very fine summary of the proceedings, editorial and photographic, and contained specially detailed articles.

DR CONOR CRUISE O'BRIEN OPENS EMC CONGRESS, MAY 1977

In opening the twelfth European Marketing Congress in the Gresham hotel, Dublin, Dr Conor Cruise O'Brien TD, Minister for Posts and Telegraphs, paid tribute to the memory of a former president of the Marketing Institute of Ireland, the late Sean Lemass.

Sean Lemass tribute

Dr Conor Cruise O'Brien said of Mr Sean Lemass that he was a statesman with a vision of what was for the good, not alone for the people of the Republic of Ireland but for all the people on the island. He was a man of progressive ideas in relation to social and economic development, and had sensitivity towards the needs and views of minorities. In addition, he had sought to open the way to constitutional reform.

Dr O'Brien went on to declare that Mr Lemass, when he met Terence O'Neill, then president of Northern Ireland, made a historic breakthrough in the direction of improving relations between the State and Northern Ireland. His example remained and it was one which could be cherished by people of all parties in Ireland.

Dr O'Brien believed that Lemass's tenure of the Marketing Institute of Ireland was the recognition, by a very practical man, of the importance of marketing to the Irish economy. He told the delegates that in Ireland, during the previous few years, the country had faced the dual challenge of recession and the final stages of the advance towards full free trade, for its emerging industrial structure. The obligations of EEC membership were severe, while industry, commerce and agriculture stayed with the task and could face the future with greater confidence.

MARKETING NEWS, MAY 1977

Marketing News, Vol. 1, No. 4, May 1977, detailed the EMC Congress programme, from the arrival of delegates on Wednesday 25 May 4 p.m., to and including the meeting on Saturday 28 May of a World Marketing Contact Group (9.00–4.00) at the Gresham hotel, Dublin.

The speakers, and subjects concerned, at the EMC Congress were:

• Financial Aspects of European Marketing

Paper 1: Mr E. Cahill, Senior Executive, Industrial Credit Company (State Development Bank), Ireland.

Paper 2: Currency fluctuations: their Effect on Marketing — Dr L. Van Driel, Chief Economist, Algemene Bank Nederland, Netherlands.

- Marketing and Labour Policies — the New Relationship

  Paper 1: Better Working Conditions — Who Benefits? — Mr J. Hallenborg, Group Staff Executive, AB Volvo, Sweden.

  Paper 2: The Business Environment — A Trade Union View — Mr P. Gresham, Manpower and Industrial Relations Adviser: National Economic Development Office, UK.

- Government Policies — their Implications for Marketing

  Paper 1: Legal Aspects of the Free Market in the Federal Republic of Germany — Dr L. Donie, Attorney-at-Law, W. Germany.

  Paper 2: The Effect of Government Policies on Marketing Decisions — Mr T. McBurnie, Managing Director, Ravenhead Glass, UK.

- Challenge of the 80s, Consumerism and the New Technology

  Paper 1: Information Labelling and Unit Pricing — Mr A. Dukes, Adviser to Mr Burke, Commissioner for Consumer Affairs, EEC.

  Paper 2: Misleading Advertising — Mr L. Kramer, Principal Administrator, Consumer Protection Division, EEC.

  Paper 3: New Manufacturing Technologies — How Marketing Can Benefit — Dr M.A. Peirce, Applied Research and Consultancy Group, Dublin University, Ireland.

The Congress dinner/cabaret was held at Jury's hotel, Dublin.

A special programme was also provided for 'accompanying persons', including the ladies in particular, not partaking in the business meetings. This included a visit to Switzer's Department Store in Dublin's most fashionable street, Grafton Street, to hear an illustrated lecture on antique Waterford Glass. After that Louis Marcus's film, *The Conquest of Light* was shown. The following day, Friday 27 May, a scenic drive took place through County Wicklow, visiting Powerscourt Gardens

TUESDAY CLUB MEETINGS, 1977

The number of Tuesday Club luncheon meetings being held by the MII, had grown so rapidly that Cathal Brugha found it possible to report on only a couple of them. One that he did report on was when Mr Albert Gubay spoke to several hundred members and students of the Institute the previous March.

To the enjoyment of the listeners he (Mr Albert Gubay) claimed he knew nothing about marketing. He told of his start in New Zealand and plans for setting up 'Three Guys Supermarkets' in Ireland.

He said they (Gubay's) would be 15–20 per cent cheaper than others were a few months previously, making him something of an enigma to all except those who had read *Marketing Decision Making — A Model Building Approach* (by Philip Kotler).

Mr Gubay claimed that he had the only fully computerised stock controlling system in the world, with the velocity of each item in stock, stock levels, etc. all measured and included as variables in computer models. Such models were used to optimise the number of products to be sold, the shelf-space to be given to each product and the throughput of each item. In concluding he informed those present that he intended to invest £7 to £10m. in Ireland.

CÓRAS TRÁCHTÁLA, INDUSTRIAL PRODUCTS, 1977

In his paper Mr Colm McDonnell, assistant chief executive of Córas Tráchtála, pointed out that CTT believed the growth rate of 15 per cent per annum in export sales postulated in the government Green Paper, was achievable but with a composition and destination of exports in 1980 very different from those of 1976.

He stated that in 1980 industrial products would provide two-thirds of our exports of manufactures, with consumer products accounting for one-third. Despite such change he felt the consumer goods industries would require a heroic effort to provide one-third of the value of total manufactured exports in 1980.

He examined clothing and footwear as two examples which were under capitalised and had come under intense pressure from imported products during the depression of the previous three years.

PRESIDENT OF EMC — MR BILL FRASER, MAY 1977

The election of Mr Bill Fraser FMII, vice-president of MII, as president of the European Marketing Council for two years was acclaimed.

Mr Richard Reid, chairman of MII, said that the Institute was proud of the honour of election of Mr Bill Fraser as president of EMC. This was an honour that had been bestowed on an Irishman for only the second time.

The agenda included the formal handing over of the 'Wilkinson Sword of Honour' by the Norwegian delegate (outgoing presidency) to the Irish EMC host.

EMC Policy proposals, May 1977

Mr W.D. (Bill), Fraser FMII, F.Inst M., newly elected president, stated that the policies of EMC, ably initiated and developed by his predecessors, would be continued, with special emphasis on the role of EMC regarding the development of the European EEC.

In addition, the education of Ireland's students and the interchange, within the European members, of such students, would be accelerated in the coming years. Assistance from Brussels for that purpose would be sought and hopefully obtained.

Mr Fraser continued by saying that contact with the World Marketing Contact Group (WMCG), bringing together all of the various organisations in countries dealing with marketing, could bring about a quick exchange of conditions in all of the major selling areas of the developed world and that had to be a priority for the next few years. In concuding, he stated that he hoped to maintain the impetus, that he would be privileged to be responsible for, during the coming years.

MARKETING EDUCATION: STUDY IN EUROPE, MAY 1977

Following a recent two-day meeting in Bavaria, Munich in May 1977, Mr Harry Woods FMII, past-president of EMC, reported that it was decided to initiate a comparative study of marketing education in Europe. It was aimed to make the results of that education, degrees, diplomas, etc. mutually recognised.

The EMC had been listed as a recognised body of the EEC and intended to make a formal proposal to have the latter endorse the aim of better co-ordinated marketing education, while asking for aid to bring that effort about.

The vice-chairman of education, Mr Eugene Quigley MMII, reported on negotiations with Trinity College, Dublin, regarding raising student graduateship to degree status. This led to a discussion on the nature of marketing courses and the importance of the syllabus.

An annual conference of lecturers and examiners, relative to the Marketing Institute examinations, was held on 10 September 1977. The presentation of student awards, graduateships and certificates, resulting from the May 1977 examinations, were made by the Minister for Labour at Trinity College, Dublin that evening. Dr D. O'Hare, director of the National Institute of Higher Education (NIHE), addressed those present. The education chairman, Mr Michael Shields, announced the special awards:

- Córas Tráchtála award for student of the year: Mr Patrick Nevin

- Albright & Wilson award for case study: Mr Anthony Boyle

- Adsell award for computer science: Mr Maitiu McCabe

- Sales Placement award for consumer motivation and behaviour: Mr Martin Bambrick

- Corning Teo award for theory and business: Ms Maria Grogan.

In the excellent *MII Directory and Diary 1978*, Mr Eugene Quigley, vice-chairman of education, outlined the entire education programme of the Institute's four-year course with the new expanded syllabus. While the MII was an examining body only, courses were available at ten centres: Athlone, Carlow, Cork, Dublin (two), Dundalk, Galway, Limerick, Sligo and Waterford. In addition, there were active student societies in Cork and Dublin. A student journal, *The Decision Makers*, was published and an annual conference held each autumn.

Fourth decade of the history of sales management and marketing in Ireland, 1977–1987

MR TOM BRADY MMII, GRAD., RIP

On the 5 August 1977 the Institute lost one of its staunchest supporters. A one-minute silence was observed at the council meeting of 8 September to commemorate the late Mr Tom Brady.

He had been a most active Institute member for many years. From the time he graduated, with the Diploma in Marketing, he had devoted boundless enthusiasm and energy to the council and to many committees, particularly the annual conferences in the previous five years and the development study group.

CII KILDARE STREET, MII OFFICES, SEPTEMBER 1977

As the lease on MII offices at Orwell Road expired, a tenancy was successfully procured at the Confederation of Irish Industries' (CII) House, Kildare Street, Dublin.

STUDENT MATTERS

A revised graduate certificate for students was designed by Mr Jack Downey and much appreciated. Mr Michael Shields attended two very successful student meetings in Cork and congratulated their branch chairman, Mr Gerard Callanan, on the work he had put in.

CORK, SPECIAL COUNCIL MEETING, OCTOBER 1977

The MII national council meeting was held for the first time in Cork on 26 October 1977. It was preceded by a branch luncheon meeting at the Metropole hotel.

The Cork Chairman produced ten new applications for membership of MII and indicated that a net profit of £150 had been produced on a successful French study course.

The opportunity was availed of to discuss how better the branch could be served and mutual ideas were agreed for further consideration.

AGM OF MII, FEBRUARY 1978

The AGM (sixteenth) of the Marketing Institute was held on 27 February 1978. Dr Pat Kehoe, a director of Irish Pensions Trust Ltd and chairman of Patrick Kehoe and Partners, Management Consultants (with offices in Dublin, Singapore and Malaysia), took over the chairmanship.

The president, Dr Tim O'Driscoll, graciously agreed to continue in office. The other officers elected were:

- Senior Vice-Chairman: Mr Pat Nolan

- Vice-Chairman of Services: Mr Jack Downey

- Vice-Chairman of Education: Mr Michael Shields

- Hon. Secretary: Mr Nial Darragh.

New title of MMII Grad.

A motion was passed at the meeting 'that a new level of membership be made available to successful students, that of Graduate Marketing Institute of Ireland, i.e. MMII Grad.'.

The MII student number was growing all the time and 350 new students had been enrolled in 1977–8, making a total since 1971 of 1,668. The actual number studying with the Institute then was 730.

A series of Saturday morning workshops were organised. The development showed that a number of graduates of other courses and disciplines were then taking part in the Marketing Institute courses.

Focus on creativity

In his speech Dr Pat Kehoe, chairman, said that the priority in the coming year would concern 'how we can become more creative' and he hoped the council would bring out an award for creativity. He also wished to see more professionalism in the Institute and more involvement with the services sector.

Pyramid selling

Mr Brendan O'Reilly chaired a committee set up to investigate pyramid selling and other unethical selling/marketing practices. It was to report back to the executive.

Graduates of MII granted membership

The decision was ratified to grant graduates automatic full membership of the Marketing Institute.

THE SEAN F. LEMASS AWARD, MARCH 1978

The Sean F. Lemass award (previously made in 1974 to the Waterford Glass Company) was awarded to the Jefferson Smurfit Group plc., on 5 March 1978.

Mr Sean D. Lemass jun., grandson of the late Sean Lemass, having been nominated by the Lemass family, made the presentation.

In the unavoidable absence of Mr Michael Smurfit, chairman and chief executive of Smurfit, who had been jetted away at the last moment to a business mission in the United States, the award was accepted by the group's financial controller, Mr Howard Kilroy.

The Institute citation honoured Smurfit, an Irish company that had, over the past years, exhibited a record of success and continued growth. The MII executive and members were proud of the consistent achievements of Smurfit and its contribution to the prosperity of Ireland.

The Sean Lemass award consists of two parts, granted:

- to the company or individual considered to have contributed to the stature of marketing in Ireland

- to an individual selected on merit to be the recipient of a cash award to be used for educational purposes or some specific project to be agreed by the award committee.

The latter award was presented to Brian More O'Farrell, a graduate in chemistry from UCD and of the College of Marketing. He was a technical sales representative with Imperial Chemical Industries, (ICI). He had been the 1976 Córas Tráchtála 'Student of the Year' award winner.

HONORARY MEMBERSHIP OF MII TO MR JOSEPH BIGGER, MARCH 1978

Mr Joseph Bigger FMII, former chief executive of MII, was awarded honorary membership of the Marketing Institute of Ireland in March 1978.

RETIREMENT OF MR BASIL LAPWORTH, APRIL 1978

It was decided to honour the retirement of Mr Basil Lapworth, vice-president of MII, at a function in Belfast on 11 April 1978.

The president, Dr T.J. O'Driscoll and Mr Derek Whelan, vice-chairman of finance, made a presentation of Tyrone Crystal to Mr Lapworth, as a memento and token appreciation of the dedicated contribution he had made to affairs of the Marketing Institute.

Thanks were expressed to the College of Marketing and Design who granted members of the Institute the privilege of access to their library, while MII members were encouraged to contribute books to the college.

IRISH GOODS COUNCIL, APRIL 1978

Co-operation was agreed with the Irish Goods Council in areas of marketing, import substitution and consumer motivation.

In the meantime, the Cork branch of MII obtained considerable press exposure regarding the 'Buy Irish/Guaranteed Irish' campaign.

OFFICIAL JOURNAL OF MII, APRIL 1978

The production of *Marketing News* by the Tara Publishing Co. was officially approved and declared as the official journal of MII, from April 1978.

UNEMPLOYMENT AND JOB CREATION SEMINAR, MAY 1978

On 23 May 1978 the newsletter, vol. 29, no. 3, of the Confederation of Irish Industry, CII, reported a speech by Mr Liam Connellan, its director general, at the Workers' Union of Ireland seminar on unemployment and job Creation.

Mr Connellan said the private sector accounted for approximately three-quarters of the people employed in the Irish economy, in sectors such as agriculture, industry, distribution and services. Further the National Economic and Social Council report no. 26, 'Prelude to Planning', stated that the overriding objections must be to realise the full potential for the growth of the Irish economy over the next ten to fifteen years.

Mr Connellan went on to say that when realising this potential, the key sectors of the economy were manufacturing, industry and agriculture and if they grew so would national output and employment. For example, an average increase of 15,000 new industrial jobs a year would be required if industry was to make its contribution towards achieving full employment.

Extensive facts and figures achieved and targets, from 1936 to date, were outlined and given by Mr Connellan. In conclusion he stated that improving productivity must not be feared while changes in technology make possible improvements in product quality and make work more fulfilling.

Ireland is a small open trading nation. It had shown that it can compete.

The current rate in industrial output and employment in Ireland was the fastest in the European Community.

METRIC CHANGEOVER, JANUARY 1980

Under the EEC 'Units of Measurement Directive', certain imperial units of measurement ceased to be authorised after 31 December 1979. They included common measurements such as yard, square inch, etc. cubic inch, etc. stone, quarter, hundredweight and degree fahrenheit.

EMC MEETING, JUNE 1978

The twenty-third annual meeting and conference of the European Marketing Council was held at Annecy, France from June 7–9 1978.

Business meetings were held at the Gillette Conference Centre at Angon, on the beautiful Lake Annecy, fifteen minutes drive from the Palace hotel Menthon, where the delegates stayed. The hotel overlooked the lake and is in one of the most scenic areas in the French Alps where there is also a small harbour adjacent for motor and sailing boats.

Delegates attended from Belgium, England, Finland, France, Germany, Holland (NCD), Ireland, Norway, Spain, Sweden, Switzerland with observers from Holland (NIMA), Portugal and USA.

The Marketing Institute of Ireland delegation included: Messrs William D. Fraser, president of EMC, Derek Whelan, (voting spokesman) and Harry Woods, past president of EMC. In addition, Mr Fergus McCormack (Allied Irish Windows Ltd, Dublin) attended as an observer.

The EMC executive members present were:

- Mr William D. Fraser (Ireland): President

- Mr Fred Th. Witkamp (Holland): Secretary-General

- Mr Leo van Nouhuys (Holland): Vice-President

- Mr Michael Neese (Germany): Vice-President

- Mr Manuel Caragol (Spain): Vice-President.

Due to health reasons the president announced with regret, the absence of Mr Tony Bellm (UK), vice-president of EMC, also Mr Roy Randolph (UK), who was recovering from a recent eye operation.

The election of officers resulted in Mr William D. Fraser of Ireland being re-elected as president of EMC, to complete two years of office. Mr Tony Bellm (UK) was re-elected as a vice-president. A proposal to nominate Mr

Tony Bellm as senior vice-president, (president-elect), was unanimously agreed.

President Fraser expressed, on behalf of EMC, gratitude to Mr Leo van Nouhuys (Holland) for his long standing and enthusiastic support. Mr van Nouhuys had just anounced his retirement.

In his report, Mr Bill Fraser said that EMC was becoming stronger by more organisations/institutes showing eagerness to obtain membership.

It was also announced that Portugal would qualify for membership next year.

Awards

The International Activities award was granted to the Marketing Institute of Ireland in June 1978 'particularly for the outstanding organisation of their international conference in Dublin last year and for Irish active participation in EMC over many years'. Mr Derek Whelan accepted the award on behalf of the Marketing Institute.

The Publication award was presented, for the second time, to the German magazine *Absatzwirtschaft*, a magazine for marketing, and in conjunction with the Deutsche Marketing Vereinigung e.v., Dusseldorf. The award was accepted by Mrs Liselotte Wagner on behalf of the publishers.

Marketing News pilot issue

Much discussion and verbal reports were given by delegates while the Irish report was accompanied by a pilot issue of their new *Marketing News* magazine.

Dutch report

A lengthy highlight report on the 'Political and Social Development in the Netherlands, June 1978', of NCD, Netherlands Centre of Directors, stated there was a swing to the right when Christian Democrats and Conservatives finally joined hands.

The report is of unusual reading particularly regarding 'Disturbances — Terrorism', which was naturally not supported by the new Dutch government. Their government had a heavy load on its shoulders to find acceptable solutions for the serious economical recession and increasing unemployment.

Portuguese report

The Portuguese submitted a five-page A4 document, setting out information in support of their probable EMC membership next year.

Business environment in France

A conference also took place at the Gillette Centre in Annecy, June 8–9. It had as its theme: 'The Business Environment in France after the 1978 General Elections'.

The first guest speaker was Mr Robert Pinard, personnel director of Gillette, France. It was particularly interesting to hear his topic, 'Sell management of time'. He stated his belief that one should build on the 'guy's coming of age', rather than old-age retirement, and create job availability.

He outlined how that was done by the Gillette. Employees were trained to prepare for retirement, at 60 years, by providing a free six weeks' course, with full pay and extra holidays in their pre-retirement year. The result led to providing a part-time position, if so desired, sometimes in a different type of business and/or the getting together, of for example, two individuals to create their own business or project.

The second speaker was Mr David Lush, managing director of Fusalp. He spoke on 'The Management Aspect'. 'The Political Aspect' was covered by third speaker, Mr Pascal Clement, Member of Parliament, Union pour la Démocratie Française.

Following lunch, a very pleasant boat trip was provided on Lake Annecy as well as a tour of the old city of Annecy and a reception at the townhall.

JAPANESE AWARD, JUNE 1978

The Japanese Economic Association announced at a Dublin reception on 27 June 1978 that they had made available a fellowship award to enable a graduate of the College of Marketing and Design, Dublin, spend some months in Japan.

The graduate would observe Japanese business methods and practices and prepare a thesis for presentation to the association.

MARKETING EDUCATION MATTERS, 1978

The College of Marketing Dublin prepared students for a Diploma in Advanced Marketing Techniques, so being eligible for the degree of M.Sc. (Mgt.) from Trinity College, Dublin.

The first award of the new fellowship was scheduled to be made to one of the twenty or so students expected to graduate in 1978, while the selection would be made by the college authorities

The chairman of the Ireland-Japan Economic Association, Mr Edgar Forster, Stokes Kennedy Crowley & Co., said that Ireland could boast of being the recipient of a higher degree of Japanese investment than any other member country of the European Community.

Mr T.P. Madden, principal of the College of Marketing, expressed appreciation to the association for their initiative and generosity.

The attendance at the meeting included Mr John McKay, chief executive officer of the Dublin Vocational Education Committee, Ald. Kevin Byrne, chairman of the college council and Mr Philip Flood, Head of the Marketing Studies Department.

FELLOWSHIP AWARDS, SEPTEMBER 1978

The awards of Fellowship were made to Messrs Jack Jones, Gerry Maher and Richard G. Tennant. They were suitably citated and acclaimed.

SALESMEN UNDER THE MICROSCOPE, 1978

The P.A. Management Consultants' updated report (of its 1971 report) *Salesman under the Microscope*, was analysed and complimented.

INDUSTRIAL MARKETING IN JAPAN, 1978

Two very interesting booklets, part of the JETRO (Japan External Trade Organisation) marketing series of eighteen, in my possession, are No. 8, *Doing Business in Japan* and No.18, *Industrial Marketing in Japan.*

The differences in behaviour of Western and Japanese businessmen are emphasised. They recommend patience in discussion, use of business cards as essential, introduction by a known third-party, if possible and also an interpreter, for all business meetings.

AGM OF MII, JANUARY 1979

Mr Patrick J. Nolan took office as MII chairman from the seventeenth AGM held on 4 January 1979. He was pleased to announce that Dr T.J. O'Driscoll had agreed to continue as president, as had Mr Bill Fraser as vice-president. Mr Jack McCluskey was elected also as a vice-president.

Other officers for 1979 were:

• Senior Vice-Chairman: Mr J. Brendan O'Reilly

• Education Vice-Chairman: Mr Michael Shields

• Vice-Chairman of Services: Mr Derek Whelan

• Vice-Chairman of Finance: Mr Patrick Nevin

• Hon. Secretary: Mr Brian More O'Farrell.

The council members were: Messrs Tony Neville, Noel Quirke, Gerry Callanan, Brian Creedon, Tom Quinn, Walter Connolly and Maitiu McCabe, and Dr Pat Kehoe.

The regional branch chairpersons were:

• Limerick: Mr Barra O'Cinneide

• Galway: Mr Brian Creedon

• Cork: Ms Lynne Glasscoe.

At the first council meeting of 4 January 1979, Mr Pat Nolan declared that the emphasis for the year would be on 'achievement'. He had written to various bodies, Córas Tráchtála Teo, IDA, Anco and the Irish Goods Council, requesting views and comments on his address to members at the MII AGM.

EUROPEAN FILE OF EUROPEAN COMMUNITIES, 1979

In 1979 the European file issues 1/79 and 2/79 of the Commission of the European Communities became available. In June 1979, for the first time in their history, the citizens of the European Community (British, Belgian, Danish, Dutch, French, Germans, Irish, Italians and Luxemburgers) would directly chose their representatives in the European Parliament.

The booklet went on further to explain the European institutions and their operation, particularly to help new voters.

The European Community had been created by three treaties:

1. The Treaty of Paris, signed on 18 April 1951.

2. Two Rome treaties signed on 25 March 1957, which set up the European Economic Community (EEC).

The 2/79 booklet referred to the hardship suffered in Europe in recent years. Increased efforts required in regional policy were defined while such redeployment would have to be co-ordinated at the community level.

Europe was no longer a matter for technocrats. It was the Europeans themselves, citizens of the community, who had to answer the major questions of the day.

The Irish address of the information offices of the Commission of the European Communities was 29, Merrion Square, Dublin 2.

NORTHERN IRELAND LIAISON, FEBRUARY 1979

The liaison between the Northern Ireland Institute of Marketing branch and the Marketing Institute of Ireland, as reported by Mr Pat Nolan, chairman of MII, enabled the establishment of closer ties. The interchange was appreciated.

MEMBERSHIP OF MII, 1979

The membership of the Marketing Institute reached 500 in February 1979.

B.SC.DEGREE, 1979

Mr Michael Shields reported that the College of Marketing had applied to Trinity College, Dublin, for permission for Institute graduates to undertake the B.Sc. Degree, on a two-year evening basis. He had appealed to Anco for finance for Institute graduates taking that programme on a one year, full-time basis, while absent from their employers.

A series of special courses on finance, research and advertising were organised to take place one night per week, for four weeks.

MARKETING HOUSE SOUGHT, FEBRUARY 1979

The senior vice-chairman, Mr J. Brendan O'Reilly, highlighted objective for a marketing house and the arranging of fundraising, consideration of legal aspects and location of a suitable premises for the Institute.

CHAIRMAN OF FELLOWS APPOINTED, MARCH 1979

Mr John D. Carroll was welcomed to the council meeting on 8 March 1979 at CII House as the newly elected chairmen of the Fellows' panel.

BRANCH RE-INAUGURATION IN GALWAY, MARCH 1979

Branch liaison resulted in Messrs Michael Shields and Brendan O'Reilly visiting Limerick and Galway, and with help from Mr Brian Creedon branch reformation for Galway was organised from 21 March 1979.

WATERFORD BRANCH INTEREST, MARCH 1979

In Waterford twelve members were interested in the formation of an MII branch.

SALE OF GOODS AND SUPPLY SERVICES BILL, 1979

A submission regarding the 'Sale of Goods and Supply Services Bill' was prepared by the Marketing Institute 'think tank' committee and submitted to the Minister for Industry, Commerce and Energy. The bill was welcomed, in principle, as an important step in improving consumer protection.

Of particular concern to the Institute were the standards of marketing practice and those of general commercial activity, while they believed consumer satisfaction to be the key to the success of individual enterprise and ultimately the prosperity of the national economy.

Important provisions included: implied terms, the defining of fitness for purpose and mercantile quality, minimum requirements for guarantees, and statements purporting to restrict the rights of buyer.

The Institute supported the sections dealing with the inertia selling practices in relation to unsolicited goods and entries in directories. However, certain implications in the bill were viewed with concern. An example related to Section 14 which provided that a finance house, financing a purchase, would be held jointly responsible with the seller for the fulfilment of the contract.

To hold a finance house liable for the actions of the seller and responsible for the quality of a product, could, it was considered, lead to a withdrawal or curtailment of finance available to certain types of traders or products. The result would distort trade in favour of older established businesses, reduce the channels of distribution open to suppliers and limit the freedom of choice of the consumer.

It was indicated by the Institute that the availability of finance facilities played a major part in the selling of a wide range of products. Any adverse effect on that availability would have serious repercussions on the sales, profitability and employment prospects of manufacturers and distributors.

CORK AGM, MAY 1979

At the Cork AGM Ms Lynne Glasscoe was re-elected chairperson for 1979–80. Members of the branch committee were: Messrs J. Cashel, S. Cowman, J. Dowling, R. Doherty, A. Harte, N. Harte, E. Irwin, G. Nagle, R. O'Kelly, A. O'Loghlan and S. Simmington.

CHAIRMAN OF LIMERICK BRANCH, MAY 1979

Mr Barra O'Cinneide was elected chairman of the Limerick branch of MII in May 1979.

EUROPEAN MARKETING CONGRESS, MAY 1979

The 'Club de Dirigentes de Marketing de Barcelona' were hosts of the thirteenth European Marketing Congress from 9–11 May 1979.

The brochure recalled the beauty of the city of Barcelona in May and also listed the chronology of the European Marketing Congresses:

- Milan: 1956

- London: 1957

- Stockholm:1958

- Berlin: 1959

- The Hague: 1962

- Barcelona: 1964

- Paris: 1966

- Brussels: 1968

- Milan: 1971

- London: 1973

- Amsterdam: 1975

- Dublin: 1977

- Barcelona: 1979.

With eleven annual 'conference meetings/AGM's' (not major congresses) having been held in some intermediary years, this gave a total of 24 years since the first EMC Congress in 1956. Barcelona 1979 was my sixteenth AGM.

The theme of the bi-annual congress was: 'Spain's Entry to the EEC'. The speakers were from France, Great Britain, Germany, Holland, Ireland, Italy and the host country, Spain.

Among the presentations made was that of Mr Colm McDonnell of Córas Tráchtála, who had been a member of MII before taking up his position in Spain. Reports of his talk were proudly recorded.

AGM of EMC

The AGM was held on the day after the congress of May 12 1979 and was chaired by Mr Bill Fraser of Ireland, the president of EMC. He welcomed the delegates and the fact that member countries (eleven of twelve) were represented at the meeting. He introduced two representatives of the Portuguese Marketing Association, as non-member observers.

The executive officers present, in addition to the president, were: Messrs Tony Bellm, Michael Neese and Rolf Back, vice-presidents; Manuel Caragol, past-president, Roy Randolph, honorary vice-president and Fred Witkamp, secretary-general.

Representing the Marketing Institute of Ireland, apart from the president Mr Bill Fraser, were Messrs Derek Whelan (voting delegate) and Harry Woods.

Apologies were received from the Greek Marketing Association, though they indicated by letter that they would like to be accepted as a member of EMC.

From papers submitted Deutsche Marketing Vereinigung e.v. of Germany informed the council that their International Chamber of Commerce had contacts with various representatives of the EEC, including a seat as an observer on the experts' committee regarding the legal protection of consumers. This was a committee created by the Council of Europe.

Portuguese marketing society, May 1979

A complete study of the Portuguese Marketing Society application, resulted in their acceptance as the fourteenth member of the European Marketing Council. Their spokesman, Mr Luizo Moutinho, expressing appreciation, declared full support for EMC and said that the Portuguese would play an active part in affairs.

Retirement of Mr Fred Witkamp

In his presidential report, Mr Bill Fraser said that he felt sad when realising that, after exactly ten years of service, the members had to say farewell to Mr Fred Witkamp as secretary-general. The latter had decided a long time ago to retire from the position.

On behalf of EMC the president expressed sincere gratitude toward Mr Witkamp for his longstanding loyalty and hard work for the benefit of EMC. It was also announced that Mr Fred Witkamp had been made an honorary member of EMC.

EMC Robert Collischon Award

The Robert Collischon award was unanimously granted to the outgoing secretary-general Mr Fred Witkamp for his longstanding and enthusiastic service to EMC.

Several members addressed their words of thanks and gratitude to him while some presents were handed to him.

Appointments

The council had approved the nomination of Mr Roger Pirot, president of DCF (France), as vice-president of EMC and elected Mr Herry W. Bakhuys Roozeboom (Holland) as secretary-general. Mr Michael Neese (Germany) was re-elected as vice-president of EMC.

EMC International activities award

For their excellent performance in organising the EMC conference in Annecy together with the annual meeting in 1978, the International activities award was granted to Dirigeants Commerciaux of France. Mr Roger Pirot of DCF was presented with the certificate.

EMC Publications award to Ireland

Mr Derek Whelan was presented with the certificate for the Publications award. This was granted to the Marketing Institute of Ireland for 'their interesting and attractive set-up' of *Marketing News*. It was judged to have been the best new publication devoted to marketing from any European country. (At that stage the magazine was only eight months old.)

New president of EMC, May 1979

Following the procedure of article 12:1 of the European Marketing Council byelaws, Mr Tony Bellm, Institute of Marketing, London, was presented as the presidential candidate, and so elected.

The minutes recall that 'on pinning down the EMC badge (i.e. past-president's) on Mr Fraser's lapel, Mr Tony Bellm expressed his appreciation, on behalf of the whole council, for all the time and effort given generously, by Mr Fraser to EMC during his two years of office'.

The new president said the UK were interested in hearing from other countries, e.g. Japan. He asked other EMC members to inform the secretary-general of other countries they too were interested in, with a view to a conference in one country of, for example 200/300 participants, with 10/20 top people on the podium exchanging ideas about various marketing subjects.

UK submission

A submission, by the United Kingdom delegation was presented by Mr Martin van Mesdag, their spokesman delegate. He deliberately presented an imbalanced picture, stressing negative aspects. The greatest problem, according to him, was the marketing of marketing.

The concepts and importance needed to be better understood by the general public, by government, by labour organisations and by business itself. He stated that there were a large number of reasons as to why the marketing of marketing was a huge problem. He confined himself to just five:

1. There was widespread ignorance and misunderstanding of marketing in industry.

2. The importance in Britain's overseas trade balance disguised an inherent weakness – much of that weakness was due to poor marketing competitiveness.

3. The prevalent preoccupation of business management, government and labour unions with the need for greater investment in industry focused on plant and machinery while ignoring investment in marketing brains and brawn.

4. Industry failed to involve marketing people in helping to improve mutual understanding in the labour/management interface.

5. The feeling of inadequacy, as an Institute, to which he had referred, highlighted two integral problems:

    • ambiguity about long-term policy

    • the mobilisation of resources to carry out a missionary task.

ADDRESS OF MR GEORGE PRIESTLEY, MAY 1979

There are five million people on this island. We should work to remove the barriers between us. Then the politicians will be forced to do what we ask them to. I myself am quite convinced that Ireland should be one economic unit.

That was the statement of Mr George Priestley, chairman of the Northern Ireland branch of the Institute of Marketing (UK) when he addressed the Tuesday Club luncheon in May 1979 in Jury's hotel, Dublin.

Mr Priestly stated that there were 1.5 million people in the North of Ireland, with almost 50 per cent of them living around the Belfast area. Trade between the North and South, percentage wise, had waned, and that according to him, should not have been allowed to happen. Mr Priestly, in asking for trade from the South, said that the marketing concept varied little between the two areas.

GALWAY UNIVERSITY COLLEGE HOSTS MEETING, JUNE 1979

In keeping with the policy of encouraging activity at regional level an Institute's council meeting was held at the Quadrangle building at University College, Galway on 8 June 1979. An enjoyable evening function in Galway, arranged by Mr Brian Creedon, was much appreciated.

The presentation of membership certificates was made to new members in the Galway area.

Arrangements were agreed to transfer MII courses in Cork to their Regional Technical College from September 1979.

Mr Michael Shields reported that 38 students had passed the graduateship examinations while a similar number had passed the certificate.

The awards decided in the graduateship examinations were to:

• Student of the Year and Best Paper in Business Policy: Ms Geraldine Glasgow

• Case Study: Ms Aoife Coffey

• Marketing Management: Mr Allan McConnell

• Consumer Motivation and Behaviour: Mr Brian P. Redmond.

FELLOWSHIP STATUS COMMITTEE, MII, JULY 1979

In July 1979 a study report was submitted to the council regarding the status of Fellowship in the Institute. The committee comprised of Messrs Jack Jones FMII, chairman, Brian More-O'Farrell MMII, hon. Secretary of Institute, Philip Flood FMII, Pat Nevin MMII, Derek Whelan MMII and Harry Woods FMII.

Six meetings were held. The main report dealt with the regulations for the award of Fellowship under certain rigid structures and outstanding service having been given to the Institute over a defined period.

MARKETING HOUSE PROPOSAL, AUGUST 1979

A proposal of Mr Michael Shields, seconded by Mr Brendan O'Reilly, was unanimously supported by the council at a meeting of 30 August 1979:

> That members of council co-operate with the marketing house sub-committee in drawing up the presentation of a report and that, if necessary,

a sum of up to £500 be made available to commission expert advice on the detailed financial arrangement from Butler Chance, (the Institute Auditors).

STUDENT AWARDS, OCTOBER 1979

The presentation of student awards was made in the Thomas Prior House, Royal Dublin Society, Ballsbridge on 31 October 1979.

It was announced that a post-graduate student was undertaking an examination of the educational records as part of a thesis.

Mr Bob Gourley became liaison officer between MII and Northern Ireland Institute of Marketing group.

AWARDS, NOVEMBER 1979

On 1 November 1979 a Scroll of Honour was presented following the well-deserved award of Fellowship, to Mr Anthony J. Neville at the President's Night dinner.

The Stephen Doyle award, for meritorious service to marketing, was presented to Mr Derek P. Whelan in recognition of his outstanding contribution to enhancing the status of the Marketing Institute.

INAUGURATION OF WATERFORD BRANCH, DECEMBER 1979

The Waterford branch of the Marketing Institute was inaugurated on 13 December 1979.

MII APPOINTMENTS, 1980

The president, Dr T.J. O'Driscoll, welcomed members and installed the incoming chairman for 1980, Mr J. Brendan O'Reilly MMII Grad., with the chain of office.

Officers for the year were announced as follows:

* Hon. Secretary: Mr Maitiu McCabe

* Senior Vice-Chairman: Mr Michael Shields

* Vice-Chairmen: Messrs Brian Creedon, Pat Nevin and John Burns.

The members of the council were: Messrs Walter Connolly, Bernard S. Fitzpatrick, Philip Flood, Brian More O'Farrell, Anthony Neville, Patrick

Nolan (immediate past chairman) Thomas Quinn and Ms Penelope Horan, together with the officers and Mr John D. Carroll, representing the Fellowship panel.

The chairman, Mr J. Brendan O'Reilly, said that the three watchwords for the year would be: 'Courtesy, Targets and Communications'.

Wilson, Hartnell & O'Reilly were retained for Public relations.

NEW ENTRY RULING FOR MEMBERSHIP, JANUARY 1980

A new condition was made to obtain membership of the Institute for those holding the MII Diploma. From now on it must be coupled with a 'minimum one year's Sales/Marketing experience'.

CORK VENUE FOR COUNCIL MEETING, FEBRUARY 1980

The Metropole hotel, Cork was the venue for the 1 February 1980 council meeting. Favourable publicity had been received through the NCEA (National Council of Educational Awards) for the 'Marketing Student of the Year' award sponsored by MII.

It was announced that an inaugural meeting for the Sligo branch had been arranged for April 1980.

A meeting was held with Mr Sean Condon of Córas Tráchtála Teo who wished the MII to advance its proposals for revised marketing courses.

JAPAN — A MARKET FOR IMPORTS, APRIL 1980

The JETRO *Facts and Finds* series no.2 of March 1980 brought the reader into the Japanese market for manufactured imports in the rapidly changing distribution channel.

In the volume JETRO (Japan External Trade Organisation) it stated that as manufactured imports to them had rapidly increased, Japan's distribution system was compelled to suit changes in its surroundings.

CHAIRMAN OF CORK BRANCH ELECTED, APRIL 1980

Mr John Cashell was welcomed to the council as the new Cork MII chairman, on his attendance at a meeting in CII House, Dublin on 23 April 1980.

PRESIDENT OF MII, APRIL 1980

An announcement that Mr Sean M. Condon, Córas Tráchtála Teo, had accepted an invitation to be the president of the Marketing Institute, in succession to Dr T.J. O'Driscoll, was gratefully received.

An agreement was reached, in principle, that the annual MII conference through the years 1981/82/83 would be a joint venture with *Business & Finance* journal.

CHAIRMAN OF LIMERICK BRANCH ELECTED, MAY 1980

The new chairman of the Limerick branch of MII was Mr Jim Dalton, who took office from their AGM on 2 May 1980.

BEHAVIOURAL SCIENCE EXAMINATION, MAY 1980

Looking back at some of the MII examination papers, I was intrigued by Question No. 4 on the Certificate in Marketing, Part 1 paper. It read: Explain the meaning of instinct, and discuss J.A.C. Brown's contention ... 'virtually, men have no instincts'.

The Chamber's Dictionary describes instinct as: 'a natural feeling or knowledge, which living things seem to have without thinking and without being taught'.

IRISH INDEPENDENT ARTICLE, MAY 1980

An excellent article on marketing careers, edited by Mr Philip Flood, was produced in the *Irish Independent* issue of 26 May 1980.

EMC MARKETING AGM, MILAN, MAY/JUNE 1980

A report of the European Marketing Council's twenty-fifth AGM and conference, held at Milan from 28 May–1 June 1980, was submitted to the MII council. Meetings had been held at the Credito Italiano Professional Trading Centre in Lesmo near Milan.

Delegates who attended from MII were Messrs J. Brendan O'Reilly, chairman of MII, Michael D. Shields, senior vice-chairman, Maitiu McCabe, honorary secretary and Harry Woods, a past-president of EMC, who deputised for Mr Bill Fraser, who was not available to travel. Thirteen countries were represented overall and welcomed by the president of EMC, Mr Tony Bellm (Institute of Marketing, London).

The president of the Milano Marketing Club, in opening the congress, referred to the political difficulties in Italy and particularly to the assassination the previous day of one of their leading newspaper editors. He stated that Italy had 1.7 million unemployed at the time, 50 per cent of whom were eighteen/nineteen years old.

The country also had the lowest growth rate in Europe — 2.83 per cent. Marketing, he concluded, had a key role to play in organising employment by working for such an end.

The first session in Milan involved three case studies and discussions on:

1. The wine industry in Italy.

2. The village of Como, as an export town, in particular Como textiles.

3. The Alfa-Romeo story — incorporating the partnership arrangement with Nissan of Japan.

EMC awards

The Robert Collischon award was presented to Ms Hellevi Olenius of the Finnish Marketing Executives Group and the Programme award presented to the Nederlands Centrum van Direkteuren. The recipients of the International Activities award were the Club de Dirigentes de Marketing de Barcelona.

Awards sheet update

Mr Harry Woods had agreed to prepare an update of the 'awards sheet' as the EMC secretary-general had stated that Mr Woods 'having consistently attended these meetings for so many years, had more knowledge of the history of EMC than anyone else'. The bound report, submitted by the Marketing Institute of Ireland delegation, was highly complimented on.

Discussion on policy of EMC

A discussion on policy and of where the EMC was heading also took place. Mr Harry Woods was given the chairmanship of a committee to discuss such matters with the spokesman of each of the other twelve countries present at Milan, and assess what was happening in each country. This was conducted on a basis of 'frank and open discussion'.

The subject was defined as: 'What are the Strict Effects on Marketing as a Result of the Wage Control System?' Much information of vital interest was gleaned particularly regarding the marketing export decisions then current.

WILKINSON SWORD DIFFICULTIES

Due to difficulties with the Italian customs and police the EMC Wilkinson Sword of Honour could not be handed over to the Italian Association during the congress.

It was agreed the 'Sword' be taken by the EMC secretary-general to Holland for the ceremony in Germany in 1981.

JAPANESE WHITE PAPER ON INTERNATIONAL TRADE, 1979

A general review of Japan's foreign trade is contained in the 193-page A4 volume *White Paper on International Trade — Japan 1979*. This was published in 1980. The document concerns:

• Part 1: The world economy at a turning point

• Part 2: New developments in Japan's economic activities abroad

• Part 3: Trade by commodity

• Part 4: Japan's foreign trade by region.

It is very informative and, of course, extensive in statistics.

JAPAN — AN OPEN MARKET, 1980

The Japanese market was wide open to the countries of the world. Prime factors, it was stated, behind the expansion in manufactured imports were the improved environment for imports. This was due to declines in import prices resulting from the yen appreciation during the previous few years.

DR T.J. O'DRISCOLL, HONORARY MEMBER MII, JUNE 1980

Dr T.J. O'Driscoll, who had been president of the Marketing Institute of Ireland for the years 1973–80 was unanimously elected an honorary member in recognition of his outstanding contribution to the Institute.

INSIGNIA FOR FELLOWS, JULY 1980

Mr John D. Carroll, chairman of the Fellowship panel, advised the council at their July 1980 meeting of an insignia for Fellows. The initial supply of the insignia had been offered to the existing Fellows for individual purchase by them. The council later decided to purchase a further supply for presentation to new Fellows, as elected, to be presented to them with their citations.

DEVELOPMENT STUDY GROUP, SEPTEMBER 1980

The president of the MII, Mr Sean Condon, proposed the formation of a development study group to review previous study and develop a medium and long-term plan. This was agreed in September 1980.

PRESIDENT'S NIGHT, OCTOBER 1980

The President's Night dinner of the Marketing Institute of Ireland was held at the Burlington hotel in Dublin on 2 October 1980.

FELLOWSHIP AWARDS, OCTOBER 1980

Mr John D. Carroll, chairman of the Fellowship panel, introduced the newly elected Fellows of the Marketing Institute of Ireland. They were:

- Mr Jack Downey: citation read by Mr Mahon Lee FMII
- Mr John Lepere: citation read by Mr Gerry Maher FMII
- Mr Pat Nolan: citation read by Mr Jack Jones FMII.

THE STEPHEN DOYLE AWARD, OCTOBER 1980

Mr Harry Woods FMII delivered a citation and made the presentation of the Stephen Doyle award to Mr Walter Connolly FMII for meritorious service to marketing over many years.

The guest speaker, Mr Desmond O'Malley TD, Minister for Industry, Commerce and Energy, was warmly welcomed and introduced by Mr Brendan O'Reilly, chairman of the Marketing Institute of Ireland.

In his toast to the president of the Institute Mr O'Malley said he was pleased to see some signs of a break in the economic gloom as people were at least talking about the end of the recession being in sight. He went on to say that in terms of both its aims and achievements, the Marketing Institute of Ireland was a prime leader among the country's business-oriented institutions and organisations. As a representative body for trade, industry and the services, it stood at the centre of things. Furthermore, he stated that its role had steadily appreciated in influence and importance, and would continue to do so, in direct proportion to economic expansion.

World recession, 1980

Mr O'Malley said the world recession was still very much with us. However, Ireland's latest export returns had exceeded expectations. Manufactured goods (excluding food, drink and tobacco) then accounted for nearly 59 per cent of total exports, i.e. January–June 1980. It was over 24 per cent greater than in the corresponding period in 1979.

During a sojourn to the United States he was deeply impressed, not for the first time, by the extraordinary goodwill manifested towards Ireland. At home, he urged, we needed to increase the sales of domestic products in the teeth of severe overseas competition.

Mr Sean Condon, in reply to the toast, thanked Mr O'Malley and reminded the guests and members that he was, in fact, the third chief executive of CTT to have become president of the Marketing Institute, his predecessors having been Mr John Haughey and Dr T.J. O'Driscoll.

He said that Córas Tráchtála, owing to its special responsibilities as the state export promotional organisation, was deeply committed to advancing the status of marketing in Irish industry and the community generally.

He was very conscious that marketing, and all it implied and required in the way of business behaviour and commitment, ranged widely beyond the frontiers of exporting into such diverse fields as importing, retailing, banking and service industries.

Other principal guests at the function included:

• Mr Jack Lynch, TD, former Taoiseach

• Mr Malachy Sherlock, director of Anco

• Dr Thomas Murphy, president of UCD, who ably replied to the toast to the guests

• Mr Roland Long, chairman of the N.I. branch of the Institute of Marketing

• Mr John Meagher, managing director of Irish Marketing Surveys

• Mr Jim Nolan, president of the Institute of Advertising Practitioners

• Mr Fred P. Hayden, president of the Association of Advertisers

• Mr Paddy McKenna, chairman of the Marketing Society.

NIHE COURSES IN LIMERICK, OCTOBER 1980

In October 1980 NIHE, Limerick provided courses for third and fourth year marketing students.

WATERFORD BRANCH, OCTOBER 1980

Mr Bryan S. Ryan, chairman of the Bryan S. Ryan group, addressed the Waterford branch of MII on 7 October 1980. He said Ireland could not afford to be caught napping by the technological revolution and this was his message to the government.

In addition he would ask their leaders to institute a national programme to ensure that competition could be competed with, in the new 'information society'. He urged that the government re-examine the VAT level at 25 per cent, which applied to a large section of the business equipment industry.

Telecommunications applauded, October 1980

A massive £650m. programme, undertaken by the Department of Post and Telegraphs, was applauded by Mr Ryan, who stated that 'in five years' time, we will have the most up-to-date telecommunications network in the whole of Europe'.

GALWAY BRANCH PROGRAMME, 1980–81

The programme of the Galway branch of MII for 1980–81 was announced by the chairman, Mr Seamus Hynes, Lydon House Ltd, to its active committee. The committee comprised: Messrs Pat Fahy, secretary, John Hickey, vice-chairman of the *Connacht Tribune*, Aidan Daly, Regional Technical College and Brian Creedon and Stephen Faller, Exports Ltd.

Chair of Marketing at Galway, 1980

The Bank of Ireland announced a Chair of Marketing at the National University, Galway. The deserved recipient was Professor James Ward, MMII.

AGM OF MII, JANUARY 1981

Following his address and review to the Marketing Institute members, the president of MII, Mr Sean M. Condon, installed the new chairman, Mr Michael D. Shields and invested him with the chain of office at the nineteenth AGM on 8 January 1981.

Newly elected to the council were: Messrs Bill Ambrose, Jack Downey and Bob Gourley.

Officers appointed were:

• Hon. Secretary: Ms Penelope Horan

- Senior Vice-Chairman: Mr John Burns

- Vice-Chairmen: Messrs Bernard Fitzpatrick, Bob Gourley and Jack Downey.

INSTITUTE OF MARKETING UK/MII, 1981

The Institute of Marketing UK conveyed, through its director Mr Peter Blood, that they would welcome discussion on the differences in the educational courses of the MII and their Institute. Mr Michael Shields agreed to commuicate on this mutual beneficial situation. An excellent liaison existed with the Institute of Marketing.

Irish marketing qualifications had the approval of the European Marketing Council, comprising 35,000 members.

MEETING OF LECTURERS AND EXAMINERS, FEBRUARY 1981

A special meeting, of lecturers and examiners, relative to the marketing courses, was held on 28 February 1981. This was attended by 26 lecturers. The breakdown was as follows:

- Dublin: College of Commerce, Rathmines: 6 and the College of Marketing and Design: 7

- Cork: Regional Technical College: 2

- Carlow: Regional Technical College: 6

- Limerick: Vocational Education Committee: 2 and NIHE: 3.

Seven examiners also participated.

The Marketing Trainee Course became the Marketing Foundation Course for 1981/82, while syllabi for the other four years were revised.

EXPORT VENTURES IN EUROPE, APRIL 1981

On 1 April 1981 the subject of a very successful meeting at the Regional Technical College in Cork was: 'Export Ventures in Europe'.

Approximately 100 people attended including Marketing Institute members, students and representatives from University College, Cork, the Irish Exporters' Association and the Institute of Materials Purchasing.

SEAN F. LEMASS AWARD, JUNE 1981

The Sean F. Lemass award was presented to Mr Michael Killeen, chief executive of the IDA, and the excellent work he did within the body was deliberated on.

Their strategy included a hard sell of the outstanding resources available in Ireland. This made compelling reading to potential investors. The dream and foresight of the former taoiseach and past-president of MII, the late Sean F. Lemass, had been made reality by the success of the IDA. Its contribution to the economy included the creation of jobs and making new skills and disciplines in high technology industries available for young Irish people.

The IDA was unanimously declared to be the worthy recipient of the highest honour the Marketing Institute of Ireland awarded.

NEW FELLOWS, 1981

Fellows elected and introduced with individual citations on President's Night, 12 June 1981, were: Messrs Robert K. Gahan, Barra O'Cinneide, Eugene P. Quigley and Derek Whelan. Their considerable individual efforts on behalf of the Institute were highly praised.

The Stephen Doyle award

For meritorious service to marketing over many years, the Stephen Doyle award was presented to Mr F. Edward James.

Senate nomination

It was also announced at the dinner that Mr Joe Dowling MMII, Cork, was the selected candidate, from the four proposed, to be the Marketing Institute nomination for the Senate election.

NEW BROCHURE FOR PROSPECTIVE STUDENTS, SEPTEMBER 1981

A new brochure for prospective students, *A Career in Marketing,* was produced, of which all colleges and concerned bodies were sent copies. Attention was drawn to the revised entry qualifications to be enforced for the academic year, 1981/82.

An introductory seminar was held in the Gresham hotel, Dublin, in September 1981.

One hundred prospective students were addressed by Messrs J. Wrynn, M. Shields, B. Gourley, J. Jennings and S. McSweeney.

The very considerable work and organisation, in educational matters, reflected particularly on the dedication of Mr Bob Gourley and Mr Brendan Wafer, vice-chairman and chairman respectively of the education committee.

STUDENT COURSE IN BOSTON, OCTOBER 1981

For some considerable time previous, the student society had worked on a proposed group visit, of personnel from the Marketing Institute, to a marketing course in Boston.

The vice-chairman of education, Mr Bob Gourley, reported that 51 bookings for the course had been made in October 1981. The credit, he said, was due to the students themselves as it had been their idea.

The result was an educational, social and financial success. Twelve students were included and Dr James Duff presented certificates to all participants.

OFFICES FOR MII, OCTOBER 1981

A lease of office premises at 12, Fitzwilliam Place, Dublin, was obtained for the Marketing Institute.

EUROPEAN MARKETING CONGRESS, OCTOBER 1981

As the chairman of MII, Mr Michael Shields, was attending the student Boston venture he could not be present at the fourteenth European Marketing Congress and AGM in Frankfurt, Germany. This commenced on 21 October 1981. It was agreed that I would again represent the Marketing Institute of Ireland.

GRADUATION CEREMONY, NOVEMBER 1981

A graduation ceremony took place on Friday 6 November 1981 at Thomas Prior House, Royal Dublin Society, Ballsbridge, Dublin. There were approximately 300 people present to honour the successful marketing students.

WATERFORD, NOVEMBER 1981

Mrs Delia Burke reported on the Waterford AGM, successfully held on 18 November 1981. She also reported that 100 persons had attended their dinner dance, which had been a most enjoyable function.

MII APPOINTMENTS, 1982

The president, Mr Sean M. Condon, kindly agreed to continue in office for 1982. As a result of the annual elections for the council he stated that he was pleased to welcome the newly elected chairman, Mr John S. Burns and place on him the chain of office. The vice-presidents, Messrs W.D. Fraser and George Priestly remained in office.

Other officers elected were:

- Mr Jack V. Downey: Senior Vice-Chairman

- Mr R.E. Gourley: Vice-Chairman of Education

- Mr Bill Ambrose: Vice-Chairman of Finance

- Mr Owen Morton: Vice-Chairman of Services

- Mr Brendan Wafer: Hon. Secretary

- Mr John D. Carroll: Chairman of Fellowship committee.

The members of the council were: Messrs Philip R. Flood, Bernard S. Fitzpatrick, Brian V. Mooney, Anthony J. Neville, John C. O'Brien, Michael D. Shields and Ms Penny Simpson.

The branch representatives were:

- Cork branch: Chairman, Mr Aidan Harte

- Galway branch: Chairman, Mr Colm Heery

- Limerick branch: Chairman, Mr James Dalton

- Waterford branch: Chairperson, Ms Delia Burke.

President's report, 1982

In his speech the president of MII, Mr Sean M. Condon, referred to the growth of awareness in Ireland of the importance of high standard professional marketing and the benefits to the economy, particularly to expanding exports. He said that the previous eighteen months or so had witnessed a new blossoming of marketing consciousness in government industry and education.

The records of the National Marketing Conferences of MII and IMI (Irish Management Institute) in 1982 had provided convincing evidence of the business sector's commitment to the advancement of marketing.

EUROPEAN MARKETING COUNCIL, 1982

MII having been a founder member of the European Marketing Council ensured the constant awareness of marketing developments in Europe and provided for the interchange of ideas between the national organisations. At that stage the EMC had 35,000 members.

DISTRICT GOVERNOR FOR ROTARY DISTRICT, 1981–82

Mr John D. Carroll, chairman of the Fellowship Panel of MII, 1981–82, was elected District Governor Select for Rotary District 116, covering the whole of Ireland, at their AGM in April 1982. In his report he recalled the extreme activity of the Fellowship panel.

STRESSES AND STRAINS OF MARKETING EXECUTIVES, MAY 1982

The guest speaker at the Fellow's dinner in the Rathgar hotel on 4 May 1982, was Dr Jack Dominion, psychiatrist in the Central Middlesex Hospital, England who spoke on the: 'Stresses and Strains of the Marketing Executive and the Role Played by the Family in Support of the Executive'.

The following day Dr Dominion gave a lecture in P.J. Carroll's theatre. More than 100 industrialists, marketing executives and their wives attended. The theatre was sponsored by P.J. Carroll's, who also kindly provided a wine reception. A vote of thanks to the speaker was proposed by Mr John Lepere.

CORK BRANCH OF MII, 1982

Continued activity was reported and thanks made to the outgoing chairman of the Cork branch, Mr John Cashell, for his 'trojan work' in the past, for the Cork branch of MII. The new chairman elected, at their AGM on 7 May 1982, was Mr Aidan Harte.

The Cork Ladies' Night had been held on 27 February 1982 — again a great success. There was good attendance from Dublin, including the president and national chairman of MII.

It was reported that an experimental 'Marketing Club' had been started in April 1982 by members and other business people meeting on Tuesday evenings at the Metropole hotel to discuss various topics.

GALWAY BRANCH OF MII, 1982

A major event in the Galway branch was, in April 1982, the course held at the Department of Marketing in UCG entitled: 'Marketing for Profit'. This ran on three successive Saturdays, with 22 people attending each day. Dr Jim

Ward, Bank of Ireland, Professor of Marketing UCG and Mr Aidan Daly, also of UCG, were the lecturers.

The branch momentum of the previous two years continued under the chairmanship of Mr Tony Broderick, who would finish his term of office on 9 June 1982.

LIMERICK BRANCH OF MII, 1982

The level of MII membership continued to be disappointing in the Limerick branch.

However a joint meeting was held with Galway and a tour of the Shannon Industrial Estate and NIHE was also conducted plus a stop at 'Dirty Nellies', well-known hostelry. A meeting with the Cork branch was planned for the future.

WATERFORD BRANCH OF MII, 1982

The Waterford branch of MII had been very active with membership growing dramatically. The chairwoman of the branch, Ms Delia Burke, and her committee worked hard in organising monthly meetings. The list of speakers included Messrs Joe McGough, Noel Sweeney, Bord Fáilte, Anthony Furlong, IBM and Michael Collins, Irish Distillers.

The Waterford members had recently completed a local survey of companies, related to the need for the marketing training of young executives. The positive results proved interesting to the Regional Technical College and it was hoped that courses in marketing would be organised by them in 1983.

A dinner dance was held 29 October and an AGM on 22 November 1982.

INSTITUTE'S CONTRIBUTION TO EDUCATION

The newly appointed national chairman of the education committee, Mr Jarlath Jennings, recalled that the Marketing Institute of Ireland was the first body in Ireland to organise a professional marketing qualification to cater for the needs of marketeers concerned with the survival and growth of their businesss.

In line with this innovative approach of the Institute, the education committee would continue the vital work embarked on by the outgoing education chairman, Mr Brendan Wafer.

Student examinations covered an area in courses over four years, culminating in graduateship. The student registrar was Ms Carol Scanlon.

AWARDS, SEPTEMBER 1982

The President's Night dinner was held in the Burlington hotel, Dublin on 21 September 1982.

Fellowships, following individual citations detailing considerable involvement in the Marketing Institute progression over many years, were conferred on:

• Mr Brian Creedon: director of Stephen Faller Ltd, Galway

• Mr J. Brendan O'Reilly: managing director of Sales Placement Ltd, Dublin.

Stephen J. Doyle award, 1982

For meritorious service to Marketing, the Stephen J. Doyle award was conferred on Mr Sean Cowman MMII, AnCo, Cork.

AGM OF MII, JANUARY 1983

At the AGM of MII, January 1983, Mr Jack Downey FMII, managing director of Janua Advertising, was appointed national chairman. The vice-presidents were Messrs Bill Fraser and George Priestly. Mr Sean M. Condon kindly agreed to continue in the office of president, until a successor was appointed.

The officers of the council were:

• Mr Philip R. Flood: Senior Vice-Chairman

• Mr Michael Hayes: Vice-Chairman of Education

• Mr Desmond J. Gilroy: Vice-Chairman of Services

• Mr Brendan Wafer: Vice-Chairman of Finance

• Mr Nial Darragh: Hon. Secretary.

The council members were: Messrs Bill Ambrose, John S Burns, Bob Gourley, Brian A. Mooney, Owen V. Morton, Michael J. McKenna, Bob J. Waddell and Ms Mary Crotty. Mr Walter Connolly was elected chairman of the Fellows' Panel.

The branch chairmen were:

• Cork: Mr Aidan Harte

• Galway: Mr John Hickey

• Limerick: Mr Matt O'Doherty

• Waterford: Mr Jim Fox.

AGM OF CORK BRANCH, JANUARY 1983

The Cork regional branch of MII held their AGM at the Metropole hotel on Friday 21 January 1983. Mr Aidan Harte was re-elected chairman. The attendance included the national chairman, Mr Jack Downey, and Mr Philip Flood, senior vice-chairman.

Mr Jack Downey's speech, 1983

The *Cork Examiner*, in its report of the branch AGM, referred to quite a few interesting points contained in the speech of Mr Jack Downey. He was a native of Toormore, near Skibbereen Co. Cork ('one of their own') and managing-director of Janus Advertising in Dublin.

Mr Downey had spoken of the Institute's achievement in marketing education, having over 1,000 registered students each year and an educational budget rapidly approaching six figures. He said it had been done without government or any other aid and was a major contribution to the future success of Irish business at home and abroad.

While jobs were important, in the short and long term, he believed that the type of industrial expansion to have was one creating a wealth base nationally, not for individuals, but for Ireland. Information-oriented and technologically-oriented industries he believed to be good but were not using our vast natural resources. He stressed the importance of a better balance which would ensure that research development and marketing were controlled within the country for a high percentage of our industrial output.

Ireland had managed to be self-sufficient, or almost, during the 1939–45 war but now he believed that the country was losing sight of its land and marine resources. To do the necessary, Mr Downey believed that the agricultural, horticultural and fisheries industries needed more marketing-oriented planning for the future.

PUBLIC PAY FREEZE, JANUARY 1983

The heading of the *Irish Independent* on 24 January 1983 read: 'Public Pay Freeze — Tax Changes Plea'.

Mr Ken Curran, special reporter, outlined what the Marketing Institute of Ireland had said in its submission to the Minister for Finance, Mr Alan Dukes, TD.

Submission to government by Marketing Institute, January 1983

The MII had referred to a public sector pay freeze; a 5 per cent limit to private pay rises and changes in PAYE. These and other radical moves, including the closure of the Whitegate Oil Refinery and the possible sale of CIE (Córas Iompair Éireann), rail and bus, to private operators, were urged by the Marketing Institute.

Business closures

A warning was given by the MII that the 700 business closures last year (1982), were just the 'tip of the iceberg' and that if there was no positive approach in the budget, a new wave of closures and redundancies would follow. Over-generous pay increases, in the previous three years, in both the public and private sectors, had been a major contributor in the recession, according to the submission.

RTÉ evening news, January 1983

A lengthy statement, from the submission of the Marketing Institute, was read on the RTÉ 1 Evening News at 6.30 p.m. on 24 January 1983.
Inter alia, the Institute submission had urged the government to:

1. Review the proposals of taxation on houses, valued at over £65,000.

2. Have electricity costs reduced by relieving ESB of rates.

3. Have financed, by the private sector, a road development programme.

The most crucial role of government was to promote enterprise, by creating an environment within which all sectors — management, labour, exporters and investors — would provide real incentive
The current taxation was certainly having an effect in 1983 and required urgent restructuring, according to the Marketing Institute.

The Irish Times reports on submission, January 1983

Citing the MII submission, *The Irish Times* issue of 24 January 1983 stated that the Institute had partly blamed the severity of the present recession on the 1982 budget.
In order to avoid matters worsening the Institute proposed that in the 1983 budget, not alone should it include a wage freeze, a reduction in the top range of VAT, but also income tax relief for export salesmen and greater incentives to work for the PAYE sector.
Excise duties, VAT and PRSI, reduced disposable income and threw retail sales into a downward spiral, reduced employment, cut government revenue and had a most depressing effect on the economy.
The Institute's submission further stated that public spending could be reduced by, among other things, obliging civil servants to contribute towards

their pensions, attracting private finance to the road building programme and adopting a more commercial approach to semi-state bodies. In addition, it saw no role for the National Development Corporation.

BORD TELECOM, FEBRUARY 1983

At the Tuesday Club meeting of 1 February 1983, Mr Tom Byrnes, chief executive of Bord Telecom, addressed those present on the subject: 'Marketing in the Public Sector'.

He expressed the Bord's annoyance at the delay in giving it a legal footing. This was the first time that disquiet had been publicly expressed on the issue. Mr Byrnes referred to 'the years which had been put into persuading and pleading with five governments to implement the recommendations made by the Post & Telegraphs Review Group nearly four years previous'.

Bord Telecom had been established as a semi-state body in 1980 to take responsibility for the running of the Irish telecommunications system from the civil service. He claimed that, in the ten years since Ireland joined the EEC, in spite of the creation of more than 97,000 new jobs — primarily by foreign investors — the net increase in industrial employment was only 7,000. Native private companies had failed to adapt to changed circumstances. There were others, however, who had grown through recession. They had three things in common:

1. They were forward-looking and internationally minded.

2. They were highly marketing-orientated.

3. They were experts in their field.

Mr Byrnes maintained that one needed to be market driven, to go out and find a niche in the market for a product or service and meet it. It had to be with a quality product, at a price which reflected its value to the customer. He believed that Ireland lay on the edge of a market 100 times its size.

Digital system, February 1983

Mr Byrnes declared that he was confident that the huge investment in the telephone system over the past three years, of over £600m., was beginning to pay off, while the switch to a 'digital' system would enable Bord Telecom to provide customers with whatever services were required.

Business & Finance, February 1983

It was reported in the 24 February 1983 issue of *Business & Finance*, that Mr Tom Garvey, chief executive of Bord Poist, agreed with the remarks made by his counterpart, Mr Tom Byrnes, Bord Telecom, condemning the long delays in putting the two boards on a legal footing and transferring responsibility from the Department of Posts and Telegraphs.

BUDGET TO ADD TO UNEMPLOYMENT, FEBRUARY 1983

Concerning the budget, the *Irish Press* pointed out that many commentators agreed that Ireland's dole queues would grow even longer — one prediction being that unemployment would reach about 250,000 within six months.

Professor John Bristow of Trinity College agreed that the budget would add to unemployment, but said that he found little alternative at that time. The rise in VAT would put the tourist industry into even deeper trouble, he believed. The results in 1983 were inevitable, following the policies pursued since 1977.

The Marketing Institute, slamming the high PAYE tax rates, stated that skilled personnel were being forced out of the country. An instance quoted was that of the PAYE tax rate of 67 per cent at £10,262 income in the Republic, compared to a 60 per cent rate at £33,069 in Northern Ireland. It was 'numbing' that for a person with a salary of £10,500, the government took £6.70 tax out of every £10 earned.

NEW PRESIDENT OF MII, FEBRUARY 1983

Mr Francis J. O'Reilly, chairman of Irish Distillers Group, also Ulster Bank Ltd and a director of other companies, kindly accepted the honorary position of president of the Marketing Institute of Ireland in February 1983. He played a major role in Irish industrial life being closely associated with various organisations.

At a reception held at Bow Lane Distillers, Smithfield, Dublin, on Tuesday 15 February 1983, he was welcomed to the position and presented with the chain of office by Mr Sean Condon, chief executive of Córas Tráchtála Teo and outgoing president.

Honorary Member of MII, February 1983

Mr Sean Condon was presented with honorary membership of the Marketing Institute of Ireland in recognition of his considerable contribution to enhancing the Institute's aims and objectives.

In accepting the office of president, Mr O'Reilly said that despite recalling the Institute's role in marketing achievements — particularly in education with over 1,000 students now registered — the importance of marketing was not sufficiently recognised and realised in Ireland.

Retail News report, 1983

Retail News reported Mr O'Reilly as saying that 'traditionally, both in industry and agriculture, Ireland had been production oriented and indeed, by and large, its production had been good, but marketing had lagged far behind'.

Mr O'Reilly had gone on to say that the scope and quality of life in Ireland would depend 'on the health and efficiency of industry and agriculture. Goods must be produced to a very high standard of quality, be competitive with other countries and then go out and be marketed properly throughout the world'.

FELLOWSHIP DINNER, MARCH 1983

The annual Fellowship dinner was held at the Irish Management Institute, Dublin on 23 March 1983. The guest speaker was Professor Harry Harrison, University College, Dublin. The attendance of 32 included 23 Fellows of the Marketing Institute. The presentation by Professor Harrison was most stimulating and provoked many questions.

NATIONAL MARKETING CONFERENCE, SEPTEMBER 1983

The fifth national MII marketing conference theme was entitled 'Imaginative Marketing'. It was sponsored jointly by the Marketing Institute and *Business & Finance*, and was held at Trinity College on 15 September 1983.

The *Irish Independent* reported that top businessmen had been told to place a greater emphasis on new ideas, rather than to depend solely on efficient management and problem solving. This advice had come from the leading international business and education consultant, Dr Edward de Bono.

At least 200 delegates from the marketing and advertising world had paid £95 each to hear from the 'guru' of lateral thinking. Dr de Bono said that business had been 'hamstrung' by the practices of the buoyant 1950s and 60s economy, where efficiency had simply maintained a steady course.

A full morning session at the conference was devoted to Dr Edward de Bono, leading consultant. He said that in the future most profitability would come from application concepts, rather than from new technology. That, he believed, opened up a whole new area of opportunity. It was not just a matter of satisfying needs but also of designing needs.

Lett & Co, September 1983

Mr James Lett, proprietor of Lett & Co. of Wexford, sellers of processed fish at home and overseas (particularly mussels) speaking at the afternoon session of the conference, said the development of his thriving business was based on international demand for the product.

In 1982 the Dutch alone consumed over 100,000 tons of mussels. The same was true for France, Denmark, Spain and Korea, with New Zealand also coming to the fore.

Spurred by the demand from the UK for Irish mussels, as far back as 1963, the company had decided to explore the possibility of mussel harvesting in Wexford. That was something that had never occurred to him before he got the request from the UK.

A mussel factory was built in 1968 and BIM (Irish Fisheries Board) was approached in 1972 to explore the possibility of mussel farming as natural stocks were running out.

Subsequently Lett & Co. produced added value product and invited customers from France and UK to visit the group's plant. Major breakthrough's included Paradoc Grangel Supermarkets and Big Gel Freezer Markets in France, and Young Seafoods and Smales in the UK.

The company had since moved into the American market, with considerable expansion expected over the next five years, as their market grew.

In 1979 the Lett's had launched a further two products — mussel on the half-shell and mussel in garlic butter. They both became successful Irish quality seafood products. It meant an enormous boost to additional employment and exports from Wexford. Ten per cent of mussel exports were in the natural state, the rest added value product, Mr Lett added.

He also stated that significant roles in the expansion were provided by BIM, Anco, the IDA and the Department of Fisheries.

Irish quality control awards, 1983

Lett's had been awarded the Irish Quality Control Association 'National Hygiene Award' for Fish Processing in 1980/81/82, while they also won the 'Supreme Award' for the total food industry in 1982.

Dublin Bay prawn

As an off-shoot of mussels, Lett's established the 'Dublin Bay Prawn' as part of its product range in 1978. In the summer of 1983 alone they sold over 250 tons of whole prawns to French and Italian supermarkets and over 200 tons of prawn-tails to the UK and Italy.

Avair, September 1983

The Irish Times of 16 September 1983 reported a 'damning indictment'of advertising agencies attributed to Mr Gerry Connolly, managing director of Avair, the Irish airline, when he addressed the Marketing Institute conference.

His feelings about advertising agencies had remained unchanged, following specific meetings with them.

Mr Connolly was unimpressed, as unless the account was sufficiently large, advertising agencies did not want to know one. He found it faster, more effective and much less costly, to develop ideas on a 'think-in' basis oneself and to use freelance people to 'dress it up'. Until someone came along and guaranteed results, Avair would continue to do it their own way, he stated.

Jameson whiskey, 1983

Mr Michael Cummins, director of sales and marketing for the home division of Irish Distilllers Ltd, explained how the company had established Jameson whiskey on the British market in the year 1981. He said the target market for the major campaign was heavier and regular whiskey drinkers, confident and experimental people, who drank specialist whiskies, and were young males from the ages of 18 to 34.

Jameson, not being Scotch was different — the real difference, of course, was being Irish. That aroused a curiosity in the target market to such an extent that one felt obliged to try it. The long-term objective was to build a clear separate personality for the brand in an over-crowded market place.

Mr Cummins concluded that their goal had been achieved as without question the direction of Irish whiskey had changed in Great Britain

Waterford Glass story, 1983

Mr Owen Kealy, chief executive of Waterford Glass, declared that their success around the world was due to marketing. They had found that great vigilance was necessary when dealing with local agents in overseas markets. Part of the success of Waterford Crystal was the care they expended to market needs.

He said there were two vital points for export conscious firms to take to heart and he emphasised the necessity of gauging the needs of the market accurately. Information should not be accepted on face value, particularly in the export market.

Sord Computer sales, 1983

Talking about the Japanese experience, Mr Patrick Scanlon, marketing manager of Sord Computer sales (the highest ranking non-Japanese member of staff with the company in Europe), having responsibility for Europe, warned that the West should not just go out and imitate the Japanese way of doing things. He pointed out that Japanese ways would have to be adapted and modified to suit Western culture, as the two were very different.

Bailey's Irish Cream success, 1983

Summing up the conference Dr de Bono said that one of the greatest marketing achievements he had witnessed was that of Bailey's Irish Cream. The producers had obviously realised that they would sell large quantities through supermarkets and mainly to women. They had also played upon a certain snob value.

Dr de Bono finally said that putting ideas to work was much more difficult and much more important than just having the ideas in the first place. His plea was that concepts should be taken more seriously than ever before. He described a concept as an organisation of experience or of action steps. It had a convenience, a purpose and coherence.

SEAN LEMASS AWARD, SEPTEMBER 1983

The Sean Lemass award was presented by the Minister for Trade, Commerce and Tourism, Mr Frank Cluskey TD, to Memory Computer Ltd. At the reception in the Burlington hotel, Dublin on 28 September 1983, Mr Frank Casey, chairman, was pleased to accept the award on behalf of the company.

Memory Computer became the fourth recipient of this major award presented by the Marketing Institute. The Minister stated that Memory Computer was a shining example of how we Irish can hold our own in a field domiciled by foreign-based companies. He went on to say that it combined an exciting blend of hardware and software facilities, and was one of the most significant of our native computer manufacturing companies.

Mr Pearse Mee, joint managing director of Memory Computer, Mr Frank O'Reilly, president and Mr Jack Downey, chairman, were at the presentation, as were the executive council and many Marketing Institute members

PRESIDENT'S DINNER, NOVEMBER 1983

The Fellowship panel organised the twenty-first President's Night dinner which was held at the Berkeley Court hotel in Dublin on Thursday 10 November 1983. Tickets were sold out well before the event and it was a night to be remembered.

Opening the evening the president of the Institute, Mr Frank O'Reilly, introduced the guest speaker, Mr Jim Fitzpatrick, chairman of the Irish Sugar Co. The latter delivered an excellent paper.

Attendance at the dinner included Lord Killanin, Mr Sean Condon, past-president, Mr Brian Patterson IMI, Mr Vivian Murray, Irish Goods Council, Dr Tim O'Driscoll, Mr Jack Downey, national chairman and Mr Bill Fraser, vice-president.

HONORARY MEMBER, NOVEMBER 1983

Mr Bill Fraser FMII, vice-president of the Marketing Institute and a founder member, was conferred with honorary membership in appreciation of his continuous efforts and outstanding dedication over so many years.

TWENTY-FIRST ANNIVERSARY OF MII, NOVEMBER 1983

Business & Finance magazine produced a *Business & Finance Souvenir Report* to celebrate the twenty-first anniversary of the Marketing Institute of Ireland, 1962–83.

MARKETING BUSINESS NEED, 1983

Congratulating the Marketing Institute on its twenty-first anniversary, an Taoiseach Dr Garret Fitzgerald TD, stated that he found it surprising that a real consciousness of the need for sophisticated marketing for all Irish goods and services was only then being fully recognised.

He was sure that, when the Marketing Institute began in 1962 that many people in the business world looked on the function as probably superficial, flashy and unscientific. However, in his opinion very few people thought that way in 1983.

He believed that marketing as a business function had become probably the biggest single need in modern Irish business. Moreover, the government was aware of the crucial need for marketing expertise. Every set of trade figures highlighted the success achieved by business, which put a high premium on the marketing function in commercial operations.

In the years ahead, Irish governments would ensure that commercial enterprises, receiving substantial public investment, would have adequate marketing and planning skills available. A new industrial policy, shortly coming before government, would be scrutinised to ensure that sufficient rating was put on the vital necessity of good marketing.

Employment creation, 1983

The president of the Institute, Mr Francis J. O'Reilly, chairman of the Ulster Bank and a director of the National Westminister Bank Plc., stated that he looked back with pride and forward with hope.

He declared that he knew that marketing men must cultivate a climate of hope to stimulate investment. Confidence lay in all those who were engaged in production, in marketing and selling, in the promotion of Ireland's exports, in developing tourism and those in the service industries, to redouble their efforts to unselfishly create employment.

Necessity of good marketing, 1983

Mr Jack Downey, chairman of the Institute stated that when the Marketing Institute was founded 21 years ago the marketeers who did so were already seasoned in good marketing practice. He said the founders did not just talk about marketing, they practised it and took action to spread the gospel. People must be left with the incentive to work harder and earn more. Looking to the future, not just 1984, 1985 or even 1986, progress as a nation had to be made into the year 2000 and beyond.

National assets needed to be fully utilised, particularly our young people, and in his opinion that was where the Institute had a lot to contribute. Its educational programme, without any outside financial help, was the cornerstone of the future.

CORK GRADUATESHIPS, NOVEMBER 1983

The *Cork Examiner* of 17 November 1983 pictorially reported the conferring of the Institute's graduateships in Marketing to Cork recipients. The presentations were made by Mr Jack Downey FMII, national chairman, (a Corkman himself), to:

• Mr John V. O' Sulliivan: G. D. Searle Ltd, Douglas, Co. Cork

• Mr Michael Halligan: Novo Ireland Ltd, Carrigaline, Co. Cork.

EDUCATING MARKETEERS, 1983

Mr Michael Hayes, vice-chairman of (Education) MII, recalled that the Marketing Institute was the first body in Ireland to organise a professional marketing qualification to cater for the needs of marketeers concerned with the survival and growth of their business.

Student numbers registered with the Institute had grown dramatically over the years, particularly from 1972, then about 200, to 1983 when over 1,000 students were studying for the various stages of the examinations. Over the previous ten-year period, the Institute had registered close to 10,000 students for its professional awards.

Lectures and tutorials were provided for registered Dublin students at the College of Commerce, Rathmines and the College of Marketing and Design in Parnell Square.

Courses were also provided at the National Institute for Higher Education, Limerick, the Regional Colleges in Carlow, Cork and Galway, Limerick Technical College and in 1983, one had just commenced in the Regional Technical College in Tralee, Co. Kerry.

Mr Hayes paid tribute to colleagues, past and present, like the vice-chairman Mr Philip Flood, who had the vision to undertake the work of business education and together initiated the programme.

MARKETING INSTITUTE MAJORS, 1983

Mr Anthony Neville FMII, wrote that it was significant that the Marketing Institute of Ireland should come of age at a time when marketing, as a topic, came so readily to the lips of politicians and media commentators. Success, in attracting major foreign investments and Ireland's exports in recent years, was attributed to skilful marketing.

Marketing talent and innovation were identified as the means of providing the jobs so desperately needed in the years ahead.

There were over 600 Marketing Institute members in 1983.

KEY TO GROWTH, 1983

Mr Sean Condon, immediate past-president of MII and chief executive of Córas Tráchtála, was critical of 'the poor state of marketing' and said, like that of some leading business authorities he named, steps had to be taken to remedy the problem.

A forthcoming White Paper on industrial policy would set out a new clear-cut approach by government to tackling the development of industry. The task was to develop industries and services so that they could secure and expand their existing bases. With such expansion of output and sale it would obtain increased employment and better living standards.

More resources were required in the area of marketing, especially in the export area. Firms, in greater number, with a marketing approach were needed to recruit qualified experienced, world-class marketing and sales personnel. Ireland should be capable of taking on and beating the competition in international markets, be it from Japan, Europe, North America or South-East Asian countries.

IRISH SUGAR COMPANY, DECEMBER 1983

The Irish Sugar Company, on an investment of only £5.5m. over almost 50 years, had managed to turn over £170m. annually, replace sugar imports and employ 3,000 people, its chairman, Mr James Fitzpatrick told those present at the dinner. He also said that the small investment had been repaid to the Exchequer many times over, while the industry had been developed without subsidy or IDA support.

PANEL TO DEVELOP RESOURCES, DECEMBER 1983

The president of the MII, Mr Frank O'Reilly, announced that the Institute was setting up a body of experts to voluntarily help entrepreneurs.

A panel of nationally known and successful people would make themselves available to offer guidance and advice to any member of the community and entrepreneurs who wished to become involved in any enterprise devoted to developing Ireland's natural resources and creating employment opportunities.

FELLOWSHIP AWARDS, DECEMBER 1983

Following citations Fellowship awards were presented to:

- Mr William Ambrose: managing director of Benelos Publications, Dublin

- Mrs Delia Burke: marketing and public relations consultant, Waterford

- Mr Geoff Beggs: general manager of Tennant & Ruttle, Dublin

- Mr John S. Burns: managing director of Birex Pharmaceuticals, Dublin

- Mr John A. Cashell: general manager of Tivoli Spinners, Cork

- Mr P. Noel M. Quirke: managing director of Quirke Lynch Ltd, Dublin.

THE STEPHEN DOYLE AWARD, DECEMBER 1983

The Stephen Doyle award for 'meritorious service to marketing' was presented by Mr Frank O'Reilly, president of the Institute, to Mr Bill Fraser FMII, past chairman (1970–71), and vice-president of the Marketing Institute of Ireland.

The citation recalled the continuous, inestimable contribution made by Mr Fraser to marketing since the earliest days, back to the formation of the ISMA (Incorporated Sales Managers' Association) group.

GOLDEN JUBILEE OF PUBLICITY CLUB, 1983

The Publicity Club of Ireland celebrated its Golden Jubilee in 1983. The chairman for this key year in the long history of the club, was Mr Donal Ó Maololaí of Córas Iompair Éireannn (CIE).

AGM OF MII, JANUARY 1984

The twenty-second AGM of the Marketing Institute of Ireland was held in Carroll's Theatre, Grand Parade, Dublin on Monday 16 January 1984 at 6 p.m.

RECORD CONFERRING, 1984

For the first time over 100 students graduated in the MII examinations. A new syllabus for the educational programme had high media exposure and steps were taken to appoint a chief executive and also acquire a computer.

MII APPOINTMENTS, 1984

In the unavoidable absence of the president of the Institute, Mr William Fraser, the vice-president, installed the chairman for the coming year, Mr Philip Flood, saying that he would certainly add prestige and impetus to the Institute.

Mr Philip Flood then addressed the meeting particularly on the economic outlook for Ireland in 1984 and the important necessary contribution which could only be made by marketing and the Institute, in particular.

He outlined the objectives for his term of office (1984) as:

* to finalise the fine work of his predecessors

* to enhance the image and awareness of the Institute

* to continue and increase the good work on the educational front

* to appoint sectoral committees regarding segments of business in MII

* to increase graduate participation and involvement in every aspect of the Institute's activities.

New additional members of the council were then announced. They were: Messrs David Manley, Michael McKenna, Bob Waddell and James Wrynn.

The new officers were declared as:

* Senior Vice-Chairman: Mr William Ambrose

* Vice-Chairmen: Mr Brendan Wafer (Education), Mr Des Gilroy (Finance), Mr Bob Waddell (Services)

* Secretary: Mr Nial Darragh

* Chairman (Fellowship): Mr Walter Connolly.

The remaining council members were: Messrs Jack Downey, outgoing chairman, Michael Hayes, David Manley, Michael McKenna, Ros O'Shaughnessy and James Wrynn, while Ms Mary Crotty and Mr Brian Mooney served initially but on resigning, were replaced by Messrs Jarlath Jennings and Alan McDonnell.

The president of the Institute, Mr Frank J. O'Reilly, kindly agreed to continue in office for 1984.

The branch representatives on the council for 1984 were:

• Cork: Mr John Donnelly, Chairman

• Galway: Mr John Hickey, Chairman

• Limerick: Mr Liam De Paor, Chairman

• Waterford: Mr Sandy Metcalfe, Chairman.

Development consultant appointed

Mr Frank Cusack was chosen and appointed development consultant to the Marketing Institute. The heightened sense of purpose, increased awareness of the work of the Institute and a huge increase in membership were largely attributed to his work and so acknowledged by the chairman of the Institute, Mr Philip Flood.

Corporate image

Under a committee chaired by Mr Jarlath Jennings, the corporate image of the MII was achieved, particularly with regard to a new logo and style of letter heading.

Submissions were made by the Institute to various sectoral bodies:

1. To the Minister for Finance, prior to the last budget: 'A Climate for Enterprise'. The submission highlighted the factor necessary to create a climate of enterprise and to resuscitate an industrial recovery, and argued for the meaningful recognition of the vital role that marketing could play in the development of the economy.

2. To the Joint Oireachtas Committee on Small Businesses the view was put forward that there must be considerable emphasis on the provision of: 'Marketing Support Services', in an integrated co-ordinated manner for small businesses. It recommended the establishment of a single National Marketing Board to be responsible for the co-ordination of all policy initiatives among the semi-state and private agencies.

3. To the Consultative Committee for Marketing: 'Improving Marketing Performance in Irish Firms'. The 25-page submission analysed the weakness of marketing in Irish companies and proposed a national marketing strategy. It showed how the general business environment could

be improved by attracting equity capital for marketing investment and by improving marketing education and training.

Overall the submissions were well received.

Minicomputer to aid administration

To streamline the administration, in both the membership and student areas, increase productivity and enhance service, a minicomputer with multiple screens and both a letter quality and dot matrix printer were acquired. In addition, a fully automated franking and letter-sealing machine were also obtained. With the new computer installed, word processing was instituted — the main priorities were the introduction of membership and student records, an examinations' and an accounting package.

FELLOWSHIP, 1984

The Fellowship dinner was held at the United Services Club, St Stephen's Green, Dublin on 21 May 1984. The guest speaker was Dr Kieran Kennedy. He addressed those present with an address on: 'Employment and Unemployment Policy for Ireland'. The topic, of particular interest at the time, provoked many questions of high quality. Dr Kennedy replied, in great detail, to some very difficult questions, resulting in an unusually late end for an Institute meeting.

CORK BRANCH MII, 1984

Despite extreme unemployment problems in the Cork area and the disastrous effect of recent major closures, the branch attitude was one of promoting both optimism and determination to improve local conditions.

Cork continued to be both innovative and energetic, under a team led by their chairman, Mr John Donnelly, well supported by Messrs Seamus Martin and John Cashell.

Membership was 65 with over 100 students and the branch headquarters were situated at the Metropole hotel.

CORK CONFERENCE, 1984

Attended by over 80 people the Cork branch conference had as its theme: 'Marketing the Key to Profit'. It was very successful and had major media coverage.

The conference was sponsored by ICI in conjunction with the MII sub-committee. Delegates present from other institutes considered it a most impressive and constructive contribution to Cork industry.

A joint venture concept, with the Institute of Purchasing and Materials Management, included a luncheon talk given by Mr Peter Barry TD, Minister for Foreign Affairs.

The meeting continued on into the late evening. Speeches from members of both institutes were included.

The students had a case study day, an annual event in the educational programme in Cork. It was a full day, well attended and was adjudicated by Dr Barra O'Cinneide of NIHE.

There was also a seminar, held at the RTC, presented by Irish Distillers Ltd and a luncheon with fellow Limerick students.

Ladies' Night surprised all by the number (250) attending, including many colleagues from Dublin and the branches.

GALWAY BRANCH REPORT, 1984

The 1983–84 season in Galway commenced with an evening meeting in October '83. This was addressed by Ms Gillian Bowler on the subject: 'Selling and Marketing Sunshine Holidays — the Agony and the Ecstasy'.

In December Mr Denis Fitzgibbon addressed the evening meeting on: 'Toyota Worldwide — A Case History'.

GALWAY'S INDUSTRY 'IN YEAR 2000', 1984

Through Galway's quincentennial year the MII branch there was led by Mr John Hickey. A very successful seminar on the theme: 'Galway's Industry in the Year 2000' was presented with Dr Michael Killeen as the principal speaker. Group discussions followed with questions to the speakers. A wide interest was shown, while much press coverage ensued. The committee appreciated the attendance of Mr Philip Flood, national chairman of the Institute, and Mr Brendan Wafer, representing council members.

The Galway branch council strongly suggested to the national council that at least two of the latter's monthly meetings should be held in regional centres, by rotation, to coincide with joint meetings of the branches.

MID-WEST BRANCH OF MII, 1984

The 1984 chairman, Mr Liam de Paor, organised a series of events and promoted awareness of the Marketing Institute in what was the smallest and youngest branch.

Their first venture of the session was a luncheon seminar on: 'Marketing Opportunities Abroad'. The guest speaker was Mr Foster Kerrison, regional manager of Córas Tráchtála. Later on a very informative meeting was held in Limerick with officers from the Cork, Waterford and Galway branches each expressing their views.

The students decided to organise a seminar on: 'Career Opportunities in Marketing'.

More than 150 attended. The speakers were Messrs Thomas Burgess and Brendan O'Reilly of Sales Placement Ltd, Michael Walton of AnCo (Dublin) and Ms Marion Deegan of Shannon Development. They felt honoured to have Mr Phil Flood as seminar chairman.

A number of other meetings of the branch also took place. They included an evening seminar on 'Electronics — How Can We Help?' The speakers, internationally known, were Messrs Bryan Lynsday and Bill Chambers; 'Yoplait — Ten Years On', was the topic of Mr Brian Milton, marketing manager of Yoplait; and a joint effort with the Exporters' Association, 'Exporting — Strategy for Success', at which Mr Andrew Crawford, commercial director of Irish Biscuits, gave a most stimulating talk.

Mr Pat Scully, branch assistant secretary, an export sales manager himself, did the group proud with his contribution.

During the year, useful contact was established with other bodies including the IMI, the Junior Chamber and the Institute for Credit Management.

WATERFORD BRANCH, REPORT 1984

Waterford continued to astound with an output and enthusiasm way beyond its apparent resources. Mr Sandy Metcalfe was a committed and energetic chairman, ably assisted by the education chairman, Mrs Delia Burke, and committee.

The speakers at the monthly lecture meetings included Prof. A.C. Cunningham, UCD, Messrs David Hedigan, CTT, Dan Hurley, Waterford County Manager and John Cunningham, *Waterford News & Star*.

A stimulating case study night was held at the Waterford RTC. This was organised by Mrs Delia Burke FMII who also acted as tutor for a six-week course in 'An Introduction to Marketing' at the Adult Education Centre. Applications were made for double the 25 places on the course.

The Institute's graduateship course was launched in October 1984 at the Waterford RTC — an undoubted reflection of the increased awareness and importance of marketing in the region.

The second annual breakfast meeting had a sell-out attendance of 35 and was addressed by Mr Jim Tuohy, general manager of Tramore Fáilte. A number of social events also took place, including the annual golf outing at Waterford Golf Club and the annual dinner.

MEMBERS' MEETINGS, DUBLIN, 1984

The 1984–85 year got off to a fine start with a well-attended presentation by Mr Cartan Finnegan, assistant general manager (Marketing) of Córas Iompair Éireann, (CIE) on the DART system. The meeting was held at the Killiney Court hotel in Dublin.

NATIONAL MARKETING CONFERENCE, SEPTEMBER 1984

The sixth National Marketing Conference, under the able direction of Mr Jack Downey and committee, probably broke all attendance records. Due to catering limitations, bookings had to be restricted to 280 participants.

The conference was held at Trinity College, Dublin on 21 September 1984. The theme of the conference, jointly sponsored by the Marketing Institute of Ireland and *Business & Finance* magazine, was 'Get Up and Grow'.

According to the opening page of the special conference brochure companies which had survived the recession in good health had, in the process, grown slimmer and fitter. Their managers, who had of necessity, become leaner, harder men, had learned more than a single trick or two about survival. In addition, most had found ways to seek growth, when those less courageous and confident sought cover. It was not that the pursuit of growth and development automatically brought them immediate or measurable results. However, those who constantly turned their performance towards improvement were the managers whose companies were always first in line for the earliest pickings.

It was clear that the booming 1960s and early 1970s were gone and attitudes of mind were most important beginning with the positive thinker, the one who looked for the bright specks in the gloom. Despite high unemployment, high taxation, and as a result reduced spending power, people were still getting married, buying houses and so forth. Businesses needed services and goods and, in both commerce and in the community, there was a demand for them. Hence the theme of the conference, 'Get up and Grow'.

There were eight main speakers. It is only possible, in this volume, to give an indication of the theme of each topic.

Toyota and beyond: Mr Tim Mahony, 1984

It was the opinion of Mr T.P. Mahony, chairman of Killeen Investments, that every success story has an element of luck. Amazingly, the harder you work, the luckier one gets.

Toyota was the origin of Killeen and remained so in 1984. Toyota grew out of his brother's retail motor business, Denis Mahony Ltd. Realising how good the Toyota product was, he and his brother, purchased Toyota (Ireland) Ltd, to develop the franchise, in 1974.

Mr Tim Mahony stated that Toyota had just been introduced into Ireland by 'the late great Stephen O'Flaherty, undoubtedly the outstanding Irish motor man of all times'. The range of vehicles comprised one model only, the original small Corolla, beloved by all.

At that time they enjoyed 1 per cent of the motor market in Ireland, that was if anyone could enjoy only 1 per cent of any market. Under government regulations it was required to assemble in Ireland all cars sold, while only by selling 5 per cent of the market was it possible to augment the range of models by bringing in other assembled Toyota models from Japan. What was a miracle in the Irish motor industry then was that from 1 per cent in January 1974, a better than 5 per cent market share achievement was made six months later.

By September that year entitlement to order assembled Toyota models from Japan was established. The result was effectively placing Toyota in Ireland on the road to success.

In September 1984, Killeen Investments had 19 per cent of the Irish market and was in second position. In the process it gave Toyota Japan the largest market share of any Japanese maker in Europe.

On take-over Toyota had an assembly workforce of 54 people. However, in order to achieve the 5 per cent market share, the plant had to go on a two-shift cycle and that increased the workforce to about 170 people. At the same time it was known that assembly would cease in 1985, at the latest. So jobs had to be provided for, by then.

In 1976 a separate company had been formed called Killeen Investments Ltd. Two engineers were recruited to the new company which was divorced from the motor operations.

After much investment, research and travel around the world, negotiation with the Foster Wheeler Energy Corporation of America, manufacturers of pressure parts for huge boilers such as those supplied to Moneypoint, Co. Clare, resulted in a joint venture with Foster Wheeler Killeen Company operating happily from Shannon, Co. Clare.

Further expansions resulted in the purchase of, over a period of seven years, the technology of the Munekata Corporation of Osaka, Japan, exclusively for Europe. The introduction came from the IDA in Japan.

Munekata was a medium-sized Japanese company employing approximately 1,700 people and engaged in the manufacture of precision plastics for the electronic industry. These related to cabinetry for television, videos, tape recorders, computer cabinets and also for the pharmaceutical industry.

A technology transfer agreement had been arrived at and signed on 10 June 1983 in Osaka. One year and one day later Plastronix Ltd was officially opened by the Minister for Industry and Commerce, Mr John Bruton TD in Santry, Dublin.

Orders were booked for twelve months ahead from prestigious companies like Panasonic, Apple, Mitsubishi and Toshiba.

At the end of 1983 a reasonably sized group of companies had evolved from originally a retail motor dealership. In 1984 they gave employment to 340 people though there were, unfortunately 213,000 unemployed in the Republic of Ireland at the time.

Lessons from the marketplace: Mr Sean Condon, 1984

Mr Sean Condon, managing director of the newly-created marketing company, IMS-Condon International, a joint venture with Irish Marketing Surveys, had himself been, from 1977 to 1984, chief executive of Córas Tráchtála (Irish Export Board). He was past-president of the Marketing Institute of Ireland, a member of the Irish Management Council and on the Taoiseach's Sectoral Development Committee.

In his presentation, Mr Condon outlined how he had selected his subject title: 'Lessons from the Marketplace'. He decided to interview a number of key individuals to comment on success and others to comment on failure. He asked various questions to each.

In the case of the failed companies the following questions were asked:

1. What were the fundamental reasons for failure?

2. Were there any relationships between the house marketing weaknesses and the company's decline?

3. What were the outstanding lessons from the marketplace?

The questions to the successful companies were, in general directly the opposite and focussed on such matters as the reasons for the company's success; development of marketing policy; and the allocation of resources.

Following discussion and written requests these were results:

Foir Teoranta

Foir Teoranta, a state-sponsored company, was established in 1972. Mr Kevin McGuinness, chief executive, explained their function was to assist manufacturing concerns, which were in danger of closing and unable to obtain financial aid from commercial sources.

It transpired that most of the questions asked by Mr Condon were already answered in a simple, yet extremely informative, brochure. Essentially, Foir Teo. could help by providing funds, in certain ways, and also executive assistance in all areas of business.

Stokes Kennedy Crowley & Co.

Stokes Kennedy Crowley & Company, (SKC), a leading national firm of chartered accountants, providing auditing, taxation and management consulting services to industrial, commercial and financial companies, state-sponsored bodies and government, originated in 1876. It is wholly Irish-owned and all of the partners then were Irish.

When asked about the fundamental reason for company failure, Mr Laurence Crowley, a partner, said it was often too glib to write off the decline in one single aspect, such as 'management weakness'. There were nearly always several contributory reasons. He would include weaknesses in the marketing field as 'important'.

Management could misinterpret the true meaning of the core business that their company was in. It should never assume that it was in a particular area of strength or technical capability. Also, when it came to change, he believed that neither the board nor management in most companies allowed enough time. 'Time,' he stated, was 'competent people and money'.

Musgrave Ltd

Musgrave Ltd, a family owned company based in Cork, had been involved in grocery distribution for over 100 years. They had 600 employees and their turnover for 1984 was projected at over £132m.

Over 60 per cent of sales came from large surface area Cash & Carrys. The first had been opened in 1972 in the Robinhood Industrial Estate in Dublin and the fifth in Belfast in 1983.

The company's wholesale division, based in Cork, accounted for 30 per cent of group sales, supplying 243 supermarkets in Munster and Leinster.

Their supermarkets formerly traded under the VG banner but a highly successful repositioning exercise had been undertaken, with the larger supermarkets coming under the Centra logo. The remaining major division in the company was its frozen operation, with depots in Dublin and Cork.

Musgrave also operated an export wholesale division, principally to the North American market and had shareholdings in Sugar Distributors Ltd and Intelligence (Ireland) Ltd, a computer software company.

The managing director of Musgrave, Mr Hugh MacKeown, put forward the single most important reason that it was a growth company. As far back as the very early 1970s, the company decided to answer the classical strategic planning question — What business are we in? They decided they were in grocery and related products, and wholesale distribution.

Mr MacKeown said he had learnt many important lessons along the way. These were:

1. Stop a failing project as early as possible.

2. Establish a clearly thought-out and cost-effective way of providing the market with what it required and then stick to it.

Musgrave Ltd continuously looked closely at what was happening in other developed countries in their line of business, particularly in USA and increasingly in Europe.

Gilbeys of Ireland

Gilbey's of Ireland, a direct subsidiary of the International Distillers and Vintners group of companies, in turn a member of the huge Grand Metropolitan Group, created Bailey's, one of the marketing success stories of the previous decade.

Bailey's Original Irish Cream Liqueur first saw the light of day only ten years previously. It had become one of the most phenomenally successful liqueur drinks in the world, a marketing 'first' and not least, a wonderful fillip to developmentally minded executives that something original could be created in and marketed from Ireland, to become the world number one.

Sales in excess of two million cases were notched up in 1984 and the product was then in distribution in 110 countries. The credit for success lay with Mr David Dand, chairman and chief executive, group marketing director, and other senior executives in Dublin. Mr Dand believed there were two fundamental reasons for the success of his company in the marketplace and they were:

1. A very basic fundamental belief in what they were doing, a deep conviction that the concept was correct and that the project would work.

2. They identified a perceived gap in the market for a product concept so new that it was indeed totally unclassified at the beginning, which brought with it, of course, some inherent benefits and difficulties — benefits by way of no competition and problems, understandably, because one was creating something brand new. As Bailey's saw it they not only had to build a brand worldwide but they had to create and build a new category simultaneously.

The three most important lessons from the marketplace in so far as Bailey's was concerned were:

1. In order to be outstandingly successful in a category one had to be first into the marketplace.

2. Premium pricing, supported by quality standards was the only worthwhile route and in fact, an important positive part of the marketing mix.

3. Pay attention to long-term planning.

Bailey's had a detailed five-year plan, rolled forward annually and also a comprehensive ten-year plan, each being updated yearly.

Assessing Ireland's assets: Mr James Delaney

The topic assigned to Mr James Delaney, president of Rand Development Corporation of San Antonio, Texas, was: 'The Role of Pathfinder in Search of Excellence'.

In his attempt to define a course of action he looked back at Ireland's assets, liabilities and pro-forma operating statement. On the asset side of the ledger he found one of the best-educated populations in western Europe with 50 per cent of the population under 25. That fact alone, he said, could provide for a firm underpinning of Ireland's social security programmes for the retiring members of its work force, for the next 40–50 years. Ireland, being English speaking, was uniquely situated in the International Time Zone. It became even more important considering the emerging opportunity of service industries, information processing and technology transfer.

In the previous fifteen years, Ireland had acquired vast and precious experience in computer science, software production and word processing — fields virtually immune from the need for natural resources. In addition, Ireland lay between two consumer markets totalling 500 million people and had access to the European Economic Community.

Mr Delaney stated that he firmly believed that Ireland could be an 'economic miracle' by 1990. However, on the liabilities side, he referred first to Professor Dermot McAleese as saying there was sufficient capital in Ireland to fund various economic incentives, due to the commendably high rate of savings (some 20 per cent of disposable income) and the enviable ratio of gross fixed capital formation to GNP.

Mr Delaney also quoted Professor Louden Ryan, in a lecture at ESRI, saying 'There is a very real danger that the degree of inequality of income distribution that is politically acceptable will become less than what is necessary to maintain economic incentives'. He also quoted Dr Ivor Kenny, from his 'Question of Balance' speech delivered in San Antonio the previous May (1983). He had said: 'The encroachment of the State into every aspect of our lives is diminishing our freedom and initiative'.

Mr Delaney went on to say that he saw little reference to marketing Ireland's products abroad. That, he felt, was the most glaring deficiency in the entire chain of commercial procedure in Irish companies. The enormous amount of goodwill that existed in the US for Ireland and the Irish people could be converted into a ready market for any number of Irish products. That could be facilitated by the establishment of an international trade mart in Dublin or elsewhere, to provide a window on Irish industry.

It was Mr Delaney's intention to continue to promote interest, in the US, particularly in developing relations with Irish businessmen, economists, academics, politicians, students, civil servants, bankers, et al. He asked those present at the conference to help his aims.

Williams Group: Mr Edmund Williams

Irish Mist liqueur had, in the 1970s, experienced growth patterns in many different countries, which were repetitive and compared favourably with market trends in the category of imported liqueurs, according to Mr Edmund Williams, managing director of the Williams Group, Tullamore, Co. Offaly.

When doing their yearly planning there had always been a lively argument about how to spend the limited sums of available advertising money. Should all of it go into the best market, which happened to be their biggest — the one with the greatest potential, the one with the best return? Or should the money be divided many ways — giving some support to the major market by trying to lessen dependency on one market by growing others and getting into new ones? The latter argument had prevailed. However in the early 1980s a number of serious problems came to hand:

- falling sales
- markets in major recession
- agents' concern with their own or major brands
- substantial mountains of inventory
- very severe fall back in orders
- resultant over-stock of raw materials for Williams
- less cash
- less profits
- less advertising.

The above represented the transformation of a company, from full optimism and expansionist attitudes, to one of gloom and constraint. Nevertheless steps were taken to secure recovery. Authority and responsibility became invested in a man who really understood both selling and marketing. His brief emerged after discussion with him and included: consolidating the principal market; examining other key markets; scrutinising agents' performance and suitability, and recommending new strategy.

He had to focus on the whole world, divide it, recommend concentration and comment on the risk of damage in secondary markets.

The main objective was to establish on a sound measurable basis in chosen markets. A defined programme of steps took place. Market surveys in the field were made.

Williams did it themselves, by continuously visiting offices, stores, bars and restaurants time and again.

From 1963 Williams had their own man living in their major market. This later increased to three men. They set out to identify a consumer profile:

1. Who are we trying to sell to?

2. Why are we trying to sell to them?

3. How do we want them to perceive the product?

4. What do we want the customers to know about it?

5. How do we want the consumers to drink the product?

With the help of the survey results, the group commenced a process of developing the market wherein they were spending, on a level sufficient to have impact in that market, when related to the activities of their competition.

There were two major points to stress. First of all there was the the need to build market strength at the right level, right at the top. The thrust should start from the boardroom and move out from there. Secondly, the key to the right marketing man, which was easier said than done, was absolutely essential to achievement.

Córas Tráchtála Teo was there to give the right information on either of the key factors. Mr Williams referred to Córas as a 'small state-sponsored body comprised of unique skills in marketing with a wealth of relevant experience'. He went on to say that everything eventually depended on the agent, who must deliver on the plan.

A number of brands jostled for market share therefore an agent had to be motivated, cajoled, coerced, persuaded to allocate the resources, especially manpower and time, to execute in the field.

He concluded by stating that all the products in the world would not sell unless investment was made to further the upsurge in exports. He quoted Mr Tony O'Reilly as saying: 'Ireland needs a strong financial war chest'.

New strategy in UK: Mr Ron McCulloch

Mr Ron McCulloch, vice-chairman of the Confederation of British Industry, (CBI), having served as chairman for two years and then as managing director of Cantrell & Cochrane, Belfast, was asked to speak to the MII conference on the subject of: 'CBI's attitudes to industrial development and the strengthening of the UK's industrial base'.

He said the undoubted main thrust of the CBI approach, over the previous few years, was to contain and reduce inflation while improving their industrial competitiveness.

First of all effort related to encouraging government to create an environment in which manufacturing industry could not only survive but grow healthily and efficiently, while retaining its rightful place as the major wealth creating employment activity in their nation. Secondly, there was a large measure of concern, with the attitudinal problem in British society, as to what was required to earn a company's living in a rapidly changing and increasingly competitive trading environment. Thirdly, they continued to assess and develop views of the balance required in social affairs in relation to the overall priorities of the UK.

In 1984 the submission to the UK government, in the budget representations to the Chancellor, was entitled 'Keep it Going' — the aim being to sustain the growth achieved in 1983 and increase competitiveness as a manufacturing nation. The CBI agreed that the service sectors (most of which comprised CBI members) played a vital part in achieving healthy exports.

The UK government was continually encouraged to further increase the involvement of everyone in encouraging enterprise, investment and innovation by developing better attitudes to business and wider share ownership by:

- improving the business expansion scheme to make business investments more marketable

- providing tax relief for share option schemes

- abolishing the investment income surcharge.

CBI had done much to secure new markets and recover old business through better design, better marketing, better salesmanship and more competitive costs.

Food Venture Fund: Mr Declan Cunningham

In assessing growth opportunity in Ireland the Food Venture Fund was set up, specifically in the food processing sector. It became a joint opportunity owned by Anglo-Irish Meats, Industrial Credit Company, Norish Food City and the Smurfit Group. The co-ordinator, Mr Declan Cunningham, described the venture capital industry as a new phenomenon.

Venture capital was then a new name for a very old and long-established activity.

It provided equity capital at the initial start-up, or early development phase, of a company. The venture capital industry had evolved to accommodate the requirements of institutional and private investors, and the cash needs of aspiring young businesses and entrepreneurs. In the United States the industry went back over 25 years, the great pioneer being a company called American Research and Development (ARD), which became an enormous investment institution on the back of its most single most famous sponsored project — Digital Equipment Corporation.

In 1957 General George Doriot of ARD gave Mr Ken Olsen $70,000. In 1971, fourteen years later, when the investment was distributed to ARD's shareholders it was valued at $350m. The year 1983 saw $4bn. contributed by investors to venture capital funds in the United States.

In Ireland venture capital activity was, as yet, very limited. There were less than ten publicly announced funds, of which Food Venture Fund was the latest.

Customer service: Mr Feargal Quinn

Growth in Superquinn, the supermarket chain, was claimed by its founder and managing director, Mr Feargal Quinn, as being based on a dedicated provision of faultless customer service.

The family owned retail chain, controlled by him, was founded in Dundalk, Co. Louth in 1960. The theme of his talk was 'Service'. The concept of service, Mr Quinn said, played a vital role in creating growth in hard times. He believed that hope for increased employment lay in the services sector. The past had failed to recognise a distinction between services of purely administrative or housekeeping nature and those of a discretionary nature.

An example of an area where the injection of a service philosophy could reach great growth was the question of customer complaints. There lay a trigger of growth because of what they could tell one about their customer. It was not a trivial issue because it symbolised the key to any effective philosophy of service — staying close to the customer.

Superquinn were proud to be a 'listening organisation'. Customers were encouraged to speak about any problem they had. A detailed report of their opinions was circulated to every head office executive, every branch manager and everyone who was concerned with planning Superquinn's marketing.

AWARDS, OCTOBER 1984

Following citations, the award of Fellowship was conferred at the President's Night function of 26 October 1984 on:

• Mr Raymond I. Joyce: Shannon-Free Airport Development Ltd

• Mr Michael D. Shields: National Institute for Higher Education, Dublin.

For meritorious service to marketing, the Stephen Doyle award was presented to Mr Nial Darragh, marketing controller of Aer Lingus, Dublin, on the same occasion.

STUDENT EDUCATION, 1984

A very comprehensive summary was contained in the annual report of MII for 1984, edited by education vice-chairman, Mr Brendan Wafer. It was a year of increased activity and intensive planning in education.

Student numbers dramatically advanced, as can be seen below:

• 1980–81: 491

• 1981–82: 700

- 1982–83: 955

- 1983–84: 1,068

- 1984–85: 1,500 (estimated).

It was found that each year the number of university graduates applying to undertake the MII graduateship increased. Such students received varying levels of exemptions, depending on their qualifications. All students had to sit Part 4.

The Marketing Institute organised a series of promotional evenings in Dublin, Cork and Galway. They were supported by a direct mail shot to the top 500 companies. It alone resulted in 1,000 enquires and registrations in excess of 600 students.

Two additional course studies commenced at the Waterford and Athlone RTCs.

Examinations were held at Dublin, Cork, Limerick, Carlow, Galway and Tralee, for a total of 822 students, (an increase of 12 per cent).

NCEA MARKETING MEDAL, 1984

For 'Best Student in Marketing' a medal and cheque was awarded in the NCEA's two-year full-time, Certificate of Business examination in July 1984. At a function, organised by NCEA, Mr Philip Flood FMII presented the award to Mr Patrick Dinan of Waterford. Mr Dinan subsequently continued his studies at the College of Marketing and Design, Parnell Square, Dublin.

GRADUATION, 1983–84

Eighty-eight graduateships and 78 certificates were presented in Thomas Prior House, Dublin, on 9 November 1984. It was necessary to have two separate ceremonies in order to accommodate the increase in numbers.

The students were addressed by Messrs Philip Flood FMII, national chairman of the Institute and Bill Fraser, FMII, vice-president. Mrs Gemma Hussey TD, Minister for Education, addressed the graduates as guest speaker and presented the graduateships to them. Mr F.J. O'Reilly, president of the Institute, congratulated the graduates and also addressed their relatives and guests.

Ms Jean Twohig received the first certificate 'Student of the Year' and a cheque sponsored by *Business & Finance* magazine. Special awards and cheques were also presented to the following (sponsors shown in brackets):

- Ms Kathleen O'Sullivan: Graduateship Student of the Year (Córas Tráchtála Teo)

- Ms Margaret Murray: Case Study (R. & A. Bailey and Co. Ltd)
- Ms Emer Brady: Marketing Management (Sales Placement Ltd)
- Ms Deirdre O'Donohoe: Consumer Behaviour (McConnell's Advertising Service Ltd.)
- Mr John Dunne: Business Policy (Janssen).

MEMBERSHIP GROWTH, 1984

The chairman of the membership committee, Mr Rory Maguire, was continuing his good work. His graph showed membership intake increase (despite continuing business depression) as going from 154 in 1983 to 210 in 1984.

Another gratifying aspect of the growing influx of members was the quality and calibre of the applicants. The Institute continued to attract high level people from semi-state bodies, associated banks, finance houses, advertising, industry and service businesses in general.

NEW PUBLICATION, 1984

A volume entitled *Marketing Management — An Introduction,* edited by Mr John A. Murray, M.Econ.Sc., MBA, Ph.D. (UCD), was published in Ireland by Gill and MacMillan Ltd, in 1984 at a price of £9.99.

DIRECT MARKETING SEMINAR, NOVEMBER 1984

In November 1984 a very successful direct marketing seminar was held in Dublin, chaired by Mr John F. Meagher MMII, executive deputy chairman of Independent Newspapers.

MII APPOINTMENTS, 1985

The national chairman of the Marketing Institute of Ireland for 1985 was Mr William (Bill) Ambrose FMII, managing director of Belenos Publications Ltd, Dublin. In accepting office he said the main aim in his programme for continuing the success of the Institute, was the fulfilment of the long hoped for acquisition of a marketing house. The premises at the time, in the basement of 12, Fitzwilliam Place, Dublin (800 square feet) placed tremendous strain on the staff to cope with the activities of the Institute and was not sustainable.

The council elected for 1985 comprised:

- Senior Vice-Chairman: Mr Brendan Wafer

- Vice-Chairman of Services: Mr Alan McDonnell

- Vice-Chairman of Finance: Mr David Manley

- Vice-Chairman of Education: Mr James Wrynn

- Hon. Secretary: Mr Nial Darragh

- Chair of Fellows: Mr Jack V. Downey.

The council members were: Messrs Aidan Daly, Philip Flood, Des Gilroy, Michael Hayes, Jarlath Jennings, Michael McKenna and Bob Waddell. Mr Sean Ennis and Mr Douglas Thornton were later co-opted to the council.
    The branch chairmen were:

- Cork: Mr Seamus Martin

- Galway: Mr Pat Fahy

- Mid-West: Mr Mike O'Donoghue

- Waterford: Mr Billy McCarthy.

The outgoing president, Mr Frank J. O'Reilly, was sincerely thanked for his outstanding contribution and support to Institute affairs during his term of office, 1983–85. Mr Bill Fraser FMII, kindly agreed to continue as vice-president.

PRESIDENT OF MII, 1985

Early in 1985, Mr Thomas P. (Tom) Hardiman was elected president of the Marketing Institute of Ireland. A former director-general of Radio Telefís Éireann (RTÉ) from 1968 to 1975, he held various appointments in the public service and embarked on a prominent successful career in industry
    In accepting office, Mr Hardiman emphasised the importance to Irish business of 'having available a good supply of young persons well trained in marketing skills'.
    Already familiar with the educational work of the Institute, he had been impressed by the level of commitment, in the students he met.
    However, he said there was an urgent need for persons skilled in marketing in industry. Moreover, industrial policy in all its aspects had been the subject of much debate in the previous few years, while many questions had been raised about public investment policy.

EDUCATION MATTERS, 1985–86

The special syllabus for the course, Graduateship in Marketing, Part 3, comprised sales management, financial management, international marketing and operations research. The aim was to introduce students to mathematical models and to show their relevance in management decision-making, particularly for marketing executives.

The final part of the course covered marketing management, case study, business policy and also consumer motivation and behaviour.

Computerisation of the education area was now complete.

MII standards were accepted internationally and a number of its foremost graduates had successfully completed MBA programmes.

GRADUATE PRESENTATION, 1985

A graduation ceremony took place on 22 November 1985. A champagne buffet was held. One hundred and twenty-one graduateships and 154 certificates were presented in Thomas Prior House, Dublin. Mr Bill Ambrose, chairman of the Marketing Institute addressed the students and guests and presented the certificates. Mr Bill Fraser, vice-president of MII, also conveyed his congratulations with words of encouragement. Mr George Bermingham, TD, Minister for State, Department of Labour and Education, presented the graduateships to the recipents.

Special awards and cheques were made (sponsors in brackets):

• Ms Bridget King: Student of the Year (Córas Tráchtála Teo)

• Mr Joseph McGrath: Case Study (R. & A. Bailey and Co. Ltd)

• Ms Leonie Brennan: Marketing Management (Sales Placement Ltd)

• Mr Adrian Murphy: Consumer Behaviour (McConnell's Advertising)

• Mr Christopher Craig: Business Policy (Janssen).

The certificate 'Student of the Year' and cheque sponsored by *Business & Finance* magazine was awarded to Mr John Ryan while Ms Sheila Gahan was runner-up.

Every graduate received a personally inscribed writing set given by A.T. Cross Ltd. This had been the practice annually for many years. Maurice Quinlan and Associates sponsored the silver for each of the six award winners.

MARKETING RESEARCH COURSE, 1985

The MII decided to initiate a programme leading to a postgraduate diploma in marketing research. The aim was to provide a comprehensive study, at the highest level, 'rooted in the theoretical aspects of marketing research and the marketing context in which the research process operated'.The course was provided in the academic year 1985–86 at the College of Marketing and Design, Dublin.

ANCO MARKETING DEVELOPMENT COURSE, 1985

In conjunction with AnCo, the industrial training authority, the Marketing Institute ran a 30-week marketing development course with twenty-one participants.

The components of the course comprised a ten-week tuition phase and a twenty-week company placement phase. It was gratifying that over 70 per cent of those who took part obtained full-time employment. Suitable host companies were selected who demonstrated a real commitment to both the trainee and the programme objectives.

NCEA MARKETING AWARD, 1985

At a function organised by the NCEA (National Council for Educational Awards) in 1985, an award of a medal was made to Ms Maureen Lynch of Limerick. The presentation of the medal and a cheque was made by Mr Bill Fraser, vice-president of MII, for her outstanding achievement of the highest mark in marketing, following her completion of the two-year full-time Certificate of Business examination.

The Limerick branch of MII had initiated sponsorship of medals and cash prizes to their outstanding students. Mr John O'Brien received a gold-plated medal for the graduateship examination and Ms Noreen Burke, a silver-plated medal for the certificate examination.

TUESDAY CLUB LUNCHEON, FEBRUARY 1985

The first Tuesday Club luncheon speaker for 5 February 1985 was Mr John F. Meagher, executive deputy chairman of Independent Newspapers, and chairman of Irish Marketing Surveys, Lansdowne Market Research and IMS-Condon.

The theme of his subject was: 'The Government and Marketing — A New Beginning'. He emphasised the changing attitudes at national level towards marketing and their implications for marketing people. Mr John Meagher's experience and understanding of marketing was widely known and respected in business and government circles. He had chaired the very successful Direct Marketing seminar in November 1984.

CONSUMER BEHAVIOUR, 1985

In 1985 my personal records show that I was particularly concerned with consumer behaviour and considered several books on the subject. Consequently I now refer to *Consumer Behaviour — A Practical Guide*, edited by Gordon R. Foxall published by Croom Helm of London in 1980.

In it he outlined the essence of consumer orientation as an integrated approach to business management. It was his opinion that the marketing message was that consumers were the arbiters of fortune in business, which through defined processes, brought forth wanted goods meriting reward.

INTENSIVE STRATEGIC MARKETING COURSE, JUNE 1985

From Sunday 9 to Friday 14 June 1985, the Marketing Institute of Ireland held an intensive strategic marketing course, particularly designed for managing directors and senior managers who had the responsibility to initiate and implement strategic planning decisions. The course was held at Trinity College, Dublin and the total cost per delegate was £1,500, with a discount of £250 for MII members. Five of the world's foremost experts on strategic marketing from the Kellogg Graduate School of Management, North-Western University, Illinois, USA, conducted the course.

The course leader was Professor Liam Fahey, co-author with Mr Philip Kotler of the best selling textbook *The New Competition*. He was joined by Professor George S. Day, Toronto University and three professors from the Kellogg School — Messrs Roy Hinton, Steve Burnett and H. Kurt Christensen.

FINANCING THE MARKETING INSTITUTE, 1985

Mr David Manley, vice-chairman of finance, believed that Marketing Institute members would be surprised to learn the amount of expenditure, in the region of £200,000, required to provide membership and education facilities in 1985.

The Institute was not favoured with direct financial support, from either government or business circles, towards its general running. By necessity, the policy adopted had to be that of self-financing.

CORK BRANCH OF MII, 1985

Mr Seamus Martin, marketing services executive of the *Cork Examiner*, became chairman of the MII Cork branch in 1985.

Cork celebrated its 800th centenary in that year which was a very progressive and successful year for the important branch of the Institute.

Their Tuesday lecture series was organised by Mr Aidan Harte and sponsored by Sales Placement Ltd. Audio-visual presentations were made by leading marketeers and academics including Messrs Michael Conlon, Cork Savings Bank, Professor Barra O'Cinneide, NIHE and Mr Aidan Daly, UCD.

In June the Tuesday Club luncheon was specially held at the Metropole hotel. The participants included the National Council, Institute members and friends. Over 30 Dublin members travelled to Cork. The guest speaker was Mr Tim Mahony, Toyota Ireland Ltd, Dublin. A highly enjoyable time was had by all and it included visits to two Cork breweries as well as a reception by Cork's Lord Mayor, Dr Liam Burke, at the City Hall. He thanked the Dublin entourage for visiting Cork in its centenary year, and spoke of local efforts to promote employment.

The national chairman of the Institute Mr Bill Ambrose, was presented with an engraved silver tray by Mr Seamus Martin, chairman of the branch.

A closer working arrangement with University College, Cork was established and further participation by their academics and under-graduates was expected in 1986.

Enrolment for Institute courses at the Cork Regional Technical College numbered 65.

The College of Commerce commenced a full-time day course for Part 1 of the MII examinations.

The student chairman, Mr Michael Power of Irish Distillers, organised many excellent functions, commencing with a Cork case study. The subject was 'Marketing in Ireland' and guest speakers included Messrs Vivian Murray, Irish Goods Council, John Tuite, Beamish & Crawford and Seamus Scally, Musgraves, Cork.

The highlight of the year in Cork was Ladies' Night which attracted an attendance of 277 members and friends at the Metropole hotel. The charity draw, in aid of the Lord Mayor's charity, produced £527 for St Patrick's Hospital, Cork.

GALWAY BRANCH OF MII, 1985

The Galway branch reported a considerable increase in the numbers attending their events during 1985. It was due primarily to the continuing high calibre of speakers and increasing awareness and interest in good marketing practice locally.

The chairman of the branch, Mr Pat Fahy, hosted three public meetings early in the year. The first of these was a presentation on public relations given by Ms Mary Finan, who placed emphasis on her practical experience with Wilson Hartnell.

Mr Michael Fingleton, managing director of Irish Nationwide Building Society, delivered a 'no nonsense' speech on the position and the future aspirations of Irish building societies (he was then chairman of the IBS Association). His remarks attracted considerable attention in the national press, to the benefit of the Institute image.

Mr Maurice Pratt, Quinnsworth, outlined the background to and implementation of Quinnsworth's marketing drives. The attendance proved to be the largest that the branch ever had at a public meeting. The informative manner of Mr Pratt was very much appreciated by the enthusiastic audience.

A one-day annual marketing seminar was held in University College, Galway in April. It was offered free to paid-up members of the branch. The University College Galway Marketing Department was thanked for again contributing their service without charge.

The 1985 programme commenced in September, with Mr Tim Phillips, Ballyfree Farms as the guest speaker. He was followed by Dr Ivor Kenny, Irish Management Institute in October and Mr Noel Gilmore, Noel Gilmore Associates in November.

Very successful social events also took place. The 'annual night out', well established in the Galway social calendar, was held in October. The national chairman, Mr Bill Ambrose, and the Cork regional branch chairman, Mr Seamus Martin, were welcomed.

To encourage and promote greater co-operation between the regional branch and marketing students locally, the president of the Students' Marketing Society in the Regional Technical College was co-opted to the committee in October 1985. At the AGM in December 1985, Mr John O'Dowd was elected regional chairman of the branch for 1986.

MID-WEST BRANCH OF MII, 1985

The chairman of the Mid-West branch of MII for 1985 was Mr Michael O'Donoghue, managing director of Mohawk Europa Ltd, Limerick. He took the chair from Mr Liam De Paor, whom the branch were sorry to lose when he was transferred, on promotion, to Cavan.

The branch decided to mark the year 1985 with a number of events especially geared towards the marketing students, as it was designated 'International Youth Year'.

A calendar of events for both members and students took place. Membership had grown from 32 to 53 though five members had been lost due to emigration.

At the Limerick School of Professional Studies there were 136 students. A 'Careers in Marketing' conference was attended by over 70 people. A conference weekend for lecturers was addressed by five lecturers from Dublin.

A gold medal for the top graduate student award was presented to Mr John O'Brien and a silver medal awarded to the top diploma student, Ms Noreen Burke. The medals were kindly sponsored by Mohawk Europa Ltd, Shannon. Allied Irish Banks sponsored a prize of £100 bursary to the top first year student, Ms Margaret O'Connell, to assist in her costs of study for 1985–86.

Mr Michael O'Donoghue was re-elected regional chairman of the branch at the AGM on Tuesday 3 December 1985 in the Greenhills hotel.

WATERFORD BRANCH OF MII, 1985

The Waterford branch held five evening meetings during 1985. The chairman of the branch was Mr Billy McCarthy.

The monthly meetings were addressed by Mr John Lennon, marketing lecturer at Waterford Regional College, formerly Professor of Marketing, Evansville, USA, Mr Gerry Grogan, chairman and managing director of Player & Wills Ireland and Mr Martin MacCabe of Creative Management Ltd. The speakers covered aspects varying from marketing in the tobacco industry, a new marketing drive in An Post and *Organising One's Time* (a video supplied by Creative Management). The Waterford third annual breakfast had Mr Bill Jaffray, managing director of Irish Mist Liqueur Ltd, with a full attendance to hear the speaker.

Over 150 people attended the fifth annual dinner dance and for the first time it was found necessary to restrict number and seek a larger venue for 1986. The guest speaker was Dr D.J. Sheridan, managing director of Atlantic Resources.

Educational matters

Progresss was made in the education drive, resulting in almost 50 students studying parts of the graduateship course at Waterford RTC. Indeed some travelled over 80 miles to attend, from Cahir, Enniscorthy etc. Educational trips were also organised for students at the Waterford RTC to Cherry Breweries, Arco Kitchens, Grants of Ireland and Digital Ireland Ltd.

Honorary membership of Institute

The branch were proud of the conferring of honorary Marketing Institute membership on Mr F. Edward James, a most deserved recognition of his services rendered to the Institute in Waterford and nationally.

It was decided that the branch would be re-named the 'South-East Region' from 1 January 1986. It would take in counties Waterford, Kilkenny, Carlow, Wexford and Tipperary S.R.

At the AGM in December, Mr David Walsh was elected regional chairman of the branch.

COMPUTER AT MII, 1985

A computer system was installed by MII during 1985, resulting in all member and student records being maintained in a computer file. All book-keeping and financial information was transferred to the system in 1986.

MII PRESS RELATIONS, 1985

Friends in the press made a major contribution to the Institute status during the year 1985. Through the influence of Mr Frank Cusack Institute activities were featured in countless press reports and many RTÉ radio and television programmes.

IMI MARKETING COURSES, 1985–86

The Irish Management Institute guide to management and training programmes, 1985/86, outlined a detailed programme of thirteen short courses in marketing and sales management.

In the foreword then Taoiseach, Dr Garret Fitzgerald TD, stated that the government recognised the need for good management in the national plan 'Building on Reality'.

The marketing management programme was the premier programme of the Irish Management Institute 'in that key function of business enterprise'. It provided managers, having major responsibility in marketing, with a comprehensive and unified development opportunity. A major feature of the programme was the involvement of each participant in an action-learning project. The programme covered four one-week sessions spread over four months. Following this, each participant continued working privately on his/her project for a further nine months. The teaching and work levels required on the programme were equivalent to a full academic year.

Successful participants were awarded the IMI Marketing Management Certificate.

The course leader was Mr Charles Carroll, BA Econ., M.Phil., senior specialist-marketing, IMI and the fee of £1,995 covered a duration of twenty days.

FELLOWSHIP AWARDS, MAY 1985

Awards of Fellowships, following citation, were conferred during President's Night on 29 May 1985 at the Burlington hotel in Dublin. The presentations were made by the President of the Institute, Mr Tom Hardiman, to:

- Dr Frank J. O'Reilly: Past-President, MII from 1983–85

- Mr Michael J. Hayes: Director of Advertising Studies, College of Commerce, Rathmines, Dublin.

NATIONAL MARKETING CONFERENCE, SEPTEMBER 1985

At the Shelbourne hotel, Dublin on 20 September 1985 the seventh National Marketing Conference was sponsored jointly by *Business & Finance* magazine and the Marketing Institute of Ireland.The theme of the conference was 'Business — Communicate for Profit'.

In the prelude to the conference papers made available to the delegate participants, the following statement was made:

> In an increasing complex world, business finds it must communicate with everybody. The successful enterprise talks, not alone to customers and suppliers but to employees, to politicians and to the community at large. Failure to communicate is now recognised as a major business failure, communicating is not an optional extra.
>
> Old-fashioned managers believed communication was a nuisance, at best. Today, effective communication is widely seen as contributing to the bottom line. Decisions taken without the full communications process are likely to be bad decisions.

Speakers at the conference represented a broad range of expertise in the area of communications, from different perspectives. The sessions were chaired by Ms Margaret Downes and Mr Robert Gahan.

Thanks were expressed to those who sponsored items including Ballygowan Springwater; Rowntree Mackintosh; Gallahers; Grants of Ireland; Cantrell & Cochrane and An Post. Appreciation was conveyed to Modern Display Artists for the construction and design of the conference display material.

Success of Waterford Glass

The first speaker was Mr Paddy Hayes, executive chairman of Waterford Glass, formerly chairman and managing director of Ford of Ireland. His paper was called 'Marketeer — Charlatan or Genius?'

It was his belief that there was a close affinity between genius and communication. He quoted that Ralph Waldo Emerson had once said: 'If a man make a better mouse-trap than his neighbour, though he build his house in the woods, the world will make a beaten path to his door'. However, time and modern communications had proved him wrong.

It was heartening that the world talked with admiration about Waterford Glass. A new skill had been created among the people of Waterford and communicated the power of ideals. This was partly due to the fact that no product must be let out of the factory unless up to standard.

Waterford Crystal was the unchallenged market leader in its field in Ireland, in the UK and, most remarkably of all, 'in the country of ruthless competition', the United States of America. It was a superb achievement right across the USA.

The ten American cities with the largest retail sales in 1984 were New York, Los Angeles, Chicago, San Francisco, Detroit, Washington DC, Philadelphia, Houston, Boston and Miami. American cities with the largest retail sales of Waterford Crystal were New York, Los Angeles, Chicago, Dallas, Houston, Washington DC, Detroit, San Francisco, Boston and Philadelphia.

Most notable was the performance of Waterford in Texas. Dallas and Houston were two of the top selling cities for Waterford Crystal. The reason for unusual success in the 'Lone Star State' was being identified in order to provide impetus to make even further advances in the US. One worthwhile target was to repeat, in other countries, the marketing success already achieved in the US and UK.

Communicating from scratch

The second paper 'Communicating from Scratch' was given by Mr John Kelleher, who was deeply involved in the communications business. He was more recently an entrepreneur, raising money from investors to back his film *Eat the Peach*. He was former controller of programmes in Radio Telefís Éireann and was currently chief executive of Strongbow Film and Television Productions.

At the outset Mr Kelleher said the date of the marketing conference coincided with the final day of shooting the feature film, *Eat the Peach*. The major proportion of its £1.7 budget had been raised from Irish shareholders. Yet eight months previously that company did not exist.

In March 1985, with the tax year in sight, Strongbow, which had been established only one month earlier, set out to try and raise approximately £1.5m. from the Irish public. The company did not reach its original target but more than 220 people subscribed for shares and Strongbow succeeded in raising just over £1m.

Despite the short offer period of three weeks, which coincided with the severe jolt to investor confidence (following the collapse of ICI), Strongbow had raised more than any other BDS company in the marketplace in that tax year — in fact, more than the others combined. It was communication that had made it possible according to Mr Kelleher, communicating the essential information and ideas to potential investors through a process of education, which in itself, became a major marketing exercise.

New and complex legislation relating to fundraising had been introduced under the Business Development Scheme in the 1984 Finance Act.

Communicating by numbers

The third paper, 'Communicating by numbers', was given by Mr John Callaghan, a managing partner of Stokes Kennedy Crowley & Co.

Mr Callaghan stated that business was measured and reported on through numbers in financial statements. Numbers provided pictures of performance at a particular point in time, or of future objectives and plans. Those pictures formed the basis of virtually all major decisions within a business and provided outsiders with the information they required in their dealings with it.

It was important that those using them examined the communication and use, or possible misuse, of financial numbers in business decision-making. That required a look at the nature of those numbers, the process by which complete business activities were measured, represented in numerical terms, and presented, in an apparently factual and precise form, as management information. He believed that a greater awareness of what was involved would lead to a more realistic and effective use of financial information and an ability to avoid some pitfalls.

He stressed his belief that numbers are absolute. They imply certainty and precision. For example, there was a world of difference in a manager stating that he had achieved a substantial increase in profit in his division and in him stating that profits had increased from £1m. to £2m. The first statement was open to any interpretation whereas the second was not.

However, that very quality of certainty was one of the reasons why decisions based on the interpretation of financial statements could often be defective There was an assumption that there was a greater security in the numbers than might actually exist.

It was important to keep in mind that the numbers were presenting a picture of the underlying business situation, which itself might be far from definite.

Mr Callaghan concluded by saying it was obvious that figures which related to the past had a different quality to those which related to the future, but even they might not have the absolute certainty sometimes ascribed to them.

Dealing with changing times

The fourth paper was entitled 'Dealing with the Changing Times' and was delivered by Mr Alec Wrafter, managing director of North Star Computers. He said that change, at that time, was not confined to the electronics industry. It was, in fact, the greatest distinguishing feature of the era we lived in. There had been, he noticed, a marked change in Ireland over the previous ten years. All around the impact of a new philosophy was seen, which he described as realism.

However, nowhere was change more evident than in the electronics industry. The birth and explosive growth, in the past decade, of the micro-computer business was an industry then estimated to produce over $6bn. of revenue in 1985. That was from sales of less than 100,000 dollars worldwide in 1975.

The pervasiveness of the electronics industry was influencing the lives of ordinary people, as could be seen by the rapid introduction of electronics in the motor industry.

The mainframe industry, born in the late 1940s, led directly to the introduction of mini-computers in the late 1950s. Today everybody knew about personal computers, leading in turn to what, in his view, could be a radically new industry itself over time.

Mentioning the multi-user micro-computer, Mr Wrafter explained that it was distinguished from the personal computer, on the one hand, by its ability to share information and resources, and the mini-computer industry on the other, by its ability to use low cost, off-the-shelf software and provide powerful computer solutions at extremely attractive prices.

Cola wars

The fifth paper entitled 'The Cola Wars — from My Side' was that of Mr Rod Malcolm, director of Creative and Promotional Services for the International Division of Pepsi-Cola, New York. His responsibilities at the time included over-seeing the division's response to the Cola reformulation activities and the development of worldwide thematic advertising.

Being his first time in Ireland, the speaker thanked Mr Jim Bradley, managing director of their local bottling company, Cantrell & Cochrane, Dublin, for inviting him to speak. Mr Malcolm then proceeded on to what was a case study of the 'Cola Wars' that had originated in North America and spread to most areas of the world. He preferred to come up to the period which covered the time from their competitor's (Coca-Cola) launch in the US of a new product formulation up to their (C-C's) most recent business results.

The speaker based his presentation on a videotape, which had been prepared for a press conference which his company, Pepsi-Cola, had conducted in eighteen cities around the world in August 1985. The tape demonstrated valid principles of proper communication for profit.

In reviewing the fifteen-minute tape for this conference, five very relevant principles of sound communication for profit were demonstrated. The tape covered the launch, in April 1985 in the United States, of a new formulation for Coke. That was after 99 years of remarkable success with its one and only formula. The tape provided some background as to why product change was deemed necessary. It summarised five points. These were:

1. Know your business.

2. Avoid over-reliance on research.

3. Explore all alternatives.

4. Be responsive to the market.

5. Do not be afraid to admit mistakes.

Regarding the latter, the speaker had virtually no doubt that the Coca-Cola company did not plan the launch and the subsequent retreat of its new product. However, it did have the strength of character to admit it made a mistake and, as a result, the consequences of the blunder might not, in the long run, be as disastrous as they potentially could have been.

Pepsi-Cola and Coca-Cola fought for their share of a $25bn. market, where one percentage point meant $250m. in sales. For 87 years the two companies had gone head to head, with Coca-Cola, in the early years, a clear leader in the struggle.

Against all odds Pepsi grew and prospered, fighting a classic marketing battle with Coke, even in the Peoples' Republic of China.

Communicating in the grocery trade

The sixth paper was given by Mr Jim Hoblyn, sales director of Irish Biscuits Ltd. It was entitled 'Communicating in the Grocery Trade'.

Mr Hoblyn stated that his brief was to discuss communications for profit, with particular reference to moving the product quickly through 'the trade', a euphemism for the grocery distribution industry.

Communication was a two-way thing — particularly true of the grocery business. Profit, in that case, meant of course, profit for the consumer. Profit for the trade was assured because without profit for them there would be no communication for the public.

The speaker talked about communicating for profit to all levels of the distribution industry — multiples, groups, direct or indirect retailers. He said elements of the Trade were bigger, much bigger, than the manufacturers were individually.

Communicating in complex companies

The seventh paper, 'Communicating in Complex companies', was given by Mr Robert Meyers, director of International Public Affairs for Allied Corporation. He said that whether one was in marketing, sales, advertising, public relations or public affairs, their business was communicating.

All of the delegates present had been affected in recent years as major businesses had marched into the international marketplace on an unprecedented scale. It constituted one of the most impressive economic developments of all time.

The job of business communications had been fundamentally altered, giving rise to challenges few would have imagined 30 or 40 years ago. The new cadre of specialised communicators had been developed to deal with the agenda of public policy issues abroad.

In Europe, the European Community, specialised agencies of the United Nations, the General Agreement on Tariffs and Trade, and other bodies, generated some of the most arcane issues yet invented by the mind of man. These included: product liability; transborder data flows; links between undertakings; product counterfeiting — the list went on and on.

New professionals monitored, reported and analysed potential impacts of proposed regulations and legislation, developed strategies to deal with the issues and then helped execute the strategies. In other words, they acted, they lobbied and they communicated. They were certainly relevant to the marketing function.

Mr Meyers stated his belief that a company which markets, advertises, manufacturers and distributes, without attention to public policy issues, was asking for trouble in the modern business environment, When Allied recently launched a new synthetic fibre, Spectra 900, the corporate and chemical sector media personnel worked with the marketing staff to organise a media event in New York. This drew, not only the trade press, but the daily and international press as well. By positioning the product, as a significant technological breakthrough, Allied communications succeeded in broadening interest in Spectra 900 significantly.

MII MEMBERSHIP INCREASE 1985–86

Membership of the Marketing Institute increased by 48 per cent, totalling 852 in October 1985. At the end of 1985 it became 933 and it was expected to elect the 1,000th member during 1986.

Heavy investment, effort and financial, showed that all Institute communications and public activities were professionally presented. This was due particularly to Mr Jarlath Jennings and his team, and the development consultant of MII, Mr Frank Cusack.

Under the chairmanship of Mr Tony Neville, a policy committee established strategic guidelines to formulate a National Marketing Council. A deputation was received by the Minister for Finance, Mr Alan Dukes TD, to discuss the annual budget submission.

Budget submission, 1985

In the latter quarter of 1985, the Institute made its annual submission to the government on their proposed 1986 budget. The deputation was received by the Minister for Finance.

While recognising the financial constraints on the government, the Institute advocated that they stimulate market-led recovery by:

• increasing marketing professionalism

• encouraging a genuine marketing orientation within companies

• improving the environment for marketing success

• developing a national strategic marketing capability.

Amongst other proposals at individual level, the submission advocated tax relief for longer term marketing courses, increased tax allowances for export personnel (similar to the UK) and increased placements of marketing graduates in companies. At company level it advocated increased capital allowances on cars, reduced VAT on meals and grant-aid for companies to establish strategic planning and marketing research functions.

The outcome of the submission was very satisfactory. Despite financial restraints on the government, VAT on meals was reduced, capital allowance on cars was raised by £500 together with some other promised supports.

JOINT MEETINGS WITH OTHER PROFESSIONAL BODIES, 1986

Meetings, of common interest to the Institute, took place with the Confederation of Irish Industry, Irish Management Institute, Public Relations Institute of Ireland and the Publicity Club. The following issues were discussed:

Finance: the professional skills of Mr David Manley, MII vice-chairman of finance, were put to good use and generously helped by Mr Paul Wallace and his colleagues at Butler Chance Auditors. Mr Manley also worked hard in bringing the computer further on stream — at that time programmed to support both member and education activities.

Services: the vice-chairman of services, Mr Alan McDonnell, brought a dynamic to the social and training activities, appreciated by members. That almost 3,000 members and guests attended Institute functions testified to the work and imagination of Mr McDonnell and his committees.

Functions: attendance at the Tuesday Club luncheons never dropped below 100, while, according to the national chairman, the visit to Cork 'probably solved the recession there'. The Ladies' Night function had been attended by

420 people in Dublin in November 1985. This was a capacity and record turnout.

Media coverage: a tribute was paid to Mr Frank Cusack, development consultant of MII, for the amount of wide media coverage of Institute activities, mainly due to his efforts.

Training committee: a training committee, under the stewardship of Mr Douglas Thornton, provided a learning service to members, an extension to educational activities. It also furnished a further opportunity to contribute to the cost of a full-time education officer.

Charitable status: the Revenue Commissioners agreed to accord charitable status to the Institute provided that members voted in favour of the necessary amendments to the Memorandum of Association at a forthcoming EGM. The accrued tax benefits would be of particular benefit to the training and education side of activities. For the achievement thanks were expressed to the Institute solicitor, Mr Larry Branigan and also to Mr Paul Wallace and colleagues, Butler Chance Auditors.

Marketing house: the premises committee, chaired by Mr Des Gilroy, completed necessary preparatory work and with the ratification of 'charitable status', began the fundraising campaign to obtain a marketing house.

Much needed facilities for members, such as training, job referral, library, database services, meeting facilities and others, could not flourish until a proper base to work from was provided.

AGM OF MII, JANUARY 1986

The 24th AGM of the Marketing Institute was held on 31 January 1986 and was well attended. At that time the Marketing Institute address was: 12, Fitzwilliam Place, Dublin, 2.

MII appointments

The chairman of the Marketing Institute elected for 1986 was Mr Brendan V. Wafer MMII, marketing and R & D manager of the National Board for Science and Technology (NBST). Previously he had responsibility for the longer term planning of the government scientific and technological institutes and agencies within the NBST.

Mr Tom Hardiman kindly agreed to continue as president of the Marketing Institute of Ireland for 1986. In his message to Institute members, he stated that industry needed continuous fixed asset investment accompanied by a parallel investment in skill assets.

Marketing was, arguably, the key skill in the competitive environment at home and abroad. It was the skill in which management was still, regrettably, very deficient.

Moreover, he believed that no amount of high technology, production expertise or commitment in the workforce could make up for an inadequacy in marketing. According to Mr Hardiman marketing, supported by production technology and suitable investment in research and development, was the key to the innovation that marked the successful company.

Other MII honorary officers elected for 1986 were:

- Vice-President: Mr William D. Fraser

- Senior Vice-Chairman: Mr Alan McDonnell

- Vice-Chairman of Services: Mr David Manley

- Vice-Chairman of Education: Mr Sean Ennis

- Vice-Chairman of Finance: Mr Garry Hynes

- Hon. Secretary: Mr Tom Freeman.

Chairmen of council committees:

- Marketing Studies Programme: Mr Douglas Thornton

- Marketing House Fundraising: Mr Bill Ambrose

- Graduate Members' Committee: Mr Conor Cunneen

- Special Project (marketing R & D): Mr Aidan Daly

- Fellows (to 29/9/86): Mr Jack Downey

- Fellows (from 29/9/86): Mr Philip Flood

- National Marketing Information: Ms Mary Egan

- Members' Social Activities: Mr John Gunnigle

- Communications: Mr Jarlath Jennings

- Membership Committee: Mr Bob Waddell

- Examinations Board: Mr James Wrynn.

Branch chairmen:

- Cork: Mr Seamus Martin

- Galway: Mr John O'Dowd

- Mid-West: Mr Mike O'Donoghue

- South-East: Mr David Walsh.

In his speech to members the chairman of MII, Mr Brendan Wafer, said that all business was about three fundamental concepts based on customers, competitors and profit. Knowing what your customers wanted, anticipating their future needs and providing better service and quality than your competitors, at a profit, were the essence of a successful business. Every other aspect of business had to be integrated into that, in a supportive way, such was the core of customer and market orientation.

Saying that marketing was approaching business from the customers viewpoint, he went on to define long-term successful companies as having two attributes:

• their customers regarded their products as being better quality than their competitors

• their customers regarded their level of service as being better also.

Mr Wafer believed that a combination of marketing tactics generated a good financial return for the risks involved.

FOOD IMPORTS, 1985

Within Ireland the loss in market share, evident from the late 1970s, had continued, particularly in food imports. These exceeded £1,000m. in 1985. In addition, indigenous companies had a very low level of sub-supply to multinationals in Ireland.

Major weaknesses were identified in market planning, market research, new product development, product/service strategy and market strategy. A survey showed that over 60 per cent of companies had no executive responsible for marketing, as distinct from sales.

The Marketing Institute was working very hard to improve marketing performance, trying to remove attitudinal, monetary barriers and disincentives, and providing professional education and training necessary at the entry stage, middle, senior management and chief executive levels.

SEAN LEMASS AWARD, 1986

On March 26 1986 the Sean F. Lemass award, for excellence in marketing, was made to the Doyle Hotel Group. The award was presented on behalf of the Institute, by Mr John Bruton TD, Minister for Finance, to Mr P.V. Doyle, managing director of the Doyle Hotel Group. The special ceremony was attended by many prominent marketing persons who paid tribute to Mr Doyle.

NCEA AWARD, 1986

The annual award for the best marketing paper in the National Council of Education awards (NCEA), National Certificate in Business Studies, was won by student Mr Adrian McGrory. The award presentation was made by Mr Bill Fraser, vice-president of MII. The recipient had studied at the RTC in Dundalk, Co. Louth.

RDS EXHIBITION, 1986

Mr Brendan Wafer, chairman of MII, was one of the judges of the Royal Dublin Society (RDS) for the New Ventures '86 exhibition in Ballsbridge, Dublin.

AMERICAN EXPRESS MARKETING AWARD, 1986

One of the judges of the American Express Marketing award, in association with *Business & Finance* magazine, was Mr Philip Flood FMII, chairman of the Fellows' committee.

PRESIDENT'S NIGHT, APRIL 1986

The President's Night dinner was held on 18 April 1986 at the Berkeley Court hotel in Dublin. The principal speaker was Mr Peter Sutherland, Commissioner of the EEC.

FELLOWSHIP AWARDS, APRIL 1986

At the President's Night dinner, following citations, awards of Fellowship were made to:

• Mr James P. Culliton: chief executive of Cement Roadstone Holdings

• Mr Aidan C. Harte: managing director of Rinear Ltd, Cork

• Mr James J. Ward: Professor of Marketing, Galway.

MARKETING HOUSE PROJECTION, MAY 1986

The Institute could no longer perform efficiently without adequate space. Further, room was also needed where members could hold a business meeting and provide relevant courses to all members. The 100 or so members, who worked voluntarily on the various committees, knew too well that the Institute could not perform efficiently from its present premises.

While MII membership had risen by 100 per cent, over the previous three years, demand for membership services had trebled.

An investigation resulted in a need for a building with at least 2,500 square feet. To provide this, a campaign was got under way from May 1986 under the chairmanship of Mr Bill Ambrose, resulting in £80,000 being secured.

While no levy was applied, members were encouraged to make some contribution to the Marketing House Building Fund. Between 5,500 and 6,000 members and guests attended 60 events organised by the MII Council and the regional branches of the Institute during 1986. It is only possible to highlight a few of the main events:

Remington, 1986

Mr Victor Kiam of Remington, addressed 100 members and guests of MII in May 1986 and promoted his book *Going for It*. He was the man who 'liked the product so much that he bought the company'.

Knappogue Castle, June 1986

While many members of MII travelled from Cork, Waterford and Galway, 53 Dublin members flew to Shannon to attend an immensely successful June Tuesday Club luncheon at Knappogue Castle.

Mr Michael Noonan TD, Minister for Industry and Commerce, addressed the gathering. Entertainment was provided by the Bunratty Singers. Lunch had been preceded by a tour of Shannon Industrial Estate and followed by a visit to the Innovation Centre. The excellent programme had been organised by the Mid-West regional branch of MII.

National Marketing Conference, September 1986

In conjunction with *Business & Finance*, the eighth National Marketing Conference was held in the Royal Hospital, Kilmainham, Dublin in September 1986. The theme was 'Back to the Future'. An innovation, a pre-conference dinner, was held in the Royal Hospital the evening before the conference.

Some of the main business activities, during 1986, covered topics such as: new product development, marketing cars, marketing financial services and sponsorship.

Annual Dublin Golf outing was held at Foxrock Golf Club, organised once again by Norman McConnell.

A fundraiser, 'Fashion and Pizza Night', for the Marketing House Fund, was held in the Blackrock Centre, Dublin. It was a tremendous success due especially to the very enthusiastic support of Superquinn staff.

COMPUTERS IN MARKEING, SEPTEMBER 1986

Speaking at the September 1986 Tuesday Club luncheon, Mr Ken Bond, managing director of Wang in Ireland, outlined some of the ways in which computers were helping his company with their marketing.

'I must make the point strongly — we do use our computers all the time. In our offices we do not own, possess, rent or use a typewriter', he said. And further his company produced more professional looking sales proposals and letters, a lot quicker and cheaper. Letters written to customers, he stated, did not need to have a copy printed — it was stored in the computer.

An extreme advantage, in having the computer, meant that mail-shots were simple, as the database could be sorted any way one wanted. A European-wide database of software products told what software house had written a system for a meat-processing plant or for a garage or for whatever. It included US software while shortly the Australian, Hong Kong and New Zealand software would be up as well.

Mr Bond informed those present that Wang in Ireland sent their product announcement magazine out by electronic mail to all their subsidiaries around the world. Electronic mail was a great way of inexpensively gathering international information. They needed to find out what the 65 computer systems installed at the New Zealand Post Office were doing. Detailed questions could be asked and responded to within 24 hours. Marketing, he said, is about knowledge and knowledge is power,

PROFESSIONAL MARKETING JOURNAL, 1986

During the year MII launched their own journal entitled *Professional Marketing*. Congratulations were extended to Mr Gerry Lawlor, editor, and his committee. The first issue was considered excellent and augured extremely well for the future.

1,000TH MEMBER OF THE MARKETING INSTITUTE OF IRELAND, 1986

A milestone in membership recruitment was passed in October 1986 when the 1,000th member to join the Institute was elected. That honour fell to Mr

Ronnie Petrie, chief executive and managing director of his family firm, Modern Display Artists. It was one of the leading companies involved in the promotion of exhibitions and conferences throughout Ireland, the UK, Europe and North America. It also coincided with being the year that Mr Petrie celebrated 25 years as a director of his company.

MARKETING INSTITUTE STAFF, 1986

In 1986 the Institute had a staff of six. Ms Sylvia Doyle and Ms Mairead Murray were responsible for members' activities, Mr Frank Cusack was the development consultant, while Ms Carol Scanlon, Ms Carole-Ann Bardon and Ms Susan Lloyd were responsible for students' and members' professional education and training. In addition Ms Rose Slevin undertook a number of very useful and practical research projects for the Institute during the year.

MARKETING STUDIES PROGRAMME, 1986

A survey was undertaken to research the ongoing training requirements for Institute members. Twenty-five per cent replied to the survey, which resulted in the establishment of the marketing studies programme.

Course subjects, tailored to members' wishes were agreed in a variety of marketing areas. The position for a course leader was advertised and this resulted in Mr Jack Downey accepting an invitation to become a consultant, on a part-time basis.

A course on strategic marketing was successfully run and other courses were planned.

STUDENT EDUCATION, 1986

There were 1,800 students registered and studying for MII courses in 1986. That meant an increase of 12.5 per cent over 1985.

BRANCH EDUCATION REPORTS, 1986

Mid-West: the Mid-West (Limerick) regional branch under the chairmanship of Mr Mike O'Donoghue, had a very active and productive year. Monthly lectures had been organised for students in the School of Professional Studies, Limerick. There were visits to RTÉ and Kilkenny Design.

At a 'Careers in Marketing' evening meeting in November 1986, a gold medal was presented to Ms Martina Clean (top Graduate Student) and a silver medal to Ms Lorraine O'Reilly (top Certificate Student). Three monetary bursary awards went to the top first year students. Mohawk Ltd and Allied Irish Banks sponsored the awards.

Cork: For the second year (1986) Mr Seamus Martin was chairman of the successful Cork branch. The members' programme included:

- a record attendance at Ladies' Night in February

- a very successful joint luncheon meeting, with the Exporters Association in March

- a second joint Industrial Credit Corporation/Marketing Institute conference in May. Its theme was 'Marketing — The Weakest Link'

- a presentation by Mr Robin Fielders of 'Close that Sale', which 220 enjoyed immensely.

With the generous support of Beamish & Crawford, Cork, new marketing graduates were provided with their scrolls in November. Mr George McKenizviss and Mr Joseph O'Gorman were presented with the best graduate and best certificate awards by Concept Marketing and Advertising.

Waterford: the chairman Mr David Walsh and vice-chairman Mr John Lennon, South-East (Waterford) regional branch ran a series of evening lectures.

Mr P. Cummins, assistant chief executive of marketing at Waterford Co-op, addressed the annual breakfast, while all present enjoyed the presentation and sampling of the Co-op's products.

The sixth annual dinner was held in October with Mr Eugene O'Neill, chief executive of Ryanair, as guest speaker. The evening was, once again, the social highlight of Waterford's business community while the proceeds of the raffle, £500, was donated to the Marketing House Fund.

In September, the branch organised a counselling night for MII students in Waterford RTC.

Galway: during 1986, under the chairmanship of Mr John O'Dowd, the western (Galway) regional branch events included:

Irish Quality Control Association seminar: in conjunction with the Irish Quality Control Association, the branch held an afternoon seminar on 'Quality and Marketing', at which 200 people attended.

Institute of Bankers' Marketing presentation: in May 1986, the branch, together with the Institute of Bankers in Ireland, organised a joint presentation on 'Marketing Money — Decisions and Implications'. The enlightening evening had an attendance of over 155 people.

374 *Marketing at the Millennium*

GRADUATESHIP MARKETING STUDIES PROGRAMME

The Marketing Institute organised a graduateship programme for new entrants to marketing, a postgraduate programme for graduates wishing to specialise and professional education and training courses for members. These were organised under the marketing studies programme. Lectures were provided by the VEC's throughout Ireland in eleven centres. A major review of the course content took place, in light of developments in marketing.

Graduateship and postgraduateship areas were the responsibility of Mr Sean Ennis, vice-chairman of education, with the assistance of Mr James Wrynn. Mr Douglas Thornton was chairman of the marketing studies' committee. The chairperson of the MII Students' Society was Ms Marion Stokes.

GRADUATION CEREMONY, 1986

Eighty-nine students received graduateships and 192 students received certificates at the ceremony in Thomas Prior House, Royal Dublin Society, on 14 November 1986.

Alderman Mr Bertie Ahern TD, Lord Mayor of Dublin, presented the graduateships, following an address by the president of the Marketing Institute, Mr Tom Hardiman.

The graduation celebration ball was held that evening at Sach's hotel.

Special awards and cheques were made (sponsors in brackets):

- Ms Barbara Patton: Student of the Year (Córas Tráchtála Teo)
- Ms Karen Flynn: Case Study (McConnell's Advertising)
- Mr Peter Brennan: Marketing Management (Sales Placement Ltd)
- Mr David Larkin: Consumer Behaviour (R & A Bailey and Co. Ltd)
- Ms Maria Murphy: Business Policy (Janssen)

The certificate 'Student of the Year' was Mr Declan Byrne sponsored by *Business & Finance* magazine and the runner-up was Ms Maeve Curtis sponsored by the Marketing Institute of Ireland. The Institute also thanked the Bank of Ireland and A.T. Cross Ltd for their generous support.

CHAIRMAN'S REPORT, 1986

In his final report of the year 1986, Mr Brendan Wafer, outgoing national chairman of the Institute, said he believed that the Marketing Institute of Ireland could become the marketing professionals of Europe. The future, while looking good, would not be simple. It would require more skill, better dedication and more innovation, but it was attainable, if wanted badly enough. The bottom line, he said, was — 'people don't have to buy from us, but we have to sell to somebody'.

While it was unfair to single out any individual, Mr Wafer felt that two people deserved special mention. These were Mr Bill Ambrose, for bringing the dream of marketing house to reality and Mr Noel Shaw who had defined the strategy that would make the Marketing Institute one of the major national institutions for the 1990s.

TUESDAY CLUB LUNCHEON NOVEMBER 1986

The speaker at the Tuesday Club luncheon on 4 November 1986 at Jury's hotel, Dublin, was Mr Craig McKinney, chairman and managing director of Woodchester Investment plc.

CHRISTMAS LUNCHEON, DECEMBER 1986

At the Institute's Christmas luncheon on 16 December 1986, the guest speaker was Mr Sam McAughtry, the well-known Belfast-based broadcaster and journalist.

SILVER JUBILEE YEAR OF MII, 1987

Mr Alan McDonnell was elected chairman of the Marketing Institute of Ireland for 1987. This was its important Silver Jubilee Year. At the time Mr McDonnell was head of marketing with Superquinn, the supermarket group.

The new chairman said that the Institute had a strong sense of fraternity and rich personal friendship was the bond that existed among its members. It was relative to the many functions held. This was one of the vibrant signs of health of an organisation.

MARKETING IRELAND, 1987

'Marketing Ireland — Our Opportunities and Strengths' was the theme selected by the Marketing Council for the Silver Jubilee Year of 1987.

Leaders of state and industry were invited to offer their views on Ireland's national strengths, and to identify the commercial opportunities that such strengths presented. There were then over 100 members who worked diligently on behalf of MII members on the various committees.

MII APPOINTMENTS, 1987

Mr Tom Hardiman kindly agreed to remain in office as the president of the Institute for 1987. In his speech he said that marketing had a particularly important role to play at that time. A professional knowledge of a company's marketplace, with good internal communications and a rapid flow of accurate information to production and finance were necessary for reducing uncertainty and minimising risk.

Furthermore, the educational activities of the Institute were of real significance in the resolving of the country's economic problems.

Mr Bill Fraser agreed to continue as vice-president of the Institute.

The council officers elected for 1987 were:

• Deputy Chairman: Mr David Manley

• Vice-Chairman of Education: Mr Sean Ennis

• Vice-Chairman of Finance: Mr Tom Freeman

• Vice-Chairman of Services: Mr Gerry Hynes

• Hon. Secretary: Mr Jarlath Jennings.

The committee chairpersons were:

• Marketing Studies: Mr Ruairí Ó Floinn

• Graduateship/Special Projects: Mr Douglas Thornton

• Fellows: Mr Philip R. Flood

• Marketing Partnerships: Mr Joseph Clancy

• Silver Jubilee Ball: Ms Sharon Parke

• Marketing Clinics: Mr John McGuire

• Marketing Information: Ms Mary Egan

• Education Development: Mr Brendan V. Wafer.

Branch chairmen:

• Galway: Mr Tom Joyce

• South East: Mr John Lennon

• Cork: Mr Ger Manning

• Mid-West: Mr Pat Moriarty.

MARKETING INSTITUTE REVIEW, 1987

It was recalled that, in the late 1950s and early 1960s, the business environment for new developments had not been very favourable. Irish industry had a number of weaknesses. There was widespread conservatism, an unwillingness to change and a lack of well-trained managers. Manufactured exports were low and mainly aimed at the UK market. There was a general lack of initiative in sales management and marketing was little understood and rarely practised. Furthermore, there was no university degree course in marketing then.

Since 1962 (establishment of MII) the Institute had gone through three major stages of development:

1. Initially the emphasis was on establishing an independent, vibrant and relevant professional institute.

2. During the 1970s the focus was on developing a degree equivalent part-time professional qualification — the graduateship of the Institute.

3. In the early 1980s the lack of public awareness of the importance of marketing was tackled. The results had been very satisfactory. The Institute was now recognised as the voice of professional marketing in Ireland. Membership had grown to over 1,000, while student numbers came to 1,500. At the public level, the importance of good marketing was widely appreciated and the government was then doubling its financial support of sound marketing practice in private companies.

On 26 January 1987 in his speech, as incoming chairman of the institute, Mr Alan McDonnell stated:

> The missing ingredient is exporting marketing support. We applaud the achievements of CTT to date, but strongly believe their role is too limited. Many indigenous enterprises could not afford the cost of international marketing, even at the most finely targeted segments, particularly as these enterprises operate from a continually weakening domestic base.
>
> We see the need for partnerships in marketing projects, between State and private enterprise. Partnerships, not to extract further demands on the restricted finances of the State, but partnerships that will profit both.

MARKETING, GOVERNMENT PLANS, 1987

In an exclusive interview with Mr Gerry Lawlor, editor of *Professional*

Marketing, Mr Seamus Brennan TD stated that radical new legislation to change the role of CTT; new private enterprise; 'trading houses'; and a central role for marketing in solving the nation's economic problems were his top priorities as Minister of State for Trade and Marketing.

Minister of State for Marketing, 1987

The first priority of the minister would be to introduce new legislation before the summer of 1987 to alter the role of Córas Tráchtála. The whole concept of marketing would be incorporated in a Bill. There would also be a strong emphasis on strategic marketing.

Mr Brennan said that his was an historic appointment. It was the first time the term 'marketing' had been used in the title of a government office since the foundation of the State. It represented a major breakthrough for the profession. He was, therefore, looking at marketing separately with a view to setting up suitable structures within his department to co-ordinate the activities of the various marketing organisations. Also he saw trade as the result of marketing and the marketing activity as leading to trade.

STUDENTS' MARKETING SOCIETY, JANUARY 1987

A new students' society committee was elected on 31 January 1987 at their AGM in the Gresham hotel, Dublin. Criticisms and suggestions from students were sought.

The committee elected was:

- Chairman: Mr Peter Doyle
- Vice-Chairman: Mr David Allan
- Secretary: Ms Mary Butler
- Education: Mr Mick McKeown
- Finance: Mr Gary Manning
- Communication: Mr Ciaran Hurley
- Case Study: Ms Nicola Garret
- Class Reps: Mr Kevin Ó Broin
- Social: Mr Neil O'Donohoe
- Programme: Mr Andrew Harries and Ms Monica Hughes.

EUROPEAN MARKETING COUNCIL, 1987

Membership of the European Marketing Council in 1987 comprised of twelve countries. These were Belgium, Finland, France, Germany, Ireland, The Netherlands, Norway, Portugal, Spain, Sweden, Switzerland and the United Kingdom. Austria (Marketing Club, Linz) were accepted observers at EMC meetings at that time.

The president of EMC in 1987 was Mr Roger Pirot of Les Dirigeants Commerciaux de France (DCF). The secretary-general of EMC was Mr Hans Kerckhoff of Nederlands Centrum van Direkteuren en Commissarissen, Amsterdam.

One of the many undertakings of EMC was the task of expressing the joint opinion of its members on matters of international marketing interest to organisations concerned and to the public in general.

MARKETING FINANCIAL SERVICES COURSE, 1987

Yet another Marketing Institute course, part of its marketing studies programme, was initiated early in 1987. This was called Marketing Financial Services. The course was specifically designed for all firms in the financial services sector, whether they were serving businesses or consumers. It was open to non-members as well as to Institute members.

While the course had particular relevance for those new to marketing their services, such as accountancy firms, it gave those who were already marketing orientated, such as banks, building societies, insurance companies/brokers, etc. an opportunity to build on their then expertise and open up new avenues of thought.

The course content was aimed at directors and partners of professional practices as well as marketing managers, marketing executives and sales managers of financial firms.

The venue for the course was the Royal Marine hotel, Dún Laoghaire, on the dates of 25, 26, 31 March and 1 and 14 April 1987. To avoid disrupting a business day, the course was held in the evenings from 4.30 to 9 p.m.

The course content was divided into five modules:

1. The Marketing Concept.

2. Marketing Information and Customer Relations.

3. Innovation.

4. Advertising and Promotion.

5. Presentation of marketing plans by each of four project teams followed by discussions.

Case studies were given to all delegates for home reading. The fee for the course was £345 for MII members and £395 for non-members, and the course director was Mr Jack Downey. Lecturers included Messrs Philip Flood, College of Marketing & Design; Michael Shields, NIHE Dublin; Patrick Kehoe, Trade Development Institute; Ruairí O'Floin, Bank of Ireland; and Douglas Thornton, Marketing Consultant.

RETAIL MARKETING COURSE, 1987

As a further part of the marketing studies programme, the Institute ran a course on retail marketing on 23 and 24 February 1987. It was a down to earth practical course relating to running a business day to day. It avoided theoretical and abstract ideas and was aimed at those who wished to improve their performance.

Lecturers were drawn from experienced practitioners. Among them were Messrs Alan Sheehy-Skeffington, Douglas Thornton, John Gunnigle, Jim Dunne (Kilkenny Design), Jack Downey, Donal Swift and Tony O'Connor. There were quite a few ladies among the 44 participants.

FORD & SON LTD, FEBRUARY 1987

Mr Hartmut Kieven, chairman and managing director of Henry Ford & Son Ltd addressed the MII Galway branch luncheon at the Ardilaun hotel on 25 February 1987.

He declared that the target of marketing was the customer, our entire *raison d'être* being the customer. In his philosophy, marketing and the customer were virtually synonymous terms and from them stemmed sales and profitability. But it was the customer who must be nurtured and cosseted and looked after to the extent that he felt one of the family. It was through the customer-driven approach that Ford's were confident that they would become market leaders once again as they entered their second seventy years in Ireland.

Mr Kieven outlined Ford's successes in Britain and Europe. In Britain they enjoyed a 27.5 per cent market share and Fiesta, Escort and Sierra models filled the top three places. Only in Ireland, of all European countries, had the market for cars actually contracted over the past decade. That was due, he said, to successive government policies. Ford had been the market leader in Ireland in the fourteen years to 1985. More recently they adopted an increased strategy in order to restore Ford to the legendary 'value for money' image.

PROFESSIONAL MARKETING, MARCH 1987

As part of its contribution to the 'Marketing Ireland' theme of the Institute for 1987, the journal of the MII, *Professional Marketing*, included a specially commissioned article by Dr A.J.F. O'Reilly, chairman and chief executive officer of H.J. Heinz, Pittsburgh, in its March/April 1987 issue.

Marketing dilemma for Ireland, 1987

Dr A. (Tony) O'Reilly said that on writing a thesis on 'The Marketing of Irish Agricultural Produce', he chanced on a definition, or rather an observation, by the great Mr Theodore Levett. It read:

> Marketing is a subject uncommonly replete with uncontrolled uncontrollables, unstandardisable and unpredictable hazards. Like politics and sex, marketing is a squishy subject.

Dr O'Reilly pointed out that the essential principles of marketing were:

- to find out what the customer wants, not only what they are actually or vocally demanding but what they would like to have, if they had the imagination to formulate their needs

- to give them what they want, if it can be done without serious moral objection and if it can be done at a profit

- to tell them that you are giving them what they want, so that they will continue to want it — and want it from you.

Two questions, Dr O'Reilly stated, should be asked in his attempts to construct what his 'Jesuit mentors would have called a perfect syllogism'. First of all: What are the recognisable Irish marks or brands that people at home and abroad are prepared to buy because they believe them to have a better quality/ value relationship than any other competition?

Of course, there is Waterford Glass, Guinness, Kerrygold, Bailey's Irish Cream, all of whom had earned international reputation. At a genetic level, there became a domestic and international awareness, but *only* awareness, of Irish linen, Irish Whiskey, Irish tweed, Irish bacon, the Irish horse and Ireland's beauty as a tourist resort.

Mr O'Reilly said that working with such excellent raw materials Ireland had failed and failed miserably and consistently to create an awareness like Gucci (Italy), Dior (France) or the Beefeater (British royal family image) in the great markets of the world and particularly in the United States. There moderate penetration would mean so much to Irish prosperity and the balance of payments. In 1986 only 380,000 Americans visited Ireland, while 2.5 million visited the UK, 1.6 million visited France and 1.5 million visited Italy.

The second question Dr O' Reilly posed was the following: If there is so little international consumer recognition of things Irish and such slender resources to effect such recognition, what can be done to change or ameliorate these circumstances?

Product development allure

In an AGM speech to the H.J. Heinz stockholders, he had discussed the often misleading allure of product development:

* Where would their beans be without the prefix Heinz or the famous 57?

* Where would Philip Morris be without the Marlboro Man?

* Where would Schweppes be without its effervescence?

* Where would American Express be if we all left home without it?

Most of those brand identities and the related consumer awareness cost millions to create and decades to mature in the public mind. Answers, Dr O'Reilly said, were subtle and multiple and would include an all-important awareness of how obviously under financed Ireland was in all areas of international marketing by the public, the trade unions, the politicians and the shareholders.

CASE STUDY COMPETITION, MARCH 1987

The twentieth annual Marketing Institute of Ireland students' case study competition got under way, in allocated rooms, at the Irish Management Institute in Sandyford, Co. Dublin.

At the official launch ten eager team captains, sponsors, guests and committee members arrived at 5.30 p.m. on 6 March 1987 to hear the formal announcement of the actual case. It was then disclosed, amid cheese and wine, that it was based on CBF, Irish Beef. Naturally the dinner following the competition included Irish beef!

Having studied the case overnight, the teams converged at 8.30 a.m. the following morning and collected their individual conference packs.

Mr Peter Doyle, chairperson of the Students' Society, introduced Ms Nicola Garret, director of the conference and the adjudication panel. The latter included Messrs Aidan O'Driscoll, Sean Ennis, author of the case study, David Manley, deputy chairman of MII, Gabriel McCarrick, manager of the Food and Drinks Department, CTT and Frank Murray, marketing executive with CBF.

Questions were distributed to each team, at varying intervals during the day. At 2 p.m. question four was made available and then the battle to regain lost points began in earnest. With the final collection of team answers, preparation was made for oral presentations, which proved to be extremely professional.

The case study questions were:

1. Assess the dominant characteristics and competitive driving forces in the Irish livestock and meat industry?

2. How is the industry evolving in product/industry life cycle terms?

3. Speculate on a medium-term and long-term business strategy for any one of the companies outlined in the case.

4. Considering its strengths and opportunities make recommendations as to how the industry should develop. In particular what role, if any, do you foresee for the government agencies involved?

The judges declared Team J, 'Smiley's People', the winners. Further Mr Declan Daly's team had gained extra points by being simple and concise in their presentations. Bronze medals were presented to Team J by Mr Gerry Donehy of Nokia Ltd, sponsors of the event.

The winning team was:

Name	College	Year
Mr Declan Daly (Captain)	Mountjoy	4
Ms Geraldine Mills	Rathmines	4
Mr David Rafferty	Mountjoy	4
Mr Donal Moriarty	Rathmines	3
Ms Monica Hughes	Mountjoy	3
Ms Katy Cuddihy	Mountjoy	2
Ms Fiona Nolan	Rathmines	2
Ms Mary Butler	Rathmines	1
Ms Sharon McDonnell	Rathmines	1
Ms Rosemary Simmons	Rathmines	1
Mr Garry Keegan	Carlow RTC	4
Mr Louis Keegan		

Mr Vivian Murray, Irish Goods Council, delivered the after-dinner speech and advocated the common sense approach to marketing. Mr Alan McDonnell, national chairman of MII, encouraged the students to be critical.

MEGAMARKETING, 1987

Mr Aidan O'Driscoll, editor of *Irish Marketing Review* and a lecturer in marketing at the College of Marketing and Design, examined the case for adding two more 'Ps' to the marketing mix. He referred to success in marketing increasingly taking on a crucial political dimension. Two then recent Irish examples illustrated the point:

1. In May 1986 a new Irish Airline, Ryanair, commenced flying the Dublin-London route. It was the result of a lengthy period of lobbying government and legislature, and tough negotiation, to secure the Irish government's permission to fly the route.

2. In January 1987 a large English tour operator, Cypriana, was granted an unconditional licence to operate a package holiday service direct from Dublin to Cyprus. Two years earlier it had applied for such a licence but found the conditions attaching commercially unacceptable.

Mr O'Driscoll asked the question: Did these examples of successful enterprise represent a kind of management by 'strokes' or a new and more determined approach to achieving commercial objectives?

Megamarketing explained

Mr O'Driscoll said that Mr Philip Kotler (Megamarketing, *Harvard Business Review*, March–April 1986, pp. 117–118) the international doyen of marketing, would have believed the latter. He saw an increasing pattern of the successful use of political muscle and public relations campaigns to achieve goals.

The two new 'Ps', power and public relations, must then be added to the marketing mix. That was called megamarketing. To understand the concept of megamarketing required a focus on certain types of 'entry barrier' to a market. That was the challenge that megamarketing, with its two Ps, attempted to surmount.

Mr O'Driscoll, went on at great length, to explain and give factual evidence of marketing and megamarketing in detailed contrast. And so, he concluded, CTT, Bord Bainne, Bord Fáilte and so on, had perhaps a megamarketing role to play.

BAILEY'S SUCCESS FORMULA, APRIL 1987

Mr David Dand MMII, chairman of Gilbey's Ireland, one of Ireland's top marketing people, addressed the Marketing Institute of Ireland, Tuesday Club at the April 1987 meeting. He stated that he was asked to continue in the Institute's theme of 'Marketing Ireland — Opportunities and Strengths', for the Silver Jubilee Year.

He wondered could you market a State as such, a State was not a consumer product, nor a piece of capital equipment. Perhaps the exception was tourism, but that was made up of many product component parts, for example transport, accommodation and even the weather.

However, in addressing the title of his talk, he was assuming, he believed correctly, that Ireland was being undersold, or under exploited on world markets. There was in fact much more available than was being put on offer. If that was not the case one would see many more Irish products in overseas markets.

He further stated that he was not an 'intellectual' marketer, but was, unashamedly, much more of a practical manager. He was an optimist by nature. It was his belief that one could market their way out of difficulties but only by the practical method. You also had to believe in the brand you were marketing.

Quality of product

Believing in quality standards and quality assurances to such a degree, Bailey's had sponsored Mr John Murphy's book entitled: *Quality in Practice*, published by Gill and Macmillan.

If the quality was right, almost half the marketing job was done. Consumers and users of products go for quality. He referred to the success of Japanese cars and how they found their market when British Leyland cars had acquired a reputation for unreliability. Therefore without getting quality right, the rest of the marketing efforts and expenditure were just a waste, and not worth doing.

There was a strong case to be made for an Irish food distribution company to operate throughout the EEC and distribute (but not sell) food products for an Irish company meeting the necessary standards of product quality and reliable service.

PIMS database, April 1987

The chief executive of the Irish Quality Control Association, Mr John A. Murphy, was asked to discuss the role of quality and in particular, complaints. For most marketing people, he said, quality was something added by the production department.

However, recently published business research, based on a database called PIMS (Profit Impact of Market Strategy) implied taking an entirely different view. The research isolated thirty key factors that influenced the expected rate of return on capital. Two of them were critical from the marketing point of view. First of all, in relation to market share — the higher the market share the better (no surprise) and secondly relative product quality. The latter was, in fact, the second most powerful factor in influencing return on capital.

Relative product quality, 1987

The database defined Relative Product Quality (RPQ), as taking into account:

• the customer's view, not the company's

• both the product and the associated services

• other competitors in the served market.

In short, quality related to everything about the product except the price, as perceived by the customers.

An EEC directive on product liability, which would be part of Irish law by mid-1988, stated that manufacturers would be strictly liable, i.e. whether it is their fault or not, for any injuries caused by defective products. Such a product was defined as 'one that does not provide the safety which a person was entitled to expect, taking all circumstances into account, including:

• the presentation of the product

• the use to which it could reasonably be expected that the product would be put.

Irish customers were traditionally reluctant to complain about a product. That was not unique as only 2 per cent of customers in the brash US bothered to complain about low-priced goods and only one in twenty complained about goods costing the equivalent of a few pounds. It was felt that it was not worth the trouble.

MARKETING AND PURCHASING, APRIL 1987

The South-East branch of the MII held a seminar on 'Marketing and Purchasing', co-sponsored with The Irish Institute of Purchasing and Materials Management. It was held at the Adult Education Centre in Waterford on Tuesday 14 April 1987.

The speakers at the seminar were: Messrs Cyril Crowley, BA, LLB, MA, solicitor, lecturer in law at Waterford Regional Technical College and John Lennon, BA, MBA, MMII, lecturer in marketing at the same college.

NATURAL GAS, APRIL 1987

Speaking to the Tuesday Club luncheon, Mr Nevin Dowling, chief executive of An Bord Ghais, summed up the impact of the most important indigenous energy resource and raw material discovered in recent decades.

The contribution of natural gas to the national economy, since it was first brought ashore in 1978, was immense in terms of reduced dependency on imported fuels, improved balance of payments, competition in the internal energy market and payments to the Exchequer. Imported oil was the main loser.

Mr Dowling stressed the environmental benefits of natural gas. It was estimated that the use of natural gas reduced the volume of sulphur dioxide released into the atmosphere by at least 87,000 tonnes. This was the equivalent of a 57 per cent reduction of what would have been emitted by a heavy oil plant.

Natural gas was ideally positioned and the marketing strategy laid emphasis on the pricing element of the marketing mix. As to strategy to be followed by the gas industry, in an effort to achieve dominance, he referred to the principles set out by Messrs Philip Kotler and Michael Porter as to the path the industry intended to take.

Fifth decade of the history of sales management and marketing in Ireland, 1987–1997

JOINT MARKETING FOR EXPORTS, MAY 1987

Mr Alan McCarthy, chief executive of Córas Tráchtála, in a special article of May 1987 in *Professional Marketing*, promoted the need for joint marketing for exports by indigenous small companies. His rationale was indisputable and he was informed that his proposals would be considered and welcomed by MII members.

Mr McCarthy also said that if a member involved in a small Irish enterprise about to enter export markets considered the new service which CTT was offering and contacted them or Mr Joe Clancy, Marketing Institute chairman of the latter's Marketing Partnerships' Committee, it would be discussed in private.

The importance of exports and exporting to the Irish economy could not be overstated, as CTT estimated that the total exports for 1986 amounted to £9.3bn., a 1 per cent volume increase on 1985. Exports accounted for some 60 per cent of Ireland's GNP and two out of every three jobs in the manufacturing industry were, to some extent, dependent on exports.

For a joint marketing project CTT would:

• act as a catalyst or co-ordinator for the formation of a group

• undertake, with the group, research into markets and assist the group in preparing a marketing plan

• provide expert assistance to the group in undertaking co-ordinated product development activities

• support the appointment of a marketing manager and sales professionals in the marketplace

• contribute financially towards the cost of establishing distribution and servicing facilities in the marketplace

• support the costs of participation in trade fairs and exhibitions

• provide advice and financial support towards the cost of promotion in the marketplace.

A joint marketing venture would provide the opportunity to strengthen marketing management for the companies involved in an overseas marketing venture. This would allow for the appointment of a full-time marketing executive and strengthen the image of the group in the marketplace.

In addition, Mr McCarthy stated that product development and technology costs would be shared and pooled and product ranges developed to be compatible and complimentary. Joint marketing co-operation would cover a wide range of activities and costs including joint market research; sharing of agents/distributors; provision of warehousing and servicing facilities; pooled costs in trade fair participation; and representation, complementary and co-operative advertising and promotion.

MENSWEAR STUDIED, MAY 1987

Mr Kevin O'Neill, a young marketing graduate, carried out some novel research into the suit buying behaviours of Irish men. His case study, 'Labels in Menswear', won him the National Student Marketing award, organised by the Irish Goods Council.

There was once a time, not long ago, when every man had a suit, and not just for Sunday. All that had changed, not just in Ireland but throughout the western world. The outlook for the Irish suit industry was bleak, particularly when Irishmen believed that foreign suits were best.

Mr O'Neill began with an examination of market share statistics for his research work. Only 12 per cent of all suits sold in Ireland were domestic brands. It seemed that while the Irish were good at making suits we were not so good at selling them. He found that. Irish manufacturers had, with the odd exception, not attempted to add value to their product. This was because Irish brands were priced, almost exclusively, on the basis of cost alone, as against value to the consumer.

There was also a lack of promotion by the Irish firms, half of whom did no advertising. Added to that there was an inordinate amount of influence by female partners over their man's choice of brand. It emerged that the retailer was a key influence in the purchase decision. Few men actually asked for a specific brand, rather that was left to the salesman. The case study showed that the role of the retailer was a key point.

Basically the idea was that a group of menswear firms working co-operatively, for example in exhibitions, could exercise greater marketing muscle. They must invest in marketing, in order to make progress by influencing the customer.

SILVER JUBILEE GOLF CLASSIC, MAY 1987

The annual MII golf outing was held at the Hermitage Club on May 1987. This was the Silver Jubilee Golf Classic. It was enjoyed by a large crowd and was a wonderfully successful day, helped by the generous hospitality and prizes provided by the sponsors, Colorman Printers.

EXPORT MARKET DATABASES, 1987

A special sub-committee of services examined the feasibility of getting a project launched to explore how information contained in export market databases could be made more readily accessible to industry, especially to smaller companies who might not be operating mainframe computers.

A partner was found to fund the initial stages of a joint project to be carried out for MII — the Department of International Marketing, UCD. The Institute was also grateful to IBM who generously put hardware at its disposal, for use in the project.

MARKETING FOR THE 1990'S, SEPTEMBER 1987

A special highlight of the Silver Jubilee year was the visit of Dr Philip Kotler who was renowned as the world's leading authority on marketing.

He first published *Marketing Management*, which was destined to become the leading textbook on marketing, in 1968. It was now in its fifth edition, having been translated into eleven languages, including Russian and Chinese.

On 10 September 1987 over 700 members, non-members and students heard Professor Kotler address the theme: 'Marketing for the 1990s.' He covered a stimulating and wide ranging programme.

HONORARY FELLOWSHIP, 1987

The award of Honorary Fellowship was conferred on Dr Philip Kotler, by the Marketing Institute of Ireland in 1987.

PRESIDENT'S DINNER, OCTOBER 1987

There was an attendance of 250 members and guests including An Taoiseach, Mr Charles J. Haughey TD, Minister for Trade and Marketing, Mr Seamus Brennan TD, Professor Michael Baker of the Institute of Marketing, UK, and other professional dignitaries at the Silver Jubilee President's Night dinner.

The celebration was held at the Royal Hospital, Kilmainham, Dublin on 16 October 1987 and was described by the media as having been an outstanding success.

Trade and marketing agencies reorganised

The gathering heard of Mr Haughey's plan for the reorganisation of the Irish trade and marketing agencies representation overseas. According to Mr Haughey Ireland's commercial representation had grown up in an unplanned manner over the years:

> As a result we are now faced with a multiplicity of offices, many of them too small to have made any real impact on the countries in which they operate. It is clearly wasteful to have Irish agencies carrying on their activities in isolation from each other, in a situation that makes it impossible for them to have proper regard for each other's interest and objectives. To this end the government has decided, in principle, that in every location abroad where our official agencies and companies are present they should be brought together in one centre.

All in all the main point of Mr Haughey's speech was that the objective was to sell Ireland and Irish goods abroad. It was clearly desirable that all Irish diplomatic missions abroad should have a much stronger commercial bias and that the government was committed to achieving this .

The president of the Marketing Institute, Mr Tom Hardiman, stated that the environment for enterprise for too long had been hampered by an unnatural and needless polarisation, which had little real basis in Irish society. An agreement made between the government and social partners was to be greatly welcomed. The Fellows and senior members of the Institute were to be found at the highest executive levels in industry and commerce. Marketing, he firmly believed, was at the very core and centre of business and he felt that support, by competent production technology and suitable investment in research and development, was the key to innovation marking the successful company.

EC market

Mr Hardiman also stressed that there was a need to get into the great internal market of the EC, a dynamic rich and vibrant market of 320 million people. In the few short years to the turn of the century, the Marketing Institute must provide greater education and training of marketing executives, Furthermore, he stated that the Institute would have to bring a strong European orientation to its work. Language skills would be most important. One could buy in any language but must market and sell successfully in the language of the customer.

National marketing plan

The preparation of a national marketing plan, recently announced in the agreement on the economic programme, was also mentioned at the dinner. It was agreed by all that it was very timely and the Institute was pleased to offer its own experienced professional members to assist the preparation of the plan.

The Sean Lemass award

The Foreign Exchange Company of Ireland (Fexco) was the recipient of the Marketing Institute's Sean Lemass award. At the dinner it was presented to the company's founder and managing director, Mr Brian McCarthy, by An Taoiseach, Charles J. Haughey.

Fexco was chosen as exemplifying a new breed of Irish enterprise, applying sophisticated technology in their pursuit of lucrative gaps in the financial services markets, at home and overseas.

The company had been formed in 1981, initially to provide bureau de change services at licensed outlets, such as hotels and department stores and mainly serving the tourist industry. A sophisticated system for handling on-board foreign exchange systems had been devised for and was in operation by the B & I line. Many other innovations included unique technology-based systems such as the tourist VAT refund system and the bureau de change management package

Early in 1987 Fexco formed a joint venture in the UK with the Bank of Scotland Plc through the vehicle of the Foreign Exchange Company (UK).

Stephen Doyle award, October 1987

Mr Bill Ambrose FMII was recipient of the Stephen Doyle award for meritorious service to marketing. It was formally presented to him by the president of the MII, Mr Tom Hardiman.

Mr Alan McDonnell, the national chairman of the Institute stated that the award was being given to Mr Ambrose in appreciation of 'his undying commitment and contribution to the Institute'.

New Fellows

Eight newly elected Marketing Institute of Ireland Fellows were presented with their scrolls by Mr Tom Hardiman, at the President's Night dinner on 16 October 1987. These were:

• Mr David Austin: executive vice-president (marketing) of Jefferson Smurfit plc.

• Mr Sean Cowman: marketing executive of AnCo

- Mr John Hickey: director of the the Connacht Tribune Ltd

- Dr Patrick Kehoe: managing director of Patrick Kehoe & Associates

- Mr Keith MacCarthy-Morrogh: deputy managing director of R & A Bailey and Co.

- Mr Bob Waddell: group general manager/director of the Gowan Group

- Mr Sean A. Walshe: managing director of Colorprint

- Mr Frank Young: managing director of Wilson Hartnell Advertising.

PROFESSIONAL MARKETING MII JUBILEE ISSUE, 1987

In producing a fine Silver Jubilee celebration issue for the Marketing Institute of Ireland, *Professional Marketing* journal teamed up with *Business & Finance* magazine.

Sports marketing, October 1987

In the celebration issue of the publication Mr Roddy Carr, managing director of Carrcorp (he was a member of a family long associated with golf and also the fashion trade) was reported as saying that nobody really knew exactly where and when sports marketing started. The real beginning, in commercial terms, as known today, started back in the 1960s. Mr Arnold Palmer, the new 'superstar' of professional golf, was emerging and there, in the right place at the right time, was Mr Mark McCormack, a young lawyer from Cleveland (who played off a one-handicap) who recognised the marketing potential of Palmer.

Within a year Mr McCormack added Jack Nicholas and Gary Player to his side and created the first television sports programme with the 'Big Three Golf Exhibition Series'. He declared that television was the way of developing and promoting his clients. It was indeed the key to the successful promotion of sports marketing as a business.

From 1960 to 1987 companies invested over $100m. into those three athletes alone, to help promote all types of products, ranging from men's suits to towels, teacups, motor cars and swimming pools.

(It is interesting to recall that in 1963 P.J. Carroll & Co., cigarette manufacturers, had been the first Irish company to sponsor a major Irish sporting event — the internationally known Carroll's Irish Open Golf Championship*).*

NATIONAL MARKETING CONFERENCE, 1987

This was jointly sponsored by the Marketing Institute of Ireland and *Business*

& *Finance* magazine. The conference was held at the Royal Marine hotel in Dún Laoghaire, Co. Dublin on Thursday 29 October1987. It was the keystone of members' events annually.

The ninth National Marketing Conference showed how steadily some success stories, corporate and individual, operated and detailed experiences of major winners abroad. The speakers at the conference and the themes they covered were:

1. Mr Seamus Brennan, TD, Minister for Trade and Marketing
    'The Government's Role in a Market Driven Economy'

2. Mr Brian Baldock, managing director of Guinness Brewing Worldwide
    'As World Markets Grow Closer, Can the Small Nation Survive?'

3. Mr Jim Lett, managing director of Lett & Co.
    'Still Flexing his Mussels — a Case Study in Success'

4. Mr David Hanly, managing director of PARC
    'Putting Irish Talent to Work Abroad — Opportunities and Pitfalls'

5. Mr Conor McCarthy, chairman of Córas Tráchtála
    'The Tourism and Leisure Industry — Are We Finally Getting It Right?'

6. Mr John Howard, marketing director of the Danish Bacon and Meat Council
    'Success in the Toughest Market of All — a Case Study'

7. Mr Eugene O'Neill, chief executive of Ryanair
    'Taking on the Well Entrenched — a Case Study in High Risk Entrepreneurship'

8. Mr Don Brennan, managing director of Morgan Stanley, New York
    'Financial Services — Niche Markets to be Exploited, even Dominated'

9. Mr Roddy Carr, managing director of Camcorp International
    'Marketing Success — the International Environment'

10. Mr Stephen Roche, World Champion Cyclist 1987
    'Managing at the Sporting Top — an Extempore Address'

The conference chairmen were Messrs Tim Mahony, chairman of Killeen Investments and Mr Michael Whelan, chief executive of Aran Energy.

Over 200 delegates were treated to what were a series of first class papers, and at a time when stock markets were teetering on the brink of chaos, had a first class account of what was happening from Mr Don Brennan of Morgan Stanley, New York.

THE NEXT 25 YEARS, 1987

Dr Tony Cunningham was given a brief by the editor of *Professional Marketing* to develop some thoughts — not on the past, but on the next twenty-five years. Looking around the historic hall of the Royal Hospital at 'the then luminaries in the Irish marketing firmament' and recognising many of the faces glowing in animated conversation at the various tables, engendered a certain amount of pride that he had had the privilege of getting to know many of them in a classroom situation, when they looked a lot younger.

Professor Cunningham wrote that he was struck by the thought that 25 years ago it would have been inconceivable to imagine that the Silver Jubilee dinner would be addressed, not only by the Taoiseach, but would have at the top table a Minister for Trade and Marketing.

Again, he pointed out that it was salutary to realise that we were only beginning to come to terms with the implications of what has to be done in order to be successful as a nation in the 21st century. He wondered how many decision-takers were aware that the Paris Chamber of Commerce invested more in business education annually than Ireland did in its total third level education. That was in addition to the massive investment by the French government in higher education.

The Sean Lemass award, presented to the Foreign Exchange Company of Ireland, demonstrated vividly that future wealth would be created by applying cerebral thinking to an internationally traded service. It would be necessary to sell problem solving to customers, rather than products. Investment in education, he stressed, required considerable expansion.

Forecast for success

He wondered, he said, what could be done to insure success in the year 2112. It was abundantly clear that in 25 years knowledge-based service industries would dominate the economic landscape. Professor Cunningham concluded that they would require highly educated people to market them successfully and that would necessitate massive investment in general, as well as marketing specific education far beyond anything traditionally considered.

MARKETING — PAST, PRESENT AND FUTURE, 1987

The immediate past-chairman of MII, Mr Brendan Wafer, marketing manager of NBST, referred to the 1950s and 1960s when Ireland decided that business education was nearly exclusively in the accounting function. He believed the country was now counting the cost — too few companies with chief executives who fully understood the need for marketing and too few internationally competitive marketing managers.

Reports on marketing over the previous five years supported his statement, while, more importantly, the market clearly showed it, i.e.:

• progressive loss of home market share over the last decade

• failure to even partially exploit the opportunities presented by the EEC

• the low level of sub-supply to many multinational companies in Ireland.

Marketing, Mr Wafer wrote, was not the most crucial function in companies. Peter and Waterman's *In Search of Excellence* (1982), and indeed similar research in Ireland, taught that company success was based on excellence in *all* management functions.

Real advantage over competitors was frequently in one function backed by an all round excellent team.

Since the recession of the early 1980s, the message was very apparent in the many liquidations — that unless management performance was improved, particularly marketing, one would go out of business.

New degree status programme

Mr Wafer went on to define the new graduateship degree status programme, illustrating, by way of a flow chart, the new course, which would comprise five stages to a final dissertation. Two formal subjects were included in relation to the area of exporting/international marketing. In addition the marketing profile of each major market for Irish companies was included for study in detail, e.g. the United Kingdom including Northern Ireland, Germany, the Netherlands, Italy, US, etc.

MARKETING INSTITUTE AS EDUCATOR, OCTOBER 1987

In his review Mr Philip Flood, past chairman of MII and chairman of fellows, said that a response to marketplace demand brought the Institute into being and it was a similar perception of a real need that set the nascent body about its educational task.

The heady days of 1962, with the 'First and Second Programmes for Economic Expansion', had directed the pace and expansionist confidence. The protectionist economic thinking of the 50s had died with little more than a whimper. The notion of marketing had been novel and not particularly well developed as a business function anywhere outside of the United States. However, marketing was now central to what the economy was attempting for itself.

Among the first objectives of the Institute, in 1962, had been the establishing of a training programme. Mr Flood recalled that:

Harry Woods was then entrusted with the task of developing an educational vehicle and he persuaded Sean Ó Ceallaigh, College of Commerce, Rathmines, Dublin, to co-operate in providing lectures to equip students for the old Institute of Marketing UK exams. A dozen or so students were enrolled in what was then a three-year programme and the course of study certainly generated its fair share of glittering prizemen: Frank Young, Cartan Finnegan, Jim Culliton, to name but a trio from the student body of those early days.

With the first tentative steps over and a couple of cohorts of graduates produced, the Institute began to think in more adventurous terms of a customised programme, more directly related to Irish needs.

Mr Flood traced the progression to the first group of students taking the new graduateship. The student awards were presented then by the Minister for Education, Mr Dick Burke TD, in a ceremony at the Shelbourne hotel, Dublin. It was reported that 'with typical panache', reciprocation was made by presenting the Minister with a piece of silver. There was much student unrest at the time, and Mr Burke expressed wry pleasure at being at the receiving end of 'something other than a brickbat'.

The graduating group, referred to, included:

• Mr Frank Davinport: IDA office, Germany

• Mr Brian O'Connor: 3M

• Mr Brian More O'Farrell: ICI Ireland

• Mr Paul Leahy: LOL Ltd

• Mr Malcolm Mitchell: College of Commerce

• Mr Greg Rogers: A.T. Cross.

Of particular note was Mr Roddy Lyons, then personal assistant to Mr Jeff Smurfit, who came to the Marketing Institute as a university graduate. He successfully completed all eight subjects, of years three and four, in a single session.

First lady MII graduate

The first lady graduate of the Marketing Institute, Ms Anne O'Doherty, was alone of her sex in that initial group. However, a feature of the Institute studies since then had been the participation rates of women and their outstanding success in the final examinations. Included were people like Ms Geraldine Glasgow, the first MII graduate to take an MBA in Trinity, who excelled.

The number of MII students registered for 1986–1987 was 1,861.

Fond memories, 1987

Implementing local policies and having complete control on educational plans and curriculum prompted the idea of setting up an autonomous Irish Institute of Marketing and Sales Management Ltd (I.Inst.MSM.) with the full support of the United Kingdom parent. On 14 July 1969, the Institute name was changed to the Marketing Institute of Ireland. A further name was registered at that time 'just in case' — The Business Institute.

Such were the opening words of Mr Bill Fraser, who had been chairman of the MII from 1970–71 and currently vice-president when he took up the story in the 1987 Jubilee Review. He detailed the progression of the Institute, including that of close contact with Northern Ireland and the UK.

Mr Fraser added that Harry Woods, who had the distinction of being chairman for two years, 1964–65 and 1965–66, had held office in education and membership, developed the educational committee with Ms Pauline Beirne, head of the School of Retail Distribution, and started day courses for students to link with the evening classes.

Branch development in the 1980s

Mr Bill Fraser referred to Mr Pat Nolan as the 'revivalist minister' who travelled the country concentrating on the Institute branches. Mr Fraser recalled that Mr John Pollock, chairman of the Northern Ireland Branch, had invited Mr Harry Wyer, chairman of MII, 1971–72, and others to his dinner. It was a renewal of close ties, which had always promised better, but continued to disappoint. He also stated that Mr Mahon Lee, with Messrs Tom Browne and Bill Deegan, at the same time, was manfully battling along in Cork with a thriving branch.

NEW COURSE, NOVEMBER 1987

In conjunction with the Department of Marketing, University College, Dublin, the MII presented a new course entitled 'Effective Marketing Strategies' at the Royal Marine Hotel, Dún Laoghaire, Co. Dublin. It was to be held on the 8, 9 and 10 of November and 22, 23 and 24 of November on Sunday evenings and full days Monday and Tuesday. The Sunday evenings, together with the two week gap from 10 November were for case study preparation. The fee for MII members was £495 and £525 for non members.

The new programme offered the opportunity for a more detailed study of the topics covered by Dr Philip Kotler in his recent one-day seminar and the previous year's introductory course on strategic marketing. It was well attended and had a strong practical orientation. Marketing management and strategy issues, likely to be faced by companies over the following three to five years, were carefully examined.

GRADUATION DAY, 1987

Friday 20 November 1987 proved to be a 'red letter' day for the Marketing Institute. His Excellency, Dr Patrick Hillery, President of Ireland, marked the Silver Jubilee year by attending the graduation ceremony in the National Concert Hall. This was an indication of the growing status in the life of the Marketing Institute of Ireland.

Two hundred and eighty students received certificates and 200 students received graduateships at the ceremony. The president of the MII, Mr Tom Hardiman, and the vice-president, Mr Bill Fraser, addressed the audience of over 1000 people.

The following received special awards and cheques (sponsors in brackets):

• Student of the Year: Ms Sheila Gahan (Còras Tráchtála Teo)

• Case Study: Mr Eugene O'Connor (McConnells Advertising)

• Marketing Management: Mr Albert Roche (Sales Placement Ltd)

• Consumer Behaviour: Ms Nuala Balfe (R. & A Bailey and Co.)

• Business Policy: Ms Geraldine Mills (Janssen).

The certificate student of the year award, presented by *Business & Finance* magazine, was won by Ms Catriona Cahill. The Institute thanked the Bank of Ireland and A.T. Cross Ltd for their continued and generous support.

Dr Hillery's speech

Addressing the award winners, graduates and certificate holders, Dr Hillery first congratulated the Institute on its Silver Jubilee and praised it on its achievements.

He stated: 'I salute it for its vigour and vision and wish it success a hundredfold in its very important mission in the years which lie ahead'. Speaking to the graduates Dr Hillery said: 'You are among the great strengths on which the future of all of us depends. We have unlimited faith in you, your skills and talents and in your will to achieve. I wish you all success as you face the challenge which beckons.'

Concluding the speeches, the president of the Institute, Mr Hardiman, stated that Ireland had the talent. Foreign companies set up in Ireland less for the grants and the low tax and more because of the availability of the adaptable and highly educated people that came from the country's third level colleges.

GRADUATESHIP, NEW PROGRAMME, 1987

The year 1987 had been one of considerable achievement in the education area for the Marketing Institute. Student registrations continued to increase. More importantly, 1987 saw the introduction of the new graduateship programme. The first holders of the new graduateship would not emerge until 1992 but the seeds were sown for an educational programme that would reflect the needs of the 1990s and beyond.

THE NEW PROGRAMME, 1987

Under the chairmanship of Mr Brendan Wafer, the educational development committee spent from September 1986 to May 1987 plotting the development and structure of the programme. The committee had been drawn from members of the Marketing Institute, lecturers in marketing from the various academic institutions, and practitioners in industry.

The end result was a programme consisting of five years of study. At the end of stage two, the student would receive a Foundation Certificate in Marketing. At the end of stage four, the student would receive a Professional Diploma in Marketing and at the end of stage five, the student would receive the Graduateship of the Marketing Institute.

Below is the trend in student registrations over the previous six academic years:

- 1981/82: 700
- 1982/83: 950
- 1983/84: 1,068
- 1984/85: 1,300
- 1985/86: 1,600
- 1986/87: 1,800
- 1987/88: 2,000.

As in previous years, the number, of university graduates and holders of professional qualifications applying to study for the graduateship continued to increase, emphasising the growth in status for the award.

OFFICERS AND COUNCIL OF MII, 1988

The officers were:

- President: Mr James P. Culliton
- Vice-President: Mr William Fraser
- Vice-President: Mr Alastair McGuckian.

The council comprised:

- Chairman: Mr David Manley, David Manley & Associates
- Deputy Chairman: Mr John McGuire, Rehab Lotteries.

Vice-Chairmen:

- Members' Services: Ms Sharon Parker, RHM Foods Ireland Ltd
- Education: Mr John Lennon, Waterford RTC
- Marketing: Mr Joe Clancy, Hunter Advertising Ltd
- Corporate Affairs: *Mr Tom Healy, Irish Stock Exchange
- Honorary Secretary: Mr Douglas Thornton, Douglas Thornton Associates
- Chairman of Fellows: Mr David Austin, Jefferson Smurfit Group.

The branch chairmen were:

- South-East: Mr Frank Conlon, IDA, South East Region
- Galway: Mr Frank Falvey, Autodata Ltd
- Cork: Mr Ger Manning, Sun Alliance Insurance
- Mid-West: Mr Tony Treacy, Texas Instruments (Irl) Ltd.

The council members were:

- Ms Cathy Carroll, Children's Research Centre
- Mr John Daly, ICL Computers (Irl) Ltd
- Mr Sean Ennis, College of Marketing & Design
- Mr Gary Hynes, Church & General Insurance Co.
- Mr Alan McDonnell, Superquinn Ltd
- Mr Ruairí Ó Floinn, Bank of Ireland
- Mr Geoff Read, Ballygowan Springwater Co.

- Chief Executive: Mr John Kerrigan.

* Co-Opted

PRESIDENT OF MII, 1988

Mr Jim Culliton FMII was inaugurated as president of the Marketing Institute at a ceremony in Dublin on Thursday 14 January 1988. He had been among the first graduates of the Institute in 1962. His career had been mainly in marketing. He had been, in turn, marketing manager of Roadstone, managing director of Clondalkin Concrete, assistant managing director of Roadstone and became chief executive of Cement Roadstone Holdings in 1974 at the age of 40.

He had developed and led the business to a position as a broadly based internationally diverse company with substantial operations in Europe and the United States. It employed 8,000 people. Currently he was chairman of the RTÉ Authority, chairman of Unidare and a director of Allied Irish Banks, Jury's hotels, Consolidated Holdings and the Agricultural Trust.

AGM OF MII, JANUARY 1988

The AGM of the Marketing Institute was held on Monday 18 January 1988 at the Berkeley Court hotel in Dublin.

It was reported in *Professional Marketing* as having been a brief, business-like affair that saw Mr Alan McDonnell hand over the chairman's chain of office to Mr David Manley MMII, principal partner of David Manley & Associates, after an outstanding Jubilee Year in office.

Accepting the president's chain of office, Mr Jim Culliton said that he had three major aspirations for the Institute in the years immediately ahead:

1. Membership should be doubled to 3,000 over the next three years, as there were many senior marketing people still outside the ranks of the Institute.

2. All students should be encouraged to become full members on completion of their studies.

3. A graduated scale of fees should be implemented for new graduates joining the Institute.

The occasion included the presentation of a special citation to Mr Tom Hardiman FMII, to mark his great contribution to the Institute during his presidency, 1985–88.

In his opening address to members of the Marketing Institute, the new president, Mr Culliton, said that there had never been a more exciting and challenging time to be a marketing professional in Ireland. The marketing landscape was generally presenting a more pleasing vista than it had for some years.

Both domestic and international factors had combined to create a set of unusually favourable circumstances. Again, sensible government policies and actions had averted a doomsday economic scenario and laid the groundwork for renewed economic progress.

Reductions in industrial costs — telephones, electricity, fuel, air transport, interest rates — lower inflation and a realistic containment of wage costs had proven a basis for making investment decisions with some degree of confidence that would result in wealth, creation and jobs.

Making marketing happen

In his speech to members Mr David Manley said that he took up office knowing the Institute had progressed and developed over the previous few years and there would be no room for complacency.

He declared the theme for 1988 as: 'Making Marketing Happen'. He restated the mission ahead as that of establishing the Marketing Institute as the premier proprietor of marketing in Ireland and detailed how that would be achieved.

Trading houses to sell Irish goods, 1988

The Marketing Institute warmly welcomed the EEC clearance for the setting up of trading houses to sell Irish goods abroad. It presented real business opportunities for the partners in them and also for Irish supplier companies. The availability of the Business Expansion Scheme funding for the trading houses was a real bonus as it made finance readily available.

It was for the members of the Marketing Institute to use their creativity in producing the result, making the trading houses concept work and so a series of regional briefings were launched in Cork, Limerick, Galway and Waterford.

Marketing house, January 1988

It was announced by the Marketing Institute of Ireland on Thursday 28 January 1988, that phase one of the fundraising campaign to purchase a permanent home had been completed.

Mr David Manley, chairman of MII, was presented with a cheque for £100,000 (first phase proceeds), which included contributions from members, the business community and proceeds of special fundraising events. The chairman of the Marketing House Funding committee, Mr Bill Ambrose, presented the cheque.

Sir John Harvey-Jones addressed a special fundraising seminar, chaired by Dr Garret Fitzgerald. Mr David Manley commented that the expansion plans, incorporating the provision of a marketing house, could then be realised.

The budget was for £250,000 with £100,000 coming from the Institute's own resources and £150,000 from the fundraising campaign. It was felt that it would not be difficult to raise a further £50,000, to conclude phase two.

CHIEF EXECUTIVE OF MII, FEBRUARY 1988

'There's a big job to be done but the environment and timing are just right', that was Mr John Kerrigan's evaluation of his new post as chief executive of the Marketing Institute, which he took over from 1 February 1988.

The most immediate of his priorities as chairman was the marketing house. He also saw as being urgent, objectives including improved services for members and students, and the marketing of marketing. There was, at that time, a national emphasis on marketing. Names like Tom Hardiman and Jim Culliton, being associated with marketing, made it acceptable.

Mr Kerrigan felt it was his job to foster the growth and authority of the Institute in size and quality. His own background, including marketing with Córas Tráchtála and the engineering division of the IDA which saw the rapid build-up of the motor components industry, employing 9,000 people in Ireland, equipped him well to chart the way forward. He himself characterised the task as 'Building on a Rising Curve'.

NATIONAL MARKETING GROUP, 1988

Previous initiatives were then reinforced by recent announcement of the formation of a national marketing group, to be chaired by Mr Seamus Brennan TD, Minister of Trade and Marketing. Top executives included in the group were Messrs Howard Kilroy, Smurfit, David Dand, Gilbey's, Alan McDonnell, Superquinn, past chairman of MII, and Eugene O'Neill, Ryanair, to mention a few.

The focus would be on the export growth of indigenous products and services through vigorous, co-ordinated, professional marketing. A publication of new strategies for the food, forestry, fish and to a lesser extent, tourism sectors, was concentrated on.

IRISH EXPORTERS' FUTURE, FEBRUARY 1988

Dr John McGuire, deputy chairman of the Marketing Institute of Ireland and head of Price Waterhouse's Marketing Consultancy Services, addressed leading Cork businessmen in February 1988, and said that the export performance of the indigenous sector had been most impressive, given the relative youth of the Irish exporting industry. Export business prospects for Irish manufacturers were excellent for the 1990s.

In 1987, indigenous manufacturing accounted for £2.2bn. or 21 per cent of total exports of £10.6bn. Predominantly foreign-owned production units accounted for £5.6bn., while the balance of £2.8bn. was made up by exports of bulk and commodity items such as mineral ores. Considering only 54 per cent of Irish companies had only been exporting since 1980, the performance was most impressive.

Dr McGuire said that many Irish exporting companies were still very much at the learning stage. Lack of experience placed them at a significant disadvantage, compared with their main competitors. In a survey of 1,500 leading European business executives, carried out by the European Management Forum, Ireland was considered to be one of the weakest of 22 OECD countries surveyed. That was particularly in relation to its sales and marketing orientation, investment in market research and product quality.

Dr McGuire lauded the government action in raising the national profile of marketing in Ireland. The recent progressive government appointment of a Minister of Trade and Marketing, the first such position to be filled by any government in Europe, was especially highlighted.

Subsequent initiatives taken by the minister included the establishment of the National Marketing Group, fostering programme and trading houses' legislation.

STUDENTS' CASE STUDY, MARCH 1988

The annual marketing case study, (21st), was held at the Irish Management Institute, Dundrum, Dublin, on Saturday 16 March 1988.

The Students' Society committee for 1988 was: David Allen, Rebecca Burrell, Alison Cowzer, Niamh Duffy, Hugh Dunn, Maureen Ennis, Orna Flannery, Nicola Garrett, Phil Hanlon, Harold Holohan, Monica Hughes, Susan Kelly, Michelle La Grue, Pamela Lynch, Ann Marie McCarthy, Amanda McConnell, Paul Nugent, Mark O'Connor, Angela O'Donoghue, John O'Regan, Jane O'Reilly, Deirdre Sheeran and David Wallis.

NEW MARKETING GRADUATES COURSE, 1988

A course of lectures for graduates of the Marketing Institute was designed and conducted by the College of Marketing and Design, Dublin. Four aspects were selected for particular examination in the course:

1. Marketing Models.

2. Buyer Behaviour Analysis.

3. Marketing Research Practice

4. Advanced Statistical Analysis.

Award winners, on completion of the course, were:

• Mr Paul Russell: marketing research in Central Statistical Office

• Ms Pauline Leahy: senior bank official in Bank of Ireland

• Ms Veronica Lynch: marketing research assistant in Aer Rianta

• Mr John Ryan: (home from the USA, looking for a job in Ireland).

Presentations were made on 2 February 1988, at St Stephen's Green Club, Dublin.

REGULATORY ENVIRONMENT IN MARKETING, 1988

Mr John Lennon, director of education of MII, prefaced an A4, 87-page, acknowledgement regarding the 'Regulatory Environment in Marketing'. He said the Marketing Institute had, three years previously, undertaken a major review of their Foundation Certificate, Professional Diploma and graduateship programme. As a consequence many new developments were introduced.

Among the changes a new regulatory environment in marketing was introduced. The intention was that marketing students be exposed to the legal and regulatory environments which affect the marketing manager in his decision making.

The emphasis generally was to provide, present and future marketing executives with sufficient knowledge about legal difficulties so that they would know when to get further advice from professionals in the law.

IRISH BREAKFAST CEREALS, 1988

Irish people were the second highest consumers of breakfast cereals, per capita, in the world. The amount spent on cereals was more than £38m. a year. Irish firms took a market share of only 15 per cent but the potential was there for considerable growth, particularly in the high quality, health sector.

These were the conclusions of a report prepared by students from University College Dublin, which won them the Irish Goods Council, National Student Marketing award for 1987. Fifty-two projects had been submitted from 103 students in seven participating colleges.

They found that Ireland's cereal consumption came second only to the UK, in Europe. Kelloggs remained the dominant firm, with a market share of about 60 per cent and Weetabix was second at 14 per cent.

The research was carried out by Messrs F.J. Malone, P. Tobin, D.R. Walsh and Robert Healy, University College, Dublin. They found that the Irish breakfast cereals market was broken down into two main segments. The main one was the 'ready to eat' segment (e.g. all 'odd' cereals such as cornflakes, brans and mueslies), while the second was the hot cereal segment, mainly porridge.

The sugar content came into serious view as Kelloggs were the dominant manufacturer in the children's cereal market. Their biggest brand then was Kelloggs Rice Crispies, which accounted for 47 per cent of the children's segment and 12 per cent of the total 'ready to eat' market.

Irish sector of cereal market

In sharp contrast to the 'ready to eat' market, the 'hot cereal' segment (12 per cent of the total breakfast cereal market — £4.5m. in 1985–6) was dominated by Irish manufacturers, with Flahavans holding a 50 per cent and Odlums a 30 per cent share of the market.

The UCD project group decided that the only segment that offered a long-term opportunity for success, for an Irish brand manufacturer, was the 'health' or bran/muesli oats segment. Irish Cereal Products then had six bran/muesli type cereals on the supermarket shelves.

It was decided to market 'Irish health' cereals. The group analysed two companies in the 'ready to eat' breakfast cereals' market, namely Tipperary Cereals and Irish Cereal Products (ICP), the latter now owned by CPC Ireland Ltd. Both had gone into receivership and were sold, as going concerns, endeavouring to establish themselves in the market.

The UCD group decided to concentrate on ICP, whose brands were positioned in the health market. The marketing strategy was questioned and followed by a number of changes. A new strategy was then adopted, including reducing the range in ICP's products.

They concluded that a critical element for success was undoubtedly a well-planned and co-ordinated promotional campaign, geared towards attaining maximum product perception among consumers.

Research methodology

Questionnaires were designed to produce knowledge before the development of a new marketing plan.

Up to 200 respondents were surveyed in fifteen Dublin multiple stores, as over 80 per cent of bran cereals and 70 per cent of muesli cereals were sold through multiples. The findings were closely analysed in such areas as: Irish product, growth in health consciousness, promotions, quality, improved promotion and packaging.

The results showed that a high quality, premium product was the requirement of the Irish target market.

YOUNG MARKETING FORMED, FEBRUARY 1988

A new forum for discussion entitled 'Young Marketing' was established for the younger members of the Institute such as final year students, recent graduates and marketing professionals.

The first meeting of Young Marketing was held at the St Stephen's Green Club, Dublin on Wednesday 10 February 1988 at 7.45 a.m. It was a breakfast meeting and was booked out.

The guest speaker was Mr Eugene O'Neill, chief executive of Ryanair, and it proved to be a very successful, informative meeting. It was sponsored by Lifetime Assurance Ltd, a subsidiary of the Bank of Ireland.

The members of the Young Marketing committee were: Ruairí Ó Floinn, Marc Thornton, Nicola Garrett, David Allan, John Diskin, Tom Kelly, Eamonn Maguire and Garry Manning.

THE SEAN F. LEMASS AWARD, 1988

In 1988 the MII decided that, for the next few years, the focus of the Sean F. Lemass award should be 1992 (the creation of the Single European Market).

In the meantime a company, showing excellence in planning and preparation for 1992, ITEC Security Products Ltd, became the worthy recipients of the Sean F. Lemass award for 1988.

IRISH PERMANENT BUILDING SOCIETY, FEBRUARY 1988

The managing director of Irish Permanent Building Society, (IPBS), Dr Edmund Farrell, addressing the MII Tuesday Club luncheon in the Berkeley Court hotel on 1 March 1988, said he believed the society would soon be able to provide a comprehensive range of financial services, which would, at least, rival those offered by the commercial banks.

Business & Finance interviewed Dr Farrell who highlighted the society's market-led approach. He stated that the customer would dictate in the final analysis what they wanted in the way of extra services. At the time the IPBS was engaged in an exercise to find out exactly what that was. Further it had technology, marketing and training expertise, second to none, and was ready for the new broader financial services marketplace. They were willing to make marketing happen and had a blueprint on which to compete — something they had been pleading for with successive governments over the previous four years.

STRATEGIC MARKETING, MARCH 1988

An intensive three-day strategic marketing programme was organised by the Marketing Institute, Córas Tráchtála and Price Waterhouse from 11–13 April 1988.

Two of the world's foremost authorities, Mr George Day, Professor of Marketing at the University of Toronto and Mr Liam Fahey, Associate Professor of Management Policy, School of Management, Boston University, presented the programme. They offered a unique blend of marketing theory and the practical experience of implementation with international blue-chip companies. Some of the concerns related to the following:

- Does your management team allocate enough resources to thinking about the future?

- What products or services will your organisation be providing in the 1990s?

- Do you know how you will score advantage over your competitors?

- What markets or segments of markets will provide your organisation with the best business opportunities in coming years?

- Is your management team aware of the established marketing frameworks and methodologies to compete in the international environment?

Remarks of some previous participants of the programme included the following:

Mr Tony Brophy, marketing manager of Showerings (Irl) Ltd stated that:

> The strategy formulation process learnt during the programme played an important role in the development of our new product 'Ritz'. It has been an outstanding marketing success and realised retail sales of £7m. in Ireland alone, in its first year'.

Mr Patrick Duffy, managing director of Moy Insulation Ltd declared:

As a chief executive, I found this programme to be particularly helpful in that it focused my mind on competitive advantage. It has helped our team to understand where we have competitive advantage and how to foster it.

Mr Chris Lowe, chief executive of Telecom Éireann Information Systems said that:

As telecommunications is such a rapidly changing business, it is of critical importance that Telecom Éireann has a strong market focus. This programme was extremely useful in providing me with the framework to monitor changes in the marketing environment, customer needs and competitor activity.

AGRESSIVE MARKETING NEEDED FOR TOURISM, MAY 1988

It was considered that tourism was the quickest area to be most cost effective way of finding and using derived prosperity in Ireland. However, returns showed, in 1988, that only 1 per cent of British tourists travelled to Ireland and there had been a considerable decline in our share of other major markets.

Action was vital as tourism would generate much needed foreign exchange and provide employment in many areas where otherwise there would be little activity. It would also provide exchequer return through taxation.

At that time the Taoiseach, Mr Charles Haughey TD, selected tourism as a priority (at one time it had been the second largest industry) and decided to change the department name to 'Tourism and Transport'. He appointed Mr John Wilson TD, a senior politician, to be the minister. A tourism task force was set up. Fares to Britain were assessed and reduced, with reductions for fares to Germany and France. This was significant as Germany then had the world's largest tourism market, even greater than the United States. The past had been against travellers coming from Australia and Japan, as Ireland was the one country not having an inclusive airfare. New arrangements were made, such as the introduction of flights from Australia to Dublin and then on to France, at the one fare. It was decided to sell Ireland's healthy, clean, non-polluted 'Isle' to tourists, without forgetting the very large 'family' market.

BORD FÁILTE, MAY 1988

Described as a most effective strategist, Mr Martin Dully (late of considerable success in Aer Rianta) took over as the executive chairman of Bord Fáilte, having been appointed in May 1988. The government directive then was to concentrate on marketing.

TOURISM TASK FORCE, MAY 1988

The chairman of Ryan Hotels, immediate past-president of the Irish Hotels' Federation and member of the tourism task force, Mr Conor McCarthy, was happy to be involved in reversing ailing tourism. His aim was to double the intake of genuine tourists (apart from visiting business people and family relatives). Previously most money spent in the UK was used on joint advertising with carriers so change meant advertising to sell seats on planes and boats. A 'Write and Invite' campaign was successfully introduced.

Mr McCarthy believed that Irish tourism interested parties were willing and able to provide the ideas and capital required for public initiatives.

MARKETING AND ENTREPRENEURS, MAY 1988

A visiting Professor at NIHE Limerick, Professor W.F. Kissner, had a special interest in the area of entrepreneurship and its education. He witnessed the economic 'revolution' in the United States at the entry of what President Regan said was the 'age of the entrepreneur'. Employment in America had increased by 17 million between 1976 and 1984. Industries created by small businesses had a growth of almost eight times that of those in large businesses during 1986.

With Ireland's greatest natural resource being her people, they created cultural areas in literature, music and politics. Yet, what was missing was a lack of direction to marketing in the business mix to spell success while competing in open markets. Further the need to achieve success demanded a development by strong orientation to marketing.

The appointment of the Minister for Trade and Marketing, Mr Seamus Brennan TD, had created a much needed impetus to state policy. Marketing methods and ideas that maximise limited resources, while combining common effort and skill, were the kind of marketing effort necessary. The need for promotional skills could not be overstated.

Ireland itself needed to be marketed.

Worldwide image that reflected Ireland's industrious, educated, workforce and technological ability, would pay a handsome return if sold by creating it at home and certainly abroad.

EDUCATION POST FOR MARKETING INSTITUTE, JULY 1988

A full-page advertisement appeared in *Professional Marketing*, July/August 1988, issue no.10, for a director of education of the Marketing Institute of Ireland. Replies were to be sent in confidence, to Price Waterhouse, Executive Selection Consultants, Dublin 2.

With the development of the Marketing Institute and the appointment of Mr John Kerrigan as chief executive, the council had decided to appoint a full time director of education.

OVERSEAS MII CONSULTANCY, JULY 1988

The Marketing Institute was invited to participate in the development of marketing in the Persian Gulf at the request of the Gulf Marketing Association. This was a further indication of status growth.

SINGLE EUROPEAN MARKET (FOR 1992)

The Internal Market Council (IMC), comprised of twelve men who met in Brussels once a month to discuss the creation of the Single European Market. At that time (July 1988) they had agreed just 50 per cent of the 200 directives to be finalised for the end of 1992.

Ireland's representative on the IMC was the Minister for Trade and Marketing, Mr Seamus Brennan TD. Their European campaign came under the Department of An Taoiseach, with his personal direction.

The first stage of the campaign was designed to create awareness. The next stage was to approach individual companies and help them adjust to Single Market conditions. The cost of advertising and public relations were estimated to be around £200,000.

Considering Ireland was a market of only 3.5 million people, directed at one of 320 million, it had a wonderful opportunity for business to aim at. Free availability to the largest and richest market in the world was the target. In the United States, in recent years, small business firms had performed better than their larger competitors and it was expected that Ireland could do the same.

IMC was set up by the twelve governments in the EC to hasten progress. For example, the mutual recognition of degrees had been achieved on a whole range of professional qualifications in the previous two-year period. What became known as 'The New Approach' accepted the individual professional's competence throughout the EC.

It also agreed on the setting up of a Central European Trademark Office while, to have one application acceptable, there would be reduced costs and greater efficiency.

The Marketing Institute was ideally placed to ensure that Irish companies geared up to take the advantage of the Single Market. MII, particularly, and other organisations such as the Confederation of Irish Industries (CII) and the trade unions, were urged to get involved and achieve the aims.

LIFTING EXCHANGE CONTROLS

The Irish Government was committed to the lifting of exchange controls by the end of 1992. A Financial Services Centre was established. New markets became available, as all government and local authority contracts throughout Europe were open to Irish tendering.

The approach to 1992 meant identifying the establishment of joint ventures which would involve technology transfers and investment in manufacturing, in for example, either or both countries. Market penetration was the key word for European distribution.

Meanwhile, improved distribution methods and requirements for more economic transport were being fully investigated. CTT focused its comprehensive information service on European markets, being linked directly to Commission databases in Brussels and Luxembourg.

ENTERPRISE DEVELOPMENT, 1988

The course development committee, headed by Mr Brendan Wafer FMII, produced a worthy volume, (102 pp.), which was entitled *Notes on Enterprise Development*. In particular, the first-year marketing syllabus was expanded to include a section on enterprise development. It introduced an understanding of the concepts and workings of entrepreneurship and enterprise development. It helped to set up a new business enterprise, for students interested in doing so

The Institute appreciated contributions to the notes provided by Mr Joseph Molony, BA, ACIS, ACMA, ASCA, Mr Patrick Scully, Grad.MII, MBA and Prof. Joyce O'Connor. The Institute was also most grateful for contributions and case history material from:

- Prof. Barra O'Cinneide, 'The Irish House', (based on material in his book: *The Case for Irish Enterprise*)

- Mr Geoff Reid, Ballygowan Spring Water Ltd

- Mr Peter Butler, Oglesby & Butler Ltd

- Mr John Burns, Birex Pharmaceuticals Ltd

- Ms Cairin O'Connor, Traditional Cheese Co.

- Mr Dick Keane, Irish Oak Carvings Ltd.

This was the first in a series of notes and books designed to assist Institute students. There were two section headings:

1. Introduction to enterprise development and sources of capital.

2.   Finding the right idea and developing a business plan for the new enterprise.

Regarding 'idea generation', the first step in the establishment of a new business enterprise, I recall an apt sum-up by a fellow lecturer and friend of mine, Mr Tom Prior: 'You say that you have identified a gap in the market, but have you checked if there is a market in the gap?'

AER RIANTA AND AEROFLOT, OCTOBER 1988

The editor of *Professional Marketing*, Mr Gerry Lawlor, told the remarkable story of the Aerofirst joint venture company between Aer Rianta and Aeroflot, the Soviet airline. The prediction was that they would be awarded, despite intense competition, the contract to build and operate Leningrad airport's first duty free shop.

Its operational success after only five months was a compliment to the speed with which the Irish got the show on the road. Some 40 Irish companies benefited from extra sales and exposed their wares to a potential five million international travellers.

DERRY, GALWAY AND MASSACHUSETTS, 1988

A tri-partite partnership, economic, social and cultural exchanges, took place between three cities. They were via Magee College, Derry, University College, Galway and the University of Massachusetts. They got together with the aim of developing a strategy to link the cities.

With the arrival in Derry in April 1987 of Mr Padraig O'Malley, McCormack Institute of Public Affairs, University of Massachusetts, work began in earnest. A comprehensive resource analysis of the Derry region was made. A four-pronged strategy to promote the link resulted in agreement:

• to use the Boston, Galway, Derry link to stimulate enterprise and increase exports

• to attract inward investments in real estate

• to attract inward investment in manufacturing

• to attract tourists.

Team-building brought about the formation of three community-based, non-profit making companies: Boston Ireland Ventures (BIV), Galway Boston Ventures (GBV) and Derry Boston Ventures (DBV), all dedicated to the achievement of economic, social and cultural integration of their cities.

For example, Derry Boston Ventures brought a handpicked team of singers and dancers who performed on a specially constructed stage in Boston's Quincy Market. That was what mainly brought Bostonians to the trade festival. Other ways of promoting exports were also under consideration.

FELLOWSHIP AWARDS

Fellowship awards were conferred during 1988 on the following:

- Dr Tom Hardiman, immediate past-president of MII

- Mr Seamus Martin, director of Concept Marketing & Advertising

- Mr John Meagher, executive deputy chairman of Independent Newspapers

- Mr Brendan V. Wafer, Eolas.

MII APPOINTMENTS FOR 1989

The president, Mr John Culliton was re-elected for 1989 and Dr John F. McGuire, managing director of Rehab Lotteries, was appointed chairman of the Institute.

Having invited all the then living past-chairmen, 28 in all, of the Marketing Institute, to contribute the highlights of their term of office, I received a few replies.

In particular, Dr John McGuire kindly acceded fully to my invitation and so I have pleasure to recall his actual contribution:

> I was most fortunate to be chairman of the Marketing Institute at a time when the Institute was going through a period of change. I was equally fortune to follow in the immediate heels of two great previous chairmen — Alan McDonnell and David Manley.
>
> Alan was the last of the 'full-time' chairmen when the Institute almost took up more time than the day job. I will always be indebted to Alan for encouraging me to take a more active role in the Institute and I have greatly enjoyed my various involvements over the past ten years.
>
> It was during Alan's period as chairman that the decision to appoint a full-time chief executive was made. That was a landmark initiative in the history of the Institute and I very well remember the meeting in the Dalkey Island hotel where the decision was made.
>
> For an accountant, David Manley was a remarkably visionary creature. With the very professional assistance of Noel Shaw, he took the Institute Council through a corporate planning process which challenged every aspect of the Institute's activities and set down a strategy which

was to serve, and did, the development of the Institute over the following three years. It is a great testament to that process that the Institute" mission statement developed at that time still remains intact today — ten years later.

David Manley was also very creative and it was his concept that the Institute should develop new 'products' which would cater for the needs of the Institute's different types of members. Out of that creativity, products such as the Young Marketing Breakfast meetings and Top Marketing Forum were born and continue to be very successful today.

I was the first chairman to have the benefit of a full-time chief executive for a full year and I greatly value the relationship which I had with John Kerrigan who made an enormous contribution to the development of the Institute. He was very ably assisted by a great team of staff who were a great support to me and worked very hard during 1989. Of these, I am glad to see my special buddies Sylvia, Regina, Suzanne and Carol Ann continuing to work in the Institute.

Good luck was on my side when the marketing house was opened during my year as chairman — another landmark development but one which had absolutely nothing to do with me. All credit has to go to Bill Ambrose and the members of the marketing house committee who worked so hard, for so many years, to deliver a home for marketing.

The 'hot' subject in 1989 was 1992. Now almost forgotten, there was huge scaremongering that Irish industry would not be prepared for the completion of the European internal market. The Institute played its role in conducting research to establish the extent to which Irish managers were preparing themselves and interpreted the results to give guidance to industry and government.

The Institute membership, in the late 1980s, experienced great growth and had reached 2000 by 1989. There were 2500 students availing of the Institute's educational programmes. They were the days when there was not the same competition to provide marketing learning as exists today. Speaking of education, I would like to acknowledge the great contribution which was made by John Lennon, now sadly deceased, to the development of the Institute's services in this area.

On reflecting on my own contribution to the Institute, I always held a strong view that more needed to be done to develop Institute activities in the Regions. In the 1980s, the Institute was very Leinster-focused and it is very heartening to see all the positive developments which have taken place to strengthen the Institute's position in the regions in recent years.

On the social front, the Marketing Institute Golfing Society, (MIGS), was born in 1989. Again, I cannot claim any credit for this initiative — it was the idea of my great friend Frank Cusack who has been so successful in managing and developing MIGS over the past years. I know that MIGS is the best loved service of the Institute with many of the members and for some, it is the only reason they are members!

One of the great hidden values of Institute membership are the friendships, both social and professional, which are formed as a result of one's involvement. For me, it has resulted in introductions to hundreds of friends who I would otherwise never have got to know.

On this note, I can record one highlight which I can claim as a personal achievement and which is unique to myself. I met my wife, Cathy Carroll, through the Institute. She was chairperson of the social committee in 1989 and was later elected to the council and served as a vice-chairman.

Now, let nobody say that the Institute does not fully satisfy the needs of its members.

REGIONAL MII APPOINTMENTS, 1989

The elected chairmen of the Marketing Institute regions for 1989 were:

- Cork: Mr Eddie Pierce, regional sales manager of Golden Pages

- South-East: Ms Margaret Donoghue, manager of Co-ops of Waterford Resource Centre

- Galway: Mr John Carroll, managing director of Comfiche Teo

- Mid-West: Mr Tony Treacy, sales manager of Texas Instruments.

In his opening address to members and students at the AGM, Mr John McGuire, chairman of the Institute, said that the council had approved the allocation of sufficient funds to ensure special emphasis on improving services to the branch areas.

PDM SPECIAL COURSES, FEBRUARY 1989

A two-day course, a PDM (Professional Development in Marketing) exclusive presented in association with the European Training specialists, Time Manager International, took place on 16 and 17 February 1989 at the Royal Marine hotel, Dún Laoghaire, Co. Dublin. The MII formed an association with Time Manager to provide the course: 'Time Management for Marketing and Sales Executives'. Over one million people in 30 countries used the internationally famous course, 'Time Manager System'.

MII WORKSHOP, FEBRUARY 1989

Together with the Irish Management Institute, MII designed a special two-day workshop to give a comprehensive overview of the steps necessary in approaching the identification, evaluation and development of exporting opportunities.

The venue was the National Management Centre, Sandyford Road in Dublin. It was to be held on 23 and 24 February 1989 from 9 a.m. to 6.30 p.m. each day. A very full programme of events included:

· **Young Marketing Breakfast**:
Mr Noel J. Toolan, head of Marketing Development, Bailey's worldwide, (sales of 3 million cases p.a.)
Venue: Stephen's Green Club, Dublin

· **Marketing the Irish Film and Television Industry**:
Mr Liam Miller, RTÉ,
Mr Russ Russell, Film Makers-Ireland
Mr John Kelleher, Strongbow Film and Television Co.
Mr Tom Kelly, EGM Television
Mr Colum Kenny, lecturer in Communications, NIHE
Ms Tish Barry, Rich Productions
Venue: Martello Room, Jury's, Dublin.

In the Cork region a case study was set by Professor Barra O'Cinneide and this was held in Fitzpatrick's Silversprings hotel, Tivoli, Cork.

SPECIAL BROCHURE, JUNE 1989

Marketing house, purpose built with the future in mind. The age of marketing has arrived. Business recognises the vital role of this most important management function, so too has government with the creation of the Office of Trade and Marketing. With the value of hindsight it seems strange that was not always so. The magnificent new headquarters — Marketing House — mirrors an entirely new status for the Institute.

Such were the opening words in the special *Business & Finance* brochure of June 1989, describing the newly built home of the Marketing Institute.

Purpose built, the marketing house, located at the South County Business Park, Leopardstown, in the south Dublin suburbs, was built to provide a highly functional and prestigious new home for the Marketing Institute.

Mr Bill Ambrose, chairman of the marketing house committee, said that when they started out fundraising, three years previously, there was a genuine core of opinion among some members and businesses that the purchase of a building by the Institute was an indulgence — an ego-trip. They felt that any resources commanded should be used to build better marketing skills and better services for members; not to buy comfortable chairs for 'bureaucratic backsides'.

However, the Institute could not afford to stand still. What with membership doubling over three years, 900 by early 1986, and the graduateship programme student numbers also doubling, to about 1,400 at the same time, it made sense to move on.

Good vision was shown in that further ground space was provided for in the lease, for future expansion. Meanwhile, one of the most important features of marketing house was the in-built conference and seminar facilities. Apart from running their own PDM courses and other meetings and events in-house, rental hire facilities were made available to members, including audio-visual equipment, such as slide and overhead projectors.

The membership of the Institute then was 1,700 and expected to reach 2,000 by 1990.

VISIT OF THE CHARTERED INSTITUTE OF MARKETING, 1989

Representatives of council of the Chartered Institute of Marketing (CIM) paid an official visit to marketing house. The chairman of the Northern Ireland branch of CIM, Mr John Edmund, and three of his council members were guests of the Marketing Institute at the February luncheon.

An official presentation was made to the Marketing Institute of a superb plaque to commemorate the opening of marketing house the previous September. Areas where the two bodies could co-operate were declared as being of mutual benefit to members. Positive and encouraging discussions took place in that area.

VIDEO LAUNCH, 1989

The Minister for Trade and Marketing, Mr Seamus Brennan TD launched the Institute's new video on marketing careers.

The video had three distinct tasks:

1. To introduce and explain the concept of marketing.

2. To describe various career opportunities in the field of marketing.

3. To describe and promote the educational programmes offered by the Institute.

It was declared as being ideally suitable for second-level students, their parents and guidance counsellors. It was available from the Marketing Institute at a price of £9.75 to MII members and students, and £11.75 to non-members. This included postage.

MARKETING AER LINGUS, 1989

Mr Cathal Mullen, chief executive of Aer Lingus, spoke about the role of marketing in the business success of Aer Lingus. He said it had been a crucial factor and reflected on the fact that over 1,000 new staff had joined the airline in the previous two years. The current success of 80 per cent growth in total traffic over the three previous years had been achieved through a strategic marketing campaign. Aer Lingus now had profits of £40m.

Mr Mullen went on to say that a cost efficiency programme had enabled the reduction of fares and a major communications campaign made staff aware of changes in the marketplace. A strategic marketing review focussed, in the first instance, on the product being offered to customers. Pricing, distribution (automated reservations etc.), promotion and their cargo business were under continuing analysis.

Mr Mullen concluded his speech by saying that winning the *The Irish Times*/PA Management award in1989 had been extremely gratifying to Aer Lingus. Furthermore, they also received encouragement in an endorsement of their management policies in the Joint Oireachtas Committee report on state-sponsored bodies.

WILTON RESEARCH AND MARKETING SURVEY OF MII, 1989

From a sample of 502 members, graduates and lapsed members of the Marketing Institute throughout Ireland, a comprehensive survey by Wilton Research and Marketing Ltd, Dublin, showed that:

* 88 per cent believed the Institute was moving in the right direction and 83 per cent were satisfied with the organisation's overall performance

* on the adverse side, while members were satisfied overall in the regions, they felt that perhaps the Institute was too Dublin orientated

* the main reasons for joining the Institute were career advancement and education.

GROWTH IN STUDENT NUMBERS,1989

Over 2,200 students sat the summer marketing examinations which took place in Dublin, Cork, Waterford, Dundalk, Galway, Carlow and Limerick. It was the largest number ever to sit the examinations and indicative of the growth in student numbers.

In Dublin the examinations were held at the Royal Dublin Society (RDS), Ballsbridge, who were able to provide sufficient space for the large number partaking.

MARKETING CAREER SERVICE, 1989

An agreement was made between the Marketing Institute and MSL International, on the provision of a new career service, called 'Marketing Careers', for members and students. It provided a service for companies seeking marketing personnel and member/students looking for career development opportunities and jobs.

PRESIDENT'S NIGHT, MAY 1989

The 27th MII President's Night was held on 17 May 1989. It was a glittering success according to the 350 members and guests who gathered to honour the president of the Institute, Mr Jim Culliton FMII.

The event took place in the magnificent surroundings of the Royal Hospital, Kilmainham, and the attendance list was considered to be like a 'Who's Who' of Irish business. The guest speaker was Mr Michael Bishop CBE, chairman and managing director of British Midland Airways, who received a presentation from the president of MII.

The proceeds of the night, including that of some 30 member companies (£10,000), were used to set up a scholarship fund to assist students, who otherwise could not do so, to study for the graduateship of the Institute.

FELLOWSHIP AWARDS, 1989

Fellowship awards were conferred on six members on President's Night. These were:

• Mr Frank Falvey: managing director of Autodata Ltd, Galway

• Mr John F. Fitzpatrick: director of the National Lottery

• Mr Desmond J. Gilroy: sales and marketing director of Berger Paints

• Mr Peter J.P. Gleeson: chairman and chief executive officer of Castle Hosiery Ltd

• Mr Alan McDonnell: chairman of the Marketing Institute, Silver Jubilee year of 1987

- Mr James Wrynn: senior lecturer in Business Policy, College of Marketing & Design

- Mr Patrick J. Wright: managing director of Smurfit Ireland, (in absentia, due business commitments).

MII POSITION ADVERTISED, JUNE 1989

Being one of the largest professional representative bodies in Ireland, with more than 1600 members and 2500 students, applications for the position of marketing executive of the Institute were invited for submission to Mr John Kerrigan, chief executive of MII.

The position required an executive who would make a significant contribution to the Institute's further development and have the ability to understand the needs of members and respond with strategic initiatives.

EC BRIEF, 1989

The Ernst & Young bi-monthly published an EC brief. In their June 1990 issue they detailed a system, which the EC agreed to adopt, to be applied to intra-community trade for a four-year period starting in January 1993. The next step should be the adoption, from January 1997, of the 'country of origin' system (i.e. the VAT is paid in the exporting country at that country's rate).

PROGRESS TOWARDS INTERNAL ENERGY MARKET, 1989

Cross-border trade in electricity and energy price comparison for industrial consumers was now possible, following agreement on two directives by the EC's Council of Energy Ministers in Brussels.

Two other draft measures — on opening up the market for gas and on the notification of energy investments of the EC interest to the EC Commission — met with strong opposition and looked likely to remain on the waiting list for adoption in order to create a single market in energy. A five-year plan, the 'Thermie' programme was agreed for the promotion of energy techniques.

All companies that make, move, or sell products in the EC would be affected by new rules on free movement of goods. EC regulations so affected would relate to licences, tariffs, drivers' hours, technical standards, tax and border procedures.

MARKETING HOUSE OPENS FOR BUSINESS, SEPTEMBER 1989

The official opening of the marketing house by the Minister of State for Trade and Marketing, Mr Terry Leyden TD, took place on 9 September 1989.

A garden party was organised to 'banish those post-holiday blues!'. Council member, Ms Cathy Carroll chaired the party planning committee. Over 500 members and guests attended which was then the largest social function hosted by the Institute. Included were the Northern Ireland chairman of The Chartered Institute of Marketing, Mr John Edmund, Mr Vivian Murray, Irish Goods Council, Mr Peter Sweeney, An Post, and Mr Maurice O'Grady, Irish Management Institute, to name just a few.

IRISHMAN CHAIRS WORLD FEDERATION OF ADVERTISERS, 1989

Mr Fred Hayden MMII, chief executive of the Association of Advertisers in Ireland, (AAI), was elected chairman, for the year 1989, of The Directors' Forum (TDF), World Federation of Advertisers, (founded in 1953).

Their network then was made up of 33 national associations of advertisers, plus seventeen corresponding members, covering a population of 1.5 billion people worldwide.

The 1989 WFA 37th general assembly was held in the Western Hotel, in the centre of the American Capital, Washington D.C. In summarising the successful growth of the TDF, Mr Fred Hayden said that although the members of the group spoke many different languages, they had one language in common — advertising!

Also, in building-up strong active member associations it was fundamental to the well-being of the WFA.

The Directors' Forum had a vital role to play in achieving this also. It was agreed that in the rapidly changing world situation, with its consequent impact on national economies, there was a need to adopt a strategy for the future in marketing and advertising.

ELITE MARKETING AWARDS, 1989

The establishment of the Dan Air Elite Marketing awards, designed to promote marketing excellence and a greater public awareness of the importance of marketing, were announced by the organisers, the Marketing Institute and Dan Air. Three awards were created:

- the Elite Marketing Director of the Year

- the Elite Marketing Executive Woman of the Year

- the Elite Marketing Man of the Year.

The prize for each award was:

- £1,000 of Dan Air tickets for the award winner

- £1,000 of Dan Air tickets for the winner's organisation

- A year's supply of specially printed 'Award' business cards.

In addition, three regional award winners in each of the five regions would receive a return Dublin/London or Cork/London air ticket and special 'Award' business cards for one year.

Following nominations the following were the 1989 recipients:

- Elite Marketing Director of the Year: Mr Richard Hoare, Lifetime Assurance Ltd

- Elite Marketing Executive of the Year: Mr Tom Browne, Allied Irish Banks Group, Marketing Department

- Elite Marketing Executive of the Year: Ms Eileen Goold, Des Wallace Travel Ltd

- Special Merit Award: Ms Ann Burns, Roadstone Dublin Ltd.

The presentations were made at a luncheon in association with Dan-Air in Jury's Dublin on Friday 6 October 1989.

IRISH MARKETING REVIEW, 1989

It was agreed that *Irish Marketing Review*, an international journal of research and practice containing thought-provoking articles, was of benefit to all marketing professionals. Therefore it was agreed to mail a copy of the journal, free of charge, to all paid-up MII members. Consequently volume 4, nos 1 and 2 were distributed in 1989. The journal was edited by Mr Aidan O'Driscoll of the College of Marketing and Design, Dublin Institute of Technology.

INTRODUCTION TO MARKETING RESEARCH, 1989

In recognition of the fact that many small and medium-sized firms lacked the expertise necessary to gather useful information, the Marketing Institute produced a new course:

'Introduction to Marketing Research'. This was led by Mr John Lennon, director of education at MII. He had, *inter alia*, been lecturing in marketing research for seventeen years and was doing so at the time in Dublin City University.

The intensive one-day seminar included lectures and practical exercises.

It showed participants methods of interpreting market research and how to avoid pitfalls

MII APPOINTMENTS, 1990

Mr David Kennedy was elected president of the Marketing Institute of Ireland for1990. He was educated at Terenure College, UCD and the Case Institute of Technology, Ohio, US. He joined Aer Lingus in 1962 and was chief executive from 1974 to 1988. He was, at the time of his election, deputy governor of the Bank of Ireland and also held many other distinguished posts. The vice-presidents elected were Messrs Bill Fraser and Alastair McGuckian and the chairman of the Institute for 1990 was Mr Richard C. Strahan.

MARKETING AT SECOND LEVEL, 1990

Mr David Kennedy, president of MII said that, bearing in mind the importance of business in our society and the dominant function of marketing in business, any review of subjects to be taught must include marketing.

'Entrepreneurship was not a suitable subject for Irish teenagers'. That was the conclusion one was likely to reach when reading the Department of Education publication: *Rules and Programme for Secondary Schools 1987/ 88 to 1989/90.*

Although four business subjects were listed for the Leaving Certificate (Accounting, Business Organisation, Economics and Economic History), nowhere in the subject descriptions or syllabus for them would be found the word 'entrepreneur'.

In 25 pages the word 'enterprise' appeared twice, but only as a description of a 'business enterprise', not as an attribute of individuals. However, more and more students were interested in business subjects at third level and were choosing business degrees at university.

Likewise in the case of MII students, shown by the number increase of 600 per cent since the early 80s, now 3,000 studying at 26 colleges throughout Ireland for the graduateship programme.

A switch in emphasis had been made by government bodies, e.g. IDA, CTT, Irish Goods Council and Shannon Development, to management development and capability in marketing in Irish businesses. CTT operated a new targeted marketing consultancy.

JUNIOR CERTIFICATE, 1992

A new Junior Certificate would replace the Intermediate Certificate from 1992.

The Business Studies syllabus produced, by giving separate sections to living and enterprise, showed a much greater awareness of the need to encourage an enterprise culture from an early age. Students, it was felt, must be made aware of the marketing dimension and its impact on all aspects of business.

CHAIRMAN OF MII, 1990

Mr Richard Strahan, was elected chairman of the Marketing Institute of Ireland for 1990. He was Managing Director of Bell Advertising Ltd and a board member of Guaranteed Irish Ltd. Under his management, Bell Advertising had established itself as a top ten advertising agency, serving international and national advertising clients.

Mr David Kennedy, president of MII, said it was an exciting time to be involved in the marketing profession. The changes in Eastern Europe, in the previous twelve months, had launched those countries firmly in the direction of market orientated economies.

The abolition of trade barriers in Europe, with the advent of the Single European Market, meant that much of the commercial world was becoming almost 'borderless' with profound marketing implications. In Ireland companies were becoming more international and the opportunities and threats, posed by 1992, were high on most corporate agendas. The concept of being 'market driven' had not reached all facets of Irish society. There was still much work to be done.

Mr Richard C. Strahan, chairman of MII, stated that in the beginning of his term, from November 1989, he had set four target areas as priorities for 1990:

1. Better communications with students.

2. Development of the regions.

3. The installation of a new computer.

4. Improvement in members' services.

Marketing would be vital for every business and also for Ireland as the SEM was approached, because without marketing there was no business. It was, he stressed, the driving force for every country.

CORPORATE PLAN, 1990

The corporate plan of the Marketing Institute included the widely recognised high standard of the graduateship programme for entry to most Master degree programmes. It provided a definite marketing qualification. The programme, then almost complete, involved the:

- capital investment of £5m.

- building of a marketing house

- appointment of a chief executive and director of education together with the strengthening of staff resources

- installation of a multi-user computer system

- expansion of the regional Institute network

- near-doubling of membership

- 70 per cent increase in student numbers

- radical overhaul and expansion of services.

TOP MARKETING FORUM, 1990

The establishment of a top marketing forum during 1990, sponsored by KPMG, Stokes Kennedy Crowley, was a quality event for senior business figures. Speakers during 1990 included:

- Mr Desmond O'Malley TD: Minister for Industry & Commerce

- Mr William Attley: joint general president of SIPTU

- Mr Tom Garvey: director of the PHARE, programme of the European Commission

- Mr Patrick Delaney: assistant chief executive of Córas Tráchtála.

FIRST AGM OF MII NORTH-EAST REGION, SEPTEMBER 1990

The North-East region of the Marketing Institute held their first AGM in the Nuremore hotel, Carrickmacross, Co. Monaghan on Thursday 27 September 1990.

Mr Michael Harbourne was re-elected chairman of the region, retaining his seat on the National Council. He stated that he was very pleased that the branch had greatly improved services for members, in addition to increasing awareness and benefits of good marketing practices. Membership had more than doubled since the start of the year.

NORTH-EAST SEMINAR, OCTOBER 1990

The MII North-East region held a 'Marketing in Action' seminar at the Sligo Park hotel on Wednesday 10 October 1990. The guest speaker was Mr R. Lynn Temple, managing director of Magee of Donegal. He presented the Magee story — an insight into international fashion branding.

Magee of Donegal, 1990

Magee of Donegal is one of the north-west regions most successful and long established industries. Magee began in 1886 as a small retail draper, on the site of the present day retail outlet in Donegal town. It is now a landmark and the name Magee is synonymous with Irish tweed and high fashion.

Prior to the 1950s, a Donegal tweed was a utilitarian fabric, course, durable and tough, used primarily for men's jacketing and overcoats to keep out the damp and keep in the heat. In the 1950s Donegal tweed was sold as a fashion fabric and labelled as hand-woven Donegal tweed to assist selling efforts on an international basis.

Mr Howard Temple spoke of how the Magee name developed rapidly in Britain, with conscious effort and considerable investment being made in projecting the image of a twisted worsted informal suit. It was hugely successful in the late 1950s and 60s and a clothing manufacturing plant was started in Donegal in 1966, aimed mainly at the Irish market.

Mr Temple gave a 'hit list' of the main factors in the development of Magee as a branded product and described how Magee made tremendous efforts to fully understand their market segment. He stressed that Magee strive to ensure that the quality of service from the company to their customers is excellent.

1992 BOOKLET LAUNCH, 1990

The Marketing Institute, in association with Craig Gardner, Price Waterhouse, published the second guide to '1992'. The booklet was launched at a press conference in the offices of the European Commission. Those present included Messrs Terry Stewart, director of the European Commission Office, Albert Reynolds TD, Minister for Finance, William McCann, managing partner of Craig Gardner Price Waterhouse and Richard Strahan, chairman of the Marketing Institute.

NATIONAL MARKETING CONFERENCE, OCTOBER 1990

The Royal Marine hotel, Dún Laoghaire, Co. Dublin, was the venue for the annual National Marketing Conference on 19 October 1990. Its theme was: 'Customer Care — Essential for Growth'. It was held in association with *Business & Finance* magazine.

Over 350 delegates attended.

The brochure for the conference emphasised that it would offer a unique insight into customer care in a wide range of business sectors. At its simplest marketing was about understanding customers and their needs, then fulfilling those needs efficiently.

It was argued that one preferred to exercise their marketing skills in the more glamorous disciplines of the profession. Ireland's natural culture militated against those very elements that went to make up modern customer care.

The theme was followed up by a customer care workshop, run through the PDM programme. The workshop was totally booked out.

A leading group of experienced speakers who understood the true value of getting customer care right, took part in the conference. It was felt that customer care was the philosophy that permeated any company in its relationships with customers, end-consumers, suppliers, management, employees and, not least, the environment.

It was an organised way of turning a customer-friendly philosophy into a system that ensured pious hope and became actual performance that differentiated one's company, its products and services, from those of competitors. The speakers and subjects are outlined below.

Morning session:

- Mr Desmond O'Malley TD, Minister for Industry & Commerce: 'The Government's Role in Attitude Change'

- Mr Gerard O'Neill, managing director of the Henley Centre Ireland: 'Global Trends in Customers' Profiles and Preferences'

- Professor David Kennedy, Professor of Strategic Marketing UCD: 'How Irish Attitudes Must Change'

- Mr Derek Prentice, assistant director of the Consumer's Association UK: 'The Customer's Perspective'

- Mr Robin Addis, managing director of Lansdowne Market Research: 'Get to Know Your Customers'.

Afternoon session:

- Mr Feargal Quinn, managing director of Superquinn: 'Case Study – Retailing'

- Mr Reggie McHugh, marketing director of Premier Dairies: 'Case Study — Business to Business'

- Mr Tim Mahony, chairman of Killeen Investments: 'The Lexus Story'
- Ms Linda Lash, director of consumer satisfaction, Avis Europe: 'Customer Care in a Service Business'
- Mr Jim Freeman, group director of Service, Whirlpool (UK): 'Advantage through Quality of Service'.

2,000TH MEMBER OF MII, 1990

Mr David Donnelly, Bank of Ireland, a 1985 graduate of the Marketing Institute, became its 2,000th member.

FOOD MARKETING, NOVEMBER 1990

Marketing News and Noticeboard, in its 8 November 1990 issue, provided a thought-provoking article by Mr Ciaran Dolan, an economist with the Irish Creamery Milk Suppliers' Association, ICMSA.

He referred to 'a case of marketing myopia to marketing utopia'. Why, he asked, had the main players in the food sector generally eschewed marketing down through the decade with such coherence? However, he contended that the reason for such aversion to marketing by the sector was totally logical. That behaviour of Irish food firms yielded maximum profit with the minimum risk faced with the given economic and institutional framework.

In essence, the market support and intervention arrangements of CAP supplanted the real market force and signals, particularly in the important milk and beef sub-sectors. He said that the myriad of reports, analysis and development plans on the food sector over the previous twenty years had tended to ignore, or failed to understand, the fundamental effect of CAP. A look at the Irish statistics would show high dependence on commodity markets and direct public intervention purchasing.

The food processing sector, he maintained was the farmer's first and largest customer. Mr Dolan believed that it was essential to retain CAP, for income guarantee reasons, while it could be retained in a way that did not crowd out marketing.

MR JOHN KERRIGAN'S NEW VENTURE, 1990

On completion of his three-year contract with the Marketing Institute, Mr John Kerrigan announced that he would set up a business resource consultancy. Meanwhile, he would remain as chief executive of the Institute until the end of March 1991.

He stated that he saw some great opportunities to work with organisations undergoing change, just as the Institute had done in the past few years. With a background in the CTT, the IDA and the Institute, as well as private industry, he could offer knowledge and experience in many businesses. In the meantime, he believed that the Institute was well placed to become even more influential in Irish business life.

RECORD NUMBERS GRADUATE, NOVEMBER 1990

A graduation ceremony for MII students took place at the National Concert Hall, Dublin on Saturday 10 November 1990. It was by far the largest graduation ceremony to date — almost 800 people received academic qualifications in marketing. Graduations were conferred on 354 men and women and a further 437 were awarded Foundation Certificates.

The joyous occasion proved that marketing in Ireland had come of age. Mr Colin McCrea, newly elected chairman of the Marketing Institute stated that it was gratifying to see the sheer numbers of highly educated young people who had selected marketing as their chosen career option and completed the rigorous study.

REGIONAL MEMBERS VISIT DUBLIN, NOVEMBER, 1990

Council members from the regions converged on the marketing house, Dublin, on Saturday 24 November 1990, for a special series of meetings on regional matters with members of the executive and Head Office staff. It was the first time ever that regional council members had come together to have the opportunity to meet their opposite numbers throughout the country. Iarnrod Éireann kindly sponsored the rail travel for the regional council members who attended the Dublin meeting.

Mr John Kerrigan, chief executive of MII, said that one of the key strengths of the Institute was the vast amount of voluntary effort which is contributed by members and this was particularly true of the regions. He went on say that in order to provide a truly national organisation, the maintenance of a high level of regional presence and membership was very important. The members of the regional council play a critical role in insuring the active and prominent position of the Institute locally.

The daylong visit consisted of separate morning meetings for chairmen/vice-chairmen, treasurers, secretaries, membership, education and PRO officers, on matters of policy and common interest. The afternoon comprised of a group meeting with the executive.

REGIONAL DEVELOPMENT

1990 was a period of intensive development in the regions with a determined push to complete the network in Ireland. In December 1990 the Marketing Institute opened its first new branch in ten years — the North-West. The branch covered counties Donegal, Sligo and Leitrim. A further establishment of a second launch in the North-East was made, covering counties Cavan, Louth and Monaghan.

CHAMBERS OF COMMERCE LINK WITH MII, 1990

A further resource was provided for the Marketing Institute, in the regions, during 1990 with the establishment of the link with the Chambers of Commerce of Ireland, Cork, Galway, Limerick and Waterford. The Chambers agreed to provide office accommodation and a permanent address for the Institute.

Four staff from the Chambers attended a course at the marketing house, familiarising themselves with the operations of the Institute. They were then able to provide both service to the relevant regional council and information on the Institute in the area. The value of regional membership was increased through more high quality events held.

FELLOWSHIPS CONFERRED, 1990

In the presence of Mr Ray McSharry MEP, European Commissioner, Fellowships were conferred on:

- Mr Brendan McGuinness: managing director of Showerings Ireland Ltd
- Dr Noel Shaw: consultant of Shaw and Co.
- Mr Douglas Thornton: managing director of Douglas Thornton Associates.

THE SEAN F. LEMASS AWARD, 1990

The Sean F. Lemass award for outstanding business achievement was presented in 1990 to Techniform Ltd.

ELITE MARKETING AWARDS, 1990

The Elite Marketing awards, sponsored by Mitsubishi Electric, for significant contribution to marketing in their business, were made, in 1990 to the following:

- Mr Niall Howard of Super Valu Supermarkets Ltd: Elite Marketing Director of the Year

- Mr Sean Kelly of Sifco Turbine Components Plc: Elite Marketing Executive of the Year.

The judging was made on the basis of a regional submission.

MII APPOINTMENTS, 1991

Mr David Kennedy was re-elected as president of the Institute for 1991. The new chairman of the Institute was Mr Colin McCrea of Córas Tráchtála. The chief executive of the Institute was Mr John Kerrigan (to 31 March 1991) and then Mr John Casey (from 1 April 1991).

The MII regional chairmen elected for 1991 were:

- Mid-West: Mr Padraig Cleary

- North-East: Mr Michael Harbourne

- North-West: Mr Cormac Meehan

- South-East: Mr John Lennon

- South-West: Mr Michael Geary

- West: Mr Aidan Daly.

The newly elected chairman of the Marketing Institute, Mr Colin McCrea, assistant chief executive of Córas Tráchtála, held management positions in the Food and Natural Resources Department in CTT's German office and in Consumer Products and Company Development departments.

NEW CHIEF EXECUTIVE, MII, APRIL 1991

Mr John Kerrigan did not resign as chief executive of the Marketing Institute until agreed, and self-appointed goals had been achieved and exceeded. As former secretary of the IDA, designing, installing and implementing organisational and administrative structures and procedures had not been a problem.

Having been involved in the IDA factory building and the new HQ project, the building of the marketing house was a return to familiar territory. His 'project management' of the building thrilled him and would be his most enduring memory.

According to the issue April 3 1991 of *MII News* he would be missed not least for his qualities but also for his unfailing courtesy.

Mr John Casey became the second chief executive of the Marketing Institute from April 1991. He was previously Director of Corporate Affairs and Membership with the then Federated Union of Employers (FUE), now the Federation of Irish Employers (FIE), from where he joined the MII. Mr Casey also held positions with Aer Lingus, the Institute of Public Administration and Price Waterhouse.

MARKETING CONSULTANCY AS A BUSINESS, 1991

At a Young Marketing breakfast meeting, Mr Darach McEvoy made a presentation entitled 'Marketing Consultancy — as a Business'. It was his belief that the emphasis in marketing consultancy was on consumer goods but that marketing for engineering and hi-tech was equally important. With good reason, the emphasis had traditionally been on agricultural goods.

The future, Mr McEvoy stated, would for prosperity, be tied to the output of engineering and hi-tech. He believed Ireland could compete globally in that area as the product and the niche-markets were much less mercurial.

As co-founder of Quaestus Consultants, in 1986, he had a background in CTT, engineering and accountancy. Most of his staff had fluency in all major European languages and had lived abroad. Quaestus believed in the thorough research of assignments, had an in-house library and access to several hundred on-line databases.

Grants had been made mainly geared toward re-equipping the manufacturing end of business. Mr McEvoy aimed to bring awareness of the non-consumer goods world.

There was a huge constituency of engineering and hi-Tech goods out there, which had been product-led until then, mainly because grants were geared toward re-equipping the manufacturing end. He believed that grants should be a catalyst towards improving overall output and stated that it was good to see structural funds being more widely dispersed towards the marketing expansion.

MII THEME FOR 1991

Emphasis on ensuring that every opportunity was taken to see that the crucial importance of marketing was understood and accepted, decided the Institute theme for 1991: 'Marketing *is* the Business'. There was also need for a much greater commitment to customer care, as the basis for profitable growth.

PROFILE OF THE UK MARKET, 1991

A second edition in 1991 of *The UK Market — A Profile*, was compiled by Ms Edel Foley, a lecturer in marketing at the College of Commerce, Rathmines, Dublin. The content of the edition covered the region, geography and population of the UK, comparatively segregated by six age groups.

At the time the UK population, including Northern Ireland, was over 57 million persons. The author provided bar-charts, which showed, amongst other things, projected population trends. Age structure, consumer expenditure, lifestyles, and international markets are among the important factors reviewed.

INTERNATIONAL FORUM, APRIL 1991

'How Management Development is a Critical Factor in Providing Companies with Sustained Competitive Advantage' was the title of the international forum presented at the Royal Hospital, Kilmainham, Dublin on 16 April 1991.

The event was open to chief executives, marketing directors and senior managers by invitation only. Dr Juan Rada, director general of IMD, Lausanne, gave the excellent presentation.

The event was sponsored by Quaestus Marketing Consultants. Being the largest specialist firm of marketing consultants in the country, they carried out confidential marketing assignments in all spheres.

Highlights of Dr Rada's presentation included:

- changes in the origin of competitive advantages, which were increasingly based on 'innovation activities' and knowledge

- significant changes in the business environment — changes which would accelerate and continue while their degree of unpredictability would also increase

- flexible and adaptive organisations being dependent on flexile and adaptable people. That would require the capacity to create learning organisations and it was there that the role of management development became critical to providing companies with sustained competitive advantage

- the question of what it meant to be international as a company and as an individual manager.

Professor John Murray of the School of Business Studies at Trinity College, Dublin, responded to Dr Rada in a presentation after lunch. A discussion was chaired, thereafter, by Dr David Kennedy, Professor of Strategic Marketing at UCD.

TOP MARKETING FORUM, 1991

Mr Niall Fitzgerald, Unilever, speaker at a top marketing forum sponsored by KPMG, Stokes Kennedy Crowley, examined the problems and signposts for Irish industry from a global perspective, with the completion of the internal market just around the corner.

In the current position he examined the plus factors: the high percentage of people in higher education and the strong adaptation powers of the economy where ample chemicals were 15 per cent of total exports and machinery nearly a third.

On the minus side, however, unemployment was around 18.5 per cent compared with 5.5 per cent in the 1960s. Ireland faced increased competition as tariff barriers fall. The onset of '1992' prompted anxiety. The growth of sophisticated/flexible production made it more economic to serve smaller markets from highly efficient low cost production centres elsewhere.

MARKET SEGMENTATION, 1991

Market segmentation explained the key part played in the Grafton Group's recent successes. Mr Howard Kilroy, managing director of Grafton Group Plc, speaking at a marketing lunch, sponsored by Dublin Crystal, said that Grafton profits had trebled and turnover risen by 74 per cent in the previous three years. They had a workforce of 730 people with a turnover of £90m. He declared that the key to that success was market segmentation and customer service.

The group consisted of three main divisions:

1. Builders' merchandising and wholesaling.

2. Manufacturing.

3. Retailing.

Each division brought its own particular ingredients to the Grafton recipe:

1. The builders' merchandising brought critical mass and market share.

2. Manufacturing brought a 10 per cent tax rate to improve EPS.

3. Retailing offered cash flow.

Chadwick's had been attempting to service, in the same branch, the building trader and as well as other customer groups, including individual householders who wished to do their own repairs and decorations. The needs of the two groups were very different. Now the Chadwick's Builders' Centre dealt exclusively with the building trade, including new locations in Lucan and Bray.

Householders' needs were met by the newly created Woodies' DIY superstore chain.

In Chadwicks further segmentation took place and service/quality became the 'differential advantage'. Management development and staff training continued on an on-going basis for about eighteen months across all branches and with every single employee exposed to the company's thinking.

THREE GOLDEN RULES OF SELLING, 1991

With Woodies' mission statement and three-year business plan, it focused on the three golden rules of selling:

1. Location, Location, Location.

2. Positioning.

3. Customer Service.

CASTLE HOSIERY, APRIL 1991

The guest speaker, at a Young Marketing breakfast in April 1991 Mr Peter Gleeson, chairman and chief executive of Castle Hosiery, said that they were the last indigenous Irish company making hosiery in Ireland.

The *Sunday Business Post* sponsored the meeting and reported that, as well as the Irish market, Castle Hosiery were major exporters to Europe, including France and Germany. The company showed its products twice yearly at the main European trade fair in Cologne. Mr Gleeson believed that in order to exhibit and supply such markets quality had to be foremost.

FINAL REGIONAL BRANCH FOR MII, 1991

The final branch, which completed the regional network of the Marketing Institute, was launched in Athlone in 1991.

The Marketing Institute had initiated a programme of regional expansion in Galway in 1988, which resulted in the launch of the North-West region in December 1989. That laid down the blueprint for further expansion in the North-East and the Midlands. The North-East had been launched in June 1990.

MII SEMINARS, SEPTEMBER 1991

The Irish Management Institute arranged, with Marketing Science International, two one-day seminars at the Royal Marine hotel in Dún Laoghaire, Co. Dublin on 5 and 6 September 1991.

Professor Philip Kotler, S.C. Johnson & Son Distinguished Professor of International Marketing at the Kellogg Graduate School of Management, North-Western University, Chicago was the presenter.

Seminar One scheduled for September 5, related to new marketing themes for the 1990s, high performance strategies and tactics for profit. The themes, for the 1990s, were: concepts; strategic; tactical; organisational and information.

Seminar Two on September 6 dealt with the successful marketing of services in the 1990s. The subjects included: the service society; concepts for analysing service organisations; steps in building an excellently managed service company; and the future of services marketing.

Participants at either seminar received a resource kit containing comprehensive reference notes and an audiotape based on Professor Kotler's book, *The New Competition*, which explained the Japanese marketing success strategies. Those attending both seminars also received a bonus videotape entitled 'Global Marketing'. It featured Professor Kotler discussing fourteen principles and the ten most common errors in global and international marketing.

FELLOWSHIP AWARDS, 1991

The Fellowship of the Marketing Institute of Ireland was conferred on 13 June 1991, following citations recalling their outstanding contribution to the Institute, on:

• Mr David Dand, chairman/chief executive of Gilbeys Ireland Group

• Mr Tom Joyce, managing director of Connacht & Court Group.

MARKET IRELAND, NOVEMBER 1991

The *Irish Independent* of Tuesday 5 November 1991 reported the new chairman of the Marketing Institute, Mr Robin Addis, as saying that Ireland had important assets — people assets — such as friendliness and trustworthiness, which could help convert customer care into a strategic advantage in the international arena. He further pointed out that it was where the input of the Marketing Institute could be drawn on, to guide Irish business to a greater appreciation of the direction for marketing Irish products and services.

He felt that the 'Made in Ireland' label did not have enough respect abroad and that there was very little international consumer recognition or appreciation of Irish-branded products. The blame for this was laid at the door of Irish businesses — too few of which were 'market driven'.

MII APPOINTMENTS, 1992

Dr David Kennedy was re-elected as president of the Institute for 1992. The vice-president Mr Bill Fraser was re-elected and the elected chairman was Mr Robin Addis of Lansdowne Market Research.

Mr Addis, managing director of Lansdowne Market Research, had previously been in the UK with Reckitt & Colman and Ford, before joining Irish Marketing Surveys in 1967. He spent two years as marketing director with Hunter Advertising (now BSB Hunter), before setting up Lansdowne Market Research in 1979.

INSTITUTE REJECTS MARKETING COUNCIL, JANUARY 1992

In January 1992 *Marketing Journal* reported that the proposal, by Mr Ian Fox, chairman of the Marketing Society, to establish a Marketing Council had been rejected by the Marketing Institute. He had said that it was an effort to reach a consensus and develop the interests of the industry.

In reply, Mr Robin Addis, chairman of the Marketing Institute, did not consider the establishment of a third organisation incorporating representative advertising bodies as a step forward. He stated: 'the Marketing Society was born out of a need to provide a forum for research practitioners. Today the Marketing Institute debated research and the carrying out of studies'.

The Marketing Institute had 3,000 members and approximately 3,000 students and was the sole examining body for professional marketing education in Ireland. It developed syllabi and provided examinations and certificates to a student body at 25 colleges throughout the country.

MS JEAN CALLANAN, 1992

The marketing director of W. & C. McDonnell, Ms Jean Callanan, joined Unilever in the UK as a graduate trainee. After four years she returned to Ireland, to a position as senior brand manager with Guinness Ireland. She rejoined Unilever as marketing director of W. & C. McDonnell in 1988.

A Graduate of University College, Dublin, Ms Callanan won a scholarship to the College of Europe in Bruges, Belgium, where she obtained a Diploma in Advanced European Studies. As deputy chairperson of MII she was chairperson-elect for 1993.

UNEMPLOYMENT, MAY 1992

Dr David Kennedy, president of the Marketing Institute, speaking at the annual dinner in May 1992, addressed the theme of unemployment. He described it as the single most important issue facing Irish society. At the time there were 300,000 unemployed.

While there were a number of democratic reasons which accentuated the high level of unemployment, he believed that lying behind a high dependency ratio was a high dependency culture.

Industrial review report, 1992

In the preface to the industrial review policy report, the theme had been picked up. It was Mr Jimmy Culliton who said:

> It is time for change, time to realise that government on their own cannot provide us with permanent secure jobs and a growing standard of living, time to accept that the solution to our problems lie in our own hands. We need to foster a spirit of self-reliance and determination to take charge of our future and as William Shakespeare put it: 'The fault lies not in our stars, but in ourselves'.

Mr David Kennedy stated that it was not easy to move from a dependency culture, where entire communities had come to accept unemployment as a fact of life. Recent financial upheavals leading to higher interest rates made the task even more daunting.

GOVERNMENT GREEN PAPER, 1992

The recent Government Green Paper was positive on education and training and set out to address the bias in the educational system against technical or vocational education.

The government also proposed to cater for the less academically skilled students over the age of sixteen.

FELLOWSHIP AWARDS, MAY 1992

The Institute was proud to welcome new Fellows, conferred following citations, at a dinner, hosted by the president of the Institute on 20 May 1992. They were:

- Mr Alan Corbett: deputy chief executive of Telecom Éireann

- Mr Aidan O'Driscoll: lecturer at the College of Marketing & Design

- Mr Raymond J. O'Keeffe: chairman and managing director of O'Keeffes.

IRELAND AS A SINGLE MARKET, 1992

At a Marketing Institute lunch Dr George Quigley, chairman of the Ulster Bank and board member of Co-Operation North stated that 'It was easy to become so pre-occupied by markets to the East — the EC and soon the European Economic Area — that we forget, both North and South, that the whole island of Ireland part of the larger European market, is our home market'. In addition, he said that, as chairman of the Ulster Bank, almost half of the IR63m it earned related to the South. He had no difficulty with the idea of Ireland as a single market, functioning to the mutual benefit of North and South.

He welcomed the progress already achieved, such as regular meetings with the councils of the CII and CBI in the North; close contact between the Chambers of Commerce movements, the proposed joint research project on the Island economy by the Economic and Social Research Unit; the NI Economic research centre; and the publication of Co-Operation North's Financial Synergies study.

He suggested that the Marketing Institute and the Institute of Marketing in the North develop some case studies of the rewards attending the success of companies, North and South.

NATIONAL MARKETING CONFERENCE, OCTOBER 1992

The theme of the fourteenth National Marketing Conference in 1992 was: 'New Products, New Markets, New Jobs'. An Taoiseach, Albert Reynolds TD, gave the opening address at Jury's hotel, Dublin on 30 October 1992. The conference was jointly sponsored by the Marketing Institute and *Business & Finance*. The speakers included:

* Professor James Barnes, Omnifax Research Ltd

* Mr Brian McCarthy MMII, managing director of Fexco

* Mr Stephen O'Connor MMII, chief executive of Waterford Foods

* Mr Jim Flannery of International Tourism Marketing

* Mr Paddy Morairty, chairman of ESB

* Mr Patrick Campbell, chairman/chief executive of Campbell Bewley.

The presentations gave examples from different sectors of Irish business, where some indigenous source of competition advantage had been developed to produce new products, exploit new markets and create or sustain jobs.

Practical experiences were examined in the context of domestic objectives and constraints in addition to international parallels in a global content. Areas of success were to the fore, such as agrifood and leisure/tourism, while specialised services and declining traditional names, which had proved unexpectedly viable, were also discussed.

MINISTER OF TRADE & MARKETING, 1992

The new Minister of State for Trade & Marketing in 1992, was Ms Mary O'Rourke, TD. On 20 November 1992, she gave an interesting and informative talk to the South- East region marketing members in Wexford. The subject was: 'The Single European Market, 1992'.

EASTERN EXCHANGES — EDUCATION TRAINING, 1992

In 1992 the Institute of European Affairs (IEA) published a booklet entitled *Eastern Exchanges* — a study report, by Ms Miriam Hederman O'Brien BL. It related to an interchange of education, training and professional formation between Ireland and Czechoslovakia, Hungary and Poland.

In 1990, while Ireland held the presidency of the European Community, a research project was undertaken, through the IDA's Killeen Fellowship, to examine the impact of educational activity involving Ireland and the three key countries of Central/Eastern Europe — Czechoslovakia, Hungary and Poland. The implications for Ireland were considered important. An outline study of the situation, between 1990 and 1992, raised issues for decision.

In honour of the late Mr Michael J. Killeen, the IDA decided to adopt its annual award for applied research to a joint fellowship in Trinity College, Dublin, on the subject of Eastern Europe. The Marketing Institute of Ireland also supported the project and a useful example of co-operation between academic, state and private institutions came into being.

THE MAASTRICHT TREATY, 1992

The solemn Declaration to the Treaty on European Union was signed at Maastricht on 7 February 1992. Having considered the terms of Protocol No. 17, to the Treaty on European Union, which is annexed to that Treaty and to the Treaties establishing the European Communities, here is the legal interpretation:

> That it was and is the intention that the Protocol shall not limit freedom either to travel between member states or in accordance with the conditions which may be laid down, in conformity with Community law, by Irish legislation to obtain or make available in Ireland information, relating to services lawfully available in member states.

At the same time the High Contracting Parties solemnly declare that, in the event of a further constitutional amendment in Ireland which concerns the subject matter of Article 40.3.3° of the Constitution of Ireland, and which does not conflict with the intention of the High Contracting Parties, herein before expressed, they will, following the entry into force of the Treaty on European Union, be favourably disposed to amending the said Protocol, so as to extend its application to such constitutional amendment in Ireland.

IRELAND'S POSITION IN MAASTRICHT TREATY, 1992

An Taoiseach, Albert Reynolds TD, stated in the foreword to *A Short Guide to the Maastricht Treaty* that the booklet explains what Maastricht is about and not about.

He stated that 'the significance of Maastricht is that it takes a major new step towards European Union — the ideal that had driven the EC for over 30 years. The Irish people will benefit massively by taking part in that forward movement. Staying out could only be devastating for us and for future generations'.

Ratification of the Treaty required a referendum, which was set for 18 June 1992. Two things had to be clearly understood. Firstly, it was not open to Ireland to vote against Maastricht and then request their partners to re-negotiate the Treaty with them. If Ireland rejected the treaty, the strong likelihood was that the partners would go ahead with the Union without Ireland. Ireland would be unable to influence decisions vital to its interests, including decisions on support funds.

Next, the Treaty was not about introducing abortion in Ireland. The Irish government negotiated, in November 1991, a special Protocol — a protection clause confirming that the Treaty would have no effect on the application in Ireland of the right to life article in its Constitution. All Irish people had a vote in the Maastricht referendum, solely on the issues affecting European Union.

SINGLE CURRENCY FOR EUROPE ENVISAGED IN 1992

One of the most important aspects of Maastricht lay in the basis for economic and monetary union in Europe before the end of the century. Ireland had been a member of the European Monetary System, since it began in 1979.

EDUCATION, VOCATIONAL TRAINING AND YOUTH, 1992

Maastricht would extend EC co-operation, including new areas, and benefit Ireland, in education, vocational training and also youth activity extension, for students and teachers; in health; consumer protection; culture and industrial research and development.

Under the Delors Package *a very* substantial increase in support to four countries, including Ireland, being most affected by the prosperity gap, was envisaged.

AGM, 1992

The 1992 AGM of the Marketing Institute was held at the Berkeley Court hotel, Dublin on Monday 9 November. The president for 1992–93 was Mr David Dand of Gilbey's Ireland. The chairman of the Institute was Mr John Fanning of McConnells Advertising Service.

It was recorded, with regret, that Ms Jean Callanan's career movement in Europe meant that she missed the opportunity to become the first woman chairperson of the Marketing Institute. She had been particularly involved in co-ordinating the preparation of the 1992/93 advance programme of events.

It was fortunate to have Mr John Fanning to take over the chairmanship, with a fine calibre of council members, to carry out the Institute's wide activities.

Mr Fanning stated that in a rapidly changing business environment, learning and training should not end with the attainment of a formal academic qualification, rather it should be a lifetime commitment.

Mr Robin Addis, outgoing chairman, referred to the success of 'market marketing' to Irish business in 1992. Also to the upgrading of *MII News* and the redesigning of the consultative register, the publication of a new industrial liaison brochure and the deepening involvement in sectors of business e.g. the food industry — by creating special interest groups to service their specific needs.

MARKETING ON THE INTERNATIONAL FRONT, 1993

On the international front, the Marketing Institute already represented ESOMAR (the European Society for Opinion and Marketing Research) in Ireland and were about to become an invited member of the European Marketing Confederation formerly the European Marketing Council. MII was also affiliated to the Chartered Institute of Marketing, UK.

On the home front joint events were now run with other professional bodies, by introducing new events and contacts, such as Design Ireland and with the Institute of Chartered Accountants and other professional bodies.

Market research had centred on a first survey of marketing intentions — the results attracted widespread media coverage and interest and had implications for all members in the Marketing Institute. An annual survey would take place to monitor change.

The newly elected president, Mr David Dand FMII, chairman and chief executive of Gilbey's Ireland Group, chairman of Grand Metropolitan Finance Ireland and a life Fellow of the Irish Management Institute, said it was of critical importance to ensure that MII members obtained the maximum value from the Institute. Everyone engaged in marketing should feel it essential to be a member of the Institute.

Mr Dand referred to the chaotic conditions that suddenly prevailed, in 1992, with the European financial crisis, and particularly for those depending on the UK market for their exports. He thanked Bord Tráchtála for their market development fund which got most businesses through in good shape. Many learned new skills in the art of 'crisis management', negotiating with both suppliers and customers to bridge the profit gap.

Dr David Kennedy, outgoing president, had been pleased to serve for three years and paid particular thanks to the three chairmen he had worked with – Messrs Richard Strahan, Colin McCrea and Robin Addis.

MEETING WITH CHARTERED ACCOUNTANTS, MARCH 1993

In partnership with the Institute of Chartered Accountants, the Marketing Institute arranged an evening meeting at the Institute of Chartered Accountants (Library), 87, Pembroke Road, Dublin on Tuesday 30 March 1993.

The MII agreed that, although marketing professionals had a key role to play, the marketing profession was not their exclusive preserve. Closeness to customer demands enabled an enterprise to achieve superiority and everyone in the organisation had a role to play.

The speakers conveyed the important relationships from their varying perspectives. They included Messrs Ron Bolger, managing partner, KPMG Stokes Kennedy Crowley; Richard Hoare, MMII, general manager of sales and marketing, Bank of Ireland, (formerly with Lifetime Assurance and prior to that with Gillette Corp. & Wilkinson Sword) and Brendan Murphy, chartered accountant, having been with IBM Ireland since 1985.

DEVALUATION OF IRISH PUNT, MARCH 1993

Following devaluation of the Irish punt, speculation was made as to what reduced percentage of Ireland's total exports would the UK market have to account for, before the punt's appreciation against sterling ceased to be regarded by the financial markets as unsustainable.

Since accession to the EC in 1973, the export dependence of Ireland on the UK market fell from two-thirds to one-third (approx.). That was still too large a proportion to prevent currency from being integrally linked with the fluctuations of sterling. To gain from the lessons of events then, a policy of product innovation and identification of market opportunities, that took account of influence on exchange rates, required development.

COMPETITIVE BENCHMARKING, 1993

A briefing presentation was made to 80 MII members by Mr Laurence K. Harper, president of Ballantrae International. He said a variety of well-established market leaders — such as IBM and General Motors — had suffered setbacks because their management had listened to what they wanted to hear.

Competitive benchmarking he described as 'the comparison of a given business function across companies designed to allow managers to understand how functional performance compared with that of other companies'. The reasons for benchmarking were:

- to provide a new stimulus to rejuvenate business
- to quantify differences in performance
- to document why differences exist
- to identify steps to catch up and surpass the best in class.

PACKAGING DESIGN, MARCH 1993

Packaging design was regarded as one of the most important marketing tools for manufactured packed products. A design management consultant, Mr Andrew Bradley, contributed a very explanatory article on packaging design, a hands on guideline for brand managers to *MII News* in March 1993. In it he said that packaging communicated hand and product values at the point of sale and continued to work long after promotional and advertising budgets were exhausted.

Other reasons why attention to package design was growing were:

- manufacturers' brands had to fight harder, with less shelf space, against retailers' own labels
- the internationalisation of markets meant packaging design must take into account national and cultural boundaries
- new materials and technology are a continuous stimulus to innovative packaging in order to boost sales, reduce costs and increase profits
- public concern with the environment and increasing legislation put pressure on manufacturers to redesign packaging to minimise waste and use materials which were biodegradable and easily recyclable.

Establishing the product scope

The scope, complexity and cost of packaging projects may vary enormously. It may be the re-design of graphics on an existing package, modifications to aspects of the pack and/or container or wrapper and new development of a pack (brand extension or new product). A design brief requires discussion, information, detail of product scope, objectives, time scale and budget.

CONSULTANCY — CASE STUDY, MARCH 1993

A case study, by Mr Pat Fahy, Creg Associates, contributed to the Marketing Institute series on consultancy projects. It examined how a planned methodical approach to identifying new products and new markets paid off.

The case relates to Mullins Engineering, who had manufactured subcontract sheet metal customised enclosures, brackets and fittings for multinational companies for nine years. The company employed eighteen people with a turnover of £8m.

MII News reported that Mr Joe Mullins was conscious of his company's dependence on the subcontract sheet metal manufacturing sector. The components he produced were used in end products which constantly shrunk in size and metal content. An alternative was to diversify into product manufacturing to reduce dependence on sub-supply, maximise his production facilities and enhance the company's abilities. He consequently engaged a consultant's help.

A new manufacturing opportunity was needed, predominantly of metal and having an electronic, hydrologic or mechanical attribute. It must include the 'know how' to enhance the company's manufacturing ability and experience; have a successful sales' record; have application in the European market; and be available by purchase, licence, joint venture or technology transfer agreement.

The vending company was not to be more than ten times larger than the client company. An English speaking company was sought with a developed economy and manufacturing technology. USA and Canada were to be the sources. A target list of approximately 500 companies was identified from a number of information sources.

A very detailed learning experience ensued on how to methodically approach a problem and devise a structured response. The end result of the findings was the expansion and development of the core business, when it was now (1993) one of the largest suppliers of value added cabinets to the Irish electronics and telecommunications sectors, employing over fifty people with a turnover in excess of £6m.

(The Marketing Institute's consultancy register is a service to business, aiming to help companies identify qualified consultants for marketing projects.)

INAUGURATION OF EUROPEAN MARKETING CONFEDERATION, APRIL 1993

The European Marketing Confederation (EMC) was formally inaugurated on 2 April 1993, by the founding members: Finland, France, Germany, Greece, Italy, the Netherlands, Spain, Switzerland and the United Kingdom.

The Marketing Institute of Ireland accepted an invitation to join the confederation (EMC). The overall objective was 'to establish a confederation which would develop marketing on a European basis and be the link and medium of expression for marketing associations in Europe'.

Full membership status was only granted to one national marketing body in each country. Individual members of such a body were automatically members of EMC.

A permanent office was set up in Brussels with a part-time chief executive and assistant.

PRESIDENT'S NIGHT, MAY 1993

Mr David Dand FMII, speaking at the President's Night dinner in May 1993 at the Royal Hospital, Kilmainham in Dublin stated that he would first ask members of the Institute to abandon a begrudged mentality and instead to stand up and be proud of the Institute achievements. Secondly he suggested the establishment of a presidential award to industry, to be for export and or for indigenous industrial development.

He said Ireland was very fortunate to have Mrs Mary Robinson, a wonderful president for the country, who continually demonstrated her commitment to the development of Ireland as a nation.

The guest speaker on President's Night was the well-known Mr Noel C. Duggan of Millstreet, (Cork), fame.

SPECIAL AWARD TO MR BILL FRASER FMII, MAY 1993

The president of the Institute, Mr David Dand, presented Mr Bill Fraser FMII with a special Waterford Glass award, in appreciation of his having been vice-president of MII for fifteen years.

THE STEPHEN DOYLE AWARD, MAY 1993

Mr Tom Prior, MMII, manager of corporate services, Conoco (Ireland) Ltd, was presented with the Stephen Doyle award for his contribution to marketing and the work and development of the Marketing Institute, over many years.

FELLOWSHIP AWARDS, MAY 1993

The Institute was pleased to welcome the following new Fellows:

• Dr Aidan Daly FMII: senior lecturer in marketing at UCG

• Mr John Daly FMII: chairman of ICI (Ireland)

• Mr Michael Geary FMII: regional manager of Bord Tráchtála, Cork

• Mr James McCauley FMII Grad.: managing direcctor of Alcast Ltd

• Mr Geoff Reid FMII: chairman of Ballygowan Spring Water Company

MR JOHN LENNON MMII, RIP, JUNE 1993

It was with the deepest regret and sympathy that members of MII learnt of the untimely death of Mr John Lennon MMII, then senior marketing lecturer at the Waterford RTC at the early age of 46.

Mr Lennon was a most likeable gentleman, of determined decision. He had been vice-chairman of education and subsequently the Marketing Institute's first director of education from 1988 to 1990. His greatest love was teaching young students and practising marketing as a very successful consultant to many national and international businesses. He had played a pivotal role in the development of the new graduateship programme and was sadly missed by all — friends, colleagues and students alike.

STUDENT YEARBOOK, 1993–94

A specially designed student yearbook for 1993–94, was introduced by Ms Catherine Kilbride, director of education, MII. It contained all the information needed by students and provided in Stage 3, the Marketing Communications Syllabus.

The title of Sales Management and Sales Promotion was changed to Management of Sales and Customer Service. Logistic Management replaced Distribution.

There were 2,500 students registered in 1993 on the graduateship programme. In addition 2,500 members represented a wide range of business sectors. Regional representation was at Athlone, Cork, Dundalk, Galway, Limerick, Sligo, Tralee and Waterford.

The annual student registration fee was £160, while at the Dublin Institute of Technology, College of Marketing & Design, for example, the course fee for 1993–94 was £195.

FELLOWSHIP BY PROFESSIONAL DEVELOPMENT AND THESIS, 1993

The Marketing Institute, in order to encourage and recognise research into Irish marketing management, set up a programme of professional development leading to the Fellowship of the Institute. The intention was to provide educational and personal development opportunities for members.

Candidates for the Fellowship needed to accumulate a minimum of 21 credits, obtained through attendance at various professional development in marketing, (PDM), courses and submission of a thesis in marketing management. Also five years proven experience was required in a marketing environment, as well as graduateship of the Marketing Institute. Specific areas were defined for the courses, with credits varying.

AGM, SEPTEMBER 1993

On 6 September 1993 the Marketing Institute of the AGM was held. The outgoing chairman, Mr John Fanning, said that it became apparent, at an early stage in his year of office, that most significant changes were taking place in the educational marketplace and advancing at such a pace as to have profound implications for the Institute.

Under the deputy chairman, Mr Jim Quinn, a strategy review committee concluded that the reduced number of students registering for the Institute's graduateship programme had nothing to do with the quality of the course but rather with demographic and marketplace issues.

In addition Mr Fanning stated that had been particularly encouraged by the strength of the Institute groups outside of Dublin.

Elections

Mr David Dand was re-elected as president of the Institute for 1993–94 and Mr Jim Quinn of Thomas Corry & Sons was elected chairman.

The newly elected chairman, Mr Jim Quinn, addressed two issues — one macro and one micro. The macro issue related to marketing in general and the micro to the Institute. He said 'the battle for marketing recognition had been won but it was no longer satisfactory that marketing people now regarded themselves as the equal of accountants and engineers in making their individual, but separate, contributions to the organisation'.

Marketing people, Mr Quinn believed, would have to define their power in organisations in terms of their capacity to make a strategic contribution and would have to orient their thinking in terms of value for the customer. Further marketing would be judged in terms of a strategic contribution to the overall goals of an organisation.

On the micro issue he felt that fragmentation of the educational market had major implications for the Marketing Institute. The graduateship had been a leading option among few alternatives. The role now would be to refocus on providing a marketing education to those who want to become marketing professionals. Change, and the pace of change, would have to be faced.

In retrospect, the number of students registered had trebled, to about 3,000, between the mid and late 1980s and had dropped a little in 1991 and 1992, to an unexpected low of 2,562 in 1993. He felt that a number of factors were involved. During the 1980s many students were interested in pursuing a course in business studies and there was now a greater availability of specialised courses, including those in private colleges and vocational educational institutes.

ANNUAL MARKETING CONFERENCE IN CORK, OCTOBER 1993

Organised by the Marketing Institute and *Business & Finance* journal, the fifteenth Annual National Marketing Conference entitled 'Marketing Through Turbulent Times', was held at Silversprings hotel, Cork, on Friday 29 October 1993.

The sponsors, who made the conference possible, were AIB, Bord Gais Éireann, Golden Pages, Guinness Ireland, Henry Ford & Son, Irish Distillers, Kerry Glass, Port of Cork and Telecom Éireann.

The opening address was given by Mr Brian Cowan TD, Minister for Transport, Energy and Communications. He said that all times were turbulent in their own way. He further stated that he believed that marketing was a process for pinpointing and seizing opportunities that always exist, no matter how tough the markets may be.

It had been a difficult year for Ireland's indigenous industry — currency instability and the increasingly competitive international markets constantly creating new challenges for Irish companies. The opening of the European borders brought Europe nearer to Ireland in many ways while the issues facing Irish business continued to be complex and perilous for the small and medium-sized enterprise.

To maximise the practical usefulness of the conference the afternoon session included a panel debate. It was chaired by Mr John Bowman, well known on radio and television. Questions varied from the effectiveness of the new County Enterprise Boards to how the media reported business affairs.

The speakers included:

• Mr John O.P. Bourke: chairman of Irish Permanent Building Society

• Mr Paddy Fitzpatrick: chairman of Fitzpatrick Hotel Group

• Mr Tony Kilduff: chairman of Reflex Investments

• Mr Des McWilliam: managing director of McWilliams Sailmakers

- Mr Edwin Nolan: chairman of Henry Ford & Son

- Ms Jane Williams: managing director of Commencements.

This was the first time the National Marketing Conference had been held outside Dublin. Delegates were welcomed from all over Ireland by Mr Seamus Hennessy, chairman of the South-West region of MII and Mr Frank Boland, president of the Cork Chamber of Commerce, who was also the conference chairman.

PUBLICATION OF CASE STUDIES, NOVEMBER 1993

The Marketing Institute published three case studies, resulting from a MII/ IMTA (Irish Marketing Teachers' Association) case study project. For the prizes offered the main winner was Ms Brenda Cullen, Graduate Business School, University College, Dublin, who prepared a case based on 'Ballygowan: Kisqua'. The runners up were Mr Gerry Mortimer, DIT, College of Marketing & Design, whose case study was entitled 'Euro-Coach Builders', and Mr John Fahy, University of Dublin, whose case study was called 'Optimeyes'.

The project had been proposed by the Marketing Institute, to combine the strength of both bodies, to produce something of value in teaching marketing. The use of case studies in marketing had increased over the previous two or three decades.

VIDEO CONFERENCE, 1993

Video conferencing was the buzz phase in business communications in 1993. Executives discovered it easier, and cheaper, to talk to colleagues in another location over the video link.

Mr Hugh Oram provided an excellent article, published in *MII News* in September 1993. He said one trade source reckoned that, with two national and one international video conferences, a company could pay for its own video conferencing system within twelve to eighteen months.

Shorts of Belfast, the aircraft manufacturers, owned by the Canadian Group, Bombardier, was a prime example. Shorts used transatlantic video conferencing, creating drastic saving on airline tickets and time for company executives.

Telecom Éireann said such a conferencing method was slowly taking on but recent technical advances meant companies could put in their own cost effective video conferencing systems to use standard telephone lines. The introduction of SDI (Switchboard Digital International) by Telecom, allowed a hook-up for voice and video transmission from Ireland to almost all the world's major commercial centres.

At the time Allied Signal in Waterford was a leader in the use of the new technology, using it to contact its US sites on a weekly basis.

AUSTRALIAN PRIME MINISTER IN DUBLIN, OCTOBER 1993

Mr Paul Keating, the Australian Prime Minister, visited Ireland in October 1993, an indication that Ireland's trading interests extended beyond the EC. What was good for world trade had then to be good for Ireland. It left more marketing opportunities, by the liberalisation of international trade and identification of market niches.

EUROPEAN MARKETING CONFEDERATION DIPLOMA, 1993

The European Marketing Confederation, (EMC), decided in 1993 to create an EMC European Marketing Diploma, to improve the quality of marketing education and to harmonise qualifications and certification. Recognition by the EC was under consideration and a syllabus under preparation, by an appointed working group.

INTERNATIONAL FORUM FOR MII, 1993

On 11 November 1993, Professor James G. Barnes, Professor of Marketing, Memorial University of Newfoundland and chairman of Omnifacts Research Ltd, presented an international forum for the Marketing Institute.

Professor Barnes said that the theory and practice of marketing had undergone great change in recent years. Many changes that took place in society had combined to create a consumer marketplace in the 1990s that was dramatically different from anything that business had faced in the past.

There was less emphasis on the marketing mix but more on creating a situation where a customer was satisfied with everything that a company had to offer. The really successful firm would be the one that could genuinely satisfy its customers, as much through how they were treated as through the products and prices that were offered.

The new model of marketing, Professor Barnes believed, had caused many companies to take a radically different view of how marketing was practised. It was contended that successful firms must turn to three Rs: building customer *relationships*, *retaining* customers and *recovering* from mistakes.

HISTORY OF THE PUBLIC RELATIONS INSTITUTE, 1953–93

The year 1993 celebrated the fortieth anniversary of the Public Relations Institute.

Mr Michael Colley, editor of the book *The Communicators — PR — The History of the Public Relations Institute of Ireland, 1953–93,* was involved in the PR Institute from its outset.

He was originally a journalist and later worked in public relations with Henry Ford & Son Ltd in Cork and with the Electricity Supply Board in Dublin for 25 years until his retirement in 1982, when he became a director of Murray Consultants Ltd. He had been honoured with the Fellowship of the PR Institute in 1979.

The first public relations person to set up an independent consultancy in Ireland was Mr Leslie Luke, a founder of PRII. Their first meeting was held in Jury's hotel (then in Dame Street) Dublin on 28 October1953.

First Irish Public Relations Officer in Europe

The first president of the PR Institute, Mr E.A. (Ned) Lawler, (1953), was the first public relations officer to be appointed in Europe. Originally there were twenty PR members, while in 1993 there were 550.

N.I. CHARTERED INSTITUTE OF MARKETING BRANCH, 1994

The Chairman's Lunch of the Northern Ireland branch of the Chartered Institute of Marketing was held at the Stormont hotel, Belfast on 8 February 1994. Members of the Marketing Institute of Ireland, including myself, were pleased to be present at the joint meeting. The chairman, Mr Gordon Orr, introduced the speaker, Mr David Fell CB, head of the Northern Ireland Civil Service, who gave an interesting outline of business affairs and future prospects for Northern Ireland.

LIFE MEMBER OF MIGS, FEBRUARY 1994

The Marketing Institute Golfing Society elected Mr Norman McConnell as an Honorary Life Member. In the worthy conferring on Mr McConnell in Woodbrook Golf Club, Mr Don Harris, MIGS Captain, said: 'This honour is in recognition of Norman's services to Institute golf since 1962'.

GRADUATION OF MII STAFF MEMBER, 1993

The graduation ceremony of Marketing Institute students for 1993 took place at the Royal Dublin Society in Ballsbrige. Ms Suzanne Carden, a member of the Marketing Institute staff, was among those to achieve the graduateship. The graduate of the year was Ms Miriam McDonald, ESB International Group.

THE US — THE PLACE FOR NEW PRODUCTS, 1994

In 1994, the United States was likely to be the marketing flavour of the year for Irish companies. Mr Hugh Oram wrote that much Irish consumer interest would focus on the US, with the World Cup finals there in the summer likely to draw as many as 15,000 soccer fans from Ireland.

Even though the World Cup would create a host of marketing opportunities for the Football Association of Ireland sponsors, headed by Opel, the US itself was likely to be the best market in 1994 for selling new products with its economy in recovery.

Mr Gerry Morrissey, North American director of An Bord Tráchtála, based in New York, said that some of the best prospects for Irish companies selling in the US would be in giftware. He stated that people in the US do not buy Irish, they buy according to their needs and that had been a very expensive lesson for a number of companies.

Quality and value for money were the key elements.

SOUTH-EAST MII REGION, 1994

Determined to make the organisation in the area of south region buzz with marketing activity, Mr Redmond O'Donoghue, sales and marketing director of Waterford Crystal, took office as region chairman for 1993–94. Membership had increased to approximately 250, covering counties Carlow, Kilkenny, Waterford and Wexford.

A feature of his programme, in addition to the endeavours to create jobs in the unemployment crisis, was for Institute members to work on a project to create greater community involvement.

TELECOM ÉIREANN — TELEMARKETING SUCCESS, 1994

Telemarketing showed a huge growth cycle in Ireland helped by Telecom Éireann tariff changes. It claimed to make Ireland the cheapest telemarketing location in Europe for overseas companies.

The Bank of Ireland, as an example, had set up to market personal loans by telephone, in its premier operation and added a second benefit — cost effective car insurance by phone. A majority of motorists, who qualified, therefore got cheaper car insurance cover.

In Europe more and more financial services were being sold to customers by telephone. This had long been the case in the US. Nearly 300 people were employed, in 1944, by Dell Computers, of which 150 worked directly in telemarketing. Many mainland European markets, besides Ireland and Britain, were being serviced by Dell, which was helping Ireland's fluency in multilingual telemarketing.

MARKETING AT CROSSROADS, MAY 1994

The theme of a special joint meeting of the Marketing Society and the Marketing Institute of Ireland was 'Marketing at the Crossroads'. This was history in the making as it was the first ever meeting of the two bodies.

A survey had been prepared by Mr Bob Smith of Coopers & Lybrand, UK, which questioned managing directors and marketing directors of 100 bluechip companies in the UK about their views on the role of marketing and of the marketing departments in their organisations.

The conclusions that emerged from the survey were deemed rather disconcerting, suggesting that, while marketing was still seen as a core philosophy, marketing departments had tended to become marginalised and remote from the crucial factors determining performance.

MII News reported that 'optimism was somewhat tempered, however, while the benefit of a marketing approach to business was acknowledged, marketing professionals must pull their socks up and ensure that their specialist contribution added value'.

Three eminent marketing practitioners led an interesting discussion that followed Mr Smith's elaboration of the points in his survey. They were Messrs Shane Molloy, managing director of Lever Brothers; Martin Corcoran, Nestle Rowntree and Redmond O'Donoghue, Waterford Crystal.

FELLOWSHIP AWARDS, MAY 1994

On the occasion of President's Night, 12 May 1994, the Marketing Institute awarded Fellowships to:

• Mr Michael Conlon: chairman of Bord Gais Éireann, Cork

• Mr Jerry Liston: chief executive of United Drug Plc

• Ms Ros O'Shaughnessy: managing director of Wilton Research & Marketing Ltd

- Mr Willie O'Reilly: general manager of marketing and human resources, AIB Group

- Mr Alan McCarthy: chief executive of An Bord Tráchtála.

The principal speaker at the dinner was Mr Tom Mulcahy, chief executive, AIB Group.

THE STEPHEN DOYLE AWARD, MAY 1994

For meritorious service to marketing and significant contribution to the success of the Marketing Institute, the Stephen Doyle award was presented to Mr Aidan Harte, marketing director of IJM Timber Engineering Ltd. He was an FMII Grad. of the Institute.

MII NEWS BOOK REVIEW, 1994

In May 1994 *MII News* published a book review of *The Rise and Fall of Strategic Planning* by Henry Mintzberg, reprinted from *The Financial Times*.

Mr Mintzberg, a mangement Professor at Montreal's McGill University, had spent twenty years campaigning around the world against the ultra-rational, mechanistic, highly detailed, and mainly top-down sort of strategic planning, popularised in the 1970s by the Boston Consulting Group and in the 1980s by Harvard Professor, Michael Porter.

Most of his criticisms of the old strategic planning school were deemed fair, if brutal. He believed it suffered from two key fallacies. The first was that it should be detached from action, with strategy decided only by top management and central staff, rather than by practising managers. The second fallacy was that planning, despite being a purely analytical activity, could create the sort of synthesis required to develop strategy. He put it this way 'Strategy-making is an immensely complex process involving the most sophisticated, subtle and at times, subconscious of human cognitive and social processes'. The Mintzberg doctrine stated that effective strategies often 'emerge' from outside events.

MARKETING TEACHERS' CONFERENCE, MAY 1994

The fourteenth annual teachers' conference was held at Trinity College, Dublin, 26 and 27 May 1994. The theme was: 'International Challenges for Marketing Education'.

The conference responded to the increasing importance of international issues in both marketing academic and practice. A panel discussion took place

458 *Marketing at the Millennium*

on how to react to the dimension of the challenges facing educators, in which some of Ireland's leading academics took part.

DIRECT MARKETING SPREADS, 1994

The spread of direct marketing became available to business of all sizes, to suit all budgets. A further use was to power efficiency drives. Supermarkets used their scanning data to decide what lines to delist and which to carry.

A study, by PA Consulting revealed similar use for internal accounting data. It claimed that 50 per cent of the FMCG lines made about 150 per cent of the profits, while a full 50 per cent of the profit was absorbed by loss-making lines. Eliminating the latter naturally made for greater profits.

The Marketing Institute involved itself in two projects designed to increase awareness of the uses of information and the impact of technology. These were a joint seminar with the Irish Computer Society and a survey with the Department of Marketing in UCD.

CREATING COMPETITIVE ADVANTAGE, 1994

A seminar was presented by Mr Christopher Lovelock for the Marketing Institute on 1 June 1994. The title was: 'Creating Competitive Advantage through Service'. It was jointly organised with the Centre for Quality and Services Management in UCD.

A number of main themes ran through all of Mr Lovelock's work. Two of them were:

1. No service business is unique. While core products vary from one type of business to another, supplementary services, such as order taking, billing etc. are common to a great many.

2. Even traditional manufacturing companies cannot prosper on the back of product quality alone. They must also offer good service such as prompt delivery and after sales backup.

MARKETING REVOLUTIONISED BY COMPUTING, JUNE 1994

The June 1994 issue of *MII News* referred to the recurring theme of the Marketing Institute during the past year as proving that marketing no longer had to prove its bona fides. The future was to prove that marketing could deliver promised benefits and results. That had been the main issue of the outgoing chairman, Mr Jim Quinn, when he took office.

A joint seminar with the Irish Computer Society took place. Both IT and marketing professionals gathered, analysed and used information as their stock in trade. The seminar debated how the marketing potential of information could be unlocked through the use of technology.

Joint events with a range of other bodies, including the Institute of Directors, MBA Association, Institute of Management Consultants and the Irish Direct Marketing Association, arose from the realisation that the overall business process was greater than the sum of the individual functional contributions.

REGIONAL ACTIVITY OF MARKETING INSTITUTE, JUNE 1994

It is worthy to recall, as an example, there were many marketing subjects and speakers, pictorially recorded in the 'Event Review' of *MII News,* issue June 1994. Here are a few, taken at random:

Organised By	*Subject/Speaker*
Marketing in Action	'Marketing the Merger Inside and Out' Mr Harry Lorton, TSB Bank
Young Marketing Breakfast	Speaker, Mr Alan Corbett, Telecom Éireann
Kerry Region	'Marketing through the Local Media' Mr Bryan Cunningham, The *Kerryman* Ms Suzanne McElligott, Radio Kerry
Midlands Region	'Rural Tourism — A Success Story' Teresa Burke, Corrib Country Co-Operative
South-West Region	Database Marketing Seminar Mr Matt Moran, An Post; Mr Gerry O'Connor President of the Irish Hotel Federation
North-West Region	Marketing Tourism — Taking Action Mr Eunan McKinney, Source Design Consultants Mr Damien Brennan, NW Regional Tourism and Ms Angela McCarthy, Four Lanterns
West Region	'Multinationals with a Marketing Base outside Ireland' Mr Pat Howard, Digital; Mr Gary Kennedy, Northern Telecom; Mr James Healy, Golden Vale
North-East Region	'Credit Control and Cash Collection' Messrs Frank Derisi and John McEvoy, Dun & Bradstreet.
South-East Region	'Sponsorships — Why they Work' Mr Enda Hogan, Irish Permanent Building Society; Mr Paddy Lynch, National Irish Bank

Mid-West Region   'The Marketing Approach to Personal Service'
                       Mr David Rowell, Mercer Fraser; Mr John
                       Lenihan, Insurance Institute

AGM MII, SEPTEMBER 1994

The 1994 AGM of the Marketing Institute was held on 5 September at Marketing House, Dublin.

The hon. treasurer, Mr Neville Galloway, reported a very healthy financial situation, showing a surplus plus a substantial reserve provided for the introduction of a new distance learning course. The surplus was mainly achieved by cost containment and control and an increase in subscription income.Mr Galloway paid a tribute to Mr John Casey, chief executive, and Ms Regina Tate, financial controller of the Institute, for their excellent commitment in controlling and processing the financial affairs.

MII appointments

Mr David Dand was re-elected president of the Institute for 1995. The chairman was Mr Tom Fennell, College of Marketing and Design.

The newly elected chairman was a senior lecturer in marketing at the College of Marketing & Design, DIT. A philosophy graduate he had taken his MBA in UCD in 1979.

In his speech he stated that 'if all of us, as individuals as well as members of corporate enterprises, focused our energies, more coherently and energetically on providing solutions to corporate and personal needs, two clearly distinguishable outcomes would result'.

He went on to state that there would first of all be increased economic activity and economic wealth. That had been the clear objective of national economic policy for many years. The attainment of the objective through the wider dissemination of marketing at individual and corporate level, was something more honoured in the speech than in the observance. Further, he believed that one of the highest human powers was the ability to understand other human beings. It was in the core of marketing. Serving the customer would add value of the highest social order if it was done with sensitivity and integrity.

MII NEW PUBLICATION, 1994

A new publication from the Marketing Institute was sent to all members, with the advance programme for 1994–95.

Edited by Ms Jane Williams, managing director of Commencements Ltd and a member of the National Council of the Marketing Institute, the booklet entitled: 'Sources of Market information' was designed as a practical guide to finding an appropriate starting point for those undertaking market research.

Wide coverage is given of the information in Ireland available at Bord Tráchtála's Market Information Centre, (MIC). The booklet extends information regarding the services of the Central Statistics Office; Forbairt; Business Information Centre, Central Library, Ilac Centre Dublin; European Community reference library etc; German Irish Chamber of Commerce & Industry; US and foreign commercial services (US and FCS); directories and yearbooks.

NEW MII CERTIFICATE IN SELLING, SEPTEMBER 1994

In considering the crucial role of the selling function, it became evident that the job of the salesperson had been overshadowed. At the same time markets and customer needs were changing faster than ever. Good sales people demanded to know how change was affecting their customers and potential customers. Surveys showed a lack of natural selling skills and that less than 5 per cent of salesmen had any recognised qualification in selling.

Hence the Marketing Institute introduced a two-year course, Certificate in Selling. The first year was to start in September 1994. The aim of the course was that salespeople should understand the functions of personal selling, appreciate its integration with the other business functions and its unique importance in a company's promotional mix.

JOINT SURVEY OF CORPORATE PURCHASING, SEPTEMBER 1994

The Marketing Institute joined with the Irish Institute of Purchasing and Materials Management and carried out the first ever comprehensive survey of corporate purchasing and materials management in Ireland.

Purchasing managers were asked about their relationship with suppliers. Questions included how they kept informed about suppliers and products; how they preferred to be contacted by suppliers; and what their major criteria for awarding contracts to suppliers was.

The importance for marketing personnel of such knowledge, about the decision-making process of potential customers, was, of course, obvious.

ADVERTISING AWARDS, 1994

Plans for the fourth annual Advertising Agency of the Year award were announced in *Marketing*, Ireland's marketing monthly, in September 1994. Based on three main criteria — growth of business in relative terms, creative achievement and financial maturity — the top agency would be selected from a final shortlist of three.

The expert panel of nine judges, a cross-section of the Irish marketing services industry, to make the winning selection, included Ms Rosamund O'Shaughnessy, MIAPI, FMII, recently elected a Fellow of the Marketing Institute.

MARKETING THE CORK REGION, OCTOBER 1994

A very interesting idea lay behind a conference, entitled: 'Marketing the Cork Region — an Integrated Strategy for Tourism and Industry'. This was organised by the Institute's council. It took place in Cork on Friday 14 October 1994.

The event, run in association with Cork Chamber of Commerce, had questions addressed, such as how the industrial development potential of Cork city and county could be marketed more effectively and how industry could be developed alongside tourism development in an integrated manner.

During the proceedings several main issues became evident:

• there was need for a shared vision

• a planning framework which integrated the two 'sides' was needed so that diverging objectives would be made visible and reconciled

• both tourism and industry, working independently, produced benefits which could help promote the other

• where conflicts existed they must be acknowledged and either elimated or minimised.

NATIONAL MARKETING CONFERENCE, 1994

The theme of the 1994 National Marketing Conference, held at Fitzpatrick Castle hotel, Killiney in Co. Dublin on 21 October 1994, was: 'Defending Brands'. The conference, in association with *Business & Finance*, was chaired by Mr Gary Joyce MMII, managing director of Dimensions.

It had been said by some management that 'the brand' was declining, dying, redefining itself, or about to be resurrected. The rapid spread of technical expertise and the speed with which manufacturers could respond to change, meant that brand owners could no longer rely on traditional defences. Customer loyalty to brands was also becoming suspect with evidence that price and value were becoming more dominant. Similarly trust in retailers might be replacing trust in brands. What was happening to brands carried lessons for all marketing people because it indicated fundamental shifts in the producer/customer relationship.

However, Dr Anthony Romeo, Head of Corporate Strategy with Unilever, said in his keynote presentation 'Brands Vs Brands: Competition is Good':

> I would argue that the challenge we are seeing to brands reflects an adjustment, occasionally painful, to a new, different and clearly more competitive marketplace. I would also argue that the challenge is in its essence — if not always in its form — healthy. In this new world brands will prosper. Customers will demand them for their real and fundamental values. Manufacturers who respond appropriately will be rewarded.

He went on to say that throughout their history brands had tried to perform three main tasks — to communicate, to differentiate and to deliver value. Brands succeeded where they did all three simultaneously and well.

New brands would be developed to meet entirely new emerging needs. The challenge was to identify the need and carry it via a brand that communicated a unique proposition to the consumers. Dr Romeo believed that brand extension had been central to the growth strategies of major companies.

Dr Romeo illustrated a number of interesting aspects of brand strategy. The withdrawal of Gibbs SR toothpaste in the UK had been replaced by a strengthened Metadent with the SR link. Such cases, he said, reflected positioning, needs, competition peculiar to each market. Again Pepsodent's powerful position in the US was a distant memory, but it now thrived as a market leader in a much faster growth market — Indonesia.

The growth of an 'own' label

John Murphy, chairman of the Interbrand Group noted that while retailers were originally drawn to an own brand strategy for financial reasons, they soon began to realise that 'own' labels could be much, much more than merely cheap alternatives to manuafcturers' brands. They came to realise too, that their buying power and their closeness to the customer placed them in a powerful position to transform the role of 'own' label in their stores.

The healthcare market

'Brands or Generics' was the title of the presentation from Mr Niall Swords, general manager of Boots Healthcare. He reminded the audience that marketing theory tells that purchase decisions involve a combination of rational and emotional considerations. Mr Swords said that brands could prosper but they had to fight to do so. The intellectual capital invested in brands had to be protected by legal means such as trademarks and patents.

Defence techniques

Several speakers addressed the role of strategies such as advertising and direct marketing in defending brands.

Mr Gary Brown of Target Marketing, introduced the concept of 'brand interactivity'. He said that communication from the brand must enter and understand the lifestyle of the customer, and be benefit driven. It must urge a response or give an opportunity for the customer to interact with the brand.

PROGRAMME OF THE MARKETING INSTITUTE, 1994–95

An elaborate full colour programme of the Marketing Institute for 1994–95 was sponsored by Smurfit Web Press, designed and produced by Creative Inputs.

The three business areas, each of which the Institute defined as contributing to the achievement of its overall objectives, were:

1.   Graduateship.

2.   Membership.

3.   Professional Development in Marketing.

Dublin

A top marketing forum series was included in the programme designed for senior Institute members by invitation only. It was an 'off the record' private encounter over dinner with a prominent speaker on an important matter of current interest.

Marketing in the Making: designed for all Institute members, was a 'go behind the scenes' to experience the reality of marketing in a specific company, in different industry sectors.

Marketing in Action: designed for middle to senior managers, comprised an in-depth look at a topical marketing issue by a top practitioner. This was to be held at Jury's hotel, Dublin at 6.30 p.m.

Young Marketing Series: (sponsored by *The Irish Times* advertising department, for 1994–5), designed for people at the beginning of their marketing careers. Breakfast meetings were to be held at the Dome restaurant, St Stephens Green Centre, Dublin at 7.45 am.

Student Marketing Forum: designed for all students, full or part time. It gave an opportunity to meet and talk with leading marketing practitioners.

Evening meetings were at 6 p.m. The sponsor for 1994–5 was Cara, the computer people.

In addition a full programme of Institute events and top speakers took place in 1994–95 in the Mid-West; West; North-West; Kerry; South-East; North-East; and South regions.

A special series of six seminars were held at Jury's hotel, Dublin (7–10 p.m.), during November/December 1994. They were sponsored by Bank of Ireland and held in association with Forbairt, Cork Enterprise Boards and EIC.

The seminars were entitled:

1. 'How to Market Yourself and Your New Enterprise Idea'. (four sessions)

2. 'EU Schemes — How Do they Assist Business?'. (two sessions)

THE IRISH PUB IN EUROPE, 1994

Mr Sean Cowman, a Graduate and a Fellow of the Marketing Institute, in an article in *MII News* Nov/Dec. 1994, said that Ireland was then in the concept business.

By this he meant creating an image of authentic 'Irishness' right at the top end of the quality market. Relating to the fact that about 2,500 Irish pubs had opened throughout Europe in the previous three years, he said that the epidemic was spreading.

Getting it right meant getting everything right on four fronts:

1. The design of the pubs.

2. Having Irish bar staff.

3. Providing Irish music.

4. Dispensing largely Irish products centred on Guinness.

If those four elements were there, Mr John Gilmore of Guinness said, 'a prime location and good management would mean a commercially very successful pub'.

The Irish Pub and The Oscar Wilde in Berlin, Kitty O'Shea's in Paris, The Fiddler's Elbow in Florence and The Shamrock Inn in Copenhagen were undoubtedly the most popular drinking spots in their own cities, where they attracted huge local as well as Irish ex-pat custom. They were becoming social venues of high sightseeing priority for tourists and visitors. The incentive for owners of existing premises was simply the immediate increase in turnover.

The concept had taken off in Germany in a big way with the sale of native German beers and other pub products and this meant that active encouragement of German breweries was assured. It was for Guinness, however, that the concept had proved a real winner. Mr Colin Brooder, managing director of Guinness Germany, said that Guinness had realised the potential that lay ahead in the Irish pub and felt that properly recreated it can perform just as well abroad as it does in Ireland. Sales in Germany were increasing at a phenomenal rate. The average Irish pub in Germany returned a profit of around 70 per cent gross and 30 per cent net, compared with 40 per cent gross and 12/18 per cent net in Ireland.

EMC GOLD BOOK 1994

The European Marketing Confederation introduced a 'Gold Book 1994', in which it recalled that the confederation had taken over the European Marketing Council in Athens, Greece, just two years previously (May 1992).

The establishment of a Secretariat in Brussels had been just a year ago (January 1993), with the opening of an office in the heart of the European Commission district in Brussels.

The EMC had declared a mission to stimulate, develop and professionalise the art of market-driven entrepreneurship, primarily in the European context, and secondly in the global context.

EMC description of marketing

The EMC description of marketing was declared in 1994 as:

> Marketing is a set of activities directed at stimulating, facilitating and expediting exchange transactions. It is also a management process of identifying, anticipating and satisfying customer requirements profitably.

In 1994 the EMC comprised of eleven national member associations, including MII, from both within and outside the EEC, which met its ethical and other criteria for membership. It represented over 150,000 marketing professionals in Europe. Many objectives were defined in detail.

Irish contributions to Gold Book

Mr John Casey, chief executive of the Marketing Institute of Ireland, contributed an article to the Gold Book. In it he said that Ireland was facing up to the challenges brought about by the ERM, from which Britain (Ireland's neighbouring country) withdrew, and to the single European market of 1993 and beyond. He defined the mission of the Marketing Institute as: 'to position the marketing profession as the crucial factor for business success'.

An excellent article, 'Ireland is the Kerrygold Country', reported Ms Caroline Palmer, Irish Dairy Board, providing a message of farm freshness that appealed throughout Europe. Ireland being one of Europe's leading producers of quality food and milk products meant that agriculture formed a very significant part of its economic activity. Dairying was one of the foundation stones of that key business. The internationally renowned Kerrygold label spaned a product range including retail dairy products, commodities and an extensive list of food ingredients. Group subsidiaries in Europe and the US also marketed a wide selection of specialised cheeses, cooked meats, fish and delicatessen-type products, for the Board. Kerrygold had become a Eurobrand, in the true sense of the word and would be a truly international brand in time.

EMC SERVICES, JANUARY 1995

The European Marketing Confederation offered a wide range of assistance to Marketing Institute of Ireland members in 1995. From its databases the EMC made available up-to-date information on a range of subjects and faxed, free of charge, for up to five pages max.

ADDED STATUS FOR EUROPEAN MARKETING DIPLOMA, 1995

In April 1995, the Marketing Institute of Ireland, a founder member of the European Marketing Confederation, comprising thirteen national member associations, representing 150,000 marketing professionals, was awarded wider European recognition. The graduateship MII was one of the first such qualifications given EMC recognition. From 1995 the parchment given to graduates reflected the European dimension.

PURCHASERS' OPINIONS OF IRISH VENDORS, 1995

A survey of corporate purchasing and materials management carried out by KPMG, Stokes Kennedy Crowley, on behalf of the Marketing Institute of Ireland and the Irish Institute of Purchasing and Materials Management (IIPMM) was extensively reported in *MII News*, Jan/Feb. 1995 issue.

According to Mr John Casey, chief executive of the Marketing Institute, the key aim of the survey was to establish the strategic importance of the purchasing function within each company/public organisation and to determine purchasers' perceptions and opinions of Irish vendors.

Some 80 per cent of respondents with foreign parent companies said that the parent would be prepared to use Irish suppliers if they could demonstrate their ability to meet the required criteria and standard. Sixty-one per cent of respondents would be willing to introduce Irish suppliers to their international contacts network.

Constraints and barriers to developing better business to business relationships between purchasers and suppliers were examined in the survey. The quantitative survey issued produced 164 respondents, while in addition, a qualitative research programme involved in-depth interviews with key purchasing managers in twenty organisations.

ADVERTISING, 1995

In *The McKinsey Quarterly* 1994, No. 3, Mr Naras V. Eechambadi stated that, despite their heightened attention to advertising spend, managers still had a hard time getting it precisely right.

No surprise, to this writer then, as it seemed for ever so that it is extremely difficult to get the right decision. So many problems arise regarding data, inappropriate performance criteria, budget decision and timing.

In his article Mr Eechambadi stated that 'advertising's effectiveness is notoriously difficult to measure, *but* accurately valuing its contribution is more important than ever'. He also believed that advertisers had over-spent during the 1980s, or they were underspending today, or both. Neither rate of spending was right — it was simply that the nature of competition, the overall performance of the economy and the role of advertising had changed from one decade to the other. Both theories, he felt were plausible and popular, while wrong.

He proceeded on to state that there was a third explanation: advert spending had become so disconnected from economic reality and from an understanding of how to evaluate an ad's 'quality', that being creative, such numbers did not reflect much other than management's willingness to open its wallet.

New approaches to thinking about advertising were anchored in effective metrics of creativity and in the economic reality of value creation. In summary, he believed, that if one could not prove that the money spent created economic value, by persuading customers to purchase their product, they should not advertise at all.

LAUNCH OF *CORK MARKETING NEWS*, 1995

Cork Marketing News was the first regional newspaper, of the Marketing Institute to be produced. It was launched in the presence of Mr Liam O'Moran, Moran & Associates, who designed the newsletter, Mr Michael Fitzgibbon, Snap Printing, Councillor Noel O'Flynn, Deputy Lord Mayor of Cork, Mr Matt Moran, regional chairman (South), Councillor Paula Desmond, cathaoirleach of Cork County Council and Mr Tom Fennell, national chairman of MII.

NEWS EXTRACTS AWARDED ACCREDITATION, 1995

A most active member and supporter of the Marketing Institute, since 1984, Mr Bill McHugh's News Extracts, a media monitoring service, was awarded the ISO 9000 accreditation. The presentation was made by Mr Tom Kitt TD.

CARA AWARD TO STUDENT, 1995

The winner of the Cara sponsored AcrNote PC, at the final student marketing forum event in March 1995, was a third year student at Tallaght RTC, Mr John Scally. The presentation was made to him in the presence of Ms Marie Lord, chairman of the Student Marketing Forum Committee, Mr Michael Rodgers, Cara Data Processing (sponsor) and Mr David Harvey who generously chaired the forum students' events.

CREATING ENVIRONMENTS, MAY 1995

A very interesting presentation was made to the Marketing Institute's West region members in May 1995 by Mr Chris Coughlan, marketing and communications manager of the Digital European Software Centre in Galway. He had been a past council member in the Institute's West and South-West regions. The subject was: 'Creating Environments for Competing in Tomorrow's World'.

He referred to the development and growth of marketing as having been very much related to, and aligned with, the progress of technology over the centuries. In particular, the application and use of communication technologies had brought about major shifts in the evolution and development of marketing theory and practice.

Mr Coughlan, in recalling the development of the printing press and through to the telephone, radio, film, television and video, said all those media communications had been exploited for their significant marketing potential. Individually and collectively they had a profound effect on the development, evolution, expertise and growth of marketing as a discipline.

Marketing personnel studied the developments in emerging technologies. Multimedia was one such emerging technology and indicated advantages within the context of competing within the marketplace. It was, he stated, a complex and synergetic set of enabling and integrating technologies that brought audio, graphics, animation and video to the desktop computer.

According to an article in *The Sunday Times*, multimedia was described thus: 'Multimedia technology is addictive because it interacts with the user and seductive because it appeals to so many senses'. Mr Coughlan believed that the advantages of multimedia, developed and used correctly, showed the potential to be the single most efficient communication mechanism that would significantly enhance the buyer's ability to understand, learn, evaluate, interact, respond and act on high volumes of complex information.

The concept, Mr Coughlan considered, was captured in the traditional saying by Lao Tse: 'You read, and you forget, You see, and you remember, You do, and you learn'.

MULTIMEDIA EXPOSURE, MAY 1995

The Multimedia Marketing Consortium director, Mr Paul Smith MIII Grad., offered (in *MII News*), the world's first series of multimedia educational programmes on marketing, produced by the Multimedia Marketing Consortium. Mr Smith gave the opportunity to MII members to gain exposure for their companies, their products and their clients.

The world's first introductory-level marketing course delivered on CD ROM had been designed in an innovative manner for use in both education and training. Twelve hours of programmes presented structural tutorials complete with tutor, slide show and video show. An assessment section allowed the user to measure his/her learning.

The programme included a 'Hall of Fame' where the world's best gurus met the user. Available, in that personalised theatre, were Japan's Mr Kenichi Ohmae, Mr Philip Kotler, Ms Rosabeth Moss Kanter, Mr Theodore Levitt and Mr Peter Doyle.

Mr Smith then invited media materials (documents, photographs, graphics, animation and video clips) of products, packaging, point-of-sale, advertisements, direct mail shots, exhibitions, conferences, customer service, meetings and more for future programmes. He gave the opportunity to Institute members, in particular.

PRESIDENT'S NIGHT, MAY 1995

The principal speaker at President's Night, held at the Royal Hospital, Kilmainham, Dublin on 10 May 1995, was Mr Nick Scheele, chairman and chief executive of Jaguar Cars. Almost 200 members and guests were at the most important get-together of the year.

FELLOWSHIP AWARDS, MAY 1995

Marketing Institute Fellowship awards were presented in recognition of significant contribution to marketing in Ireland. The 1995 Fellowship recipients were:

- Ms Gillian Bowler: Budget Travel
- Dr Cathal Brugha: University College, Dublin
- Mr Garry Hynes: Church & General Insurance
- Mr Denis Lucey: Dairygold Co-Operative Society
- Mr Pat O'Mahony: Allied Irish Bank
- Senator Feargal Quinn: Superquinn.

GRADUATE APPOINTED AS MII MARKETING EXECUTIVE, MAY 1995

Having been a member of the Marketing Institute staff since 1988, Ms Suzanne Carden (MII Grad. in 1993) was appointed marketing and membership executive of the Institute in May 1995.

STRATEGIC MARKETING NEWSFLASH, MAY 1995

In May 1995, the European Marketing Confederation commenced an information service known as the strategic marketing newsflash. It contained short summaries on key European issues of interest to marketers.

A full database printout, of any of a list of articles, was available to MII members (on fax request to the Institute).

CONSULTANTS' REGISTER, MARKETING SEMINARS, MAY 1995

A series of marketing seminars, to be presented by members of the Institute's marketing consultants' register, was launched by Mr Enda Kenny TD, Minister for Tourism and Trade. The project had the support of Forbairt and other state agencies.

The first of the seminars, designed to increase awareness of the range of assistance available to business, was held in Galway on 17 May 1995. Those present included Mr Edwin Whittaker, chairman of the Consultants' Register Committee; Mr Brendan Geraghty, chairman of the West region of the Marketing Institute; and Mr Martin Boyle, West regional director of Forbairt.

MARKETING INSTITUTE MEMBERSHIP, JUNE 1995

At the end of June 1995, the Marketing Institute membership reached an all time high of 2,570.

ROLE OF HONOUR, JULY 1995

The first person to be admitted to the Marketing Institute's newly established Role of Honour was Mr Philip Flood FMII, a foundation member. The ceremony took place at a dinner held in his honour to mark his retirement, from the Dublin Institute of Technology, College of Marketing and Design, and to acknowledge his immense contribution to the professional and educational work of the Institute over many years.

98FM DUBLINER OF THE MONTH, JULY 1995

Mr Michael Coote FMII, chairman of the Alzheimer Society of Ireland, a founder member of the Marketing Institute, was awarded the National Irish Bank, Classic Hits 98FM Dublin Award of the Month in July 1995.

MII AGM, SEPTEMBER 1995

The 34th AGM of the Marketing Institute was held at the marketing house, in Dublin on 4 September 1995.

Prior to the commencement of the meeting, the chairman, Mr Tom Fennell, requested those present to observe a moment's silence in memory of Mr Leslie Whitehead and Mr Sean Condon, a founder member and past-president of the Institute respectively. They had died during the past year.

The president of the Institute, Mr David Dand, said that he was happy to accept an invitation to serve a third year as president and congratulated the Institute on its record membership numbers, its new range of educational activities and it's sound financial situation. Mr Tom Fennell, outgoing chairman, said he believed that the Institute was undergoing a time of great change.

He gave a summary, of the previous highly successful year, and said that none of the developments would have taken place without the support of the president or the many current members and office holders past and present throughout the country. He regarded what he said as a special mark on the buoyancy of the Marketing Institute.

Mr Fennell said it was his pleasant task to hand over the chain of office to the incoming chairman, Mr Roger Jupp. Mr Jupp, in accepting office, said that he looked forward to the opportunity to work with Messrs David Dand

and Bill Fraser, as president and vice-president respectively, during their final year in office.

MII APPOINTMENTS

The council of the Marketing Institute elected for 1996 comprised:

- President: Mr David Dand FMII
- National Chairman: Mr Roger Jupp MMII, Lansdowne Market Research
- Deputy Chairman: Mr Redmond O'Donoghue MMII, Waterford Crystal
- Hon. Secretary: Mr Conor Cunneen
- Hon. Treasurer: Mr Neville Galloway
- Vice-Chairpersons: Ms Sheila Gahan and Mr David Nea.

The out-going chairman, Mr Tom Fennell, remained as an ex-officio member of the executive committee.

The regional chairmen elected for 1995–96 were:

- Kerry: Mr Michael Friel MMII, Forbairt
- Mid-West: Mr Tadhg O'Brien MMII, Power Convertibles
- North-East: Mr Aidan Devenney MMII Grad., Forbairt
- North-West: Mr Seamus Bergin MMII, North Western CBS
- South: Mr Declan Lordan, MMII Grad., The O'Shea Group
- South-East: Mr Albert Ellis MMII, Albert Ellis & Associates
- West: Mr Declan O'Connor MMII, Marketing Quality Assurance Ireland.

MII GRADUATE ON EUROPEAN BUSINESS TEAM, SEPTEMBER 1995

The Marketing Institute Graduate of the Year 1994, Ms Sandra Hickey, started her career in marketing with a year in Germany, having been selected by Mr Arnold O'Byrne for a twelve-month stint with General Motors there. The German town, Russelheim, where she worked as a marketing specialist, is literally known as the 'Opel town'. That is because most of the employment in the area is supplied by Adam Opel AG, owned by General Motors, Europe.

She found the complex huge and was overwhelmed by the size of the place — the company even had its own railway line for transporting employees and freight throughout the grounds.

Ms Hickey stated that what she came across in practice she already knew in theory from her studies and she would not have got the job without the Institute's course in the College of Marketing and Design, Dublin.

IRELAND ON-LINE, SEPTEMBER 1995

A composite brochure mini-pack, produced by Ireland On-Line, Furbo, Co. Galway in September 1995, was mailed to Institute members. It contained material relating to the worldwide electronic mail, internet and a range of Irish information services. They indicated their mission was to make it as easy as possible for people and businesses in Ireland to benefit from the latest global computer networking technology

Full details of electronic mail (email) were set out, as a typed message from one's own computer arriving at the other computer within minutes, even to the far side of the world, meant saving money and time. The saving meant that there was no need for long-distance calls or expensive faxes or no more time wasted trying to reach someone who was out.

Further explanations of services that were given related to the World Wide Web, newsgroups, Gopher, Telnet, FTP (File Transfer Protocol) and education and learning (unrestricted by geographic location) — an idea then only being explored, but expected to have far reaching implications in the future.

PROFESSIONALISM *IS* THE MESSAGE, 1995

The Marketing Institute national chairman, Mr Roger Jupp stated that marketing in Ireland was at an intriguing period of its development. Ireland, and more specifically the companies operating in it, faced a wide range of threats to survival and prosperity. The challenges for organisations were wide-ranging and included:

- issues accelerating globalisation and the reduced scope/rationale for local differentiation

- the pressures that brand proliferation and competition could bring to bear

- the arrival of new forms of competition in the marketplace

- international media fragmentation

- the scale of investment needed to support successful brands in the marketplace.

The pace of change was 'hotting up' and it could be seen that the issues needed to be faced more rapidly. Nevertheless, Mr Jupp believed that marketing opportuinites existed. The ethos of a company had to be driven by customer satisfaction, even if customers themselves might not be rational in their requirements and might not envisage that manufacturers/distributors/retailers had to make sufficient profits from their activities to ensure they could satisfy their customers.

NATIONAL MARKETING CONFERENCE, OCTOBER 1995

The National Marketing Conference for 1995 of the Marketing Institute, in association with *Business & Finance*, took place at the Royal Marine hotel in Dún Laoghaire Co. Dublin on Friday 20 October.

The theme of the conference was: 'Marketing — the Driving Force for Strategic Change'. The patrons of the conference were AIB; Esat Telecom and Ford and the sponsors were Aer Lingus, DMA (Direct Marketing Association) and Waterford Crystal. The conference chairmen were Mr John Bowman, RTÉ and Mr Redmond O'Donoghue, vice-chairman of MII.

The conference was set to analyse and answer developments of change. Loyal customers must be created through long-term relationships, but brand loyalty was a thing of the past, it was said.

Keynote address

The keynote conference address was given by Professor John A. Murray, University of Dublin. He proposed turning the assertion in the conference title into a question.

That he did because he was not clear that marketing's promise and potential, as a driving force for change, had been, or necessarily would be, realised. Professor Murray said the wholesale restructuring of businesses and industries and their strategic redirection, during the past fifteen years, had been overwhelmingly managed by colleagues in finance.

The principal healthy sign that he found in marketing was that it was increasingly puzzled and worried about its state. Out of that worry he hoped would grow rejuvenation, a renewal that would put it in a pivotal position in respect of business growth and expansion.

The Marketing Institute view was that it needed to consolidate its strength, and perhaps continue to evolve its tactics, as the business philosophy that was, by definition, oriented towards growth and expansion. The ultimate yardstick would always remain the creation of added value.

A number of stimulating papers were given at the conference. Below are a sample of these.

Designing the market organisation

This was delivered by Dr Eddie Molloy, director of Advanced Organisation and Management Development.

According to Dr Molloy the shift from functional or specialist logic to process-based designs was perhaps the most far reaching and definitive transformation then taking place. At that time key processes like supply chain management, new product management, market development or customer satisfaction necessarily required marketing people to work in much closer cooperation across functions.

A new approach to segmentation

This paper was given by Ms Barbara Patton, head of marketing at Irish Permanent.

Ms Patton outlined a segmentation exercise which her company had conducted recently based on a basic demographic variable — gender.

Research had been conducted into the female market exclusively, the objective being to find out if the difference in gender gave rise to any characteristics relevant to financial services. Two had emerged. The first was financial independence or dependence and the second was having or not having children.

Unlucky for some: seven problems facing the millennial brand owner

This paper was delivered by Mr John Fanning, managing director of McConnells Advertising Services. He referred to the 'rampant retailer and the post modern consumer'. He also stated that above all, the millennial brand owner should ignore the siren voices of the fin de siècle Rasputins offering universal solutions and continue to have faith in the tried and trusted disciples of the marketing philosophy.

(Unfortunately it was not possible in this volume to record, in detail, the very interesting facts, figures and information that unfolded in the speakers' papers, however, *MII News* Nov/Dec. 1995 Vol. 8 No. 6, contains some.)

IMJ MARKETING AND ADVERTISING MAGAZINE, 1995

The IMJ marketing magazine, *Guide to Marketing & Advertising 1995*, recalled its establishment in 1974. An IAPI Business Readership Survey in 1995 showed that IMJ was read by 23 per cent of Ireland's top chairmen/ managing directors and 49 per cent of marketing directors.

Every two years the IAPI Business Readership Survey provided an update on the reading habits of the country's top business executives. In 1995 the survey, by Irish Marketing Surveys, was enlarged to include three new job categories — personnel, production and IT managers.

The Irish Times was the top business newspaper and *Business & Finance* the top business magazine, and IMJ was declared the top marketing and advertising magazine for 1995.

CHAIRMAN OF AIMRO, 1995–96

Mr Robin Addis, past chairman of the Marketing Institute and executive chairman of Lansdowne Market Research, was elected chairman of AIMRO — the Association of Irish Market Research Organisations. This was the body which represented the interests of the market research profession in Ireland.

LAUNCH OF MQA01, 1995

In December 1995, in the presence of the Minister for Tourism and Trade, Mr Enda Kenny TD, Mr Declan O'Connor, MQA Ireland, Mr Roger Jupp, chairman of MII and Mr John Casey, chief executive of the Institute, the MQA01, marketing quality assurance specification, in Ireland was launched.

The Marketing Institute agreed, henceforth, to be associated with MQA Ireland in promoting MQA01 as a best practice blueprint for marketing, sales and customer service.

MR DAVID HANLY OF RTÉ, DECEMBER 1995

The Christmas marketing lunch was a very pleasant social affair in The Great Room, Shelbourne hotel, Dublin on 8 December 1995.

The guest speaker was Mr David Hanly of RTÉ. Born in Limerick, Mr Hanly had been in Bord Fáilte before joining RTÉ, where he worked in News Features and as presenter of Morning Ireland for the previous ten years. He also presented a series of television programmes called Hanly's People.

NEW PDM PROGRAMME, 1996

In January 1996 the Marketing Institute was pleased to announce that Dr Cathal Brugha FMII of University College Dublin's Michael Smurfit Graduate School of Business, had accepted the invitation to act as course leader on an exciting new programme. The programme was called Professional Development in Marketing, (PDM).

TELEMARKETING JOBS, 1996

One of the job creation success stories in Ireland in recent years was that of telemarketing. The greatly improved telecommunications system, together with a talented skills pool, led international service companies to base their telemarketing centres in Ireland.

A threat to this was a proposed new European directive, following a debate about the citizen's entitlement to privacy. The point concerned being disturbed at home at seven o'clock during dinner. Concern existed then as to what an EU ban on 'cold-calling' would mean for business. In Brussels there was a sense that market research could be an intrusion.

A proposal was drawn up for a European Foundation for Freedom of Information, by the Financial Advisory Committee of ESOMAR. Describing the background to the initiative, the president of ESOMAR, Mr Helmut Jung, said that there was a conflict of values in public opinion that was increasingly affecting legislation. ESOMAR envisaged that the function of the Foundation would reach out far beyond the immediate market research industry to governments and society as a whole.

Consumers' fraud prevention act, 1996

In the USA, following a crackdown on fraudulent telemarketing in 1993, there now existed the Telemarketing and Consumers Fraud Prevention Act. It required telemarketers to inform telephone contacts up front that they are selling something.

GRADUATE INTERVIEW, 1996

The 1995 graduate of the year was Ms Monica Walsh MMII Grad., a twenty-six year old trained accountant and treasury manager with Golden Vale, Charleville, Co. Cork.

In her position she worked in the area of foreign exchange and debt management. Having completed her accountancy finals in 1990, she was with Deloitte & Touche. She started her marketing course in 1992, attending class two nights per week, at the Cork RTC.

Regarding the main development for the future she believed that it was customer service. Customers were changing and more demanding and the need was to react, from the top down, quickly to the demands of clients.

MR EOIN GRIMES, MMII GRAD., MBS, 1996

Having graduated from the Marketing Institute in 1993, Mr Eoin Grimes MMII

Grad., obtained his Master's in Business Studies from the Michael Smurfit Graduate School of Business in January 1996.

Congratulations were extended to Mr Grimes, advertising manager of the Bank of Ireland, who achieved a first class honours masters degree, specialising in marketing, and came second in his class.

MARKETING INSTITUTE IN CYBERSPACE, JANUARY 1996

The arrival of the Marketing Institute of Ireland in cyberspace in January 1996, enabled it to offer members additional services and allow promotion of the Institute in new ways.

First of all, members could now email the Institute at mii@iol.ie. Secondly, a home page was created for the Institute on the World Wide Web at http://www.failte.com /mii/. This would promote membership of the Institute and include information about the educational services and programme of events. Finally, commencing with the Jan/Feb. 1996 issue of *MII News*, Mr Conor Madden of Interact, would edit a regular column, alerting members to relevant marketing information which could be assessed via the Internet. Items for inclusion in the column were to be sent to him at email sales@interact.ie or fax (091)-590365.

MARKETING INFORMATION ON THE INTERNET, 1996

Mr Conor Madden, sales and marketing manager of Interact, an Internet services company, provided a hand held approach to the internet. Interact specialised in training and marketing companies and their products on the internet.

His first column (*MII News*, Jan/Feb. 1996) explained that the internet was 'a big place where it could take some time to get the information one looked for'. Members would be regularly informed in the *News* as to where useful marketing information could be found on the web. The column would point readers in the direction of appropriate sites. Furthermore he stated that a search engine should always be used when seeking information. A particular useful one was 'Savvysearch'. It could be assessed at: http:// guaraldi..cs..colostate.edu2000/AgentMania/form. It would point out the direction of sites which held information on conventional type marketing information and sites holding information on how an organisation could market itself by using the internet.

IRISH VICE-PRESIDENT OF EMC, 1996

Mr Roger Jupp, national chairman of MII was elected a vice-president of the

European Marketing Confederation at its General Assembly in Helsinki on 16 December 1995.

Mr Jupp told *MII News* that he regarded his election as a tribute to the role the Institute had played in the European arena. He was delighted with the honour and the opportunity it afforded the Marketing Institute to influence international professional marketing activities.

CORK PR SEMINARS, 1996

Some leading Cork PR and media personnel were brought together by the Marketing Institute to present a series of three seminars on Public Relations in Marketing.

The seminars were sponsored by the Bank of Ireland and organised in association with the Cork Business Association.

The MII chairman of the South region, Mr Declan Lordan, was pleased to welcome Ms Ann Mooney, AM Media; Mr Tom MacSweeney, southern correspondent with RTÉ; Mr Sean O'Sullivan, sales and marketing consultant with F & V Sheehan Auctioneers; Mr Ray Doherty, president of the Cork Business Association; Mr Joe O'Brien, sales and marketing manager of the Bank of Ireland; Mr Neil Prenderville, programme director of 96FM; and Mr Robin O'Sullivan of O'Sullivan PR during the active series.

CASE STUDIES IN MARKETING, 1996

Edited by Professor Anthony C. Cunningham, Professor James J. Ward and Ms Catherine Kilbride, *Case Studies in Marketing*, was published by Oak Tree Press in 1996 at a price of £14.95. The book was the product of a competition sponsored by the Marketing Institute and run in conjunction with the Irish Marketing Teachers' Association.

IDMA/MII JOINT SEMINAR, 1996

A special joint IDMA/MII seminar on 'The Future is Customer Loyalty' was held at the Royal Marine hotel, Dún Laoghaire, Co. Dublin on Thursday 8 February 1996. The speakers gave a practical, no-nonsense and often fascinating, insight into how one could develop a successful customer loyalty programme for their company.

The panel of speakers and subjects were:

• 'Winning a Lifetime of Loyalty'
  Mr Gary Brown, managing director of Target Marketing

- 'Your Future is Your Database'
  Mr Michael McGowan, marketing manager of Kompass Ireland

- 'Strategies for Success'
  Ms Susan Bourke, director of direct marketing in Watermarque Integrated Marketing

- 'Prospecting for Gold'
  Mr Mark Cassin, managing director of Direct Marketing Association

HIGHER DIPLOMA IN MARKETING PRACTICE, UCD, SPRING 1996

In the early 1980s Professor Cunningham and two UCD colleagues, the late Professor Bernard Moran and the current Dean, Professor Frank Bradley, were approached by the International Trade Centre in Geneva, the UN agency involved with Third World development, to devise a pilot programme in consultancy skill development. It was to enable marketing advisers in developing countries to assist companies to build their export business.

The concept was piloted in the Philippines and an early version was tested in Thailand.

An improved version was later tested in Jamaica. It was decided to run a similar programme in Dublin, while it coincided with Professor Cunningham's developing interest in action learning, an area he had been researching with colleagues in UCD. In a combination of both, the first version of the UCD Higher Diploma in Marketing Practice programme was created.

The underlying objective of the programme was that participants learn their profession through practising it in a supportive environment. Anco funded the early years of the programme. It was subsequently converted to a self-financing, National University of Ireland accredited, postgraduate diploma programme — the UCD Higher Diploma in Marketing Practice (HDMP) programme. Later it became more complex and comprehensive.

The programme is unique, being a continuous experiment. It is not a placement programme. Halfway through their first assignments, graduates are given another, and halfway through that, they get a third, and so forth. The support they get from the network of management, tutors, mentors and consultants is critical, adding immensely to both their personal and professional development.

MSC IN MARKETING, 1996

The Graduate School of Business for many years had been concerned about education for senior managers in Ireland. Involvement was intensified through the establishment of the Advanced Management Programmes (AMP) division within the Graduate School. Activities were housed in a well-equipped dedicated facility at Management House on the Blackrock Campus, Dublin.

The MSc in Marketing was specially designed to address the critical issues faced by every marketing manager in attempting to marry the objectives and resources of the organisation with the needs and opportunities in the marketplace.

Having, over the previous twenty years, graduated about two thousand students over a rigourous four years study, many graduates were keen to study further.

Working jointly with the Smurfit Graduate School of Business in University College, Dublin, the Marketing Institute now promoted the unique Master's programme. The curriculum embodied the most advanced concepts in marketing, being oriented towards the intensive development of professional skills in marketing.

LAUNCH OF STRATEGIC MARKETING PROGRAMME, MAY 1996

The Strategic Marketing Programme for Growing Business was jointly launched by the Marketing Institute and An Bord Bia, in May 1996. The objective of the programme was to foster the marketing potential of smaller businesses in the food and drink sector and to harness the experience and expertise of senior Institute members in helping to achieve that.

Among those present at the launch were Mr Muiris Kennedy, Bord Bia; Mr Tommy Boyle, Tipperary Cuisine Ltd; Mr Jimmy Cass, Erin Foods and Mr John Casey of the Marketing Institute.

The first programme was composed of ten member companies who became involved as company advisers. Seminars were also included in the programme on such topics as: 'Making Presentations to Buyers' and 'New Product Development'.

Mr Jimmy Cass, a member of the Institute's panel of advisers for the project, was joined by:

• Mr Michael Finegan: Kraft Jacobs Suchard

• Mr Camillus Dwane: Irish Distillers Group Ltd

• Mr Michael Carey: Irish Biscuits Ltd

• Mr Keith MacCarthy-Morrogh: Findlater (Wine Merchants) Ltd

• Mr Bernard Kinlay: Ace Consultants

• Mr Kieran Rumley: Batchelors Ltd

• Mr David Fitzgerald: Avonmore Foods

• Mr Conor Cunneen: CPC Foods (Irl) Ltd

• Mr David Dand: president of the Marketing Institute.

IRISH HORSERACING AUTHORITY, 1996

It was no secret that the Irish horse racing industry had come through difficult times, with attendances and income falling over a number of years. The Irish Horseracing Authority (IHA), formed just two years previously to replace the Racing Authority, had a five-year plan to reshape the industry while marketing was going to play a vital part, not only in selling Irish racing to foreign investors and racegoers but also to the domestic market.

Mr Matt Mitchell was appointed marketing director of IHA, an industry employing almost 25,000 people, directly and indirectly, and worth aproximately £60m. He stated:

'Our objective is to raise the level of awareness and knowledge of marketing within the industry so that we are more conscious of the needs of the consumer.'

MR JACK DOWNEY, RIP, JUNE 1996

Mr Philip Flood FMII, in an appreciation of Mr Jack Downey in *MII News* May/June 1996, wrote:

When the history of the Institute comes to be written, the contribution of Jack Downey will be written large.

In its early days, before the establishment of a full-time secretariat, the chairman and officers of the day were expected to and, it could be said, did work in a full part-time capacity for the Institute. Officers had at least one committee meeting each week, in addition to development work during business hours, as well as bi-monthly executive and council meetings. The chairman would expect to put aside at least two days per week full-time on Institute business. It was the age of enthusiasm and on such generosity the solid foundations of the Institute were greatly enhanced.

Jack Downey was indeed the exemplar of such unhesitating willingness to foster and develop the Institute, a role in which he played a major and significant part. He began his advertising career in London in 1957 and was one of the first to acquire formal qualifications in the newly emerging discipline in marketing. After his return to Dublin in 1970, he joined the Institute and was elected to the council in 1976, becoming vice-chairman for the years 1977 and 1978. Jack was elected a Fellow of the Institute in 1980. Re-elected to the council in 1981, he again became vice-chairman until his election as chairman in 1983.

Members on council and in the various committees, in those heady days of ambition and dynamism, will witness that it was through Jack's capable leadership that the restructuring of the Institute was begun. As

far back as 1981, he chaired a sub-committee to put in place a chief
executive and to find the money to do so — a strategy that was only
completed some years later.

The heightened sense of purpose, increased awareness of the work
of the Institute and the huge increase in membership can largely be
attributed to his sense of dedication and achievement. In this, his outstanding work for the Institute lives on.

Jack Downey was a big man in every way, big in stature, big in
heart. Modest in recalling his notable achievements, his was a gracious
amiable kindness that showed a true generosity of spirit and charity
that overcame the insensibilities of others. In later years, his expertise
and his innate sense of professionalism was spent encouraging young
graduates wishing to enter the advertising and marketing professions.

May the gentle giant rest at peace in his native Goleen, West Cork,
not far from the house he had recently built to retire to, overlooking the
Atlantic. May the glow of his warm spirit and his endearing smile always shine on us from his well-earned Heaven.

COTHU, 1996

The findings of the National Arts Sponsorship Survey were presented for the
first time in 1996 by Cothu, the Business Council for the Arts, in association
with the sponsors Farrell Grant Sparks, Corporate Finance and Consulting.

A graphic brochure showed the total picture in growth and finance obtained for sponsorship to be 40.8 per cent in 1995 (compared to 1993) and
totalling IR£7.4m. (1995). The encouraging performance took place against a
background of flourishing artistic activity, of increasing state funding and of a
new recognition, within government, of the role of the arts in cultural and
economic terms.

A detailed survey report, available to purchase from Cothu, provided a
wealth of data on arts sponsorship and an invaluable source of reliable information for marketing and communications professionals, and of course, art
managers.

WINNING CONSUMER MARKETING STRATEGIES, 1996

One of the world's foremost experts on marketing consumer goods, Mr Camillo
Pagano, former executive vice-president of Nestlé, Switzerland, presented a
senior management seminar for Marketing Institute members. The presentation dealt with the subject of 'Winning Consumer Marketing Strategies'.

The world had become smaller as travelling had become easier and
transport and means of communication had become much faster. Access to

information was also improving. Today's consumers were exposed to new cultures and consequently mixing cultures. The levels of standards of living and attitudes towards health and environment in the western world were still quite different. Consquently, Mr Pagano believed that the motto: 'think global, act local' was highly pertinent.

Global brands

The distinction between global brands, which were sold worldwide by way of different marketing campaigns appropriate to each territory, and global brands, sold universally via standardised marketing, was important. The first nearly always made sense, the second needed certain conditions to be successful. There was a risk of lowest common denominator marketing, or 'global bland'. Four conditions gave the answer, as to whether global marketing made sense:

1. The markets should have developed the same way from country to country.

2. Consumer targets should be similar in the various markets.

3. Consumers needed to share the same product wants and needs around the world.

4. A desirable quality for a global food brand was that it must be its own yardstick.

Socio-demographic changes

In the next ten years, Mr Pagano said there would be a number of very important socio-demograpic changes of western world societies. Those changes were closely related to the evolution in social and individual values that characterised western society:

- a return to conservative ideas

- a rejection of the 1980s legacy

- a demand for differential value growth of altruism

- a search for balance and moderation.

Some of the trends were well established but their potential not fully exploited. Others were just emerging.

Evolution in the structure of society

The traditional family stereotype, father breadwinner, etc. represented about 6 percent of society in the USA. A broader definition — two parents and children — was still only 24 per cent of US households. In Europe the figure was between 30 and 50 per cent. The picture was further complicated because of less permanence in relationships.

THE WEB, JULY 1996

According to the Alta Vista home page:

> Transversing the internet has always been a bit like exploring outer space. One could wander indiscriminately and make many useful discoveries. Just as easily though, hours (thankfully not years) could pass with nothing of value to show for the effort.

Mr Conor Madden, sales and marketing manager of Interact, the internet marketing and training company, in an article in *MII News* of July/Aug. 1996, asked the question if one needed information from the net, how was it found. More importantly, if people wanted to do business on the net, how were they to find you.

The World Wide Web, he stated, is packed with over 30 million web pages, and so the odds between somebody stumbling across your website and somebody never even knowing that your website existed, took no genius to work out. That being so, a solution was required for some sort of way to find one. Due to the manner in which the internet had evolved, there was no set or indexed structure to it.

Mr Madden, however, pointed out that all was not lost. He said that although there was no way to control the structure of the internet, it was being navigated, recorded and indexed by mechanisms called 'Search Engines'. A search engine tracts the web, keeping record of sites that are there, new sites and the wording contained on each of those sites.

An example of this shows that when looking for 'marketing' information, simply by typing in 'marketing' the search engine returns with sources on the internet where it found references to the word 'marketing'. A relevant choice can then be made. Further, if one wanted a more specific reference, say 'Marketing and Ireland', search engines would return with results from your search within seconds of you sending it. Probably the best news was that the use of search engines for the most part was free of charge.

It became increasingly necessary to use search engines when using the internet, due to the sheer vastness of the information which 'cyberspace' contained.

The Alta Vista search engine (run by Digital) was extremely efficient yielding excellent results on most searches, conducting over 10 million searches daily for people around the world. Savvy Search was a search engine which searches the other search engines, increasing the accuracy of ones search. There were also other major searching engines including Web Crawler.

KERRY MARKETING AWARDS, JULY 1996

In a successful effort to promote the marketing and awareness of indigenous business in the country, the Kerry region of the Marketing Institute devised and inaugurated two new awards. The first award for manufacturing in the Kerry region was won by Holden Leather Goods, while the first 'Women in Tourism' award went to Ms Marie Quinlivan of Destination Killarney. The awards were sponsored by Forbairt, Bank of Ireland and *The Kerryman*, and promoted by the Marketing Institute.

Ms Marie Quinlivan, general manager of Destination Killarney (the marketing arm of the Gleneagle Group) outlined her marketing experience and findings in the US, UK and at home. This included the handling of the extremely successful Showtime Express package, run in conjunction with Irish Rail, which brought 150,000 'bednights' to eight hotels and six guest houses in Killarney, since it was set up in 1989.

Dingle couple are 'Holden' their own in the craft world

The manufacturing award winner, Holden Leather Goods, was set up by husband-and-wife team, Conor and Jackie, so that they could get away from the busy thoroughfares.

They had been office working in London and decided to get back to Ireland, and set up their own business.

Holden Leather Goods was built up on an excellent reputation for high quality goods, such as wallets, popular bags and belts. Each item was hand finished and lined in distinctive green suede, with silk pockets and double penloops. Supplies of goods were provided for corporate customers. Penhaligon's, the London perfumers taking a customised collection of leather assessories to sell in Harrods, Knightsbridge and Saks, Fifth Avenue, New York.

All the merchandise was made available directly from the Burnham workshop (the old Burnham schoolhouse) or from the Holden's shop in Dingle, An Sparán Síoda.

Selected retail outlets around Ireland who they supplied, included the new specialist leather department upstairs at Weirs of Grafton Street, Dublin.

AGM, SEPTEMBER 1996

Prior to the commencement of the AGM of the Marketing Institute, the chairman of the Institute, Mr Roger Jupp, requested those present to observe a moment's silence in memory of Fellows, Messrs Dick Tennant and Jack Downey, a founder member and past chairman of the Institute respectively, who had died during the past year.

The 35th AGM of the Marketing Institute was held at Marketing House, Leopardstown, Dublin 18, on Tuesday 10 September 1996.

The outgoing president of MII, Mr David Dand, said that each year at that time, he always though of graduation day and the importance of the Institute's educational activities.

Last November 200 young people, and some not so young, had received their graduuateship parchments from him. At the time he had commented on the business challenges facing the graduates and the ways in which their newly acquired skills would need to evolve in response.

Mr Dand recalled that in the 1950s Mr Peter Drucker had said that every company had only two basic functions: marketing and innovation. Merely being customer oriented was not enough, nor was marketing skill. Constant innovation was also necessary to deliver better value to customers in the competitive marketplace. It was now understood that marketing, like quality, was a total organisational commitment.

Mr Roger Jupp, outgoing chairman, reviewed the year particularly detailing the educational advancement and provisions available, including the MSc in Marketing and the new Certificate in Selling, available by distance learning.

On the international stage, his own election as one of the three vice-presidents of the European Marketing Confederation last December, had given him the responsible education portfolio — representing an acknowledgement of the Marketing Institute's very real credentials in that context.

MII GRADUATES CONFERRED WITH EMC DIPLOMA

Those conferred with the Institute's graduateship in November 1995 received tangible European recognition in that they were automatically conferred with the European Marketing Confederation Diploma in Marketing. This was the first ever time this had come about.

ROLL OF HONOUR, 1996

Congratulations together with the presentation of a Roll of Honour were extended to Messrs Bill Fraser FMII and Michael Coote FMII, who were celebrating their 50 years of membership of the Marketing Institute and its predecessors (Irish Institute of Marketing and Sales Management and the Incorporated Sales Managers' Association).

MII APPOINTMENTS

The council of the Marketing Institute for 1996–97 comprised:

- President: Mr John O.P. Bourke
- National Chairman: Mr Redmond O'Donoghue
- Deputy Chairman: Mr David Nea.

Executive committee:

- Ms Mary Crotty MMII: director of Mary Crotty Public Relations
- Mr Don Harris MMII: managing director of Airtime
- Mr Roger Jupp MMII: managing director of Lansdowne Market Research.
- Hon. Secretary: Mr Conor Cunneen MMII Grad., manager of Caterplan, CPC Foods
- Hon. Treasurer: Mr Gerry Mortimer MMII, College of Marketing & Design
- Chairman of Fellows' committee: Mr Anthony Neville FMII Grad., OHM Group.

Regional chairpersons:

- South: Ms Paula Cogan MMII, Jury's hotel
- South-East: Ms Ann Cusack MMII, Granville Hotel/Woodstown House
- Kerry: Mr Michael Friel MMII, Forbairt
- North-East: Mr Shane Hill MMII, HBA Distribution
- West: Mr Myles McHugh MMII, Iarnrod Éireann
- Mid-West: Ms Vera Murray MMII, Vera Murray & Associates
- North-West: Mr Pat Scanlon MMII, Market Scan Ltd.

The Marketing Institute was pleased to welcome its new president, Mr John O.P. Bourke, BCL, BL, FCA, non-executive chairman of Irish Permanent and chairman of the Gensis Corporation.

In his speech, the president recalled when he addressed the National Marketing Conference in Cork in 1993 on the topic: 'Thinking about Marketing in Turbulent Times'. It brought to mind the contrast with the business environment today. Business was now booming with living standards rising. Much had been due to investment in physical infrastructure and in the educational system, greater productivity and business efficiency.

In accepting office as national chairman, Mr Redmond O'Donoghue, chief executive of Waterford Crystal, also director of Waterford Crystal Ltd, Waterford Wedgwood Plc, Stuart Crystal and E. Flahavan & Sons Ltd, said that business was largely about competing for scarce resources, in order to win necessary marketing investment. Marketers needed to be able to prove that they could husband those resources effectively by increasing the success of key marketing programmes. He told members that a price had to be paid in terms of investment of personal time and urged commitment.

In writing the introduction to the Programme of Events for 1996/97, Mr O'Donoghue stated that he knew he was undertaking a formidable challenge but was greatly encouraged by the widespread voluntary support which the programme demonstrated.

As the first national chairman from one of the regions and a past regional chairman, he was especially heartened by the geographical spread of the programme, reflecting the national character of the Institute — one of its most precious assets.

MR BILL FRASER STEPS DOWN, SEPTEMBER 1996

Mr Bill Fraser announced his retirement as vice-president of the Marketing Institute at the AGM, September 1996. He was sincerely thanked by his colleagues for his long and dedicated contribution to the Institute, right from the early days of the Incorporated Sales Managers' Association back in 1947.

A tribute was written by Mr Philip Flood FMII and recorded in *MII News,* (Nov./Dec. 1996 issue). In it Mr Flood stated that it was hard to remember when Mr Fraser was not vice-president of the Institute.

It was the sincere wish of colleagues that Mr Fraser would long remain with the Institute, 'so that we can be exhilarated with the largesse of his immense experience, his wise and timely counsel and his valued friendship'.

NATIONAL CONFERENCE, 1996

The National Marketing Conference, in association with *Business & Finance*, was attended by a capacity audience in the Royal Marine hotel, Dún Laoghaire on Thursday 17 October 1996. It was opened by the conference chairman, Dr Mary Lambkin, Head of the Marketing Department, UCD Graduate School of Business.

The sponsors were Aer Lingus; BTIS University of Limerick; PostGEM; Topaz; UCD Marketing Development Programme and Waterford Crystal. The conference patrons were AIB, Ford and Esat Telecom.

Conference speakers were asked to compare the indigenous with the international experience; to contrast the approaches of the mature with the emerging business; to see if different commercial sectors approached this question in different ways and to get state of the art views and opinions from those who made specialist studies, as consultants and academics.

SUPREME COURT VS MARKETING, 1996

In his keynote address Mr Redmond O'Donoghue, national chairman of the Institute and chief executive of Waterford Crystal, quoted a rather startling example of an unsuccessful marketing programme.

On 12 June 1996, five judges of the Supreme Court ruled that an advertising programme, costing hundreds of thousands of pounds, was not proven to have materially affected the outcome of the divorce referendum. Without discussing the rights or wrongs of the referendum itself, it was a serious indictment of the effectiveness of an advertising campaign, costing half a million pounds. It had been determined, in law, not to have influenced the outcome of what was a very close referendum.

After further definition, Mr O'Donoghue wondered just how business measured the effectiveness of marketing programmes. If one could not prove the effectiveness of marketing programmes, one would not attract the scarce resources, the oxygen that business needed.

He went on considering and defining the needs that arose and concluded by saying that 'if you can't measure it, you can't manage it'. Marketing, he said, was no exception to that rule, in fact it is an area of high priority for measurement.

MARKETING RENAISSANCE REQUIRED, 1996

Dr Anthony Freeling, McKinsey Company, Inc., took the view that achieving marketing effectiveness would only be met by marketers who tackled the changing requirements of the marketplace with new creativity, new skills and almost certainly, new organisation structure — a true marketing renaissance. Organisations, he said, also need the capability to integrate all of the potential marketing levers into a coherent marketing relationship approach. Delegates were urged to question whether current organisational structures helped companies meet the challenges raised by the need for new skills.

Revitalising performance, Aer Lingus

Mr David Bunworth, director of sales and marketing at Aer Lingus, spoke about the radical overhaul which his company's marketing and sales effort had had to undergo in facing up to the turmoil of the aviation marketplace; how a competitive environment caused an organisation to be very ill prepared for battle; and where timing of events could often be a cruel element in its ability to handle such eventualities.

In discussing the role of marketing, in the measurement of effectiveness, he asserted that marketing must drive the organisation to question itself, for example:

- what are we good at and what are we doing well and vice versa?

- is it relevant to our marketplace and is it adding value?

- what do we need to do in terms of product and service quality to further differentiate our brand from our competitors?

- how do we benchmark ourselves to best practice and ensure continuous improvement?

One of the major marketing initiatives, which Mr Bunworth spoke about, was the development of a brand vision, as a tool to communicate, a corporate vision to the staff of the airline that would relate back in the delivery aspects of a product and service to passengers.

Shareholder value is the measure, Clydesdale Bank

Mr Paddy Lynch, head of marketing and consumer services at Clydesdale Bank, stated the theme of the conference — the relationship between marketing activity and business effectiveness — was absolutely vital within the financial services industry worldwide. In particular, it was the role of marketing in building and differentiating brands and enhancing shareholder value within financial services that would be the pivotal test of the said relationship.

He developed the theme that 'marketing campaigns should only be initiated on the basis that they will impact positively on shareholder value and should be measured accordingly'.

Thumbs down to food marketing, Genesis Corporation

The focus of the paper presented by Mr Michael O'Rourke, director of Genesis Corporation Ltd, was on the effectiveness, or otherwise, of marketing in the Irish food industry. It was necessary, he suggested, to grasp the major challenges facing Irish food companies in order to provide a benchmark for any discussion on relative performance vis-à-vis marketing effectiveness. He took the approach to endeavour establish the enormous void that existed between the aspiration and the reality for a consumer driven food industry.

Mr O'Rourke concluded by saying that marketing's most difficult task was the funding, testing and launching of profitable new products. There was evidence to suggest that Irish food companies moved far too quickly into the product development and concept testing stage.

MAP PROGRAMME FOR LEDU, NOVEMBER 1996

In November 1996 the Marketing Institute of Ireland certified the Marketing Awareness Programme, (MAP), for Northern Ireland's local enterprise development unit, (LEDU).

Among those present at a meeting highlighting that the MAP programme could lead the way to worldwide marketplaces for Northern Ireland small business, were MAP participant, Ms Jane McCallum of the Newtownabbey-based company, Personnel and Safety Service, LEDU business development director, Mr Kevin McCann, and Mr John Casey, chief executive of MII.

Mr McCann said that over 250 businesses had already benefited from MAP, the status of which had been confirmed by formal accreditation from the Marketing Institute. In addition to the practical benefits the programme offered, participants received the added benefit of the award of a prestigious Certificate in Marketing Practice.

FINANCIAL TIMES LISTS IRISH INTERNET COMPANY, NOVEMBER 1996

Interact, the Galway-based internet marketing and web design company, became the first, and so far only, Irish internet company to be included on *The Financial Times,* (FT), list of recommended web designers.

The London branch of Interact had been working with the paper in the UK and authorised design web sites for its UK server. Currently the FT London site had registered over 30,000 accesses per week. Another development was the design of their first Gaeltacht website for the television facilities company, Telegael.

MARKETING STRATEGIES, 1996

Mr David Doyle had held diverse roles in marketing and financial control in Paris since 1975. He was a graduate in Marketing and Statistics from the Dublin Institute of Technology and Trinity College, Dublin, as well as holding the graduateship of the Marketing Institute.

Differentiated Marketing Strategies: A Cost Nightmare, is adapted from the second edition of his book: *Cost Control — A Strategic Management Guide,* (co-published by Kogan Page and the Chartered Institute of Management Accountants, London).

The book has also been published in French, German, Bulgarian, Polish and Indonesian.

A review in *MII News*, Nov/Dec. 1996, said that in recent years, policies aimed at product proliferation and market diversification, with sales spread over multiple markets (both geographical and segmental), had only made the task of identifying cost factors considerably more difficult.

Differentiated marketing (i.e. new product variations, new markets and diversification) added up to customer satisfaction, but the economics of such a strategy needed to be reappraised.

Following an extensive ABC (Activity Based Costing) exercise, a leading Japanese consumer electronics group discovered that only 20 per cent of working hours, put in by marketing staff, were directly related to business. Many functions were being duplicated, while the company had grown too large to function effectively.

FELLOWSHIP AWARDS, 1996

The award of Fellowship, for outstanding dedicated services to the marketing profession and to the Institute, was conferred in December 1996 on:

• Mr Richard Burrows: chairman, Irish Distillers

• Professor Tony Cunningham: University College, Dublin

• Mr Anthony Gannon: chairman, Cylon Controls Ltd

• Mr Fred Hayden: regulator, Premium Rate Telephone

• Mr David Manley: managing director, Newmarket Consulting Ltd.

MARKETING INNOVATION, 1997

In 1996 Dr Sean McCarthy was appointed chairman of the Irish Advisory Group on Innovation to review the EU Innovation Programme. He was a board member of EACRO (European Association of Contract Research Organisation). As managing director of Hyperion, his company was a contract research organisation specialising in energy technologies, energy auditing and renewable energy systems.

The Jan./Feb. 1997 issue of *MII News* recorded Mr McCarthy's description of the innovation process and in the process, highlighted the role of the marketing professional. Dr McCarthy presented examples of how marketing professionals could participate in public and privately funded research and development programmes.

He said that 'innovation is the commercial exploitation of an invention' as it covers not just new products but new services (tourism, health care, etc.) and new processes (or methods). To understand the innovation process it was first necessary to understand the 'invention part' and then to add to it the 'commercialisation part'.

THE IRISH MARKET — A PROFILE, JANUARY 1997

The Irish Market — A Profile, the fifth edition of the invaluable standby of managers, marketers and students, was published in January 1997 by the Marketing Institute. It was referred to as 'a treasure trove of facts and figures, not just about the Irish consumer market, but about the Irish economy and Irish society'.

BORD FÁILTE'S NEW MARKETING PROPOSALS, JANUARY 1997

Bord Fáilte's international marketing director, Mr Noel Toolan, unveiled new marketing proposals in a presentation to a Marketing Institute meeting in Galway, in January 1997. The annual amount of earnings from tourism was then £2.3bn., representing 8.5 per cent of GDP, almost all of which was retained in the country. It was the top generator of wealth for Ireland.

However, Mr Toolan stated that new challenges were taking place and Bord Fáilte was now facing increased competition. Countries like Vietnam and Morocco were also expanding their industries and spending huge money on advertising budgets. There were three steps to the 'Total Tourism Marketing' approach:

1. Business was to be redefined from maximising visitor numbers to maximising visitor revenue.

2. Segmentation research showed that the US, UK and European markets each generated about 30 per cent of tourism revenue. Further analysis was required to set priorities for scarce resources, extend the season and disperse revenue around the country.

3. Customer contact was vital. Communicate the right message to the right people to get them to spend the right type of money at the right time of year in the right places.

'Total Tourism Marketing' was not just a logo. It was a commercial way forward where Northern Ireland and the Republic had joined under the one identity to sell themselves abroad.

DIRECT LINE TO CUSTOMER CARE, JANUARY 1997

For the sophisticated and demanding customer a quick and efficient service is of vital importance. In Ireland the growth in the use of customer carelines was a result of companies' reponse to customer demands and also manufacturers' commitment to service.

Most of the larger companies like Kelloggs, Coca Cola and Lever Brothers had carelines. Telecom Éireann's head of telemarketing services, Ms Dorothy O'Byrne, stated that the main benefits of carelines are that 'carelines send out signals to customers that you want to develop a dialogue'. The customer can contact you free, or at low cost and the lines give immediate feedback and so record customer satisfaction.

In the US, 90 per cent of products carry a careline, while the number in Ireland at that time was less than 1 per cent. Irish customers were, however, embracing teleculture enthusiastically.

MITSUBISHI ELECTRIC IRELAND, JANUARY 1997

At the Martello Room in Jury's hotel, Dublin on 23 January 1997, Mr Fergus Madigan, president of Mitsubishi Electric Ireland, told of the success of the company he had established back in 1981. It was now the most successful Mitsubishi company in the world, in terms of market share and enjoyed market leadership in most of the product sectors in which it competed.

Mr Madigan maintained that the success was driven by a combination of classic branding and powerful marketing of all its products. The most recent illustration of the tremendously effective formula was Mitsubishi's entry into the fiercely competitive PC market.

PROMOTING CROSS BORDER TOURISM, JANUARY 1997

Two leader companies, in County Louth and South Down/Armagh, came together to look at the establishment of a community tourism initiative. County Louth, as one of the six southern counties bordering Northern Ireland was often referred to as 'the wee county' as it covered the smallest county area in the Republic of Ireland. The county has some of the finest scenery in Ireland, including the Cooley peninsula and Carlingford in the north to Drogheda, the gateway of the Boyne valley in the south.

The Louth tourist action plan was produced and looked on from a critical angle in relation to tourism. Consultants who undertook the report recommended, and highlighted, a strategic approach. The region was identified as a core area and fully defined.

THE OFFICE OF REGULATOR, JANUARY 1997

The recently appointed regulator of premium rate telephone services, covering the 1,500 range of numbers, was Mr Fred Hayden, newly elected Fellow of the Marketing Institute. Mr Hayden was born in Castledermot, Co. Carlow and was from a farming background and it had been his intention to teach at one time.

The office of regulator had been set up eighteen months previously and he had been appointed on the nomination of the director of consumer affairs and the approval of the Department of Transport, Energy and Communications with the agreement of Telecom Éireann. It was established to ensure that the services were running according to the code. The regulator drew up the code and adjusted or reviewed it in conjunction with the other players in the field — Telecom Éireann and the service providers. The availability of services to the public included weather forecasting, commercial competitions, astrology, tarot area, tourism information and helplines.

Mr Hayden believed that the growth of different techniques in marketing and the concentration today on consumer requirements were probably the most important elements of change. Also marketing had more recognition due to the availability of communication methods, varying from the media to below the line activities.

MARKETING STUDENT OF THE YEAR

Mr Tom Halpin, marketing executive of the Irish Energy Centre, was awarded the Student of the Year Diploma 1996. Originally from Drumcondra, Dublin, he studied in Árd Scoil Rís before completing a degree in electronic engineering at UCD.

His career based him far and wide, and he was experienced in a variety of engineering and marketing areas. Despite that he never got a hankering to move out of Ireland permanently.

Saving on energy

Mr Halpin's appointment as marketing executive to the Irish Energy Centre (IEC) was in August 1995. He is responsible for managing the centre's promotional activities, including advertising, PR, design and major information events, such as Energy Awareness Week and the Energy Show.

The IEC is an EU funded joint initiative of the Department of Transport, Energy and Communications, and Forbairt. It has a mission to promote and support energy efficiency in all sections of the economy. The work programme is defined until 1999 and the IEC has £21m. worth of funding to achieve £50m. savings in the yearly energy bill, which totals over £36bn. annually.

MR DAVID DAND, INSTITUTE PRESIDENT, 1992–1996, RIP

It was with the most sincere regret to learn of the demise of Mr David Dand, a long standing and revered member of the Marketing Institute and its predecessor, the Incorporated Sales Managers' Association.

Of Mr David Dand, Mr Redmond O'Donoghue MMII, national chairman
of the MII, said:

> There are gentlemen, there are businessmen and there are friends. David
> Dand was all three. His outstanding achievement, for his company, and
> for his country, was bringing Bailey's Irish Cream to the world. But
> David was much more than an extraordinary salesman; he was a so-
> phisticated business manager who fully understood that he must use
> the assets of the business in the most effective way.
>
> He continuously achieved this goal with outstanding success, with
> a great sense of fun and with his unique style.

MAKE USE OF THE NET, MARCH 1997

The idea of interacting with customers via the net was something new in 1997.
One way of raising awareness and helping marketers to conceive more mature internet strategies was called the ICDT — information, communication,
distribution, transaction — model. Each of the four approaches has a different
set of aims, investments and organisational objectives.

New sites

Marketing 1:1 (www.marketing1to1.com), the Connecticut-based company
run by gurus Martha and Don Peppers, set up an extensive and content-rich
website so that users could order books or subscribe to the company's newsletter, *Inside 1:1*, which covers a range of marketing and web-related business
issues.

Advertising and Marketing Review (www.ad-mkt-review.com) contains
articles on copyright, intellectual property and trouble-shooting digital video.

Marketing CD Roms, March 1997

The first series of multimedia educational programmes on marketing was produced by the Multimedia Marketing Consortium. The Marketing CD ROMs
are an aid to learning about marketing in a completely new way. Thoughts can
be compared with ordinary people, top marketing managers and world gurus.
One can go as far as exploring a particular item and its related examples in the
vast layers of hyperlinks.

A visit can be made to the Hall of Fame where Theodore Levitt, Rosabeth
Moss Kanter, Kenichi Ohmae, Philip Kotler and Peter Doyle reveal the se-
crets of marketing success.

Video browsers can be used to see marketing managers, from Coca Cola
to Concorde and Microsoft to Manchester United, explain how they do it for

real. Further information is available from Mr Paul Smith, MMII Grad., London Guildhall University, 84, Moorgate, London EC2M 6SQ.

CASE STUDY ROUTE TO MII GRADUATE MEMBERSHIP, APRIL 1997

The Marketing Institute offered from April 1997 its four-year graduateship programme final year students at DIT, RTC and VEC colleges as well as by distance learning, to simply take a one-day case study examination. Successful candidates would then be admitted to graduate membership of the Institute, using the designation MMII Grad.

ORGANISATIONAL CHANGE, MAY 1997

Mr Martin Sorrell, chief executive of the WPP Group, the world's largest advertising and marketing services company, addressed Institute members in May 1997 about structures and processes involving significant organisational change developed by clients in response to environmental changes. He gave examples of free trade, communications, technology and travel, and the need for corresponding response from the marketing services industry.

People in advertising and marketing services were probably the most conservative profession that his clients had to deal with, probably more so than lawyers, investment bankers or management consultants. In fact, their organisational structures were very similar to 80 years ago — functionally driven, silo-like structures that failed to communicate as effectively and efficiently as they should in the increasingly competitive world.

Something like 80 per cent of advertising in the newspapers was interactive, in the sense that it demanded a response from the customer through a box number, telephone number, coupon or classified advertisement. What was new, he said, was the power of the new technologies. The new electronic means of communication had facilitated the development of new technologies more radically than before — a critical issue for marketing services. Business had become global because of competitive pressures.

IRELAND'S FIRST EMAIL DIRECTORY, JUNE 1997

E-Search, Ireland's email directory on the web: HTTP://WWW.ESEARCH.IE, was launched in 1997. Almost 2,200 people registered their addresses and the number was climbing. Registrations were a mixture of business and personal.

Irish people at home and abroad registered their email address and other optional information fields. The directory could be searched by any combination of first name, second name or organisation. The search could be narrowed by county/state, country or organisation. It was free to register and search in the directory as E-Search got its return through advertising on the site.

Unlike most American directories, E-Search did not sweep the internet and populate the database without the permission of the owner of the address. All registrations were either by the owner of the address through the website or by E-Search with the consent of the person. Neither did E-Search pass on mailing lists to any third party.

WEB ADVERTISING, JUNE 1997

In 1997 advertisers wondered how many times a web page was read or how many visitors to a website clicked on the advertisement to get more information. For electronic publications and eventually traditional media there could have significant implications. Websites with the highest number of visitors, such as search services, could charge a premium if large numbers of their users were sufficiently attracted to click on advertisements. The internet publishing industry, for instance, expected a new form of targeted direct marketing with advertisers paying a bounty to web publishers who could deliver readers from specific demographic groups.

PRESIDENT'S NIGHT, JUNE 1997

The President's Night function, highlight of the Marketing Institute year, was held at Trinity College, Dublin on 13 June 1997. It was the members' tribute to their president and the annual forum for the presentation of Institute awards. The evening was hosted by the president, Mr John O.P. Bourke, with guest speaker Mr Paddy J. Wright FMII, president and chief operations officer of Jefferson Smurfit Plc.

Fellowship awards, June 1997

The Fellowship awards, for outstanding service to the Marketing Institute and the profession of marketing in Ireland, were presented, following citations, to:

- Mr David Bunworth FMII: director of sales and marketing, Aer Lingus

- Mr Pat Fahy FMII: principal of Creg Associates, Limerick

- Mr Fergus Madigan FMII: president of Mitsubishi Electric Ltd

- Dr John McGuire FMII: managing director of Rehab Lotteries Ltd

- Mr Patrick J. Nevin FMII Grad.: chief executive of the Jones Group Plc

- Ms Barbara Patton FMII Grad.: head of marketing, Irish Permanent Plc.

The Stephen Doyle award, 1997

Mr Robert Gahan FMII, Seirbhís Thelifís na Gaelige, was presented with the Stephen Doyle award, for meritorious service to marketing and to the development of the Institute.

Part 6

Into the millennium, 1997 – 2000

WOMEN RISING IN THE SALES FORCE, MAY 1997

Are women better at selling than men? They were certainly taking the world of sales by storm in 1997. The *Evening Herald* of 29 May 1997 carried an article by Mr Brendan O'Reilly FMII headed: 'Who's a Better Seller?' Mr O'Reilly went on to say that the latest figures showed an astonishing rise in saleswomen, which, if continued at the same pace, would soon eclipse their male counterparts.

Mr O'Reilly, chief executive of recruiter, Sales Placement, said 'women, by and large, have a different approach to selling than men. For a start they are better listeners — one of the most important aspects of selling They will weigh up and analyse selling situations very carefully'. The pharmaceutical/healthcare sector had the highest proportion of women in sales, though it would be changing with the fast growing information technology sector catching up. The average basic salary for a sales representative in Ireland was nearly £19,000, with bonuses and commission on top. The percentage of women working in sales positions had grown from 4 per cent in 1982, to 26 per cent in 1990, to 33 per cent in 1996.

IRISH MARKETING TEACHERS' ASSOCIATION, 1997

In May 1997 the annual Irish Marketing Teachers' Association conference acclaimed Professor Anthony Cunningham's contribution to marketing in Ireland. Among those present at the IMTA conference were: Prof. William K. Clarke, University of Ulster; Prof. James Lynch, University of Leeds; Prof. Michael Baker, University of Strathclyde; Prof. Mary Lambkin, University College, Dublin; Prof. David Carson, University of Ulster and Prof. John Murray, Trinity College, Dublin.

CHANGING THE BOOK MARKET, JUNE 1997

Mr Derek Hughes MMII, group managing director of Hughes Book Services, (HBS), was invited to attend the renowned Insead business school in Paris, where he took part in the owners/directors programme. In 1995 HBS had won the award of European Entrepreneur Member of Europe's 500 dynamic entrepreneurial companies. Mr Hughes adopted some blueprints from the programme for HBS with plans to implement others in the future.

He had worked for fifteen years with the company, set up by his father, and developed an awareness of the needs and desires of the book buying public. His plan was to open up a number of retail units throughout the country. At the same time he said the book market was changing and new challenges faced it.

A third company, Hughes Media Services, was set up in 1996. This was a national wholesale distributor of audio and video products. A 24-hour delivery service to all points of Ireland was made available. Booksales in supermarkets had grown. The retail end had been very successful and the first store was at Nutgrove Shopping Centre, Dublin, which was opened in 1984.

At Dublin Airport they opened four units in 1985, with other openings at St Stephen's Green in 1990, Lisburn in Northern Ireland in 1993 and Frascati Shopping Centre in Blackrock, Dublin, in 1996. The opportunity to move into retailing involved a high standard of customer service. The key development was technology.

Book buying changed

According to Mr Hughes the book-buying public had changed in the previous ten years. They now wanted a specialist bookshop, while Irish publishers were taking a bigger slice of the cake. The industry needed to encourage children to read at an early age because then they would continue to do so.

Parents also had a key role and needed the backup of the educational system.

IRISH COMPANIES COME 'ON-LINE', JUNE 1997

An EU initiative was launched to bring Irish companies on line to the commercial benefits of multimedia and the internet. Research found that 61 per cent of Ireland's top 500 companies felt they needed to be better informed about the internet, with 59 per cent of the same group wanting more information on multimedia in order to be in a position to benefit commercially from the technologies.

The second Irish internet/multimedia survey had been carried out, by the Dublin based Nua Ltd, for MIDAS.NET. They were released at the launch of MIDAS.NET Ireland, a new nationwide help-desk for multimedia and the internet. It was funded under the European Commission. The help included nationwide seminars, roadshows, exhibitions and training programmes introducing the internet, multimedia, CD-ROMS and on-line, especially to small companies that had not yet ventured on-line.

Government initiatives to help Irish companies

Ms Maryse Collins, marketing manager, of the renowned Kenny's bookshop in Galway, said that her company generated approximately £65,000 in sales on the internet in 1996 and expected to top £100,000 in 1997.

Mr Alan Dukes TD, Minister for Transport, Energy and Communications, outlined government initiatives to help Irish companies take advantage of on-line services. These included the liberalisation of the telecommunications sector and the introduction of a special system of tariff regulation for services not subject to effective competition. Mr Dukes stated that this meant putting a 'price cap' on Telecom Éireann's tariffs, which would result in a reduction of their prices by around 35 per cent in real terms, by the year 2000 when the market would be opened up.

AMERICAN MARKETING ASSOCIATION IN DUBLIN, 1997

Probably the world's largest body of marketing academics, the American Marketing Association,(AMA), came to Dublin in June 1997 to run a major conference in conjunction with the Michael Smurfit Graduate School of Business at University College Dublin. It was the first time the AMA had been involved in a major conference outside the USA for fifteen years. The overall theme was contained in the conference title: 'New and Evolving Paradigms: the Emerging Future of Marketing'.

There were three sub-conferences in areas of marketing undergoing fundamental change. These were: Services Marketing; Relationship Marketing and Marketing Communications.

Unlike most conferences, which the AMA solely sponsored, it was co-sponsored by the Graduate School of Business at University College, Dublin.

It was considered very important in terms of positioning UCD as one of Europe's leading schools.

The proceedings of the conference, edited by Dr Tony Meenaghan, were published on CD-ROM format. This was also a first for the AMA and saved delegates from having to carry home several weighty volumes. Co-chairing the conference were Professor Mike Etel of Notre Dame, Professor Stan Madden of Baylor University, Texas and Dr Tony Meenaghan, University College, Dublin.

Overall some 340 delegates from 27 countries attended in the Burlington Hotel, Dublin from 12–15 June 1997. The AMA regarded it as one of its most successful ever conferences.

The Gala dinner was a highlight and was held in the O'Reilly Hall of University College, Dublin.

MARKS & SPENCER'S FIRST TV ADVERTS, JULY 1997

The UK's biggest retailer, Marks & Spencer, launched its first TV advertising campaign —to promote financial services — in July 1997.

They did it because many customers were unaware of their financial service products. At this time the company had no plans to advertise M&S food and clothing.

M&S now sells unit trusts, personal pensions, standard term assurance and personal loans, being one of the first store groups into the financial services sector.

IRISH DESIGN AWARD, JULY 1997

There were 1700 entries from eighteen European countries to a major European competition. Despite this heavy competition an Irish annual report was awarded a gold medal. The report was designed by Kunnert & Tierney and printed by an Irish printer, City Print. The hosts and sponsors of the competition were SAPPI Europe (South African Pulp and Paper Industries), one of the largest paper manufacturers in the world.

The Pfizer Irish Pension Scheme Annual Report, was entered by the Cork-based designers for the McNaughton paper design and print awards in Ireland. Having won the design section of the competition, the winning piece was then put forward for the SAPPI Europe awards.

The gold medal was presented by Mr Franz Neudeck, managing director of SAPPI Europe. The winning report then went to the world competition in Capetown, South Africa in September.

After the presentation, Ms Elaine Tierney, director at Kunnert & Tierney, said: 'the strategic importance of such an award did much to highlight, in the European marketplace, the quality of work being achieved in Ireland'.

ROLE OF MARKETING IN SOCIETY, 1997

The Marketing Institute's north-west regional council organised an essay competition, sponsored by Forbairt, for transition year and fifth year students of secondary schools in the region. Students were asked to write an essay entitled: 'The Role of Marketing in Society' and provide their own ideas on what they thought marketing was, whether marketing was good or bad and use examples to back up their views.

The prize-winning essay (from Ms Rebecca Strain) brought out many examples relating to quality, brand, promotional offers, sponsorships and so forth. She said, amongst other things, that: 'when you think about it, marketing has a huge role in society' and 'marketing existed because people demand knowledge about the newest and the best products'.

The winners were:

- 1st: Ms Rebecca Strain, Loreto Community School, Milford, Co. Donegal
- 2nd: Ms Elaine Giblin, St Patrick's College, Ballina, Co. Mayo
- 3rd: Mr Richard Kilfeather, Sligo Grammer School, The Mall, Sligo.

SELLING THE IRISH ABROAD, AUGUST 1997

Ms Cathryn Hargan MMII Grad., sector manager of Bord Bia, introduces potential buyers to the qualities of Irish food and drink. Her job, in the consumer foods division of Bord Bia, centres around marketing and facilitating the introduction to foreign buyers.

In December 1994, the Irish Meat Board, CBF, and the food promotion responsibilities of An Bord Tráchtála were transferred to a single organisation — Bord Bia. It co-ordinated promotional effort and marketing expertise to what is Ireland's largest indigenous industry.

The organisation's international operating structure comprises units in Dublin, Dusseldorf, London, Madrid, Milan, Moscow, New York and Paris. The Dublin office of An Bord Bia has less than fifty employees while more than half of them are engaged in market development activity, supporting marketing staff based overseas.

Their marketing incentive and strategic market development schemes provide companies with grants for various marketing activities, including market research, travel, the recruitment of marketing graduates and attendance at courses and seminars. Also available is financial assistance if a company needs a consultant to help draw up a marketing plan. In return the companies give increased employment and exports.

STEP INTO MARKETING, 1997

'Step into Marketing', a self-directed learning programme, was devised by the Marketing Institute for transition year students in second level schools. The programme had been successfully pilot-tested, during 1996–97, in the Sacred Heart Secondary School, Clonakilty, Co. Cork, and certificates were awarded to twenty-two students in June 1997. It had since been launched nationally.

The method includes:

- a self-directed learning programme — students working on their own through eight units
- a learning pack which teaches, tests and provides feedback

- a member of staff who acts as supervisor and checks that the students are progressing satisfactorily — the supervisor needs no marketing expertise

- support from the Marketing Institute for the supervisor through the provision of workshops

- an award from the Marketing Institute of a 'Step into Marketing' certificate to all candidates who complete the programme satisfactorily.

The material for the programme was written by Mr Sean Cowman FMII, a marketing instructor in FÁS, Cork, and run in partnership with CEED Ltd.

MII AGM, SEPTEMBER 1997

The 36th AGM of the Marketing Institute was held at Marketing House, Leopardstown, Dublin 18 on Thursday 4 September 1997.

In his speech the outgoing chairman, Mr Redmond O'Donoghue said that there had been both high points and low points in the past year. The most significant low point by far was the death of the Institute's former president, Mr David Dand. The high points were many, including record membership levels, excellent financial results, the programme of events, the strength of the regions, the expanding suite of educational programmes and the initiation of the strategic review process.

MII appointments

Mr John O.P. Bourke was re-elected as president for 1997–98. The chairman was Mr David Nea MMII, director of Cawley Nea. The following executive council officers were announced:

- Deputy Chairman: Mr Gerry Mortimer MMII

- Hon. Secretary: Mr Myles McHugh MMII

- Hon. Treasurer: Mr David Mooney MMII Grad.

- Vice-Chairpersons: Mr Ciaran Conroy MMII Grad. and Ms Barbara Patton MMII Grad.

- Chairman of Fellows: Mr Anthony Neville FMII Grad.

The outgoing chairman, Mr Redmond O'Donoghue, remained as an ex-officio member of the executive committee.

Mr David Nea said that he was fortunate to become chairman at a time when the Institute was in such a healthy strong state. He took the view that the country's positive business environment presented both challenges and opportunities and he intended that to be the focus of his attention in continuing the work on the strategic initiative, referred to by his predecessor.

Chairpersons for regions, 1997–98:

- Kerry: Mr Niall O'Loingsigh MMII, John M. Murphy (Tralee)

- Mid-West: Mr John B. Ryan MMII, Telecom Éireann

- South: Mr Ray Walsh MMII, Ray Walsh Associates

- South-East: Mr Pat Loftus MMII, IDA Ireland

- North-East: Mr Malachy Magee MMII, Irish Life

- North-West: Ms Paula Lawlor MMII Grad., Professional Merchandising & Marketing Services

- West: Mr Norman Rochford MMII, John F. Rochford & Co.

National council members: Tony Amoroso MMII (Smurfit), Paula Cogan MMII (Jury's), Mary Crotty MMII (Mary Crotty PR), John Diskin MMII Grad. (Momentum), Valerie Hannigan MMII Grad (*Finance* magazine), Don Harris MMII (Airtime Ltd), Michael Hayes MMII (Gilbey's) and Bill McHugh MMII (News Extracts).

Business Person award, September 1997

Business & Finance, 11 September 1997 issue, reported that Mr Redmond O'Donoghue, chief executive of Waterford Crystal, was declared *Business Person of the Week*. An interim profit of £6.7m. on sales of £70.3m. for the six months to the end of June 1997, had just been reported.

MARKETING CRUCIAL FACTOR, 1997

In 1997 the Marketing Institute's survey of Ireland's top marketers, was undertaken to update that of 1992. It allowed the Institute to better understand the attitudes, concerns and priorities of senior managers currently responsible for the marketing function in Ireland's leading companies. The survey was carried out for the Institute by Lansdowne Market Research Ltd.

A listing of the top 1,000 companies (compared to 500 in 1992) was made with a random selection of 628 heads of marketing. The response was 38 per cent with 236 completed questionnaires recorded.

The belief of 90 per cent of the heads of marketing was that marketing *is* the key factor for success. Yet, two out of three still felt that marketing was not taken seriously enough in Irish companies. They felt that business in Ireland would benefit more from people with a marketing background becoming chief executives. It was felt also that government and semi-state bodies should do more to promote marketing in Ireland. More than eight out of ten believed marketing was becoming more influential in their company.

The survey confirmed that the 'Celtic Tiger' was alive and well. More than half believed European Monetary Union, EMU, would have a positive impact on their company. About nine out of ten felt that Irish companies invested too little time in training their people in marketing. That comparison with 1992 was unchanged.

EUROPEAN MONETARY UNION — EMU IMPLICATIONS, 1997

Changes in banking and the financial services industry continued to make a rapid and increasing impact in 1997. Globalisation, and most importantly, new technology were presenting new challenges. Economic and Monetary Union (EMU) would further accelerate the process.

The preparations, over the ensuing eighteen months, would be a critical issue for financial institutions in their preparation for EMU. It was likely that Ireland would be in a position to join EMU at its commencement on 1 January 1999.

Mr Philip Halpin, chief operating officer of the National Irish Bank, who had given presentations and published articles and papers on the subject of EMU a few years ago, gave an impressive talk entitled: 'European Monetary Union — Implications for Irish Business'. This took place in the Dome Restaurant, St Stephen's Green Shopping Centre, Dublin on 17 September 1997.

A native of Dublin, Mr Halpin was a graduate of UCD and lectured in economics at the College of Marketing, University of Gezira, Sudan and the Irish Institute of Public Administration.

REVIEW OF MARKETING AND BUSINESS, 1997

In the 1997 brochure review Mr John Bourke, president of the Marketing Institute, said the contrast between the early and late 1990s provided an opportunity to reflect on different approaches to achieving business success. He pointed to the core distinctions which a marketing orientation brought to a business. One approach was based on squeezing more and more output through greater efficiency; the other was based on taking advantage of improved prospects to grow and expand. Switching from the macro economic picture to the micro economic perspective of an individual enterprise would make the point more easily understood.

He believed that business might have many objectives in building success but two were likely to dominate. He referred to those to do with profit (net income, EPS) and those to do with growth (sales and market share). Financial measures alone could create barriers to achieving balanced financial and marketing strategies over time. Problems arose when financial measures based on realising short-run profit result in bad marketing decisions, such as cutting back on investment in new products or neglecting to develop new market segments. On an encouraging note, he finished by saying that 'good marketing continues to be relevant throughout the business cycle'.

INNOVATIVE MARKETING, 1997

The National Marketing Conference, in association with *Business & Finance,* took place at Industry Centre, University College, Dublin, on 16 October 1997. The conference patrons were Esat Telecom, Ford and the Irish Permanent Building Society. The chairpersons at the conference were: Ms Karen White, Esat Telecom and Mr Michael Duffy, Bord Bia.

The chairman of the organising committee, Mr John O.P. Bourke (president of MII) wrote in the Sept./Oct. 1997 issue of *MII News* that of all the business functions marketing was most likely to suffer from a crisis of identity. Marketers were constantly urged to make their effectiveness more measurable, creating the need for their activities to become quantifiable and there was no denying the necessity for the discipline. Other business colleagues were still more likely to turn to marketers, when the spark of creativity, of imagination and of spontaneity was likely to make the difference.

Innovative marketing continued to be the most exciting of business activities and the year's National Marketing Conference presented a range of case histories, analyses and studies, which showed that fresh thinking, in response to both new and traditional business challenges, was both widespread and effective.

The keynote address at the conference was given by Mr Colin Storm, deputy managing director of Guinness Brewing Worldwide (GBW). Until recently he had been managing director of the Guinness Ireland Group. He provided 'a thumbnail sketch' of the strategy followed by GBW in pursuit of its vision of being the world's best brewer and marketer of top quality beer brands.

For the previous four years, the company had been targeting the same four objectives. The first was to cover the world by growing the sales of Guinness stout around the globe and secondly to go for growth in their full portfolio markets such as Ireland, Malaysia, Spain and Nigeria where they offered a full range of brands to meet consumers' tastes. The third aim was to do it better through improved quality and finally to build on success by increasing profits at the same time as making an ever-greater investment in marketing.

Guinness Irish pub concept

The Guinness Irish Pub concept was a prime example of how Guinness connected with consumers and responded with an innovative solution. It had become a personal obsession for one of Guinness's Irish managers who wanted to extend the 'experience' of an Irish pub outside Ireland.

Mr Storm said that innovative marketing might mean developing a new brand or product that was fundamentally different but it might equally be about finding new and original ways of presenting and marketing an existing product that had been around for years. It might even mean a combination of small changes which together added up to a new and exciting way of meeting consumer needs.

Marketing — A European perspective

Ms Jean Callanan, Unilever Italia Spa, echoed one of Mr Storm's points. Her conclusion, from a review of innovation, was that successful innovation was driven by an individual of a very small close team of people with a clear vision, enthusiasm and determination to succeed. She stressed that it could not be done by a large committee or people with different agendas. To facilitate this, Unilever Ice Cream and Frozen Foods had developed the concept of the international brand manager. This allowed for the single-minded championing of an innovation.

Marketing a global professional services firm

Mr Richard O'Reilly, marketing director of Anderson Consulting Ireland, identified integration as being 'the factor to transform the various sparks of creativity into business enhancing innovations'. For larger organisations, he said, marketing success would depend on three key indicators of integration:

- how well various marketing initiatives were integrated with one another so that they were mutually reinforcing

- how well these activities were integrated with the business and how well the business was integrated with them

- how well the knowledge capability and best practice was leveraged across the marketing organisation.

Furthermore he stated that integration was achieved through the organisation of marketing activity and marketing professionals were diffused within the organisation rather than centralised.

New marketing — the new technologies

Mr John Leftwitch was named vice-president of European Marketing for Microsoft Corporation in 1997. In that position he was responsible for marketing Microsoft products and service offerings to the complete spectrum of personal computer users and channels of distribution in western and eastern Europe.

He told the conference delegates how new technologies, such as the internet, were revolutionising marketing communications and gave examples of global businesses such as the professional services and tourism. Retailing and banking were being transformed by new marketing strategies.

Mr David Nea, founding partner of Cawley Nea, Advertising and Marketing Ltd, and national chairman of the Marketing Institute, responded to the challenges of the marketing services industry and shared his views on how it should be done.

NEW WEBSITE ADDRESS OF MARKETING INSTITUTE, NOVEMBER 1997

The Marketing Institute's new virtual domain internet website address became: www.mii.ie. It brought the Institute into line with the best practice in such an important area of its promotional activity. Also added was an important new 'links' facility. To check this out one went to the Institute home page and clicked on the links icon. The purpose of this was to provide direct access to sources of information, advice, services etc. of interest to marketing personnel.

GRADUATION DAY, NOVEMBER 1997

The graduation day on 29 November 1997 was again the highlight of the year for marketing students. In the Foundation Certificate examinations, 230 qualified, with 188 obtaining the Diploma and 155 Graduateship of the Institute.

Before the presentation ceremony, the president, Mr John Bourke and the chairman, Mr David Nea, hosted a lunch in Fitzers Cafe to honour those students who excelled in the examinations. In addition to the prizewinners, the guests included lecturers from the colleges of the winning students. The sponsors of the awards also attended as well as representatives of the companies where the winners worked. The Institute invited the latter in order to give due recognition to the partnership between education and business.

Mr Bourke, president of the Institute, presented the parchments and congratulated the successful students and their families who provided the moral support. Mr John Casey, chief executive of the Institute, encouraged the graduates to take up the invitation to become members of the Marketing Institute.

The award winners were:

• Graduate of the Year: Ms Susan Jesper

- Marketing Finance award: Ms Julie Jones
- Marketing Management and Strategy award: Ms Orla Fleming
- Management of Sales and Customer Service award: Mr Gerard D'Arcy
- Marketing Communications award: Mr Noel Mullen
- International Marketing Management and Strategy award: Mr Finn McGuirk
- Services Marketing award: Ms Sinead Flynn
- Certificate Student of the Year: Ms Susan Daly.

WEBSITE VALUE TRIANGLE, DECEMBER 1997

Jointly organised by the Marketing Institute and the Irish Internet Association, a seminar was held entitled: 'The Internet: Marketing Success Stories'.

Mr John O'Shea, managing director of Webfactory, described the concept of the website value triangle. He drew a diagram of a triangle showing, in ascending order, awareness, information, interaction and transaction. His descriptions included:

- awareness: increasing awareness of the existence of the company

- information: the website becomes a channel for informing visitors of products, services and general company data. The site can become the repository of the most up-to-date information and be a valuable reference point

- interaction: at this level the internet medium's advantages are being utilised. Valuable customer feedback and market research can be garnered which can lead to improvements in customer service level. Customers may request service calls, installations, quotes, etc.

- transaction: visitors undertake transactions with the site, which may include purchasing goods. Benefits include lower cost of sales, distribution and processing.

ADVERTS ON THE WEB, DECEMBER 1997

A full-screen advertisement that pops up when you visit a website was among the latest innovations on the internet. This was called the 'intermercial'. Already being run on 'push' services that deliver content automatically to internet users, they are five to ten second animated advertisements.

ENTREPRENEURS — CHANCERS OR GANGSTERS?, DECEMBER 1997

Mr Dan Flinter, chief executive of Forbairt, spoke at a South-East region meeting, of the Marketing Institute, on the subject of: 'Towards an Enterprise Culture'. He informed the audience that historically Ireland did not produce a high percentage of entrepreneurs. It had a poor record at producing and nurturing those precious individuals who created, sustained and grew a business. They were positively looked down on. The Irish attitude to business creators had been to describe them as 'gangsters' and 'chancers' if they failed.

He went on to say that 50 per cent of business start-ups failed. In the United States they looked upon business failure as part of the education of an entrepreneur. No academic business course could simulate the kicks and blows endured during business failure.

However the attitude in Ireland was thankfully changing. Mr Flinter said people had been encouraged by the examples of Irish business creators such as Green Isle Foods, Monaghan Mushrooms, and in the South-East, Kent Manufacturing, Fish Distributors South-East Ltd and Alcast Ltd.

BOOM TIME IN LIMERICK, 1997

The third largest city in the Republic of Ireland is Limerick. It has a population of about 52,000. Over the last ten years more than £200m. had been invested in the city. 1997 proudly marked its Charter 800. The Charter 800 celebrated the granting of the first charter to be given the right to elect a mayor. It was in the time of the Crusaders, King Richard the Lionheart and the legend of Robin Hood, that Limerick was granted its first charter in 1197.

There were many reasons for Limerick to celebrate in 1997. In November 1997 the opening of a Rugby Heritage Centre weekend saw the celebration of World Spirit of Rugby weekend. There was also the Charter 800 fashion awards for mediaeval, military and lace designs, with the best of Limerick fashion on show. The industrial sector had grown by over 33 per cent in the 1990–95 period. Some 8,700 new jobs had been created in the previous two years. The fastest growth had been in the electronics and instrument engineering sectors. Shannon Development had helped to create new jobs. In the previous year 1,255 jobs were created through business expansion and the arrival of new industry, through guidance of the IDA.

Established by the Chamber of Commerce, Limerick, as part of its Business and Local Affairs Forum, a report was carried out by LEFG (Local Economic Factors Group). The main purpose of the report was to enhance the performance and welfare of the retail community in the greater Limerick area.

Marketing training in Limerick

Limerick was very well serviced with marketing courses at the Limerick Regional Technical College and Limerick Senior College and the Batchelor of Business Studies (BBS) had a marketing specialisation at the University of Limerick. Graduates qualify for the case study route to graduate membership of the Marketing Institute.

CODE OF PRACTICE, 1998

The Marketing Institute set out details of its Code of Practice in *MII News*, Jan./Feb. 1998. The Code of Practice is a regulation of the Institute. Some of the main items include:

Professional responsibility

All members are answerable to the council of the Institute for any conduct which, in the opinion of the council, constitutes a breach of the code. All members have responsibility to their employers or clients, to customers, to colleagues, to the marketing profession and to the general public.

Professional conduct

At all times members shall conduct themselves as persons of integrity and observe the principles of the code. Other undertakings of members arise under headings of: Instruction to others; Injury to others; Honesty; Professional competence; Conflict of interest; Confidentiality of information; Securing and Developing business and other relevant Codes of Practice.

The council of MII will always accept other relevant Codes of Practice, as a minimum level to be expected of members of the Institute, unless it has determined to the contrary, and informed members of its decision.

The most important aspects of the other relevant codes relate to: advertising, sales promotion, market research, public relations and marketing. The various bodies under each heading having been listed. For example under marketing, the Direct Marketing Code of Practice (Irish Direct Marketing Association), International Code of Marketing Practice (International Chamber of Commerce) are the referred to bodies outside the Marketing Institute of Ireland.

Enforcement of the Code

The relative areas referred to are the role of the individual member; misuse of the code; procedures for handling complaints and consequences that will/may follow.

The Marketing Institute thanked the Chartered Institute of Marketing (UK) for its support and guidance in the preparation of the Code of Practice.

CORK REGION MARKETING, JANUARY 1998

Cork Region Marketing was set up in April 1995. This was a Cork city and county, public and private sector tourism marketing initiative. It followed a conference on marketing in Cork in October 1994 organised by the Marketing Institute in association with the Cork Chamber of Commerce.

An attendance of 150 included representatives of local authorities, government bodies, industry and tourism.

The conference conclusion was that, while many individual tourism products in the Cork region were being marketed, the region was not being promoted as a single entity. A steering group translated the views into a cohesive co-operative marketing plan.

According to Ray Walsh, chairman of the Marketing Institute South-West region, Cork had a number of natural strengths. He provided examples of the many areas within the county with a very high tourism profile and a highly diversified landscape with a high quality environment.

Opportunities were seen for the growth of visitors from Britain and overseas.

The possibilities of incorporating funding and investment in a co-ordinated marketing effort were looked into, as were the securing of major international events with a consequent development of high yield incentive business for the region.

Cork has always regarded itself as the alternative capital in Ireland. Cork city was now a thriving centre for business, cultural and social activity. A testimony to that was Southern Advertising, the only agency outside of Dublin making the national newspapers of Ireland list of top advertising agencies. It was ranked No. 13 with expenditure of £832,163. That figure was for the period January–June 1997, and indicated that Southern's annual expenditure for 1998 should be about £1.6m.

By giving clients a free marketing service, the managing director of Southern Advertising, Mr Manus O'Callaghan said 'we get paid through media commission and not from the client, that being the unique selling point, and it has proved a very popular point'.

BARRY'S BAKERY, JANUARY 1998

Established in 1912, Barry's Bakery in Midleton, Co. Cork, a business of the independent Irish baker, spelled its marketing success story of survival in 1998, even with the growth of chains in Ireland, such as Tesco and Marks & Spencer.

Mr John Barry set up the bakery in 1912, something of an institution in Midleton and the Cork region. The managing director in 1998 was Mr John Roche, chartered accountant and grandson of the founder. In 1994 Mr Roche purchased the bakery from his uncle. At the time they had only one van on the road (there were nine vans in the 'heyday').

Society wanted easy and long-lasting foods, leaving little shelf space for bread/confectionery that had no preservatives. First of all Mr Roche had to get that longevity into the bakery products. After sixteen months doing tests the required results were achieved. Barry's developed two confectionery products and a bread which were launched on the Irish and European markets. The Irish Whiskey cake and the Irish Cream Liqueur cake were produced. Mr Roche opted for packaging that reflected the Irishness of the product and included a short history of the company. The missing link was found to be *marketing*.

Now Ms Maire Curtin took up the challenge and became the first marketing manager appointed to the bakery. While her degree was in research science she had always been interested in marketing throughout her college years. Barry's targeted their products at the UK, France and Germany as part of the speciality food sector.

MARKETING AND THE EURO, 1998

Mr Jean-Marie Van Houwe, director-general of EMC, the European Marketing Confederation, stated that during meetings with marketers in Europe, there was more and more evidence that a large number of enterprises, in particular SME's, had not yet addressed the complex technical questions of the changeover to the Euro.

He went on to say that it was the claim of the chartered accountants that the sales and marketing department must be the driver of the implications in their company of the move to the Euro, not the personnel, nor the production nor the financial department. In or out most companies would be confronted with the Euro as from January 1, 1999. The Euro would have important commercial repercussions and the most affected of all would be the distribution chain.

Mr Van Howe believed that to plan for the changeover a project team should be set up, with members of the various departments affected, in order to review the impact for one's company. The ideal team leader should be an experienced marketer.

A VISION OF IRISH RETAILING 2010, 1998

Mr Steve Costelloe was the general manager of Marks & Spencer (Ireland)

Ltd. He had been appointed to that position in October 1997, having spent ten years as general manager of M & S Lisburn, where they have their largest Food Store, Sprucefield. It is the biggest shop on the island of Ireland.

Mr Costelloe was chairman of the Northern Ireland Education Business Partnership and vice-chairman of 'Business in the Community'. In 1977 he was awarded an MBE for Services to Education. He had 26 years experience in retailing, including working in store development in Head Office for four years.

He gave a very interesting and informative evening talk to Marketing Institute members and guests in The Martello Room, Jury's Hotel, Dublin on 2 February 1998. This was the eighteenth year of Marks & Spencer Ireland trading in Dublin, with another successful store in Cork, and plans to open further stores later in the year, including Liffey Valley.

Mr Costello said that their introduction to the Irish market had been a forerunner in their expansion into Europe. Many lessons were learnt, with the first few years being difficult. The structure of Irish retailing he said was about customers — right goods, right time, right price.

MARKETING IN ACTION, MARCH/APRIL 1998

The 'Marketing in Action' programme of the Marketing Institute meetings, sponsored by the *Irish Independent* during March/April 1998 were held at The Martello Room, Jury's hotel, Dublin. The well-attended meetings were chaired by Mr Vincent Wall of the *Irish Independent*.

Strategies for moving a successful Irish technology company into the future

The speaker on Monday 6 April 1998 was Mr Colin Newman, vice-president of marketing and a director of Iona Technologies.

Founded in 1991, to help organisations facing the challenge of making software work together, Iona Technologies was a major indigenous success story. Their flagship product, Orbix, was the culmination of over a decade of research. They are listed on both the US Nasdaq and the Irish Stock Exchange. Iona Technologies set itself up for the challenges of the new millennium by creating strategic industry partnerships.

Observations on cultural differences — a market researcher's viewpoint

On Wednesday morning 15 April 1998 a marketing breakfast meeting was held at the Dome Restaurant, St Stephen's Green Shopping Centre, Dublin. It was sponsored by *The Irish Times*.

Mr Phelim O'Leary, a director and founding partner in 1985, of Behaviour & Attitudes, a leading Irish market research company, addressed students, members and guests on the subject: 'Observations on Cultural Differences — A Market Researcher's Viewpoint'.

Mr O'Leary, a psychologist, was a specialist in qualitative research and its development. He favoured the use of the whole range of disciplines in the analysis of research data. Also he had a particular interest in communications research and in the area of cultural differences and their implications for marketing strategies. His company utilised both qualitative and quantitative methods.

In his talk, he drew on his experience with relation to the issues referred and their relevance to contemporary marketing approaches.

NCEA GOLD MEDAL, APRIL 1998

Mr Dermot Ahern TD, Minister for Social Community and Family Affairs, presented a gold medal for the best student nationally in the NCEA Certificate in Marketing, to Mr Paul Woods of Drogheda, Co. Louth.

Mr Peter Fuller, Dundalk RTC, Mr Malachy Magee, chairman of the North-East region, Mr John Casey, chief executive of the Marketing Institute and Ms Mary Sheridan, assistant registrar of the NCEA, were also present to honour the occasion.

LANGUAGE REGISTER FOR TELESERVICES, FÁS, 1998

A brochure produced by FÁS, with the assistance of The European Commission, EURES- European Employment Services, outlined the language register for teleservices sector. It defined a FÁS service to employers seeking staff with foreign language skill and invited applicants fluent in one or more languages, in addition to English, to apply for registration .

Applicants were assessed and contacted a number of times per year in order to ensure that the register would be up to date. Companies establishing telemarketing operations in Ireland, along with existing companies, found the register of particular assistance when recruiting staff. The service was free of charge.

MAXIMISING NATURAL TOURISM RESOURCES, MAY 1998

Three leading figures in the Galway tourism industry provided discussion during an eventful evening aboard the *Corrib Princess* in May 1998. The trio referred to were Ms Paula Carroll MMII, director of sales and marketing,

Ashford Castle hotel, Mr Brian Flynn MMII, regional tourism manager, Ireland West Tourism and Ms Kathleen McDonagh, director of Go West. Despite bad weather there was an excellent attendance of members from the Institute's West region.

It was said that Ireland was fortunate to have an abundance of natural resources in its countryside. Tourism was one of the most significant revenue generating sectors in Ireland. While the *Corrib Princess* made its way up the river and into the lake, the speakers outlined how they had successfully developed and marketed specific natural resources.

Ms Paula Carroll of Ashford Castle hotel, told about the challenges of providing a product or service that could compete in a worldwide market to ensure a year round occupancy for an award winning five star hotel.

Ms Kathleen McDonagh, owner of the *Corrib Princess*, said that in the late 70s she became aware of a 'niche' in the market for a formalised form of transport to and from the Aran Islands. She founded Aran Ferries in 1980, operating from Rossaveal and carried 300 passengers in the first year. It became a highly successful company and was now carrying 75,000 passengers a year. Having left Aran Ferries in 1995, in addition to becoming owner of Corrib Tours, she co-founded Go West in 1995.

Mr Brian Flynn of Ireland West Tourism, stated that the challenge for everyone was to market and sell the West in the off season. Granted it had EU funding which contributed to the development of tourism products catering for visitors all the year round. In the three-year period 1995–1997 EU funding influenced a total investment of £66.1m. in the marketing of Irish tourism.

INSTITUTE IN LEONARDO DA VINCI PROGRAMME, MAY 1998

The Maastricht Treaty, while fully respecting the responsibility of the member states for the context and organisation of their national vocational training systems, requires, under Article 127, that the European Community should implement a vocational training policy which supports and complements the actions of the member states. The name given to the programme, which fulfils the requirement of the treaty, is Leonardo Da Vinci.

In 1996, the European Marketing Confederation successfully applied for funding under the programme for a project entitled: 'Towards the development of a European Marketing Training Benchmarking Standard and European Core Curriculum'. Phase one, involving the Netherlands, Sweden and the UK was completed in January 1998. Phase two, saw the Marketing Institute of Ireland as a partner with Belgium, Finland, France, Greece, Czech Republic and Hungary.

There were three elements to the phase of the project. It was hoped to finally lead to the point where a list of core subjects would be drawn up, which are essential to any marketing course. Two additional pieces of information would need to be elicited:

1. The extent of regional and national differences which, quite properly, exist.

2. Suggestions for updating current national programmes.

With the EMC, the Marketing Institute had applied for funding for Phase 3. The title of the proposed project was: 'Spreading Marketing Training Standards through Traditional and Distance Learning'. The outcome became a European core curriculum for marketing.

NEW FELLOWS' CHAIRMAN, MAY 1998

Mr Robert (Bob) Gahan FMII, chairman of RTÉ Commercial Enterprises Ltd, became the newly elected Chair of Fellows of the Marketing Institute in May 1998.

PRESIDENT'S NIGHT, MAY 1998

The guest speaker at the Marketing Institute's President's Night dinner on 19 May 1998 was Sir George Bull, joint chairman of Diageo Plc. The dinner held at Trinity College Dublin, was hosted by the president of the Institute Mr John Bourke. Radio Telefís Éireann were the sponsors. The distinguished guests included the British Ambassador, Her Excellency Veronica Sutherland.

In his speech Sir George said 'there's no denying some of the fun has gone out of marketing compared with my early years in the job. It's monstrously difficult launching new brands. Huge advertising budgets do not guarantee either availability in store or movement out of store. 'Me-too' products measure their life cycle in weeks'.

He said also that he foresaw relationships between industry and society continuing to evolve, as society with access to almost limitless information would pry and probe into the workings of every significant business and continually ask the question: Does this organisation contribute to our society or just exploit it?

In conclusion, Sir George stated that first class marketing would be of critical importance to the success of business in the future and that nothing could question the value of marketing.

FELLOWSHIP AWARDS, MAY 1998

Fellowships for the significant contribution to marketing, following citations, were presented to:

- Mr Richard Martin: Flogas Ireland Ltd
- Mr Richard C. Strahan: Bell Advertising
- Mr Tony Brophy: Guinness Ireland Ltd
- Mr Neville Galloway: RNAN Ltd
- Mr Patrick Howard: Thermo King, Europe
- Mr Colm Molloy: Radio Telefís Éireann
- Ms Sheila Gahan: Wilson Hartnell Public Relations
- Dr Pat Keenan: T. P. Whelehan Son & Co.
- Mr Robin Addis: Lansdowne Market Research.

THE STEPHEN DOYLE AWARD, MAY 1998

For meritorious service to marketing and his contribution to the development of the Institute over many years, the Stephen Doyle award was presented to Mr Michael Hayes FMII Grad., director of Advertising Studies, Dublin Institute of Technology, (DIT), Aungier Street, Dublin.

FIRST TRANSITION YEAR CERTIFICATES, MAY 1998

Having had the pilot programme, Step into Marketing, in Clonakilty in 1997, the first transition year students on the programme were awarded their certificates in May 1998. At Ard Scoil na nDeise in Dungarvan, County Waterford, all twenty-four girls were presented with their certificates by Ms Catherine Kilbride, director of education. Ms Kilbride congratulated them, their teacher, Ms Margaret Dennehy and their principal, Ms Margaret O'Brien, herself a graduate of the Institute.

Ms Catherine Kilbride paid particular tribute to Ryan's Super Valu, who sponsored the entire programme, stating that it was a very farseeing initiative on their part and evidence of their strong marketing culture.

WORLD MARKETING CONGRESS, JUNE 1998

The World Marketing Congress was held in Tokyo in June 1998 to coincide with the fortieth anniversary of the Japan Marketing Association. There were over 1100 delegates there from 32 countries around the world. Of the total Japan supplied 900. Over 100 made the journey from North America and Europe. Many of the (former) tiger economies of South East Asia were represented at the conference.

On his return Mr Roger Jupp FMII, managing director of Lansdowne Market Research Ltd, a former chairman of the Marketing Institute and currently vice-president of the European Marketing Confederation, gave a detailed report of the conference.

Creativity and innovation had been the broad themes addressed throughout the two days, which incorporated parallel sessions from the second day, splitting the overall conference into four separate groups. Having been a speaker at one of the parallel sessions, Mr Jupp said it would have been impossible to report on the other three. However, he said, the essence of the speeches fell into two neat groups. First of all, the broad economic issues underpinning marketing and secondly, the impact of the internet and other IT developments on marketing practice and thought.

Japan had experienced the most prolonged recession in its post-war history and was clearly finding it difficult to adjust to its current difficulties. Generally known as a very middle-class society, Japan had a high disposable level of income. What was mystifying current Japanese commentators was the 'maturity of customer demand'.

A Dentsu lifestyle survey, reported on by Mr Hiroe Suzuki, showed that six out of ten Japanese consumers had no interest in acquiring fashion items, interior goods, cars or PCs, having opted instead for 'none of these', as a choice in a key question in the study. It indicated how severely Japanese consumers were reassessing their needs in this time of relative austerity.

DIRECT MARKETING IN IRELAND, JULY 1998

The first book to address the powerful direct marketing approach to business in an Irish context, edited by Ms Mary Lalor and Mr John Keane, was *Direct Marketing Ireland: Theory and Practice*, published in 1998.

Ms Lawlor was a lecturer in marketing at Dublin Institute of Technology, (DIT) and Mr Keane MMII was managing director of PHS (Ireland) Ltd, a company specialising in direct marketing consultancy and service.

There are contributions in the book from over forty practitioners and academics, making it an excellent overview of the tools and techniques required for successful direct marketing strategies.

IRISH TRADE BOARD INTERNET SERVICE FOR EXPORTERS, JULY 1998

The Irish Trade Board announced the addition of a major new search facility to its website to help international buying teams to connect with competitive suppliers from Ireland. It described the new facility as the most advanced offered by any government, trade promotion organisation worldwide.

The new service became available at www.irish-trade.ie, which can be searched through five major international languages. It enables buyers to identify potential suppliers through a multi-layered search facility using tens of thousands of product categories drawn from the internationally accepted Kompass indexation system. It leads buyers to comprehensive data about Irish suppliers with links to their websites.

WEST REGION BUSINESS MARKETING AWARDS, JULY 1998

The marketing awards for business in Galway, Mayo and Roscommon — for Excellence in Marketing Practice and for Innovation in Marketing — were presented to the winners by the Minister for Public Enterprise, Mrs Mary O'Rourke TD. She was the guest of honour of the Marketing Institute's West region. The scheme was sponsored by the Bank of Ireland, the *Connacht Tribune*, Marketing Quality Assurance and Galway Irish Crystal.

The winners of the award for 'Excellence in Marketing Practice' were Carraig Donn Industries Ltd, Westport, Co. Mayo. Their success abroad included the fact that the Carraig Donn label is involved with such matters as the accomplishments of the Irish soccer team, the proliferation of Irish pubs and the triumph of Riverdance. The Westport plant products are known throughout Europe.

The winner of the 'Innovation in Marketing' award was Loughaunrone Health Farm, Oranmore, Co. Galway. Ms Margaret McNulty, manager/owner of Loughaunrone Health Farm, spotted a business opportunity in the trend to healthier life styles that had been triggered by stress-induced illnesses, low energy levels and lack of motivation.

She returned from Australia in 1992, and with her training and experience her husband and herself transformed what was then a dilapidated farm into a thriving health farm.

Their success had already been honoured in 1996 as a health retreat and deer farm, when they were named regional winners in the 'Development Farmers of the Year' competition and in 1997 they became regional winners in the 'Family Farm of the Year'.

VIRTUAL COMMUNITY WEBSITE FOR MARKETERS, JULY 1998

One of the first professional bodies in Ireland to utilise the internet to promote its activities was the Marketing Institute, in July 1998. In the previous few months, they overhauled and redeveloped the original site to create a unique resource, a second-generation website, known as a virtual community for marketers in Ireland who wanted to get information about any aspect of their profession. The development of the Marketing Institute virtual community was facilitated through sponsorship by the *Sunday Tribune*.

A virtual community is one large interactive site bringing together internet users with a common interest to discuss current topics and ideas, share resources and in general, benefit from the specialised focus of the community. It features interactive elements creating the opportunity for on-line discussion.

A key to the success of a virtual community is information content. It can be provided in a number of ways for example: original information, linkages, and interaction.

The Marketing Institute stated that, given its very distinctive focus, virtual community would quickly become the foremost electronic channel of communication to everyone connected with the marketing profession in Ireland for obtaining information, for targeting messages and for the supply of services.

MII AGM, SEPTEMBER 1998

The president of the Institute, Mr John Bourke, kindly agreed to continue in office for 1998–99. Mr Gerry Mortimer MMII, Dublin Institute of Technology, (DIT), Faculty of Business, was elected chairman for 1998–1999. Ms Barbara Patton FMII Grad. of Irish Permanent Plc was elected as deputy chairperson. Mr David Nea MMII of Cawley Nea was the past-chairman.

The council members elected for 1998–99 were:

- Mr Tony Amoroso MMII: Smurfit Web Press

- Ms Paula Cogan MMII: Jury's hotel

- Mr Ciaran Conroy MMII Grad.: Waterford Crystal Ltd

- Mr John Diskin MMII Grad.: Momentum Financial Services Ltd

- Mr Sean Dorgan MMII: UCD Marketing Development Programme

- Mr Tommy Dunne, MMII Grad.: An Post

- Ms Valerie Hannigan MMII Grad.: Fintel Publications Ltd

- Mr Michael Hayes MMII: Gilbeys of Ireland

- Mr Martin McEvoy MMII: McEvoy Associates

- Mr Bill McHugh MMII: News Extracts Ltd
- Mr Myles McHugh MMII: Iarnrod Éireann
- Ms Monica Murphy MMII: Iarnrod Éireann
- Mr Norman Rochford MMII: John F. Rochford & Company.

Regional chairpersons:

- North-West: Ms Paula Lawlor MMII Grad., Professional Merchandising Services
- North-East: Mr Gerry Moan MMII, Optimum Results Ltd
- Kerry: Mr Paul Morgan MMII Grad., Trustees of Muckross House
- West: Mr Declan O'Connor MMII, Declan O'Connor Consultancy
- South-West: Mr Andrew O'Neill MMII, Anglo Irish Bank
- South: Mr Gerry Owens MMII: EBS Building Society
- Mid-West: Mr John B. Ryan MMII: Telecom Éireann
- Chairman of Fellows' committee: Mr Robert K. Gahan FMII, Seirbhísí Theilifís na Gaeilge.

Strategy 2000

The outgoing chairman Mr David Nea said that one of the most gratifying aspects of his term of office was that there had been many positive messages to communicate to the public. He referred to the redeveloped and launched Institute internet website, providing a virtual community.

Various projects, he said, had been taking place against the backdrop of the Strategy 2000 initiated by his predecessor, Mr Redmond O'Donoghue. This was designed to enhance public perception of the Institute by the year 2000.

Implicit in this was the confidence that the educational and membership services, provided by the Institute, were already in the front rank, while their value needed to be communicated more effectively to the various audiences.

The financial result of the year, to 30 June 1998 showed a healthy surplus recorded, bringing the balance sheet reserve to £271,000, establishing financial stability to give increased confidence to face the continuing challenges of the future. Strength was reflected in Institute membership, now 2,750.

Enterprise Ireland

The president of the Marketing Institute, Mr John Bourke, said in his annual report, that during the year the Institute had issued several public announcements and made direct representations to departmental officials about the decision to establish Enterprise Ireland. This was the single state agency into which was merged the previously separate Forbairt, Irish Trade Board and the business training element of FÁS.

From a marketing viewpoint, this development had to be, in effect, more than an elegant restructuring of organisations. The new support agency needed to retain a sharp focus on the real business needs of the enterprise sector. Having established the Institute's point of view the president wished the development well.

The underlying issue was the need for all possible resources, private and public, to be directed towards anticipating and meeting the challenges of the marketplace. Education, Mr Bourke said, was the foundation on which almost all future prosperity would be built. Much of the success of the economy had stemmed from education. It came from knowing how to locate and place critical pieces of information and how to organise understanding into forms that others would understand.

GERRY MORTIMER MMII, CHAIRMAN, SEPTEMBER 1998

Marketing News, the Marketing Institute magazine, on Sept./Oct. 1998 reported in an interview with Mr Kyran Fitzgerald, how the new chairman of the Institute, Mr Gerry Mortimer had spent a well-earned August break in France in the knowledge that he would hardly have time to draw his breath in the coming months.

Mr Gerry Mortimer lectured at the DIT, Faculty of Business, in Dublin and also acted as a consultant to a wide range of corporate clients. His job, as chairman of the Marketing Institute, involved helping to run the organisation which now had almost 3,000 members spread throughout Ireland.

The new chairman vowed to find ways to see the Institute take steps to have a greater input to policy issues at national level, particularly for those involved in the world of marketing. In the interview he stated his belief that:

> Marketing is becoming ubiquitous. Everyone, willingly or unwillingly, is becoming involved in marketing. If it is a profession, and I believe it is, it is also becoming an adjunct to lots of other professions. There is now an opportunity for the Institute to involve people who, up until now, would not have thought of themselves as being in marketing.

Asked about Ireland's investment driven recent economic boom and increased global activity, and how this impacted on the Institute, he said:

> Institute members are now working in a much more diverse range of countries, in response to which the MII had developed its distance

learning activities. This year, for example, there were exam centres for Institute students in places as far apart as Bermuda, the US, Saudi Arabia and Madrid.

The old dictum that suppliers should never have more than 20 per cent of their business with one customer was now dead. Spreading risk was no longer a runner, in many cases. A supplier should deepen the relationship to such an extent that the customer could not really do without them.

The interview concluded with his view that it was imperative to develop a strong voice on the issues of importance to people in marketing.

MARKETERS WITH BOTTLE, SEPTEMBER 1998

The cover story of *Marketing News,* Sept./Oct.1998, related to the changing face of Ireland's booming drinks' industry. It stated that 'with a fast growing economy and a growing number of young adults, the beer market is growing, but there are some worrying signs that the long-term prospects of that end of the drinks' market could be cloudy'.

Mr Brendan Behan once said 'work is the curse of the drinking class'. Those immortal words still stood as a contempt-filled swipe at the great army of healthy livers who would dare to threaten the livelihood of the army of brewers, distillers, salespeople and marketers drawing a living out of the promotion of products which bond, as well as divide, fostering both conviviality and dissension.

The drinks industry competes, in an increasingly crowded leisure market, for the attention and approval of a discerning body of consumers. Gone are the master brewers and proud publicans of the 1950s. Drinks' companies spend heavily on sponsorships and research. The beer industry is still in a commanding position with a 65 per cent share of the alcoholic drinks' market, followed by spirits 20 per cent, wine 10 per cent and cider 4.6 per cent.

Wine is no longer the preserve of the wealthy. Consumption has spread over all age and social groups. There was a 57 per cent increase in the number of wine drinkers, over the previous seven years, with a current trend of growth 15 per cent a year. Comparatively, there is still room for considerable growth in the sale of wine in Ireland. Market research has become more and more vital, in the drinks' industry, as companies seek to assess the impact of various promotional activities.

CHANGING FOCUS OF BUSINESS, SEPTEMBER 1998

Mr Colin Gordon MMII, managing director of C & C (Wholesale) Ltd, stated that on the face of it, suppliers to the consumer market never had it so good. In the western world, consumers were living twice as long as their great grand-parents, they were better off and more educated. They had better communications, more product information, more legal protection and higher quality of purchases than ever before. Also they had a range of methods to which to action their purchases — all the way from the 'cashless' society to phone banking, electronic shopping, the internet and a vast array of highly competitive ever-more professional high-street retail outlets. There were also more goods and services on which to spend greater wealth — green field innovations such as home computers, satellite TV, mobile phones and so forth.

However, Mr Gordon went on to say that the situation was made more complex by some of the advantages. The world was made smaller by improved communications, due to faster and more frequent travel as well as satellite broadcasting. Thus came the advent of internationalism, global branding, one-world business strategies and a sense of sameness.

Boundaries between countries could become blurred and the divides between industries and brand identities hazy, right through to the differences in all walks of life, with male/female distinctions even being reduced at an alarming rate.

Family breakdown was now seen as leading to increased crime. The trend was toward confusion. However, a paradox existed where the causes of change were beginning to force consumers to rethink their behaviour.

The globalisation of brands was forcing consumers to re-examine how they want to be differentiated, how they could express themselves as well as concerns about such issues as health and the environment.

Mr Gordon believed that tomorrow's successful business leaders would be a unique blend of marketing, accounting and service practitioners. The face of business would be focused on how to build some stability and predictability in a fiercely changing world. The recognition of the impact of such changes needed to be made clear to shareholders, stockholders and observers. He ended his speech with the opinion that successful people in this business world would be those best able to create the right balance between stability and change.

CASES IN MARKETING, SEPTEMBER 1998

Edited by Professor James J. Ward, the book, *Cases in Marketing,* was the product of the third case study competition sponsored by the Marketing Institute. The eleven cases published would prove excellent teaching materials for use with final year undergraduate and postgraduate marketing students. They were published by the Marketing Institute at a price of £14.99. The cases are all of Irish companies and cover a wide range of industries:

• *Plasma Ireland*: Messrs Don O'Sullivan/John O'Sullivan

- *Cheeverstown Industries Ltd*: Mr Donal Rogan
- *The Rose of Tralee*: Messrs J. Cyril Gavaghan and Gene O'Donnell
- *Tourism Brand Ireland*: Mr Alex Gibson
- *Multi-Level Marketing in Tourism:* Mr John Milliken
- *The City of Derry Airport:* Mr Tony Johnston
- *Alpha Bank: Student Retail Banking:* Ms Laura Cuddihy and Ms Aileen Kennedy
- *Foinse*: Ms Ann Torres
- *EuroCoach Builders II*: Mr Gerry Mortimer
- *APSO: A marketing Plan:* Mr Gerry Mortimer
- *Irish Biscuits*: Ms Brenda Cullen.

INTERNET — OPPORTUNITY OR THREAT, OCTOBER 1998

The 5 October 1998 'Marketing in Action' meeting was held at The Martello Room, Jury's Hotel, Dublin. The subject, one of the issues and initiatives for the new millennium, was: 'The Internet — Opportunity or Threat for the High Street Retailer?'

Mr Stuart Coulson, technology director and co-founder of Gradient Solutions, designed and delivered technology and communications solutions for over 60 large travel vendors including Thomas Cook, Aer Lingus, KLM, Delta, Thomson Holidays and Ryanair. In discussing how travel agents and, by definition, High Street retailers, could embrace the internet and the intranet, and use them as building blocks for their business, Mr Coulson said: 'In the not too distant future, the Irish travel market will resemble the US market more and more as travel agents become consultants in travel management — and charge for their advice and their time'.

The concept of travel agents in the US had practically ceased to exist. They now specialised in travel arrangements. The traditional travel agent faced significant threats from technology and from major lifestyle changes. This not just because of the internet as the travel industry was changing dramatically — the latest buzz word being 'disintermediation'. This is meant to mean that anyone can sell to anyone, for example, airlines sell directly to consumers, tour operators own airlines, and so on.

He also stated that elements of the travel industry had gained from the internet. An example was that of the Marriot Hotel Group with internet bookings for next year, 1999, accounting for between 15/20 per cent of their business, compared to 7 per cent for this year, 1998, and 3 per cent for last year. In that case, the internet had facilitated a full audio-visual experience for the consumer, by showing pictures of hotel rooms.

However another speaker, Mr Gerry Benson, president of the Irish Travel Agents' Association, believed that internet usage by consumers in Europe to directly book holidays, was slow. He believed that the internet would never replace the travel agent or High Street retailer. Some 55 per cent of access to the internet was travel related, but very few booked through the internet and he felt that travel customers liked to see a human face when they handed over an average of £1000.

NATIONAL MARKETING CONFERENCE, OCTOBER 15 1998

The theme of the National Marketing Conference, held in Jury's hotel, Dublin on 15 October 1998 was: 'The Elusive Customer — New Problems, New Opportunities'.

The chairman of the conference committee, Mr John O.P. Bourke, president of the Marketing Institute, stated that a core marketing edict had always been 'Know Your Customer'. The techniques for doing this were improving everyday but at the same time the marketplace was becoming more fragmented, making it harder to reach customers through the usual channels. Changing lifestyles and demographics continuously created new opportunities for products and services.

The speakers' presentations covered a diverse range, examining a marketplace where the habits, tastes and lifestyles of customers, and the means of communicating with them, were changing more rapidly than ever before.

Who owns the customer?

Mr Adrian Hegarty, managing director of Friends First, in his paper: 'Who Owns the Customer?', gave examples of change related to the financial services sector. He said that new entrants to the sector, such as the major retailing chains, had brought a fresh approach to the market. Their objective was to give the customers what they wanted and they realised that what the customer really valued was price and speed of delivery, not a 'relationship'.

Innovation explosion

Mr Roger Jupp, managing director of Lansdowne Market Research, said that marketers were facing a world where wealth is as much generated from being 'best at something important to the customer' as it is from physical products. It was clearly demonstrated that the shift to services was one of the most fundamental aspects of change. Examples referred to related to some of the richest people in the world — Messrs Rupert Murdoch, Steven Spielberg and Bill Gates — who were now in the service industry.

'Maybe' means 'maybe'

Ms Julie Weeks, director of research at the National Foundation for Women Business Owners in the US, referred to women-owned businesses as an emerging market opportunity. Men and women making decisions, particularly purchasing, showed significant differences in their ways. Women tended to take more time and think about options. They also took outside advice and were more likely to emphasise values. Men tended to make decisions more transactional/price oriented. Men when they said 'maybe' mean 'no' but women who said 'maybe' meant 'maybe'.

Database marketing

Mr Andrew Street, chief operating officer of Dunne's Stores, Ireland's largest retailer, gave some examples of database use.

He said that in the Cornelscourt store 500 high spenders in grocery were identified who were not shopping for textiles. A great textile offer, having a very high takeup, was mailed to that group. Once stimulated, a good percentage of those customers became regular textile customers. Choosing the right store locations, he believed, was one of the critical decision uses of the database.

No average consumer

The marketing director for Mars Benelux, based in Holland, Ms Fiona Dawson, spoke about the snacking market in Europe. It was no longer what had been an easy identification of their average consumer, he or she, where they came from and what their interests were. The reason, she said, was that there was now no such thing as the 'typical' family.

Ms Dawson stated that nowadays less than 20 per cent of families were married couples living with their children. Moreover, fewer than 30 per cent of today's adolescents will have lived together with both parents prior to adulthood.

There was much discussion about the emergence of a new breed of 25–35 year old 'solitary' lifestyle emerging, representing a new target for the confectionery marketer.

Brand extension the key

The background of a paper from Mr John Foley, sales and marketing director of Waterford Crystal, related to a corporate imperative towards continuing strong growth. To sustain growth was indeed the challenge, by ensuring that existing customers were retained and new 'elusive' customers found.

Repositioning the company's product range in the United States was a major plank in the strategy developed to meet the objective. In the US the market for gifts was a massive $7bn. and that primarily led the company into the whole new exciting world of brand extensions.

Additional contributions

Other contributions to the conference referred to major changes, described as a marketer's dream and a TV time buyer's nightmare, that were now taking place in the media frameworks. These were described as being such an integral part of the network of marketing communications. Speakers included Mr James Morris, chairman of TV3 and Mr Stephen Stokes, project director of Ireland BSkyB.

CONSULTANTS' REGISTER, OCTOBER 1998

In October 1998 the Marketing Institute announced the appointment of Mr Paul O'Kelly MMII as the new chairman of their Consultants' Register. Mr O'Kelly was a senior partner with O'Kelly Sutton, accountants, marketing and management consultants.

The Consultants' Register is the Marketing Institute's body of approved professional consultants and is confined to professional consultants and professional practices. It was established to provide the definitive and authoritative source of marketing assistance to Irish business and was committed to maintaining a high level of standards within the profession. Its primary aim was to create awareness amongst companies to position the marketing profession as the crucial factor for business success.

QUEENSLAND MARKETING EVENT, NOVEMBER 1998

The Queensland marketing event of the year was held on Friday 13 November 1998 at the Brisbane Sheraton hotel. It was entitled: 'Mega Trends Beyond 2000'.

The conference related to how technology, globalisation, the world economy and changes in consumer behaviour, brought about by dynamic social patterns, would effect business. The impact of those trends would cut across all industries. Whether an organisation provided services, or produced goods, in either the private or public sector, it needed to meet the coming trends.

The Australian Marketing Institute, AMI, assembled speakers from around Australia and designed the programme to meet marketers as well as business decision-makers. It combined a balanced content of theory illustrated by real-life case studies and successfully implemented marketing strategies.

There were four sessions in all and as I was in Brisbane myself at the time and have the attractive detailed brochure, I have included below a sample of the activities as it involved far too much to record everything.

* Session 1: Recognising the Trends

* Session 2: Developing Your Strategy for the Future

* Session 3: Marketing Tools for Beyond 2000

* Session 4: Implementation Case Studies: Companies that Have Surfed the Trends.

The case studies included:

Energex: 'Rebranding and Re-Engineering a Billion Dollar Monolith', a case study of why Energex re-branded from SEQEB and their vision for the future.

Cash Converters: 'Capitalising on trends for success', the largest chain of second-hand good stores in the world with stores in Australia, UK, France, Canada, USA, NZ, South Africa, Spain, Holland, Germany and Ireland.

ADVERTISING AWARD, NOVEMBER 1998

A review made of criteria for the eighth annual 'Advertising Award of the Year' included, for the judges consideration, developments in the area of on-line and multimedia initiatives undertaken by agencies on behalf of clients. Ireland's monthly magazine, *Marketing,* organised the judging process on three main standards:

1. Agency growth in real terms.

2. Creativity.

3. General overview.

Mr Michael Cullen, editor of *Marketing*, said it was important that the technological changes impacting on the advertising industry be reflected in a major competition.

The panel of eight judges to select the 'Agency of the Year' was chaired by Mr John Casey, chief executive of the Marketing Institute, and comprised of Mr Liam Holland, *The Irish Times*; Mr Pat Kiely, TV3; Ms Kristi O'Sullivan, Adshel; Mr Tim Healy, Mercator Marketing Research; Ms Melanie Morris, *d'SIDE* magazine, Mr Dave Hammond, Today FM; Ms Eithne Ryan, Carlton Screen Advertising and Mr Des Whelan, WLR FM.

R. & A. BAILEY STORY, DECEMBER 1998

A further meeting in the 'Marketing in Action' issues and initiatives for the new millennium, was held at The Martello Room, Jury's hotel, Dublin on 7 December 1998.

The evolution of the Bailey's brand, from an Irish cream drink of twenty years ago to today, was fully outlined by Ms Aldagh McDonagh, worldwide marketing director of R. & A. Bailey. Through a number of strategic and creative examples, she demonstrated the various evolutions that the brand had gone through and how the brand and the business were undergoing another stage of evolution, as it entered the millennium.

DR T.J. O'DRISCOLL AND MR EUGENE QUIGLEY, RIP

It was with sincere regret and sympathy that the Marketing Institute recorded the deaths of Dr T. (Tim) J. O'Driscoll, past-president 1973–80 and Mr Eugene Quigley, a long standing dedicated committee member, who had been a Fellow since 1981.

BANKS RELUCTANCE TO USE INTERNET, JANUARY 1999

The *Sunday Independent* of 7 February 1999 headlined an article by Mr Kevin Moore entitled 'Record Numbers Go On-line but Banks Averse to Electronic Commerce'.

He said the latest statistics showed the Irish people of all ages were using the Internet and World Wide Web in record numbers. The sole exception was the country's 'grey-suited conservative bankers'.

Data revealed, by Nua Internet Surveys, showed that in the year ending 31 December 1998, 15 per cent of the adult population (350,000 people) were 'on-line' compared to 200,000 the previous year and 2,000 in 1994. According to Mr Moore while the figure was estimated to reach 700,000 by the end of the year 2000, one group still refused to move into the new millennium — Irish banks.

Nua was based on Merrion Road, Dublin 4 and was set up in 1995. It won the top award in Europe for business development the following year and was voted into the 35 top internet developers in the world in the US in 1998. In a *Guardian* poll, Nua was voted one of the top websites.

Mr Moore went on to say that the group was critical of the major banks who made £1.75 bn. in profits between them in 1998 but who 'refused to use the internet to develop commerce or accept credit card deals'. The fears of Irish banks (apparently of widespread fraud or other abuses) might be eased by the better use of encryption technologies. This was the belief of Mr Mark Cawley, consultancy services manager of Ireland On-Line.

A spokesman for Public Enterprise Minister, Mrs Mary O'Rourke TD, who had the charge of developing internet services, said it was hoped to have legislation on the use of encryption and digital signatures through the Oireachtas by the end of the year.

TAKING ON THE SUPERMARKET GIANTS, 1999

It was reported in the *Irish Independent* of February 1999, that for the first time since the early 1970s, the independent sector actually held the lion's share of the Irish grocery market and the balance of the power had been re-stored to the market with no one operator or sector dominating. This was the opinion of Ms Anne Dunphy, marketing director of SuperValu-Centra, speak-ing at a Marketing in Action meeting in Dublin.

The Musgrave Group had, over the previous twenty years, headed a lot of the remarkable revival in Ireland's independent grocery sector. The multiples held 64 per cent in July 1986 as against a combined SuperValu-Centra figure of just 6 per cent while overall independents had 36 per cent. By November 1998 figures showed a much-changed picture. The multiples' share was down to 49.9 per cent, while SuperValu-Centra's share was up to 23.6 per cent and the independents' total came to a healthy 50.1 per cent

Ms Dunphy said that her company was actively supporting the campaign to prevent the development of out-of-town superstores in Ireland. She pointed out that kind of development had left 42 per cent of towns and villages with-out a grocery store of any kind in the UK.

FROM A BUILDING SOCIETY TO A BANK, MARCH 1999

Mr John Smyth, group managing director of First Active Plc, in a presenta-tion to the Marketing in Action evening meeting at the Martello Room, Jury's hotel, Dublin on 1 March 1999, described and illustrated the challenges and opportunities in transforming the mutual First National Building Society to First Active, a Plc trading on the stock exchange.

The flotation of one of Ireland's biggest building societies, First National, provided the right opportunity for an overhaul of the company's corporate image and Mr Smyth said:

> Corporate identity can be a key element in the future development of a business and for First Active it was far more than just a name change. It was a powerful tool to signal a clear change to the marketplace that we were setting new standards and increasing the company presence and share of voice with our competitors.

The message appeared to successfully reach the public with 68,000 of the 70,000 members who voted indicating their support for the flotation.

Mr Smyth's career had encompassed lending and branch management, personnel, group operations, development and company secretary. He joined First Active in 1972 following a career in estate agency. *Inter alia*, he was chairman of Irish Mortgage and Savings Association from 1995–96.

OMA POSTER AWARDS, MARCH 1999

The eighteenth OMA poster awards took place on 25 March 1999, celebrating outdoor creativity over the previous year. There were over 700 entries, leaving the jury with a difficult task. The Grand Prix winner was McCann-Erikson for their Bank of Ireland GAA sponsorship campaign.

Other winners included:

• Cawley Nea: C&C Club Orange campaign

• CDP: Ocean Communications

• Amv, London: Dunlop 'Hairpin' design

• Irish International: Dillon's Black and White 'Chasers'

• Peter Owens: MDL's VW 'Old Man'.

TECHNOLOGY AND CONSUMER SATISFACTION, MARCH 1999

Ms Bairbre Doran MMII Grad. BA (Hons) HRM, marketing manager of the Sercle Group, provided a feature article in the *Marketing News* March/April 1999 issue. Her subject related to the impact of technology on customer satisfaction.

For the benefit of the consumer, the world of banking, and indeed commerce in general, had been to the fore in increasing the use of technology. The financial services sector faced a challenge from the US financial organisations whose access to advanced information technology threatened to give them a critical advantage over those in Ireland that failed to keep up.

As competition heated up, the importance of billing and customer care systems in competing and offering attractive products and services could not be underestimated. Most business today was technically based. New delivery channels ranged from satellite banking, in Africa and the Caribbean, to internet banking across the globe. By the year 2000, the volume of data on the global telecommunications infrastructure would exceed voice traffic, according to the Price Waterhouse Coopers 1999 technology report.

US giant AT&T had lost market share by not having a flexible billing system in the deregulated market in the 1990s. Competitors had re-packaged discount billing systems for family and friends and made serious inroads into long distance market share before AT&T were able to re-engineer its information and billing systems.

First ever international agreement to be digitally signed

America endorsed Ireland as the potential e-commerce hub of Europe when President Clinton used an Irish company's software to digitally sign a communiqué document with the Taoiseach, Bertie Ahern TD, the first ever international agreement to be digitally signed.

The future, Ms Doran believed, would see information being placed online which would allow customers help themselves through interactive web software. People would be able to track usage, sort out queries and request new services online. Web-enabled technologies would also be a major factor in delivering transparency in the marketplace.

PROGRAMMING FOR RTÉ, APRIL 1999

Ms Helen Shaw, director of Radio Telefís Éireann, RTÉ radio, was the guest speaker at the marketing breakfast meeting in the Dome Restaurant, St Stephen's Green Shopping Centre, Dublin on 21 April 1999. She gave a very interesting graphic talk on programming for RTÉ in an evolving multimedia context.

Mr Gerry Mortimer, chairman of the Marketing Institute, Mr Liam Holland, *The Irish Times* (sponsor) and Mr John Casey, chief executive of MII, were present together with a good representation of Institute students and members.

IRISH JOBS PAGE WEBSITE AWARD, MAY 1999

The Irish Jobs Page, http://www.exp.ie, Ireland's longest running website for recruitment, went from strength to strength. Celebrating its fourth anniversary, May 1999, the site was honoured with the first ever award for electronic media, at the 1999 Irish Direct Marketing Awards.

While four years would seem very young to other industries, in terms of the internet recruitment, it was a milestone. When the site was established, the internet was used primarily as a tool for this in the IT industry. Today, with access to the internet much more widespread, jobs were advertised across all disciplines.

PRESIDENT'S NIGHT, MAY 1999

President's Night of the Marketing Institute, the highlight of the year, again represented the members' annual tribute to their president and was the forum for the presentation of the Institute's awards.

The guest speaker at the dinner in The Great Hall, Trinity College, Dublin, on 6 May 1999, was Mr David Went, chief execuive of Irish Life & Permanent. Other principal guests included Mr John Edmund, national chairman of the Chartered Institute of Marketing (UK) and Mr Jim McAnlis, chairman of the Chartered Institute of Marketing (NI).

Fellowship awards

Fellowship awards, in recognition of significant contribution to marketing in Ireland and to the Marketing Institute over a number of years, were presented to:

- Mr Tom Prior: Prior & Associates

- Mr Arnold O'Byrne: Opel Ireland Ltd

- Mr Colin Gordon: C&C Ireland Ltd

- Mr Redmond O'Donoghue: Waterford Crystal Ltd

- Mr John Fanning: McConnell's Advertising Services Ltd

- Mr Noel Hynes: Shelbourne Park Stadium

- Mr Seamus Scally: Musgrave Ltd

- Mr Michael Maughan: Oglivy & Mather Group Ltd.

UK FINANCIAL SERVICES, MAY 1999

Mr Peter Sunderland, director of Reactive Ltd, joined Abbey National in 1983 and held a number of positions including regional director. He moved on to head Abbey National, which he rapidly expanded. A direct marketing department was set up with six linked call centres, which sold the whole range of the company's products. Included in this were mortgages, where they were the clear market leaders.

A recognised authority within the industry, Mr Sunderland, left Abbey National in 1997 to establish a new company, Reactive Ltd. Subsidiaries of Reactive include a call centre consultancy which advises major PLC's on call centre strategy and management.

MARKETING CASE STUDY COMPETITION AWARDS, MAY 1999

In 1992 the Marketing Institute, at the Irish Marketing Teachers' Association conference, undertook to sponsor a case writing competition. The object was to encourage academics (and others) to write case studies of Irish companies which could be used in marketing education. The method of sponsorship would be to give prizes to the winners one year and the following year to publish the cases in book form. This would be an investment of £8,000 in all.

The result of the fourth competition, which comprised eight finalists, was announced at the IMTA conference in the Tallaght Institute of Technology in May 1999. The first prize went to Mr Don O'Sullivan, NUI-Cork who, with Mr John O'Sullivan of Act Venture Capital, wrote a case on Qumas, a software company. Ms Edel Foley, Dublin Institute of Technology, was awarded second prize for her case on Blooming and the third prize went to Ms Ann Torres, NUI-Galway, for Judy Greene Pottery.

THE LITTLE RED BOOK, MAY 1999

Marketing Institute members were invited to update themselves about internet advertising with *The Little Red Book* and obtain a free copy by contacting ICAN. That I did and found the 40-page book, introduced by Mr Ian Fox, chief executive of the Institute of Advertising Practitioners in Ireland, IAPI, very interesting.

Mr Fox said he found himself engaged today in a whole range of matters relating to electronic data on a national and European level and could see that, as the internet developed, it could well dominate communications in the future. The book explains and helps one to stay at the vanguard of contemporary and future communication techniques.

Mr Damian Ryan, chief executive of ICAN, looked back at the Irish scene and explained the power and potential of the internet from a media perspective.

He stated that the main attribute of the internet was the ability to host and foster a 'one to one' relationship between individuals or between advertisers and individuals. This was something that no other media had managed to achieve to the same degree.

THE CHANGING FACE OF IRISH ADVERTISING, 1999

The cover story in *Marketing News*, May/June 1999, concerned the 'Changing Face of Irish Advertising — New and Improved'. It stated that Ireland's booming economy was attracting international investment into local agencies in advertising in a big way.

The launch of the Euro focussed peoples' minds on the emergence of a single European market which threatened to change the way advertisers and their clients did their business. Spending on the internet would be the transformation with websites being set up by Irish firms. The growth of education, knowledge of technology and increase in consumer awareness and demands, were some of the social changes affecting the way advertising agencies set about collecting their earnings. Advertising was not now about fast moving consumer brands but integrated with communications media and skills, such as design. Change was the order of the day. Total branding in concerns was leading to more industry concentration. There had been a noticeable trend toward direct marketing techniques with response devices, such as freephone, appearing in more ads.

Telecom Éireann, in 1998, were the biggest spenders in advertising, about £9m., followed by the traditional leaders, Proctor & Gamble and Guinness, £7.6m. and £7.2m. respectively. Dunnes Stores was next with £5m., then the ESB and Kelloggs with about £4.5m. each. Last year, 1998, the total expenditure was up by almost 10 per cent, just £400m., according to the latest IAPI figures.

Outdoor advertising, in 1998, as a result of investment in both illumination and new product development opportunities, had an increased share in advertising expenditure, with 20 per cent of the revenue being that of new advertisers, revealing it as a media strength.

MARKETING INSTITUTE WEBSITE, 1999

The Institute website, http://www.mii.ie, was originally established in 1996 to supply information to members via the internet. Now firmly established it was receiving on average 20,000 hits per month. The website was supported by Interact; Irish Marketing Surveys; Creative Inputs; AIM and DDFH &B. Its main sponsor was the *Sunday Tribune*.

The site project managers, Interact, developed a searchable database of companies engaged in marketing services, e.g. advertising agencies, PR consultants, marketing research consultants, graphic designers, printers, etc. (For further information – e-mail gpat@interact.ie.)

RELATIONSHIP MARKETING, JULY 1999

Relationship marketing is not something that one can pay 'lip service' to or classify in the 'nice to have' category, according to Mr Tony McSweeney, director of sales and marketing with the VHI, (Voluntary Health Insurance Board).

Bringing a successful product to the market was the most difficult challenge facing marketing people as the long hours involved clearly testified. However, if it was designed around the customer and was delivered at a time and place that best suited needs, a new product stood a greater chance of success.

One of the great marketing successes of recent years had been the customisation of retail petrol stations. Marketers had recognised the potential of motorists, standing on a petrol forecourt for five minutes or more, and created an environment that delivered retail products and services at a time and place that suited the needs of their customers.

A recent article suggested that in 1988 Ireland had 673 garages with retail outlets, while the number in 1999 was over 1,800. Those outlets employed 1,700 people of which 80 per cent were fulltime.

Does relationship marketing really work?

Mr McSweeney went on to say that three years previously, in preparation for the oncoming deregulation of the private health insurance market, VHI commissioned research to identify the product/service distribution and delivery requirements of its Group Scheme Network. At that time, 1996, it comprised of over 6,000 companies and organisations. Among a mass of data, received from over 1,000 responding companies, two strategic distribution issues clearly stood out:

1. A single point of contact between the VHI and the Group Scheme was a pre-requisite.

2. All services, namely claims and administration, should be localised to the nearest regional office.

ELECTRONIC COMMERCE MARKETING, JULY 1999

Dr Chris Coughlan was strategic planning and e-commerce manager at Compaq Computer International, European Software Centre, Galway.

In the feature article of *Marketing News*, July/August 1999 issue, Dr Coughlan discussed why e-marketing and e-commerce should not be considered as separate entities by companies conducting e-business. A vast amount had been written about the internet. It first began with e-mail, then moved to the next phase, the World Wide Web and now the latest internet development 'e-commerce', was consuming vast amount of articles, debate and discussion.

Different businesses were at different stages in the new media revolution. The more progressive and experienced in using the new media were beginning to explore and implement e-commerce solutions. Dr Coughlan said that e-commerce was currently at a similar stage of development and state of use as the World Wide Web was four years ago.

Dr Coughlan described the definition of electronic commerce as 'the act or the collective set of activities involved in the buying and selling of goods and services in an electronic environment'. However, he said, it was not as simple as that, as the electronic environment was dynamic and would continue to change over time, due to its dependency on the innovative use and application of technology.

IRELAND'S NET GAINS, E-COMMERCE, JULY 1999

The *Evening Herald* of 12 July 1999 reported that Ireland's future opportunities lay in the world of electronic commerce, which it was well equipped to take advantage of. It stated that our tax policy, as well as an educated workforce and increased government spending on the telecommunications infrastructure were the key tools in the area.

Ireland was extremely attractive as a location for e-commerce, according to Mr Patrick McSweeney of tax consultants, HLB VF Nathan. In addition, overheads were cut out by the fact that when business was carried out over the internet there was no need for large offices.

The possibilities of cyberspace, as a growth area for Irish business, was outlined by the head of the Bank of Ireland's internet business, Mr Noel Hindley. He told how the bank was developing new business strategies such as the first internet offshore banking service, Fsharp. The new service would go 'on line' in September 1999 and, he said, was set to revolutionise offshore banking, and would initially target Irish and UK expatriates. Based on the Isle of Man, the resource was expected to have a potential market size of £1.7m. and be defined as English speaking with 'investable personal assets' of sterling £15,000. Research had found that over 60 per cent of English speaking expats would prefer to use the internet to traditional channels when conducting offshore banking

AGM, SEPTEMBER 6 1999

The thirty-seventh AGM of the Marketing Institute was held on Monday 6 September 1999 in Marketing House, South County Business Park, Leopardstown, Dublin 18.

Mr William (Bill) Fraser, RIP

Before the start of the meeting the chairman, Mr Gerry Mortimer, announced with sincere regret, the death earlier that day of Mr Bill Fraser, a founder member, fellow, past chairman and past vice-president of the Marketing Institute.

A short silence was observed as a tribute to Mr Fraser's memory.

A marked increase in the numbers of marketing students seeking graduateship as a top-up professional qualification, having already obtained academic qualifications, was reported by the outgoing chairman, Mr Gerry Mortimer. Students studying through the distance education programme accounted for 10 per cent of all students registered.

The Marketing Institute council elected for 1999–2000 were:

- President: Senator Feargal Quinn
- Chairperson: Ms Barbara Patton
- Deputy Chairperson: Mr Martin McEvoy
- Hon. Treasurer: Mr David Mooney
- Hon. Secretary: Mr Myles McHugh
- Chairperson of Fellows: Mr Robert K. Gahan
- Chief Executive: Mr John Casey.

The council members were: Paula Cogan, Ciran Conroy, J.P. Donnolly, Sean Dorgan, Tommy Dunne, Miriam Hughes, Gerry Mortimer; Camillus O'Brien; Tom O'Toole and Norman Rochford.

Regional chairpersons:

- Mid-West: Mr Pat Cahill
- South: Mr Richard Crotty
- North-West: Ms Paula Lawlor
- North-East: Ms Jackie O'Connell
- West: Mr Declan O'Connor
- Kerry: Ms Gene O'Donnell
- South-East: Mr Peter Roche.

First lady chair of MII, September 1999

Ms Barbara Patton became the first lady to chair the Marketing Institute of Ireland. A Fellow and graduate of MII, she was head of the Irish Permanent, marketing department. In her incoming speech she stated that her key objective would be to convey to the broader marketing community that sense of energy and dynamism when one is closely involved, as she continued to be, in Institute affairs.

Having completed his three-year term of office, the president of the Institute, Mr John Bourke, said he had been impressed with the work of the Institute, which had made a significant contribution to the professionalism of Irish business. In accepting the invitation to succeed Mr John Bourke, as president, Senator Feargal Quinn paid tribute to Mr Bourke and to the Institute for its part 'in improving the appreciation of the role of the customer in business'.

ENCOUNTERING CHANGE, OCTOBER 1999

The annual national Marketing Institute conference, in association with *Business & Finance* magazine's conference division, was held at the Burlington hotel, Dublin, on Thursday 10 October 1999. The conference theme was: 'Encountering Change'.

Ms Barbara Patton, chairperson of the conference organising committee, said:

> Change has many dimensions. It can cause disruption. But it can offer opportunity to those who can turn circumstances to their advantage. It can bring the fear of failure. But it can open the door to success through creativity and innovation.

The conference itself had a changed format — a change which the delegates found stimulating and refreshing.

Challenge it was agreed was not new. Between 1975 and 1995, sixty per cent of the companies on the Fortune 500 were replaced. The common situation for new entrants on the list, irrespective of the industry, was that they either created new markets or recreated existing ones. It meant those companies had been led by people constantly searching for new opportunities. It was marketers who, by inclination and training, were best equipped to undertake the task.

Distinctions between categories that were once discrete were becoming blurred. Extremes cited saw banks, once places to leave your money and/or get a loan, now selling you insurance and handling the sale of your investment shares — which one can do in the middle of the night, via the Internet. Even more dramatically, financial services could be bought, not only in a bank, but in the supermarket. Consumers now had a choice of communication needs, be it by cable, telephone or computer-based.

Speakers at the conference included:

• Mr Noel Toolan: Founder of Brand Aid

• Dr Gordon Campbell: Internationale Spar Centrale BV

• Mr Conrad Free: P4 Consultancy

• Mr Lee Thompson: Yahoo, UK & Ireland

• Ms Maureen Gaffney: Trinity College, Dublin

• Mr Ian Jeffers: Cablelink.

The conference was chaired by Ms Maeve Donovan of *The Irish Times* and patrons Irish Permanent, Compaq, Ocean and Mercedes-Benz.

TREASURY MARKETING INTO THE MILLENNIUM, OCTOBER 1999

The largest international bank in Ireland is Citibank, having been established in 1966, (33 years ago), and the biggest employer in the IFSC. Citycorp, the parent company of Citibank and Travellers Group, a major US insurance and financial services institution, announced an agreement to merge and form Citigroup Inc. The merger was finalised in October 1998 establishing Citigroup as the world's leading financial services conglomerate.

Mr Brian Hayes, director of treasury and structural products marketing in Ireland, addressed members, students and guests of the Marketing Institute at the Dome Restaurant, St Stephen's Green Shopping Centre, Dublin, on Wednesday 20 October 1999. It was a very interesting meeting which concerned his involvement in marketing foreign exchange, derivatives, securitisation, leasing and other structural financial products.

MR MICHAEL COOTE, RIP

On 24 October 1999 it was learned with sincere regret that Mr Michael Coote, a founder member and fellow of the Marketing Institute, died. Mr Coote was president of the Alzheimers' Society of Ireland and had been elected as the first life member of Age Action Ireland at their AGM on 8 July 1999.

IRISH INTERNET SERVICE PROVIDER, NOVEMBER 1999

The first Irish internet service provider, (ISP), operated by a 'content' company, rather than a telecommunications company, went live on 3 November 1999, offering a virtual e-commerce marketplace as well as traditional ISP services.

A joint venture between *Buy & Sell*, a free paper, and Stentor Communications — buyandsell.net — gave the opportunity to suppliers to place advertisements 'on-line' and make bids for products using their credit cards. Access to news, sports, traffic, stocks and shares information, free e-mail, web access and web space was provided by link-ups with other companies. Lines were leased from Eircom to provide the service. Stentor also offered a new form of call-card on the site, enabling subscribers to log on and buy time for phone calls on the net.

THE LITTLE RED BOOK 2000, SECOND EDITION

ICAN (Internet Communications and Advertising Network) in association with IAPI (Institute of Advertising Practitioners of Ireland) produced a second edition of *The Little Red Book 2000*. Mr Ian Fox, chief executive of IAPI, referred to the first edition, launched October 1998, as now being a collector's item. It may well have been, not alone Europe's, but the world's first such directory of commercial websites.

The book included an alphabetical list of almost 60 websites, with wide data, actively seeking on-line advertising revenue in the Irish market. The internet population was estimated then at 400,000.

ENTERPRISE IRELAND — TAKING YOUR BUSINESS ON-LINE, 1999

Enterprise Ireland produced a concise volume, for 29p, relating to how to take your business on-line. It defined the internet multitude of uses thus:

> You can search for answers to almost any question one can think of, send messages and documents across the world in an instant, shop for goods and services in another continent, visit art galleries, play games, chat, download free software or even gamble.

Crucially, the internet has become an invaluable business tool used to sell and market products, and deliver support services. Also to acquire customer feedback through inviting comment and surveys, to publish data and for everyday correpondence. Enterprise Ireland point to the internet fast becoming as integral to business as the telephone. Contact can be made at: www.enterprise-ireland.com/e business Email:gary.morrissey@enterprise-ireland.com.

MR JOHN M. LEPERE, RIP

The death of Mr John M. Lepere was learnt with sincere regret and sympathy. Mr Lepere had been a member of the Marketing Institute since 1966 and was awarded the Fellowship in 1980.

INTO THE MILLENNIUM

For the future, into the millennium, one of the certainties is that the internet is here to stay in business. It is another marketplace, just as mediums of retail, wholesale and cash and carry are. A registered trademark is essential to protect one's goodwill. It is anticipated that within a few years everyone will be represented on the internet. Yes, change is the order of the future — the millennium.

Appendix 1

INCORPORATED SALES MANAGERS ASSOCIATION:
PAST CHAIRPERSONS AND PAST PRESIDENTS
— 1947–1962

Year	Past Chairmen	Past Presidents
1947	H.N.B. Palmer	none
1948	H.N.B. Palmer	—
1949	Donald MacKenzie	—
1950	Derek Black	—
1951	D. Bolton Thom	—
1952	Leslie V. Whitehead	—

Irish group (ISMA) became a branch in 1953

Year	Past Chairpersons	Past Presidents
1953	Leslie V. Whitehead	Senator E.A. McGuire
1954	C.W. Chesson	Senator F.M. Summerfield
1955	C.W. Chesson	Lord Killanin
1956	C.W. Chesson	Lord Killanin
1957	Tom Moran	Lord Killanin
1958	Bill Fraser	David D. Frame
1959	Stephen J. Doyle	David D. Frame
1960	Michael Coote	Sir Basil Goulding
1961	Brian M. Murphy	Sir Basil Goulding

Irish branch (ISMA) ceased in 1962

Appendix 2

THE MARKETING INSTITUTE OF IRELAND — PAST CHAIRPERSONS
AND PAST PRESIDENTS — 1962–2000
(founded July 1962 — initially named Irish Institute of Marketing
and Sales Management)

Year	Past Chairpersons	Past Presidents
1962	Brian M. Murphy	Thomas Murray
1963	Norman McConnell	Thomas Murray
1964	Harry V. Woods	John Haughey
1965	Harry V. Woods	John Haughey
1966	Joseph Bigger	John Haughey
1967	Aubrey N. Fogarty	Sean Lemass
1968	Gerry Maher	Sean Lemass
1969	Leslie Thorn	Sean Lemass
1970	Bill Fraser	Sean Lemass
1971	Harry Weir	Dr J.F. Dempsey
1972	John D. Carroll	Dr J.F. Dempsey
1973	Denis Fitzgibbon	Dr T.J. O'Driscoll
1974 (July/Dec.)	Joseph C. McGough	Dr T.J. O'Driscoll
1975	Joseph C. McGough	Dr T.J. O'Driscoll
1976	Anthony J. Neville	Dr T.J. O'Driscoll
1977	Richard Reid	Dr T.J. O'Driscoll
1978	Dr Pat Kehoe	Dr T.J. O'Driscoll
1979	Patrick J. Nolan	Dr T.J. O'Driscoll
1980	J. Brendan O'Reilly	Dr T.J. O'Driscoll
1981	Michael D. Shields	Sean M. Condon
1982	John S. Burns	Sean M. Condon
1983	Jack V. Downey	Francis J. O'Reilly
1984	Philip Flood	Francis J. O'Reilly
1985	William Ambrose	Thomas P. Hardiman
1986	Brendan V. Wafer	Thomas P. Hardiman
1987	Alan McDonnell	Thomas P. Hardiman
1988	David Manley	John P. Culliton
1989	Dr John F. McGuire	John P. Culliton
1990	Richard C. Strahan	David Kennedy
1991	Colin McCrea	David Kennedy
1992	Robin J. Addis	David Kennedy

Year	Past Chairpersons	Past Presidents
1993	John Fanning	David I. Dand
1994	Jim Quinn	David I. Dand
1995	Tom Fennell	David I. Dand
1996	Roger Jupp	David I. Dand
1997	P. R. O'Donoghue	John O. P. Bourke
1998	David Nea	John O. P. Bourke
1999	Gerry Mortimer	John O. P. Bourke
2000	Barbara Patton	Senator Feargal Quinn

Appendix 3

FELLOWS OF THE MARKETING INSTITUTE OF IRELAND

Name	Date Awarded	Name	Date Awarded
Norman McConnell	1965	Sean A. Walshe	1987
Harry V. Woods	1965	Frank Young	1987
F. Edward James	1971	Dr Philip Kotler (Hon)	1987
Jos. C. McGough	1974	Dr Tom Hardiman	1988
Philip R. Flood	1974	Seamus Martin	1988
Harry A. Wyer	1974	John Meagher	1988
John D. Carroll	1977	Brendan V. Wafer	1988
Mahon Lee	1977	Frank Falvey	1989
Gerry F. Maher	1978	John Fitzpatrick	1989
Jack J. Jones	1978	Desmond Gilroy	1989
Anthony J. Neville	1979	Peter Gleeson	1989
Patrick J. Nolan	1980	Alan McDonnell	1989
Robert K. Gahan	1981	Paddy Wright	1989
Dr Barra O'Cinneide	1981	Douglas Thornton	1990
Derek P. Whelan	1981	Brendan McGuinness	1990
Brian Creedon	1982	Tom Joyce	1991
J. Brendan O'Reilly	1982	Alan Corbett	1992
William Ambrose	1983	Aidan O'Driscoll	1992
Geoff Beggs	1983	Raymond J. O'Keeffe	1992
Delia Burke	1983	Aidan Daly	1993
John S. Burns	1983	John F. Daly	1993
John A. Cashell	1983	Michael Geary	1993
P. Noel M. Quirke	1983	James McCauley	1993
Raymond Joyce	1984	Geoff Reid	1993
Michael D. Shields	1984	Michael Conlon	1994
Frank J. O'Reilly	1985	Jerry Liston	1994
Michael J. Hayes	1985	Ros O'Shaughnessy	1994
James P. Culliton	1986	Gillian Bowler	1995
Aidan C. Harte	1986	Dr Cathal Brugha	1995
James J. Ward	1986	Garry Hynes	1995
Sean Cowman	1987	Denis Lucey	1995
Dr Patrick Kehoe	1987	Pat O'Mahony	1995
Keith MacCarthy Morrogh	1987	Senator F. Quinn	1995
Bob Waddell	1987	Richard Burrows	1996

Name	Date Awarded	Name	Date Awarded
Dr A. Cunningham	1996	Richard C. Strahan	1998
Anthony Gannon	1996	John Fanning	1999
Fred Hayden	1996	Colin Gordon	1999
David Manley	1996	Noel Hynes	1999
David Bunworth	1997	Michael Maughan	1999
Pat Fahy	1997	Arnold O'Byrne	1999
Fergus Madigan	1997	R. O'Donoghue	1999
Dr John McGuire	1997	Tom Prior	1999
Patrick J. Nevin	1997	Seamus Scally	1999
Barbara Patton	1997	Conor Cunneen	2000
Robin Addis	1998	Frank Dolphin	2000
John Hickey	1987	Maeve Donovan	2000
Tony Brophy	1998	Anne Dunphy	2000
Sheila Gahan	1998	Tom Fennell	2000
Neville Galloway	1998	Roger Jupp	2000
Patrick Howard	1998	Liam Meaney	2000
Dr Pat Keenan	1998	Jim Quinn	2000
Richard Martin	1998	Jack Restan	2000
Colm Molloy	1998	Alf Smiddy	2000

Appendix 4

HONORARY MEMBERS OF THE MARKETING INSTITUTE OF IRELAND

Senator Prof. R. Conroy
Dr A.C. Cunningham
J.G. Dunne
Philip Flood
Dr T.P. Hardiman
J. S. Henderson
F.E. James
Prof. David Kennedy
John T. Kerrigan
Mr C. Lambrinopoulis, Hellenic Institute of Marketing
Mr P. Malliaris, Hellenic Institute of Marketing
Norman McConnell
Joseph McGough
Prof. John Murray
Dr A.F.J. O'Reilly
Dr F.J. O'Reilly
Dr T.A. Ryan
Dr M.J. Smurfit
Harry V. Woods
Harry A. Wyer

Appendix 5

THE MARKETING INSTITUTE OF IRELAND

The Sean F. Lemass Award

Year	Company
1974	Waterford Glass Company
1978	Jefferson Smurfit Group
1981	Industrial Development Authority
1983	Memory Computer
1986	The Doyle Hotel Group
1987	Foreign Exchange Co. of Ireland
1988	ITEC Security Products
1990	Techniform Ltd
2000	Riverdance, The Company

Appendix 6

THE MARKETING INSTITUTE

The Stephen J. Doyle Award

Year	Recipient
1971	Sean F. Lemass (posthumously)
1972	Harry V. Woods
1973	Prof. A. C. Cunninghan
1974	Michael H. Coote
1975	Philip R. Flood
1976	Joseph C. Bigger
1979	Derek P. Whelan
1980	Walter Connolly
1981	F. Edward James
1982	Sean Cowman
1983	Bill Fraser
1984	Nial Darragh
1987	Bill Ambrose
1993	Tom Prior
1994	Aidan Harte
1997	Robert K. Gahan
1998	Michael J. Hayes
2000	Anthony J. Neville

Index of Names